SYBEX READY REFERENCE SERIES

LOTUS 1-2-3® DESKTOP COMPANION

Greg Harvey

SYBEX®

SAN FRANCISCO · PARIS · DÜSSELDORF · LONDON

SYBEX Ready Reference Series
Editor in Chief: Rudolph S. Langer
Managing Editor: Karl Ray
Series Editor: Barbara Gordon
Editor: Kay Nelson

Book and cover design by Thomas Ingalls + Associates.
Technical drawings by Nancy Webb.

Hardcover: Library of Congress Card Number 86-63454
ISBN 0-89588-385-6
Softcover: Library of Congress Card Number 87-72900
ISBN 0-89588-501-8
Printed by Haddon Craftsman
Manufactured in the United States of America
10 9 8 7 6 5 4 3 2

PURPOSE	FUNCTION	MENU COMMANDS
To insert new rows in the worksheet	To insert new rows above the cell pointer's current row position:	/**W**orksheet **I**nsert **R**ow (indicate the number of rows to be inserted by typing in their cell addresses or pointing with the ↑ key) **Return**
To delete columns or rows from the worksheet	To delete a column or columns from the cell pointer's current column position: To delete a row or rows from the cell pointer's current row position:	/**W**orksheet **D**elete **C**olumn (indicate the number of columns to be deleted by typing in their cell addresses or pointing with the arrow keys) **Return** /**W**orksheet **D**elete **R**ow (indicate the number of rows to be deleted by typing in their cell addresses or pointing with the arrow keys) **Return**
To copy data or formulas in cells	To copy entries in cells (including formulas, numbers, and labels):	/**C**opy Enter range to copy FROM: (indicate the cell or cell range you want copied) **Return** Enter range to copy TO: (indicate the first cell where you want the data copied to) **Return**
To move cell entries to a new area of the worksheet	To move entries in cells (including formulas, numbers, and labels):	/**M**ove Enter range to move FROM: (indicate the cell or cell range you want moved) **Return** Enter range to move TO: (indicate the first cell where you want the data moved to) **Return**
To keep areas of the worksheet on the screen when scrolling	To freeze the rows above the cell pointer's current row position: To freeze the columns to the left of the cell pointer's current column position: To freeze both the rows above and the columns to the left of the cell pointer's position:	/**W**orksheet **T**itles **H**orizontal /**W**orksheet **T**itles **V**ertical /**W**orksheet **T**itles **B**oth
To split the display screen into two windows	To split the display at the cell pointer's current row position (duplicating the column border): To split the display at the cell pointer's current column position (duplicating the row border):	/**W**orksheet **W**indows **H**orizontal /**W**orksheet **W**indows **V**ertical Press the Windows function key (**F6**) to move the cell pointer from window to window.
To save a worksheet	To save a spreadsheet in the current directory the first time: To save a spreadsheet in the current directory that has been saved before:	/**F**ile **S**ave (type in file name) **Return** /**F**ile **S**ave **Return** **R**eplace (If you want to save the spreadsheet under a different file name, type in the new name before pressing Return.)

Table of Contents

PREFACE

The Lotus 1-2-3 Desktop Companion was designed to meet an unfulfilled need. The idea behind this book is simple: whenever you find yourself "stuck"—a function isn't working as planned, a command is producing unpredicted results, or a macro refuses to give up its bugs—you need a single source of information that can quickly help you solve the problem at hand so that you can get on with your work.

When this book was in its planning stages, my editors and I looked carefully at alternatives for organizing its material. At first, the alternatives appeared straightforward: either a dictionary reference alphabetically listing the commands and functions or a topical reference covering the commands and functions in general discussions.

From these, we came up with a third, the one that has been used in this book: a topical reference that introduces particular Lotus 1-2-3 features and functions by discussion, but also includes very specific and structured reference entries where appropriate. The arrangement of these reference entries was dictated by their nature. If the reference entries consist of Lotus 1-2-3 commands, they follow the order in which they are found on the command menus. If the reference entries consist of functions or macro commands, they are arranged either as they are most often used or by strict alphabetical listing.

SCOPE OF THE BOOK

This book is a complete reference that covers all aspects of using Lotus 1-2-3, either Release 1A or Release 2.01. Where the versions diverge most, separate discussion sections are provided, one for Release 1A users and another for Release 2 users. Where the versions differ only in minor ways, these differences are pointed out in the discussion. When a command or function is available only in the newest version, it is noted as Release 2 only.

Organization and Layout

Part 1 contains an overview of Lotus 1-2-3, including the specific differences between its versions, its applications, its design, and its user interface. The remaining parts represent the major functions of the program. They are presented as follows:

Part 2: Covers all spreadsheet commands arranged by the common tasks of creating, editing, and formatting worksheets. Also included are chapters on working with cell ranges and file operations.

Part 3: Covers the use of formulas and @ functions in worksheets. A chapter covering the general use of formulas is followed by individual chapters covering related groups of @ functions. A final chapter in this part looks at models, error trapping, and methods of recalculating formulas.

Part 4: Discusses data management in Lotus 1-2-3. This part is divided into chapters covering database management, statistical data functions in the form of frequency distribution and linear regression analysis, and sophisticated data calculation in the form of matrix algebra and data tables.

Part 5: Covers all aspects of creating and using Lotus 1-2-3 graphs. In addition, this part discusses enhancing graphs through the use of add-on products.

Part 6: Discusses Lotus 1-2-3's printing features. Chapters cover producing written reports from spreadsheets and databases, and printing and plotting graphs.

Part 7: Covers the creation and use of macros. The first chapter discusses the general planning, creating, and debugging of macros in the context of keystroke macros; the second covers the use of Lotus 1-2-3's macro command language.

Part 8: Discusses using Lotus 1-2-3 in combination with other application programs. Two chapters stress data sharing either by means of ASCII files or direct file translation.

The majority of the chapters are organized into two distinct sections: discussions that include techniques and applications for the commands or functions, followed by reference entries for each command or function previously examined. It is not necessary to read the more explanatory material to obtain the information you need to use a particular command or function. The technique and application discussions are enrichment material that gives you some extra hints and design considerations. The meat of the book, however, is contained in the reference entries.

You will often come upon keystroke macros in the context of a particular discussion or in a reference entry. Each macro includes a suggested name. This name appears to the left of the keystrokes necessary to build the macro (including any required apostrophes to have the keystrokes accepted as labels). To enter the macro, place the pointer in an out-of-the-way section of the worksheet and enter the macro exactly as it is shown. Remember that to activate the macro you must use the /Range Name Labels Right command. To do this, position the cell pointer in the cell that contains the macro name, type **/RNLR,** and press the Return key.

Acknowledgments

A project of this magnitude would not have been possible without the expertise and cooperation of a great many people. I was fortunate throughout in having top-quality people to support and guide me at every turn. This list of thanks is heartfelt and only begins to repay those involved:

To Shane and Joshua, without whose constant support I couldn't have completed the manuscript.

To Phil Friend and John Shepard at TEK/LINK, who supported and encouraged this effort in every way possible and also generously allowed me to use some of our training materials in this book.

To the instigator of it all, Dr. Rudolph Langer, who helped me so much in clarifying the fundamental design and purpose of this project. And to Karl Ray, whose behind-the-scenes action kept all the machinery working.

To Kay Nelson, who edited the text, helped me plan and design many of its elements, and contributed her usual excellence and vision to every aspect of this book and still found time for much-appreciated hand holding.

To Barbara Gordon, who not only did an outstanding job of overseeing and keeping this entire project on track but also weeded out the ambiguities in the manuscript and, most important to me, gave so generously of her natural humor and her warmth.

To Joel Kroman, whose technical edit provided many insights into the workings of Lotus 1-2-3 that I have been able to share with the reader. To Chuck Ackerman, who provided all kinds of assistance from getting required software to providing moral support; to Dianne King, who energetically pursued and provided the last-minute software needed; to Gwenyth Swain, who caught all those little things in final edit that matter so much, and to Jonathan Kamin, who provided the excellent glossary of error messages in Appendix A.

To Olivia Shinomoto, who processed all these words; to Brenda Walker, who did an excellent job of typesetting an enormous amount of complex material on a short schedule; and to Sharon Leong, who pasted up all these pages.

To Ann Leach, who worked so hard and did such a fine job on the index, one of the most demanding yet important parts of the book.

Finally, I wish to express my thanks to Lotus Development Corporation for furnishing me with copies of their software for this project.

Greg Harvey November 8, 1986

PART 1

PRELIMINARY CONSIDERATIONS

No longer is there just one Lotus 1-2-3. Today, there are two versions in common use in the business world: the original Release 1A program and the updated Release 2. Although they share a common command structure, Release 2 now offers considerably more commands and functions. Part 1 gives an overview of these differences and discusses how they can affect your work. It also provides detailed instructions on installing and configuring your system for each version of the program. Here you will also find basic information about how Lotus 1-2-3 uses the IBM PC keyboard and an overview of how the command menus are organized.

Chapter 1 presents an overview of Lotus 1-2-3, comparing and contrasting the major differences between Release 1A and Release 2. You will also find a discussion of techniques used to design efficient and economical spreadsheets as well as some suggestions for practical applications of Lotus 1-2-3 spreadsheets.

Chapter 2 contains specific instructions and detailed information on configuring either version of Lotus 1-2-3 for your computer system. You will probably refer to this information only to perform the initial installation when you first purchase the program or when you acquire new hardware such as a new monitor or printer.

Chapter 3 contains basic reference information on how Lotus 1-2-3 uses the keyboard and screen display. You may need this information if you are still getting used to working with Lotus 1-2-3. This chapter also contains macros that allow you to enter numbers from the 10-key number pad while automatically advancing the cell pointer either across the row or down the column.

Chapter 4 gives an overview of the purpose and function of each of Lotus 1-2-3's command menus. It also contains a series of figures containing menu maps to help orient you as you perform complex or new command sequences from various menus. (You will also find all of these maps reproduced in Appendix A in case you need to refer to them quickly.)

CHAPTER 1

An Overview of Lotus 1-2-3

An Overview of Lotus 1-2-3

The immense popularity of Lotus 1-2-3 stands as a testament to its success in integrating spreadsheet, business graphics, and database management to provide an abundance of powerful features with unending business applications. This handbook will focus on how program functions are related to applications as it presents each component of the program. You will be able to see not only how a command or function works but also when and where it can be best applied to various business problems. For to make full use of all that Lotus 1-2-3 has to offer, you need to have a thorough understanding of the mechanics involved as well as a very definite sense of how they can and do work together.

The first part of this chapter compares and contrasts the two versions of Lotus 1-2-3, Release 1A and Release 2. This information is useful if you are thinking of upgrading to Release 2, just beginning to work with Release 2, or working in an office where both versions still coexist.

Next, your role as a Lotus 1-2-3 user is examined. Design considerations become important if you do anything beyond simple data entry. This section begins to explore how you, as a designer, can make maximum use of the features at your command. You will find this discussion especially valuable if you are just beginning to use the program to develop your own applications.

The final section deals with the wide range of possible applications for Lotus 1-2-3. It addresses the many different ways the program is being used by professionals in all walks of business. It can get you thinking about things you can accomplish with Lotus 1-2-3 that you might not have already planned.

LOTUS 1-2-3—RELEASE 1A AND RELEASE 2

There are really two separate, though very much related, versions of Lotus 1-2-3: Release 1A and Release 2 (technically Release 2.01). The differences between them are significant in some instances and quite minor in others. If you continue to use Release 1A, you will find that some of the material covered in particular sections in this book does not apply to your situation. Whenever possible, this book handles significant differences between the two versions by providing two separate sections, one specifically tailored to Release 1A and the other to Release 2. This is the case, for example, when discussing program installation in the next chapter and creating macros in Part 7. Other, more minor differences in syntax or variation in usage are described side by side when a specific command or feature is discussed.

The development of Release 2 is very much an evolutionary change in the basic Lotus 1-2-3 program. The program has been expanded in three areas: hardware support, additional commands, and new built-in functions. Each of these areas reflects changes in new hardware that has come on the market and the increasing sophistication of computer users that has occurred since the original Lotus 1-2-3 (Release 1A) was released in 1983. Table 1.1 contrasts the major changes between the two versions of the program. New Release 2 features not available in Release 1A are summarized in Table 1.2.

Compatibility: Release 1A to Release 2

Worksheets created with Release 1A are generally compatible with Release 2 and can be loaded directly by using the /File Retrieve command. All macro commands in Release 1A are supported in Release 2, and most formulas in 1A worksheets will function in Release 2 without any modifications.

When the new version of Lotus 1-2-3 was originally released, users encountered some compatibility problems when loading Release 1A spreadsheets that contained formulas in which labels (character strings) were mixed with values. These incompatibilities were subsequently cleared up when Lotus Development corporation come out with the most current Release 2.01.

	RELEASE 1A	**RELEASE 2**
Memory	192K RAM minimum 640K RAM maximum	256K RAM minimum 4 MB RAM maximum
Operating system	DOS 1.10 or 2.XX	DOS 2.XX or higher
Processing	8087 not supported Label carries numeric value of zero	8087 and 80287 fully supported Label carries string value (different from numeric value)
Spreadsheet size	524,288 maximum cells (A1 to IV2048) 1–72 column width Smaller worksheets in RAM; memory allotted to all blank cells in active worksheet area.	2,097,152 maximum cells (A1 to IV8192) 1–240 column width Larger worksheets in RAM; memory not allotted to blank, unformatted cells in active worksheet area.
Database size	32 fields maximum 2047 records maximum	256 fields maximum 8191 records maximum

TABLE 1.1: Lotus 1-2-3, Release 1A and Release 2—Physical Comparison

Release 1A and Release 2 File Name Extensions

Worksheets created in Release 2 are given the file name extension .wk1 to keep them separate from those created in Release 1A, which are given the extension .wks. The first time you save a worksheet created with Release 1A with the /File Save Replace (/FSR) command of Release 2, the program automatically changes its file extension to .wk1. You will hear a beep and see the message "File will be saved as .wk1." The only way to override this modification and leave the extension as .wks, so you will have two versions of the same worksheet saved on your data disk, is to press the Esc key and type in the file name with a .wks extension.

It is never a good idea to use this method or the DOS RENAME command to change these file name extensions. They are there to alert you to

- Additional /Global menu commands—/Global Zero to suppress the display zeros in the worksheet and /Global Column Hide to hide the display of columns of information (see Chapter 7)
- Additional /Range menu commands—/Range Value (see Chapter 6) and /Range Transpose (see Chapter 7)
- New /System command to temporarily exit to DOS (replaces File and Disk Manager options on the Lotus Access System Menu in Release 1A; see Chapter 9)
- Additional financial functions—@CTERM, @SLN, @DDB, and @SYD (see Chapter 13)
- New date functions—@NOW (replaces @TODAY in Release 1A) and @DATEVALUE (see Chapter 14)
- New time functions—@TIME, @TIMEVALUE, @SECOND, @MINUTE, and @HOUR (see Chapter 14)
- Additional logical functions—@ISSTRING and @ISNUMBER (see Chapter 15)
- New set of string functions (see Chapter 17)
- Additional special functions—@@, @CELL, @CELLPOINTER, @COLS, @INDEX, and @ROWS (see Chapter 18)
- Additional /Data menu commands—/Data Matrix, /Data Regression (see Chapter 21), and /Data Parse (see Chapter 29)
- Exploded pie charts and new pattern and color selection for graphs (see Chapter 24)
- Page breaks at any point within a worksheet (see Chapter 25)
- Printer setup codes in cells to mix printing enhancements (see Chapter 25)
- New macro command language similar to Symphony's (see Chapter 28)
- Direct export and import of data to and from dBASE III (see Chapter 30)
- LICS (Lotus International Character Set) graphic characters possible in worksheets by using the Alt-F1 (Compose) key and appropriate code number (see Appendix B)

TABLE 1.2: Release 2 Features Not Available in Release 1A

differences in the way the worksheets are stored on disk. Changing the file name extension does not affect the underlying differences between the Release 1A and Release 2 formats, and it could later confuse you or your fellow workers about the origin and compatibility of these files.

Compatiblity: Release 2 to Release 1A

Worksheets created in Release 2 are not compatible with Release 1A. To load worksheets carrying the .wk1 extension, you must first use the Release 2 Translate utility to translate a Release 2 worksheet to a Release 1A format.

In addition, some areas may need to be modified before the translation if the resulting worksheet is to function properly. (For details on what must be modified and how to perform a Release 2 to Release 1A translation, see Chapter 30.)

Differences in Spreadsheet Size

In Release 1A, the spreadsheet is 256 columns by 2048 rows. However, you cannot fully utilize all of these cells because of the way the program handles memory and because of its addressable limit of 640K of RAM.

In Release 2, the spreadsheet has been increased to 256 columns by 8192 rows. While it is doubtful that you could ever use all of the cells in this expanded spreadsheet, you can use a lot more of them because of changes made to the way the program manages memory and its support of expanded memory boards. By using these add-on cards, it is theoretically possible for Lotus 1-2-3 to access up to 4 megabytes of RAM above the IBM PC's main memory limit of 640K. (For more information on using expanded memory cards, see "Release 2 and Expanded Memory" in Chapter 2.)

Differences in Memory Management

Release 2 has been redesigned to take advantage of a sparse matrix array that uses memory much more efficiently than Release 1A. Only cells containing labels, data, or formulas occupy RAM. With the same amount of computer memory, you can build much larger worksheets in Release 2 than in Release 1A. Release 2, unlike Release 1A, does not allot any main or expanded memory to blank, unformatted cells that occur in the active worksheet area. It may be possible to use almost the entire worksheet, depending upon the application you have designed.

An Exercise: Comparing Memory Usage

If you use Release 1A of the program, you can do a simple exercise that graphically demonstrates worksheet size. In a completely blank worksheet, go to the very last cell of the spreadsheet by pressing End-→ and then End-↓. Then enter the number **123** in cell IV2048. As soon as you press Return, you receive the "Memory Full" error message. Even though this is the only entry in the entire worksheet, its position in the last cell makes the entire spreadsheet active. Because this version allots some memory to all of the blank cells (all 524,287 of them) within the active area, you run out of memory.

In Release 2, you can complete this exercise without any trouble, even though you are making the entry in cell IV8192. Release 2 uses no more memory to make an entry in cell A1 than it does in IV8192.

Limitations on Worksheet Size

In either version, how large a worksheet you can create given the amount of memory in your system depends largely on the type of cell entries you make. Simple numeric entries and labels take up less memory than calculations by formulas or functions. As most worksheets consist of an uneven combination of input values, labels, and calculations, there is no simple formula for determining the amount of memory that will be required for any given application.

Determining Available Memory in Release 2

Release 2 has an on-screen status indicator that lets you know when you are almost out of memory. The message "MEM" flashes when the amount of available memory drops to 4K, which is just about the time you are in danger of receiving a "Memory Full" error message. (You can also see how much memory is still free while you are building a worksheet by using the /Worksheet Global Status command.)

Whenever you see the MEM indicator, save the worksheet. You may have to release some of the memory by eliminating any expendable items such as range names or graphs that are no longer needed. After deleting all the unneccesary items you can, save the worksheet and then retrieve it again to free the memory no longer used by the items you eliminated. If doing this doesn't free sufficient memory, split the spreadsheet into smaller, separate worksheets (for specific information on how to do this, see /File Xtract and /File Combine in Chapter 9).

Determining Available Memory in Release 1A

If you are using Release 1A, there is no way to determine that your memory is almost used up before you receive the "Memory Full" error message. Your chances of running into this situation are much greater than in Release 2 because of the way this version treats blank cells. When you receive the error message, save your worksheet and then retrieve it again; this frees some memory. Then try to reduce the size of the active area by deleting all of the extraneous blank cells and any expendable data. Save the worksheet and retrieve it again. If this does not free enough memory to allow you to complete your spreadsheet, you can split it into smaller worksheets (for specific information on how to do this, see /File Xtract and /File Combine in Chapter 9).

Memory Considerations with Databases

Databases created with Lotus 1-2-3 usually require large amounts of memory, especially when they have many fields. The more fields in your database, the fewer records you can accommodate. Though Release 2 will allow you up 256 fields (as many fields as there are columns), it is generally much better to limit the number of individual fields, even if this means that you have to construct and maintain separate, somewhat redundant, database files. Because all the data in the database must be loaded into RAM, the amount of memory in your computer is the prime factor that ultimately determines how large a database you can maintain.

The User as Spreadsheet Designer

When you are new at designing with Lotus 1-2-3, you are hampered primarily by a lack of experience. It is only as you continue to work with the product that you learn some of the more subtle design techniques that can help you create more efficient applications.

Thinking of yourself as a Lotus 1-2-3 designer is important: it forces you not only to look at which function or command you will use but also to grasp the implications of its usage. Before you can create any application, you must be able to conceptualize what the application is to accomplish and how it is to go about it. Your understanding of the design principles involved determines in large part how successful your resulting application will be. Depending on your background in working with spreadsheet programs, you may find that this is the hardest aspect of Lotus 1-2-3 to master.

Designing Economical Spreadsheets

A common example of the difficulty of grasping underlying principles of spreadsheet design occurs when a user, newly trained in the mechanics of the spreadsheet, sets out to build an application for the first time. At this point, the mechanics of pointing, using cell references, basic Lotus formula construction, and common functions like @SUM are well understood. However, less well understood is how to identify the data variables involved in the application and use them to attain economy in the design.

The result is often a spreadsheet that works well as a one-time application but fails to be of much use in performing continued "what-if" analysis. One reason this occurs is that the user is not yet sophisticated enough to separate the data variables from the rest of the model, thus ensuring that the entry of numeric values in the worksheet is kept to a minimum so that any subsequent changes in assumptions can be accomplished with a minor amount of revision. Although some applications, like databases, make little use of data variables, there are also many that demand it, like spreadsheet templates. Knowing when this type of economy is feasible and how best to achieve it is one of the design tasks that confronts any serious Lotus 1-2-3 user.

Example: Using a Formula to Copy a Source Cell

A simple example demonstrating design economy is shown in Figures 1.1 and 1.2. Here you need to bring forward an entry made in one cell of the worksheet to a new area. It might seem that the easiest way to do this would be to use the /Copy command, which has been used to bring forward the value input as 345 in cell A1 to cell A4. A better strategy, however, is to construct a formula that copies whatever is input in the source cell. This technique was used to copy the value of A1 to C1 by constructing the simple formula +A1 in cell C1.

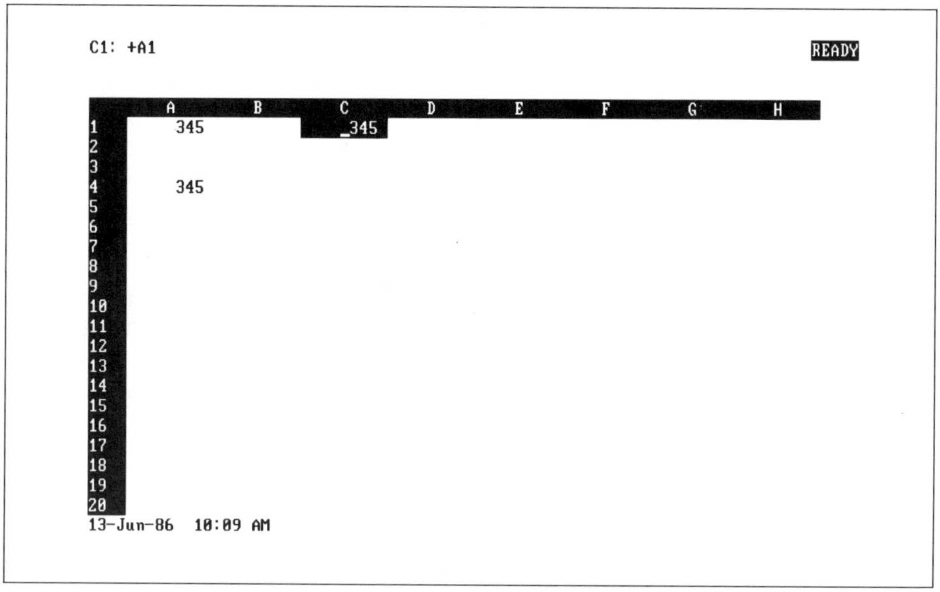

FIGURE 1.1: Bringing forward a value in the worksheet. The value entered in cell A1 was brought forward by using the /Copy command in A4 and the simple formula +A1 in C1. As a result, the value in C1 is still dynamically linked to that in A1, while the value in A4 is static.

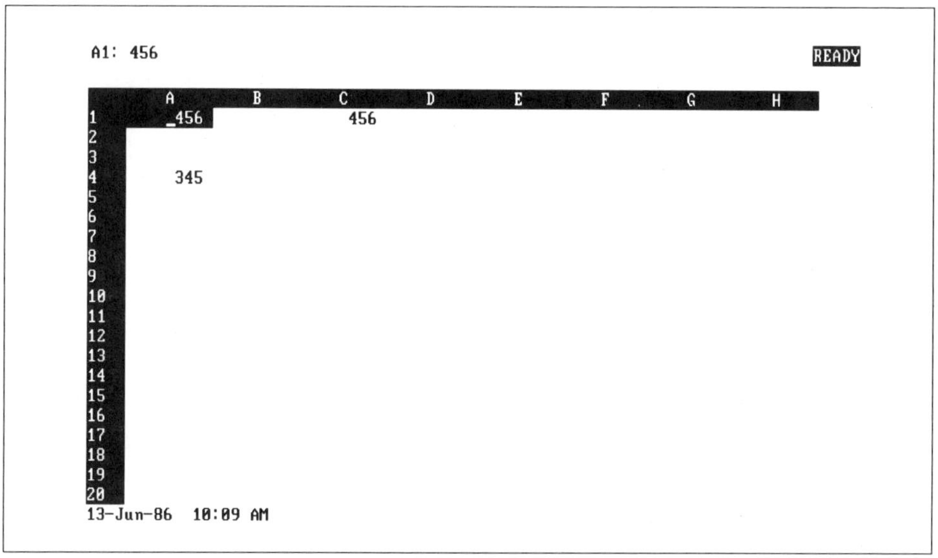

FIGURE 1.2: The effect of updating the original value in A1. Because the value in C4 is linked by formula to that in cell A1, it was automatically recalculated as soon as a new value was input in A1. Notice that the copied value in A4 has not changed.

See what happens in Figure 1.2 when the original value is changed. A new value of 456 was entered into cell A1. Immediately upon input, the value of C1 was recalculated, demonstrating the dynamic dependency that exists between these cells because of the formula. Notice that the value of the copied value in A4 remains unchanged. If the /Copy command is used throughout a worksheet to bring forward necessary values, these all have to be recopied or updated manually to reflect the new assumption correctly.

While this represents a very simple example, it illustrates part of the problem that new users face when they begin to design applications in Lotus. The problem superficially seems to be "how do I *copy* the value (or label) from this cell?", so the user immediately thinks of the /Copy command. The second strategy really only becomes apparent when the problem is expanded to "how do I *copy* the value from this cell and *ensure that no error results if its value changes?*" Seen in this light, the more subtle aspect of using formulas to set up dynamic dependencies between cells makes it the superior choice.

Example: Designing for "What-If" Analysis

Figure 1.3 is a good example of designing a worksheet with an eye toward economy in terms of user input and continued "what-if" scenarios. It contains a payment schedule showing the various payments required at different loan amounts for a spread of interest rates. Constructing this table required only seven literal inputs for the entire worksheet (including the title and three labels) and the use of five formulas (the @PMT function was entered in cell B8 and copied throughout). Only the three cells C3 down to C5 have been left unprotected to allow for changes in assumptions (new beginning principal, interest rate, or term). This is because all of the data in the payment table is dynamically linked through formulas to the data variables contained in these three cells. A change made in any one of these cells cascades down through the payment table like dominos falling in a line.

Someone new to designing in Lotus has a natural tendency to want to enter each principal and interest rate in the table manually (that is, as literal values). Instead, both are derived with two simple formulas. The first brings forward the values entered in the input cells to the beginning of the table. In cell A8, this is entered as **+C3** and in cell B7 as **+C4.** To

B8: (F2) PR @PMT($A8,B$7/12,$C$5*12) READY

	A	B	C	D	E	F	G	H
1		Payment Schedule for Simple Interest Loans						
2								
3	Begin. Prinicpal		$150,000					
4	Interest Rate		9.00%					
5	Term (in years)		30					
6								
7		9.00%	9.25%	9.50%	9.75%	10.00%	10.25%	
8	150,000	1206.93	1234.01	1261.28	1288.73	1316.36	1344.15	
9	150,500	1210.96	1238.13	1265.49	1293.03	1320.75	1348.63	
10	151,000	1214.98	1242.24	1269.69	1297.32	1325.13	1353.11	
11	151,500	1219.00	1246.35	1273.89	1301.62	1329.52	1357.59	
12	152,000	1223.03	1250.47	1278.10	1305.91	1333.91	1362.07	
13	152,500	1227.05	1254.58	1282.30	1310.21	1338.30	1366.55	
14	153,000	1231.07	1258.69	1286.51	1314.51	1342.68	1371.03	
15	153,500	1235.10	1262.81	1290.71	1318.80	1347.07	1375.52	
16	154,000	1239.12	1266.92	1294.92	1323.10	1351.46	1380.00	
17	154,500	1243.14	1271.03	1299.12	1327.39	1355.85	1384.48	
18	155,000	1247.17	1275.15	1303.32	1331.69	1360.24	1388.96	
19	155,500	1251.19	1279.26	1307.53	1335.99	1364.62	1393.44	
20	156,000	1255.21	1283.37	1311.73	1340.28	1369.01	1397.92	

13-Jun-86 10:17 AM CALC

FIGURE 1.3: This simple payment schedule for a range of loan amounts at various interest rates on a 30-year loan requires only three data variables supplied by the user: beginning principal, interest rate, and term in years. The range of loan amounts, interest rates, and resulting monthly payments for each are all derived by formulas.

increment the principal by $500, the formula **+A8+500** was entered in A9 and then copied down to A20. To increment the interest rates by a quarter of a percent, the formula **+B7+.0025** was entered in C7 and then copied across the row to G7. (The /Data Fill command was not used for the same reason /Copy was not used in the example above.) Then the @PMT function, as shown in Figure 1.3, was entered in B8 and copied both down and across the rest of the table (a two-dimensional copy).

Figure 1.4 shows how this design is able to accommodate changes as part of "what-if" analysis. The beginning interest rate and length of the term have both been changed to determine their effect on the resulting payments. Any of these three variables can now be modified without requiring any additional revision to the worksheet. If the payment schedule had not been designed in this way, the spreadsheet would have limited use for further analysis. It would either have been restricted to the first set of assumptions, or it would require a good deal of continual manual revision to be used for further analysis.

C5: U 30 READY

	A	B	C	D	E	F	G	H
1		Payment Schedule for Simple Interest Loans						
2								
3	Begin. Prinicpal		$175,000					
4	Interest Rate		7.50%					
5	Term (in years)		30					
6								
7		7.50%	7.75%	8.00%	8.25%	8.50%	8.75%	
8	175,000	1223.63	1253.72	1284.09	1314.72	1345.60	1376.73	
9	175,500	1227.12	1257.30	1287.76	1318.47	1349.44	1380.66	
10	176,000	1230.62	1260.89	1291.43	1322.23	1353.29	1384.59	
11	176,500	1234.11	1264.47	1295.09	1325.99	1357.13	1388.53	
12	177,000	1237.61	1268.05	1298.76	1329.74	1360.98	1392.46	
13	177,500	1241.11	1271.63	1302.43	1333.50	1364.82	1396.39	
14	178,000	1244.60	1275.21	1306.10	1337.25	1368.67	1400.33	
15	178,500	1248.10	1278.80	1309.77	1341.01	1372.51	1404.26	
16	179,000	1251.59	1282.38	1313.44	1344.77	1376.36	1408.19	
17	179,500	1255.09	1285.96	1317.11	1348.52	1380.20	1412.13	
18	180,000	1258.59	1289.54	1320.78	1352.28	1384.04	1416.06	
19	180,500	1262.08	1293.12	1324.45	1356.04	1387.89	1419.99	
20	181,000	1265.58	1296.71	1328.11	1359.79	1391.73	1423.93	

18-Jun-86 03:42 PM

FIGURE 1.4: The payment schedule has now been subjected to "what-if" analysis to see the effects of a change to principals and interest rates. This change required only the entry of **175000** and **.075** in cells C3 and C4, respectively, and the use of the F9 key to recalculate the entire table.

Using This Handbook to Create Good Designs

You will see many of these kinds of examples illustrating various types of design techniques as you use this handbook. Wherever possible, the command or function in question is presented from two viewpoints:

- How to use it properly (the mechanics)
- How it can be applied in building applications (the design principle)

As you use the handbook to look up specific information, first concentrate on understanding what the command does and how it is commonly used. Then think about the ways you plan to use the command or function in your application. See if any of the hints and techniques presented in the book can help you accomplish what you need to do more efficiently. In this way, slowly, but surely, the more subtle aspects of the program will come into focus and your design skills will increase.

Applications for Lotus 1-2-3

There is almost no industry or line of business that has not found countless ways to put Lotus 1-2-3 to work. While the spreadsheet may have once been considered a special tool for the accounting and bookkeeping department, today it is just as important in a business's personnel, marketing, sales, planning, and production departments. There are few, if any, aspects of business that can't benefit by the capabilities of Lotus 1-2-3.

Financial, Statistical, and Mathematical Functions

In addition to the traditional financial analysis tools, Lotus 1-2-3 contains a group of powerful statistical functions that are often of much more use to those involved in the sciences (both applied and social sciences of all types) than they are to those involved in financial analysis. For those working in the applied sciences, Lotus 1-2-3 has even more specialized mathematical and trigonometric functions.

Database Management Functions

Lotus 1-2-3 also integrates database management functions with its spreadsheet. This makes the product useful for an extremely broad audience with diverse needs. Needing to track and maintain bodies of information is a part of almost all jobs. Applications can entail both the traditional record-keeping functions using databases of information as well as those geared to statistical data analysis, which has greatly been enhanced in Release 2 with the inclusion of the /Data Matrix and /Data Regression commands.

Table 1.3 lists many of the major categories of applications for Lotus 1-2-3. It presents *kinds* of templates and models that can be created rather than one-time applications, which are too numerous to include here.

Third-Party Templates for Lotus 1-2-3

Instead of creating all of your own applications from scratch, you can purchase and use ready-made templates and models marketed for Lotus

Finance

- Income statement
- Balance statement
- Financial ratio analysis
- Sensitivity analysis
- Depreciation analysis—straight line, double-declining balance, and ACRS
- Capital equipment replacement
- Lease-versus-buy decisions
- Portfolio analysis
- Source and use of funds
- Forecasting sales, profit, and cash flow
- Breakeven analysis
- Budgets—sales, production, cash, etc.
- Fixed-assets decisions

Tax Planning

- Organization of new business and income tax—proprietorship versus corporation, etc.
- Profit versus cash flow and income tax
- Depreciation decisions and income tax
- Personal income tax templates—1040 and required schedules
- Tax tables

Marketing and Sales

- Marketing and advertising budget
- Pricing decisions—cost-plus versus marginal pricing
- Analyzing market potential—statistical analysis of surveys, questionnaires, industry data, census, maturity curve, etc.
- Sales, share-of-market, source-of-sales analyses
- Quotation analysis
- Distribution-channel analysis
- Sales forecasts—linear regression models
- Seasonal forecasts

TABLE 1.3: Common Lotus 1-2-3 Applications

Manufacturing
• Hiring plans • Bill of materials • Quality control • Job logs • Product planning and development—learning-curve analysis • Inventory forecasting
Real Estate
• Amortization and payment schedules—fixed and variable rate • Investment analysis • Rent-versus-buy decisions • Property management—costs of utilities, vacancies, etc.
Record Keeping
• Sales register • Check register • Invoice system • General ledger • Accounts receivable, accounts payable, and payroll • Vacation-accrual and sick-leave schedules • Lists for tracking customers, sales leads, etc. • Expense registers and appointment scheduling

TABLE 1.3: Common Lotus 1-2-3 Applications (continued)

1-2-3 by third-party vendors. These are available for a wide range of custom applications for anything from standard types of financial planning to more specialized applications like farm management. There are currently so many templates on the market that you can probably find several that will fit your needs. Many of these are geared to different-sized companies, from large corporations to small and medium-sized businesses.

Customizing Templates

Of course, the biggest benefit of using ready-made templates is that they save you from having to take time to develop them yourself. However, you may locate an application template that seems to be just what you need, only to discover that it does not follow practices that your company prefers or your specific needs demand. Although you can customize these templates, you should try to make sure that they are set up basically the way you want them, or you will end up taking almost as much time to modify them as you would take to create your own from scratch.

Choosing the Right Template for You

You should try to get as much specific information as possible about what a template does and how it is used before you purchase it. Sometimes you can get part of this information from product reviews in computer magazines, especially *Lotus,* which is devoted entirely to information on products by Lotus Development Corporation. You can also try to contact the manufacturer of the template directly and discuss its fine points. Most of these products are marketed by small companies that are more than willing to discuss your needs.

Summary

This chapter has looked at three areas:

- An overview of Lotus 1-2-3 comparing the two versions of the product
- Your role as a Lotus 1-2-3 user with a view toward designing applications with the product
- Custom applications for the program

If you are interested in learning more about any one of these topics, use the following guide to find related topics you are interested in.

For more specific information on new features in Lotus 1-2-3 Release 2:

- Chapter 2, "Installing and Customizing Lotus 1-2-3"
- Chapter 5, "Creating Worksheets"—/Worksheet Global Zero and Column Hide

- Chapter 6, "Editing Worksheets"—/Range Value
- Chapter 7, "Formatting Worksheets"—/Range Transpose
- Chapter 8, "Working with Cell Ranges"—/Range Name Table
- Chapter 9, "File Operations"—Passwords and /System
- Chapter 13, "Financial Functions"—@CTERM, @SLN, @DDB, and @SYD
- Chapter 14, "Date and Time Functions"—@NOW, @DATEVALUE, and all time functions
- Chapter 15, "Logical Functions"—@ISSTRING and @ISNUMBER
- Chapter 17, "String Functions"
- Chapter 18, "Special Functions"—@@, @CELL, @CELLPOINTER, @COLS, @INDEX, and @ROWS
- Chapter 22, "Data Distribution, Matrix, and Regression Commands"
- Chapter 24, "Creating and Using Graphs"—pie charts
- Chapter 25, "Printing Reports"—printer control codes and page breaks in the worksheet
- Chapter 28, "The Macro Command Language"
- Chapter 29, "Importing and Exporting ASCII Files"—/Data Parse
- Chapter 30, "The Translate Utility"—dBASE III and Lotus 1-2-3
- Appendix B, "LICS Chart"

For more information on designing with Lotus 1-2-3:

- Chapter 19, "Spreadsheet Models, Error Trapping, and Recalculation"

INSTALLING AND CUSTOMIZING LOTUS 1-2-3

Installing and Customizing Lotus 1-2-3

This chapter summarizes how to install Lotus 1-2-3 on your computer system and configure it to work with the hardware you are using. Because the specific procedures for installing and customizing Lotus 1-2-3 are different in Release 1A and Release 2, they are presented separately.

If you are using Release 2, pay particular attention to the section describing the ways you can customize some of the program defaults. Also, if you are planning on using Release 2 with expanded memory boards, look at the section on Release 2 and Expanded Memory.

Installing Lotus 1-2-3: An Overview

Lotus 1-2-3 was designed specifically for the IBM PC and compatible computers running the PC/MS-DOS operating system. The systems it runs on can consist of several different hardware configurations. The installation procedures allow you to specify what equipment you are using.

Monochrome or Color Monitor

The difference between monochrome and color configurations is important because of Lotus 1-2-3's graphics program. If you want to be able to see the graphs created with the program on your monitor, your computer must have graphics capabilities. If you have a monochrome monitor, you may need to purchase a graphics adapter card, such as the Hercules Graphics Card. This add-on board allows you to display Lotus 1-2-3 graphs on a monochrome monitor.

Defining Alternate Equipment

For Lotus 1-2-3 to run properly on your equipment, you must tell it during installation the type of computer and the kind of display configuration you are using. Lotus 1-2-3 stores different configuration files referred to as *drivers* that cover the various combinations. During installation, you tell the program which drivers to use.

In Release 2, you can define alternative sets of drivers so that you can use your copy of the program on various computers, each with slightly different display configurations. To do this with Release 1A, you have to reinstall the program using a new set of drivers required by the configuration of the new computer.

Floppy Disk or Hard Disk Storage

An IBM PC system can use various storage devices. If you have two floppy disk drives, the left-hand drive is called drive A and the right-hand drive is called drive B. In a configuration with one floppy disk and a hard disk, the floppy drive is called drive A and the hard disk is usually called drive C.

The major difference between the two systems is that a hard disk user generally stores the entire software program in its own directory on drive C and stores data files in subdirectories. This eliminates the need for disk swapping between the various Lotus 1-2-3 program disks and makes the program run a little faster.

Under Release 1A's copy-protection scheme the System Disk, which is the only one that is copy protected, cannot be copied entirely onto the hard disk. In Release 1A, the System Disk must be in drive A whenever you start up the program, regardless of your storage configuration. Release 2, though still copy protected, allows you to copy all of the System Disk files onto the hard disk with a new installation command and thus boot Lotus 1-2-3 entirely from drive C (see "Making Lotus 1-2-3 Bootable from the Hard Disk" later in this chapter).

The Default Data Directory

With either release, an important part of the installation procedure tells the program where your data files are located by setting the default directory. The program uses that drive (usually B or C) and any directories you specify when it saves and retrieves the data files that you create.

Printers and Plotters

The last component of your computer system that is important to Lotus 1-2-3 is the type of printers, plotters, or both, that you use to produce hard copies of your reports and graphs.

Lotus 1-2-3 has two printing functions: one that prints spreadsheets from within the Lotus 1-2-3 program itself and another that prints graphs from the PrintGraph utility, which is part of the Lotus Access System. You may have just one printing device that you use with both programs (if you have a dot-matrix printer, for example), or you may have two (or more) devices, one for printing worksheets and the other for printing graphs. This would be the case if you use a letter-quality printer for worksheets and a pen plotter for graphs. In Release 2, you can specify more than one printer model when you install the program.

Printers and plotters differ in the type of interface they use to communicate with the computer—either a parallel interface designated as LPT (line printer), which a dot-matrix printer generally uses, or a serial interface designated as COM (communications), which a plotter or letter-quality printer uses. You can have two of each of these kinds of devices connected to your system. (Although by using DOS you can have three parallel devices, one plugged into the LPT1 port, the second in LPT2, and the third in LPT3.) If you have two serial devices, one is in the COM1 port and the other is in COM2. Lotus 1-2-3 has to know what kind of printers and plotters you are using as well as which of these ports they use.

Installing Lotus 1-2-3 Release 1A

Normally, installing Lotus 1-2-3 is a one-time procedure that you go through when you first purchase the product. Release 1A is no longer sold, so it is assumed that if you are using this version, you have already gone through the installation procedure at least once.

The Program Disks (Release 1A)

Release 1A consists of the following five program disks:

1. System Disk (original)
2. System Disk (backup copy)
3. Utility Disk
4. PrintGraph Disk
5. Tutorial Disk

The System Disk contains all the Lotus 1-2-3 program files needed to load the program. Because it is copy protected, a backup copy of this disk is provided for you to use if the original becomes damaged. None of the other disks are copy protected.

If you use Lotus 1-2-3 on a hard disk system, a System Disk must be in drive A when you start up the program. If you use Lotus 1-2-3 on a two-disk system, this disk should remain in drive A even after you start the program. You will receive instructions on the screen to replace it with either the Utility or PrintGraph Disks whenever they are required.

The Utility Disk contains the Lotus 1-2-3 driver files as well as those needed to perform certain kinds of data transfer using the Lotus Access System.

The PrintGraph Disk contains the files required to print the graphs that you create with the system. This disk is needed only when you choose the PrintGraph Menu, which is also located in the Lotus Access System.

The Tutorial Disk provides a series of interactive tutorial lessons that introduce you to the major features of Lotus 1-2-3.

Making Backup Copies (Release 1A)

Always use only backup copies of the Utility, PrintGraph, and Tutorial Disks. If you need to make more backup copies, use either the Disk-Copy option on the Disk-Manager Menu from the Lotus Access System or the DOS COPY command from the operating system. (If you need to refresh your memory on how to use the DOS COPY command, refer to Table 2.6 at the beginning of the section "Installing Lotus 1-2-3 Release 2.")

Installing DOS System Files (Release 1A)

If you are using Lotus 1-2-3 on a two-disk-drive system and have not yet copied the DOS system files onto your Lotus 1-2-3 System Disk so that you can load the operating system from the System Disk when you start up your computer, use the procedures in Table 2.1.

Reinstalling Lotus 1-2-3 Drivers (Release 1A)

You may need to reinstall the Lotus 1-2-3 drivers when you purchase new hardware or when you must reinstall the entire program on drive C of a hard disk system. In either situation, you will have to reinstall the appropriate drivers from the Utility Disk onto each of the remaining program disks or, if you have a hard disk, onto the directory containing all of the Lotus 1-2-3 programs. Table 2.2 summarizes the instructions for doing this on a two-disk-drive system, and Table 2.3 presents the procedure for a hard disk system.

1. Place a copy of your DOS disk in drive A and your original System Disk in drive B.
2. Turn on the computer and enter the current date and time when prompted for them.
3. Enter the following command:

   A>B:INSTALL <Return>
4. Remove the System Disk from drive B and replace it with the backup System Disk. Then repeat step 3.
5. Take these same steps to copy the DOS system files onto any working copies that you have made of the Utility and PrintGraph Disks. (This is not necessary for the Tutorial Disk.)

TABLE 2.1: Installing the DOS System Files on the Lotus 1-2-3 Release 1A Program Disks

1. Place the Utility Disk in drive A and turn on the computer.
2. After entering the current date and time, choose the most appropriate configuration from those listed below, type in the command that follows it, and press Return (↵):
   - If you have a monochrome monitor with a monochrome adapter card, type

     A>MONO B: <Return>
   - If you have a monochrome monitor with a Hercules Graphics Card, type

     A>HERCULES B: <Return>
   - If you have a color monitor, type

     A>COLOR B: <Return>
   - If you have a monochrome monitor with a Color/Graphics Adapter, type

     A>B&W B: <Return>
   - If you have both a monochrome and color monitor with an adapter that supports each, type

     A>BOTH B: <Return>
   - If you a Compaq computer, type

     A>COMPAQ B: <Return>
3. After you enter one of these commands, the program will instruct you to place the remaining program disks, one by one, in the target drive, which is drive B.
4. You can then remove your Utility Disk from drive A. You should put write-protect tabs on each of your program disks.

TABLE 2.2: Installing Lotus 1-2-3 Drivers on a Two-Disk-Drive System (Release 1A)

Configuring the Default Printer and Drive (Release 1A)

To view or modify the default settings for your printer or the drive and directory where your worksheet files are saved, you must be in Lotus 1-2-3. To set up a default graphics printer or plotter as well as set the text printer and the default drive, enter the program by using the startup command **lotus** instead of **123.** It takes you into the Lotus 1-2-3 program via the Lotus Access System Menu. To start Lotus 1-2-3 from here, simply highlight the 1-2-3 option and press Return. Table 2.4 shows the Default Menu

1. Turn on your computer and enter the date and time (if necessary).
2. Use the Change Directory command to make the directory containing your Lotus 1-2-3 programs current:

   C>CD\123 <Return>

   (Substitute your name for this directory if it is something other than \123.)
3. Delete all existing driver files:

   C>DEL *.DRV <Return>
4. Change the current drive to A:

   C>A: <Return>
5. Place the Utility Disk in drive A and choose the most appropriate configuration from those listed below. Then type in the command that follows it:
   - If you have a monochrome monitor with a monochrome adapter card, type

     A>MONO C: <Return>
   - If you have a monochrome monitor with a Hercules Graphics Card, type

     A>HERCULES C: <Return>
   - If you have a color monitor, type

     A>COLOR C: <Return>
   - If you have a monochrome monitor with a Color/Graphics Adapter, type

     A>B&W C: <Return>
   - If you have both a monochrome and a color monitor with an adapter that supports each, type

     A>BOTH C: <Return>
   - If you have a Compaq computer, type

     A>COMPAQ C: <Return>
6. After you enter one of these commands, the program processes your program files. Once it has finished, you will be prompted to interrupt this procedure by pressing Ctrl-C.
7. Remove the Utility Disk from drive A and make drive C current by typing **c:** and pressing Return.

TABLE 2.3: Installing Lotus 1-2-3 Drivers on a Hard Disk System (Release 1A)

options and their default settings for Release 1A. To change any of the settings in this table you must issue the command /Worksheet Global Default (/WGD).

THE PRINTER OPTION

You use the Printer option to set up the type of printer interface, margin settings, page length, and single-sheet or continuous-feed paper. Printer control codes are used to obtain special print enhancements like compressed mode or boldface type. You can override the margins, page length, and

/Worksheet Global Default Printer		
Interface	1 Parallel 2 Serial 3 Second Parallel 4 Second Serial	(LPT1—default) (COM1) (LPT2) (COM2)
Auto-LF	No (default) Yes	
Left	4 columns	
Right	76 columns	
Top	2 lines	
Bottom	2 lines	
Page-Length	66 lines	
Wait	No (default) Yes	
Setup		
Directory	B:\	
Status	Displays all settings currently in effect.	
Update	Stores any changes to made to the Printer or Directory settings on the System Disk.	
Quit	Returns you to the Lotus 1-2-3 spreadsheet.	

TABLE 2.4: Lotus 1-2-3 Release 1A Default Menu Options and Settings

printer control code settings during a session by using the /Print Printer Options command (see Chapter 25).

To change the printer port from the default setting of parallel, choose the Interface option and type the appropriate number. If you find that your printer is also double-spacing when you print your worksheets, use this command and change the Auto-LF option from No to Yes.

Under most circumstances, you will not need to permanently change any of the other printer default settings. You can easily change them as needed by using the /Print Printer (or File) Options command. Any changes made to these settings with the /Print command stay in effect only during your work session with Lotus 1-2-3. (If you wish to make changes to these values, see /Print Printer Other in Chapter 25 for information on how this is done and the permitted range of values for each setting.)

The Directory Option

The Directory option sets up the default directory where Lotus 1-2-3 will store and retrieve data files each time the program is started. You can override it during a session by using the /File Directory command (see Chapter 9).

If you are using a hard disk system, you will want to use this option to change the default drive from B:\ to C:\. You can also designate a subdirectory where you usually keep all of your data files, such as C:\123\DATA (see also /File Directory in Chapter 9).

Saving Your Changed Settings

Once you have finished making the changes to the default configuration settings, make sure that you choose the Update option before you use the Quit command to return to the spreadsheet. If you overlook this step, your changes will not be saved on the System Disk. You can return to this menu and make other changes at any time during a Lotus 1-2-3 session.

Configuring the PrintGraph Device and Directories (Release 1A)

To view or make changes to the default graphics device or directories where your graph files (saved with the /Graph Save command and given the extension .PIC) or the Lotus 1-2-3 graphics program files are kept, you must use the PrintGraph option on the Lotus Access System Menu. To access this menu system, exit from Lotus 1-2-3 (enter **/QY**). If you initially typed LOTUS as the startup command instead of 123, you always exit the program through the Lotus Access System (if you did not, then type **lotus** and press Return). Choose the PrintGraph option on this menu. (You can also start PrintGraph directly from DOS by typing **graph.**)

Figure 2.1 shows the default configuration for the directories and the graphics device in the column at the far right. To change these, first choose the Configure option on this menu. Table 2.5 shows you the options on the Configure Menu.

CHANGING DIRECTORIES

To modify the directories, choose the Files option on the Configure Menu. Choose the Pictures option to change the drive and directory where Lotus 1-2-3 looks for graph files saved with the extension .PIC. To change the setting, type in the drive and directory, such as C:\123\BUDGETS.

```
Copyright 1982, 1983 Lotus Development Corp.  All Rights Reserved.          MENU
--------------------------------------------------------------------------------
Select  Options  Go  Configure  Align  Page  Quit
Specify Hardware setup
================================================================================
 SELECTED GRAPHS  COLORS              SIZE     HALF            DIRECTORIES

                  Grid:      Black    Left Margin:      .750   Pictures
                  A Range:   Black    Top Margin:       .395   B:\
                  B Range:   Black    Width:           6.500   Fonts
                  C Range:   Black    Height:          4.691   A:\
                  D Range:   Black    Rotation:         .000
                  E Range:   Black                             GRAPHICS DEVICE
                  F Range:   Black    MODES
                                                               Epson FX80/1
                  FONTS               Eject: No                Parallel
                                      Pause: No
                  1: BLOCK1                                    PAGE SIZE
                  2: BLOCK1
                                                               Length   11.000
                                                               Width     8.000
```

FIGURE 2.1: The PrintGraph screen and Main Menu options (Release 1A). This screen displays the default directories and device driver and interface settings. You choose the Configure option to change these default settings. To save them permanently on the PrintGraph Disk, use its Save Replace option before you exit the PrintGraph Menu.

OPTIONS		DEFAULTS	COMMENTS
Files	Pictures	B:\	Set default drive and directory that contains graph files.
	Fonts	A:\	Set default drive and directory that contains fonts files.
	Quit		Return to Configure Menu.
Device			Select printer or plotter to use by marking it from list of device drivers.
Page	Length	11.000	Length of printed page in inches
	Width	8.000	Width of printed page in inches—can set to 13.6 for 132-column printer
	Quit		Return to Configure Menu.
Interface	1	Parallel	Parallel interface from LPT1
	2	Serial	RS232C serial interface from COM1. Set baud rate as follows: 1 = 110 2 = 150 3 = 300 4 = 600 5 = 1200 6 = 2400 7 = 4800 8 = 9600 9 = 19200
	3	Second Parallel	Parallel interface from LPT2
	4	Second Serial	RS232C serial interface from COM2. Set baud rate as shown above for option 2.
Save	Cancel		Do not save setting changes.
	Replace		Save setting changes.
Reset			Return to default settings.
Quit			Exit Configure Menu and return to PrintGraph Menu.

TABLE 2.5: The Configure Menu Options (Release 1A)

Choose the Fonts option on the Configure Menu to change the drive and directory where Lotus 1-2-3 looks for the PrintGraph files that control the different lettering styles, or fonts, that you assign to your graphs before printing (see Chapter 26). These files are located on the PrintGraph Disk. If you have a hard disk, these will be on drive C along with all of the other program files. For example, if your Lotus 1-2-3 files were located in a directory named \123, change this setting by entering **C:\123.** Then choose the Quit option to return to the Configure Menu.

Changing the Graphics Device

To change the graphics device (the printer or plotter) you are using, choose the Device option on the Configure Menu. Figures 2.2 and 2.3 show the various types of printers and plotters that are listed under that option. To select a new device, use the ↓ or ↑ keys to move the cursor to the printer or plotter desired. Press the space bar to mark it with a # symbol; then press Return (marked Enter on this screen). Notice that when you select an IBM or Epson dot-matrix printer, you can choose between different densities that affect the darkness of the printed graph.

```
Copyright 1982, 1983 Lotus Development Corp.  All Rights Reserved.          POINT
--------------------------------------------------------------------------------
Select graph output device

================================================================================
          Type of Graphic Output
   -----------------------------------------
   Anadex 9620A Silent Scribe Printer         [Space] bar moves mark
 # Epson FX80 Printer, Single Density Mode    [Enter] selects marked device
   Epson FX80 Printer, Double Density Mode    [Escape] exits
   Epson FX80 Printer, Triple Density Mode          without changing device
   Epson FX80 Printer, Quad Density Mode      [Home] goes to beginning of list
   HP 7470A Plotter                           [End] goes to end of list
   IBM Graphics Printer, Single Dens. Mode    [Up] moves cursor up
   IBM Graphics Printer, Double Dens. Mode    [Down] moves cursor down
   IBM Graphics Printer, Triple Dens. Mode     List will scroll if cursor moved
   IBM Graphics Printer, Quad Density Mode     beyond top or bottom of display.
   Epson MX80 or MX100, Single Dens. Mode
   Epson MX80 or MX100, Double Dens. Mode
   Epson MX80 or MX100, Triple Dens. Mode
   NEC 8023 Printer
   Okidata 82A or 83A Printer
```

FIGURE 2.2: The first part of the library of device drivers supported by Release 1A. The default device, the Epson FX-80 printer, is indicated by the # symbol preceding it.

Using a Serial Port; Selecting a Baud Rate

If you select a device that does not use the first parallel interface (connected to LPT1), you must also use the Interface option on the Configure Menu. If the device is connected to a serial port, you must also select a baud rate (the speed at which data is sent in characters per second). Check your printer or plotter manual to determine the fastest speed at which it can send data. If you cannot locate this information, try setting the baud rate at 1200, option 5.

Saving Your Changed Settings

After you change any of the settings on the Configure Menu, you can save them permanently on the PrintGraph Disk or just use them for the current printing session. The Save Replace option makes the new settings the permanent defaults, and they will be in effect whenever you use the

```
Copyright 1982, 1983 Lotus Development Corp.  All Rights Reserved.          POINT
--------------------------------------------------------------------------------
Select graph output device

================================================================================
          Type of Graphic Output
 ------------------------------------------
   HP 7470A Plotter                            [Space] bar moves mark
   IBM Graphics Printer, Single Dens. Mode     [Enter] selects marked device
   IBM Graphics Printer, Double Dens. Mode     [Escape] exits
   IBM Graphics Printer, Triple Dens. Mode          without changing device
   IBM Graphics Printer, Quad Density Mode     [Home] goes to beginning of list
   Epson MX80 or MX100, Single Dens. Mode      [End] goes to end of list
   Epson MX80 or MX100, Double Dens. Mode      [Up] moves cursor up
   Epson MX80 or MX100, Triple Dens. Mode      [Down] moves cursor down
   NEC 8023 Printer                             List will scroll if cursor moved
   Okidata 82A or 83A Printer                   beyond top or bottom of display.
   Okidata 93, 92 or 84 Printer
   Prism 80 or 132, Single Density Mode
   Prism 80 or 132, Double Density Mode
   Strobe 100 Plotter
   Sweet P Plotter
```

FIGURE 2.3: The rest of the library of device drivers supported by Release 1A. To set a new default device, you use the ↑ and ↓ keys to move the highlight to it. Then press the space bar and Return (marked Enter on this menu). Press Esc to return to the Configure Menu without making any changes.

PrintGraph Utility in the future. The Reset option allows you to set all of the changes you have made during this session back to the default settings. For information on using the other PrintGraph Menu options and printing your graphs, see Chapter 26.

Installing Lotus 1-2-3 Release 2

The installation program for Release 2 is a menu-driven program that prompts you for all the information it requires to customize Lotus 1-2-3 to your hardware. After making backup copies of your program disks or copying them onto your hard disk, you have only to run this program. You can rerun this program at any time afterwards by choosing the Install option from the Lotus Access System Menu. This makes it easy to inform the program about changes you may make to your hardware. The following sections give you specific information about running the installation program.

The Program Disks (Release 2)

Release 2 consists of the following six program disks:

1. System Disk
2. Backup System Disk
3. Utility Disk
4. PrintGraph Disk
5. Install Library Disk
6. A View of 1-2-3 Disk

The original System Disk contains the program necessary to load Lotus 1-2-3 into the computer's memory. Because it is copy protected, a backup System Disk is provided in case the original becomes damaged.

The Utility Disk contains the Install program, which you use to configure Lotus 1-2-3 to your hardware and program files, as well as the Translate utility, which you use to transfer data between Lotus 1-2-3 and other application files.

The PrintGraph Disk contains the program files required to print the graphs that you create with the system.

The Install Library Disk contains a library of driver files that configure Lotus 1-2-3 to the type of display and printers you are using. You use this disk along with the Utility Disk when you run the Install program.

The last disk, called A View of 1-2-3, contains an interactive tutorial program that acquaints you with the basic features of Lotus 1-2-3 and how they work. If you have never used Lotus 1-2-3, go through the Introduction and Sample Session demonstrations. If you have just upgraded to Release 2, take the time to go through the New Features demonstration.

Making Backup Copies (Release 2)

The four program disks other than the two System Disks are not copy protected, so you can use the DOS COPY program to make backups of them. Table 2.6 shows you the steps for making these backup copies on a two-drive system. Make your backup, or working, copies before running the Install program.

1. Place a copy of your DOS system disk in drive A and turn on the computer. Enter the date and time as prompted.
2. Format four new or recycled disks in drive B by using the DOS FORMAT command as follows:

   A>FORMAT B:/V <Return>
3. Label your four newly formatted disks as follows: Utility Disk, PrintGraph Disk, Install Library Disk, and A View of 1-2-3 Disk. You can also mark them as backups by adding "BAK" or "backup copy" or "working copy."
4. Replace the DOS system disk in drive A with the Lotus 1-2-3 Utility Disk.
5. Put your newly formatted disk marked Utility Disk in drive B.
6. Type the following command, making sure that you add a space after the word **copy** and the designation **a:*.***:

   A>COPY A:*.* B:/V <Return>
7. When the copying is finished, remove both the master Utility Disk and your new working copy from drives A and B, respectively. Repeat this same procedure with the PrintGraph, Install Library, and A View of 1-2-3 Disks.

TABLE 2.6: Making Backup Copies of the Lotus 1-2-3 Release 2 Program Disks

Copying COMMAND.COM to the Program Disks (Release 2)

There is insufficient room on the Release 2 System Disk to include all the DOS system files on it. You will not be able to start your computer with the Lotus 1-2-3 System Disk in drive A, as you may have become accustomed to with the earlier version. Instead, you will have to use a separate working copy of the DOS disk to load these operating system files and then replace it with the Lotus 1-2-3 System Disk each time you turn on your computer to work with the program.

There is room, however, to copy one of the DOS system files called COMMAND.COM on the Lotus 1-2-3 System Disk. By doing so, you can return to the DOS prompt without getting an error message when exiting the program. Copy this file onto both copies of your Lotus 1-2-3 System Disk as well as onto your backup (working) copies of the four other program disks. Follow the instructions given in Table 2.7.

Copying the Program on a Hard Disk (Release 2)

If you will be using Lotus 1-2-3 with a hard disk, you will want to copy all of the program files into a directory on drive C. Many people find it convenient to name this directory \123 and place it directly beneath the root directory (called C:\). However, if you are upgrading to Release 2 and were previously using Release 1A on the hard disk, you probably already have a C:\123 directory containing the Lotus 1-2-3 files for this version. In this case, you should remove all of the Release 1A program files in this directory before you copy the Release 2 files into it.

1. Place a working copy of your DOS system disk in drive A.
2. Place the Lotus 1-2-3 System Disk in drive B. Make sure that it does not have a write-protect tab.
3. Type the command as follows, making sure that you add a space after the word **copy** and after the designation **a:command.com**:

   A>COPY A:COMMAND.COM B:/V <Return>
4. Replace the Lotus 1-2-3 System Disk in drive B with the backup System Disk and enter the same command. Repeat this procedure for your four remaining program disks.

TABLE 2.7: Copying the COMMAND.COM Program to the Lotus 1-2-3 Release 2 Program Disks

In the rare case that you wish to keep both versions of the program on the hard disk, you will have to create a new directory with a different name on drive C. Most of the time, however, continuing to use both versions is not a good idea, considering all the new features that Release 2 offers and the incompatibilities between the two versions' files (see "Lotus 1-2-3—Release 1A and Release 2" in Chapter 1).

To copy the Lotus 1-2-3 program on your hard disk, follow the instructions in Table 2.8.

Equipment Inventory (Release 2)

The next step is to use the new Install program to configure Lotus 1-2-3 to the hardware you are using. Before you run the Install program, it is a good idea to take an inventory of your system. You will need to supply the following information:

- The make of your computer—such as IBM PC, IBM PC AT, IBM 3270-PC, Compaq, AT&T 6300, and so forth.
- Type of monitor and display card—such as color monitor with Color/Graphics Adapter, enhanced color monitor with EGA (Enhanced Graphics Adapter), monochrome monitor with Monochrome Adapter, monochrome monitor with Hercules Graphics Card, and so forth.
- Type of text printer(s)—such as Diablo 630, Epson FX-80/100, IBM Graphics Printer, HP LaserJet, and so forth.
- Type of graphics printer(s) and/or plotter(s)—such as Epson FX-80/100, IBM PC Graphics Printer, Amdek Amplot II Plotter, HP 7470A Plotter, and so forth.

Configuring the Default Printer(s) (Release 2)

When you install Release 2, you can designate more than one type of text printer and graphics printer for use in Lotus 1-2-3. Later, you designate which text printer to use with the /Worksheet Global Default Printer Name command (see "Customizing Lotus 1-2-3 Release 2" later in this chapter). You can designate which of your graphics devices is to be used from the PrintGraph Menu that is accessed from the Lotus Access System Menu (see Chapter 26). If you have only one printer that you use for text

If you are upgrading to Release 2 and you already have a Lotus 1-2-3 directory containing Release 1A program files on drive C:

1. Turn on the computer and make your Lotus 1-2-3 directory current by entering

   C>CD\123 <Return>

   (Substitute the name you have given to this directory if you named it something other than \123.) Obtain a directory listing by typing **dir** to make sure you are in the directory containing the Release 1A files before you go on to the next step.
2. Delete all of the Release 1A files by entering

   C>DEL *.* (confirm this by typing y and pressing Return)

   Then proceed to step 5.

If you have not used Release 1A and have not yet created a directory for your Lotus 1-2-3 program files:

3. Turn on the computer and use the MKDIR command to create a new Lotus 1-2-3 directory as follows:

   C>MKDIR C:\123 <Return>
4. Make this new directory current by entering

   C>CD\123 <Return>
5. Place the Lotus 1-2-3 System Disk in drive A. Enter the following command, making sure that you add a space after the word **copy**:

   C>COPY A:*.*/V <Return>
6. Remove the System Disk and replace it with the one of the other four Lotus 1-2-3 program disks (the order is not important) and repeat the copy command listed in step 5. Repeat this procedure until you have copied all of the files from the Utility, PrintGraph, Install Library, and A View of 1-2-3 Disks.
7. If you wish, you can also create a subdirectory for data files beneath the \123 directory that now contains the program files. To do this, enter the following commands:

   C>CD\ <Return>
   C>MKDIR c:\123\DATA <Return>

   You can create as many subdirectories as you need by giving the same MKDIR command as shown above, substituting a name you provide for **data.**

TABLE 2.8: Copying the Lotus 1-2-3 Release 2 Program Files onto a Hard Disk

and graphics, as might be the case if you use the HP LaserJet or some kind of Epson dot-matrix printer, you do not have to make any changes to either of these defaults.

During the installation procedure when you give the program all of this information about the hardware you are using, your responses tell Lotus 1-2-3 which drivers to use. At the end of the process, these drivers are saved in a special file named 123.SET unless you give it another name. The file named 123.SET is always used as the default whenever you use Lotus 1-2-3.

Defining Additional Configurations (Release 2)

In Release 2 you can store more than one hardware configuration (or driver set) on the System Disk in separate files that carry the extension .SET. This allows you to use Lotus 1-2-3 on different computers that do not have the same hardware configuration. For instance, you could set up your Lotus 1-2-3 System Disk so that it will work with both your IBM XT at work, using a monochrome monitor with a Hercules Graphics Card, and with your Compaq portable computer at home. To do this, you create two of these files and save the one for the IBM XT under the default file name 123.SET and the other under the name COMPAQ.SET.

When you enter the file names for additional driver sets, you do not have to add the .SET extension; the program does this automatically for you. When you use Lotus 1-2-3 on a computer that requires the alternate driver set, you start the program up by giving the startup command plus the file name of the alternate driver set. For instance, to start Lotus 1-2-3 on your home computer in the example given above, you would enter the startup command as **123 compaq.**

Because the free space on the Lotus 1-2-3 System Disk is limited, keep the number of driver sets you create to a minimum. If you use the program on only one system, it is best just to save that driver set on the System Disk under the default name 123.SET.

Storing Additional Configuration Files

If you need different configuration files and you don't have enough room to save all of them on the System Disk, you can save them on a blank, formatted disk. Make sure that you back up all of the .SET files stored on the System Disk on this blank disk as well.

To save extra driver set files on this disk, replace the System Disk with it when the program asks you to put the System Disk in drive A to save the newly named driver set file. When the program tells you to replace the System Disk with the PrintGraph Disk, press Esc to return to the Install Menu.

Starting the Program with Another Configuration

To start Lotus 1-2-3 on a different computer using one of these extra driver sets, delete one of unneeded the driver files on the System Disk and replace it with the driver set file you want to use. To use the program again on your original computer, you must delete this extra driver set and replace it with the original driver set file required to run it.

Using the Install Program (Release 2)

To complete the installation process, follow the steps outlined in Table 2.9 if you have a two-disk-drive system and those in Table 2.10 if you have a hard disk system. Make sure that you understand the appropriate

1. Place your working copy of the Utility Disk in drive A and type the following command:

   A>INSTALL <Return>

2. At the Main Menu (shown in Figure 2.4), press Return to select First-Time Installation.
3. When prompted, replace the Utility Disk in drive A with your working copy of the Install Library.
4. Follow the step-by-step instructions that prompt you to respond to various questions about the hardware you are using. Press F1 if you need on-line help.
5. If you are creating only one driver set, save it under the default file name 123.SET. If you have several driver files, give each a different name no more than eight characters long. You will be prompted to save these files on the System, PrintGraph, and A View of 1-2-3 Disks in succession.
6. When you have finished defining and saving the driver set, you can look at its contents by pressing F10. Figure 2.5 shows you the way this information is displayed on the screen.
7. Return to the Main Menu and choose the Exit Install Program option.

TABLE 2.9: Using the Lotus 1-2-3 Install Program on a Two-Disk-Drive System (Release 2)

response to each of the questions the program asks of you. Figure 2.4 shows you the Main Menu of the Install program, which appears when you start this program.

1. Make sure that the directory containing your Lotus 1-2-3 program files is current and then enter the following command:

   C>INSTALL <Return>

2. At the Main Menu (shown in Figure 2.4), press Return to select First-Time Installation.
3. Follow the step-by-step instructions that prompt you to respond to various questions about the hardware you are using. Press F1 if you need on-line help.
4. If you are creating only one driver set, save it under the default file name 123.SET. If you have several driver files, give each a different name no more than eight characters long.
5. When you have finished defining and saving the driver set, you can look at its contents by pressing F10. Figure 2.5 shows you the way this information is displayed on the screen.
6. Return to the Main Menu and choose the Exit Install Program option.

TABLE 2.10: Using the Lotus 1-2-3 Install Program on a Hard Disk System (Release 2)

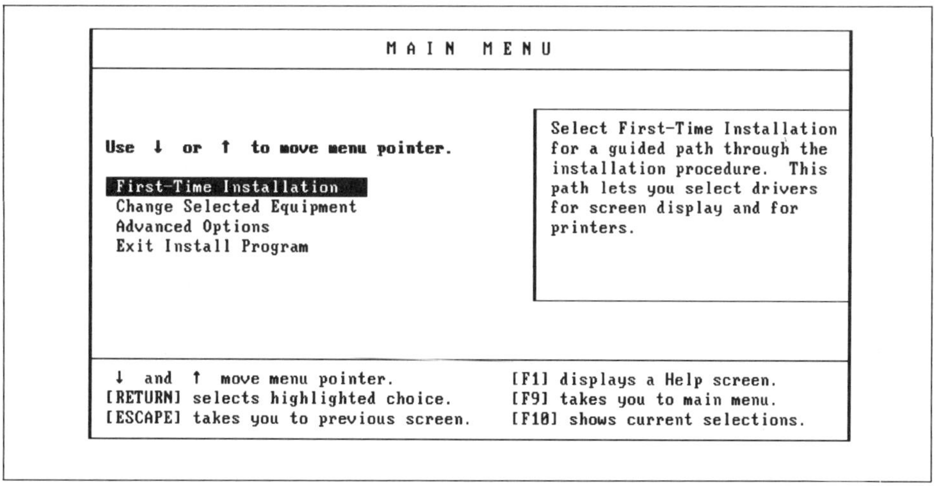

FIGURE 2.4: The Install Main Menu. In addition to selecting the first option, which you use the first time you are configuring Lotus 1-2-3 to your hardware, you can select Change Selected Equipment to update equipment changes on the default driver file. You can also select Advanced Options, which allows you to modify driver settings or change the program's sorting.

Changing Hardware (Release 2)

If you change your hardware (for example, by replacing your monochrome monitor with a color monitor and Color/Graphics Adapter), you can use the Install program to make the appropriate changes to your driver file. At this point you do not need to run the Install program from the operating system prompt. Instead, you can start it by choosing the Install option from the Lotus Access System (enter **lotus** as the startup command).

Advanced Options: Changing the Sort Order in the Spreadsheet (Release 2)

The Advanced Options choice on the Main Menu allows you to change the sorting order that the /Data Sort command uses to order your spreadsheet data and database records (see Chapter 20). As you can see in Figure 2.5, the default is Numbers first (after the heading Collating). There are

```
------------------ Current selections in 123.SET ------------------

Text Display          COMPAQ Display·
Graph Display         IBM or COMPAQ Hi-Res·
Keyboard              IBM Keyboard·
Printer Int.          IBM Printer Interface·
File Trans.           IBM PC or compatible·
Collating             Numbers first·
Math Unit             Coprocessor Floating Point Driver·
                      Software Floating Point Driver
Text Printer          Epson·FX, RX, and JX series; LQ-1500·
                      IBM·Quietwriter or Graphics Printer·
Graph Printer         Epson·FX and RX series
                      IBM·Graphics Printer

------------------ Press [ESCAPE] to continue ------------------
```

FIGURE 2.5: Viewing the contents of a driver set. This figure shows the current selections in effect for the default driver file, 123.SET. There are two monitor display settings, one for displaying data in the spreadsheet and the other for graphs. The Collating setting controls the sorting order for spreadsheet data and database records. You can change the Numbers first default by selecting Advanced Options from the Install Main Menu. Also notice that the same two printers were designated both text and graphics. The printer type listed first in both cases is used as the default device when printing worksheets or graphs.

three options for Collating: ASCII, Numbers first, and Numbers last. When you use either Numbers first or Numbers last, Lotus 1-2-3 does not differentiate between uppercase and lowercase letters in the range to be sorted. With Numbers first, all numerical entries in the range are placed before labels arranged in ascending sort order. Just the opposite is true if you change it to Numbers last. In ASCII sort order, numbers are placed before uppercase letters, and lowercase letters follow uppercase.

To modify the Collating default, select Advanced Options from the Main Menu of the Install program. Figure 2.6 shows the screen that appears. Highlight the Collating option on this screen and press Return. This takes you to a Collating Sequence screen that contains the three choices ASCII, Numbers first, and Numbers last. To make a different sort order the program default, you merely highlight it and press Return.

Making Lotus 1-2-3 Bootable from the Hard Disk (Release 2)

Lotus 1-2-3 Release 2 allows you to copy the hidden copy-protection files that the program usually looks for on the System Disk onto drive C. After

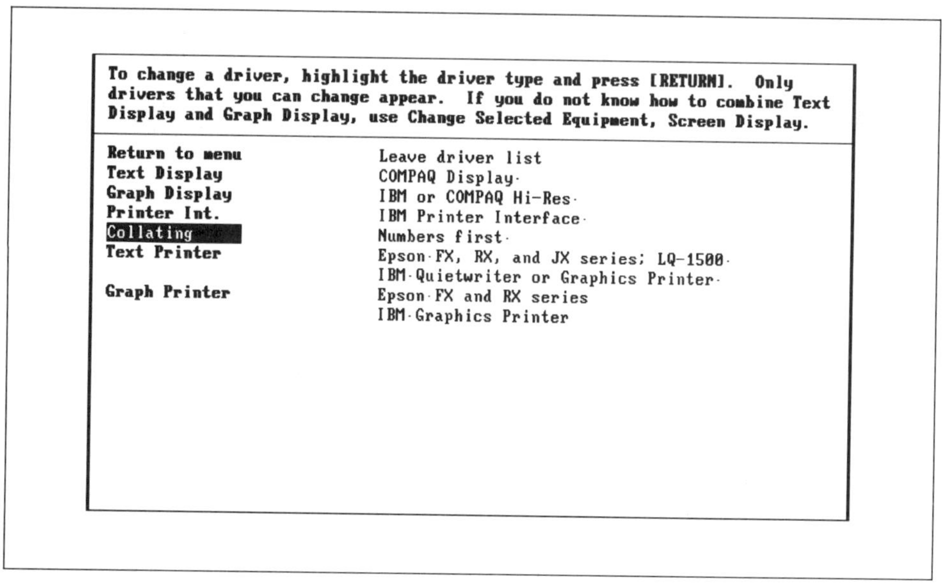

FIGURE 2.6: The Advanced Options screen. From this screen, you can modify the driver settings listed here, change the sorting order Lotus 1-2-3 uses, or both. The three choices for Collating are ASCII, Numbers first, and Numbers Last.

you do this, you will be able to start Lotus 1-2-3 directly from the hard disk without having to have your System Disk in drive A.

To do this, the System Disk should be in drive A and the directory containing your Lotus 1-2-3 program files should be current. Then type the appropriate command as follows:

C>copyhard <Return>

You will be prompted through the routine. Make sure that your System Disk does not have a write-protect tab on it.

In Case of Hard Disk Problems . . .

Once you have used one of these routines to transfer the copy-protection files onto your hard disk, you can no longer use your System Disk to load Lotus 1-2-3. If something happens to your hard disk (such as a crash that necessitates replacing the hard disk), use your backup System Disk to copy the program files back onto drive C. If you have to take your disk in for repairs, use the COPYHARD /U command to remove the copy-protection files and to make your System Disk functional again.

Also note that you cannot use the DOS BACKUP and RESTORE commands or a similar backup system with a streaming tape to archive and then restore your files to drive C. Doing so makes it impossible to boot Lotus 1-2-3 from the hard disk and forces you to rely on your backup System Disk (your only functional copy) to use the program.

Customizing Lotus 1-2-3 Release 2

You can customize Lotus 1-2-3 in many ways by using the options on the Default menu. To reach this menu, you use the command /Worksheet Global Default (/WGD). Table 2.11 presents the options and default settings on this menu. Figure 2.7 shows the screen that presents information about the current default settings. You access this screen by issuing the command /Worksheet Global Default Status (/WGDS).

Whenever you start up Lotus 1-2-3, the program looks for the default configuration in a file named 123.CNF on the System Disk. This file contains settings that control the following:

- The printer you are using and its interface
- The margin settings, page length, and whether you are using single sheets (Wait) or continuous-feed paper in printing

COMMAND SEQUENCE	MENU OPTIONS	COMMENTS
/Worksheet		
Global		
Default		
Printer		
Interface	1 Parallel	(default)
	2 Serial	
	3 Parallel 2	
	4 Serial 2	
	5 DOS Device LPT1:	(Choices 5–8 are virtual devices for networks)
	6 DOS Device LPT2:	
	7 DOS Device LPT3:	
	8 DOS Device LPT4:	
Auto-LF	No	(default)
	Yes	
Left	4 columns	
Right	76 columns	
Top	2 lines	
Bottom	2 lines	
Pg-Length	66 lines	
Wait	No	(default)
	Yes	
Setup	(blank)	(default). You can specify control characters to be sent to your printer prior to printing.
Name		Select new text printer by name (the first text printer selected with the Install program becomes the default).
Quit		Return to Default Menu.
Directory	A:\	Set default drive and directory for saving and retrieving data files.
Status		Display current defaults.
Update		Save changes made to default settings.

TABLE 2.11: Lotus 1-2-3 Release 2 Default Menu Options and Default Settings

COMMAND SEQUENCE	MENU OPTIONS	COMMENTS
Other		
International		
Punctuation		Select punctuation for numbers and arguments of functions.
Currency		Select currency symbol as prefix or suffix of number or change the symbol (such as $) used to represent currency.
Date		Select default date format.
Time		Select default time format.
Quit		Return to Default Menu.
Help		
Instant		Quick help access—help files must remain in program drive.
Removable		Slower help access—help files can be removed from program drive.
Clock		
Standard		Uses DD-MMM-YY date and HH:MM AM/PM time format.
International		Uses MM-DD-YY date and HH:MM 24-hour clock format.
None		Suppress time and date on screen display.
Quit		Return to Lotus 1-2-3 spreadsheet.

TABLE 2.11: Lotus 1-2-3 Release 2 Default Menu Options and Default Settings (continued)

- The drive and directory where your Lotus 1-2-3 worksheets and graphs are to be saved and retrieved
- Default settings for the display of currency, punctuation in numbers, dates, and time
- The configuration for accessing the on-line help facility

You can customize all of these settings from the Default Menu.

```
A1:                                                              STAT

  Printer:                                 International:
    Interface..... Parallel 1                Punctuation..... A
    Auto-linefeed. No                              Point Dot
                                                Argument Comma
    Margins                                    Thousands Comma
       Left 4      Top 2
      Right 76  Bottom 2                     Currency........ $ (Prefix)
                                             Date format D4.. A (MM/DD/YY)
    Page length... 66                        Time format D8.. A (HH:MM:SS)
    Wait.......... No
    Setup string..
    Name.......... IBM Quietwriter or Graphics Printer

  Directory at startup: C:\123\DATA

  Help access method: Removable

  Clock on screen: Standard


23-Jun-86  03:43 PM
```

FIGURE 2.7: The Default Status screen. To access the information displayed on this screen, issue the command /Worksheet Global Default Status (/WGDS). Unlike Release 1A, Release 2 displays the name of the default printer (below Setup) as well as the type of interface. This screen also gives you information about the date, time, currency, and numerical punctuation formats currently in effect.

Customizing the Text Printer and Interface

If you specified more than one text printer during installation, the first one you selected becomes the program default. To make another printer the default printer, select Printer Name from the Default Menu. Lotus 1-2-3 assigns numbers to each of the printers you select. It also shows you the name of the printer associated with each number. To select a new default device, type the appropriate number.

If the new printer does not use the same interface as the previous default printer, use the Interface option to change it. In Release 2, this menu has eight options. Options 1 to 4 correspond to the numbers used in Release 1A: (1) a parallel interface connected to LPT1; (2) a serial interface connected to COM1; (3) a second parallel interface connected to LPT2; (4) a second serial interface connected to COM2. The options numbered 5 to 8 refer to virtual devices that you assign and access through DOS on a local area network.

If you select one of the serial interfaces, you must also supply the baud rate (the transmission speed in characters per second). There are nine possible baud rates to choose from (refer back to Table 2.5). You must also set your printer to 8 bits, no parity, and 1 stop bit (except at 110 baud, which requires 2 stop bits).

PRINT FORMATS

The Printer Menu also contains many options for controlling the formatting of your printing. After making changes to these setings, use the Quit option to return to the Default Menu.

Line Feeds The Auto-LF option controls whether a line feed is automatically given after every carriage return (advances the paper one line). Because most printers do not give this signal, the default value is No. If your reports come out double spaced, change this setting to Yes.

Margins You can set new margin values for the left, right, top, and bottom margins. The left and right margins can be set anywhere from 0 to 240 and the top and bottom margins from 0 to 32. You will usually make temporary changes to these settings by using the /Printer Print (File) Options command (see Chapter 25) rather than change them permanently with the Default Menu. The same is true of the Pg-Length option, which sets the number of lines per printed page. The default is 66, which is standard for an 8½ by 11-inch page. You can change this value to anywhere from 10 to 100.

Pause after Printing If your printer takes only single sheets of paper as opposed to fan-folded paper with holes for a tractor feed, change the Wait option on the Printer Menu from its default of No to Yes. This instructs Lotus 1-2-3 to pause after printing each page to allow you to add another sheet of paper.

Print Enhancements The last formatting option on this menu is Setup. It allows you to add special control codes for printing enhancements like italics, compressed print, and the like. You usually specify these through the /Printer

Print (File) Options Setup command (see Chapter 25) unless you have control codes that should be used on every Lotus 1-2-3 report you produce.

Changing the Default Directory (Release 2)

You use the Directory option on the Default Menu to tell Lotus 1-2-3 where you usually want the program to save your worksheets and retrieve your data files. The default setting is the one from which you start the program (drive A in a two-drive system and drive C in a hard disk system).

If you want to save your data files on a subdirectory of the Lotus 1-2-3 directory, you should change the default directory by entering the complete path name of where your files are stored, such as **C:\123\DATA.** If you are using a two-disk-drive system where you keep your data disks in drive B, change the drive to B:\. When you use this option, press Esc to clear the line of its current drive and directory.

Changing Other Formatting Options (Release 2)

The Other option on the Default Menu (/WGDO) allows you to control a number of formatting options. Three groups of default settings are controlled from this menu: International, Help, and Clock. The first and last choices regulate default entry and display formats in the worksheet for the punctuation used in numbers and functions as well as for currency, date, and time. The second, Help, controls the method for accessing on-line help screens and is discussed in the next section.

Punctuation in Numbers and Functions

With the International option, you can change the type of punctuation used when formatting ranges of numbers in the worksheet (see /Range Format in Chapter 5) as well as the type of punctuation used when entering functions (Chapters 11–18). There are eight combinations from which to choose, shown in Table 2.12. The first option, A, is the default setting. It uses the American system of separating thousands with a comma and decimal places with a period. It also uses commas to separate arguments in any Lotus 1-2-3 function (this punctuation is used in all the examples and figures in this handbook). The other common punctuation for numbers

OPTION	THOUSANDS SEPARATOR	DECIMAL SEPARATOR	EXAMPLE	ARGUMENT SEPARATOR	EXAMPLE
A	Comma	Period	1,500.25	Comma	@DATE(86,2,1)
B	Period	Comma	1.500,25	Period	@DATE(86.2.1)
C	Comma	Period	1,500.25	Semicolon	@DATE(86;2;1)
D	Period	Comma	1.500,25	Semicolon	@DATE(86;2;1)
E	Space	Period	1 500.25	Comma	@DATE(86,2,1)
F	Space	Comma	1 500,25	Period	@DATE(86.2.1)
G	Space	Period	1 500.25	Semicolon	@DATE(86;2;1)
H	Space	Comma	1 500,25	Semicolon	@DATE(86;2;1)

TABLE 2.12: Punctuation Options on the International Menu (Release 2)

favored in some European countries is just the opposite of the American system. It uses the period to delimit thousands and the comma to delimit decimal places. As you can see from Table 2.12, you can choose between several permutations involving a mix of different argument and number delimiters. Note that the A–H options on the Lotus 1-2-3 menu display these punctuation symbols in the order of decimal separator, argument separator, thousands separator. This order has been changed in Table 2.12 to make it easier to understand their effect in the worksheet.

CURRENCY FORMATS

You can also control the symbol used to denote currency when you assign the currency format to ranges in the worksheet (/Range Format Currency), as well as whether it is placed before or after the number. The default is the $ symbol, which always precedes the number. To change to a new currency symbol like the pound or yen, enter its code from the Lotus International Character Set (referred to as LICS) using the Compose key (Alt-F1). These codes are shown in Appendix B of this handbook along with instructions on how to enter them. If, for example, you change the currency to the pound symbol by entering its LICS code, you could also change the default from prefix to suffix if you want this symbol to come after the amount, as in 340£.

Date Formats

The Date option controls the date formats in the worksheet, /Range Format D4 or /Range Format D5 (see Chapter 5). The difference between these two displays is illustrated in Table 2.13, which shows the four choices on this menu. Format D4 differs from D5 only in its inclusion of two digits for the year in the display. Option A is the program default. Any change that you make affects how you enter the arguments for the @DATEVALUE function (see Chapter 14).

Time Formats

The Time option works like the Date option. It controls either /Range Format D8 or /Range Format D9 (see Chapter 5). The only difference between D8 and D9 is that D8 displays the seconds as well as the hours and minutes. Lotus 1-2-3 uses the format D9 for displaying the time in the clock at the bottom of the spreadsheet. Option A is the program default. Any change that you make to this setting affects the arguments for the @TIME function (see Chapter 14). Table 2.14 shows the choices for this option.

The Clock option affects the on-screen clock display that Lotus 1-2-3 includes at the bottom of the spreadsheet. If you do not want the current date and time displayed, choose the None option. The default is the first option, Standard. It displays the date and time as 22-Sep-86 and 3:45 PM, respectively. You can change it to the International option, which places the month before the day and year and uses a 24-hour clock instead of the

OPTION	DATE FORMAT (D4)	EXAMPLE	DATE FORMAT (D5)	EXAMPLE
A	MM/DD/YY	10/20/87	MM/DD	10/20
B	DD/MM/YY	20/10/87	DD/MM	20/10
C	DD.MM.YY	20.10.87	DD.MM	10.20
D	YY-MM-DD	87-10-20	MM-DD	10-20

TABLE 2.13: Date Format Options on the International Menu (Release 2)

OPTION	TIME FORMAT (D8)	EXAMPLE	TIME FORMAT (D9)	EXAMPLE
A	HH:MM:SS	11:45:30	HH:MM	11:45
B	HH.MM.SS	11.45.30	HH.MM	11.45
C	HH,MM,SS	11,45,30	HH,MM	11,45
D	HHhMMmSSs	11h45m30s	HHhMMm	11h45m

TABLE 2.14: Time Format Options on the International Menu (Release 2)

AM/PM convention. In the example above, it would change the display to 09/22/86 and 15:45. If you change the International Date default, it also affects the International clock's time display.

Accessing Help (Release 2)

The Help option allows you to choose between two methods, Instant and Removable, for accessing Lotus 1-2-3's on-line help screens. The default is Removable, in which the help file is closed when you leave help screens and return to the spreadsheet. This means that you can remove the disk containing help files during your session. It also means that help access is slower than with the Instant method. If you use Lotus 1-2-3 on a two-disk-drive system, leave this default set to Removable.

With the Instant help method, the help file stays open after you use the help facility the first time. This gives you faster access to the various help screens during your session in Lotus 1-2-3. Choose the Instant option if you use the program on a hard disk system.

Saving Your Changed Printer, Directory, or Other Menu Settings (Release 2)

After you make any changes to the options on the Printer, Directory, or Other menus, choose the Update option to save your changes before you select the Quit option to return to the spreadsheet.

Customizing PrintGraph Defaults (Release 2)

To change the default graphics device or directories where your graph files (those saved with the /Graph Save command and given the extension .PIC) or Lotus 1-2-3 graphics program files are kept, use the PrintGraph Menu from the Lotus Access System. To access this menu, start the program with the command **lotus** rather than **123.** The PrintGraph option is the second one on the Lotus Access System Menu. You can also start the PrintGraph program directly from DOS by typing **pgraph.** If you use this command to start it, the PrintGraph program files must be accessible. If you are using a two-drive system, the PrintGraph disk must be in drive A; if you are using a hard disk, the PrintGraph files must be located in the current directory.

THE PRINTGRAPH MENU

The PrintGraph Menu contains six options. You use the second one, Settings, to change the graphics or default directories.

Figure 2.8 shows you the Settings Menu options as well as the information on the default PrintGraph screen. Notice that the program defaults in effect are shown in the right column under HARDWARE SETUP. The Graphs and Fonts directories are both in the root directory of drive A.

The Graphs-Directory Option To change hardware setup entries, select the Hardware option from the menu. Then, to change the drive and directory where your graph files are saved, use the first option, Graphs-Directory. If you are using a two-disk-drive system, change this default to B:\. If you are using a hard disk system, you may want to change it to the directory where you store your data files on drive C:, unless you store all of your graphs on a data disk in drive A. For example, you might set it to C:\123\DATA if this is where most of your graph files are saved.

The Fonts-Directory Option To modify the default directory where Lotus 1-2-3 looks for the graph files that control the various lettering styles or fonts that you can assign to graphs before printing, use the Fonts-Directory

```
Copyright 1985 Lotus Development Corp.  All Rights Reserved.  Release 2   MENU
Set directory containing graphs
Graphs-Directory  Fonts-Directory  Interface  Printer  Size-Paper  Quit

  GRAPH        IMAGE OPTIONS                         HARDWARE SETUP
  IMAGES        Size                  Range Colors    Graphs Directory:
  SELECTED       Top         .395  X                    A:\
                 Left        .750  A                  Fonts Directory:
                 Width      6.500  B                    A:\
                 Height     4.691  C                  Interface:
                 Rotate      .000  D                    Parallel 1
                                   E                  Printer Type:
                Font               F
                 1  BLOCK1                            Paper Size
                 2  BLOCK1                              Width        8.500
                                                        Length      11.000

                                                     ACTION OPTIONS
                                                      Pause: No   Eject: No
```

FIGURE 2.8: Release 2 PrintGraph Settings Menu options and the PrintGraph defaults. This screen shows the Settings options running from Graphs-Directory to Size-Paper. You can use these options to configure new default directories for graphs and the fonts files and graphics printers. Notice that the current defaults are displayed under HARDWARE SETUP in the right column.

option. Leave it as A:\ if you are using a two-disk-drive system. If you are using a hard disk, change it to the directory on drive C that contains all of your Lotus 1-2-3 program files, such as C:\123.

Changing the Default Graphics Device To change the default graphics device, choose the Printer option from this menu. It will take you to a list of the printers and plotters you indicated you had when you ran the Install program. To select a new default printer, move the cursor highlight to it and press the space bar to mark it; then press Return to select it. The PrintGraph display screen is then immediately updated to show your new selection.

Changing the Interface Option If you select a device that uses a different interface, you must also change the Interface option. If the printer or plotter requires a serial interface, you must specify the baud rate, just as you do for a text printer with a serial connection. There are nine possible baud rate settings (refer back to Table 2.5 to review them). Specify the data bits as 8, parity as none, and stop bits as 1 (unless you set the baud rate to 110, in which case you should set the stop bits to 2). Check your printer manual to determine the fastest setting your printer will work with. If you cannot find this information, try 1200 baud (option 5).

Just as with text printers, Release 2 supports four new interfaces called DOS DEVICE LPT1 to LPT4 (choices 5 to 8). These represent virtual devices that are generally used to connect printing devices over a local area network. Only the first four choices represent physical devices that might be connected to your computer (known as LPT1, COM1, LPT2, COM2).

Saving Your Changed Settings

When you have finished making changes to the default printer and directories, use the Save command to have them permanently updated in the PGRAPH.CNF file. This is the file that Lotus 1-2-3 opens to get the default settings whenever you use the PrintGraph program. If you wish to use your settings only for one printing session, do not use the Save option. Once your graphs have been printed, use the Reset option to set all of these defaults back to their original settings (saved in the .CNF file). For information on using the other PrintGraph Menu options and printing your graphs, see Chapter 26.

Installing Hardware to Boost Performance in Release 2

If you have been using Release 1A for some time and have recently upgraded to Release 2, you may be considering purchasing a math coprocessor and an expanded memory board so that you can boost calculation speed. You will also be able to enlarge some of the spreadsheet models you created in Release 1A and create even larger worksheets as you use Release 2. If so, the following sections give you a brief overview of the functions of these hardware additions and how they work with Lotus 1-2-3.

Release 2 and the Math Coprocessors

The new version of Lotus 1-2-3 supports the use of Intel's 8087 or 80287 math coprocessors to decrease processing time for math-intensive spreadsheet applications. If you are using an IBM PC or compatible computer equipped with an 8088 microprocessor, purchase the 8087 chip. If you are using an IBM PC AT or compatible equipped with an 80286 microprocessor, purchase the 80287 chip.

Often referred to as "number crunchers," these chips work with the 8088 or 80286 microprocessor whenever you use an application involving floating-point arithmetic (decimal numbers). Whenever a calculation involving floating-point arithmetic is called for, the math coprocessor kicks in and performs the calculation. This process takes place in a fraction of the time it would take if the regular microprocessor alone had to do the calculating.

Installing these math chips is very simple. The IBM PC and IBM PC AT already contain sockets on their motherboards for these chips. All that is required is locating the proper socket and snapping the chip into place. As for how much of a decrease in calculating time to expect, it depends upon the type of calculation called for in the spreadsheet. Benchmark figures from Intel indicate that formula calculations involving multiplication, division, @SUM, @MAX, and so forth can take place anywhere from 1.5 to 3 times faster, while those involving some of the financial, logarithmic, and trigonometric functions can take place from 5 to 10 times faster than is possible without the use of the math coprocessor.

Release 2 and Expanded Memory

Release 2 supports expanded memory up to 4 MB when you use boards that meet the Lotus/Intel/Microsoft Expanded Memory Specification (abbreviated LIMEMS). This specification allows the IBM PC and compatibles to utilize RAM beyond the 640K limit imposed by the DOS operating system developed by Microsoft. You can populate each expanded memory board with up to 2 MB of memory. You can add two such boards to your computer and have Lotus 1-2-3 take advantage of this additional memory.

Types of Memory

Three terms are used when discussing RAM in the IBM family of personal computers: conventional memory, expanded memory, and extended memory. *Conventional memory* refers to the RAM recognized by the DOS operating system, extending from 0 to 640K. *Expanded memory* ranges from 640K to 8 MB of RAM. Expanded memory refers only to the IBM PC and compatible computers that use the Intel 8088 microprocessor. Lotus 1-2-3 can use only half of the possible expanded memory, up to 4 MB. *Extended memory* refers only to IBM PC AT and compatible computers that use the Intel 80286 microprocessor. It ranges from 1 to 16 MB. Present versions of DOS for the IBM PC AT are as yet incapable of utilizing all of the RAM supported by the 80286 chip and, of course, Release 2 is still only able to access up to 4 MB of this RAM.

Expanded Memory and DOS

The Lotus/Intel/Microsoft EMS uses a technique called *memory paging* whereby memory above 640K is divided into segments referred to as *pages*. It keeps track of the addresses of the memory in these pages by using some of the conventional memory. But this loss of conventional memory is slight compared to the overall memory gain. DOS is always unaware of the existence and addresses of this memory. Even after you have installed a fully populated expanded memory board, DOS will tell you your system has only 640K.

Other Standards

The LIMEMS standard for expanded and extended memory cards is not the only standard that has been developed. A rival specification called the AST/Ashton-Tate/Quadram specification is also available on the market. Fortunately, it is compatible with the LIMEMS standard and will, therefore, work with Release 2. If you purchase an expanded memory board that conforms to this standard rather than the LIMEMS, be aware that Microsoft could make changes to its DOS operating system that do not support it. This will surely not be the case for the LIMEMS standard, which Microsoft has endorsed.

Installing an Expanded Memory Board

Installation of an expanded memory board requires a free slot in your personal computer. You can purchase just the board and install the memory chips yourself, or you can buy the board fully populated. If you buy just the board, you can purchase either 64K or 256K of memory chips to install on it. You cannot mix these chips, and you will need to use 256K chips if you want to have the full 2 MB of memory possible. These boards also come with a software program that controls the expanded memory's use. To be able to use the new memory, you will have to use the program to configure your DOS CONFIG.SYS file on your system disk. Boards like Intel's AboveBoard supply a menu-driven program for setting up the expanded memory drivers on your DOS system disk. This procedure is very similar to using Lotus 1-2-3's Install program to install its driver sets.

If you do not have 640K on your computer when you purchase an expanded memory board, you must allot some of its 2 MB of RAM to filling out the conventional memory. For example, if you still only have 512K on your system, you will have to designate 128K of the expanded memory as conventional memory. You do this by setting switches; the process is explained in the documentation that comes with the board.

How Lotus 1-2-3 Uses Expanded Memory

Lotus 1-2-3 uses expanded memory to store only three types of spreadsheet entries: labels, formulas, and decimal (floating-point) numbers. It stores integers along with the driver sets, range names, formats, and graph settings used in the spreadsheet in the conventional memory below 640K. Because conventional memory is used to store so much about the spreadsheet, you can run out of conventional memory long before you have used up all of your expanded memory. Once this happens, you no longer have access to the expanded memory: you see the MEM indicator and are back in the same predicament that you would be in if you were using only conventional memory (see "Differences in Spreadsheet Size" and "Differences in Memory Management" in Chapter 1). This means that you probably can't make use of much more than 2 MB of expanded memory, even though the theoretical limit is 4 MB.

SUMMARY

This chapter discussed how to install and customize Lotus 1-2-3 to work with your computer system and all of its hardware. With Release 2, you have many options for customizing the program to use it on different computers and change format options for numbers, arguments in functions, dates, and times.

For topics related to the discussions in this chapter, use the following references.

For information on setting printer defaults in the worksheet:

- Chapter 25, "Printing Reports"

For information on setting other PrintGraph options and printing graphs:

- Chapter 26, "Printing and Plotting Graphs"

For information on setting a new default directory for one session:

- Chapter 9, "File Operations"

For information on formatting cell ranges using the date and time formats:

- Chapter 14, "Date and Time Functions"

LOTUS 1-2-3 AND THE IBM PC

Lotus 1-2-3 and the IBM PC

This chapter covers how you use Lotus 1-2-3 with the IBM PC keyboard and how program information is displayed on your screen. The first section discusses the functions assigned to the various keys; the second section presents the way Lotus 1-2-3 handles the on-screen display of the worksheet.

If you are new to Lotus 1-2-3, you need to understand both of these aspects thoroughly in order to use the program effectively. If you have used Release 1A for some time and have just upgraded to Release 2, you will find that changes in keyboard usage and on-screen display are minimal (there is a change in the function of Alt-F1 and the addition of an on-screen clock), and you probably will not have to use this chapter except as an occasional reference to a specific aspect of keyboard use or on-screen display.

However, if you have not yet set up macros to facilitate using the numeric keypad for data entry, you may want to use those shown in Figure 3.5 and discussed in the section "Macros for Numerical Data Entry with the 10-Key Number Pad." These macros allow you to make numerical entries either down columns or across rows with the Num Lock key activated.

Lotus 1-2-3 and the IBM Keyboard

Because Lotus 1-2-3 was designed specifically for use with the IBM PC, it makes full use of its peculiar keyboard arrangement. This keyboard is divided into three distinct areas:

- An extended typewriter keyboard following the standard QWERTY key arrangement for the letter and punctuation keys as well as the special keys Esc, Ctrl, Alt, Caps Lock, PrtSc, Num Lock, and Scroll Lock
- The ten special function keys numbered from F1 to F10, usually located in two columns at the left of the keyboard
- The cursor/numeric keypad located on the right of the keyboard (you must press Num Lock to enable the numeric keypad)

These three areas are shown in Figure 3.1. Lotus 1-2-3 accomplishes three basic functions through these areas:

- Entering data and formulas by using the typewriter keys or numeric keypad
- Moving the spreadsheet pointer or editing cursor by using the cursor keypad
- Issuing commands to add to, save, print, and control the appearance of the worksheet by using the typewriter keys or the special function keys (see Chapter 4)

Special Uses for the Extended Typewriter Keys

Figure 3.2 highlights the typewriter area keys that have special assignments in Lotus 1-2-3. The most important key assignment is that of the forward slash (/) key, located at the right end of the bottom row of letter keys. It is used to activate the Lotus 1-2-3 command menu and make it visible on the screen.

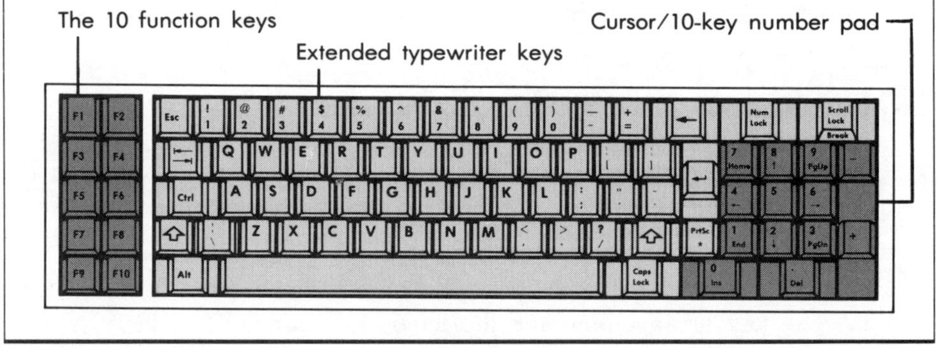

FIGURE 3.1: The three areas of the IBM PC keyboard: the ten function keys, the extended typewriter keys, and the cursor/numeric keypad. The typewriter letter and punctuation keys are arranged in the standard QWERTY arrangement with some modifications. Some new symbols have been added: the square and curly brackets (right of P), the accent grave and tilde (right of '), and the backslash and broken vertical line (left of Z). This area also includes the special shift and function keys Esc, Ctrl, Alt, Caps Lock, PrtSc, Num Lock, and Scroll Lock. The cursor/numeric keypad functions as a cursor-movement keypad, with the exception of the minus (−) and plus (+) keys on the far right, unless Num Lock is activated.

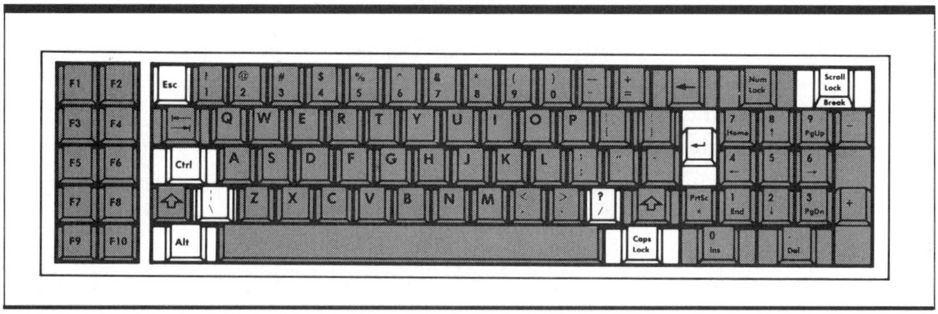

FIGURE 3.2: Special key assignments for the typewriter keys in Lotus 1-2-3. The most important key in Lotus 1-2-3 is /, which brings up the command menu. The Esc key cancels a specific selection and backs you up one menu level. The Ctrl-Scroll Lock (Break) key combination returns you immediately to READY mode. The Alt key is most often used in combination with a single letter key to invoke macros. The major use of the \ key is in combination with a single character to enter that character across the entire width of a cell as a repeating label. The ↵ key is referred to as either the Enter or Return key. It is used to complete data entry or to carry out selected menu commands.

The Esc Key

To cancel a command, you use the Esc key. It also has the effect of backing you out of various menu levels all the way to READY mode, where you can once again move the pointer and enter data into cells (see "The Mode Indicators" later in this chapter for a discussion of spreadsheet mode and status indicators).

The Break Key

A faster method of deactivating the command menus and returning immediately to READY mode is to hold down the Ctrl key and press the Scroll Lock key (located in the upper-right corner of the keyboard). This key combination is referred to as the Break key (and is labeled as such on the front face of the Scroll Lock key). It does not function as a program interrupt in Lotus 1-2-3.

The Backslash Key

Lotus 1-2-3 also has some special uses for the backslash key (\) located immediately to the left of the Z key on the same row that contains the forward slash. Most commonly, it functions as the signifier of a repeating label. Whatever character is typed immediately after the backslash is repeated across the entire width of the cell. It is used most often to add a horizontal line of single or double underscores by using the hyphen (\-) or the equal sign (\ =). In macros, it is used as a special macro name prefix—as in **\E,** which signifies that the macro is invoked by pressing Alt and the letter E. This key can also be used in assigning titles to graphs where the title is supplied by the contents of the cell being referenced—as in **\A1,** where cell A1 contains the title of the worksheet that is also used as the title of the graph you are defining.

THE ALT KEY

The Alt key is used primarily to invoke macro commands stored in the worksheet. It is used in combination with a particular letter key that has been defined as the macro name. This macro name is placed in a cell immediately to the left of the first one containing the macro keystrokes and commands. You enter the macro label with the \ prefix, as in the \E example above, but you also enter an apostrophe (') before the backslash to indicate that this is a macro label and not a repeating label. You then issue the /Range Name Labels Right command to tell Lotus 1-2-3 which cell contains the macro instructions saved under this range name (for more information on setting up macros, see Chapter 27). Once you depress the Alt key and the desired letter key, Lotus 1-2-3 follows all of the keystrokes and commands in the macro.

The Alt key is also used in combination with the function key F1 in Release 1A to execute macros one step at a time when you are debugging them (see Table 3.3). In Release 2, this key combination assignment was changed to Alt-F2. In Release 2, Alt-F1 enters a LICS screen character in the worksheet (see Appendix B) and is referred to as the Compose key.

THE RETURN (ENTER) KEY

The Return key is most often labeled on IBM PC and compatible keyboards as ↵. The Return key is also referred to as the Enter key in Lotus 1-2-3, which hints at its real function in this program. While labeling it the Return key is more appropriate in word processing (where it functions as a carriage return to signify the end of a paragraph), many IBM-compatible keyboards have taken to marking this key "Return" in place of the ↵ symbol. Reference to it as the Enter key in non-word processing programs is also fading fast (for example, where the Release 1A documentation refers to pressing ENTER, Release 2 now refers to pressing RETURN). This handbook will consistently refer to this key as the Return key. In Lotus 1-2-3, it functions either to complete data entry into a cell or to invoke a command selected from the command menu.

The Caps Lock Key

The last typewriter key of mention is the Caps Lock key. While its function in Lotus 1-2-3 is consistent with its use in other application programs, its usage is often a source of confusion for the new Lotus 1-2-3 user. Unlike on a standard typewriter, where the comparable key is called Shift Lock, activating Caps Lock does not shift any of the punctuation keys or top-row number keys while capitalizing all of the letter keys. This means that even after activating Caps Lock, you often have to use one of the Shift keys when you need to use a shifted symbol, as when entering the function @NOW.

Keys that Move the Spreadsheet Pointer and Editing Cursor

When discussing moving around the spreadsheet, it is important to differentiate between the spreadsheet cursor and the editing cursor. The *spreadsheet cursor* is the highlighted block that extends across the entire width of a cell, marking it as the current cell where data can be entered. It can be moved only when the program is in READY mode. The *editing cursor* is the single blinking underscore marking the character that currently can be edited. It can be accessed only when the program is in EDIT mode. To avoid confusion between these two, it is convenient to refer to the spreadsheet cursor as the *cell pointer* or *spreadsheet pointer* or even just the *pointer.* Following this convention then allows us to use the term *cursor* for the editing cursor, which is available only in EDIT mode.

Figure 3.3 highlights the keys that move the cell pointer around the worksheet, and Table 3.1 explains their usage in READY mode. You make simple one-cell movements in the four directions by pressing the appropriate arrow key. Larger jumps are accomplished in a variety of ways.

FIGURE 3.3: Spreadsheet pointer movement keys. The scrolling functions of Tab (or Ctrl-→) and Shift-Tab (or Ctrl-←) are called Big Right and Big Left, respectively. F5 is called the Goto key. It takes the pointer directly to a cell named either by a cell address or range name.

KEY	IN READY AND POINT MODES	IN EDIT MODE
Home	Moves pointer to cell A1.	Moves cursor to the first character on the entry line.
↑	Moves pointer up one cell.	
↓	Moves pointer down one cell.	
←	Moves pointer left one cell.	Moves cursor left one character.
→	Moves pointer right one cell.	Moves cursor right one character.
End		Moves cursor to the end of the entry line.
End-↑	Moves pointer up the column to the beginning of a cell range or to row 1, if it is empty.	
End-↓	Moves pointer down the column to the end of a range or to row 8192 (2048 in 1A), if it is empty.	
End-←	Moves pointer across the row to the beginning of a cell range or to column A if it is empty.	
End-→	Moves pointer across the row to the end of a cell range or to column IV, if it is empty.	
End-Home	Moves pointer to the last active cell in the worksheet.	

TABLE 3.1: The Spreadsheet Pointer and Editing Cursor-Movement Keys

KEY	IN READY AND POINT MODES	IN EDIT MODE
PgUp	Moves pointer up one screen.	
PgDn	Moves pointer down one screen.	
Tab (→|)	Moves pointer one screen to the right—same as Ctrl-→ (also called Big Right).	Moves cursor five characters to the right.
Shift-Tab (|←)	Moves pointer one screen to the left—same as Ctrl-← (also called Big Left).	Moves cursor five characters to the left.
Scroll Lock	Freezes pointer in relative position while scrolling the screen display; displays SCROLL status indicator when activated.	
Num Lock	Activates numbers on the 10-key numeric pad and disables cursor and editing functions; displays NUM status indicator when activated.	
Note: In LABEL and VALUE modes, the spreadsheet pointer movement keys also complete data entry in the current cell before moving the pointer to the next cell as designated above.		

TABLE 3.1: The Spreadsheet Pointer and Editing Cursor-Movement Keys (continued)

Moving the Spreadsheet Pointer

Lotus 1-2-3 relies heavily on the cursor keys to move the pointer around the worksheet. Because most IBM-compatible keyboards combine these keys with the 10-key number pad, it is usually impractical to use Num Lock for data entry because it disables all the shared cursor functions.

The Home and End Keys To take the pointer to cell A1 from anywhere in the worksheet, you simply press the Home key. To take the pointer to the last used cell in the worksheet, press the End key and then the Home key. This cell varies according to how much of the spreadsheet has been used in your work. It is called the *last active cell* of the worksheet. Whenever you press the End key, the status indicator END is displayed on the screen.

The End and Arrow Keys The End key is also used in combination with the arrow keys. When it is used with one of the arrow keys, the cell pointer behaves in one of two ways: it either moves in the direction of the arrow to the extreme edge of the spreadsheet if there are no cell entries in its path, or it moves to one of the edges of the cell range it encounters or is already located in. The End and arrow keys are most often used in POINT mode to highlight in one step an entire block of cells as the range in one direction.

The F5 (Goto) Key The function key F5, called the Goto key, can take the cell pointer to any specific cell in the spreadsheet. After you press it, you are prompted to type in a cell address. You can give the address either by column letter and row number or by range name. If you type in a range name, Lotus 1-2-3 takes the pointer to the cell in the upper-left corner of that range.

Other Pointer Movements Other pointer movements shown in Figure 3.3 and outlined in Table 3.1 are made in conjunction with scrolling the screen display. These functions are discussed in the section "The Lotus 1-2-3 Screen Display" later in this chapter.

Moving the Editing Cursor

Table 3.1 shows that some of the same keys used to move the cell pointer also move the cursor in EDIT mode. Figure 3.4 highlights the location of these keys on the IBM PC keyboard.

The F2 (Edit) Key The function key F2 brings the contents of the current cell to the entry line for editing. Once you have pressed this key, the cursor is positioned after the very last character.

The Home and End Keys To move the cursor to the very first character in one jump, you simply press the Home key. This is very useful when you only need to add an apostrophe or one of the other two label prefixes to the line to change the entry from a value to a label. To move the cursor directly to the end of the line, you press the End key.

FIGURE 3.4: Cell entry editing keys. F2 is the Edit key. It brings the literal contents of the current cell to the second line on the Control Panel for editing. The editing cursor is then located at the end of the contents. Insert mode is on (it is disabled with Ins) and the Backspace key is destructive. Pressing Home takes the cursor directly to the beginning of the line. Tab moves the cursor five spaces to the right, and Del erases the character at the cursor. Pressing Return enters the edited contents into the cell.

The Tab and Shift Keys To move in smaller jumps, use either the Tab key or a combination of the Shift and Tab keys (called Backtab). Pressing the Tab key moves the cursor five characters to the right of its current position. Holding down one of the Shift keys and then pressing Tab moves the cursor five characters to the left.

The Backspace and Del Keys Use the Backspace key to delete characters to the left of the cursor's present position. Because Backspace is destructive, use the ← key to move the cursor to a new position without destroying existing characters. Pressing the Del key erases the character at the cursor's position. Lotus 1-2-3 is in insert mode until you press the Ins key (the status indicator then reads OVR) so that you can type in any new characters without disturbing those to the right of the cursor's position. Table 3.2 gives a quick reference list of the editing functions assigned to these keys.

Function Key Assignments in Lotus 1-2-3

As mentioned earlier in this chapter, Lotus 1-2-3 has specific functions for all ten of the IBM function keys. Table 3.3 shows you the names and usages assigned to these keys as well as the modes in which they operate.

KEY	IN EDIT AND FILES MODE
Backspace	Deletes character to left of cursor.
Ins	Switches editor from insert mode (default) to overtype mode, displaying the OVR status indicator. Press the Ins key a second time to return to insert mode.
Del	Deletes character at current cursor position.
Esc	Clears data entry line but does not return you to READY mode. In FILES mode, it clears the file name but not the subdirectories listed before it. Press Esc a second time to clear these when you want to enter a new drive, directory, and file name.

TABLE 3.2: Lotus 1-2-3 Editing Key Assignments

KEY	MEANING	USAGE	MODE
F1	Help	Accesses on-line, context-sensitive help.	
F2	Edit	Brings the contents of the current cell to the entry line for revision. Pressed a second time, it switches between EDIT and VALUE or LABEL modes.	EDIT
F3	Name	Displays a list of defined range names for selecting in POINT mode only. Pressed a second time, it gives a full-screen display of range names.	POINT
F4	Absolute	Switches between relative, mixed, and absolute cell references in POINT mode only. The order is as follows: first time—absolute (such as $F$4); second time—mixed as relative column, absolute row (such as F$4); third time—mixed as absolute column, relative row (such as $F4); fourth time—relative (such as F4).	POINT
F5	Goto	Moves the spreadsheet pointer directly to a particular cell specified by either a cell address or a range name.	READY

TABLE 3.3: Lotus 1-2-3 Function Key Assignments

KEY	MEANING	USAGE	MODE
F6	Window	Switches the spreadsheet pointer from one window to the other.	
F7	Query	Repeats the previous /Data Query command, such as Find, Extract, or Unique.	
F8	Table	Repeats the previous /Data Table command, such as 1 or 2.	
F9	Calc	Recalculates the worksheet in READY mode; in EDIT mode, converts the formula contents of a cell to its currently calculated value.	READY EDIT
F10	Graph	Draws the most recently defined graph.	
Alt-F1	Step [1A]	Executes a macro command one keystroke at a time (used to debug large macros—press Break to interrupt and F2 to edit). Displays STEP status indicator (Release 1A only).	
Alt-F1	Compose [2]	Used with other specified characters to produce LICS graphics or foreign-language symbols (Release 2 only).	
Alt-F2	Step [2]	Executes a macro command one keystroke at a time (used to debug large macros—press Break to interrupt and F2 to edit). Displays STEP status indicator (Release 2 only).	

TABLE 3.3: Lotus 1-2-3 Function Key Assignments (continued)

Only F1 in Release 1A and F1 and F2 in Release 2 are used in combination with the Alt key as well as alone. All of the others are only used alone.

The most important of these keys are F1, F2, F5, F6, F9, and the combination of Alt-F1 (and Alt-F2 in Release 2); these functions do not have alternative methods on the Lotus 1-2-3 command menu. To help you remember the assignments for all these useful functions, the program contains a plastic function key overlay as well as a Quick Reference listing them all.

GETTING HELP

The F1 function key allows you to access on-line help messages at any time while using the program. This help is context sensitive, meaning that Lotus 1-2-3 will display a help message screen tailored as much as possible to where you are in the program. For instance, if you have just selected the Range command menu with /R and then press F1, the help screen displayed discusses the various Range commands.

Release 2 of the program has made this on-line help quite a bit more extensive than it is in Release 1A. In addition to getting context-sensitive help, you can also select an option to display an index of all the Lotus 1-2-3 help topics. You can get more information about any topic. Figure 3.5 shows you all the topics available from this Help Index screen.

As discussed in Chapter 2, in Release 2 there are two methods of accessing this on-line help: instant and removable. If you choose the Instant help option from the /Worksheet Global Default Help command, the help file remains open after the first time you press F1, making subsequent requests for help much faster. This method of help access is possible only if you are

```
A1:                                                                  HELP

Help Index              Select one of these topics for additional Help.

Using The Help Facility              How to Start Over
Errors and Messages                  How to End a 1-2-3 Session
Error Message Index
                                     Moving the Cell Pointer
Special Keys                         Cell Entries
Control Panel                        Erasing Cell Entries
Modes and Indicators
                                     1-2-3 Commands
                                     Command Menus
Formulas
@Functions                           Column Widths
Cell Formats -- Number vs. Label
                                     Macros
Operators                            Function Keys

Ranges                               Menus for File, Range, and Graph Names
Pointing to Ranges                   File Names
Reenterng Ranges
10-Jun-86  04:26 PM
```

FIGURE 3.5: The Lotus 1-2-3 Help Index screen in Release 2. This screen contains 25 topics, many of which have several help screens of their own that explain the subject in detail. To get help about a specific topic listed here, use the arrow keys to move the pointer to it and press Return. To return to the spreadsheet, press the Esc key once.

using a hard disk system where the help files are stored along with all the other Lotus 1-2-3 program files (see the section in Chapter 2, "Customizing Lotus 1-2-3 Release 2," for more information on this topic). When you have finished using the help screens, pressing the Esc key returns you to the spreadsheet in READY mode.

OTHER FUNCTION KEYS

The rest of the function keys are used to invoke various commands during the program's use. These command functions are listed in Table 3.3; you will find them discussed in detail in various sections of the book that deal with the use of these and other related commands.

Macros for Numerical Data Entry with the 10-Key Number Pad

While many users are proficient at numerical entry from a 10-key number pad and would prefer this method, everyone usually ends up doing numeric entry using the top-row number keys, because Lotus 1-2-3 relies so heavily on the cursor keys to move the spreadsheet pointer to new areas in the worksheet.

To get around this, you can use the program's macro facility to create two separate macros for entering numeric data down a column or across a row. These are shown in Figure 3.6; they will work in either Release 1A or Release 2. The one for entering data down a column is called Alt-C (labeled \C), and the one for entering data across a row is called Alt-R (labeled \R). After entering the labels and keystrokes as shown, use the command /Range Name Labels Right (/RNLR) and press Return with the pointer in the label cell for each macro. (Refer to Chapter 28 if you are unsure where to locate these macros in your worksheet.)

1. To use the Alt-C macro, position the pointer at the beginning of the column where you want to input numerical data and press Num Lock (you should see the NUM status indicator at the bottom-right corner of the screen). Press Alt-C.
2. Enter the first number and press Return. The pointer automatically advances to the next cell down the column.
3. Enter the second number and press Return.

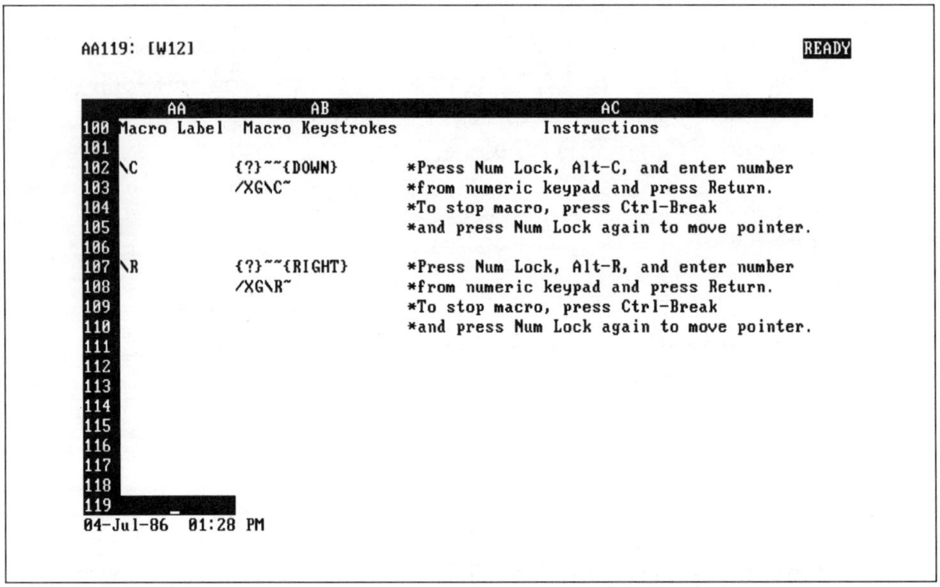

FIGURE 3.6: Macros for using the 10-key number pad to do numerical data entry in a worksheet. The Alt-C macro allows you to do numerical entry down a column with Num Lock activated. The Alt-R macro does the same across a row. In Release 2, you could use the {BRANCH} macro command in the second line of each macro. In Alt-C, enter it as {**BRANCH** **C**} and in Alt-R, {**BRANCH** **R**}.

4. When you have finished entering all of the data for that column, press F5 and enter the cell address of the top of the next column, or press Num Lock again to enable the cursor functions and move the pointer to it.
5. To deactivate the macro when you have finished your numerical input, press Ctrl-Scroll Lock (Break). In Release 2, the first time you press this combination you will hear a beep and the program will go into ERROR mode. To clear the macro, press Break a second time or press the Return key. In Release 1A, you only have to press the Break key once to halt the macro. The CMD status indicator then disappears from the bottom of the screen.

You use Alt-R in a similar way. The only difference is that you must position the pointer at the beginning of the row before you press Num Lock and then press Alt and **r** to start the macro. You will be entering data from left to right as the macro advances the pointer to the next cell to the right.

THE LOTUS 1-2-3 SCREEN DISPLAY

When you first start up Lotus 1-2-3, the only things visible on the screen are the current cell reference in the upper-left corner, the border displays showing the column letters and row numbers in two reverse-video bands, and the clock showing the current date and time (in Release 2). From here, you are free to begin a new worksheet or retrieve one that has already been saved.

Figure 3.7 shows the screen display after a worksheet has been retrieved. Each of the components is called out. The first three lines of the screen are referred to as the Control Panel. In this figure, the forward slash key (/)

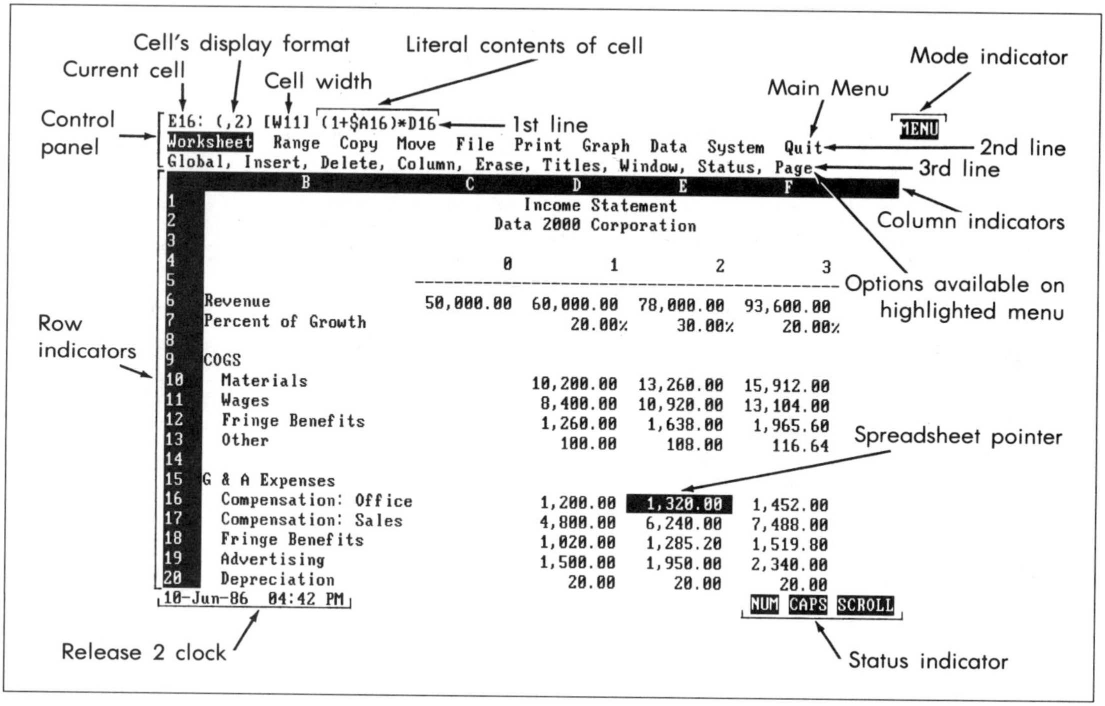

FIGURE 3.7: Components of the Lotus 1-2-3 screen display. The Control Panel takes up the first three lines of the screen display. The first line shows the address of the current cell, its literal contents, and any formats assigned to it. At the far right of this line is the mode indicator. The second and third lines contain the command menus and their options in MENU mode. In EDIT mode, the second line contains the literal contents of the current cell for editing. Columns are indicated by letters listed across the fourth line, with the number of columns visible dependent upon their width. Rows are indicated by numbers listed vertically; 20 rows are always displayed. The 25th line of the screen displays a clock showing the current date and time on the left (Release 2 only), error messages, and the status indicators, shown as NUM, CAPS, and SCROLL in this figure.

has been pressed to bring the main command menu options to the second line in this area.

The Control Panel

The first line of the Control Panel gives you valuable information about the current cell (the cell containing the spreadsheet pointer). In the example shown in Figure 3.7, this is cell E16. After providing the address of the pointer in the worksheet, this line gives you information about the cell's contents. If the cell is blank, nothing is listed after the colon.

If the cell has been formatted or protected, or if its column width has been altered from the default setting, this information is then listed before the cell's literal contents. In Figure 3.7, the comma format with two decimal places has been assigned to E16, shown by the (,2). Column E has also been widened from the default of 9 characters to 11, shown by the [W11] that follows. If this cell had been protected, a [P] would also have been included on this line (if global protection were enabled and the cell were then unprotected, it would be indicated by [U]).

After listing any information about display formatting, changes to the cell width, and security status, Lotus 1-2-3 displays the contents of the cell just as they were entered. The only exception occurs when you have input a label without first typing of one of the label prefixes (', ^,"). In such a case, the contents of the label are displayed with an apostrophe automatically added by the program itself. In Figure 3.7, cell E16 contains the formula (1 +$A16)*D16.

The Mode Indicators

The only other information displayed on the first line of the Control Panel is the mode indicator at the far right. Table 3.4 gives you a full listing of all the possible mode indicators and explains the significance of each. They convey important information about how Lotus 1-2-3 will interpret and react to any input you make from the keyboard. In Figure 3.7, this indicator shows as MENU, reminding you that a command menu is currently being accessed and that any characters typed from the keyboard at this time will be interpreted as menu selections. If you try to make entries that are not valid in this context, Lotus 1-2-3 beeps at you.

MODE	MEANING
READY	Lotus 1-2-3 is ready to accept data entry in the current cell or a menu command. You must be in READY mode to enter data in the current cell.
LABEL	Lotus 1-2-3 will enter your current entry as a label. This mode is activated whenever the first character you type is an alphabetical character or punctuation symbol other than those reserved for values (see VALUE).
VALUE	Lotus 1-2-3 will enter your current entry as a value. This mode is activated whenever the first character you type is a digit from 0 to 9, a mathematical operator (+,–), or a punctuation symbol (@,#,/,().
POINT	Lotus 1-2-3 will indicate the extent of a range in the worksheet if you use the cursor keys ←, →, ↑, or ↓. This mode is activated when you press one of these arrow keys instead of typing in a cell address to indicate the beginning of the range.
EDIT	Lotus 1-2-3 has brought the literal contents of the current cell to the second line of the Control Panel, allowing you to revise its contents. This mode is activated when you press F2. When you first enter data into a cell in VALUE mode, the program automatically switches to EDIT mode if you try to complete an invalid entry. When you indicate a range in POINT mode, it switches to EDIT mode if you press something other than one of the arrow keys.
ERROR	Lotus 1-2-3 is indicating that you have made some kind of data entry or command sequence error. This mode indicator flashes on and off until you clear it by pressing Esc or Return. In the rare event that neither of these keys works, press Ctrl-Scroll Lock (Break).
WAIT	Lotus 1-2-3 is indicating that it is currently busy. This mode is activated when you issue a command that requires processing, such as recalculating the worksheet or saving a file. The indicator flashes on and off during processing. When it has finished, the program automatically returns to READY mode.
MENU	The Lotus 1-2-3 Command Menu is activated (you have pressed /). The only data entry accepted is either one of the initial letters of the command options currently listed on the second line of the Control Panel or a valid entry in response to a specific command prompt. Pressing Esc backs you up one menu level until you reach READY mode. Pressing Ctrl-Scroll Lock (Break) returns you immediately to READY mode.
HELP	The Lotus 1-2-3 on-line help is activated (you have pressed F1). Press Esc to return to READY mode.

TABLE 3.4: Lotus 1-2-3 Mode Indicators

MODE	MEANING
FILES	Lotus 1-2-3 is currently displaying a listing of files. This mode is activated when you issue any one of the commands on the File menu. If you wish to return to READY mode, press Esc as many times as necessary or press Ctrl-Scroll Lock (Break).
FIND	Lotus 1-2-3 is currently involved in a /Data Query Find operation. This mode is activated by either typing /DQF or pressing F7 if the previous /Data Query operation was the same.

TABLE 3.4: Lotus 1-2-3 Mode Indicators (continued)

MENU MODE

Whenever you are in MENU mode and one of its menus occupies the second line, the third line of the Control Panel displays all the menu selections available if the option currently highlighted should be selected, or, if there are no options, the Control Panel displays instructions on its usage. In Figure 3.7, the third line of the Control Panel contains the options available to you if you select the Worksheet menu. Pressing the Esc key at this, the Main Menu level, returns the mode to READY and causes the menu options on both of these lines to disappear. It is only in READY mode that you can move the cell pointer to new cell locations and enter data into them.

LABEL AND VALUE MODES

As soon as you begin to enter data into a cell, the mode indicator changes to either LABEL or VALUE mode. Until you press Return or one of the arrow keys, this data is displayed only on the second line of the Control Panel and can be edited by using any of the editing keys. When you press Return or an arrow, the label or value is entered into the cell and can be modified only by locating the pointer in the cell and pressing F2, the Edit key.

The program assigns either LABEL or VALUE mode by assessing the content of the first character you type. If an alphabetical character is the first typed, Lotus 1-2-3 goes into LABEL mode. Once in this mode, you can then enter any combination of alphabetic, numeric, or punctuation symbols as part of the label. If a digit, arithmetic operator, or a special punctuation symbol (see Table 3.4 for a listing) is entered first, the program goes into VALUE mode.

When you are in VALUE mode, you are prevented from adding any alphabetical characters or characters not specifically reserved for use in Lotus 1-2-3 functions and formulas. If you do, Lotus 1-2-3 beeps at you and immediately goes into EDIT mode when you try to enter anything into the cell. It also moves the editing cursor to the first position in the entry where an illegal character was typed. This is a signal that you should locate and revise the input by deleting any unwanted alphabetical characters or punctuation. After you delete the character or characters in question, press Return to enter the value in the cell.

EDIT Mode

Lotus 1-2-3 also goes into EDIT mode automatically when you press the Return key if the value you have input consists of a formula or function that contains any syntax errors. It locates the cursor at the first position in the line where it detects an error. More often than not, these errors are caused either from a typographical error that occurred when you entered the function name or from forgetting to add some necessary punctuation, such as a comma delimiter or right parenthesis.

The Spreadsheet Work Area

The spreadsheet column letters and row numbers highlighted in reverse video mark the top and left borders of the worksheet area on the screen. When you first enter a blank worksheet, eight columns from A to H and twenty rows from 1 to 20 are displayed. The cell pointer cannot go above row 1 or to the left of column A. Any attempt to take the pointer beyond these limits results in Lotus 1-2-3's beeping at you.

At this point you can move the spreadsheet pointer and enter data in the areas only down and to the right of these borders. As you move into new areas of the worksheet, the border displays are updated immediately to keep you apprised of your relative position. If you do not modify any column widths, Lotus 1-2-3 will always display an area consisting of 160 cells. If you change column widths, the number of cells you see will vary.

Scrolling

Because this area represents only a very small part of the overall size of the spreadsheet, Lotus 1-2-3 provides many ways for you to scroll the screen display to bring new areas into view:

- The Tab key scrolls the display left by 80 characters.
- The Shift-Tab key combination scrolls the display right by 80 characters.
- The PgDn key scrolls the display up 20 rows.
- The PgUp key scrolls the display down 20 rows.
- The Goto key (F5) moves the cursor to a specified address. It also places this new cell in the upper-left corner of the screen.

Windows

You can also use Lotus 1-2-3's window capabilities to split the display either horizontally or vertically. When windows are unsynchronized, you can bring separate areas of the same worksheet into the display area. This allows you to compare and work on two different areas of the spreadsheet without having to keep moving the pointer between them. You can use the Scroll Lock key to freeze the pointer in its relative position in its window while you use the arrow keys to scroll a new area into position on the screen. (For information on how to use the Window commands, see Chapter 8, "Working with Cell Ranges.")

The Last Line of the Lotus 1-2-3 Display Screen

The last line of the display screen displays a clock at the left (in Release 2 only), any of the program's error messages, and the status indicator. The clock gives the current date and time supplied to the system at startup—either what you entered at the DOS prompt or what was entered automatically from a battery-operated clock/calendar on one of the add-on boards in your computer. (You can eliminate the clock from the screen display by using the command **/WGDOCN.**)

Immediately to the right of the on-screen clock, Lotus 1-2-3 displays any error messages. Before you see the error message, Lotus 1-2-3 beeps at you and the mode changes to either EDIT or ERROR. Appendix C at the end of this handbook contains a complete alphabetical listing of the program's possible error messages. Whenever you receive one of these and the mode has changed to ERROR, press the Return key or the space bar to clear the message and return to READY mode.

The Status Indicators

On the far right of the last line of the display, Lotus 1-2-3 displays status indicators (see Table 3.5). These usually appear when the Ins, Caps Lock, Num Lock, or Scroll Lock keys have been pressed.

INDICATOR	MEANING
CAPS	Caps Lock is activated, shifting all alphabetical characters you type to uppercase (not the top-row numbers or punctuation on the keyboard). Press the Caps Lock key a second time to disable it.
NUM	Number Lock is activated. Numbers or the period will appear whenever you press one of the keys on the 10-key numeric pad. Press the Num Lock key a second time to disable it.
SCROLL	Scroll Lock is activated, freezing the spreadsheet pointer in its relative position on the screen. Press the Scroll Lock key a second time to disable it.
OVR	Insert mode (the program default) has been disabled and overtype mode activated. In EDIT mode, anything you enter replaces existing characters instead of pushing them to the right. Press the Ins key once to activate overtype mode and a second time to return to insert mode.
END	The End key has been depressed and Lotus 1-2-3 is waiting for you to press one of the arrow keys or the Home key to move the spreadsheet pointer (refer to Table 3.1 for specific movements). Press Esc to cancel.
CALC	Lotus 1-2-3 is in manual recalculation mode, and you have entered new data into formulas that need to be recalculated by pressing F9. You activate this indicator by typing **/WGRM** and updating formulas in the worksheet.
CIRC	Lotus 1-2-3 is in natural recalculation mode (the program default), and you have entered a formula containing a circular reference. This status indicator does not appear when you have changed the recalculation mode to columnwise, rowwise, or iteration.

TABLE 3.5: Lotus 1-2-3 Status Indicators

INDICATOR	MEANING
CMD	Lotus 1-2-3 is currently processing a macro command that you activated by pressing the Alt key and typing the letter assigned to it as a range name. Press Ctrl-Scroll Lock (Break) to cancel macro operation.
STEP	STEP mode has been activated by pressing Alt-F1 in Release 1A or Alt-F2 in Release 2. Any macro (keystroke or command) activated thereafter will be processed a single step at a time. Press the Return key to proceed to the next step. Once you have activated STEP mode and a particular macro, the status indicator changes to SST (see below).
SST	Lotus 1-2-3 is currently processing a macro command in STEP mode. Press Ctrl-Scroll Lock (Break) to cancel the step.
MEM	(Release 2 only) The amount of available memory for Lotus 1-2-3's use has fallen below 4K. This status indicator continues to flash on and off as you work. At the first sign of it, you should save your worksheet by using the /File Save command. If you continue to build your worksheet, you will soon receive a Memory Full error message (see Appendix C), making it impossible to continue to add data without eliminating some of your work.

TABLE 3.5: Lotus 1-2-3 Status Indicators (continued)

The other group of status indicators lets you know when a macro has been invoked. The most common indicator of this type is CMD, which tells you that the macro you selected is in effect. With some macros, you must press Ctrl-Scroll Lock (Break) to stop the macro and remove the CMD status indicator. If you have used the Step key (Alt-F1 in Release 1A or Alt-F2 in Release 2), you will see either the STEP or SST status indicator as the program processes each step of the macro instructions. You must then press the Return key to continue or the Break key to cancel the macro's execution.

A new status indicator has been added to Release 2. It is the MEM status indicator, which lets you know that the memory available to Lotus 1-2-3 is getting low (see Chapter 1). Like the WAIT and ERROR mode indicators, this status indicator flashes on and off continuously until you do something about it.

Summary

This chapter covered the way Lotus 1-2-3 interacts with the IBM PC. First it looked at the ways Lotus 1-2-3 uses the IBM keyboard to communicate with the user. Then it analyzed the components of the program's screen display and the important information contained there.

For related topics, refer to the chapter references that follow.

For more information on using command menus:

- Chapter 4, "The Lotus 1-2-3 Command Menu System"

For more information on values and labels in the worksheet:

- Chapter 5, "Creating Worksheets"

For more information on editing cells:

- Chapter 6, "Editing Worksheets"

For more information on windows and scrolling:

- Chapter 8, "Working with Cell Ranges"

For more information on creating and using macro commands:

- Chapter 27, "Keystroke Macros"

For a listing of Lotus 1-2-3 error messages:

- Appendix A, "Lotus 1-2-3 Error Messages"

For a listing of the LICS characters:

- Appendix B, "LICS Chart"

CHAPTER 4

THE LOTUS 1-2-3 COMMAND MENU SYSTEM

The Lotus 1-2-3 Command Menu System

This chapter gives you an overview of the Lotus 1-2-3 command menu system: how it is set up, how to use it, and what commands are attached to each of its menus. You can peruse this information to find out how the menu system is laid out as well as to locate a particular set of commands that you need to use in building your spreadsheet, database, or graph.

The chapter begins with a section on how to navigate the Lotus 1-2-3 menu system. Individual sections that outline the potential uses for the Main Menu selections and many of their suboptions follow. The intention is not to provide in-depth discussions of each menu command and option but rather to orient you to Lotus 1-2-3's menu system. Certain commands are discussed in greater detail elsewhere in this handbook; you will be referred to those sections throughout the chapter as well as in the listing of further references at the end of the chapter.

Navigating the Lotus 1-2-3 Menu System

Lotus 1-2-3 menus are referred to as *ring menus* or *ribbon menus*. Each command or menu name available is laid out horizontally. Though these selections all begin with a different initial letter, their order from left to right is not alphabetical.

Selecting Menu Options

You always have two methods of selecting a particular menu option: either by pointing to it with the → or ← keys and pressing the Return key or by typing the initial letter of the command word. The second method facilitates menu selection and is generally preferred by users of all types and skill levels. Choosing menu options by typing the letter sequence is much faster than using the pointing method, because you do not have to press the Return key.

If you use the pointing method, you will get a good idea why the Lotus 1-2-3 menu system has been dubbed a ring menu. When the cursor highlight reaches the last menu option on the line, it immediately returns to the first option. If you keep the → or ← key depressed, it appears as though the highlight is traveling around the menu selections in what appears as a circle or a ring.

Menu Levels

Lotus 1-2-3's menu system consists of various levels, each with its own options. Only one menu selection, System, on the top line or Main Menu, is not attached to any suboptions. It represents a new DOS shell command in Release 2 that takes you immediately to the operating system prompt. The rest of the commands have at least one set of options attached to them, and most have many more. Figure 4.1 shows the Main Menu options as they appear on the screen when you first start up Lotus 1-2-3.

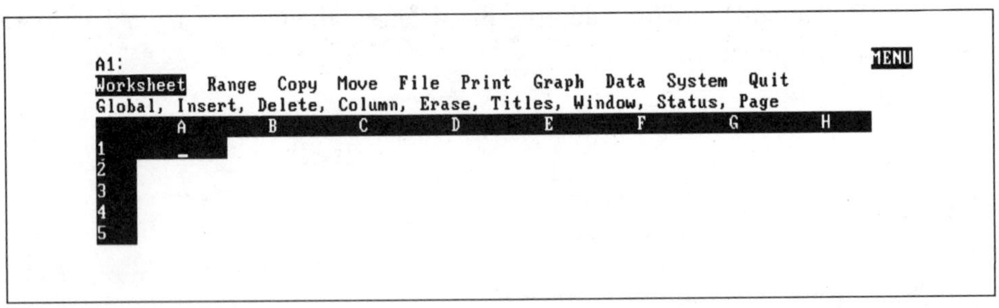

FIGURE 4.1: The Lotus 1-2-3 Main Menu, which is activated by pressing /. Ten options are available on this menu (nine in Release 1A, as the System option is not present). You select a command (option) listed here by typing its first letter (in this case either W, R, C, M, F, P, G, D, S, or Q) or by pressing the arrow keys to move the highlight to it and then pressing Return. In this figure, pressing Return selects the Worksheet command and makes all the options listed on the line below available to you.

Once you select one of the options on the Main Menu, any suboptions associated with it become available. These are then displayed on the second line, replacing those from the prior menu. This technique for descending the hierarchy of menu levels as you refine your command is consistent throughout the program. In the case of the Worksheet, Range, File, and Data options on the Main Menu, the third line of the Control Panel contains the entire listing of suboptions associated with each of these choices, in the order in which they are available.

With the remaining options on the Main Menu and those you see on subsequent menu levels, this third line contains only a short description of what the currently highlighted menu command does rather than an entire listing of the options available from it. This relationship is illustrated in Figure 4.2, where you can trace the complete menu path of the command /Range Format Date Time (/RFDT) as it would appear on the screen at each level.

Backing Up

To back up one menu level from any given point in the hierarchy, you press the Esc key. When you are at the Main Menu level and press Esc, the mode switches from MENU to READY, and you are once again free to move the cell pointer and make further entries into the spreadsheet. If you find that you are descending a menu path in error, you can either press Esc to back up to the level you meant to begin with, or you can press Ctrl-Scroll Lock (Break) to return immediately to READY mode.

If You Make Errors in the Menu Path

Starting down the wrong menu path is most often the result of transposing letters when you type the first letters of the commands. The most common transposition is the letters R and F. Typing **/RF** for Range Format is quite different from typing **/FR** for File Retrieve. If you mean to choose the command Range Format but instead type **FR,** you will find yourself being prompted for a file name instead of seeing the familiar list of display formats. If you no longer need to look at the format options and don't even look up at the Control Panel, you may even find yourself at that point typing in a letter of the format option you want, such as **c** to select the Currency format. Of course, Lotus 1-2-3 takes this character to indicate

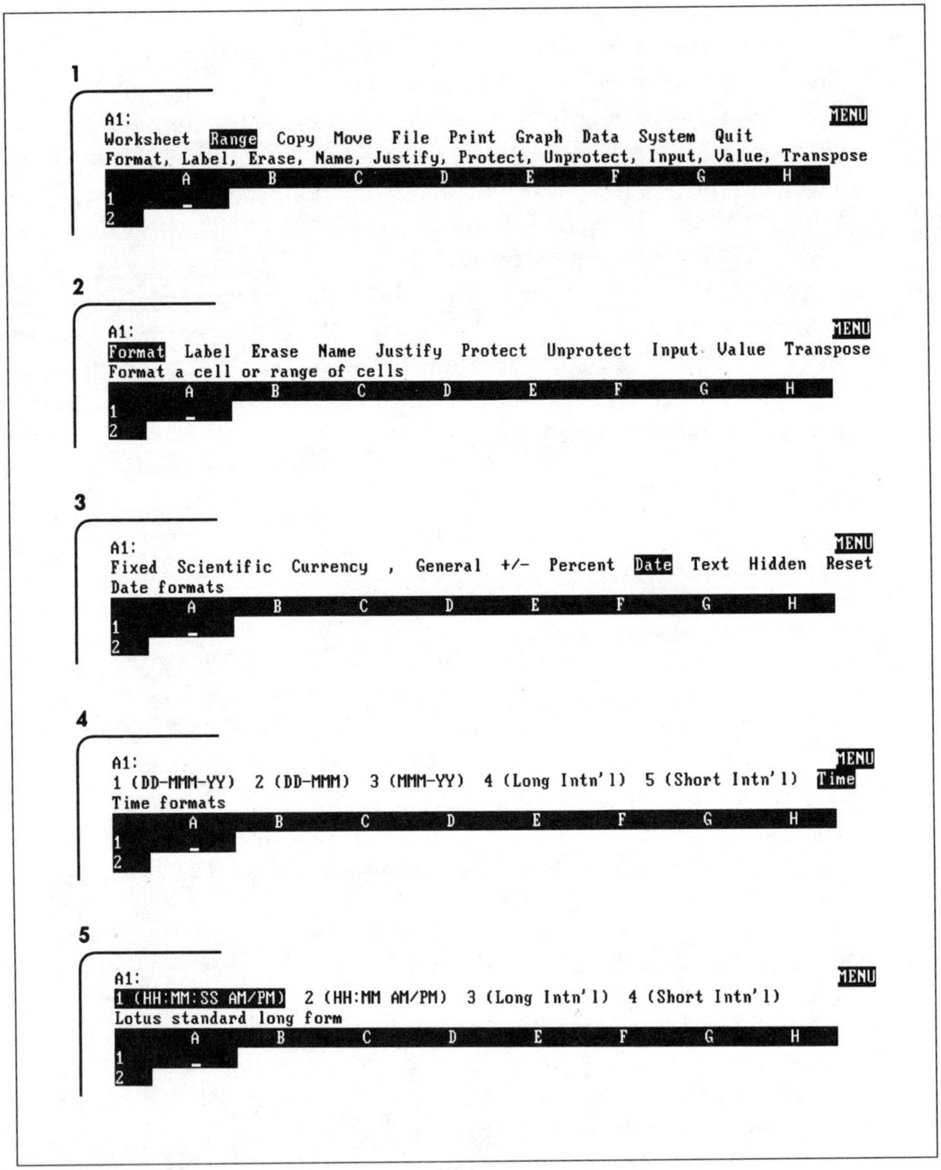

FIGURE 4.2: The menu screens as they appear when invoking the command /Range Format Date Time (/RFDT). (1) The Main Menu options appear after you type **/**. The Range options are displayed on the third line because Range is highlighted. (2) The suboptions on the third line in (1) are brought to the second line when you type **R** (or press Return). Format is then chosen from this menu by typing **F.** (3) The format options are now displayed. From here, Date is chosen by typing **D.** (4) The date options are now displayed. From here, Time is chosen by typing **T.** (5) The time options are now displayed, allowing you to select the appropriate one by number.

part of the file name instead of the Currency format. When you discover your error (in this example when you press Return to accept two decimal places and Lotus 1-2-3 beeps at you), you may find it easier just to press Break and start the sequence all over again than to begin pressing the Esc key to back up until you reach the Main Menu.

THE WORKSHEET MENU

The Worksheet Menu contains commands that affect the entire Lotus 1-2-3 spreadsheet. The options attached to this menu are illustrated in Figure 4.3 (all commands new to Release 2 are shown in boldface type).

/Worksheet Global

The first option, Global, is used to modify the default settings for your whole worksheet. From it, you can change any of the default settings listed in Table 4.1, which are in effect when you begin work on a new worksheet. Any changes made to these settings are saved as part of the file when you save your worksheet with the /File Save command. To see what global settings are currently in effect at any time during a session, give the command **/WS.**

/WORKSHEET GLOBAL DEFAULT

You can change the default printing device as well as the printing settings and directory by using the Default option on the Global Menu. The greatest differences between the menu options on the Worksheet Menu in Release 1A and Release 2 occur on the Default Menu. An entire new series of defaults has been added to the new version under the Other option on this menu. If you use Release 2, you will find all of these options discussed and illustrated in Chapter 2.

Unlike the other Global options, you must save any changes you make to the program settings from the Default Menu by using the Update option. The Default Menu also differs in that you use the Quit option to return to READY mode (though you can also back out by pressing Esc). (You will find this same situation when you use a number of other menus, like the Print, Graph, Data Query, Data Regression, and Data Parse menus, as well as some of their submenus.)

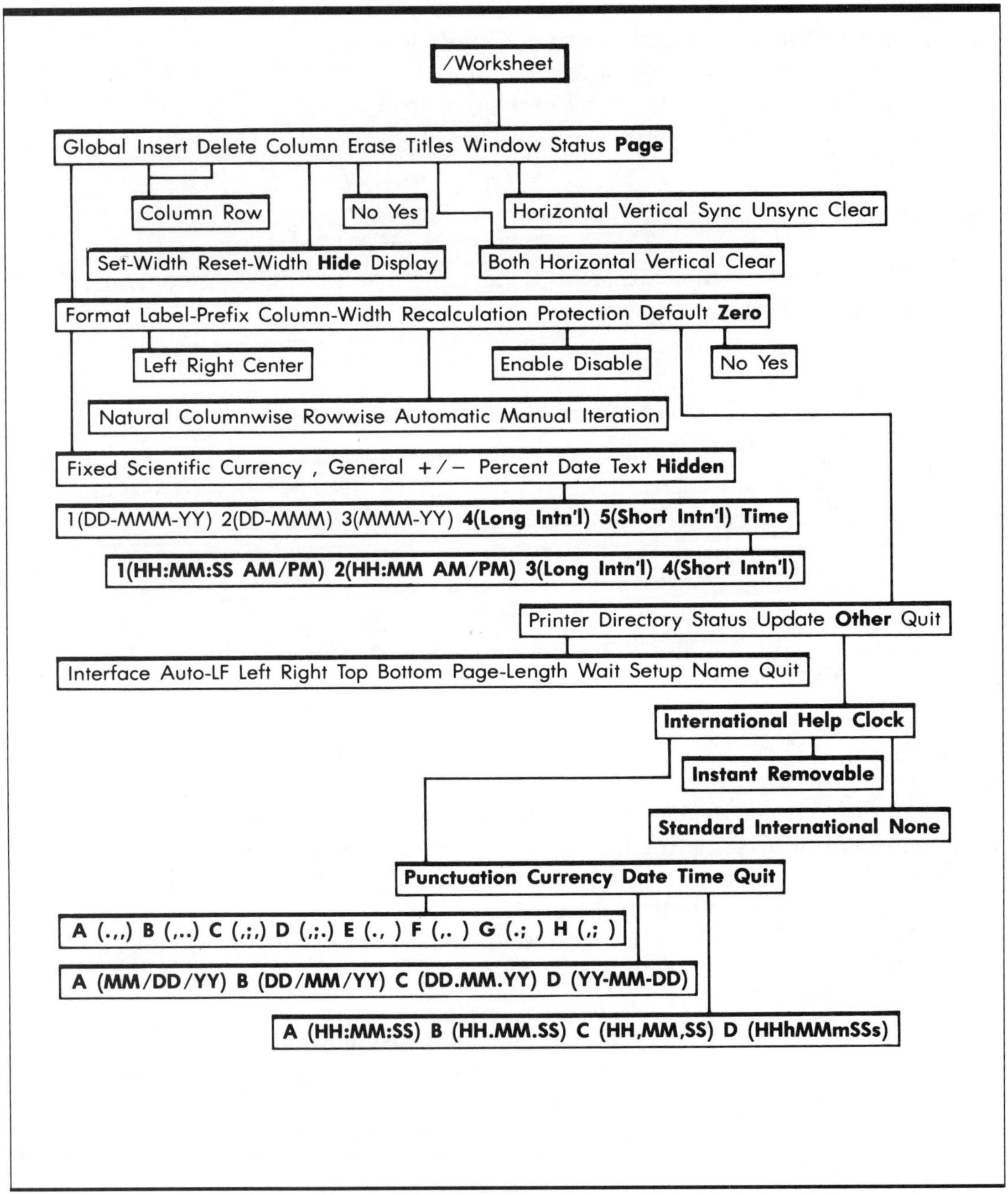

FIGURE 4.3: The Worksheet Menu is one of the most involved in Lotus 1-2-3. Options that you select from it affect your entire worksheet. The Global options are used to set new worksheet defaults.

COMMAND	VALUE	COMMENTS
Format	General	Can be changed to any of the other display formats available.
Label-Prefix	Left (')	Can be changed to Center (^) or Right (").
Column-Width	9 (characters)	Can be set to a value from 1 to 240 (1 to 72 in Release 1A).
Recalculation	Natural, Automatic	Natural can be replaced with Columnwise or Rowwise; Automatic can be set to Manual.
Protection	Disable(d)	Can be set to Enable.
Default	(Various)	Settings for printer, directory, display formats, Help method, and Clock display (Release 2) can be changed.
Zero	No	Can be set to Yes to suppress the display of zeros.

TABLE 4.1: Global Default Settings for Lotus 1-2-3

/Worksheet Global Zero

/Worksheet Global Zero allows you to suppress the display of zeros throughout the spreadsheet. It is often useful when printing a worksheet where the display of cells of zeros throughout adds nothing to its overall legibility. There is, however, no comparable Range command that would allow you to suppress the display of zeros in a particular range of cells.

/Worksheet Global Format Hidden

The /Worksheet Global Format Hidden command suppresses the display of all cells in the worksheet that have not been previously formatted with a /Range Format option. When this is on, you can tell that a particular cell has data in it only by moving the cell pointer to it and looking at its literal contents on the first line of the Control Panel. This, of course, will not allow you to see the calculated results of any formulas, because they are shown only in the worksheet. Lotus 1-2-3 Release 2 provides a comparable Range command for hiding the display of particular ranges, /Range Format Hidden. You will often find this new command quite useful. It is discussed later in this chapter.

/Worksheet Insert, Delete

The Insert and Delete options are used either to add or to delete entire columns and rows in the spreadsheet. They should be used with care, especially if you are working with a worksheet that you didn't design. Many people use these commands almost as the equivalents of the /Move and /Range Erase commands, although in fact they behave quite differently. Remember that when you delete a column or row with the /Worksheet Delete command, you erase it not only in the area visible on the screen but all the way from row 1 to 8192 or column A to IV.

/Worksheet Column

The Column option allows you to change column widths, hide columns, or display hidden columns. These options are discussed in more detail in Chapter 5, "Creating Worksheets."

/Worksheet Erase

The Erase option clears from RAM the worksheet currently in memory. If the worksheet has not been saved previously, it will be lost after you give the /Worksheet Erase Yes (/WEY) command. Be careful not to confuse this command with the /File Erase command, which deletes a specified worksheet file from disk. If you wish to load a new worksheet from disk to replace the one currently in memory, you do not need to use /WEY to clear the one in memory first. Accessing the command /File Retrieve will do the equivalent before loading your new worksheet.

/Worksheet Titles, Window

The Titles and Window selections are often used together to control the worksheet display. They offer almost the same options. The Titles command freezes column labels in the horizontal direction, row labels in the vertical direction, or both. The Window command splits the display into two viewing areas that you can size as you wish. You can split the display either horizontally at a particular row number or vertically at a particular column letter.

/Worksheet Status

This command displays a variety of information about available memory and certain global settings. It is discussed in greater detail in Chapter 5, "Creating Worksheets."

/Worksheet Page

There is a new addition, called Page, at the end of the Worksheet Menu in Release 2. Using the /Worksheet Page command allows you to enter a printer control code to start a new page at any row in the worksheet.

THE RANGE MENU

The Range Menu commands affect ranges of cells within the worksheet. You define the size and location of the range of cells to be included. The options available on this menu are shown in Figure 4.4.

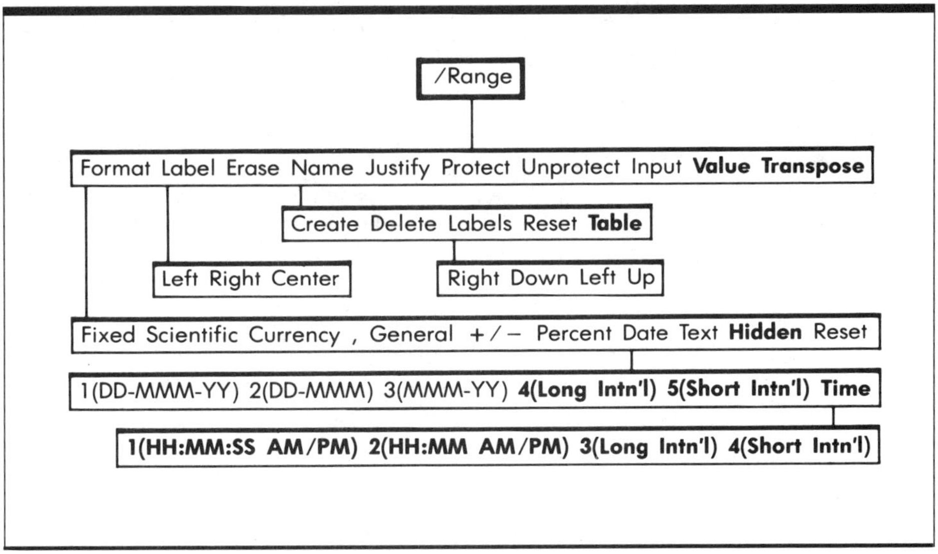

FIGURE 4.4: The Range Menu is one of the most often used in Lotus 1-2-3. The extent of the range to be affected by the particular command selected must be defined by cell addresses unless you have previously used the /Range Name command to define and name the range you wish to use. Range commands like Format and Unprotect take precedence over /Worksheet Global commands in effect. The /Range Erase command is the only way to delete a cell's contents in a range. Value and Transpose are new Release 2 options.

This chapter discusses some procedures used for working with the Range commands, including the Range commands that are new in Release 2. For detailed discussions of other Range commmands, see the list at the end of the chapter.

Defining a Range of Cells

When you define a range to be affected by a particular Range command, you must use the cell addresses unless you have already named the range with the /Range Name Create command. You can either type in the cell addresses or use pointing to highlight the range.

Anchoring the Pointer

If you use pointing, you do not have to use the period key as an anchor; all Range commands are naturally anchored from the position of the pointer. In fact, if you find that the pointer is not located properly to highlight the entire range, you must press Esc to unanchor the pointer in order to be able to relocate it. Then type a period as you would when pointing out a range with the /Copy or /Move commands.

Format Precedence

Ranges whose displays are formatted with the /Range Format options supersede changes to the global worksheet format. Compare Figures 4.5 and 4.6. In Figure 4.5, two ranges of values have been entered into the sample worksheet. Range 1, extending from B6 to B8, has not been formatted with /Range Format. Range 2, extending from D6 to D12, has been formatted with /Range Format Currency (/RFC2). In this figure, the global format default setting is still General, which is the program default when beginning a new worksheet. This accounts for the various numbers of decimal places displayed in range 1.

Figure 4.6 represents the same worksheet with the same two cell ranges. The only difference is that the global format has been changed to Fixed with one decimal place (/WGFF1). Range 1, which has not been formatted with the /Range Format command, is immediately affected by this new global format, while range 2 is not. To format this range to the new global format, use the /Range Format Reset command on it (**/RFR D6..D12**).

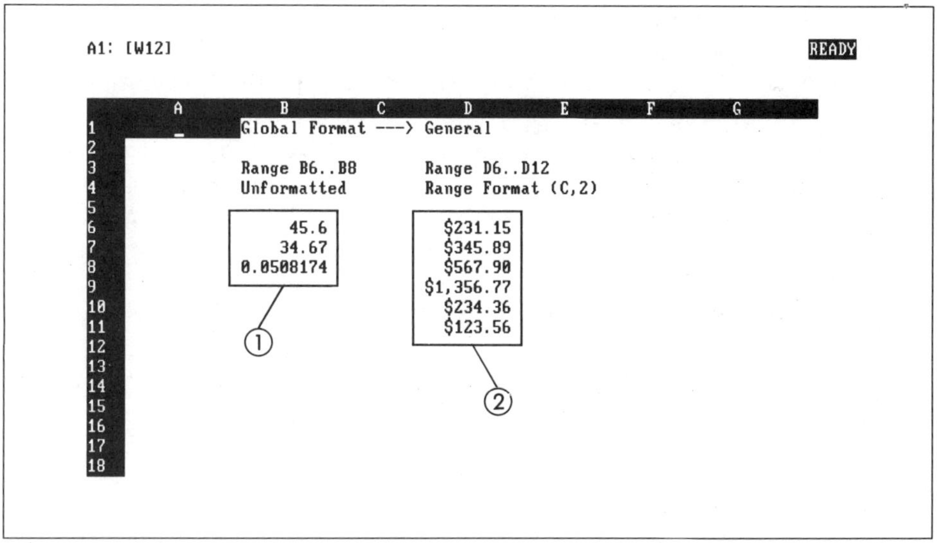

FIGURE 4.5: Two ranges of values in a worksheet where the global format is still the program's default setting of General. Because the format is General, range 1 displays decimal places as input or required by calculation (in B8, the calculated result fills the entire cell width). Range 2 has been altered with the /Range Format command to Currency with two decimal places, overriding the General global format.

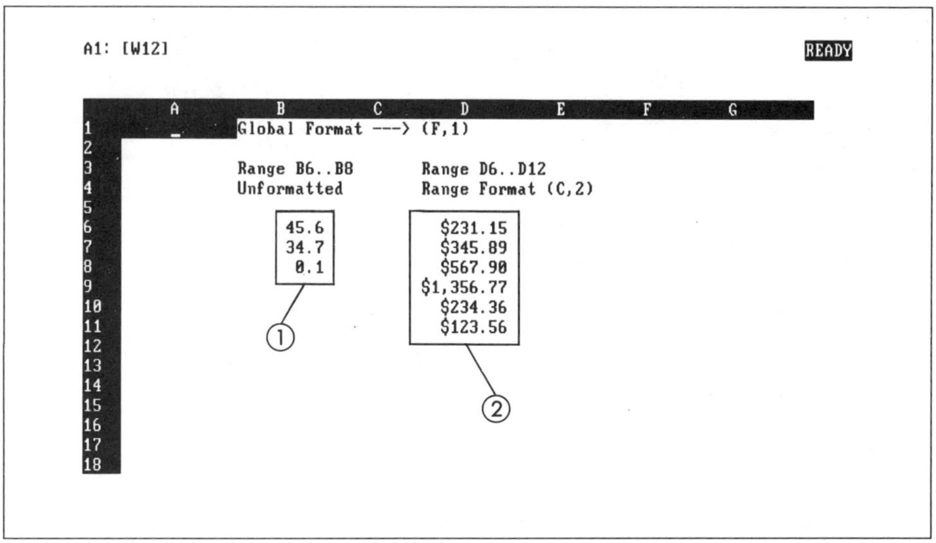

FIGURE 4.6: Effect on the same two ranges after changing the global format to Fixed with one decimal place. This new format affects range 1 by rounding up the values as required to display one decimal place. Range 2 is unaffected by the modification to the global format. It will continue to display the (C,2) format until the /Range Format command is used again to change it.

This precedence also holds when you set protection or hide cell ranges in your worksheets. For example, if you enable global worksheet protection, all cells in the spreadsheet are affected except those cell ranges that have been unprotected with the /Range Unprotect command. The only way to protect these cells is to use the /Range Protect command on them. If you set the global format to Hidden, all cell displays will be suppressed except those that have been formatted with one of the /Range Format options.

New Range Commands (Release 2)

Several new commands have been added to the Range Menu in Release 2. In Figure 4.4 these are indicated in boldface type.

/RANGE VALUE

The Value command converts the literal contents of a cell calculated by a formula or function into its resulting value. This relieves you of having to write a macro or use the /File Xtract Values command to do such conversions. If you are still using Release 1A, you can do the same thing by using /File Xtract Values to copy the range into a new file and then use the /File Combine Copy Named/Specified-Range command (/FCCN) to copy it back into your worksheet.

/RANGE TRANSPOSE

The Transpose command is one that Lotus 1-2-3 users have wanted for a long while. It allows you to transpose the position of data in columns to rows and data in rows to columns. You may often find yourself entering values (including formulas) or labels down a column, only to decide that they would be better placed across a single row. This command allows you to make this transposition easily. Its use is fully covered and illustrated in Chapter 7, "Formatting Worksheets."

/RANGE NAME TABLE

The other two new Release 2 commands worthy of note are /Range Name Table and /Range Format Hidden. You use /Range Name Table to have Lotus 1-2-3 build a table of all the ranges that you have named with the /Range Name command. It constructs a table listing these names in alphabetical order. It also includes a second column that gives you their cell addresses. This is most useful when you want to get a listing of all the available macro commands for use in the area of the spreadsheet where you are currently working.

/Range Format Hidden

As discussed above, /Range Format Hidden is a new counterpart of the /Worksheet Global Format Hidden command; it suppresses the screen display of specified ranges in the spreadsheet. It is quite useful when you do not wish to include particular sections of the worksheet in a printed report or when you need to suppress the display of sensitive data as you work on the worksheet.

The Copy and Move Menus

The Copy and Move Menus do not have suboptions attached to them as do the Worksheet and Range Menus discussed above. However, they both require user input in the form of cell ranges before their commands are carried out.

/Copy and /Move Prompts

Both /Copy and /Move display the same kind of prompt when you first invoke them. With the /Copy command, the prompt is

Enter range to copy FROM:

With the /Move command, it is altered slightly to

Enter range to move FROM:

The cell range you enter can consist of either the cell addresses of the range or a range name you previously defined with the /Range Name Create command. This is the source range, that is, the one to be either copied or moved, depending upon which command you are using.

When you enter the range and press Return, the same type of second prompt is displayed. When using the /Copy command, it is

Enter range to copy TO:

In the case of the /Move command, it appears as

Enter range to move TO:

As with the first set of prompts, you can enter this range by using either the cell addresses of the range or its name. It is, however, very rare that you will use a range name, because you seldom name an empty range of cells before a copy or move operation has been completed. If you are designating a named range that already holds data, be aware that the new data copied or moved into this range will overwrite the existing contents of these cells. Most often, you will use /Copy or /Move only to go to new, blank areas of the spreadsheet.

In both cases, the range you enter at the TO prompt represents the destination range, that is, the cell location where the copy is to be made or the range is to be moved. However, unlike when you defined the source range, you do not need to designate more than the address of the cell in the upper-left corner of this destination range. Lotus 1-2-3 will make the copy or move from this point on, using as many cells as it needs.

Using Pointing

When you designate the source and destination ranges for the /Copy or /Move command, you can use cell pointing rather than typing in their addresses (the merits of cell pointing as a design technique are discussed in Chapter 8). When you use pointing, remember that unlike with /Range commands, the beginning of the TO range is not automatically entered at the pointer's current position. You must type a period to anchor the TO range when pointing out a range larger than a single cell.

Using the /Copy and /Move Commands

The uses for the /Copy and /Move commands are discussed and illustrated in Chapter 7, "Formatting Worksheets." In addition, the subject of using the /Copy command when making copies of formulas is covered in Chapter 10, "Working with Formulas and Functions." Here you will find a complete discussion of when to use relative, mixed, and absolute cell references in making copies.

The File Menu

The File Menu controls all worksheet file functions, including save, load (called Retrieve), delete, the cut-and-paste options, extract and combine, directory listings, and importing ASCII files. These functions affect every kind of Lotus 1-2-3 file except graph files, which can be saved and retrieved only from the Graph Menu. Figure 4.7 shows you the options and setup of the File Menu.

File Extensions

Lotus 1-2-3 automatically assigns three file extensions to differentiate the file types it recognizes and uses:

- Worksheet files, whether they contain spreadsheets or databases, carry the extension .WK1 (.WKS in Release 1A). It is added to the file name you give when you save a worksheet with the /File Save command.

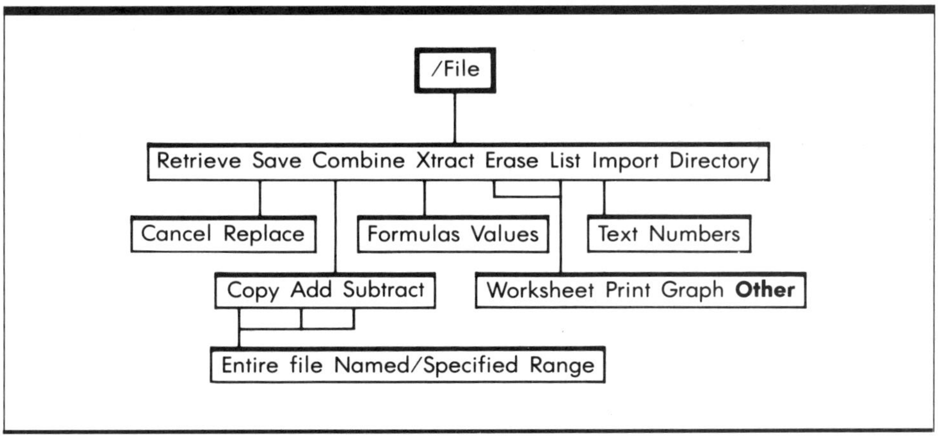

FIGURE 4.7: The File Menu controls all aspects of file handling for all types of Lotus 1-2-3 files except graph files. In addition to using this menu to save and retrieve your worksheets, you also use it to import any ASCII files into the spreadsheet. The /File Combine and Xtract commands are used for cut-and-paste operations between worksheets. The /File Erase command allows you to erase files. The /File List command gives a listing of any of your Lotus 1-2-3 files on the current directory, and /File Import allows you to import standard ASCII files into your spreadsheets. /File Directory enables you to make a new directory current.

- Graph files carry the extension .PIC. It is added to the file name you give when you save a graph with the /Graph Save command.
- ASCII files carry the extension .PRN (for Print files). It is added to the file name you give when you save a worksheet in ASCII format with the /Print File command.

/File Retrieve

The /File Retrieve command loads a saved worksheet into memory. You must load a worksheet if you wish to work on it or print it. This command erases any worksheet currently in memory before it loads the designated file. The command always displays the worksheet files saved in the current directory on the third line of the Control Panel. In Release 2, this listing is in alphabetical order.

To choose a file, you can move the highlight to it and press Return. Most often, this list will extend beyond the width of the screen display. Continuing to press the → key scrolls new file names into view. You can also bring up a directory-style file listing by pressing F3 (Retrieve). Or you can just type in the name of the file (the entry line clears when you begin to type).

In Release 1A, only files with the extension .WKS can be loaded into the program. In Release 2, you can load worksheet files that carry your own extensions (listed only by the /File List Other command), though to do this you must type in their complete file names. Lotus 1-2-3 will not display them when you use the /File Retrieve command, so you cannot use the pointing method to select them. To load a file saved in ASCII format into the Lotus 1-2-3 spreadsheet, you must use the /File Import command (see /File Import earlier in this chapter).

/File Save

The /File Save option saves not only all of the data entered in your worksheet but also all of the current settings, including graph and defaults and display formats as well as the last position of the cell pointer. Because Lotus 1-2-3 does not automatically save your worksheets when you exit the program, you can lose all of your work if you use the /Quit command without first issuing /File Save.

The first time you save a worksheet, you are prompted to give it a file name. In Release 2 of the program, you can also password-protect the file by designating a password after you enter the file name. (Be careful when you assign passwords, because there is no way to retrieve the worksheet later without knowing the exact password you assigned to it. For a full discussion of how to use this option, see Chapter 9, "File Operations.")

When you save this same worksheet later, Lotus 1-2-3 suggests the file name you assigned. If you press Return rather than enter a new file name, you are then prompted with Cancel and Replace. New users sometimes become confused by these prompts and choose the default, Cancel, in preference to Replace (which really means update). Doing so fails to save any work added since the last time the /File Save command was used.

/File Combine, Xtract

The /File Xtract and /File Combine commands allow you to do cut and paste operations between worksheets, using either the entire file or just specific ranges within it. The /File Combine command has three options: Copy, Add, and Subtract. Choosing Copy means that the data brought in at the current cell will overwrite any existing data. If you choose Add or Subtract, all numerical values in the same cells will be totaled using either addition or subtraction (text in both worksheets will be left untouched). This is Lotus 1-2-3's method for doing spreadsheet consolidations (see Chapter 19).

When you use the /File Xtract command, you must designate not only the range to be saved and a new file name but also whether to extract and save your formulas. As mentioned earlier, using the Values option of this command allows you to convert formulas to their calculated values.

/File Erase, List

You can use the /File Erase and /File List commands to obtain a directory listing of any of the three types of data files by using the options Worksheet, Print, and Graph attached to the Erase and List options on the menu illustrated in Figure 4.7. A new option, Other, has been added to this menu in Release 2. It allows you to get a listing of (or delete) all files on the data disk, even those that do not carry any of the three file extensions automatically assigned by Lotus 1-2-3.

/File Import

The /File Import command will not display any file that does not have the .PRN extension. If a file has no file extension or carries an extension other than .PRN, you must enter the complete file name to import it. You can also use the DOS RENAME command to add the .PRN extension to it.

There are two options, Text and Numbers, on the Import menu. With the Numbers option, the program searches the file for all numerical data and text enclosed in pairs of quotes. It disregards any other data. With the Text option, each separate line of the file is placed into an individual cell of the worksheet. These cells display as long labels extending from the current cell down the column to as many cells as there are lines of text in the original file. To separate particular data items in the label and place them in their own cells, you can use the /Data Parse command (see Chapter 29) if you are using Release 2.

/File Directory

The /File Directory command lets you view and/or change the current drive and directory where data files are stored. Making a new drive and directory current remains in effect only until you exit the program. To set a new, permanent default directory, you must use the /Worksheet Global Default Directory command (/WGDD).

When you save or retrieve a worksheet in Release 2, you can always change to the directory in which it is located simply by designating the complete path name when you enter the file name. For example, if the current directory is C:\123\DATA, you could retrieve a worksheet named ORDER987 stored in the directory \ACCTS by entering **C:\123\ACCTS \ORDER987** in response to the prompt for the file to be retrieved. Then, if you wished, you could save a copy of it in the \DATA directory by altering its file name to **C:\123\DATA\ORDER987** after giving the /File Save command. In Release IA, you must make a directory current in order to save or retrieve files in it.

Using the /File Commands

All the File Menu commands with the exception of /File Import are discussed and illustrated in Chapter 9, "File Operations." The /File Import command is covered in Chapter 29, "Importing and Exporting ASCII Files."

THE PRINT MENU

The Print Menu controls all aspects of printing Lotus 1-2-3 worksheets. This includes printing sections of spreadsheets as well as printing reports from your Lotus 1-2-3 databases. It does not, however, include the printing of graphs, which is handled exclusively by the PrintGraph utility (separate from the Lotus 1-2-3 program). The options and layout of the Print Menu are shown in Figure 4.8.

Notice that these options are concerned with defining the parameters for the printed report, including the range of cells, formatting options, and whether to print the cells as displayed or to print the formulas used in them. The printing device and the type of interface are designated from the /Worksheet Global Default Printer command (see Chapter 2). Any other printing defaults, with the exception of whether to use single-sheet or continuous-feed paper, can be controlled from the Print Menu. Settings made from this menu stay in effect only during the current work session. When you start Lotus 1-2-3 again, the global printing defaults will be in effect again.

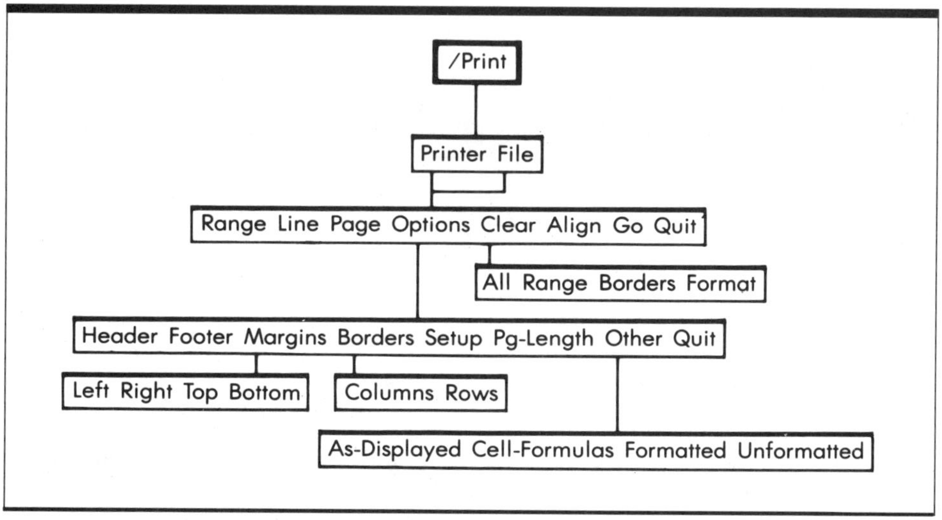

FIGURE 4.8: The Print Menu is used either to obtain a hard copy of the worksheet in memory or to create a new ASCII version of that worksheet on disk. It controls all aspects of report printing except setting the printing device and its interface, which is controlled by the /Worksheet Global Default Printer command. To print graph files, you use the PrintGraph option on the Lotus Access System Menu.

/Print Printer, File

The first options you receive after invoking the /Print command are Printer and File. To obtain a hard copy of the worksheet in memory, choose Printer. To create a new ASCII file version of the worksheet in the current directory, choose File. After that, the major options of the Print menu are presented.

Setting Print Options

This menu is a "sticky" menu, meaning that after you define various parameters with its options, you are always returned to it. For that reason, the menu provides a Quit option to return you to READY mode.

You will often need to use many of the options on this menu to set up all of your printing parameters before you issue the Go command to begin printing. This type of menu setup saves you from having to type the initial letter sequence **/PP** (or **/PF**) repeatedly before the letter of each menu option. You will run into this type of menu in Lotus 1-2-3 whenever there might be a need to use several options on a single menu before you issue a command. Notice in Figure 4.8 that a Quit option is also listed on the Options Menu, indicating that this is true at that level of the Print Menu hierarchy as well.

Using the /Print Commands

All of the Print Menu commands are discussed and illustrated in Chapter 25, "Printing Reports." To obtain information on setting up the printer defaults, see Chapter 2, "Installing and Customizing Lotus 1-2-3."

THE GRAPH MENU

You use the Graph Menu to design, display, and save all the graphs that you generate from the data in your spreadsheets or databases. The many options on this menu are shown in Figure 4.9. Lotus 1-2-3 supports five different graph types that can use up to six different data variables defined by their cell ranges in the worksheet. The data variables are designated by the letters A through F.

In Release 2, you can use a B data-variable range to designate what kind of shading to use for the different segments of the pie and to explode various segments of it. The A data-variable range contains the data that generates and sizes the pie segments themselves.

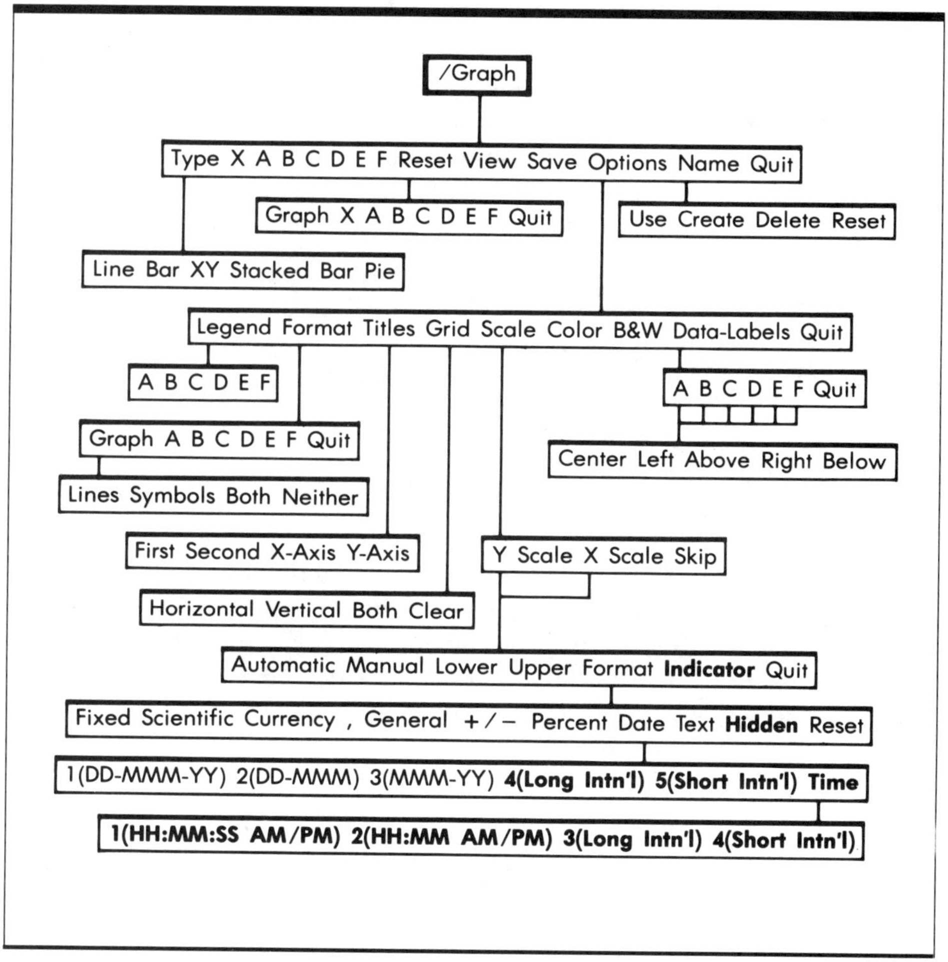

FIGURE 4.9: The Graph Menu is used to generate and save all of the graphs you create from your spreadsheet and database data in Lotus 1-2-3. You can use five different graph types. All of them except pie charts can have up to six data variables (A to F) defined by range in the worksheet. You can save up to eight separate graph settings, though you must name them with the /Graph Name Create command and save them with your worksheet. To be able to print graphs, you must also save them with /Graph Save. Lotus 1-2-3 gives all of these graph files the extension .PIC (for picture file).

Defining and Saving a Graph

You can define up to eight different graphs to be saved in a single worksheet file. The general procedure is as follows:

1. Create your graph by using the various options on the Graph Menu and then name it using the /Graph Name Create command.
2. After generating and naming your graph, save it as part of the worksheet using the /File Save command.
3. If you want to plot or print your graph using the PrintGraph utility, save it in a separate graph file using the /Graph Save command. When you enter a file name for it, do not use an extension. The program automatically saves it with the file extension .PIC.

If you do not name a graph before you create a new one, you will lose it. Lotus 1-2-3 always keeps only the most recent graph settings as the current graph. This graph is the one that is displayed any time you press the Graph function key (F10), when in READY mode.

Displaying Graphs on the Screen

To display graphs on the screen, your computer must be equipped with some sort of graphics device. If your system has an IBM monochrome monitor, you can purchase a special monochrome graphics adapter like the Hercules Graphics Card. If you do not have this or a Color/Graphics Adapter (and a color or composite monochrome monitor), you can still generate graphs from this menu and print them with the PrintGraph program, though you will have no way to preview them on the screen.

Using the /Graph Commands

All of the Graph Menu commands and options are discussed and illustrated in Chapter 24, "Creating and Using Graphs." To learn about printing and plotting your graphs, see Chapter 26.

THE DATA MENU

The functions of the commands on the Data Menu are among the most varied on Lotus 1-2-3's Main Menu. These options and their layout on the

Data Menu are illustrated in Figure 4.10. This menu handles at least five distinct functions:

- Automatic generation of sequences of numbers in a worksheet, using the /Data Fill command
- Multiple formula calculation in the spreadsheet using the /Data Table commands
- Database management, using the /Data Sort and /Data Query commands
- Statistical analysis, using the /Data Distribution command (and the /Data Matrix and /Data Regression commands if you are using Release 2)

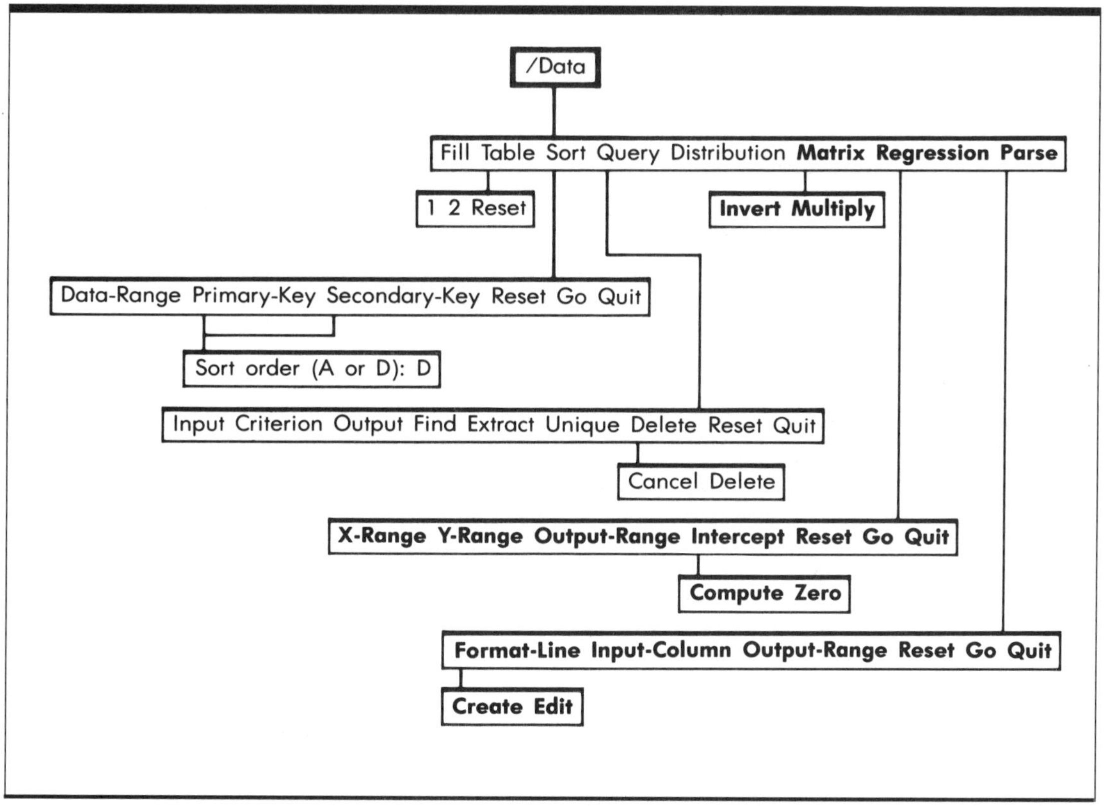

FIGURE 4.10: The functions provided by the commands on the Data Menu are among the most varied of any Lotus 1-2-3 menu. The /Data Fill command automates the generation of number sequences in the worksheet. The /Data Table commands extend and automate "what-if" analysis. The /Data Sort and Query commands maintain Lotus 1-2-3 databases. The /Data Distribution, Matrix, and Regression commands provide powerful statistical data analysis. The last command, /Data Parse, breaks up long strings of ASCII data imported with the /File Import command into separate cells in the worksheet.

- Splitting long label entries in single cells into separate cells containing individual items, using the /Data Parse command (Release 2 only)

/Data Fill

The first command, /Data Fill, automatically generates sequences of numbers in worksheets or databases. To create the sequence, you enter the range of cells to be numbered, enter the beginning number, enter a number by which each succeeding cell is to be incremented, and indicate the highest or lowest number allowed. The increment, or step, you use can be a positive or negative number.

/Data Table

The /Data Table commands are used in situations that call for multiple calculations using one or two input variables. There are two separate commands, /Data Table 1 and 2, that make it possible to extend and automate "what-if" analysis in one part of the worksheet. In most cases, these commands can be used as powerful alternatives to having to subject the spreadsheet model to various new assumptions by manually revising the input cells on which they depend.

/Data Sort, Query

The /Data Sort and /Data Query commands are often used together to maintain the Lotus 1-2-3 databases that you have created. The /Data Sort command can be used to sort any data in the worksheet in either ascending or descending order. In Release 2, you can change the sort order by using the Install option located on the Lotus Access System Menu (see the "Advanced Options: Changing the Sort Order in the Spreadsheet" section in Chapter 2 for details).

The /Data Query commands allow you to locate particular records in the database or copy those that meet specified criteria to a new range in the worksheet. The /Data Sort command is covered in Chapter 20, "Creating a Lotus 1-2-3 Database," and the /Data Query command is covered in Chapter 21, "Database Operations."

Data Analysis Commands

Statistical data analysis has been greatly enhanced in Release 2 of Lotus 1-2-3 with the addition of the /Data Matrix and /Data Regression commands to the /Data Distribution command. The /Data Distribution command allows you to create a frequency distribution table that condenses large amounts of data grouped in ranges. The resulting frequency distribution table can then be graphed by using Lotus 1-2-3's graph facilities.

The new Release 2 commands /Data Matrix and /Data Regression provide you with powerful statistical functions. With the /Data Matrix command, you can solve systems of simultaneous linear equations in a matrix. You have the option of either inverting or multiplying the matrix. The largest matrix you can use is a square 90 columns wide by 90 rows deep.

The /Data Regression command provides you with a means to do simple or multiple linear regression analysis involving up to 16 independent variables. This function is used to establish whether any correlations exist between what are determined to be the independent and dependent variables in a statistical sampling. Determining the quantitative relationship between the two can sometimes provide a powerful way to estimate the value of the dependent variable in relation to the values of the independent variables. All three of these statistical commands are discussed and illustrated in Chapter 22, "Data Distribution, Matrix, and Regression Commands."

/Data Parse

The /Data Parse command is used with ASCII files that are imported with the /File Import command. This command provides an easy way to separate into individual cells items brought into Lotus 1-2-3 as long labels in single cells. It is most often applied to database data that is imported. When the /File Import Text command is used to transfer data, each record is stored in an individual cell down the rows. The /Data Parse command (*parse* means to break down into parts) allows you to define each field item and place it into its own column, as is done with any Lotus 1-2-3 database. Its use is discussed and illustrated in Chapter 29, "Importing and Exporting ASCII Files."

THE SYSTEM AND QUIT MENUS

The /System command is new to Release 2. It provides a means for temporarily exiting directly to the operating system, where you can use DOS commands like FORMAT, COPY, DELETE, RENAME, and so on. As soon as you type **/s,** you receive the operating system prompt and a message telling you to type **exit** to return to Lotus 1-2-3.

If you use Lotus 1-2-3 on a two-disk-drive system, you will be logged onto drive A. If you have not copied the COMMAND.COM file onto your Lotus 1-2-3 System Disk, you will receive the message "Cannot invoke DOS" (see Chapter 2 for details on how to copy this file). If this happens, press Esc and replace the Lotus 1-2-3 System Disk with a copy of your DOS disk.

If you use the program on a hard disk system, you will be logged onto drive C and the directory containing the program files (usually C:\123). To use the external DOS FORMAT command, you will have to first use the change directory command (cd\DOS) to make the directory containing your DOS files current, unless you keep a copy of FORMAT.COM in your Lotus 1-2-3 directory (or unless you tell DOS where FORMAT.COM is located by using a PATH command).

Using the /System Command

When you use the /System command, you cannot load other memory-resident programs into memory (even external DOS utilities like PRINT or SETCLOCK). This command is not intended to be a switching program like Microsoft Windows, which allows you to load different application programs into RAM and then shift back and forth between them. Be sure that you never load a RAM-resident utility like SideKick or Note-It (commonly called *TSRs* for programs that terminate and stay resident) after you exit to DOS with the /System command. It is intended only as a replacement for the disk file utilities that are no longer included on the Release 2 Lotus Access System Menu as they are in Release 1A.

Always load such RAM-resident programs from DOS before starting up Lotus 1-2-3. If you load other software into RAM, you will not be able to reenter Lotus 1-2-3 by using the exit command. Your computer will probably crash, though it may be possible to get back to the DOS prompt without having your system freeze up. Always save your worksheet before intentionally using the /System command. If you type **/s** when you mean to type **/fs** and find yourself suddenly in DOS, you will not be able to save your worksheet. If this happens, type **exit** right away to return to Lotus 1-2-3.

It is also dangerous to use the /System command to terminate a TSR program before you enter Lotus 1-2-3 to try to free up more memory for your worksheet. This creates a gap in RAM, which usually makes it impossible either to return to Lotus 1-2-3 or to prevent a system crash. If you need to free memory to increase the size of your worksheet, save the worksheet and then use the /Quit command to return to the operating system. Once there, give the appropriate command to terminate the TSR and then start up the program again.

Using the /Quit Command

The /Quit command is the only way to exit Lotus 1-2-3 and permanently return to the DOS operating system. When you use this command, you are prompted with No and Yes. Pressing Return at this point will return you to the spreadsheet. You only have to type **y** to exit. Be sure that you have used the /File Save command to save your worksheet in its most recent form before you give the /Quit command (/QY). Once you invoke it, all data in the computer's memory will be cleared.

SUMMARY

This chapter has covered the layout of the Lotus 1-2-3 command menus as well as outlined their general uses. In the chapters ahead, you will find each of these commands described by itself with instructions on how to use it as well as common examples illustrating its potential applications. Also, when possible, macros that facilitate the use of the particular command have been included so that you can incorporate them into your own worksheets as you use the program.

To locate the chapter containing the particular commands you are interested in, use the following reference table.

For more information on /Worksheet commands:

- Chapter 5 /Worksheet Global Format, Label-Prefix, Column-Width, Protection, Zero, /Worksheet Column
- Chapter 6 /Worksheet Erase
- Chapter 7 /Worksheet Insert, Delete

- Chapter 8 /Worksheet Titles, Window
- Chapter 19 /Worksheet Global Recalculation
- Chapter 25 /Worksheet Page

For more information on /Range commands:

- Chapter 5 /Range Format, Label, Protect, Unprotect, Input
- Chapter 6 /Range Erase, Value
- Chapter 7 /Range Justify, Transpose
- Chapter 8 /Range Name

For more information on the /Copy command:

- Chapter 7 Copying cell ranges
- Chapter 10 Copying formulas with relative, mixed, and absolute cell references

For more information on the /Move command:

- Chapter 7 Moving ranges around the worksheet

For more information on the /File commands:

- Chapter 9 /File Retrieve, Save, Combine, Xtract, Erase, List, Directory
- Chapter 29 /File Import

For more information on the /Print commands:

- Chapter 25 /Print Printer Range, Line, Page, Options, Clear, Align, Go, Quit,/Print File Range, Line, Page, Options, Clear, Align, Go, Quit

For more information on the /Graph commands:

- Chapter 24 /Graph (all menu commands)

For more information on the /Data commands:

- Chapter 20 /Data Fill, Sort
- Chapter 21 /Data Query

- Chapter 22 /Data Distribution, Matrix, Regression
- Chapter 23 /Data Table
- Chapter 29 /Data Parse

PART 2

SPREADSHEET COMMANDS

The Lotus 1-2-3 spreadsheet is undoubtedly the most important component of the program. Part 2 discusses its use in terms of creating spreadsheets (Chapter 5), editing worksheets (Chapter 6), formatting worksheets (Chapter 7), working with cell ranges (Chapter 8), and worksheet file operations (Chapter 9). It is in this part of the handbook that you will find most of the reference entries for the /Worksheet and /Range command menus.

Chapter 5 discusses techniques for creating a spreadsheet, including the topics of designing, doing data input, formatting the display of cells, and protecting the final spreadsheet from further change.

Chapter 6 focuses on editing an existing spreadsheet, either by modifying the contents of the cells, reentering them, or by deleting them entirely. It also discusses how to transform formulas into their calculated values, and how to transform labels into values and back again.

Chapter 7 is concerned with worksheet formatting. These topics include techniques for adding and deleting columns and rows from a spreadsheet, copying and moving cell ranges, and combining and separating cell entries. (Note that this chapter does not discuss setting up and changing cell display formats by using the /Range Format or /Range Label commands; this information is found in Chapter 5.)

Chapter 8 examines cell ranges: what they are and how they are used. Here you will find techniques and command references for naming ranges, setting up title areas, and working with windows.

Chapter 9 concentrates on file operations within Lotus 1-2-3. This includes saving and retrieving a worksheet file, password protection (in Release 2), listing files by type, and changing directories. It also contains information on using the File and Disk Manager programs in Release 1A and using the /System command in Release 2. Finally, it discusses how to combine and perform consolidations between worksheets by using the /File Combine commands.

CHAPTER 5

CREATING WORKSHEETS

Creating Worksheets

This chapter discusses techniques used in designing and creating new worksheets. It first presents several topics that you may find useful, depending on your level of experience with the program:

- A section on design considerations discusses issues that confront you when you first start a new spreadsheet model.
- A section on spreadsheet labels and values looks at the way Lotus 1-2-3 evaluates initial entries into cells and the problems you may encounter.
- Another section covers techniques for making data input in worksheets easier and quicker.
- A final section deals with worksheet protection methods.

Following these discussions is detailed information on the /Worksheet and /Range commands that you commonly use when you build a new worksheet. These individual reference entries are arranged in the order they occur on the Lotus 1-2-3 menus.

Design Considerations for New Worksheets

When you create a new worksheet, you need to think about several things before you begin your work in the Lotus 1-2-3 spreadsheet itself. First, you must consider whether the worksheet you are about to create is to serve as a template for building application worksheets or is to be a one-time application model that may or may not be subjected to extensive what-if analysis.

If it is to be a template, you may need to spend more time on the preliminary design than with a one-time model. Start by laying out the basic design on paper. As you do this, contemplate what functions the worksheet must serve and how it will actually be used in the office. Part of these considerations include the skill levels of those who will be using it.

If the worksheet will require a great deal of data entry and later updating that will be done by less-experienced Lotus 1-2-3 users, you will need to consider what to protect in the worksheet and, perhaps, how to guide the operator in his or her work. If you are creating a really complex application, you may even find it necessary to include macros that automate and protect the integrity of the data input.

Documenting the Worksheet While Designing It

It is always important to make sure that the spreadsheet is well documented. This oftens spells the difference between an application whose assumptions can be checked for correctness, and therefore used in confidence, and one that cannot. You may even find that in time you will not remember what you based certain input values on or the reason you chose to use particular functions. Also, having each spreadsheet well documented allows it to be revised and expanded fairly easily as assumptions change, especially if this is to be done by others not involved in the original design.

When you document a worksheet, it is helpful to assign descriptive range names to as many of the cell entries as possible. For instance, contrast the effect of seeing the formula

INT_RATE_EARNED*BEG_BAL

as opposed to

B8*B50

for calculating the interest earned in an account as the literal contents of a cell labeled Interest Earned.

In the first example, using descriptive range names allows you to comprehend immediately whether the formula is correctly constructed. The drawback of this method is that it does not tell you where the cells named INT_RATE_EARNED and BEG_BAL are located in the worksheet. You can determine this only by looking at the cell labels for B8 and B50, respectively. In fact, part of the process of thoroughly documenting your spreadsheet is to make sure that your cell labels are correct and reflect as much as possible the range names you have assigned to the cells that they refer to.

Also regarding labels, make sure that they are not too short or cryptic unless space is at an absolute premium. It may be tempting to abbreviate to cut down on the amount of typing and keep the column width narrow, but too much abbreviating is really not a good idea. Labeling is an important part of documenting a spreadsheet's functioning. After all, the labels are really the primary means of identifying a worksheet's contents. They allow you and others concerned to spot any oversights or incorrect assumptions quickly.

Steps in Creating a New Worksheet

Even if you are creating a one-time-only application (or one that appears so at the outset), you should try not to rush into designing on the screen and building on the fly. Although it may seem like this can save valuable time, you will usually end up doing many revisions, often major, that you could have avoided by taking time with preplanning. Many of these revisions are the most basic and persistent kind, such as having to move and rearrange ranges continually to make room for parts of the spreadsheet that you did not originally plan space for as you built the application. Worse yet are those revisions to formulas that require you to rework the fundamental layout of the spreadsheet.

Below is a general outline of the series of steps that you should routinely follow when creating a new worksheet:

1. Determine the shape of your worksheet and try to estimate its size. Will it be shallow in rows and wide in columns, or narrow in columns and deep in rows? From this decision, and from any sketches you have made of the spreadsheet, determine the number of panels (i.e., display screens of 8 columns by 20 rows, or 160 cells) you will need.
2. Copy in the macro library file containing the construction macros that you normally use when you build new spreadsheets (/FCCE). Locate this file in a new part of the worksheet so that it is below and to the right of the panels where you will begin construction.
3. Use the /Range Name commands to activate your construction macros in the new worksheet.
4. Return to the first panel and begin entering all the headings you need. Make sure none of these labels are so abbreviated that they could be misinterpreted by someone else using the worksheet.

5. If the application calls for it, or if it helps you to construct the formulas you need, enter sample data in key cells before you construct the major formulas required.
6. As you construct your primary formulas, always be mindful of when and how they may be copied. Think about when it is necessary to use relative, mixed, and absolute cell addresses so that you can copy these formulas in the worksheet later.
7. Whenever appropriate and helpful for documenting the working of the spreadsheet, name the cells or ranges of cells that contain the primary formulas (using /Range Name Create—/RNC). Then refer to these range names in other dependent formulas you create (remember, though, that a range can be only relative or absolute in a formula; it does not admit mixed addresses).
8. Copy the formulas as required throughout the worksheet.
9. Format the worksheet's display. Widen and narrow columns to improve legibility.
10. If the worksheet is to serve as a template, erase the sample data from it. If required, protect the entire worksheet with /Worksheet Global Protect Entire (/WGPE) and then unprotect all of the input cells with /Range Unprotect (/RU).
11. Save the worksheet under a unique name. If you wish, you can first remove the construction macros by using /Range Erase (/RE).

As with any guidelines, there are times when your application will not only benefit from but will require that you not follow them verbatim. Nevertheless, you will find that most applications are best designed and created by following the steps outlined above. (For one notable exception, see "Methods for Inputting Dates in the Worksheet" below.)

Using Worksheet Construction Macros

Almost every user of Lotus 1-2-3 keeps a file containing his or her favorite keystroke macros that make creating a new spreadsheet faster and easier. As noted in the design guidelines above, you should bring this file into the new worksheet at the very beginning. Figure 5.1 shows you these basic construction macros and their location. In this figure they are located starting in cell Y61 (three screens over and three down from A1) to give plenty of working space in either direction. If more working room is required for

```
AD61:                                                                  READY

        Y            Z                 AA        AB        AC          AD
61  \C         {?}~~{DOWN}       <--Enter numbers in column
62             /XG\C~                from 10-key pad
63
64  \R         {?}~~{RIGHT}      <--Enter numbers across row
65             /XG\R~                from 10-key pad
66
67  \E         /RE~              <--Erase current cell
68
69  \W         /WCS{?}~          <--Widen column
70
71  \U         \-~/C~.{RIGHT}    <--Add row separators
72
73  \V         ^:~/C~.{DOWN}     <--Add column separators
74
75  \D         @DATE(86,{?},{?})~ <--Auto date entry
76             /RFD1~/WCS10~
77
78  \S         /FS~R             <--Save file under same name
79
80  \P         /PPR{?}~AGQ       <--Print worksheet
07-Jul-86  09:34 AM
```

FIGURE 5.1: A typical set of construction macros that are useful when creating a new worksheet. This set is stored in a worksheet file named MACROLIB. It is read into a new worksheet with the /File Combine Copy Entire <macrolib> command (/FCCE <macrolib>). Then the range Y61..AA80 is named MACROS with /Range Name Create (/RNC) and the individual macros are named with /Range Name Labels Right (/RNLR <Y61..Y80>).

the spreadsheet itself, this range of macros can be moved a little further down or over (or both, if necessary).

When you begin a new worksheet, bring the file containing these macros into it by using the /File Combine Copy Entire (/FCCE) command. Then use the /Range Name (/RN) command to activate the macros in the new worksheet. Give the entire range of construction macros a range name like MACROS in case it should have to be moved down or over to stay out of the way of the spreadsheet itself.

In this file you can also keep descriptions of the macros available and the Alt-key combination for invoking them. This "help" screen is shown in Figure 5.2. Give it a range name like MENU and then activate the macros: locate the cell pointer back in cell Y61 and use the /Range Name Labels Right (/RNLR) command on the range Y61..Y80 to name the macros themselves and activate them in the worksheet. Save the worksheet with the name you intend to give it; then return to A1 and begin to build the worksheet itself.

```
AE61: ^|                                                                    READY

      AE    AF    AG              AH                         AI       AJ
61    |_    \C    |    <--Enter numbers in column            |
62    |           |       from 10-key pad                    |
63    |           |                                          |
64    |     \R    |    <--Enter numbers across row           |
65    |           |       from 10-key pad                    |
66    |           |                                          |
67    |     \E    |    <--Erase current cell                 |
68    |           |                                          |
69    |     \W    |    <--Widen column                       |
70    |           |                                          |
71    |     \U    |    <--Add row separators                 |
72    |           |                                          |
73    |     \V    |    <--Add column separators              |
74    |           |                                          |
75    |     \D    |    <--Auto date entry                    |
76    |           |                                          |
77    |           |                                          |
78    |     \S    |    <--Save file under same name          |
79    |           |                                          |
80    |     \P    |    <--Print worksheet                    |
07-Jul-86  09:35 AM
```

FIGURE 5.2: Descriptions of the macros in the construction set and their associated names. This menu was created by copying the first column (Y) containing the macro labels and the third column (AA) containing descriptions of their use to columns AF and AH, respectively. Whenever you need to refer to the macros available while building the new spreadsheet, press F5 and enter the range name MENU to view its contents.

You will probably want to follow similar steps in preparation for creating your worksheets. All of the construction macros shown in Figure 5.1 as well as some others not shown there are listed and explained under the various references detailing the use of their associated command. You may want to look them up in the index and include them in your own construction macro file, if you have not already created one for yourself.

LABELS VERSUS VALUES IN LOTUS 1-2-3

Lotus 1-2-3 recognizes two kinds of data entries in worksheet cells: *labels* begin with an alphabetical character or particular punctuation symbol, and *values* begin with a number, mathematical operator, or some symbol that denotes a function (@) or is reserved for values. While most of the time this is a convenient aid to swift data entry, it is sometimes necessary to circumvent the system.

Forcing a Value to Be Considered a Label

These are the most common occasions for turning what Lotus 1-2-3 would normally consider a value into a label:

- When you enter a column or row heading that begins with a number, such as 1987 Budget Projections. In this case, Lotus 1-2-3 goes into VALUE mode when you type **1** and changes into EDIT mode as soon as you press the Return key to enter the label. You cannot mix text with numbers in cells unless you are in LABEL mode.
- When you enter a fixed number of hyphens to be used as underscores that have not been entered as a repeating label (\-). Lotus 1-2-3 takes this as a string of minus signs and goes into EDIT mode. You cannot enter more than a single minus sign without following it with either a number or a cell reference.

Label Prefixes; Formatting Labels

In these cases, you must preface the entry with one of Lotus 1-2-3's label prefixes: '(apostrophe) for left justified, ^ (circumflex) for centered, and " (quotation marks) for right justified. The default is left justification for all labels that are not entered with a label prefix. As a rule, most people find it most convenient and appropriate to use the apostrophe (') as the label prefix when they have to force Lotus 1-2-3 into LABEL mode. This is because the display of left-justified labels extends across blank cells to the right if the label is longer than will fit in the current cell width.

If you know that you want the label centered or right justified at the time you enter it, you can go ahead and use the appropriate prefix character in place of the apostrophe. However, you can also accomplish the same thing by using the /Range Label Center (/RLC) or /Range Label Right (/RLR) commands. These are even more convenient for centering or right justifying labels in cells because they can be applied to an entire range of cells at one time rather than one cell at a time. They also make data entry easier because the apostrophe is an unshifted character located on the home row, while the circumflex and quote are both shifted characters.

Some data-entry operators adopt the technique of pressing the space bar before all entries that should be labels but are interpreted by the program as values. Although prefacing an entry with a blank space also activates LABEL mode, it has a different effect on the entry. Pressing the space bar not only ensures that subsequent characters will be accepted as a label but also indents the first character of the label one space. If you later want to center the cell contents, this blank will be included. On the whole, it is much better to use the apostrophe rather than the space bar to force your entry to be accepted as a label. Reserve the use of the space bar for when you really want to set off a label by indenting it.

Forcing a Label to Be Considered a Value

The most common situation in which you need to turn what Lotus 1-2-3 normally considers a label into a value is when you enter a formula that begins by referencing a specific cell address, such as B3 + B4. Because the first character typed is alphabetical, referring to a column letter, Lotus 1-2-3 goes into LABEL mode. Although the program will accept your entry as a label, it cannot calculate the formula; it can only enter its contents into the cell.

To get around this, you must start the formula with a mathematical symbol that will put the program into VALUE mode before you enter the column letter of the cell reference. The plus sign signifying addition is used because it has no effect on the resulting calculation. Using the plus sign is required only when the cell reference is not prefaced with some other value symbol such as −, (, $, or #. When any of these characters precede the cell address, VALUE mode is automatically activated.

Values are always right justified in the cell. In fact, looking at whether a cell's contents are right justified is often a way to tell whether a particular cell entry has been entered as a value or a label. This method of differentiation is not foolproof, however, because you can also right justify labels either by prefacing a label with the quote or by using the /Range Label Right (/RLR) command.

Determining Whether a Cell Entry Was Made as a Label or a Value

The only way to be sure whether a particular entry has been entered as a value or a label is to move the cell pointer to the cell and examine the literal contents on the first line of the Control Panel. All label entries display one of the label prefixes before the characters that make up the entry displayed in the cell. Values entered as literals do not carry any of these prefixes. And, of course, values entered as formulas display the contents of the formulas.

Release 2 of Lotus 1-2-3 includes the functions @ISSTRING and @ISNUMBER, which test the contents of cells to determine whether they contain labels or values. These functions are useful in formulas and macros where the kind of cell entry determines how you will process the formula or macro. They are described in Chapter 15, "Logical Functions."

LABELS VERSUS VALUES IN A DATABASE

Taking into consideration how Lotus 1-2-3 interprets the first character you enter is important not only in the spreadsheet but also when working with Lotus 1-2-3 databases. The same limitations in terms of labels and values apply. They most often arise when you enter data in the address field of a database. Many addresses begin with street numbers, which naturally make the program go into VALUE mode. This means that you must preface street numbers with an apostrophe. When you have others who are not very experienced in using Lotus 1-2-3 doing data entry in a database, be sure to alert them to this potential problem and how to avoid it.

DATA INPUT TECHNIQUES

There are a few techniques that you can to use to make your job easier when you have a lot of data input to do in a spreadsheet. This section discusses two techniques: one for making text and numerical data entry more efficient and the other for making it easier to do date entries that require the special @DATE function.

Methods for Efficient Spreadsheet Data Input

Chapter 3's section "Macros for Numerical Data Entry with the 10-Key Number Pad" presents two macro commands, one for inputting numbers down columns and the other for inputting numbers across rows. While you may not wish to use these macros because you are more comfortable doing numerical data entry from the top-row keys, you will still find it more efficient to input your data either vertically or horizontally.

When you enter data (numeric or text) in the spreadsheet, you can speed up the process substantially by pressing the appropriate arrow key instead of pressing the Return key to complete the entry into the current cell. This has the advantage of moving the cell pointer to the next cell where you need to enter data. If you use the Alt-C or Alt-R macros, the spreadsheet cursor moves in the correct direction when you press Return.

Regardless of the method, you should establish a pattern of either going down the rows and then up to the beginning of the next column or going across the columns and then down to the beginning of the next row. You can automate this zig-zag pattern of data entry if you are using the Alt-C and Alt-R macros. With the Alt-C macro, you simply add a macro that takes the cursor back to the beginning of the column and then over to the right one cell, automatically positioning the cell pointer in the proper position for continuing data entry without requiring you to disable Num Lock and use the arrow keys. You can create a similar macro to work with Alt-R to take the cell pointer to the start of the current row and then down one cell.

When you use these macros, you do not have to inactivate the Num Lock key. After the cell pointer has been repositioned, invoke either Alt-C or Alt-R and continue data entry. The actual contents of the macros are given in Table 5.1.

To reposition the pointer when doing data entry down a single column:

Label	*Macro Contents*
'\t	**{UP}{END}{UP}{RIGHT}**

The first {UP} positions the cell pointer at the end of the column of entries. Then {END}{UP} takes it to the very top (thus, Alt-T) of the column and {RIGHT} moves it over to the new column. This macro will not work properly if you skip a row before entering data down the next column. Also, if the column heading is the first cell in the column, you must append the command {DOWN} to the end.

To reposition the pointer when doing data entry across a single row:

Label	*Macro Contents*
'\b	**{LEFT}{END}{LEFT}{DOWN}**

The first {LEFT} positions the cell pointer at the end of the row of entries. Then {END}{LEFT} takes it to the very beginning (thus, Alt-B) of the row and {DOWN} moves it down to the next row. This macro will not work properly if you skip a column before entering data across the next row.

TABLE 5.1: Macros for Repositioning the Pointer during Data Entry

Methods for Inputting Dates in the Worksheet

Entering a series of dates in a new worksheet with the @DATE function is very tedious. To help with this kind of entry, you can either use a macro command (see the @DATE entry in Chapter 14) or enter the first date and then copy it to all of the following cells. You can then edit each date to make it correct.

Earlier in the design guidelines it was suggested that you should save display formatting ("prettying up" the spreadsheet) until after you have built all the formulas and completed all the necessary data entry into your input cells. While this holds true in many cases, you should do just the opposite in date entry: copy a single date and then edit the contents of the copies. Widen the column and format the first date entry before you copy it down or across a range of cells, because the date format is copied along with the serial date. As you edit each date, you can tell whether you have revised it correctly as soon as you press Return or the appropriate arrow key. This is not nearly so easy to see if you are looking at serial date numbers.

PROTECTING THE COMPLETED WORKSHEET

Once you have finished creating, formatting, and checking out the operation of your spreadsheet, you may wish to protect certain areas in it from further modification. The first step in this process is to protect the entire worksheet with the /Worksheet Global Protection Enable command (/WGPE). Doing this prevents you from making changes to any cell in the spreadsheet.

Next, you use the /Range Unprotect (/RU) command to disable the protection for any cell ranges that must be left open to further revision. This usually involves only the input cells in the spreadsheet, that is, those that are used as variables in the dependent formulas you have constructed.

In many of the templates that you create, these cells are the ones that must be loaded with data in order to create an actual working spreadsheet. In some models, these cells are the ones that contain the basic assumptions that must be revised in order to subject the worksheet to further what-if analysis.

You can also apply protection to some database applications. Unprotected cells can be limited to a special range that holds the input cells for each field. Once the operator has finished data entry in each of them for a single record, a macro is used to check the data and then add it to the database.

The benefit of using such a system for adding records is that there is no chance that the central database itself can be corrupted during data entry. This means that data-entry operators who are not very familiar with the workings of Lotus 1-2-3 can still do the basic data-entry task. Later, more skilled Lotus 1-2-3 users can perform the query and maintenance operations required. During these operations, global protection is lifted by using the /Worksheet Global Protection Disable (/WGPD) command.

Lotus 1-2-3 also offers another command that you can use along with protection to aid the more inexperienced Lotus 1-2-3 user in basic data entry. This is the /Range Input (/RI) command. After you enable global protection and then unprotect selective ranges, you can use /Range Input to limit the cell pointer to only those cells in the worksheet that are unprotected. After you use this command, the pointer will move only to these unprotected cells.

THE /WORKSHEET COMMANDS COMMONLY USED IN CREATING WORKSHEETS

The following commands are often used when you create a new worksheet. They are presented in the order they are found on the Lotus 1-2-3 menu system.

/Worksheet Global Format

MENUS

/Worksheet
Global
Format
Fixed Scientific Currency , General +/− Percent Date Text Hidden

FUNCTION

This command sets a new global display format for the worksheet. It affects all values in the worksheet not previously formatted with /Range Format. The default setting when you begin a new worksheet is General. Regardless of the global format you choose from this menu, Lotus 1-2-3 stores each numerical value to a precision of 15 decimal places. Changing the display format in the worksheet itself does not affect this precision.

In General format, numbers with more than 15 digits are automatically converted to scientific notation. If the number of digits in a value is greater than the number of characters in the column width minus one, the program also converts the value into scientific notation. Any zeros entered after the decimal point are not displayed.

USAGE

To set a new global display format, type **/WGF** and then choose the desired format from the menu options that appear.

FIXED—/WGFF

The Fixed format allows you to choose the number of decimal points to be displayed in values in the worksheet. You can select a number between 0 and 15. The default suggested by the program is 2. In this format, values are presented as X.XX. To set a new value, enter the number of digits and press Return.

SCIENTIFIC—/WGFS

The Scientific format displays all values in exponential notation. You can specify the number of decimal places to be displayed before the exponent as a number between 0 and 15. The default suggested by the program is 2. In this format, values are presented as X.XXE+XX. To set a new value, enter the number of digits and press Return.

CURRENCY—/WGFC

The Currency format displays all values in a dollar-and-cents format in which a dollar sign precedes numbers, commas separate thousands, and negative numbers are in parentheses. The default number of decimal places is 2. You can show any number of decimal places between 0 and 15. In this format, values are presented as $X,XXX.XX. To set a new number of decimal places, enter the number of digits and press Return.

In Release 2, you can change the currency symbol used in this format as well as the thousands and decimal-point delimiters by using the /Worksheet Global Default Other International command (/WGDOI). Any changes made to the Punctuation and/or Currency options that appear after you use this command are picked up when you choose the Currency format (see "Customizing Lotus 1-2-3 Release 2" in Chapter 2 for details).

THE COMMA (,) FORMAT—/WGF,

The Comma format displays values in the same way as the Currency format, except that it does not preface the value with a dollar sign. The default number of decimal places is 2. In this format, values are presented as X,XXX.XX. To change the number of decimal places, enter a number between 0 and 15. Any changes made with the /Worksheet Global Default Other International command are also reflected in this format.

GENERAL—/WGFG

The General format is the Lotus 1-2-3 global default at startup. You choose this format to change the global format back to General after you use one of the other options listed on the menu. In this format, values are presented as X.XX or X.XXEXX. To set this format, you simply type **/WGFG** (for /Worksheet Global Format General) and press Return. Unlike the Scientific format, this format gives you no control over the number of decimal places displayed before the exponent. It is always 2 when the General format is in effect.

THE +/− FORMAT—/WGF +

The +/− format is referred to as a horizontal bar graph format. It converts all values into a corresponding number of pluses or minuses. Zeros are displayed as a decimal point. In this format, values are presented as + + + or − − −. To set it as the global format, you simply type **/WGF +** and press Return. There are no further options to be selected.

PERCENT—/WGFP

The Percent format displays all values as percentages by multiplying the value by 100 and adding a trailing percent sign (%). The default number of decimal places is 2. In this format, values are presented as X.XX%. To set the global format to Percent, type **/WGFP** and the number of decimal places between 0 and 15; then press Return. Any changes made to the International Punctuation command are also reflected in this format.

DATE—/WGFD

The Date format displays all values in the worksheet in one of the date formats you specify after selecting this command. These formats include 1(DD-MMM-YY), 2(DD-MMM), and 3(MMM-YY). In Release 2, there are two other formats, 4(Long Intn'l) and 5(Short Intn'l). The default for these displays are MM/DD/YY and MM/DD, respectively.

Finally, the Release 2 Date format selections include a Time option attached to a menu with these four options: 1(HH:MM:SS AM/PM), 2(HH:MM AM/PM), 3(Long Intn'l), and 4(Short Intn'l). The Long International date format is just like format 1 except that it uses a 24-hour clock instead of the AM/PM notation. The Short International format is just like format 2 except for its use of a 24-hour clock. You can modify the punctuation and style of these formats by using the International Date and Time menus (/WGDO).

TEXT—/WGFT

The Text format displays all formulas used in the worksheet in place of their calculated values. Where literal values have been used, the program uses the General display. To set the Text format as the default, type **/WGFT** and press Return. There are no further options associated with this format.

HIDDEN (RELEASE 2 ONLY)—/WGFH

The Hidden format suppresses the display of all cells in the worksheet. Their contents are displayed only on the first line of the Control Panel when the cell pointer makes the individual cell current. Because only cell contents, not calculated values, are displayed on the Control Panel line, you cannot see their calculated values (derived from formulas); you can see only the formulas.

EXAMPLES

The /Worksheet Global Format commands affect values in the spreadsheet in the same way that /Range Format commands do. For examples of each display format, see Figure 5.5.

SEE ALSO

/Range Format

/Worksheet Global Label-Prefix

MENUS

/Worksheet
Global
Label-Prefix
Left Right Center

KEYBOARD ENTRY

/WGLL /WGLR /WGLC

FUNCTION

This command changes the label default of left justified to either right justified or centered in the cell. It is referred to as Label-Prefix because it automatically adds either the quote (") for right justification or the circumflex (^) for centering before any entry completed while the program is in LABEL mode (for a discussion of LABEL mode, see Chapter 4).

USAGE

You will usually leave the Lotus 1-2-3 global label prefix set to the apostrophe because only left-justified labels are displayed in adjacent blank cells to the right when they are longer than the column width. In worksheets in which the majority of labels should be right justified in their cells, use the /WGLR command. In worksheets in which the majority of labels should be centered in their cells, use the /WGLC command.

Be aware that when you enter a label that requires you to add a label prefix (refer back to the section "Forcing a Value to Be Considered a Label" in this chapter), you will have to use either the " or ^ instead of the apostrophe to maintain consistent label formatting.

You can modify any cell or range of cells that already contains label entries formatted to the new global setting by using the /Range Label command with either of the other two options not specified as global. You can also type a different label prefix character to change the formatting of a label display as you are entering it. Either method allows you to override the default setting whenever required in the worksheet.

SEE ALSO

/Range Label

/Worksheet Global Column-Width

MENUS

/Worksheet
Global
Column-Width

KEYBOARD ENTRY

/WGC <number of characters>

FUNCTION

This command changes the width of all of the columns in the entire worksheet (from A to IV) from the default width of 9 to a new setting of your choice. In Release 1A, the setting can be anywhere from 1 to 72. In Release 2, it can be anywhere from 1 to 240.

USAGE

To set a new global column width, issue the command **/WGC** and type in the new number of characters or press either the → or ← key to use pointing to increase or decrease the width. After you press Return, all columns will be set to the new width. To modify a particular column to a different width, use the /Worksheet Column Set-Width command.

SEE ALSO

/Worksheet Column

/Worksheet Global Protection

MENUS

/Worksheet
Global
Protection
Enable Disable

KEYBOARD ENTRY

/WGPE /WGPD

FUNCTION

This command protects the entire worksheet from further revisions of any kind. Once global protection has been enabled, no one can edit, delete, reformat, or in any way change the contents of the cells entered when creating the spreadsheet or adding new entries in other areas. Any attempt to add new entries or edit existing ones results in the program going into ERROR mode. The user also receives the error message "Protected cell." Lotus 1-2-3 indicates that protection has been enabled by adding the abbreviation P before the display of the cell's literal contents on the first line of the Control Panel.

USAGE

To set global protection, type **/WGPE** and press Return. To remove it, type **/WGPD** and press Return.

Global protection is used on completed spreadsheets and templates to protect the majority of the worksheet from further change. After you enable global protection, you can then unprotect particular input cells by using the /Range Unprotect (/RU) command. From then on, you can make any what-if analysis in confidence that the template is safe from inadvertent changes.

If you need to make revisions to part of a spreadsheet that has been globally protected, use the /Worksheet Global Protect Disable command (/WGPD) to lift the protection. After making any required changes, globally protect the worksheet once again with /WGPE.

EXAMPLES

For an example of setting global protection in a spreadsheet, see Figure 5.6.

SEE ALSO

/Range Protect and /Range Unprotect

/Worksheet Global Zero (Release 2 Only)

MENUS

/Worksheet
Global
Zero

KEYBOARD ENTRY

/WGZ

FUNCTION

This command suppresses the display of all zero values throughout the worksheet. It is useful when you want to print a spreadsheet without having the report cluttered with zeros.

USAGE

To suppress the display of zero values in the worksheet, type **/WGZY** (for Yes). All zeros visible on the screen will be blanked out as though the cells were empty. Take care when you activate the /Worksheet Global Zero command that you do not mistake the cells with zeros for empty cells and add new data in them or copy or move ranges over them. You may want to use the /Range Protect command to prevent this possibility. To make zeros visible once again, type **/WGZN** (for No).

EXAMPLES

Figures 5.3 and 5.4 show the effect of using the /Worksheet Global Zero command on a typical spreadsheet template. In Figure 5.3, income and expenses have been projected only for the first and second quarters of the upcoming year. As a result, the third- and fourth-quarter income and expenses columns still display their original zero values.

Figure 5.4 shows the effect of activating the global suppression of zeros by using the /Worksheet Global Zero Yes command on these two columns. Notice, however, that even though these cells now appear to be blank, the literal contents of the current cell (D6) shows that this cell still carries the value of zero. Blanking out the display of zeros across these two columns helps make the income statement easier to read.

```
D6: (,0) [W10] 0                                                          READY

        A               B          C          D          E          F
1   Data 2000 Corporation
2   Projected Income Statement
3
4                    1st Qtr    2nd Qtr    3rd Qtr    4th Qtr    Year
5
6   Sales            500,000    550,000          0          0 1,050,000
7   COGS             200,000    220,000          0          0   420,000
8                ---------------------------------------------------
9   Gross Profit     300,000    330,000          0          0   630,000
10               ===================================================
11  Total Expenses   100,000    110,000          0          0   210,000
12               ===================================================
13  Operating Profit 200,000    220,000          0          0   420,000
14  Interest Expense  10,000     10,000          0          0    20,000
15               ---------------------------------------------------
16  Taxable Profit   190,000    210,000          0          0   400,000
17  Income Tax        51,300     56,700          0          0   108,000
18               ---------------------------------------------------
19  Net Income       138,700    153,300          0          0   292,000
20               ===================================================
13-Aug-86  03:07 PM
```

FIGURE 5.3: A projected income statement displaying two columns of zero values. In this example, figures have not yet been entered into the columns containing the income and expenses for the 3rd and 4th quarters, so they currently display all zero values. Contrast the appearance of this worksheet with that of the one in Figure 5.4, where global zero suppression has been activated.

```
D6: (,0) [W10] 0                                                    READY

      A              B         C          D          E          F
1   Data 2000 Corporation
2   Projected Income Statement
3
4                   1st Qtr   2nd Qtr    3rd Qtr    4th Qtr    Year
5
6   Sales           500,000   550,000      _                1,050,000
7   COGS            200,000   220,000                         420,000
8                   ---------------------------------------------------
9   Gross Profit    300,000   330,000                         630,000
10                  ===================================================
11  Total Expenses  100,000   110,000                         210,000
12                  ===================================================
13  Operating Profit 200,000  220,000                         420,000
14  Interest Expense  10,000   10,000                          20,000
15                  ---------------------------------------------------
16  Taxable Profit  190,000   210,000                         400,000
17  Income Tax       51,300    56,700                         108,000
18                  ---------------------------------------------------
19  Net Income      138,700   153,300                         292,000
20                  ===================================================
13-Aug-86   03:07 PM
```

FIGURE 5.4: The same projected income statement after activating global zero suppression by entering **/WGZY.** As a result, all of the zero values previously displayed for the 3rd and 4th quarters have vanished. You might think that these cells were now empty if it were not for the 0 displayed as the literal contents of the current cell (D6). To make the zero values reappear, you would enter **/WGZN.**

/Worksheet Column

MENUS

Release 1A	*Release 2*
/Worksheet	/Worksheet
Column-Width	Column
Set Reset	Set-Width Reset-Width Hide Display

KEYBOARD ENTRY

/WCS /WCR	**/WCS /WCR /WCH /WCD**

FUNCTION

The original /Worksheet Column-Width command has become /Worksheet Column in Release 2. In both, the first option allows you to make a spreadsheet column wider or narrower than the current global column width setting (9 characters is the program default unless modified). This new width can be anything from 1 to 72 in Release 1A and from 1 to 240 in Release 2.

You use the second option, Reset or Reset-Width, to change the column width back to the global default for any columns you have previously modified with the Set or Set-Width options.

In Release 2, two more options are available on this menu. The Hide option makes the display of the specified column of the worksheet invisible. You use the Display option to redisplay any column masked by the use of the Hide option.

USAGE

To Set Column Widths

To set a new column width, position the cell pointer anywhere in the column and give the command **/WCS.** You can set a new width for only that particular column. You can either type the number of characters for the new width or point with the → or ← keys. To reset the column back to the global default, place the pointer anywhere in the column and use the reset option, /WCR.

Suggestions on Setting Column Widths

You often need to reset the width of columns to improve the legibility of your worksheets. Whenever the current column width is too narrow to display its contents, Lotus 1-2-3 places a string of asterisks (******) in the cell. This often occurs when you format a date entry to Date format 1 (DD-MMM-YY) in a cell that has been set to the default of 9 characters; Date format 1 requires a minimum width of 10.

You can also use the /WCS command to widen columns to display entire labels that are otherwise truncated by the data in the column immediately to the right. In addition, you will sometimes find this command effective for narrowing a column that functions only to display a set number of blank spaces between two columns containing data.

Whenever you alter the column width from the global default, Lotus 1-2-3 places the number of the new setting in brackets that precede the literal contents of the cell, such as [W15] for a column set to 15 characters. To change all of the column widths in the entire worksheet, use the /Worksheet Global Column-Width command.

To Hide and Display Columns (Release 2 Only)

To hide the display of all data in a column in the worksheet, position the pointer anywhere in that column and give the command **/WCH.** The letter of the hidden column is no longer shown in the border area. You can hide a range of columns by typing the address of the range or by pointing to the cells.

To redisplay a hidden column, use the Display option (**/WCD**). When you use this option, Lotus 1-2-3 displays an asterisk after the letter of all hidden columns in the border area. To unhide a column, first display it; then move the pointer to one of its cells and press Return. To unhide a range of columns, you can either use pointing or specify the range address.

Suggestions for Using Hidden Columns

Hiding columns is an effective way to mask the display of columns temporarily during printing or to hide sensitive information from other users who may work on the spreadsheet. Remember that a hidden column affects all of the rows in that column from 1 to 8192.

Whenever you issue a command like /Move, /Copy, /Range Erase, /Range Format, and so forth, all hidden columns that can be viewed on the screen are temporarily unhidden. Their column letters are followed by asterisks. This prevents you from issuing a command that could harm or otherwise affect the data in these columns.

To hide only particular cells in a range rather than entire columns, use the /Range Format Hide command.

MACRO

Alt-W, a Macro for Setting the Column Width

Label	*Macro Contents*
'\w	**'/WCS{?}~**

This macro issues the command to change the column width of the column containing the cell pointer. It waits for you to either type in the number or use the ← or → keys to set the width. You only need to press Return once after setting the new column width by either method.

SEE ALSO

/Worksheet Global Column-Width
/Range Format Hide

/Worksheet Status

MENUS

/Worksheet
Status

KEYBOARD ENTRY

/WS

FUNCTION

This command displays the amount of available memory as well as the global parameters in effect, including method of recalculation, global display format and label prefix, and global protection status.

USAGE

The Status command gives you vital statistics on the global conditions in the worksheet. In Release 2, more information has been added to the command, and, consequently, it uses a full screen. The information included on the worksheet status screen differs from the earlier version only in that Release 2 includes statistics for the amount of expanded memory, presence of a math coprocessor, circular references in the spreadsheet, the number of iterations set, and the status of zero suppression.

Otherwise, the status commands in both releases give information on the amount of conventional memory (the only kind supported by Release 1A), the method and order of recalculation, the global cell display for values and labels, the global column-width setting, and the status of global protection.

Most of the time you use this command to obtain a reading on the amount of memory still available as you build your spreadsheet. In Release 1A, using the /Worksheet Status command is the only way you have of determining whether the available memory is getting critically low. Release 2 has added the MEM status indicator that alerts you to this condition while you are still working.

Although using the /Worksheet Status command provides an easy method for obtaining information at a glance on certain global default settings, Lotus 1-2-3 provides other clues in the worksheet itself for getting this information. Nevertheless, if you work on a computer shared with fellow workers, it is valuable to use this command when you begin a new worksheet to see whether any of the global defaults have been altered with the /Worksheet Global commands.

To use this command, you simply type **/WS.** Lotus 1-2-3 then displays the information. If you wish, you can use the Shift-PrtSc key combination to obtain a hard copy of the status screen. To return to the spreadsheet, press the Return key. Doing this takes you immediately back to READY mode.

EXAMPLES

Figures 5.5 and 5.6 illustrate the use of the /Worksheet Status command in Release 1A and Release 2, respectively. Notice that the additional information displayed in the Release 2 status screen is now laid out in a full-screen format. The mode indicator is also STAT (for status) in Release 2, while it remains MENU in Release 1A.

While most of the information presented in these two sample screens is the same, there are some notable differences. For one thing, Release 2 now gives the available conventional memory statistic in a slightly different way. In addition to giving the number of bytes, it now gives you the percentage of memory that is free. If the percentage falls to 4 percent or less, Lotus 1-2-3 alerts you by flashing the MEM indicator while you are working on the spreadsheet.

Also, in the Release 2 status screen, the statistics on the type of recalculation in effect in the spreadsheet include not only the method and order, as in Release 1A, but also the number of iterations set with the /Worksheet Global Recalculation Iteration command. As you can see, the default of the program is 1. In cases of circular references, whose presences are now noted in the Release 2 status screen, this number would be set much higher to try to resolve the circular references (see Chapter 19 for information on recalculation methods and circular references in the spreadsheet).

```
                                Label     Column    Avail                  MENU
  Recalculation      Format     Prefix    Width     Memory    Protect
AUTO       NATURAL   (G)        '         9         474773    OFF
            A                B          C          D          E
1   Data 2000 Corporation
2   Projected Income Statement -- 1988
3
4                      1st Qtr     2nd Qtr     3rd Qtr      4th Qtr
5
6   Sales            350,000.00  385,000.00  423,500.00   465,850.00
7   COGS             140,000.00  154,000.00  169,400.00   186,340.00
8                    ------------------------------------------------
9   Gross Profit     210,000.00  231,000.00  254,100.00   279,510.00
10                   ================================================
11  Total Expenses    70,000.00   77,000.00   84,700.00    93,170.00
12                   ================================================
13  Operating Profit 140,000.00  154,000.00  169,400.00   186,340.00
14  Interest Expense   5,000.00    5,000.00    5,000.00     5,000.00
15                   ------------------------------------------------
16  Taxable Profit   135,000.00  149,000.00  164,400.00   181,340.00
17  Income Tax        36,450.00   40,230.00   44,388.00    48,961.80
18                   ------------------------------------------------
19  Net Income        98,550.00  108,770.00  120,012.00   132,378.20
20                   ================================================
```

FIGURE 5.5: The /Worksheet Status command in Release 1A. In this figure, a sample spreadsheet has been loaded before taking the status reading. None of the global defaults—including automatic recalculation, the natural method of recalculation, the General global display format, apostrophe label prefix, column width of 9, or protection off—have been changed. Compare the amount of available memory after loading this worksheet with that in Figure 5.6. Though the spreadsheets are identical, the difference is caused primarily by the smaller amount of memory required to load Release 1A.

Because of changes to the new version, the status screen in Release 2 now gives you information on whether the program detects the presence of expanded memory and a math coprocessor. If you have installed either of these devices and the status screen still indicates None, you should investigate the problem (one method is to check whether other software that supports this hardware also fails to detect its presence). The status screen also tells you whether zero suppression has been turned on with the /Worksheet Zero command.

SEE ALSO

/Worksheet Global Format
/Worksheet Global Label-Prefix
/Worksheet Global Column-Width
/Worksheet Global Recalculation
/Worksheet Global Protection
/Worksheet Global Default Status
/Worksheet Global Zero

```
-                                                                 STAT

     Available Memory:
       Conventional..... 406065 of 419584 Bytes (96%)
       Expanded......... (None)

     Math Co-processor:  (None)

     Recalculation:
       Method........... Automatic
       Order............ Natural
       Iterations....... 1

     Circular Reference: (None)

     Cell Display:
       Format........... (G)
       Label-Prefix..... '
       Column-Width..... 9
       Zero Suppression. Off

     Global Protection:  Off

 02-Aug-86  09:14 AM
```

FIGURE 5.6: The /Worksheet Status command in Release 2. In this figure, the same worksheet as in Figure 5.5 was loaded before issuing the status command. In the Release 2 version of this screen, the statistics about the worksheet include additional information about expanded memory, the presence of a math coprocessor, circular references, and zero suppression. Notice that the amount of free memory is stated not only in bytes but also as a percentage of the total amount of memory still available.

THE /RANGE COMMANDS COMMONLY USED IN CREATING WORKSHEETS

You often need to control the parameters affecting smaller, select areas of the worksheet. For this reason, most of the /Worksheet commands have direct counterparts in /Range commands that allow you to change a particular range of cells. These commands are presented in the order they are displayed on the /Range menus.

/Range Format

MENUS

/Range
Format
Fixed Scientific Currency , General +/− Percent Date Text Hidden Reset

FUNCTION

This command sets a new display format for a range of values that you designate. Regardless of the display formats available from this menu, Lotus 1-2-3 stores each numerical value to a precision of 15 decimal places. Changing the display format in the worksheet itself does not affect this precision.

USAGE

To set a new range format, type **/RF** and then choose the desired format from the menu options that appear. Enter any necessary parameters and then designate the range of cells to be formatted either by typing in their cell addresses or by using pointing.

FIXED—/RFF

The Fixed format allows you to choose the number of decimal points to be displayed in values in the range. You can select a number between 0 and 15. The default suggested by the program is 2. In this format, values are presented as X.XX. To set a new value, enter the number of digits, indicate the range, and press Return.

SCIENTIFIC—/RFS

The Scientific format displays the values in the range in exponential notation. You can specify the number of decimal places to be displayed before the exponent as a number between 0 and 15. The default suggested by the program is 2. In this format, values are presented as X.XXE+XX. To set a new value, enter the number of digits, indicate the range, and press Return.

CURRENCY—/RFC

The Currency format displays the values in the range in a dollar-and-cents format in which a dollar sign precedes numbers, commas separate thousands, and negative numbers are in parentheses. The default number of decimal places is 2. You can show any number of decimal places between 0 and 15. In this format, values are presented as $X,XXX.XX. To set a new number of decimal places, enter the number of digits, indicate the range, and press Return.

In Release 2, you can change the currency symbol used in this format as well as the thousands and decimal-point delimiters by using the /Worksheet Global Default Other International command (/WGDOI). Any changes made to the Punctuation and/or Currency options that appear after you use this command are picked up when you choose the Currency format (see "Customizing Lotus 1-2-3 Release 2" in Chapter 2 for details).

THE COMMA (,) FORMAT—/RF,

The Comma format displays values in the same way as the Currency format, except that it does not preface the value with a dollar sign. The default number of decimal places is 2. In this format, values are presented as X,XXX.XX. To change the number of decimal places, enter a number between 0 and 15, indicate the range, and press Return. Any changes made with the /Worksheet Global Default Other International command are also reflected in this format.

GENERAL—/RFG

The General format is the Lotus 1-2-3 global default at startup. You would choose this format to change the format of the range back to General after you have used one of the other options listed on the menu. In this format, values are presented as X.XX or X.XXEXX. To set this format, you simply type **/RFG,** indicate the range, and press Return. Unlike the Scientific format, the General format gives you no control over the number of decimal places displayed before the exponent. It is always two when the General format is in effect.

Note: You can use the /Range Format Reset command to return a range to its current global format.

THE +/− FORMAT—/RF +

The +/− format is also referred to as the horizontal bar graph format. It converts all values in the designated range into a corresponding number of pluses or minuses. Zeros are displayed as a decimal point. In this format, values are presented as + + + or − − −. To set this format, you simply type **/RF +** , indicate the range, and press Return.

PERCENT—/RFP

The Percent format displays the values in the range as percentages by multiplying each value by 100 and adding a trailing percent sign (%). The default number of decimal places is 2. In this format, values are presented as X.XX%. To set the format to Percent, type **/RFP,** type the number of decimal places between 0 and 15, indicate the range, and press Return. Any changes made with the International Punctuation command are also reflected in this format.

DATE—/RFD

The Date format displays the values in the range in one of the date formats you specify after selecting this command. These formats include 1(DD-MMM-YY), 2(DD-MMM), and 3(MMM-YY). In Release 2, there are two other formats, 4(Long Intn'l) and 5(Short Intn'l). The defaults for these displays are MM/DD/YY and MM/DD, respectively.

Finally, the Release 2 Date format selections include a Time option attached to a menu with these four options: 1(HH:MM:SS AM/PM), 2(HH:MM AM/PM), 3(Long Intn'l), and 4(Short Intn'l). The Long International date format is just like format 1 except that it uses a 24-hour clock instead of the AM/PM notation. The Short International format is just like format 2 except for its use of a 24-hour clock. You can modify the punctuation and style of these formats by using the International Date and Time options (/RFD and /RFDT).

TEXT—/RFT

The Text format displays all formulas in the range in place of their calculated values. Where literal values have been used, the program uses the General display. To set the Text format as the default, type **/RFT,** indicate the range, and press Return.

HIDDEN (RELEASE 2 ONLY)—/RFH

The Hidden format suppresses the display of all cells in the range. Their contents are displayed only on the first line of the Control Panel when you make the individual cell current. To hide a range, type **/RFH,** indicate the range, and press Return.

Reset—/RFR

The Reset command returns the range of cells designated to their original global format. To use this command, type **/RFR,** indicate the range, and press Return.

EXAMPLES

Figure 5.7 shows how the various display format options available as part of the /Range Format command affect the same value in a worksheet. In cell C7, the result calculated by multiplying the values in A1 by A2 (their display is blanked out by the use of /Range Format Hidden) is shown in General format. This formula was then copied to all of the other cells in columns C and F, each of which was formatted with a different /Range Format option.

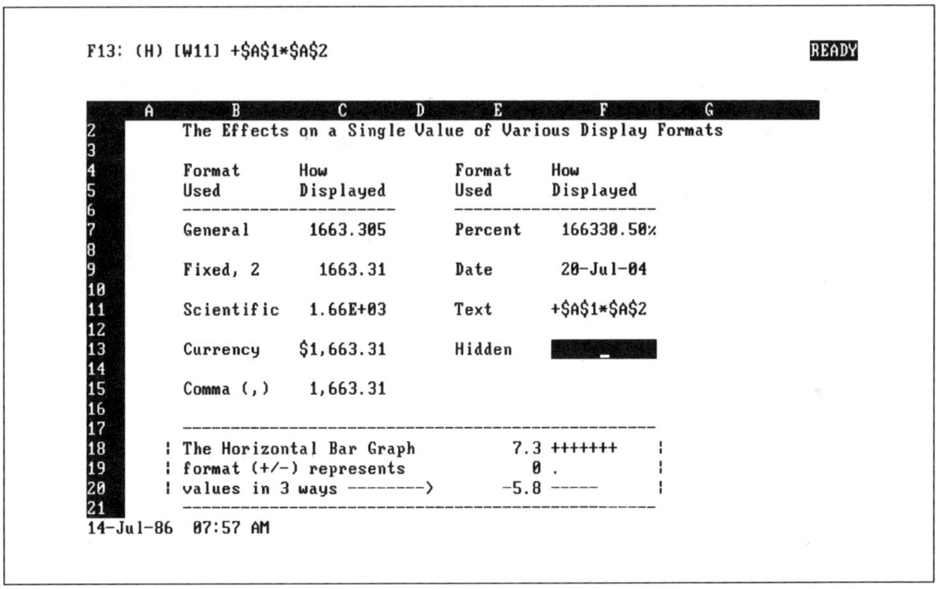

FIGURE 5.7: The effects of using the various /Range Format options on a single value and the horizontal bar graph format representations. In the upper part of this figure, a single calculated value, 1663.305, was copied and subjected to various range format options. In each case, the default number of decimal places or default setting (e.g., Date format 1) was used. In the last example, you can see that this cell is not empty by looking at its literal contents in the Control Panel.

The lower boxed section in this figure shows how the horizontal bar graph format (+/−) affects three small input values—one positive, one zero, and one negative. Notice that even though the positive and negative values were not whole numbers, in the graph format they have both been rounded down. The first value, 7.3, is represented by seven pluses, and the value −5.8 is represented by five hyphens.

SEE ALSO

/Worksheet Global Format

/Range Label

MENUS

/Range
Label
Left Right Center

KEYBOARD ENTRY

/RLL /RLR /RLC

FUNCTION

This command changes the justification of labels in a designated range. Most often, this involves changing the labels in the range from the default of left justified to either centered or right justified. Whatever new option is chosen overrides the global label prefix in effect or the /Range Label option last used to format the labels in the range.

USAGE

To change the justification of all labels in a particular range in the worksheet, type **/RL** and either **L** for left justified, **R** for right justified, or **C** for centered. Indicate the extent of the range and then press Return.

You will often find it more convenient to use the /Range Label command to format column and row headings in the spreadsheet after you have entered them than to type in the appropriate label prefix while entering them. This command is used to center column headings over the data in multiple columns.

EXAMPLES

For an example of using the /Range Label Center format, see Figure 5.5.

SEE ALSO

/Worksheet Global Label-Prefix

/Range Protect

MENUS

/Range
Protect

KEYBOARD ENTRY

/RP <range>

FUNCTION

This command protects a particular range of cells in the worksheet from further modifications of any kind. Once a range has been protected, no one can edit, delete, reformat, or in any way change the contents of the cells entered within its boundaries. Also note that protected ranges cannot be copied or moved to new places in the worksheet.

USAGE

Use the /Range Protect command to preserve particular areas of the worksheet from any further changes when global protection is not in effect. To protect a particular range, move the cell pointer to the beginning of the range, type **/RP,** indicate the extent of the range, and press Return.

This command is often used to protect ranges that contain important and complex formulas as you continue to build your spreadsheet. It prevents you from inadvertently erasing or modifying those ranges as you work.

Another important application for Release 2 users is to protect those cell ranges that contain zeros whose display has been suppressed with the /Worksheet Global Zero command. You will often want to protect these ranges because you may forget that they are not actually blank. You could mistakenly add new data in them if you do not protect them with /Range Protect.

SEE ALSO

/Worksheet Global Protection
/Range Unprotect

/Range Unprotect

MENUS

/Range
Unprotect

KEYBOARD ENTRY

/RU <range>

FUNCTION

This command removes the protection status from those ranges that have been previously protected with either the /Worksheet Global Protection Enable or the /Range Protect commands. All data in unprotected ranges in a worksheet with global protection in effect is displayed in high intensity to set it off from the rest of the protected data. Whenever a cell within this range is current, it also displays the code U before its literal contents on the first line of the Control Panel.

USAGE

You often use this command after setting up global protection throughout the worksheet. It is applied to all ranges in the spreadsheet that contain input cells whose data must be updated to do further what-if analysis. It can also be coupled with the /Range Input command to restrict the cell pointer to only those cells that have been unprotected with this command (see /Range Input below).

EXAMPLES

Figure 5.8 shows a simple loan payment schedule that is globally protected except for three input cells, C3, C4, and C5. First, protection for the entire worksheet was activated by issuing the /Worksheet Global Protection Enable (/WGPE) command. The cell pointer was then moved to cell C3, and the range C3..C5 was unprotected by issuing the /Range Unprotect (/RU) command.

These three input cells are all displayed in high intensity on the screen (shown in boldface in this figure) to indicate that they are unprotected. Notice the contents of cell C3 in the first line of the Control Panel. The U stands for unprotected.

Because only these three cells are unprotected, no changes can be made to any other cell in the worksheet. To view the payments for a different principal, interest rate, or term, all the user has to do is move the pointer to

```
C3: (C0) U 175000                                                        READY

      A          B          C          D          E          F          G
1                 Payment Schedule for Simple Interest Loans
2
3  Beginning Principal  $175,000
4  Interest Rate            9.00%
5  Term (in years)            25
6
7                   9.00%      9.25%      9.50%      9.75%     10.00%     10.25%
8        175,000  1468.59    1498.67    1528.97    1559.49    1590.23    1621.17
9        175,500  1472.79    1502.95    1533.34    1563.95    1594.77    1625.80
10       176,000  1476.99    1507.23    1537.71    1568.40    1599.31    1630.43
11       176,500  1481.18    1511.51    1542.07    1572.86    1603.86    1635.07
12       177,000  1485.38    1515.80    1546.44    1577.31    1608.40    1639.70
13       177,500  1489.57    1520.08    1550.81    1581.77    1612.94    1644.33
14       178,000  1493.77    1524.36    1555.18    1586.22    1617.49    1648.96
15       178,500  1497.97    1528.64    1559.55    1590.68    1622.03    1653.59
16       179,000  1502.16    1532.92    1563.92    1595.14    1626.57    1658.23
17       179,500  1506.36    1537.21    1568.29    1599.59    1631.12    1662.86
18       180,000  1510.55    1541.49    1572.65    1604.05    1635.66    1667.49
19       180,500  1514.75    1545.77    1577.02    1608.50    1640.20    1672.12
20       181,000  1518.95    1550.05    1581.39    1612.96    1644.75    1676.75
14-Jul-86  07:21 PM                                        CALC
```

FIGURE 5.8: Loan payment schedule showing the use of global protection with an unprotected input range. In this schedule, only the three cells that contain inputs for the beginning principal, interest rate, and term can be modified in any way. The table is safe from any change except through recalculation with new input values.

each of the input cells to be modified, type in the new values, and press F9 to recalculate the table. Even though the table itself is protected from direct revision, it can still be updated by recalculating its formulas.

SEE ALSO

/Worksheet Global Protection

/Range Input

MENUS

/Range
Input

KEYBOARD ENTRY

/RI

FUNCTION

This command restricts the cell pointer to only those cells that have been unprotected. This makes for faster data entry because the spreadsheet cursor can move only to those cells in which the data operator needs to enter data. Also, while /Range Input is in effect, none of the Lotus 1-2-3 worksheet commands are operational. This prevents an inexperienced data operator from activating a potentially dangerous command sequence while entering data.

USAGE

You use this command in a spreadsheet that is globally protected except for specific ranges of cells that have been unprotected (with /RU) to allow new data input or revisions to take place. To use the /Range Input command, position the cursor at the beginning of the range of unprotected cells, type **/RI,** indicate the extent of the range, and press Return.

This command stays in effect only until the operator presses the Esc key. After executing the command, the cell pointer can move only to the range or ranges specified. Pressing the Home key takes the pointer directly to the first input cell in the range instead of to cell A1 (unless A1 has been designated as the first input cell). Pressing the End key takes the pointer to the last input cell in the range. After executing /Range Input, the Lotus 1-2-3 command menu is deactivated and cannot be accessed until you press Esc or Return in READY mode. The only function keys that are operative during its execution are F1 (Help), F2 (Edit), and F9 (Calc).

Because this command remains in effect only until the operator presses the Esc or Return key in READY mode, you may wish to create a keystroke macro that can be used any time the spreadsheet has been retrieved and the operator is ready to enter or edit the data. Such a macro is included below.

Note: The /Range Input command behaves much like the F5 (Goto) function key in that it not only locates the pointer in the first cell of the range but also repositions the worksheet so that this cell then occupies the upper-left corner of the display screen. Sometimes this is not desirable because it prevents the operator from viewing a necessary part of the protected spreadsheet. To prevent this, include several columns to the left of those containing the actual input cells as part of the input range. As long as the cells in these columns to the left are protected, the cell pointer will still be restricted to only those cells that have been unprotected in the enlarged input range (see the example below).

EXAMPLES

Figure 5.9 shows the same loan payment schedule as is shown in Figure 5.8. Here, the /Range Input command has been used to designate the three cells C3, C4, and C5 as the input range. Notice that this has shifted the display so that C3 is now in the upper-left corner of the screen. In so doing, it has cut off the view of the two leftmost columns so that it is no longer possible to view the principals on which the payments are calculated.

To use the /Range Input command to restrict the cell pointer to the range C3..C5 and still be able to view all of the table, the input range would have to be enlarged to A1..C5. But because only the three cells C3..C5 have been unprotected in this enlarged input range, the cell pointer would still be restricted to them until the user presses Esc or Return in READY mode.

C3: (C0) U 175000 READY

	C	D	E	F	G	H	I	J
3	$175,000							
4	9.00%							
5	25							
6								
7	9.25%	9.50%	9.75%	10.00%	10.25%	10.50%		
8	1498.67	1528.97	1559.49	1590.23	1621.17	1652.32		
9	1502.95	1533.34	1563.95	1594.77	1625.80	1657.04		
10	1507.23	1537.71	1568.40	1599.31	1630.43	1661.76		
11	1511.51	1542.07	1572.86	1603.86	1635.07	1666.48		
12	1515.80	1546.44	1577.31	1608.40	1639.70	1671.20		
13	1520.08	1550.81	1581.77	1612.94	1644.33	1675.92		
14	1524.36	1555.18	1586.22	1617.49	1648.96	1680.64		
15	1528.64	1559.55	1590.68	1622.03	1653.59	1685.36		
16	1532.92	1563.92	1595.14	1626.57	1658.23	1690.09		
17	1537.21	1568.29	1599.59	1631.12	1662.86	1694.81		
18	1541.49	1572.65	1604.05	1635.66	1667.49	1699.53		
19	1545.77	1577.02	1608.50	1640.20	1672.12	1704.25		
20	1550.05	1581.39	1612.96	1644.75	1676.75	1708.97		
21								
22								

14-Jul-86 07:21 PM CALC

FIGURE 5.9: The effect of using the /Range Input command to restrict the cell pointer to the three input cells in the loan payment schedule. When the command was issued, the input range was designated as C3..C5. This shifted the screen display, making C3 the first cell visible. The cell pointer is now restricted to these three cells that have been unprotected (with /RU). Pressing Home will take the printer to C3, while pressing End will take it to C5. Pressing Esc or Return while the program is in READY mode will release the cell pointer and shift the screen display back to the way it is shown in Figure 5.8.

MACRO

ALT-I, A RANGE INPUT MACRO

Label	*Macro Contents*
'\i	**'/RI{?}~**

This macro issues the /Range Input command and waits for the operator to designate the range of cells to be affected. To use it, make sure the cell pointer is located at one of the corners of the range and press Alt-I. You can indicate the range either by typing the cell address or by pointing. After you define the range, press Return to complete the command. If you expect other data-entry operators to use this macro before doing data entry, be sure to instruct them in how to indicate the extent of the data-input range.

SEE ALSO

/Worksheet Global Protection
/Range Unprotect

SUMMARY

This chapter has covered various techniques and commands used for creating new spreadsheets. You can use the following references to locate related topics from other chapters in this handbook.

For information on making revisions to your spreadsheets:

- Chapter 6, "Editing Worksheets"

For information on using the other /Range commands:

- Chapter 7, "Formatting Worksheets"
- Chapter 8, "Working with Cell Ranges"

For more information on entering data into a database:

- Chapter 20, "Creating a Lotus 1-2-3 Database"

For more information on creating and using keystroke macros:

- Chapter 27, "Keystroke Macros"

CHAPTER 6

EDITING WORKSHEETS

EDITING WORKSHEETS

This chapter discusses editing the contents of a Lotus 1-2-3 spreadsheet once you have partially or completely created it. In this chapter, you will find techniques for the following:

- Editing data that you have already input into a cell
- Making new space in the worksheet by deleting ranges of cells
- Converting formulas into their calculated values
- Converting labels to formulas and back again

It is convenient to convert formulas to their calculated values whenever you need to edit a version of a spreadsheet so that it will not be subject to further what-if analysis. Converting labels to formulas and back again is useful when you need to make copies of formulas that do not contain the absolute cell references.

After these general discussions, you will find detailed information on using the specific commands commonly required when you edit worksheets. They are listed in the order they appear in the Lotus 1-2-3 command menus.

Because Lotus 1-2-3 contains no row or column copy or move commands, you will find the copy and move operations discussed with range commands in Chapter 7, "Formatting Worksheets." That chapter also covers adding and deleting columns and rows in the worksheet.

EDITING THE CONTENTS OF THE WORKSHEET

You will often need to revise particular cells in a worksheet that you have created. Sometimes you may just need to fix errors you made when typing in labels or values in cells. At other times you may find that you need to change the formulas you have created either by changing their underlying assumptions or by expanding them in some way.

Reentering versus Editing Data

Once you have entered either a label or a value into a cell of the worksheet, you have two alternatives for editing that entry. If it is short, simply enter a new label or value in the cell and press either Return or the appropriate arrow key. This replaces the old cell contents with your new label or value.

If the entry is fairly long and requires only minimal editing, you can press the F2 (Edit) key. It brings the literal contents of the cell to the second line of the Control Panel, where the cell entry can be revised. If the cell contains a label, the label prefix that either you or Lotus 1-2-3 assigned to it is included. You can edit the label prefix just like any other character on this line. In fact, if you wish to change the cell's contents from a label to a value, all you have to do is delete this one character and press Return.

Depending upon how good a typist you are, you may prefer to reenter the revised contents of the cell rather than go into EDIT mode to make the changes. When to use which method is usually a matter of personal taste. The only time when editing the cell's contents through EDIT mode is far superior to retyping the entire entry is when you have a large number of cells in a column or row that all require slight modifications, such as revising the value of the month and day in a range of @DATE entries. In such a situation, it is more efficient to revise the arguments by pressing F2 and making the simple and repetitive changes required than it is to retype the entire function.

Insert Mode

As soon as you press F2, Lotus 1-2-3 goes into EDIT mode. You can then use the program's editor to make any necessary changes. Whenever you are in EDIT mode, the editor is always in insert mode. Any new text or numbers that you enter do not overwrite existing text located to the right of the cursor.

If you wish to get out of insert mode to type over many characters, press the Ins key. The status indicator OVR appears at the bottom of the screen to remind you that you are no longer in insert mode. Doing this is sometimes the easiest way to get rid of large sections of a line, because the Lotus 1-2-3 line editor does not provide a delete-word function.

Positioning the Editing Cursor

You can move the cursor character by character by using the → or ← keys. The cursor is always initially located at the end of the entry, even if the entry is longer than the screen display. To take the cursor immediately to the beginning of the line, press the Home key. Pressing the End key from this position (or from anywhere else within the line of text) takes the cursor to the end of the line.

To move shorter distances, you can press the Tab key to move the cursor five spaces to the right or the Backtab key (Shift-Tab) to move it five spaces to the left.

Adding New Characters to the Entry Line

If all you wish to do is add to the entry in some way, you simply position the cursor at the place in the text where you want to make the addition and start typing. When you press Home, the cursor moves to the beginning of the entry, in front of the label prefix. If you are adding text to a label, remember to press the → key before you add your new text. Otherwise, the label prefix will be pushed behind the characters that you add and will become part of the displayed text when you press Return.

If you make a mistake when typing a revision, you can press the Backspace key to rub out unwanted characters to the left of the cursor's present position.

Deleting Characters from the Entry Line

To delete characters from the line, you can move the cursor to them and press the Del key as many times as are required to erase them. The Del key deletes only the single character above the cursor. There is no way to delete larger sections of text, such as deleting a word or deleting to the end of the line. Also, Lotus 1-2-3 does not provide an undo function. If you delete too many characters, you have to retype them.

Deleting Data in the Worksheet

There is only one way in Lotus 1-2-3 to delete data that you have already entered in a cell: use the /Range Erase command. Pressing the space bar and then pressing Return *appears* to have the same effect as using /Range Erase (the literal contents and the display of the cell both appear blank), but it in fact enters a blank space character in place of the characters that were entered previously. And, because a blank space entered into an empty cell carries a string value, not a value of zero, using this method could cause ERR values to occur in any formulas that refer to these cells.

You are always safer using the /Range Erase command to delete any unwanted cell entry. To make using this command easier when you need to erase only a single cell, most users include in their worksheets a macro to reduce the number of keystrokes from four to two. You will find this macro included in the /Range Erase reference at the end of the chapter.

Transforming Formulas to Their Calculated Values

After you have edited a spreadsheet, you may want to maintain a copy of it that is not subject to further revision. For example, you may have a spreadsheet whose calculations are to be included in quarterly or yearly reports. Once all of the spreadsheet's figures and formulas have been thoroughly checked, you can convert them into values to ensure that no further what-if analysis can occur.

Converting Formulas to Calculated Values in Release 1A

To convert formulas to values when working with Release 1A, you must use the /File Xtract command with the Values parameter. To do this, position the cell pointer at the beginning of the range (or at the beginning of the entire spreadsheet, if you need to convert all of its formulas).

Issue the /File Xtract command using the Values option (**/FXV**) and then give the file you are about to create a new, but related, name. You will usually want to append a special character to the original file name that indicates that it has been converted to values. For instance, if the original file name was ISQ4.WKS for a fourth-quarter income statement, you could name the new extracted worksheet file ISQ4V.WKS to differentiate it from the original.

Then indicate the range to be extracted either by using cell addresses or by pointing. When you have finished and press Return, Lotus 1-2-3 creates a new worksheet that consists only of values.

Converting Formulas to Calculated Values in Release 2

To convert formulas to values in Release 2, you can use the /Range Value command in place of /File Xtract Values (which still works exactly as described above). This command converts any result calculated by a formula into a static value that is not subject to further recalculation. Its use is fully discussed in the /Range Value entry at the end of this chapter.

Alt-V, a Macro for Converting Formulas to Calculated Values

You can construct the following simple keystroke macro to convert a single formula into its calculated value.

Label	*Macro Contents*
'\v	**{EDIT}{CALC}~**

The Alt-V macro returns the contents of the current cell to the editing line, where the formula is calculated. Once the formula has been calculated in EDIT mode, only the result remains as the cell entry.

Converting Labels to Value Entries and Back Again

You sometimes need to edit a formula or group of formulas so that you can copy them to new places in the worksheet. For example, you may have entered a particularly complex formula without making its cell references absolute because you did not foresee a need for copying it when you originally constructed it.

In such a circumstance, you have two alternatives:

- You can make the formula's cell references absolute by adding dollar signs ($) to each reference and then copy the formula to its new position in the worksheet.
- You can edit the formula by converting it into a label, copying it to its new position, and converting it back to a value in both its new and old positions.

In the second case you can construct two simple keystroke macros to aid in this kind of operation: the first to convert the value to a label and the second to convert the label back to a value. These macros are defined in the two sections that follow. Figure 6.1 illustrates the use for these macros in editing and refining your worksheets.

Alt-L, a Macro for Converting Values into Labels

The following macro command quickly converts a single value, whether it consists of a literal value or formula, into a label.

Label	*Macro Contents*
'\l	**{EDIT}{HOME}'~**

The Alt-L macro edits the current cell by taking the cursor to the beginning of the cell contents on the editing line, where it adds the apostrophe

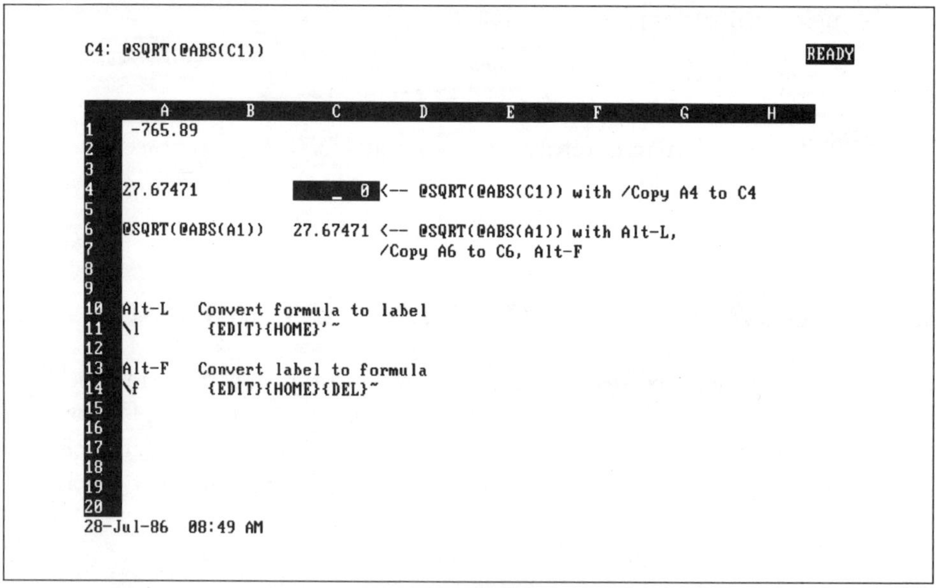

FIGURE 6.1: Copying a formula to a new part of the worksheet by first converting it to a label, copying it, and then converting it back to a formula. The formula for calculating the square root of the negative entry in A1 was entered in both A4 and A6. The formula was then copied to C4 with the /Copy command, where because of its relative cell reference, it was adjusted to find the square root of C1. To avoid this, the two macros shown in the figure were used to copy the formula from A6 to C6. First, Alt-L was used in A6 to convert the formula to a label (as shown). Then the /Copy command was used to copy the new label to C6. Finally, Alt-F was used to convert the copied label back into its original formula.

label prefix and presses Return to enter the same contents as a label. In place of the calculated value, Lotus 1-2-3 displays the contents of the formula as a label. (If you use Alt-L on an existing label, it will add a duplicate label prefix to the label.)

Alt-F, a Macro for Converting Labels into Values

The following macro converts any single label into a value. This macro works only on literal values or valid formulas that have been entered as labels or converted to labels, as with the Alt-L macro described above.

Label	*Macro Contents*
'\f	**{EDIT}{HOME}{DEL}~**

The Alt-F macro edits the current cell by taking the cursor to the beginning of the cell contents on the editing line, where it deletes the label prefix and presses Return to enter the contents as a value. In place of the formula as a label in the cell, Lotus 1-2-3 displays the calculated value.

/WORKSHEET COMMANDS COMMONLY USED IN EDITING

When you finish and save your work with one spreadsheet and then wish to create a new spreadsheet, you use the /Worksheet Erase command. This command clears the first worksheet from memory, allowing you to build your next application. You can also use this command to abandon a spreadsheet that you have begun but that you do not wish to save. You can then start over again with a clean worksheet.

/Worksheet Erase

MENUS

/Worksheet
Erase
Yes No

KEYBOARD ENTRY

/WEY /WEN

FUNCTION

The /Worksheet Erase command clears the current worksheet file loaded into Lotus 1-2-3 from the computer's memory.

USAGE

The /Worksheet Erase command has two options: No, which is the default, and Yes. If you access this command by mistake, press the Return key to cancel it and stop the worksheet from being cleared. This is especially important to remember if you have not yet saved the worksheet by using the /File Save command.

To clear the worksheet, the entire command is /Worksheet Erase Yes. You enter it as **/WEY** (this is also the way to enter it in any macros in which clearing the current worksheet is required). This command is needed whenever you wish to clear the current worksheet to begin work on a new spreadsheet. It is not required if all you want to do is load another worksheet file into memory. The /File Retrieve command automatically clears the current worksheet before loading the new file you indicate.

Do not confuse this command with /File Erase. The /File Erase command deletes the worksheet file from the disk, whereas /Worksheet Erase deletes it only from memory. As long as you have saved the worksheet previously during the session, you can load it again by using the /File Retrieve command after you use /Worksheet Erase. This is not the case when using /File Erase.

MACROS

Most users do not create a /Worksheet Erase Yes macro because it is far too easy to "zap" a worksheet that you have not yet saved by accidentally typing its range name letter in error when you access a construction macro. Nevertheless, the /WEY keystrokes are often used in more complex macros, especially in custom menus that require a "clear and continue" option.

SEE ALSO

/Range Erase
/File Erase

/Range Commands Commonly Used in Editing

You may often need to use two /Range commands when you edit your worksheets. By far the most important is the /Range Erase command, which is the only way to delete a cell entry when you do not wish to replace its contents. The /Range Value command is a Release 2 command that eliminates the need to use /Range Xtract Values to convert formulas into their calculated values.

/Range Erase

MENUS

/Range
Erase

KEYBOARD ENTRY

/RE <range>

FUNCTION

The /Range Erase command deletes the contents of the current cell or a range of cells, beginning with the current cell.

USAGE

Using the /Range Erase command is the only to way to delete a cell's contents without replacing them with something else. To use the command, position the cell pointer in the cell to be deleted or at the beginning of the range of cells to be deleted, type **/RE,** indicate the extent of the range, and press Return.

Its use is different from that of the /Worksheet Delete Column and Row commands. Though these /Worksheet Delete commands also erase any cell entries located in the columns or rows specified, they do not work on partial ranges of cells. When you use these commands, all data located in the column or row is lost. The /Range Erase command provides the only method in Lotus 1-2-3 for deleting partial columns and rows.

Note: Be careful when you use /Range Erase; Lotus 1-2-3 does not have an undo function. If you delete a range of cells in error, you will have to reenter it or, if possible, retrieve the worksheet again.

MACROS

ALT-E, A MACRO FOR ERASING A SINGLE CELL

Label	*Macro Contents*
'\e	**'/RE~**

This macro erases the entry in the current cell. When you press Alt-E, the cell's contents are erased. Using this keystroke combination is far easier than typing **/RE** and pressing Return each time you need to delete only one cell's contents.

Note: Do not use Alt-E (designated \e) as the name for this macro if you are using Lotus 1-2-3 on an IBM 3270 PC. This computer reserves the Alt-E key combination; it cannot be given to any Lotus 1-2-3 macro command. You can rename this combination Alt-R (\r) for remove. If you are using Alt-R for adding data across rows as suggested in Chapter 3, you can rename that macro Alt-H (\h) for horizontal.

SEE ALSO

/Worksheet Erase

/Range Value (Release 2 Only)

MENUS

/Range
Value

KEYBOARD ENTRY

/RV
Enter range to copy FROM: **<range>**
Enter range to copy TO: **<range>**

FUNCTION

The /Range Value command converts a range of formulas in a worksheet to their currently calculated values.

USAGE

This command makes it unnecessary to use the /File Xtract Values command for converting formulas to their calculated values. It is useful whenever you need to freeze the values derived by the formulas in your spreadsheet, as is often the case when the completed worksheet is to serve as a permanent business document, such as a part of a formal report.

Its use is similar to the /Copy command in that the /Range Value command prompts you first for the range to copy from and then for the range to copy to. If you do not want to copy the range to a new location in the worksheet, you simply indicate the same range of cells in response to both the FROM and TO prompts.

Copying the range to a new location allows you to maintain two copies of the same formulas—the original, which is still subject to further what-if analysis, and a new range in which the formulas are calculated and converted to their present numeric values.

EXAMPLES

Figures 6.2 and 6.3 illustrate the use of the /Range Value command by contrasting a data table before and after issuing this command. In this example, the same range is given to both the copy FROM and copy TO prompts. This has the effect of destroying the original formulas during their conversion.

An alternative is to use this command to copy the entire data table to a new location in the spreadsheet. You could then name the new table by using the /Range Name command and print the range whenever it was required in final reports. That way, the original formulas could still be used to generate new tables for data gathered at a later date.

MACROS

Though it is easy to capture the /Range Value command keystrokes and store them in a macro, most users do not bother because the command is

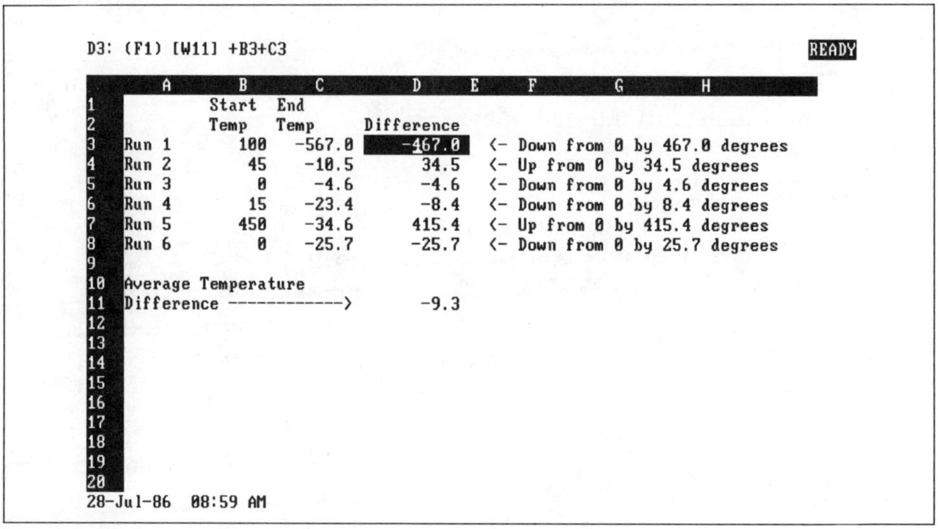

FIGURE 6.2: A data table whose formulas are to be converted to their presently calculated values with the /Range Value command. Currently, the range of cells D3..D11 contains formulas that derive and average the temperature differences input into columns B and C.

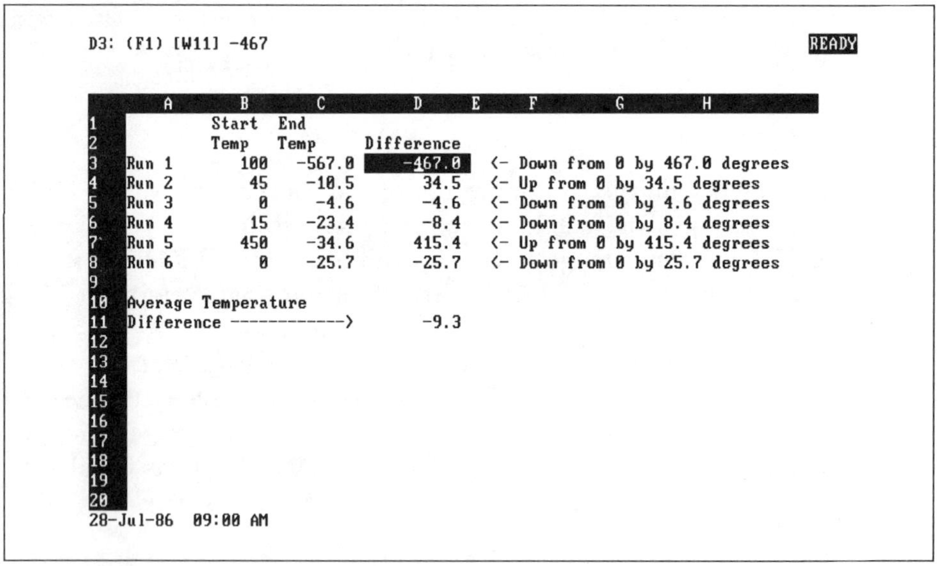

FIGURE 6.3: The effect of using /Range Value on the data table in Figure 6.2. Because the same range (D3..D11) was designated as the source and destination of the copy, all the formulas in column D have now been converted to literal values (contrast the literal contents of D3 [−467] with that in Figure 6.2 [+B3+C3]). The results calculated in this table are essentially frozen as though all data had been input manually.

not frequently used. See instead the keystroke macro for converting a single formula to its calculated value, listed earlier in the chapter in the section "Alt-V, a Macro for Converting Formulas to Calculated Values."

SEE ALSO

/File Xtract

SUMMARY

This chapter has discussed various techniques for editing the contents of your spreadsheets. The following references contain suggestions for obtaining information related to commands and topics addressed in this chapter.

For information on label prefixes in a label entry:

- Chapter 5, "Creating Worksheets"

For more detailed information about the /File Xtract command:

- Chapter 9, "File Operations"

For information on constructing formulas with absolute cell references for copying:

- Chapter 10, "Working with Formulas and Functions"

For information on constructing menu macros:

- Chapter 28, "The Macro Command Language"

FORMATTING WORKSHEETS

FORMATTING WORKSHEETS

Two kinds of formatting occur in a worksheet:

- Formatting entries within their cells
- Formatting cells within the worksheet

This chapter contains information about the latter kind of formatting, including adding (inserting) and deleting new columns and rows, copying and moving ranges, changing relative column-row positioning (transposition), and formatting labels across cell ranges.

For information about formatting entries within their cells, refer to the discussions and reference entries in Chapter 5, "Creating Worksheets."

ADDING NEW COLUMNS AND ROWS

It is quite common when you create or edit worksheets to discover that you need to make room for new columns or rows of data previously overlooked or later required. In such cases, you can use Lotus 1-2-3's /Worksheet Insert command to add either new columns or new rows at the cell pointer's position. When you do so, it is important to remember that this command affects the entire worksheet.

For instance, when you insert a single column at the cell pointer, all data in columns to the right is shifted over one column to the right to make room for the new blank column. This movement affects not only those columns visible on the screen but also all columns from row 1 to row 8192 (or 2048 in Release 1A). The same thing happens when you add a new row to the worksheet. The data in rows below the cell pointer is shifted down one row from column A all the way to column IV.

It is therefore possible that adding a new column or row can separate data ranges in other unseen areas of the spreadsheet with a new blank column or row. It could, for example, result in splitting columns or rows that you had intended to keep together in a data table. You cannot insert a row or column if the last row or column in the worksheet contains any filled cells. Such an operation results in the program's trying to push the data in the last row out of the worksheet area. You get the message "Cannot Move or Copy data beyond worksheet boundaries".

How Lotus 1-2-3 Adjusts Cell References

Lotus 1-2-3 automatically adjusts all cell references in formulas whenever you insert a new column or row. To illustrate this, assume that you have used the @SUM function to add a column of figures down column X in your spreadsheet. The formula in cell X12 reads @SUM(X3..X10). You then add a new blank row to the worksheet by issuing the command /Worksheet Insert Row with the cell pointer in A7 and pressing Return (inserting just a single row).

After adding the new row, you move the cell pointer to X3 to examine the effect of this operation on the figures totaled in column X of the spreadsheet. You find the figures separated by a blank cell at X7. You also find the @SUM formula located in cell X13. If you move the cell pointer to that cell, you see that its contents now read @SUM(X3..X11). This automatic adjustment is illustrated in Figures 7.1 and 7.2.

Notice that because a blank cell carries a zero value, the total is not affected by the addition of this blank cell in the range of figures. However, because the newly inserted row splits the column of figures in two at X7,

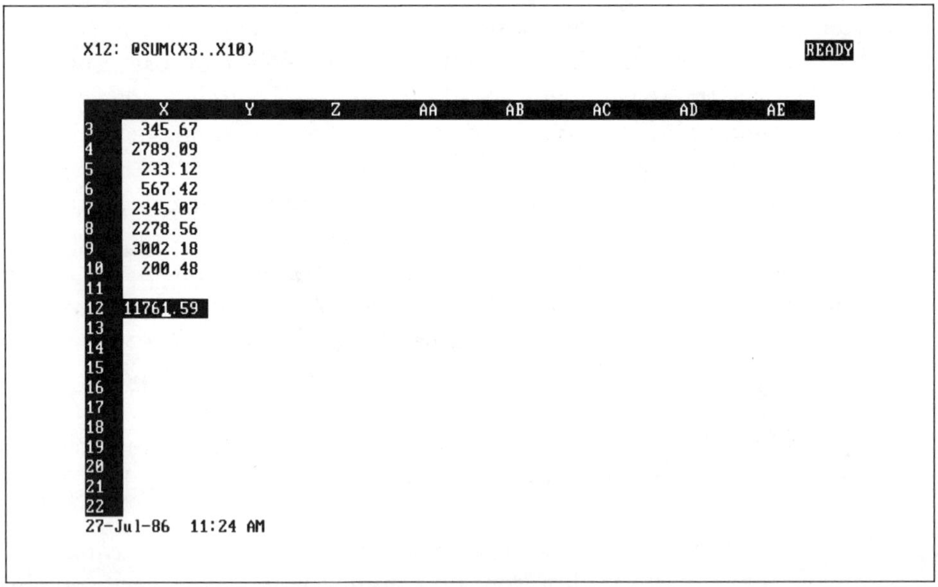

FIGURE 7.1: A column of figures about to be split by using the /Worksheet Insert command to add a new row in row 7. Note that the formula in X12 contains a formula that uses the @SUM function to total the range extending from X3 to X10. Contrast this to the adjustment made after inserting the row in Figure 7.2.

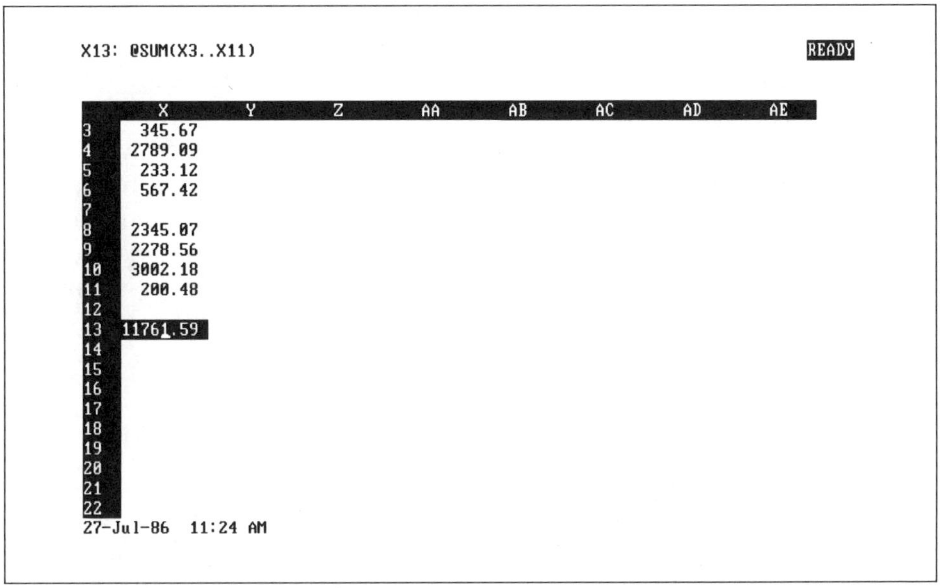

FIGURE 7.2: The same column of figures after inserting a blank row at row 7. Notice that the range specified in the @SUM function was automatically adjusted to accommodate the new row, for it now reads @SUM(X3..X11). All data from X7 down was pushed down and the cell references were adjusted. Also note that the addition of the blank row makes it appear as though there are two separate groups of figures.

the figures now appear to be organized into two separate data ranges instead of a single column of figures.

To rearrange the display of this range without having to remove the new row 7 (assume that its addition is vital to the part of the spreadsheet in columns A to J), you need to use the /Move command. This command moves the range X8..X13 to X7, healing the split in this range while retaining the new row throughout the rest of the worksheet (for more information on using the /Move command, see "Copying and Moving Ranges in the Worksheet" and the /Move reference entry later in this chapter).

As you can see from this simple example, making additions to columns and rows with the /Worksheet Insert command can cause new formatting problems in distant parts of the worksheet. If you are working on a spreadsheet that you did not create, you should examine its contents beyond the screen display where you need to make your additions.

A quick method for determining what other ranges may be affected by column or row insertion is to take the cell pointer across the row using the End and → keys or down the column using the End and ↓ keys. Each time you use this combination, the cell pointer jumps from the beginning of one data range to the beginning of the next. When no other block of data is located in the row or column, the cursor jumps to the extreme limits of the worksheet, either the last column or the last row.

If you find from this excursion that you will have to do a lot of rearranging in these areas after inserting the new columns and rows, you might look into the amount of work required to rearrange your data with the /Move command and create adequate space to accommodate the information you need to add. Choose moving over inserting if it looks like this operation will require less work because you won't have to do a lot of clean-up work in other affected ranges.

Inserting Blank Columns as Spacers

The /Worksheet Insert Column command provides a means for spacing data that otherwise would appear too close together because of the way Lotus 1-2-3 formats values and labels in their cells. Because values are always right justified in their cells, they are separated only by a single trailing space from left-justified labels placed in columns immediately to their right. You run into this same situation whenever you use the /Range Label Right command to put right-justified labels in a column next to one containing left-justified labels.

If you cannot use the /Range Label command to center or right justify the labels in the column to the right (often they are too long), the only way to add more spaces between the values and the labels is by inserting a new column. After inserting the column, you narrow it to the number of spaces you want between the displayed values and labels. When you use this technique, be aware of the possible effects it can have on data in columns and rows that are not visible on the screen. Figures 7.3 and 7.4 illustrate how you can use the /Worksheet Insert Column command to add spaces between displayed entries.

Deleting Columns and Rows

Although you must exercise extreme care when using the /Worksheet Delete commands, they do provide an effective way to delete unneeded columns and rows while simultaneously reformatting the worksheet. Whenever you delete a column or row in a worksheet, all of the data ranges

```
B7: [W10] 'Smith                                                        READY

     A     B         C        D E     F        G      H       I     J
1  Date:27-Jul-86
2                             VACATION ACCRUAL
3                             Dept's 10 - 12
4
5    ID  Last      First    M  Dept   Date   Unused Accrual  Days  Total
6    No  Name      Name     I  Code  Hired    Days   Rate     TD   Days
7  1073  Smith     Thomas   A.   12 02-Oct-83   0.0  0.0275   5.7    5.7
8   534  Drew      Mary     J.   10 24-Mar-81   5.0  0.0411   8.5   13.5
9  1233  McGill    David    P.   10 04-Jan-84   2.5  0.0275   5.7    8.2
10 1407  Farner    Kenneth  E.   12 20-Apr-85   0.0  0.0137   2.8    2.8
11  788  Kaye      Peter    A.   11 16-May-82   8.0  0.0275   5.7   13.7
12  233  Smith     Sandra   B.   12 13-Feb-80  10.0  0.0411   8.5   18.5
13 1066  Olsen     Phillis  G.   12 17-Apr-83   5.0  0.0275   5.7   10.7
14 1289  Tudor     Carol    M.   10 03-Dec-84   3.5  0.0137   2.8    6.3
15 1004  Nelson    Steven   F.   11 02-Jun-84   0.0  0.0275   5.7    5.7
16 1415  Watson    Sean     A.   10 05-Jul-85   0.0  0.0137   2.8    2.8
17 1059  Allen     Holly    M.   11 18-Mar-83   2.0  0.0275   5.7    7.7
18
19
20
27-Jul-86  11:33 AM
```

FIGURE 7.3: A Lotus 1-2-3 database with a column of numbers and column of labels back to back. In this figure, column A contains identification numbers that are right justified in their cells. Column B contains last names that are left justified. Their label prefix cannot be changed from left justified because all the spaces in this column may be required to accommodate long last names. The only way to add additional spaces between the ID numbers and the last names is to insert a new column, as shown in Figure 7.4.

affected by the deletion are automatically adjusted to reflect their new locations. Using these commands provides a quicker method for erasing certain data ranges: you do not have to perform two separate operations, first erasing the data with /Range Erase and then reformatting the spreadsheet with /Move to remove the blank spaces left by your deletions.

However, because the /Worksheet Delete commands affect the entire worksheet area, their use is potentially more dangerous. It is easy to forget about columns or rows of data in distant areas of the spreadsheet that will also be erased along with those in the screen where you are currently working.

Whenever you delete a column with /Worksheet Delete Column, the program erases any data that exists in that column from row 1 to 8192 (2048 in Release 1A). Likewise, when you delete a row with /Worksheet Delete Row, the program erases any data that exists in that row from column A to IV.

Unlike the /Worksheet Insert command, the /Worksheet Delete commands let you do great harm to your model if you delete columns and rows that contain data essential to certain formulas or macros you have

```
B7: [W3]                                                            POINT
Enter column width (1..240): 3

     A   B      C          D      E F       G        H       I        J      K
 1 Date:     27-Jul-86
 2                                  VACATION ACCRUAL
 3                                  Dept's 10 - 12
 4
 5   ID      Last       First      M  Dept   Date    Unused Accrual  Days  Total
 6   No      Name       Name       I  Code  Hired     Days   Rate     TD   Days
 7  1073  _ Smith      Thomas     A.   12 02-Oct-83   0.0   0.0275   5.7    5.7
 8   534     Drew       Mary       J.   10 24-Mar-81   5.0   0.0411   8.5   13.5
 9  1233     McGill     David      P.   10 04-Jan-84   2.5   0.0275   5.7    8.2
10  1407     Farner     Kenneth    E.   12 20-Apr-85   0.0   0.0137   2.8    2.8
11   788     Kaye       Peter      A.   11 16-May-82   8.0   0.0275   5.7   13.7
12   233     Smith      Sandra     B.   12 13-Feb-80  10.0   0.0411   8.5   18.5
13  1066     Olsen      Phillis    G.   12 17-Apr-83   5.0   0.0275   5.7   10.7
14  1289     Tudor      Carol      M.   10 03-Dec-84   3.5   0.0137   2.8    6.3
15  1004     Nelson     Steven     F.   11 02-Jun-84   0.0   0.0275   5.7    5.7
16  1415     Watson     Sean       A.   10 05-Jul-85   0.0   0.0137   2.8    2.8
17  1059     Allen      Holly      M.   11 18-Mar-83   2.0   0.0275   5.7    7.7
18
19
20
27-Jul-86  11:34 AM
```

FIGURE 7.4: The database after a blank column has been inserted to act as a spacer between the data in the ID No and Last Name fields. To accomplish this, the cell pointer was first positioned in column B and the /Worksheet Insert Column command was issued. The blank column added was then narrowed from nine to three spaces with the /Worksheet Column Set-Width command.

constructed. If a key input cell or reference cell is taken out as a result of using these commands, ERR values may suddenly appear throughout your model.

In addition, macros that you rely on, especially complex command macros that control data input or report generation, may cause havoc the next time they are used. It will be all the worse if these resulting errors don't show up until you need a report produced from the spreadsheet in a hurry or your data-entry operator goes to add or update data, especially if that person is not yet skilled enough in using Lotus 1-2-3 to deduce the cause of the error and figure out a quick fix.

Before you delete columns and rows, check out the entire width of the row or length of the column to make sure that no essential data will be affected by the deletion. To move quickly to the end of the row or rows that you want to delete, use the End-→ key combination discussed earlier. If there is no data in the row other than what you see on your screen, the cell pointer will jump to the last column, IV. To check the length of the column, use the End and ↓ keys in the same way.

If you find data that would have been destroyed by using the /Worksheet Delete command, determine how difficult it would be to use the /Move command to relocate the data outside the columns or rows to be deleted.

You will not have to worry about destroying part of your macros with the /Worksheet Delete command if you have located them in an area down and to the right of the area containing spreadsheet data. This position is beyond the reach of any usual row or column deletion. For specific information about locating your macros in this area, see Chapter 27, "Keystroke Macros."

COPYING AND MOVING RANGES IN THE WORKSHEET

When you work on the final formatting of your worksheets, you will often need to copy and move entire tables or parts of columns or rows of data. Lotus 1-2-3 does not have a command that will copy or move an entire column or row, so you have perform these operations on ranges of cells.

Copying Cell Ranges

When you make a copy of ranges, remember that all of the formulas that contain cell-relative references will automatically be adjusted to their new positions. (See Chapter 10, "Working with Formulas and Functions," for a full discussion of absolute versus relative cell references.) This can sometimes cause problems if you do not also copy the formulas that these references depend on. Most of the time, you can use this situation to good advantage to move work that relies on the same type of formulas and shares similar, if not the same, headings and layout. Figure 7.5 illustrates such a situation.

Remember when you use the /Copy command that any data existing within the destination range will be overwritten and thus lost. If you need to locate a copy between existing ranges of data, you will either have to add some blank columns or rows to accommodate the copy or move the endangered data range to a new, safe location in the spreadsheet before you perform the copy operation. Be especially aware of hidden ranges. You may want to protect hidden cells temporarily.

```
D13: (F1) [W11] +B13+C13                                          READY

       A         B        C          D    E       F        G        H
1               Start    End
2               Temp     Temp     Difference
3    Run 1        100    -567.0      -467.0   <- Down from 0 by 467.0 degrees
4    Run 2         45     -10.5        34.5   <- Up from 0 by 34.5 degrees
5    Run 3          0      -4.6        -4.6   <- Down from 0 by 4.6 degrees
6    Run 4         15     -23.4        -8.4   <- Down from 0 by 8.4 degrees
7    Run 5        450     -34.6       415.4   <- Up from 0 by 415.4 degrees
8    Run 6          0     -25.7       -25.7   <- Down from 0 by 25.7 degrees
9
10
11              Start    End
12              Temp     Temp     Difference
13   Run 1                              0.0   <- Up from 0 by 0.0 degrees
14   Run 2                              0.0   <- Up from 0 by 0.0 degrees
15   Run 3                              0.0   <- Up from 0 by 0.0 degrees
16   Run 4                              0.0   <- Up from 0 by 0.0 degrees
17   Run 5                              0.0   <- Up from 0 by 0.0 degrees
18   Run 6                              0.0   <- Up from 0 by 0.0 degrees
19
20
27-Jul-86   11:27 AM
```

FIGURE 7.5: In this figure, a table for recording and calculating differences between temperature data taken during various test runs was developed at the top of the worksheet (A1..H8). In preparation for adding new data from a second set of test runs, the Lotus 1-2-3 /Copy command is used to bring forward the labels and essential formulas into the lower part of the worksheet (A11..H18). The entire range A1..H8 is copied into the lower part of the worksheet. Run data in B13..C18 is then erased (/RE) so that new data can be input. Formula references are automatically adjusted during the copy operation to reflect their new locations. As soon as the next batch of test results is added, all of these formulas will be recalculated automatically.

Moving Cell Ranges

As discussed earlier, rearranging cell ranges with the /Move command is often superior to inserting and deleting columns for making your required formatting changes. This is because moving ranges affects only those cells designated as the source in the local area of the spreadsheet in which you are working. Just as when using the /Copy command, you must be careful that you do not move the data to a location in the spreadsheet that already contains data of its own, because the incoming range always overwrites the existing one. Be especially aware of hidden ranges; protect hidden cells before making extensive moves.

When moving ranges, you sometimes will find that you are required to perform at least two move operations to rearrange the data as you would like:

1. First, you relocate a range of cells that is in the way of the arrangement you want.
2. Second, you actually move the range you want to move to its newly desired location.

You have to perform the same kind of two-step operation when you want to exchange the positions of two data ranges. This situation is illustrated in Figures 7.6 to 7.9.

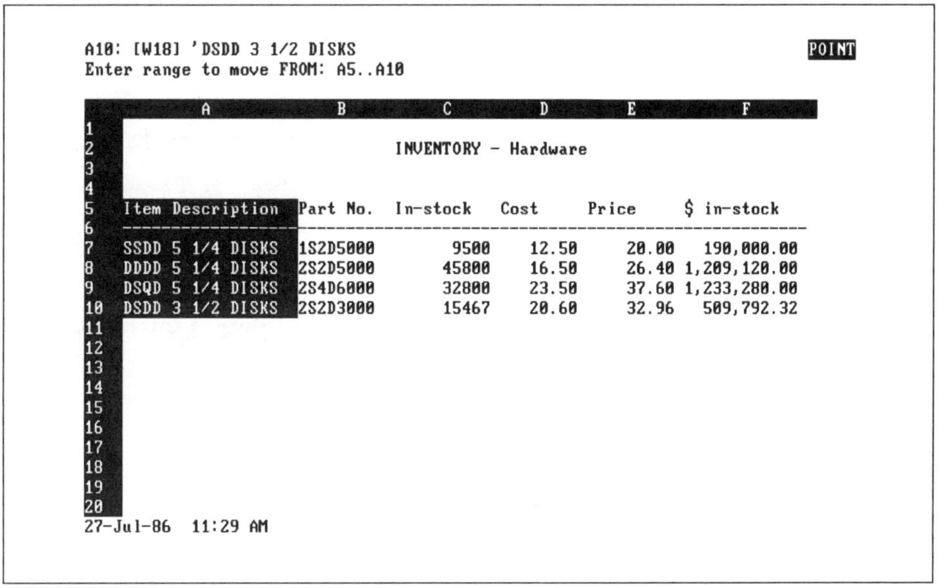

FIGURE 7.6: An inventory database in which the user has decided to exchange the positions of the Item Description and Part No. fields. Because data has already been added, the /Move command will be used a number of times so that no data reentry will be required.

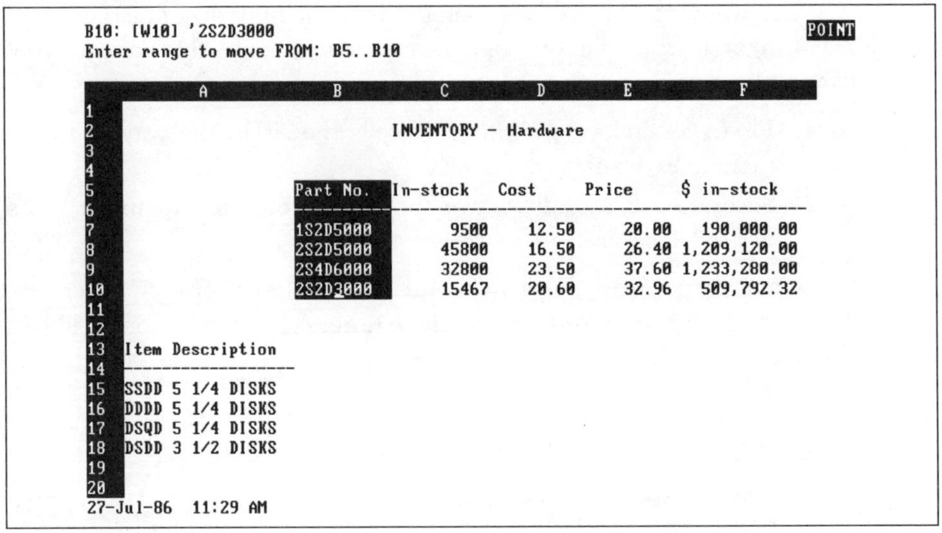

FIGURE 7.7: After the first move operation, the Item Description field name and the associated data have been temporarily moved down from A5 to A13 in preparation for moving the Part No. field name and data over from column B to column A. This was done to save item descriptions from being destroyed by the incoming part number data.

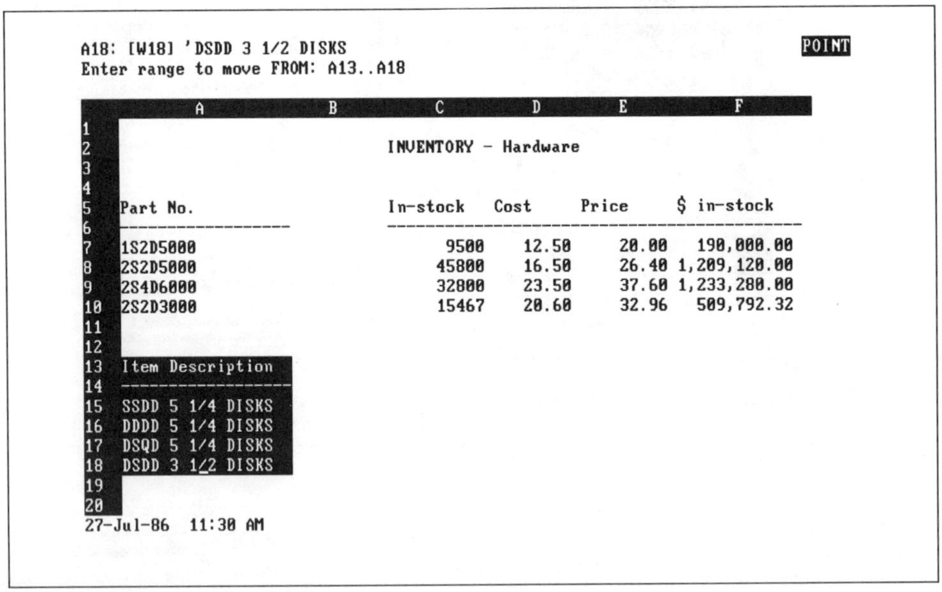

FIGURE 7.8: After the second move operation, the Part No. field name and its data have been moved over one column to the left. This leaves room in column B, into which the item description data, now temporarily located in A13, can be moved.

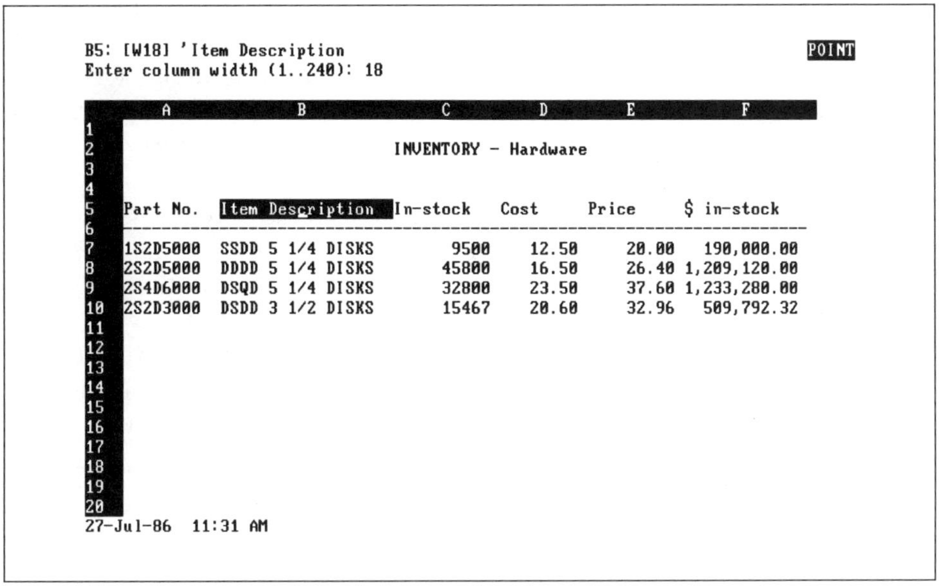

FIGURE 7.9: The revised database with the Part No. and Item Description fields interchanged. All that was required was a third and final move operation that relocated the Item Description field name and data from their temporary position in column A to their final position in column B. Finally, the /Worksheet Column Set-Width command was used to narrow and widen columns A and B, respectively, to display all of their data.

Using /Range Transpose (Release 2 Only)

Occasionally, after setting up a data table in the spreadsheet, you realize that it would have been preferable to have interchanged its vertical and horizontal axes. If you are using Release 2 of the program, you can sometimes use its / Range Transpose command to make such a change automatically.

This command represents a special kind of copy operation that transposes the alignment of the data as it copies it. For instance, when you use it to copy a row of labels entered across a row, the labels will be arranged vertically down a column from the beginning of the destination range. You can also use this command to horizontally arrange data entered vertically. It works well when the cell ranges specified contain only labels and literal values, but usually it is not successful with ranges that contain formulas. This is because cell references are automatically adjusted during transposition, but their references are skewed, resulting in inaccurate calculations or, much more commonly, ERR values.

Figure 7.10 illustrates the problem. A table comparing the net profit for five years has been set up in the range A3..F8 with the headings for the years running vertically down column A and the headings for the financial figures running horizontally across the columns. This table would be more effective if it did not read from left to right across each row but rather down each column.

The /Range Transpose command is then used to copy and move the labels and data into the preferred arrangement in the range A11..F16 of the spreadsheet. As you can see in Figure 7.10, this tranposition worked fine with the column and row headings and all of the values that were input into the table, but it failed when it came to transposing the formulas successfully. As a result, cell references were thrown out of kilter (the formula +B4−C4 in the first table has become +IV14−A14 in the second),

```
B14: (,2) [W15] +IV14-A14                                               READY

       A           B          C          D            E           F
 1
 2
 3 Year     Pre-Tax Profit SL Deprec Tax Profit   Income Tax Net Profit
 4          1    56,700.00  1,600.00   55,100.00  14,877.00  40,223.00
 5          2    76,250.00  1,600.00   74,650.00  20,155.50  54,494.50
 6          3    94,500.00  1,600.00   92,900.00  25,083.00  67,817.00
 7          4   103,560.00  1,600.00  101,960.00  27,529.20  74,430.80
 8          5   115,875.00  1,600.00  114,275.00  30,854.25  83,420.75
 9
10
11 Year                  1          2           3          4          5
12 Pre-Tax       56,700.00 76,250.00   94,500.00 103,560.00 115,875.00
13 SL Depre       1,600.00  1,600.00    1,600.00   1,600.00   1,600.00
14 Tax Prof            ERR       ERR         ERR        ERR        ERR
15 Income T      14,877.00 20,155.50   25,083.00  27,529.20  30,854.25
16 Net Prof            ERR       ERR         ERR        ERR        ERR
17
18
19
20
27-Jul-86  11:34 AM
```

FIGURE 7.10: Using the /Range. Transpose command to rearrange a data table that contains labels, values, and formulas. The second data table was created in two operations by using /Range Transpose. In the first, the range A3..A8 was given as the source range to copy from, and the cell A11 was given as the destination range to copy to. This resulted in having the years that ran down column A in the original table run across the top of the newly copied data table. In the second operation, the source range was given as B3..F8 and the cell A12 was given as the start of the destination range. In the new table, this resulted in a vertical arrangement in columns of all of the data arranged across rows in the original table. Wherever formulas were used in the first table, ERR values are displayed in the second because of the tranposition of their cell references.

and ERR values are returned in all of the calculated cells in the second table (rows 14 and 16) that contain formulas for deriving the taxable profit and net profit.

Figure 7.11 shows the same data tables as in Figure 7.10, only without the ERR values in the second table. In this case, all of the formulas in the first table were converted to values with the /Range Value command before using /Range Transpose to create the second. Using this technique is the only way to be sure of avoiding problems that result from transposing cell references in formulas.

```
A12: [W8] 'Pre-Tax Profit                                                  READY

         A          B           C           D           E          F
1
2
3   Year     Pre-Tax Profit SL Deprec Tax Profit   Income Tax Net Profit
4          1      56,700.00  1,600.00   55,100.00  14,877.00  40,223.00
5          2      76,250.00  1,600.00   74,650.00  20,155.50  54,494.50
6          3      94,500.00  1,600.00   92,900.00  25,083.00  67,817.00
7          4     103,560.00  1,600.00  101,960.00  27,529.20  74,430.80
8          5     115,875.00  1,600.00  114,275.00  30,854.25  83,420.75
9
10
11  Year                  1         2           3          4          5
12  Pre-Tax       56,700.00 76,250.00   94,500.00 103,560.00 115,875.00
13  SL Depre       1,600.00  1,600.00    1,600.00   1,600.00   1,600.00
14  Tax Prof      55,100.00 74,650.00   92,900.00 101,960.00 114,275.00
15  Income T      14,877.00 20,155.50   25,083.00  27,529.20  30,854.25
16  Net Prof      40,223.00 54,494.50   67,817.00  74,430.80  83,420.75
17
18
19
20
27-Jul-86   11:35 AM
```

FIGURE 7.11: Using the /Range Transpose command to rearrange a data table that contains only labels and values. To avoid problems with cell references becoming jumbled during transposition, as illustrated in Figure 7.10, the /Range Value command was first used in the original table on the range B4..F8 to convert all the formulas it contains to their calculated values. This time, all of the labels and data were successfully transposed when the same two /Range Transpose operations were used. All that is required in this spreadsheet is to widen column A so that its headings are displayed and to move it to the position of the original table (effectively erasing the original table).

Formatting Labels with /Range Justify

Lotus 1-2-3 provides a single command to format labels across cells in the spreadsheet. While the /Range Label command can be used to change the alignment of labels within their cells, the /Range Justify command can be used to change their alignment across adjacent cells. It gives you a method for controlling the width of each label's display without requiring you to break it up and enter it in sections in separate cells. This is accomplished in a manner somewhat like the word-wrap function in word processors. It is often used to limit the display of long labels that overflow into adjacent blank cells in the same row by forcing them down into adjacent vertical cells.

The way this command works is illustrated in Figures 7.12 and 7.13. In Figure 7.12, a long label that will be used to annotate figures in a sales table has been entered into cell A1. The label extends horizontally across row 1 all the way from A1 to G1. To limit the display, the /Range Justify command is used. This command word-wraps a long label into a specified range, in this case A1..B1. Figure 7.13 shows the result of issuing the command. The label is limited to columns A and B and runs vertically from row 1 to row 4.

Notice that in this example using /Range Justify is somewhat like transposing a long horizontal label into a narrow vertical label. It is as though Lotus 1-2-3 were a word processor with a right margin of 240 characters

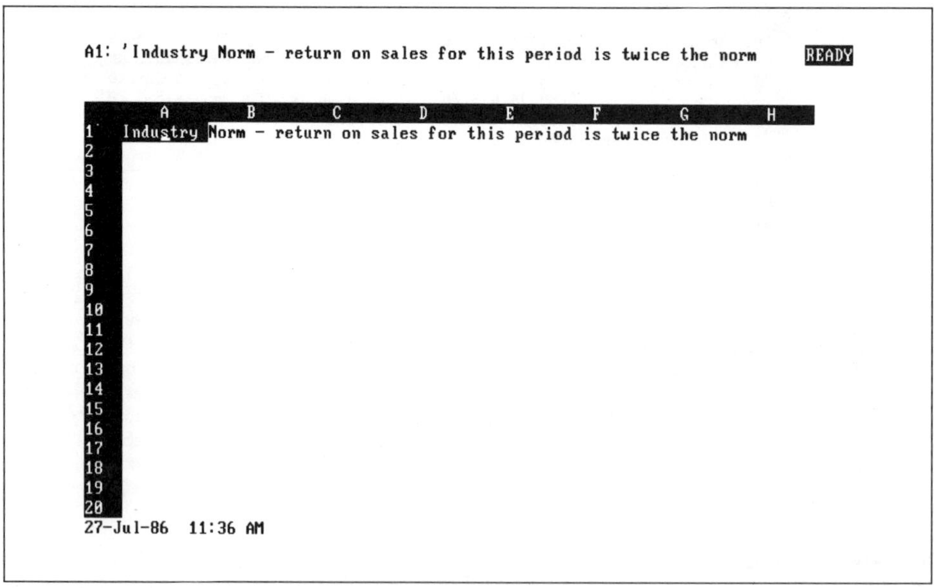

FIGURE 7.12: A long label is entered into cell A1. Because the adjacent cells to the right in the row are empty, it is displayed across the row from column A to column G. Assuming that the note is to run down the left side of a table of figures to be added, it can be easily reformatted with the /Range Justify command (see Figure 7.13).

```
A1: 'Industry Norm -                                          READY

     A         B         C         D         E         F         G         H
1    Industry Norm -
2    return on sales
3    for this period
4    is twice the norm
5
6
7
8
9
10
11
12
13
14
15
16
17
18
19
20
27-Jul-86  11:36 AM
```

FIGURE 7.13: The long label entered into cell A1 after reformatting with the /Range Justify command. The range indicated was restricted to A1..B1; therefore the program wrapped any words that would extend beyond B1 down to the next row. The label is now displayed in the range A1..B4, even though it is still entered only in cell A1.

and that you had set a new right margin of 18 (the combined width of columns A and B) by using the /Range Justify command.

This command can also be used in an opposite way to display labels that have been individually entered down a column in adjacent cells horizontally across a single cell. It works, however, only if the cell is wide enough to display all of the characters included in the individual cells. This application is discussed in the following section on concatenating labels.

Using /Range Justify to Concatenate Labels in Release 1A

Release 2 of Lotus 1-2-3 includes new methods for handling character strings so that they can be concatenated (added together) by using the & (ampersand) operator. In Release 1A of the program, the /Range Justify command accomplishes the same result.

How this works is illustrated in Figure 7.14, in which employee names are stored in parts in three separate columns (fields) of a Lotus 1-2-3 database. In this figure, column A contains the first name, column B the middle

```
D6:                                                                   SST POINT
Enter justify range: D6..D6

     A       B   C       D                  E  F          G            H
1   FName    MI  LName   Full Name                  Peter
2   Thomas   A.  Smith   Thomas A. Smith            A.
3   Mary     J.  Drew    Mary J. Drew               Kaye
4   David    P.  McGill  David P. McGill
5   Kenneth  E.  Farner  Kenneth E. Farner
6   Peter    A.  Kaye
7   Sandra   B.  Smith
8   Phillis  G.  Olsen
9   Carol    L.  Tudor
10  Steven   F.  Nelson
11
12  \J           /RNCplace~{RIGHT}{RIGHT}~
13               /XI@COUNT(place)=0~/RNDplace~/REG1~/XQ
14               /C~G1~{right}
15               /C~G2~{right}
16               /C~G3~{right}
17               /RJG1~/CG1~~
18               /RNDplace~
19               {DOWN}{LEFT}{LEFT}{LEFT}
20               /XG\J~
                                              STEP
```

FIGURE 7.14: Using the /Range Justify command to concatenate labels in Release 1A. This macro takes the three parts of the full name (first name, middle initial, and last name) and combines them into a single label in the Full Name field. It first copies the individual entries to three temporary cells arranged vertically adjacent to one another in G1..G3. In this figure, the three parts of Peter A. Kaye's name have been copied to these particular cells. The /Range Justify command is then issued with only cell G1 as its range. It brings Peter's middle initial and last name into G1. Once this is done, the macro copies the full name into the appropriate cell in column D (D6 in this case). The macro continues to process all of the names in the database until it encounters a blank row indicating the end of the database. In Release 2, the same thing could be accomplished with a simple formula using the & operator to concatenate the names into one entry in column D (for example, entering the formula **+A2" "&B2&" "&C2** in cell D2).

initial, and column C the last name. To combine these separate cell entries into a single label in column D in a new Full Name field, a macro has been created using /Range Justify to do the concatenation.

The macro creates a single label out of three separate labels as follows:

1. First, each part of the name is copied from its horizontal listing in columns A, B, and C in the database to a vertical listing in three adjacent cells (G1..G3 in this example).
2. The cell pointer is then located in the first of these cells (G1) and the /Range Justify command is given with only the current cell (G1) as its range. This causes the program to bring the two parts of the full name entered in the cells directly below it (G2 and G3) into the current cell (G1), which already holds the first name.

3. The combined full name is then copied to its permanent position in the appropriate cell in column D, the Full Name field.

Note that the macro refers to the three cells into which the parts of the names are copied by cell address rather than by range name. This is required because /Range Justify deletes any range name it encounters. If you use this macro in applications of your own, make sure that the column containing the cell where the parts of the label are concatenated with /Range Justify (G1 in this example) is wide enough to display the entire new entry. If it is not, /Range Justify will not combine all of the parts. Only as much of the combined labels as can be displayed in the width of the cell will be concatenated.

Using /Range Justify to Parse Labels in Release 1A

The /Range Justify command can also be used in Release 1A to split up long labels into individual cells, an operation referred to as *parsing.* (In Release 2, a new command—/Data Parse—has been included, thus making this technique unnecessary.) Such an operation is often required when importing into Lotus 1-2-3 data generated in other applications such as stand-alone database management systems. When imported with /File Import, the data is copied into the worksheet as long labels, usually in column A.

To be used effectively in a Lotus 1-2-3 database, these long labels must then be broken apart (parsed) into individual data items and copied into individual columns so that they can be manipulated with the /Data Query commands. To automate this procedure, a macro that uses the /Range Justify command can be created.

This macro and its application are illustrated in Figure 7.15. This figure shows the opposite of the procedure depicted in Figure 7.14. Here, each person's full name is entered in column A as a long label whose display spills over into column B. The macro operates by first copying each name into cell E25, which has been narrowed to a width of only three characters. Once the /Range Justify command is issued using this extremely narrow cell as its range, the name is split into three vertically adjacent cells (E25..E27 in this case).

The macro then copies the new contents of each of these vertically arranged cells into three adjacent cells in a single row (F25..H25 in this example), where they are then copied as a single range back into the

```
E27: 'Tudor                                                      SST POINT
Enter range to erase: E27..E27

       A    B     C          D          E F         G        H
24  Full Name
25  Steven  W.   Smith                  CarCarol  L.        Tudor
26  Barry   L.   Johnson                L.
27  Doris   M.   Olsen                  Tudor
28  David   P.   McGill
29  Carol L. Tudor
30  Peter A. Kaye
31
32
33  \P      /RNCplace~{RIGHT}~
34          /XI@COUNT(place)=0~/RNDplace~/REF25..H25~/XQ
35          {GOTO}E25~/Cplace~~
36          /RJ~
37          /C~{RIGHT}~
38          {DOWN}/C~{RIGHT}{RIGHT}{UP}~
39          {DOWN}/C~{RIGHT}{RIGHT}{RIGHT}{UP}{UP}~
40          /REE25..E27~
41          {GOTO}place~/CF25..H25~~
42          {DOWN}/RNDplace~
43          /XG\P~
                                        STEP
```

FIGURE 7.15: Using the /Range Justify command to parse labels in Release 1A. The macro listed here first copies the long label entered into column A into a very narrow cell, E25. The /Range Justify command is then issued, using this cell alone as the range. It breaks up the label into the three adjacent cells, E25..E27. The contents of each of these are then copied to cells F25, G25, and H25, respectively. This range is then copied to the appropriate row in column A, where it replaces the original long label. In this figure, the macro has already parsed the first four names in column A and is operating on the fifth, Carol L. Tudor. It has just copied the three parts of her name split up into cells E25..E27 with /Range Justify into cells F25..H25. Next, it will copy this range to cell A29. The macro will continue until it reaches the blank cells in row 31. This operation can be performed without such a macro in Release 2 by using the /Data Parse command.

appropriate row in column A. This overwrites the original long label entry, leaving the successfully parsed name in the first three columns of each row.

If you use this macro in your own applications that require parsing long labels, note that you must use cell references rather than range names for those cells that will contain the parts of the label split with /Range Justify. This is because the /Range Justify command automatically deletes all range names assigned to the cells that it affects.

Note: The macros shown in Figures 7.14 and 7.15 are located below the data they operate on only to illustrate both their contents and operations in a single figure. In actual spreadsheet applications, they would not under any circumstances be located in the same area as the data they operate on.

WORKSHEET COMMANDS COMMONLY USED IN FORMATTING

The most commonly used commands for rearranging the structure of a worksheet are /Worksheet Insert and Delete. Both of these commands affect the entire worksheet. You may dislocate or erase data in distant parts of the spreadsheet if you do not use them carefully.

/Worksheet Insert

MENUS

/Worksheet
Insert
Column   Row

KEYBOARD ENTRY

/WIC
Enter column insert range: **<range>**
/WIR
Enter row insert range: **<range>**

FUNCTION

This command inserts entire new columns or rows in the worksheet.

USAGE

The /Worksheet Insert command has two options, Column and Row. To add a new column or range of columns from the current cell pointer's position, enter the command **/WIC.** The program will supply the current cell address as the default (though it takes into consideration only the column letter). To add more than a single new column, you can then indicate a range by highlighting a group of adjacent columns with pointing or by typing in the range addresses. The procedure for adding a new row or range of rows with this command is similar. You merely enter the command as **/WIR** and proceed as described above.

As soon as you press the Return key after indicating the range with either command, the program inserts the blank column(s) or row(s) at the cell pointer's position. A row is inserted above the specified row range; a column is inserted to the left of the specified column range. The data located in cells displaced by the insertion of new columns or rows is automatically moved to new locations. All of the cell references in any formulas are adjusted to reflect the new addresses.

If you wish to add blank cells in only a portion of a column or a row, you must use the /Move command.

EXAMPLES

For an illustration of the use of the /Worksheet Insert command and its effect on existing data, refer to Figures 7.1 and 7.2. For an illustration of inserting a new column to act as a spacer between columns of adjacent data, refer to Figures 7.3 and 7.4.

SEE ALSO

/Move

/Worksheet Delete

MENUS

/Worksheet
Delete
Column Row

KEYBOARD ENTRY

/WDC
Enter range of columns to delete: **<range>**
/WDR
Enter range of rows to delete: **<range>**

FUNCTION

This command deletes entire columns or rows from the worksheet.

USAGE

The /Worksheet Delete command has two options, Column and Row. To delete a column or range of columns from the current cell pointer's position, enter the command as **/WDC.** The program will supply the current cell address as the default (though it takes into consideration only the column letter). To delete more than a single new column, you can then indicate a range by highlighting a group of adjacent columns with pointing or by typing in cell addresses. The procedure for deleting a row or range of rows with this command is similar. You merely enter the command as **/WDR** and proceed as described above.

As soon as you press the Return key after indicating the range with either command, the program deletes all of the data contained in the column(s) or row(s) from the cell pointer's position. The data located outside the column(s) or row(s) is automatically moved to new locations. All of the cell references in any formulas are adjusted to reflect the new addresses.

Of course, if any of the cell references in the remaining formulas refer to data that was deleted, zeros, error values, or circular references may suddenly appear in some of them. Before using the /Worksheet Delete commands, you should always exercise the precaution of first saving the worksheet if it has never been saved before.

If you wish to delete data in only a portion of a column or row, you must use the /Range Erase command.

SEE ALSO

/Range Erase

RANGE COMMANDS COMMONLY USED IN FORMATTING

Two /Range commands can be useful when you need to reformat cell entries in the worksheet. The first, /Range Justify, works on labels and can be used to modify their display across columns or down rows. The second, /Range Transpose, is a new Release 2 command that allows you to invert the vertical and horizontal arrangement of labels and values as they are copied to a new area of the worksheet.

/Range Justify

MENUS

/Range
Justify

KEYBOARD ENTRY

/RJ
Enter justify range: **<range>**

FUNCTION

This command reformats label entries so that they fit within the justify range indicated.

USAGE

The /Range Justify command reformats labels so that they are justified within the width of the cells included in the range you specify. To narrow a long label entered into a single cell, position the cell pointer in that cell and issue the /Range Justify command (**/RJ**). Then indicate the extent of the range where you want the label to appear by pointing or typing the cell addresses. After you press Return, the text will be reformatted to stay within this range using new rows as required to display all of the labels.

This command can also be used to combine separate labels entered into vertically adjacent cells. To combine an entry, position the cell pointer in the first cell of the range and then widen the cell to display all of the combined label. Issue the /Range Justify command (**/RJ**) and give the current cell as the justify range by pressing Return. The program will then display in the first cell all of the labels in the adjacent cells. If there is insufficient room, not all of the labels will be combined.

EXAMPLES

For an illustration of how the /Range Justify command works on long labels in a spreadsheet, refer to Figures 7.12 and 7.13. For illustrations of how to use /Range Justify to concatenate and parse labels, refer to Figures 7.14 and 7.15.

SEE ALSO

/Data Parse

/Range Transpose (Release 2 Only)

MENUS

/Range
Transpose

KEYBOARD ENTRY

/RT
Enter range to copy FROM: **<range>**
Enter range to copy TO: **<range>**

FUNCTION

This command makes an inverted copy of the source range (copy FROM:) data in the destination range (copy TO:).

USAGE

The /Range Transpose command is used to copy and simultaneously transpose data that has been entered down columns in the source range so it is arranged across rows when copied to the destination range or, vice versa, to transpose data that runs across rows so that it runs down columns.

The transposition will not, however, be completely successful if the data in the source range includes formulas that use cell references. These become skewed in the copy and usually result in ERR values. To avoid this, you can use the /Range Value command to convert all formulas to their calculated values before issuing the /Range Transpose command.

To copy and invert a column of labels and values, issue the command **/RT,** indicate the extent of the source range in response to the copy FROM prompt either by pointing or by using cell addresses, and press Return. When you indicate the source range, be sure that the order given is from top to bottom. Then indicate the first cell of the destination range, either by pointing to it or by typing in its address, and press

Return again. The copy of the data will be displayed from left to right across the row of the destination range in the same order as it was entered down the column in the source range.

To copy and invert a row of labels and values, issue the command / **RT**, indicate the extent of the source range in response to the copy FROM prompt either by pointing or by using cell addresses, and press Return. When you indicate the source range, be sure that the order given is from left to right. Then indicate the first cell of the destination range, either by pointing to it or by typing in its address, and press Return again. The copy of the data will be displayed down the column of the destination range in the same order as it was entered from left to right across the row in the source range.

When you use the /Range Transpose command, remember that any existing data in the area required by the copy will be destroyed by incoming data.

EXAMPLES

For illustrations of how the /Range Transpose command works, refer to Figures 7.10 and 7.11.

Copying and Moving Cell Ranges

Because Lotus 1-2-3 does not have a command to copy or move a column or row, you perform these operations on cell ranges. The /Copy command copies cell ranges, leaving the original range or ranges in place. The /Move command moves cell ranges from one location in the worksheet to another.

/Copy

MENUS

/Copy

KEYBOARD ENTRY

/C
Enter range to copy FROM: **<range>**
Enter range to copy TO: **<range>**

FUNCTION

This command makes a copy of the data included in the source range (copy FROM:) in the destination range (copy TO:).

USAGE

The /Copy command is used to make copies of cell ranges from one area of the worksheet to another. When copying labels and values, Lotus 1-2-3 makes an exact copy. When copying formulas that contain relative cell references, it makes a relative copy in that all cell addresses are automatically adjusted, reflecting the direction of the copy. Absolute cell references are not changed. You can override the relative addressing default when you copy formulas to make all or part of the formula copy absolute. For a complete discussion of relative, mixed address, and absolute formula copying, see Chapter 10.

The command prompts you for two inputs: the source of the copy in response to the prompt "Enter range to copy FROM:" and the destination of the copy in response to the prompt "Enter range to copy TO:". In practice, this allows you to make three types of copies in the worksheet: one to many, one to one, and many to many. Each is described below.

THE ONE-TO-MANY COPY

In the one-to-many copy, the source range is a single cell entered by cell address or range name. You can indicate a cell address by typing in the address or by pointing. The destination range is made up of a block of multiple cells. These, too, can be indicated by entering cell addresses or by pointing. If you are using pointing, remember to anchor the range by typing a period.

The one-to-many copy is most commonly used for copying a single formula to other cells. You must take into consideration relative versus mixed or absolute cell addressing when you create the original formula to be copied. The copy can be done in one or two dimensions, as illustrated in Figure 7.16, which shows three examples of the one-to-many copy.

THE ONE-TO-ONE COPY

The one-to-one copy differs from the one-to-many copy only in that the source range and destination range are both single cells. This type of

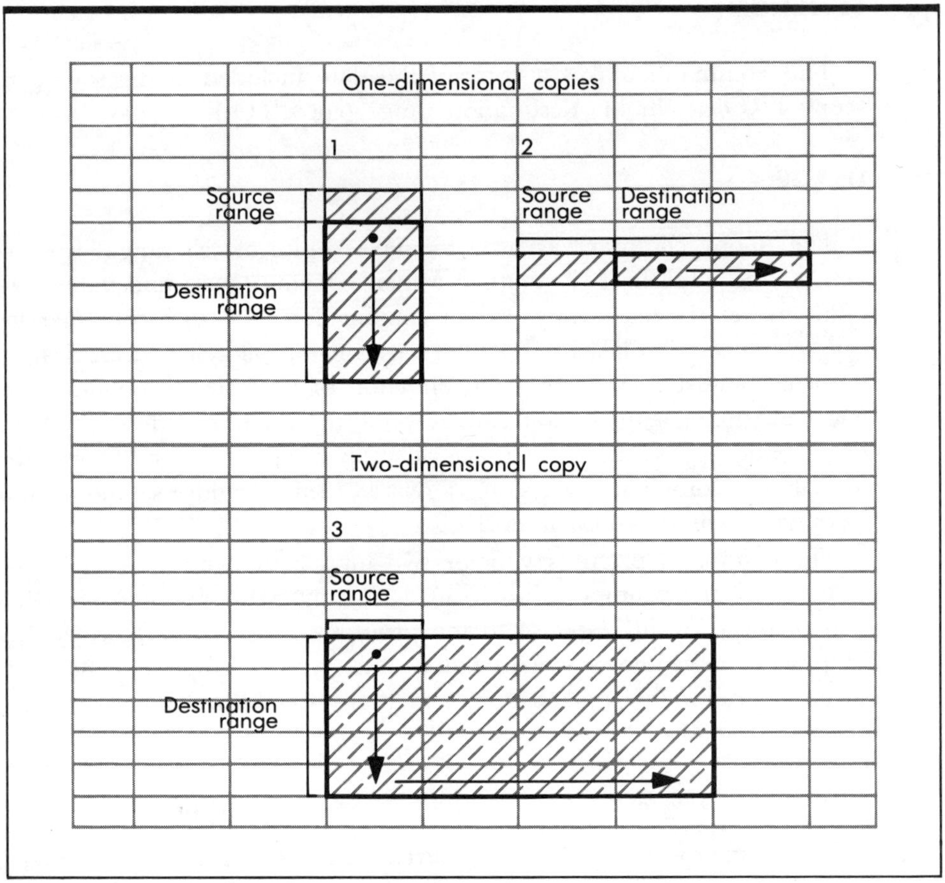

FIGURE 7.16: The one-to-many copy in the worksheet. Copy 1 in this figure shows a vertical copy of the contents of one cell to the five cells directly below it. If pointing is used, after designating the first cell as the source, the cell pointer is moved down one cell and the period is typed to anchor the range. Then the ↓ key is pressed to extend the range down. Copy 2 shows the same kind of one-dimensional copy, only in the horizontal direction. Copy 3 shows a two-dimensional one-to-many copy. Here the source is designated as a single cell in the upper-left corner of the range. It is also included as part of the destination range. In pointing, the range is anchored with the period on the first cell; the ↓ key is used to bring the range down, and the → key is used to bring it across.

copy is used most often to copy a spreadsheet title or heading from one area of the worksheet to another.

However, when you need to bring forward the contents of one cell to a new area of the worksheet and you want the copy to remain dynamically linked to its source, do not use the /Copy command. In such cases, create a formula in the new cell, preceding the source cell's address with a plus sign. For instance, to bring forward the contents of cell A1 to AB20, locate the pointer in AB20 and enter the formula **+A1.** That way, any updating done in A1 will also be done in AB20.

THE MANY-TO-MANY COPY

The many-to-many copy is used when you wish to bring forward a range of cell entries, which may include any combination of labels, literal values, and formulas. In this kind of copy, the source range of cells must be arranged in a contiguous block (see Chapter 8 for more information on cell ranges in Lotus 1-2-3). When entering the source range, you can designate it either by cell addresses or by range name. When designating cell addresses, you can type in the cell addresses or use the pointing method. If you use pointing, type a period to anchor the range.

After designating the extent of the source, you indicate the location of the destination range by designating only its first cell (the one in the upper-left corner of the range). Lotus 1-2-3 will make the copy from this point on, filling in the rest of the copied cells as necessary. This kind of copy is illustrated in Figure 7.17.

EXAMPLES

For an illustration of the use of the /Copy command to bring forward previously entered labels and formulas, refer to Figure 7.5.

SEE ALSO

"Relative, Mixed, and Absolute Cell References in Copying Formulas" in Chapter 10, "Working with Formulas and Functions"

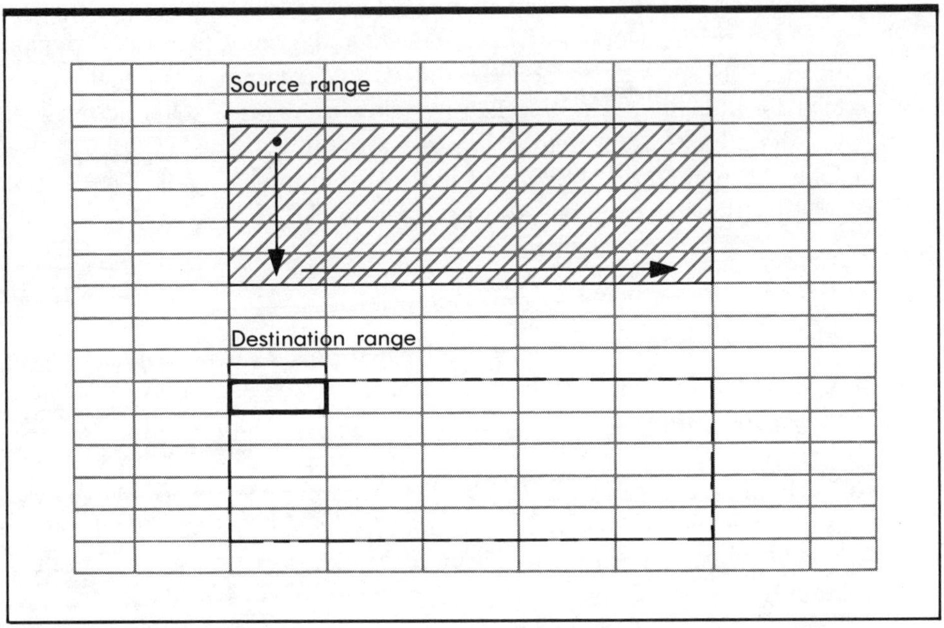

FIGURE 7.17: The many-to-many copy in worksheet. Here the source range of the copy consists of a range that extends down many rows over several columns. This range is designated as the range to copy from. In pointing, use the period to anchor the range on the cell in the upper-left corner before using the arrow keys to extend the range. Only the first cell of the destination range is designated in response to the copy TO prompt. The broken lines show the extent of the cells copied from the original range after the Return key is pressed.

/Move

MENUS

/Move

KEYBOARD ENTRY

/M
Enter range to move FROM: **<range>**
Enter range to move TO: **<range>**

FUNCTION

This command relocates the data included in the source range (move FROM:) to the destination range (move TO:) in the worksheet.

USAGE

The /Move command is used to move cell ranges from one area of the worksheet to another. Formulas that contain references to cells in the range that has been relocated with the /Move command are automatically adjusted to reflect the cells' new position in the worksheet.

In use, the command prompts you for two inputs: the source of the range to be relocated in response to the prompt "Enter range to move FROM:" and the new location of the range in response to the prompt "Enter range to move TO:".

When indicating the range to be moved, you designate it by cell addresses or by range name. When designating cell addresses, you can either type in the cell addresses or use pointing. If you use the pointing method, type a period to anchor the range before you extend it with the appropriate arrow keys.

When indicating the new location of the range, you need only designate the position of the first cell (the one in the upper-left corner of the range). Lotus 1-2-3 fills in the rest of the cells included in the range as necessary.

EXAMPLES

For an illustration of how to use the /Move command to exchange data in two columns, refer to Figures 7.6 to 7.9.

SUMMARY

This chapter has discussed various techniques that you can use to format cell entries within the spreadsheet. The following references contain suggestions of where to go to obtain additional information related to the commands specifically discussed as well as to the general topic of formatting spreadsheets.

For information about formatting labels and values in their cells:

- Chapter 5, "Creating Worksheets"

For information about deleting portions of columns and rows:

- Chapter 6, "Editing Worksheets"

For information about designating cell ranges in Lotus 1-2-3:

- Chapter 8, "Working with Cell Ranges"

For information on when to use relative, mixed address, and absolute cell references when copying formulas in a spreadsheet:

- Chapter 10, "Working with Formulas and Functions"

For information on concatenating labels and other related string functions in Release 2:

- Chapter 17, "String Functions"

For information about parsing labels in Release 2:

- Chapter 29, "Importing and Exporting ASCII Files"

CHAPTER 8

WORKING WITH CELL RANGES

Working with Cell Ranges

This chapter discusses Lotus 1-2-3 cell ranges: what they are, how to designate them, and how to make effective use of them. It also takes up the important subject of naming ranges: how named ranges are used and how their use can aid in spreadsheet design and maintenance. Finally, the windowing and titles functions are illustrated, demonstrating how they can help you work with isolated cell ranges in a large spreadsheet.

After these discussions, all of the commands examined are listed as reference entries in the order they are found in the Lotus 1-2-3 command menus. Also included are keystroke macros to facilitate creating and deleting numerous range names.

Because the /Range Name commands are used extensively in creating macros, you may want to examine the /Range Name reference entry and read about its use in this chapter before you try to use Chapters 27 and 28, which take up the subject of creating Lotus 1-2-3 macros.

Cell Ranges in Lotus 1-2-3

A cell range in Lotus 1-2-3 can be as small as a single cell and as large as the memory of your computer can hold. It is designated in all commands and functions that use cell ranges by a double period between two cell addresses. (You have to enter only one period when you indicate a cell range; Lotus 1-2-3 supplies the second period for you.) The default range is always a single cell using the address of the current cell. For example, if the cell pointer is located in A1, the program designates the range as follows:

A1..A1

If only the single address of A1 is displayed after the prompt, you know that Lotus 1-2-3 is not using a cell range but is using a single cell address instead. The difference is significant when you use the pointing method to extend the range. If you see only a single cell address displayed, you know that you have to type a period to anchor the range before you can use the arrow keys to extend it.

Valid Cell Ranges

Figure 8.1 illustrates four examples of valid cell ranges in Lotus 1-2-3. In order for a cell range to be valid, its shape must be rectangular. Range 1 is the smallest possible range, consisting of a single cell. It is designated by B2..B2 rather than just B2. Lotus 1-2-3 automatically creates single-cell ranges consisting of the current cell as the default response to any of the prompts you see when you use the /Range commands, although the

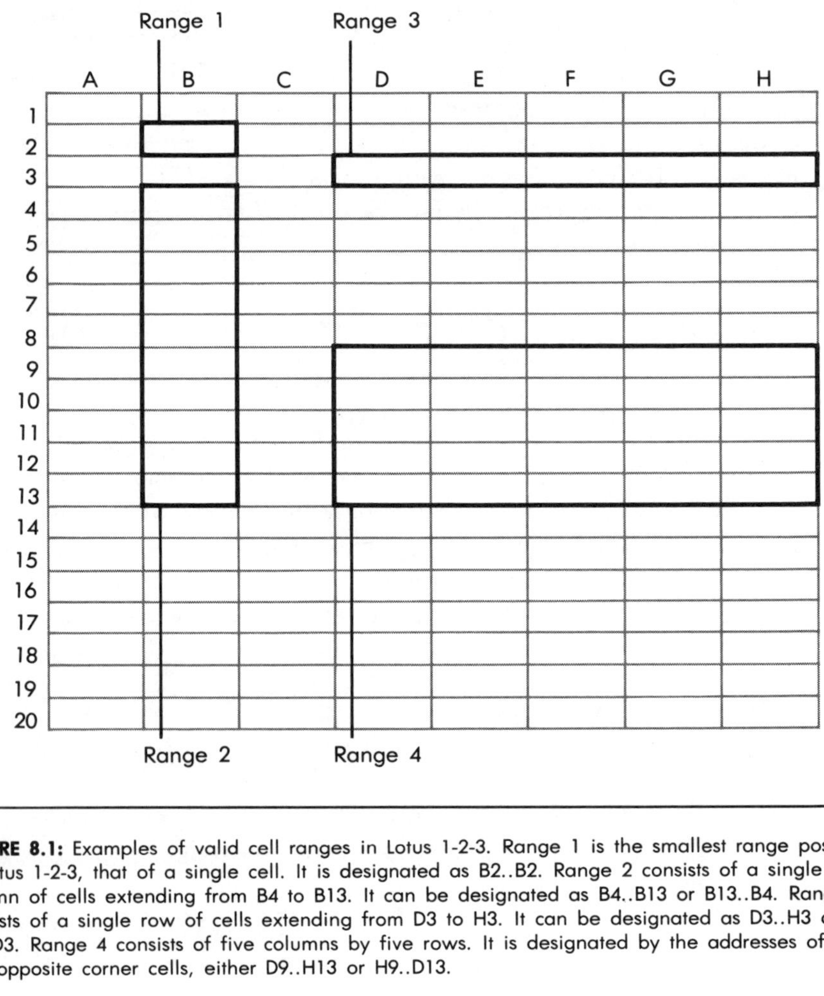

FIGURE 8.1: Examples of valid cell ranges in Lotus 1-2-3. Range 1 is the smallest range possible in Lotus 1-2-3, that of a single cell. It is designated as B2..B2. Range 2 consists of a single column of cells extending from B4 to B13. It can be designated as B4..B13 or B13..B4. Range 3 consists of a single row of cells extending from D3 to H3. It can be designated as D3..H3 or H3..D3. Range 4 consists of five columns by five rows. It is designated by the addresses of the two opposite corner cells, either D9..H13 or H9..D13.

program expects that you will usually designate a cell range larger than a single cell when you use these commands.

Range 2 in Figure 8.1 illustrates a range that consists of only a single column of cells. It can be defined as either B4..B13 or B13..B4. Range 3 illustrates a range that consists of a single row of cells. It can be defined as either D3..H3 or H3..D3. Notice that in the case of a single column or row of cells, the cell range is designated by the address of the first and last cells. Lotus 1-2-3 always considers the topmost or leftmost cell as the beginning of such a range, regardless of the order the cell addresses are given when the range is defined. Most people follow the same convention as Lotus 1-2-3 by naming the top or leftmost cell first, but you may want to vary this, depending on which direction you are working in.

Range 4 in Figure 8.1 illustrates another common cell range shape. This one includes several columns and rows. In this particular example, the range is square, consisting of exactly five columns across by five rows deep. If a range consists of several columns and rows, it is defined by using the cell addresses of opposite corner cells. Lotus 1-2-3 always considers the upper-left cell as the beginning of the range, regardless of the order of the corner cell addresses you use in its definition. In this example, you could define the range by entering **D9..H13, H13..D9, H9..D13,** or even **D13..H9.**

Cell ranges like Range 4 in Figure 8.1 that consist of several columns and rows always contain complete columns and rows within their corner cells. For example, if you reduced the size of Range 4 by a single row, it would then consist of five columns and four rows. In other words, there is no way to create a range that consists of four rows in the first three columns and two rows in the next two columns.

Designating Cell Ranges

Whenever Lotus 1-2-3 requires you to enter a cell range, you have two ways to designate its location and extent:

- You can type in the appropriate cell addresses, separated by a period.
- You can point to the cells by using the appropriate arrow keys.

The second method is generally considered to be superior to the first because it eliminates the possibilty of incorrectly designating a cell range by making a simple typing error. It also cuts down on spreadsheet errors, because with pointing it is almost impossible not to include all of the cells that need to be incorporated in the range. This can happen quite easily when you try to "eyeball" correct cell addresses before typing them in a congested spreadsheet.

When you use pointing to designate a range with one of the /Range commands, all you need to do is press the appropriate arrow keys to extend the range as required. Lotus 1-2-3 provides constant visual feedback by displaying the extent of the range with highlighting as you press the arrow keys. This is sometimes referred to as "painting" a range in Lotus 1-2-3.

However, some commands that require ranges do not always automatically anchor the range at the current cell as the /Range commands do. In commands like /Copy and /Move and in procedures for designating graph variables or ranges to be printed, anchoring is not completely automatic. In such cases, you must first type a single period to anchor the range at the current cell. The Lotus 1-2-3 prompt will change from displaying a single cell to a single cell range (for example, from B2 to B2..B2) as soon as you press the period key.

Once you have anchored the cell range, use any of the four arrow keys to highlight its extent. Where you anchor the range is important: you should always first determine which cell is the first (or last) or is one of the four corners of the range you want to specify. Then move the cell pointer to it and enter a period to anchor it.

If you anchor a range in the middle, it will be impossible to indicate the entire range in one operation. If you find yourself in such a predicament, press the Esc key to unanchor the range. Then move the cell pointer to the appropriate corner cell and type the period again to anchor the range.

Note: You can also use the Esc key to unanchor a range that is automatically supplied by Lotus 1-2-3. For instance, if you activate the /Range Format Currency command before you locate the pointer at the beginning of the range to which it is to be applied, press Esc to unanchor the range. You can then reanchor it with the period after you move the pointer to the appropriate cell.

Commands and Applications That Require Cell Ranges

Many commands and applications in Lotus 1-2-3 require you to designate cell ranges. Apart from the obvious examples of all of the /Range commands, many other commands also work with cell ranges.

Cell ranges are required when using the /Copy and /Move commands. They are needed in defining graphs, in using /Data Sort and /Data Query with database applications, and in printing spreadsheets either to the printer or to a file. On the /File menu, ranges are required when you use the /File Combine and /File Extract commands.

Even some of the /Worksheet commands require designating ranges—when using the Insert and Delete commands, for example. These /Worksheet command prompts ask for the range of rows or columns to be included when using /Worksheet Insert Row or /Worksheet Delete Column. You must define them just as any other valid cell range in Lotus 1-2-3.

All of the principles describing the naming of cell ranges laid out in this and the following sections apply when you use any of the Lotus 1-2-3 commands that require cell ranges as a part of their input and definition.

Naming Cell Ranges

Lotus 1-2-3 allows you to assign a name to any valid cell range in the worksheet. This is done from the /Range Name menu by using either the Create or Labels command. There are a number of important applications for range names when building a spreadsheet or database. These and their general use are discussed in the following sections.

Conventions in Naming Cell Ranges

When you name cell ranges, it is important to keep in mind these few guidelines:

- Make range names as descriptive as possible. Though you may still be forced to use some abbreviations, you should be able to avoid really cryptic names.
- Do not use more than 15 characters. If you assign a longer name, it will be automatically truncated after the fifteenth character.
- Do not begin your range name with any mathematical operators (+, −, *, /) or valid cell addresses (A1 to IV8192). Their use will confuse Lotus 1-2-3, especially if the range name is used when constructing a formula or with the Goto function key.
- Make each range name unique. If you assign a duplicate range name, it will be used only to designate the most recent cell range, which in effect deletes the range name for the original cell range. Whenever you are assigning a new range name, Lotus 1-2-3 displays a listing of all range names you have used. Check this list to avoid duplication.

- Lotus 1-2-3 does not distinguish between uppercase and lowercase letters included in the range name. It considers the range names TOT_SALES and Tot_Sales to be the same.
- Lotus 1-2-3 allows you to assign different range names to the same cell range in a spreadsheet. This means that if you are just trying to rename a cell range, assigning a new name will not replace the old one. The only ways to delete a range name are to use the /Range Name Delete command or to reuse the range name by assigning it to another cell range.

Creating a Named Range

There are two ways to assign a name to a cell range:

- Use the /Range Name Create command.
- Use the /Range Name Labels command.

These commands differ in use and somewhat in application.

Using the /Range Name Create Command

The /Range Name Create command allows you to assign a range name to an entire cell range. Once you have named a specific range with it, you can use this name in place of cell addresses when you use any Lotus 1-2-3 command that requires a cell range. If the name range consists of only a single cell, you can give its range name in place of the cell address when you use it in formulas or functions that allow arguments consisting of only a single cell.

Using range names created with this command offers several benefits:

- You can use the Goto function key (F5) to move the cell pointer directly to the beginning of the range (its upper-left corner cell) by giving the range name assigned to it instead of entering a cell address.
- You can add and delete data within the named range, and Lotus 1-2-3 will automatically update the addresses of the range as long as you do not delete the cells that define the limits of the range by using the /Worksheet Delete Column or Row commands. If you delete either of these corner cells, Lotus 1-2-3 displays ERR values in all formulas that contain references to the range. Once a range

name has been replaced by an ERR value as the function's argument, you must change it manually in EDIT mode even if you have restored and renamed the cell range.

- You can easily relocate named ranges to new sections of the worksheet. All you have to do is move the cell pointer to the new location, type in the range name in response to the prompt for the range to move from, and press the Return key.
- When you use pointing, you can include a named range in response to any prompt for a cell range by selecting it from a listing of all assigned range names. You simply press the Name key (F3), highlight the name desired, and press the Return key.
- Using range names assigned to either single cells or larger ranges in spreadsheet formulas provides an excellent means for documenting the functions of those ranges in the formulas.

Using range names can help you eliminate costly spreadsheet errors as you create and refine your applications. Range names also tend to make it easier for other people who are not directly involved in constructing spreadsheets to understand and use them. Finally, using range names helps you update and revise spreadsheets quickly because the range names indicate the contents of your spreadsheets.

Revising a Named Range

Figures 8.2 and 8.3 illustrate how Lotus 1-2-3 handles revisions to a named range. In Figure 8.2, a table analyzing the potential profits for six new product mixes (of which only the first five are visible in this figure) has already been named PROFIT ANALYSIS by using the /Range Name Create command. In cell A15, the /Range Name Table command was used to display the range name and its current cell range. Notice that even though this range was named by entering the cell addresses A9..G3, Lotus 1-2-3 designates the range PROFIT ANALYSIS as A3..G9 in the table it has created.

In row 11 of this same figure, additional data for determining the return on the fixed cost was entered. This data needs to be included in the PROFIT ANALYSIS table in the row right above Dollar Profit. To accomplish this, the cell pointer is moved up to A9 and a new row is inserted with the /Worksheet Insert Row command. The range A11..G11 is then moved to the new row 9.

```
A15: [W24] 'PROFIT ANALYSIS                                              READY

                  A                B        C        D        E        F
 1
 2
 3 Mix Numbers                     1        2        3        4        5
 4 Fixed Cost                200,000  250,000  210,000  195,000  210,000
 5 Break-even Volume          46,300   65,000   51,500   72,300   38,000
 6 Est. Unit Sales            44,000   67,200   50,000   86,500   41,200
 7 Volume above Break-even   (2,300)    2,200  (1,500)   14,200    3,200
 8 Unit Contribution            4.00     4.00     4.00     5.00     5.00
 9 Dollar Profit             (9,200)    8,800  (6,000)   71,000   16,000
10
11 Return on Fixed Cost      -19.87%   13.54%  -11.65%   98.20%   42.11%
12
13
14
15 PROFIT ANALYSIS          A3..G9
16
17
```

FIGURE 8.2: The range named PROFIT ANALYSIS with a range name table showing its location. In this figure, a new row of data determining the return on fixed cost in row 11 must be added to the named range. The new data is to be located in the row right above row 9, which contains the dollar profit. To do this, a new row is inserted at row 9 and the range A11..G11 is moved there. (See Figure 8.3 for the effect this revision has on the named range.)

```
A15: [W24] 'PROFIT ANALYSIS                                              READY

                  A                B        C        D        E        F
 1
 2
 3 Mix Numbers                     1        2        3        4        5
 4 Fixed Cost                200,000  250,000  210,000  195,000  210,000
 5 Break-even Volume          46,300   65,000   51,500   72,300   38,000
 6 Est. Unit Sales            44,000   67,200   50,000   86,500   41,200
 7 Volume above Break-even   (2,300)    2,200  (1,500)   14,200    3,200
 8 Unit Contribution            4.00     4.00     4.00     5.00     5.00
 9 Return on Fixed Cost      -19.87%   13.54%  -11.65%   98.20%   42.11%
10 Dollar Profit             (9,200)    8,800  (6,000)   71,000   16,000
11
12
13
14
15 PROFIT ANALYSIS          A3..G10
16
17
18
19
```

FIGURE 8.3: The range named PROFIT ANALYSIS with a range name table showing its new location after adding a row of data. The /Range Name Table command was issued a second time in the same location. Lotus 1-2-3 automatically updated the cell addresses of the range from A3..G9 to A3..G10 to include the new row inserted in the table.

Figure 8.3 shows the spreadsheet after this move has been accomplished and the /Range Name Table command has been given a second time (a range table is not automatically updated to reflect changes made to named ranges). It now shows that the PROFIT ANALYSIS range extends from A3..G10. Lotus 1-2-3 automatically updated the addresses of the named range.

This method for revising named ranges without having to rename them works fine as long as you do not delete the beginning and ending cells (A3 and G9 in Figure 8.2). However, you could still delete the contents of these cells by using the /Range Erase command. It makes no difference to the program if these key cells contain data or are blank.

If, however, you wanted to insert the Return on Fixed Cost line in the last line of the PROFIT ANALYSIS table, you would have to rename the range to include this new line as part of the named range. Lotus 1-2-3 can automatically update a named range only as long as row and column insertions and deletions occur within the boundaries of the cell addresses originally designated for the named range.

THE EFFECTS OF DAMAGING A NAMED RANGE

Figures 8.4 and 8.5 illustrate what happens if you inadvertently delete part of a named cell range that holds either of its corner cell addresses. In Figure 8.4, the range of figures containing the fixed costs for the various product mixes is given the range name COST. A range name table has been created in A16..B16 showing the cell addresses of this range as B2..B7.

To determine the total and average of the fixed costs, two formulas using the statistical functions @SUM and @AVG were entered. Instead of giving the cell range by address as the arguments for these two functions, the range name was used, so these formulas were entered as **@SUM(COST)** and **@AVG(COST),** respectively.

Figure 8.5 shows what happens to these formulas after the last row of the range has been inadvertently deleted by using the /Worksheet Delete Row command. Not only has the program returned an ERR value for the total and average formulas, but it also now shows this same value as the location of the COST range. Notice that in changing the cell range location to ERR, Lotus 1-2-3 has also substituted ERR as the argument for each of the two formulas.

```
B9: (,0) [W10] @SUM(COST)                                          EDIT
@SUM(B2..B7)

        A            B        C        D         E          F         G
1   Mix Numbers   Fixed Cost
2        1          200,000 <--
3        2          250,000     |
4        3          210,000     |<---Range Name COST
5        4          195,000     |
6        5          210,000     |
7        6          225,000 <--
8                 ----------
9   Total         1,290,000 <-- @SUM(COST)
10                ==========
11
12  Avg. Fixed Cost  215,000 <-- @AVG(COST)
13
14
15  Range Name Table (/RNT)
16  COST          B2..B7
17
18
19
20
30-Jul-86  01:09 PM
```

FIGURE 8.4: An example showing the use of range names in formulas. Here the range name COST is assigned to the fixed-cost figures. The range table created by Lotus 1-2-3 shows that this range presently extends from cells B2 to B7. Instead of entering these addresses (by typing or pointing), COST was typed in as the arguments of both the @SUM and @AVG functions.

Even after you restore the fixed cost for the sixth mix in row 7 and redefine the COST range as B2..B7 when you rename it, you will still have to edit the contents of both the @SUM and @AVG functions manually. This points out the one major drawback of using range names instead of cell addresses in functions and formulas. If you had not used range names in the formulas, you would not have to edit their arguments.

Using the /Range Name Labels Command

The /Range Name Labels command allows you to assign range names to adjacent cells in any of the four cursor directions. It differs significantly from the /Range Name Create command:

- You can assign multiple range names in one operation.
- You borrow the range name from a label that is already in an adjacent cell instead of typing it in.

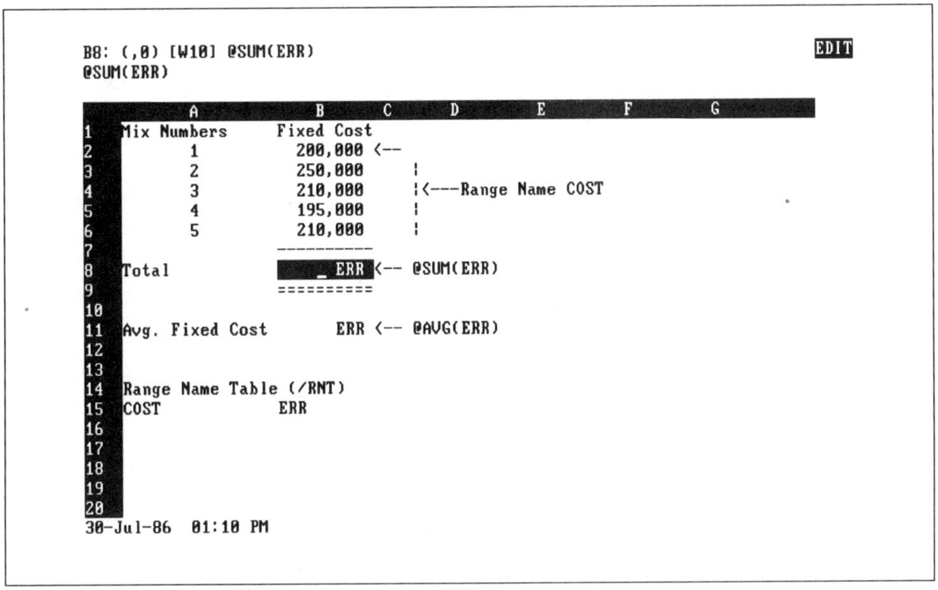

FIGURE 8.5: The effect of deleting the last row of the named range on the formulas using its range name. Here the last row of the COST range was deleted by using the /Range Delete Row command. As a result, the range name table now shows the location of COST as ERR. The substitution of ERR as the argument for each of the two functions caused the ERR values for the total and average figures. To rectify this situation, you must rename the range B2..B7 as COST after restoring the lost data and then manually edit the contents of the two formulas, substituting COST for ERR. This is not the case if cell addresses are used in the formulas in place of the range name or if only the *content* of B7 is deleted with the /Range Erase command.

The uses for this command are varied but tend to fall into three broad applications:

1. The /Range Name Labels command is most frequently used for locating and naming macro keystrokes and commands in the spreadsheet. Because of the structured approach to creating and documenting macros, its variation, /Range Name Labels Right (/RNLR), is the one used exclusively for this application. The macro name is listed in the first column, the first line of the macro keystrokes is listed in the second adjacent column, and the documentation of the macro's function is listed in the third column. Using the /Range Name Labels Right command then provides a quick, easy method for assigning the names listed in the first column to the first cell of the macro immediately to its right. (See Chapter 27 for a more complete discussion and examples of this application.)

2. The /Range Name Labels command is also used to assign the row labels in the first column of a spreadsheet to designate the first column of data immediately to its right. It can likewise be used to assign column labels to the first row of data entered directly beneath the labels (see 3 below).
3. This command is often used in Lotus 1-2-3 databases to assign the field names (column headings) to the data in each of the fields in the first record (row). You can then construct criteria formulas by using the assigned range name rather than the cell address as the test cell. (See Chapter 21 for a complete discussion and examples of this application.)

Note: If the labels in the cells to which you apply the /Range Name Labels command are longer than 15 characters, Lotus 1-2-3 recognizes only the first 15 characters, including any spaces, and ignores the rest of the characters in the label. If this results in an undecipherable range name, use the /Range Name Create command to enter an appropriate name manually.

Deleting Range Names

Lotus 1-2-3 provides two means for deleting range names assigned by either the /Range Name Create or the /Range Name Labels commands:

- To delete a single range name, use the /Range Name Delete (/RND) command. When you are prompted for the name of the range to erase, you can type in the name or point to it in the list of assigned range names that the program displays and then press the Return key.
- To delete all of the range names assigned anywhere in the worksheet in one operation, use the /Range Name Reset command (/RNR). Because this command eliminates all range names in use at the time, use it judiciously. You will probably use the /Range Name Delete command most often to eliminate unnecessary range names one by one.

Whenever you erase range names by either method, Lotus 1-2-3 automatically converts the range names used in your formulas to their appropriate cell references. Deleting a range name therefore has no adverse effect on the data that was contained in the range or in formulas to which the cells are referenced.

Creating a Table of Range Names in Use (Release 2 Only)

Release 2 of Lotus 1-2-3 has added a new /Range Name command option, Table, which allows you to obtain a tabular listing of all range names assigned to ranges in the spreadsheet. This command provides a means to view not only all of the range names in use but also their locations. Range locations can be helpful as a guide to which areas are clear to expand into as you design a spreadsheet.

There are two things to note about the /Range Name Table command:

- First, when you specify the range (by beginning cell only) where the table is to be located, be sure that this area is empty of data, because the range table will overwrite existing data just as the /Copy and /Move commands do.
- Second, the range table created is just a snapshot of the range names in use at the time you issue the command. The table is not automatically updated as you continue working and assign new range names. To update it, you must reissue the command, which creates a new range table.

WORKING WITH WINDOWS AND TITLES

Lotus 1-2-3 provides two /Worksheet commands that can make your work easier when you are working with cell ranges in different areas of the spreadsheet:

- The /Worksheet Window command splits the display screen into two views of the same worksheet.
- The /Worksheet Titles command freezes parts of the spreadsheet on the screen, in effect creating new worksheet borders.

Because you will often use these commands together when you work with isolated cell ranges in different parts of the spreadsheet, their uses are discussed and illustrated together.

Using the /Worksheet Window and Titles Commands

The /Worksheet Window command allows you to split the screen either vertically or horizontally at the column or row of your choice. You will usually find it most convenient to split the screen into roughly equal halves.

When you create equal horizontal windows (/Worksheet Window Horizontal—/WWH), the cell pointer should be in row 11 when you give the command. When you create equal vertical windows (/Worksheet Window Vertical—/WWV), the pointer should be in column E. After splitting the display in either direction, you use the F6 (Window) function key to move the cell pointer between the two windows.

When you split the screen into two windows, you can decide whether to unsynchronize their scrolling. The default of the program is synchronized movement in the direction of the window split (horizontal windows scroll in sync right and left with the Tab and Backtab keys, while vertical windows scroll up and down with the PgUp and PgDn keys).

You will often find it more advantageous to unsynchronize the windows' movements (/Worksheet Window Unsync—/WWU), especially when you want to view two remote cell ranges side by side in the worksheet so that they appear one on top of the other in a horizontal window. This can also be useful when you need to line up two cell ranges that are located in widely different rows so that they appear on your screen as though they are across from one another in a vertical window.

In addition to using windows to overcome the limited size of your monitor display, you can also use the /Worksheet Titles command to "freeze" titles and headings on the screen so that they don't disappear when you scroll isolated ranges into view. Lotus 1-2-3 allows you to make titles out of either column headings (/Worksheet Titles Vertical—/WTV), row headings (/Worksheet Titles Horizontal—/WTH), or both (/Worksheet Titles Both—/WTB), which in essence creates a new corner of the worksheet.

Though you cannot move the cell pointer into an area that has been made into a title by using the arrow or scrolling keys, you can still move into such an area by using the Goto function key (F5). Once you have located the cell pointer within the titles area, you can move it with the arrow keys.

When you work with windows and titles, it is often expedient to use the Scroll Lock key to make the cell pointer stationary as you scroll new areas into view. Whenever you press the Scroll Lock key, the SCROLL status indicator appears at the bottom of the screen to remind you that the pointer is locked in the current cell; when you try to move the pointer you will actually scroll the spreadsheet.

You usually create windows and titles in a worksheet so that you can visually compare widely separated ranges of cells. You can manually update data in one window using data displayed in the second window, view the effect of changing assumptions in one part of the model on another part in what-if analysis, or simply view earlier parts of the model as you continue to construct your worksheet in new and distant locations.

VERTICAL WINDOWING WITH TITLES

Figure 8.6 illustrates a situation in which a projected income statement for the five-year period from 1988 to 1992 has been completed. Separate income statements for each succeeding year are located side by side, separated by a blank column. Unfortunately, when the worksheet was created, no range names were assigned to any of the projected figures.

To assign range names to key cells in the yearly totals column for each income statement, a vertical window was created in column D. To keep the item headings in column A and the column headings in rows 1 to 4 displayed during this procedure, these areas were made into titles by locating the cell pointer in B5 and issuing the /Worksheet Titles Both command. Likewise, the column headings in rows 3 and 4 of the second window were

```
F19: (,2) [W13] +TAX PROFIT88-INCOME TAX88                              READY

          A               F           G    M              N
1  Data 2000 Corporat                   1
2  Projected Income S                   2
3                       1988            3   1989
4                       Year            4   Year
5                                       5
6  Sales              1,624,350.00      6 2,320,500.00
7  COGS                 649,740.00      7   928,200.00
8                     ------------      8 ------------
9  Gross Profit         974,610.00      9 1,392,300.00
10                    ============     10 ============
11 Total Expenses       324,870.00     11   464,100.00
12                    ============     12 ============
13 Operating Profit     649,740.00     13   928,200.00
14 Interest Expense      20,000.00     14   140,000.00
15                    ------------     15 ------------
16 Taxable Profit       629,740.00     16   788,200.00
17 Income Tax           170,029.80     17   212,814.00
18                    ------------     18 ------------
19 Net Income           459,710.20     19   575,386.00
20                    ============     20 ============
30-Jul-86  08:12 AM
```

FIGURE 8.6: Using windows and titles to compare year-end figures and assign range names to isolated ranges in a series of projected income statements. In this spreadsheet, two vertical windows have been created to view the yearly figures for two income statements. Vertical and horizontal titles were also created in column A and rows 1–4 so that the item and column headings will always be visible as new columns containing subsequent yearly figures are scrolled into view.

made into titles with the cell pointer in this window in row 5 when the /Worksheet Titles Horizontal command was issued.

Next, with the cell pointer in the first window and Scroll Lock engaged, column F in the first income statement was brought into view and the range names required were added to this range and individual cells within it. The cell pointer was then jumped to the second window, where the spreadsheet was scrolled until the next year's figures were in view. The process can continue until all the year-end figures are scrolled into view and the ranges are named.

During this process, not only can you compare figures and make quick spot checks, but you can also assign range names with the item and column headings always in view. After you have named all of the ranges and converted their formulas into values, you can copy them to a new table that compares all the projected year-end figures to one another and then graph this table. Because you can refer to these ranges by name while working in the new area, you can create the new table much faster than if you had to move back and forth between the isolated cell ranges.

Horizontal Windowing in a Database

Figure 8.7 illustrates the use of horizontal windows for facilitating queries in a Lotus 1-2-3 database. In this case, the criterion range is located to the side of the database that uses columns A to J for its fields. The output range is located directly below the criterion range, so both use columns L to U. (Lotus 1-2-3 database management is discussed in detail in Chapters 20 and 21.)

To help the user create formula criteria for extracting a particular subset of the records, the screen display was first split horizontally at row 7 by using the /Worksheet Window Horizontal command (/WWH). Next, the cell pointer was moved to the lower window and the scrolling of the windows was unsynchronized by using the /Worksheet Window Unsync command (/WWU). This made it possible to move the criterion and output ranges so that they appear aligned beneath the field names and the first two records in the database.

Doing this allows the user to validate the results of the test cell without having to scroll back and forth constantly between the two cell ranges. In this example, the windows are not equal in size because the user is concerned only with the field names and the first record in the database and therefore wants to have more of the extracted records visible.

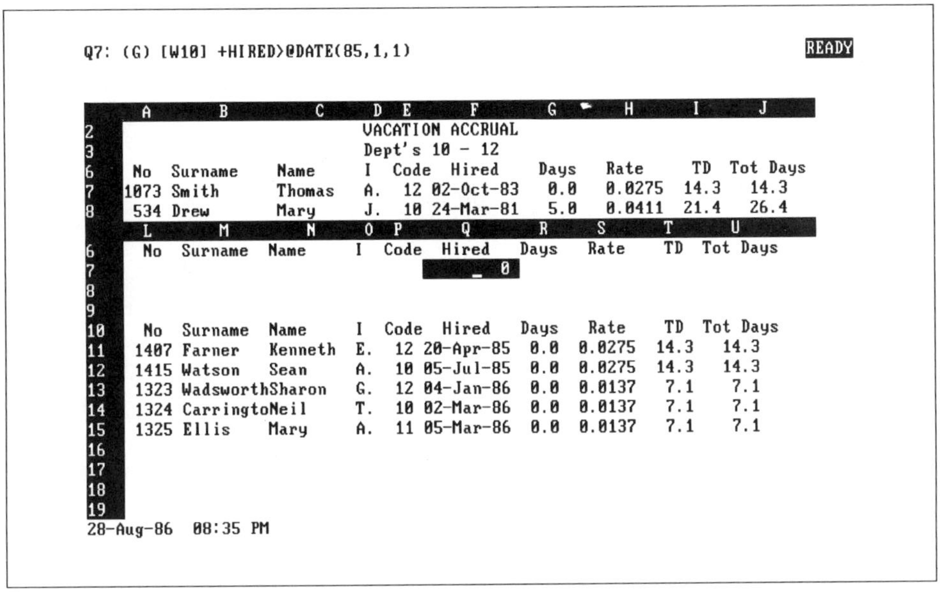

FIGURE 8.7: Using windows to query a Lotus 1-2-3 database. Because the fields extend across columns A to J, the criterion range is created to its right in columns L to U. To assist in setting up and validating formula criteria that will be used to extract a subset of the records, a horizontal window is created. By unsynchronizing the windows, the criterion range and the output range, located directly beneath it, can be aligned with the field names and data visible in the first two records of the database. This allows the user to easily check the results of each formula criterion against the contents of the test cells, making sure that everything is correct before proceeding with the /Data Query Extract operation.

THE RANGE NAME COMMANDS

Using the /Range Name commands to give descriptive names to the cell ranges you work with makes it unnecessary to refer to their locations by cell addresses. When range names are assigned to input cells and ranges that are referenced in formulas, they also help document the workings of your spreadsheets.

Lotus 1-2-3 allows you to name ranges in two ways: assigning a name to the entire range by entering its first and last cell address with /Range Name Create or assigning a label contained in one cell as the name for an adjacent cell in one of the four cardinal directions with /Range Name Labels.

This latter method is the one used most often to name macros and tell Lotus 1-2-3 where the beginning of the range containing its keystrokes and macro commands is located in the spreadsheet.

/Range Name

MENUS

Release 1A	*Release 2*
/Range	/Range
Name	Name
Create Delete Labels Reset	Create Delete Labels Reset Table
Right Down Left Up	Right Down Left Up

KEYBOARD ENTRY

/RNC
Enter name: <**name**>
Enter range: <**range**>

/RND
Enter name: <**name**>

/RNL
Right Down Left Up
Enter label range: <**range**>

/RNR ↵

(Release 2 only)
/RNT
Enter range: <**range**>

FUNCTION

These commands assign the name you enter to any valid cell range in the spreadsheet. The range name is then saved with the spreadsheet and can be used in place of cell addresses in commands that require cell ranges as inputs. If you name individual cells (the smallest Lotus 1-2-3 range), you can use their names in formulas and as arguments of functions that allow only single values.

USAGE

Two /Range Name commands—Create and Labels—can be used to name ranges in the spreadsheet. To delete an individual range name, you use the /Range Name Delete command. To delete all range names in use in a worksheet at once, you can use the /Range Name Reset command. Release 2 also provides a new command, /Range Name Table, that creates an alphabetical listing of the range names with their cell addresses.

/Range Name Create

The /Range Name Create command prompts you for two things: the range name and the cell addresses of the range. The range you input can be up to 15 characters long. It should not begin with any valid cell address or mathematical operator. You can include spaces between the words, though it is common practice to use underlines.

The range input can be any valid Lotus 1-2-3 cell range. The program will suggest the current cell address as the range (as in A1..A1). You can enter the location of the range to be named either by typing in the addresses of its first and last cells or by pointing. As with the other /Range commands, Lotus 1-2-3 automatically anchors the range at the current cell. If you wish to use pointing and do not want to begin the range at the current cell, press Esc to unanchor the range.

Lotus 1-2-3 allows you to give more than one name to the same cell range. Different range names can be given to overlapping cell ranges with this command. However, if you assign the same name to two different cell ranges, it will recognize only the last-named range by that name.

Whenever you type **/RNC** to name a new range, Lotus 1-2-3 displays an alphabetical listing of all range names currently in use. If you are using Release 1A, you can use this method to verify whether the name you are planning to assign is in use. If you intend to use an assigned name for a different range in the spreadsheet, you can use the → and ← keys to move the highlight to the name and select it by pressing the Return key.

As soon as you assign a range name to a cell range with this command, the range name appears in the literal contents of all formulas that contain references to it.

/Range Name Labels

The /Range Name Labels command allows you to use labels already entered in the spreadsheet as names for ranges located in adjacent cell ranges. This command has four options, each corresponding to one of the four cursor directions:

- Right names cell ranges in the columns directly to the right of the labels.
- Down names cell ranges in the rows directly beneath the labels.
- Left names cell ranges in the columns directly to the left of the labels.
- Up names cell ranges in the rows directly above the labels.

To name a cell range with this command, locate the cell pointer in the cell that contains the label you wish to assign as the range name and type **/RNL.** Then choose the appropriate direction option either by typing its initial letter or by moving the highlight to it and pressing the Return key.

You will then be prompted for the cell range containing all of the labels you wish to use as range names. You can indicate this cell range by typing in the cell addresses or by pointing to them. If you are using only the label in the current cell, simply press the Return key.

Note: The application of the /Range Name Labels command differs considerably from that of the /Range Name Create command. The labels you assign as range names must be in cells adjacent to those to which the name is assigned. Also, because you do not input the range name yourself but are using labels already entered in spreadsheet, you may find that these labels exceed the 15-character limit. In such a case, the program recognizes only the first 15 characters as the unique label.

Deleting Range Names with the Delete or Reset Options

To delete an individual range name in use, you issue the /Range Name Delete command. As when using /Range Name Create, Lotus 1-2-3 will display an alphabetical listing of the range names you have already created. Although you can type in the name to be deleted, it is easier to use the → key to move the highlight to it and press Return.

When you wish to delete all the range names you have created at once, use the /Range Name Reset command. This command has no prompts associated with it. To use it, you simply type **/RNR.** After issuing the command, all range names are immediately lost, and the only way to retrieve them is to rename them with the appropriate /Range Name command.

As soon as you delete range names with either of these commands, all formulas that contain references to their assigned ranges revert back to cell addressing. Instead of the range name being displayed in the literal contents, you will then see only the cell addresses.

/Range Name Table (Release 2 Only)

This command allows you to create a table of all range names currently in use. It creates a two-column table in the spreadsheet in the cell range you indicate. The first column of this table contains an alphabetical listing of the range names. The second column indicates their present location by cell addresses. If the range was created with /Range Name Create, both the beginning and ending cell addresses will be shown (as B3..H4, for example). If the range was created with the /Range Name Labels commands, only the single cell address will be shown.

Just as with the /Copy and /Move commands, a range table overwrites any existing data that is located in the range indicated. You need to indicate only the beginning cell address of the range for locating the table. Lotus 1-2-3 will fill in the table from that point, using subsequent cells as needed.

Be aware that the table created with this command is static. As you continue to work in the spreadsheet and assign new range names, you will need to reissue the /Range Name Table command if you wish to keep the table current.

This command can be used to keep track of available space in the spreadsheet. It is also useful for creating a key to the macro names that are in use. It provides a more convenient reference than checking with the /Range Name Create command because more range names can be displayed in the worksheet than on a single line in the Control Panel. You can even give a range name to the beginning cell in the range table so that you can use the Goto function to go to it and update it quickly, if necessary.

EXAMPLES

Figures 8.8 and 8.9 illustrate common applications for the /Range Name Create and Labels commands. For an example of assigning a range name to ranges larger than single cells, refer to Figures 8.2 and 8.3. For an illustration of what happens to formulas constructed with range name references when the range referenced is damaged, refer to Figures 8.4 and 8.5. For an example of how to use the /Range Name Labels Right command to name macros in the spreadsheet, see Chapter 27, "Keystroke Macros."

```
B10: (T) [W29] +VOLUME_OVRBE1*UNIT_CONTRIB1                                   NAMES
Enter name:
$PROFIT1          BE_VOLUME1        UNIT_CONTRIB1    UNIT_SALES1       VOLUME_OVRBE1
                  A                                  B                       C
1
2
3  Mix Numbers                           1                        2
4  Fixed Cost                                       200000        250000
5  Break-even Volume                                 46300         65000
6  Est. Unit Sales                                   44000         67200
7  Volume above Break-even +UNIT_SALES1-BE_VOLUME1          +C6-C5
8  Unit Contribution                                    4             4
9  Return on Fixed Cost    +$PROFIT1/BE_VOLUME1             +C10/C5
10 Dollar Profit           +VOLUME_OVRBE1*UNIT_CONTRIB1 +C7*C8
11
```

FIGURE 8.8: Range names assigned to single cells in the spreadsheet with the /Range Name Create command. This figure compares two columns of formulas whose display formats have been changed to Text to display the formulas in their cells. In column B, notice how the range names assigned to cells B5 to B10 help to document their function in the formulas in which they are used. Contrast this to the formulas in column C, where cell references are still used. This application for range names can help quite a bit in documenting the workings of your spreadsheets.

```
Q7: (G) [W10] +HIRED>@DATE(83,1,1)#AND#TOT DAYS<15                            READY

     A      B           C        D E      F         G         H        I      J
2                                VACATION ACCRUAL
3                                Dept's 10 - 12
6    No   Surname     Name       I  Code  Hired     Days      Rate     TD  Tot Days
7   1073 Smith        Thomas     A.   12 02-Oct-83   0.0     0.0275  14.3   14.3
8    534 Drew         Mary       J.   10 24-Mar-81   5.0     0.0411  21.4   26.4
      L     M           N        O  P      Q          R         S        T
6     No   Surname   Name        I  Code  Hired      Days      Rate     TD
7                                               1
8          Range Name Table (/RNT)
9          CODE      E7
10         DAYS      G7
11         HIRED     F7
12         I         D7
13         NAME      C7
14         NO        A7
15         RATE      H7
16         SURNAME   B7
17         TD        I7
18         TOT DAYS  J7
```

FIGURE 8.9: Range names assigned to all of the fields in the first record of a Lotus 1-2-3 database with the /Range Name Labels Down command. In this database, the field names of each field in the first record were assigned as range names. To accomplish this, the pointer was located in A6, **/RNLR** was typed, and the name was given as A6..J6. The results of using this command were then documented by the range table that was created in the range B9..C18. It was then possible to enter the criterion formula in Q7 (shown on the first line of the Control Panel) by using these range names instead of cell references. This makes the phrasing of the criterion formulas used in data queries more natural and easier to follow.

MACROS

The /Range Name Create and /Range Name Delete commands are often incorporated into macros (see Chapter 27), although the command sequences used to invoke the commands are not usually made into keystroke macros. Nevertheless, if you find yourself creating and deleting a lot of range names in your spreadsheet, you might want to use the following keystroke macros to cut down on the amount of typing required during this process.

The /Range Name Labels Right command is most often used in assigning a macro name to its associated keystrokes and macro commands. Because range names assigned with this command are not copied when a macro library file is combined into a new worksheet, sometimes it is beneficial to enter a keystroke macro to facilitate renaming all of the macros brought into the new worksheet as well as any that you create during your work session.

ALT-N, A MACRO FOR CREATING RANGE NAMES

Label	*Macro Contents*
'\n	**'/RNC{?}~{?}~**

To use this macro, position the cell pointer at the beginning of the cell range you wish to name and then invoke the macro by pressing Alt-n. Type the range name and then press the Return key. In response to the prompt to enter the range, type the cell addresses or use pointing to indicate the range's location. Then press Return.

ALT-D, A MACRO FOR DELETING RANGE NAMES

Label	*Macro Contents*
'\d	**'/RND{?}~**

To use this macro, press Alt-d and then use the → key to move the highlight to the range name you wish to erase. Then press the Return key.

ALT-R, A RANGE NAME LABELS RIGHT MACRO

Label	*Macro Contents*
'\r	**'/RNLR{?}~**

To use this macro, position the cell pointer in the cell that contains your first macro label and invoke the macro by pressing Alt-r. Use the ↓ key to include all of the macro labels in this column; then press the Return key. All of the macro keystrokes in the first cell to the right of each macro label are now named with the label on the left. You can now invoke any macro listed there by holding down the Alt key while typing the letter key of the macro label.

THE /WORKSHEET WINDOW AND TITLES COMMANDS

The reference section for the /Worksheet Window and Titles commands follows. The /Worksheet Window commands not only give you the ability to split the display screen into two viewing areas but also let you bring two isolated areas of the same worksheet into the same display. Doing this makes it simple to compare two data ranges not normally visible in a single viewing area.

The /Worksheet Titles commands are often used with the Window commands to make it easier to keep titles and headings locked in place on the screen as you scroll cell ranges into view. They can also be used effectively in situations that do not call for the use of windows but do require scrolling through large ranges of data.

/Worksheet Titles

MENUS

/Worksheet
Titles
Both Horizontal Vertical Clear

KEYBOARD ENTRY

/WTB /WTH /WTV /WTC

FUNCTION

This command locks the columns to the left or rows above the cell pointer's current position in place on the display screen.

USAGE

The /Worksheet Titles commands are most often used to keep important row and column headings in place on the display screen. Doing this allows you to scroll through large areas of the spreadsheet to examine all necessary data and still have the pertinent headings visible for reference.

Once a group of columns or rows has been designated as titles with these commands, the cell pointer will not enter these areas unless you use the Goto function key (F5). Even when you use Goto, Lotus 1-2-3 does not really allow access to this area. Instead, it gives you access to the data ranges contained in the titles area by duplicating them in the area right below or to the right. (Any editing changes made in the duplicated columns or rows are transferred to the designated titles area.) This leads to a very confusing screen display, like the one shown in Figure 8.10. The only way to get rid of this double display is to use the /Worksheet Titles Clear command (/WTC).

```
A1: [W18] 'Data 2000 Corporation                                              READY

          A                  A              B           C           D
1   Data 2000 CorporatData 2000 Corporation
2   Projected Income SProjected Income Statement -- 1988
3
4                                        1st Qtr     2nd Qtr     3rd Qtr
1   Data 2000 CorporatData 2000 Corporation
2   Projected Income SProjected Income Statement -- 1988
3
4                                        1st Qtr     2nd Qtr     3rd Qtr
5
6   Sales              Sales           350,000.00  385,000.00  423,500.00
7   COGS               COGS            140,000.00  154,000.00  169,400.00
8                                      ------------------------------------
9   Gross Profit       Gross Profit    210,000.00  231,000.00  254,100.00
10                                     ====================================
11  Total Expenses     Total Expenses   70,000.00   77,000.00   84,700.00
12                                     ====================================
13  Operating Profit   Operating Profit 140,000.00 154,000.00  169,400.00
14  Interest Expense   Interest Expense   5,000.00   5,000.00    5,000.00
15                                     ------------------------------------
16  Taxable Profit     Taxable Profit  135,000.00  149,000.00  164,400.00
01-Aug-86  09:23 AM
```

FIGURE 8.10: Using the Goto function to take the cell pointer into a titles area. Originally, column A and rows 1–4 were designated as titles with the /Worksheet Titles Both command. The command Goto: A1 was then issued. In response, Lotus 1-2-3 duplicated the restricted column and rows so that two columns A and two sets of rows 1–4 now appear. Though doing this allows you access to the titles area to make editing changes, it results in a very confusing display. You can correct it only by using the /Worksheet Titles Clear command.

Note: When you use the /Worksheet Titles commands after you have split the display with one of the /Worksheet Window options, the titles affect only the window that contains the cell pointer at the time you issue the Titles command. This allows you to set up different titles areas in each window you have created.

/WORKSHEET TITLES BOTH

The Both option designates both the columns to the left and the rows above the cell pointer's current position (i.e., the current cell) as titles in the spreadsheet. In effect, this creates new borders for the spreadsheet, making the current cell the Home position. Pressing the Home key will take the pointer to this cell rather than cell A1, as is usual.

Use this option when you want to freeze columns as well as rows of headings on the screen. You must first locate the cell pointer in a cell directly below the row (or rows) as well as directly to the right of the column (or columns) to be included. Then issue the command by typing **/WTB.** There is no need to press the Return key. After you issue the command, you will be unable to move the pointer either up or left into the newly created titles area.

/WORKSHEET TITLES HORIZONTAL

The Horizontal option makes titles out of the rows that are located above the cell pointer's position when you issue the command. It is useful when you want to lock only column headings on the screen. This command is often applied to Lotus 1-2-3 databases to keep the field names in view when you scroll vertically through the records.

To use the Horizontal option, locate the cell pointer anywhere in the row right below the rows you wish to include in the titles area. Then type the command **/WTH.** There is no need to press the Return key. After you issue this command, you will be unable to move the pointer up into this area.

/WORKSHEET TITLES VERTICAL

The Vertical option makes titles out of the columns immediately to the left of the cell pointer's position when you issue the command. It is useful when you have item headings running down a single column that you wish to remain on the screen when you scroll horizontally through the data in your spreadsheet.

To use the Vertical option, locate the cell pointer in the column immediately to the right of the column (or columns) you wish to include in the titles area. Then type **/WTV.** There is no need to press the Return key.

/Worksheet Titles Clear

The Clear option clears any titles that have been created in the full-screen display or in the window in which the cell pointer is located. To issue it, type **/WTC.** There is no need to press the Return key. Once you have issued this command, you can move the cell pointer into any cell that was previously restricted by using the arrow keys or the appropriate pointer-movement keys. Using the Goto function key (F5) will no longer duplicate the headings that were in the titles area.

EXAMPLES

For an example of using the /Worksheet Titles Both and Horizontal commands, refer to Figure 8.6. It illustrates their use combined with vertical windowing in a spreadsheet. For an illustration of what happens when you use Goto to move the cell pointer into a titles area, refer to Figure 8.10.

SEE ALSO

/Worksheet Window

/Worksheet Window

MENUS

/Worksheet
Window
Horizontal Vertical Sync Unsync Clear

KEYBOARD ENTRY

/WWH /WWV /WWS /WWU /WWC

FUNCTION

This command splits the Lotus 1-2-3 worksheet display area into separate viewing areas along either a horizontal or a vertical axis of your choice, effectively creating two windows on the data contained in a single spreadsheet.

USAGE

The /Worksheet Window Horizontal and Vertical commands are used to split the worksheet display at either a specific row (horizontal windowing) or a specific column (vertical windowing). To move the cell pointer back and forth between the windows you create with these commands, you press the Window function key (F6).

Note: Once you have created the windows you need, you will often find it advantageous to use the Scroll Lock function to make the cell pointer stationary as you scroll new parts of the spreadsheet into view in a particular window. This is easier than having to move the pointer with the arrow keys in the direction opposite to the way you want the spreadsheet to scroll (i.e., using the ↓ key to bring data ranges up into view).

Creating Horizontal Windows

To use the Horizontal option, position the cell pointer anywhere in the row where you want the split to occur and type the command **/WWH.** Lotus 1-2-3 will then duplicate the regular spreadsheet border display from this row down. It will contain the same column letters visible in the first window and as many of the same row numbers as the size of the window allows.

To create two horizontal windows of roughly equal size, position the cell pointer in the eleventh row of the spreadsheet display before you issue the command. If you have trouble creating a horizontal window, press the Home key to take the cell pointer to A1 and then move it down to the appropriate row. Then scroll into view the areas of the spreadsheet that you wish to work with. All horizontal scrolling with the Tab or Backtab keys is synchronized automatically in horizontal windows unless you use the /Worksheet Windows Unsync option (see below).

Creating Vertical Windows

To use the Vertical option, position the cell pointer anywhere in the column where you want the split to occur and type the command **/WWV.** The screen is split to the left of the cursor. Lotus 1-2-3 then duplicates the regular spreadsheet border display from this column over. It will contain the same row numbers visible in the first window and as many of the same column letters as the size of the new window allows.

To create two vertical windows of roughly equal size, position the cell pointer in the fifth column of the spreadsheet display (if you have not changed the column widths from their default value of 9 spaces). All vertical scrolling with the PgDn or PgUp keys is synchronized automatically in vertical windows unless you use the /Worksheet Windows Unsync option (see below).

Synchronized versus Unsynchronized Windows

Once the display screen has been divided into windows in one direction or the other, you have the option of also using the /Worksheet Window Unsync option. The program default is synchronized scrolling in the direction of the window split.

If you are working with vertical windows, pressing the PgDn key will scroll both window displays the same 20 rows down. If you are working with horizontal windows, pressing the Tab key will scroll both window displays the same amount of columns to the right. The same synchronized effect (but in the opposite direction) takes place if you use the PgUp or Backtab keys.

To bring a different area of the worksheet into view in the two windows, you use the /Worksheet Window Unsync command. This is usually done by positioning the cursor in the second window and typing **/WWU.** From then on, you can scroll to new parts of the spreadsheet in the second window while the same area remains displayed in the first window. If you need to return to synchronized scrolling, use the /Worksheet Window Sync command (**/WWS**).

/Worksheet Window Clear

To clear either kind of window and return to a single spreadsheet display, use the Clear option by typing **/WWC.** It immediately clears the second border display and returns you to a full-screen display of the area shown in the top or left window.

When you use this command, any titles area that you have created in the second window is also automatically cleared. However, if a titles area has been set up in the first window, it will remain in effcct until you use the /Worksheet Titles Clear command (see above).

EXAMPLES

For an example of horizontal windowing created with the /Worksheet Window Horizontal command, refer to Figure 8.7, which illustrates its use when querying a Lotus 1-2-3 database. For an example of vertical windowing created with the /Worksheet Window Vertical command and using the /Worksheet Window Unsync command, refer to Figure 8.6.

SEE ALSO

/Worksheet Titles

SUMMARY

This chapter has discussed the concept of a Lotus 1-2-3 cell range and has presented techniques and applications for using range names, windows, and titles areas to make working with ranges easier as you construct spreadsheets. The following reference section will lead you to related topics where you can find out more about when and how cell ranges are used.

For information about changing and controlling the display formats of cell ranges:

- Chapter 5, "Creating Worksheets"

For information about copying and moving cell ranges within a spreadsheet:

- Chapter 7, "Formatting Worksheets"

For information about saving cell ranges in separate files:

- Chapter 9, "File Operations"

For information about using cell ranges in formulas:

- Chapter 10, "Working with Formulas and Functions"

For information about cell ranges in Lotus 1-2-3 databases:

- Chapter 21, "Database Operations"

For information about using cell ranges in creating graphs:

- Chapter 24, "Creating and Using Graphs"

For information about printing specific cell ranges in a spreadsheet:

- Chapter 25, "Printing Reports"

For information about using range names in macros:

- Chapter 27, "Keystroke Macros"

CHAPTER 9

FILE OPERATIONS

File Operations

This chapter deals with all file operations in Lotus 1-2-3 except those involving the /File Import command. If you require information on how to use this command to bring in data in an ASCII file, see Chapter 29, "Importing and Exporting ASCII Files."

The topics in this chapter include saving and retrieving worksheets, obtaining directory listings, combining files, and extracting specific cell ranges by creating separate files for them. The discussion on combining files will be of particular interest if you need to perform consolidations on a group of worksheets.

Information about preparing data disks from within Lotus 1-2-3, deleting unwanted files, and making backup files is included in its own section, "File Maintenance Operations," which discusses the File Manager and Disk Manager options of the Lotus Access System. Because you use the /Quit command to access the Lotus Access System Menu from within a 1-2-3 spreadsheet, the use of the /Quit command is also presented in this chapter.

If you are using Release 2, you may be interested in the subject of assigning passwords to protect your worksheets. This information is in the section "Using Passwords to Protect Spreadsheet Files." Also, you may want to become familiar with the new /System command that allows you to exit Lotus 1-2-3 and enter DOS temporarily to format new data disks; this topic is covered in "Using the DOS Shell Command (/System) in Release 2."

Following discussions on each of these topics, you will find reference entries containing detailed information on each command. They are presented in the same order as they appear on the /File menu. In the /File Save entry, you will find a very handy macro for saving and continuing work on a worksheet.

SAVING AND RETRIEVING SPREADSHEETS

The two most basic /File commands are /File Save and /File Retrieve. The /File Save command (/FS) not only writes the data and formulas you enter into a worksheet in a disk file but also saves all of the current settings, including the display formats used; the range names assigned; the print, graph, and database ranges and settings defined; and even the cell pointer's current location.

When you load a worksheet with the /File Retrieve command (/FR), the program first clears any worksheet already in memory and then reads all of this information into the computer's memory.

Saving Your Worksheets

To have permanent copies of the worksheets you create with Lotus 1-2-3, you must save them in disk files with the /File Save command. The first time you use this command on a worksheet, the program will prompt you to enter a file name. The directory where the file is to be saved is supplied by the default directory that Lotus 1-2-3 is currently using. Unless you have changed the default directory by using the /Worksheet Global Default Directory command (see Chapter 2), this directory is the one where the Lotus 1-2-3 program files are located: A:\ for two-drive systems and C:\Lotus or C:\123 (depending on your directory name for Lotus 1-2-3), for a hard disk system. (For information on changing the default directory during your work session, see the section "Changing the Current Directory" later in this chapter.)

When you give a Lotus 1-2-3 worksheet a file name, you must obey all DOS file naming conventions. Basically, this means that you are limited to an eight-character file name that cannot include spaces (replace them with the underscore character), periods (except to denote the beginning of a three-character file name extension), or other reserved characters (see Table 9.1 for specifics). Any letters you use in a file name are automatically converted to uppercase, regardless of how you enter them.

Lotus 1-2-3 automatically appends its own file name extension to the file name you enter. This extension varies according the version of the program you are using. Release 1A worksheets carry the file name extension .WKS (to denote a worksheet file type), while Release 2 worksheets carry the extension .WK1. All you have to enter is the file name itself—the first eight characters (or fewer) without the file name extension.

PERMISSIBLE CHARACTERS	RESERVED CHARACTERS
Letters A–Z (all lowercase letters in uppercase)	Space (replace with the underscore)
Digits 0–9	
!	*
@	+
#	=
$	[
%	]
^	:
&	;
(	"
)	?
_	/
-	¦
{	\
}	<
'	>
`	
.	

TABLE 9.1: Lotus 1-2-3 File Name Character Restrictions

Note: Release 2 allows you to add your own file name extensions when you save worksheet files. To do this, you must enter the complete file name, including a period and the extension you wish to use. Because the /File Retrieve command lists only worksheets that carry the .WK1 or .WKS extensions, you will have to enter the complete file name each time you wish to load such files. You can, however, use the /File List Other command to obtain a directory listing that includes these files.

Once you have saved a worksheet and then use the /File Save command to save subsequent work and edits on that worksheet, Lotus 1-2-3 will supply the file name you originally gave to the file. If you want to save your changes under the same file name, you accept the name the program supplies by pressing Return. Lotus 1-2-3 then supplies two further choices, Cancel and Replace. Choosing the Replace option will save your updates in the file. The Cancel option (the default) is supplied in case you access the command by mistake and want to return to the spreadsheet without saving the file.

To save the edited worksheet under a new file name, type in a new name over the existing name. To save the edited worksheet in a new directory, press Esc three times and then type in a new path name.

Using Passwords to Protect Spreadsheet Files (Release 2 Only)

If you are using Release 2, you can include a password when saving the file. This password must be entered each time you retrieve the worksheet, which means that if you don't know the password assigned to a file, you will not be able to load it successfully. While such protection limits access to those entrusted with the password, it can also prevent you from using your own spreadsheets if you forget the passwords you have assigned to them.

To assign a password to a file, press the space bar and type **p** after entering the file name. Lotus 1-2-3 then prompts you to enter the password (refer to Table 9.2 on the rules for assigning and using passwords). As you

- Passwords can contain up to 15 characters.
- Passwords are case sensitive. For example, the following are all different passwords even though they contain the same letters:

  FEO FEo Feo feo fEo feO
- To assign a password to a file, enter the file name followed by a space and the letter **p**.
- To enter a password, type it from the keyboard in response to the prompt. As you enter the characters, each one is masked by a rectangle in reverse video. This allows you to monitor the number of characters entered but not their content.
- To complete the save operation, you must verify the password you just entered by duplicating it (both the sequence of the characters and their case), or Lotus 1-2-3 will abort the save operation. The characters of the password you enter for verification will also be masked during input.
- To change the password assigned to a file, use the /File Save command. Press Esc twice and reenter the file name. Then press the space bar, type **p**, and enter a new password. Use the /File Erase command to delete the original password-protected file (you will be required to enter the original password to complete this erase operation).
- To abandon the use of password protection, use the /File Save command. Press the Backspace key to delete the [PASSWORD PROTECTED] message. Then press the Return key and type **r** to use the Replace option.

TABLE 9.2: Rules for Password-Protecting Files

enter it, each character is masked on the screen by a rectangle so that no one can see the characters you type. You can see only the number of characters used.

After you press the Return key, you receive a second prompt to verify the password you just entered. Type in the password a second time, exactly as you originally entered it. If the two passwords do not match in every detail, Lotus 1-2-3 will abort the save operation, and you will have to start over by reissuing the /File Save command.

If both passwords match, Lotus 1-2-3 saves the file. When you go to retrieve the file after that, you will always be prompted to enter the password after you give the file name. Failure to enter the password exactly as you assigned it will abort the /File Retrieve operation.

When you save a password-protected file again, you will see the message [PASSWORD PROTECTED] following its file name. If you accept this file name and use the Replace option, all updates will be saved under the same file name and will use the same password.

If you no longer wish to have the file password protected, press the Backspace key to delete the [PASSWORD PROTECTED] message and then press Return. This saves the file under the same name but without password protection. To remove the password and save the file under a new name, press Esc twice to delete the message and the file name; then enter a new name without supplying a password.

Password-Protection Issues

Restricting access to certain worksheet files by assigning passwords to them provides an effective way to secure sensitive data. However, when using password protection you should carefully consider the question "Who in the company must have access to the file and under what conditions?"

First of all, it is very important that you take steps to ensure that the password will not be forgotten. A critically important spreadsheet could be lost if you do not remember the exact password you assigned to it. Though you may be sure that you will always remember a password when you first assign it, this often proves to be more difficult than you expect, especially as you create more and more worksheets under similar file names and with only slightly different passwords.

To guard against this, you can keep a written list of file names and their passwords. Then you must take steps to secure this list from unauthorized distribution, or you will end up providing a direct guide to all the restricted files you use as well as the means to access them.

The second question to consider is "Who in your department or group is authorized to have access to specific password-protected worksheets and is therefore entitled to know the passwords assigned to them?" To answer this question you must explore the personnel hierarchy of your group as well as the conditions under which the data in protected worksheets might be required.

For instance, if while you were away from the office a need arose to produce a report from one of your password-protected worksheets, could you be certain that someone else in the office would be able to produce it? To answer this question in the affirmative, you would have to be certain that someone else familiar with Lotus 1-2-3 knows that the file requires the use of a password as well as the exact password to use.

Often, the best way to deal with both problems is to combine their solutions. You could do this by working out a system whereby only the department head or manager keeps a written list of all protected files and their passwords produced by anyone in the group.

If you do not remember a password you have assigned to one of your own files, you could then go to the department manager to consult the list. Or if you are away from the office and someone else in your group has to use one of your protected files, the manager could provide the password. This method maintains control of who is cleared to use sensitive data files and also provides a backup system for preventing loss of a password (and therefore access to a spreadsheet).

Retrieving Files

Worksheet files must be loaded into the computer's memory before you can make editing changes or print the files. You load files by using the /File Retrieve command. All worksheet files saved in the current directory are listed in alphabetical order across the third line of the Control Panel as soon as you type /FR.

The screen display can accommodate only five file names in Release 2. This is because Release 2 displays the entire file name, including the extension. In Release 1A, eight file names can be accommodated on the screen because no extensions are displayed. All of the files in the directory are listed on subsequent screens. You can scroll through the listing to find the file you want. Table 9.3 illustrates various key combinations you can use to move the cursor highlight through the file listing. In addition, in Release 2 you can press F3 to display a full-screen listing whenever Lotus 1-2-3 is displaying a large number of file names or is prompting you for a file name.

KEY	FUNCTION
→	Moves the highlight to the next file name in the list (one to the right).
←	Moves the highlight to the previous file name in the list (one to the left).
Home	Moves the highlight directly to the first file in the list.
End	Moves the highlight directly to the last file in the list.
Tab or Ctrl-→	If the highlight is on the first file of the list when you press the Tab or Ctrl-→ keys, it moves right, directly to the fifth file of the first group displayed on the screen. Thereafter, pressing the Tab or Ctrl-→ keys scrolls the screen display as it jumps the cursor highlight to every fifth file name. (These keys do not work in Release 1A.)
Shift-Tab or Ctrl-←	The opposite of Tab; it jumps the cursor highlight five file names to the left, scrolling the screen display as necessary. (These keys do not work in Release 1A.)
↑	If the highlight is on the ninth file of the list (Release 1A) or the sixth file of the list (Release 2) when you press the ↑ key, it moves left, directly to the first file. Thereafter, it continues to scroll the screen as it jumps the cursor highlight to every eighth (Release 1A) or fifth (Release 2) file name.
↓	The opposite of ↑; it jumps the cursor highlight eight (Release 1A) or five (Release 2) file names to the right, simultaneously scrolling the screen display.
Note: Because Release 2 includes the file name and its extension in this list, only five file names can be seen on the screen at one time. If you are using Release 1A, you see eight file names per screen instead.	

TABLE 9.3: Cursor Highlight Movements through a File Listing

To select a file, move the highlight to its name and press the Return key. The program displays the flashing WAIT mode indicator until the file is completely loaded into memory. You can retrieve only one worksheet at a time. To work on more than one spreadsheet, you must use the /File Combine commands to bring one worksheet into the other (see the section "Combining Worksheets and Performing Spreadsheet Consolidations" later in this chapter).

To retrieve a new worksheet when one is already loaded into memory, use the /File Retrieve command. After you select the new file, Lotus 1-2-3 automatically clears the original file before loading the new one. To clear a file that you have retrieved so that you can begin a new worksheet, use the /Worksheet Erasc Yes command (/WEY).

If you do not use the /File Save command to write any revisions or additions (made since your last save operation) to the file before you use the /File Retrieve or /Worksheet Erase Yes commands, these changes will be lost.

Changing the Current Directory

The current directory where Lotus 1-2-3 saves files or retrieves them is set by the /Worksheet Global Default Directory command (see Chapter 2). If this command has not been used to change the default directory, Lotus 1-2-3 will use the same directory as its does to locate its program files at startup.

With a two-drive system, the directory A:\ (or the drive from which you started 1-2-3) is made the default. You will probably want to change it to B:\. If you are using a hard disk system, you will probably use subdirectories that you may need to modify from time to time.

To change the current directory during a work session, use the /File Directory command. Unlike the /Worksheet Global Default Directory command, the current directory set with this command is only temporary. It remains in effect only until you change it again or exit Lotus 1-2-3.

To check which directory is current, type **/FD**. If you do not need to change the directory, press the Return key. If you wish to change it to use files in another directory, type in the name of the other directory. The directories in which you keep Lotus 1-2-3 data files may vary, depending on the type of file hierarchy used in your office. For instance, your office might maintain a hierarchical system like that illustrated in Figure 9.1, or you might use one more like that shown in Figure 9.2.

If you are using the type of hierarchy illustrated in Figure 9.1 in which data files created with Lotus 1-2-3 are saved in separate directories beneath the LOTUS directory, you would use the full path name to change data file directories with the /File Directory command.

For instance, assume that C:\LOTUS\MASTER is the default directory at startup and that Joe wishes to make the \ACCTS directory current. He would then enter the path name **C:\LOTUS\ACCTS** at the prompt for the current directory seen after he typed **/FD**. If later during the same session he wanted to start working with files in his own client directory, he could reissue the /File Directory command and enter the new current directory as **C:\LOTUS\JOE\CLIENT**.

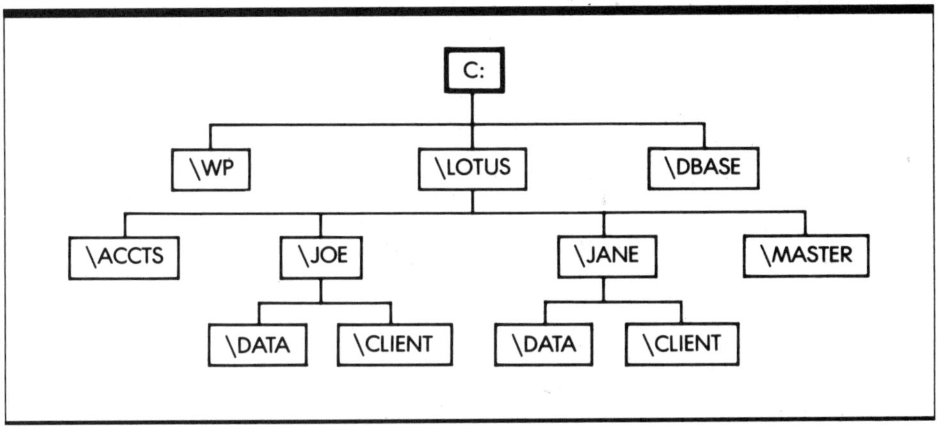

FIGURE 9.1: Typical file hierarchy with data file subdirectories below the Lotus 1-2-3 program file directory. In this type of file organization, all Lotus 1-2-3 files are kept in subdirectories of the \LOTUS directory. The \MASTER directory is the default directory at startup (C:\LOTUS\MASTER). To make another subdirectory current, the user of this system would use the /File Directory command and enter the appropriate path name. For example, to make Jane's \CLIENT directory current, she would enter **C:\LOTUS\JANE\CLIENT.**

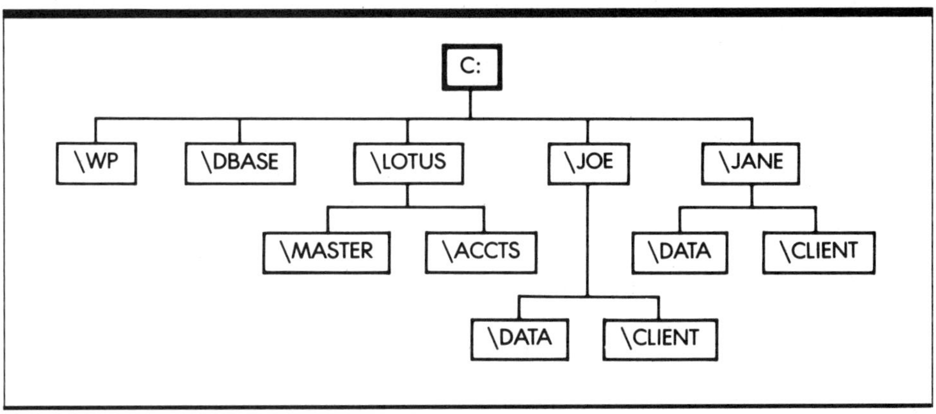

FIGURE 9.2: File hierarchy with data file directories on the same level as the Lotus 1-2-3 program file directory. In this type of file organization, not all Lotus 1-2-3 files are kept in subdirectories of the \LOTUS directory. Rather, each individual user, such as Joe and Jane, maintains his or her own Lotus 1-2-3 data files in personal directories. The \MASTER directory is still the default directory (C:\LOTUS-\MASTER). To make a directory current, the /File Directory command is used. For example, to make Jane's \CLIENT directory current here, she would enter **C:\JANE\CLIENT.**

However, if Joe just needed to retrieve a single worksheet file from Jane's personal directory, he wouldn't have to use the /File Directory command. He could simply specify its location as part of the file name he enters with the /File Retrieve command. For instance, to retrieve Jane's worksheet called REGION4.WK1 from her \CLIENT directory, Joe would enter the name of the file to be retrieved as **C:\LOTUS\JANE\CLIENT\REGION4**. If after reviewing the file's contents Joe decided he wanted to keep a copy of it in his client directory (which is still current), he could just rename it REGION4 after pressing Esc twice to delete its suggested file name.

If the office had set up a file system more like the one illustrated in Figure 9.2, in which the data file directories are on the same level as the program files, the change-directory operations described above would have to be only slightly altered. For instance, when first accessed during a work session, the /File Directory command would still display C:\LOTUS\MASTER as the Lotus 1-2-3 default directory, and it could still be replaced with C:\LOTUS\ACCTS. However, when Joe wants to change the current directory to his own client directory in this system, he would enter **C:\JOE\CLIENT** after he issued the /File Directory command.

The only thing to remember is that your worksheet file will be saved in whichever directory is current if you enter only the file name without preceding it with the entire path name. If you use the /File Retrieve command and do not find the worksheet file you wanted, it may not be in Lotus 1-2-3's current directory.

FILE MAINTENANCE OPERATIONS

From within the program, you can accomplish many routine file maintenance operations, such as obtaining a directory listing of all Lotus 1-2-3 files, deleting unneeded files, and even formatting new data disks.

There is a major difference between the way the two versions of the program permit you to format new data disks. In Release 1A, you must use the Lotus Access System, while in Release 2, you must use the /System command and issue the FORMAT command directly from the DOS prompt. Each of these methods is outlined in the sections that follow.

Obtaining a Listing of Files

To obtain a directory listing of any Lotus 1-2-3 files, you use the /File List command. Three options are associated with this command in Release

1A: Worksheet, Print, and Graph. To these three, Release 2 has added an additional option, Other, which allows you to get a listing of all files, even those that do not carry the .WK1 (Worksheet), .PRN (Print), or .PIC (Graph) extensions.

Note: The /File List commands in Release 1A display at the top of the screen the amount of available storage space still left in the current directory or on the data disk, while those in Release 2 do not include this information. Instead, Release 2 file listings give you statistics on the file's size in bytes and the date and time of creation of each file as you move the cursor highlight to it. To obtain the amount of available storage space in Release 2, you must use the /System command and obtain a directory listing with the DOS DIR command.

Lotus 1-2-3 subdivides the directory listings according to file type by using the DOS global wildcard character (*) along with the particular file name extension. When you choose to see the worksheet files in the current directory by using the command /File List Worksheet, the program uses the pattern *.WKS.

The Release 2 /File List Worksheet command has been expanded to include both the global and single-character wildcards, as in *.WK?. The question mark single-character wildcard allows it to include both .WKS (created in Release 1A) and .WK1 (created in Release 2) worksheet files in its listing.

When you issue the /File List Print command, the program uses the pattern *.PRN to give you a listing of all ASCII files that have been created with the /Print File command and automatically given the extension .PRN. Similarly, you obtain a listing of all graph files in the current directory by using the /File List Graph command. In this case, the program uses the search pattern *.PIC (for Picture file, the extension given to all graphs saved with the /Graph Save command).

In Release 2, you can also perform these kinds of directory listings by entering the same search patterns with the DOS DIR command after you temporarily exit the program with the DOS shell command (/System). You can also use these search patterns with either version before starting up Lotus 1-2-3 or after permanently exiting the program (/Quit Yes) to view specific groups of data files and to determine the amount of storage space remaining.

THE /FILE LIST OTHER COMMAND (RELEASE 2 ONLY)

Because Release 2 allows you to add your own file name extensions in place of .WK1 when saving worksheets, it provides a new /File List command option, Other, to allow you to obtain a directory listing of these files. When you use the Other option, Lotus 1-2-3 uses the search pattern *.*, which results in a listing of all files in the current directory.

Deleting Files

To delete an unwanted file from the current directory or data disk, you use the /File Erase command. This command offers the same options available when using the /File List command, employing the same search patterns to group files by worksheets (*.WKS in Release 1A and *.WK? in Release 2), ASCII text (*.PRN), graphs (*.PIC), or all types (*.* in the Release 2 Other option).

After you choose the file type, the program displays a single line listing of all files of that type, just as it does when you use the /File Retrieve command. (You can use the cursor highlight movements described in Table 9.3 to locate the specific file to erase.) After you select the file to delete, Lotus 1-2-3 asks for confirmation with its No (cancel the erase operation) or Yes (go ahead and delete the file specified) options. Once you type **y**, the file is deleted and cannot be retrieved again with Lotus 1-2-3.

Because this method of deletion allows you to erase only a single file at a time, you will find times when it is much more efficient to use the DOS DEL or ERASE commands with the appropriate wildcard characters to delete a particular group of Lotus 1-2-3 files or all data files in the directory.

Using the DOS Shell Command (/System) in Release 2

Release 2 provides the /System command to allow you to access DOS temporarily to use such commands as FORMAT, DIR, COPY, DEL, CHKDSK, CD, MD, and the like from within the Lotus 1-2-3 worksheet. As soon as you type **/s**, you are returned to the DOS prompt in the current directory. While it is safe to use these types of DOS commands from the shell (the operating system), you cannot start any other application or DOS command that terminates and stays resident in RAM. This includes utility programs like SideKick as well as the DOS commands PRINT, GRAPHICS, and MODE (see "The System and Quit Menus" in Chapter 4 and the /System reference entry at the end of this chapter for more details).

To reenter the Lotus 1-2-3 worksheet at any time from the DOS prompt, type **exit** and press Return. Never turn off the computer after you use the /System command if you have a spreadsheet in RAM that has either never been saved or contains edits that have not yet been saved.

Note: Anyone using Release 2 should become familiar with the functioning of the /System command and how to reenter Lotus 1-2-3 after invoking it. It is extremely easy to access this command unintentionally by transposing the F and S when you enter the command /FS to save a file with /File Save. A new user may become unsettled when suddenly he finds himself at the DOS operating prompt instead of having his file saved. If he does not understand how to return to Lotus 1-2-3 or panics, the spreadsheet in RAM could be lost.

FORMATTING DATA DISKS FROM THE DOS SHELL

To prepare new data disks when using Lotus 1-2-3 on a two-drive system or to back up data disks when using a hard disk system, you must use the DOS FORMAT command. You can do this with the /System command if you find yourself in a situation in which you have no prepared data disks available to save a spreadsheet you have created.

As soon as you are at the operating prompt, you can change to the directory containing the FORMAT command and use it to prepare a new data disk. When you are finished, return to Lotus 1-2-3 by typing **exit** and pressing Return. Then save your worksheet on the newly formatted disk.

MAKING BACKUP COPIES

You can also use the /System command to make backup copies of your data files while you are still in the Lotus 1-2-3 worksheet. When you do this, you can use the DOS DIR command to obtain a listing of all or a specific group of files. You can also use the DOS MD command to create a new directory to hold the backup files and then use the DOS COPY command to copy them to it. More commonly, you will use the COPY command just to copy your data files located on drive C or B to a backup disk in drive A.

Using the File Manager and Disk Manager in Release 1A

Release 1A provides two menu-driven programs, File Manager and Disk Manager, as part of its Lotus Access System to help you maintain your data files without having to use DOS commands. These options are available only from the Lotus Access System Menu (accessed by using **lotus** as the startup command rather than 123.) To use these programs from the Lotus 1-2-3 worksheet, you must use the /Quit command.

THE FILE MANAGER PROGRAM

When you use the File-Manager option, you must first indicate the letter of the drive that contains your data files (called the source disk). After doing this, you will see the following options:

Copy Erase Rename Archive Disk-Drive Sort Quit

The Copy, Erase, Rename, and Sort options on this menu perform the same functions as the identically named DOS commands. The Archive option allows you to make a copy of a file under a new file name on the same disk. The Disk-Drive option makes another drive current, so you can switch from drive A back to drive C, for example.

The Sort option can be used to sort the file directory temporarily by file name, extension, date, or size of file in either ascending (A–Z, 0–9) or descending (Z–A, 9–0) order. Its options and use are very similar to those of the Lotus 1-2-3 /Data Sort command.

When using the Sort option, you use the Primary Key option to designate which of the four items listed in the directory you want the listing sorted on. If you wish, you can also designate one other item as a secondary key to further order duplicate listings. For instance, if you want the directory listing ordered by date, you would use another item like file name as the secondary key because many files could have the same date, but each has a unique file name. After you designate the keys, use the Go option to have Lotus 1-2-3 perform the sort.

If you wish to perform a different sort on the same directory listing, you can use the Reset option to clear all previously designated keys and then designate new ones. To return to the File Manager options, use the Quit option.

Be aware that your sorted directory remains sorted only during the rest of your session with the File Manager program. Using this program makes no permanent changes in the way your Lotus 1-2-3 data files are listed when you use the DOS DIR command or how they appear when you use the File Manager options on subsequent occasions. Nevertheless, sorting your files with this utility before using such other options as Copy and Erase can make it a great deal easier for you to locate files.

When you use the Copy or Erase options, the program allows you to mark a number of files before it performs the designated operation. This saves time by allowing you to make the copies or deletions in one batch rather than forcing you to repeat the command for each file. To mark a file, move the highlight to it and press the space bar. You will see the number symbol (#) before each file name marked this way. To unmark a file, press the space bar a second time. Once the files have all been marked, press the Return key to carry out the command.

When you wish to return to the Lotus Access System Menu, use the Quit option.

The Disk Manager Program

The Disk-Manager menu options appear as follows when you access this program from the Lotus Access System Menu:

Disk-Copy Compare Prepare Status Quit

The Disk-Copy and Compare options function exactly as the similarly named DOS commands, DISKCOPY and DISKCOMP. The Disk-Copy option copies all of the files on the disk in drive A to the disk in drive B. If the disk in drive B has not been formatted, the program will format it before copying the files.

The Prepare option is the equivalent of the DOS FORMAT command. It used to format new disks out of the box or reformat old ones that contain files you no longer need to save. When you use the Prepare option, you will find that Lotus 1-2-3 always expects the disk to be formatted to be located in drive B. If you are using a hard disk system with only drives A and C, it will successfully format a disk in drive A (as logical drive B). However, if your system has two disk drives and a hard disk, you must place the disk to be formatted in physical drive B. If you ever give the go-ahead to prepare a disk and then realize that you gave it in error, press Ctrl-C (or Ctrl-Scroll Lock) to abort the formatting process.

The Status option is the equivalent of the DOS CHKDSK command. It tells you the amount of free space on a disk as well as the amount of memory available to the computer. Use the Quit option whenever you want to return to the Lotus Access System Menu either to return to DOS or to enter Lotus 1-2-3.

Combining Worksheets and Performing Spreadsheet Consolidations

The /File Combine command is extremely important for performing any number of manipulations that require the use of multiple worksheet files. It provides the only way in Lotus 1-2-3 of linking related data stored in separate files for whatever reasons (space constraints due to limited memory or organizational priorities, for example). It can be used to create new composite worksheets or for temporary lookup and comparisons.

The /File Combine command has three options: Copy, Add, and Subtract. With any one of these, you can use the entire file or a just a specified range within it. The /File Combine Copy command works just like the /Copy command in that any existing data in the range where the file is copied to is overwritten and thereby destroyed.

However, the /File Combine Add and Subtract commands do not overwrite existing data: they provide a specialized consolidation in which existing numeric values are summed with those in the incoming file wherever they overlay each other exactly.

If you use the Add option, the values calculated or entered in the incoming file are summed. If the Subtract option is used, the negatives of these values in the incoming file are summed (providing the equivalent of the subtraction operation). Text entries in the incoming file are ignored when either the Add or Subtract option is used. For illustrations of how these three options work, see Figures 9.3 and 9.4 in the /File Combine reference entry later in this chapter.

Applications for the /File Combine Copy Command

The Copy option is used whenever an entire worksheet or some part of it must be combined with another worksheet. Possible situations include the following:

- Bringing in lookup tables maintained in separate files to use in the spreadsheet you are currently building or updating
- Joining data ranges stored in separate files so that you can generate graphs that require all of them
- Combining smaller worksheets created by several individuals using different computers into one complete model

- Combining database records entered by several individuals on different computers into a central Lotus 1-2-3 database file
- Copying a set of construction macros from a macro library file when beginning a new worksheet

One example of a common application for this command is to keep all lookup tables, such as those containing prices, in their own files; one person has the responsibility of keeping these tables up to date. Each person who needs the data in these tables to use with @LOOKUP functions and related formulas copies the file containing the appropriate table into the new worksheet. This ensures that all spreadsheets are using the same price information and also prevents the chance of input error that could occur if each user manually entered the table into each application. It also allows for easy updating when prices change.

The /File Combine Copy command is not used when you need to add data in files created with some application other than Lotus 1-2-3. In such cases, you use the /File Import command. Depending on the program used to create the data, you may also have to perform some sort of translation before bringing it into a worksheet file with this command (see Chapters 29 and 30).

Keep in mind when you use the /File Combine Copy command that you must locate the data contained in the incoming file in a blank area of the worksheet so that it will not destroy existing data during the copy procedure.

Applications for the /File Combine Add and Subtract Commands

The /File Combine Add and Subtract commands are used to perform spreadsheet consolidations. Any spreadsheet created from a template or constructed with an identical layout can be consolidated into other spreadsheets by using the /File Combine Add command.

For instance, it is common practice to take yearly budgets produced by various department heads using a standard template and consolidate them into a company-wide budget. The same thing is done with income statements constructed individually for each division within a corporation. Each of these separate worksheet files is totaled, and the /File Combine Add command is used to produce a final budget or income statement.

If after performing a consolidation you wish to delete any one set of values, you use the /File Combine Subtract command, giving the name of the worksheet whose values are to be subtracted.

Saving Parts of Worksheets in New Files

The /File Xtract command (/FX) copies a data range in a spreadsheet into its own separate file. As with the /Data Query Extract command, the term *extract* means that the data is copied rather than removed from the worksheet.

The /File Xtract command is often combined with the /File Combine Copy commands for a kind of cut-and-paste operation. For instance, you may set up a data table that you want to save as a file of its own. In this case you would use the /File Xtract command to copy it into its own file. If you then wanted to include that data table in another spreadsheet, you would open the second spreadsheet and use the /File Combine Copy command to copy the new file containing the table into it.

Whenever you use /File Xtract, Lotus 1-2-3 automatically copies the range specified in the source file to the range beginning at cell A1 in the new file. If you had copied the range containing the table directly to the second spreadsheet by using the /File Xtract command, it would overwrite any existing data that it overlayed in the first part of the spreadsheet. By bringing the table in from its own file with /File Combine Copy, you avoid overwriting any data by specifying that the table be copied into a blank area of the worksheet.

The /File Commands

The /File command reference entries in this section contain all of the options found on the /File Menu, with the exception of /File Import. Because the function of this command is to import ASCII files into a Lotus 1-2-3 worksheet, it is included in the reference section of Chapter 29, "Importing and Exporting ASCII Files." The rest of the /File command reference entries are listed in the order they are found on the Lotus 1-2-3 /File Menu.

/File Save

MENUS

/File
Save
Cancel Replace

KEYBOARD ENTRY

/FS

FUNCTION

This command saves a Lotus 1-2-3 worksheet in a disk file under a file name of your choice.

USAGE

The first time you use this command to save a worksheet, you must supply a unique file name consisting of no more than eight characters and an optional extension (in Release 2) if you want one other than .WK1. If you wish to save the file on a disk in a drive other than the default drive or in a directory other than the current directory, type in the complete path name as part of the file name. (If you are using Release 1A, Lotus 1-2-3 will not allow you to save a file in a directory other than the current directory.) Worksheets saved in Release 1A are automatically given the file name extension .WKS, while those in Release 2 are given the extension .WK1.

If you are using Release 2, you can enter your own file name extension. If you do, you must enter the complete file name including the period and extension. The program will not automatically display worksheets that do not carry either the .WKS or .WK1 extension as part of their file names.

In Release 2, you can also add a password consisting of up to 15 characters of your choice. To password-protect a file, press the space bar and type **p** after you enter the file name. You will then be prompted to type in the password. You must verify it by retyping it exactly as you originally entered it, or Lotus 1-2-3 will abort the save operation.

After you have saved a file the first time, Lotus 1-2-3 will supply this file name as the default whenever you save the file again. To accept the file name, press the Return key. You will then see the choices Cancel and Replace, with Cancel as the default setting. To save the file, type **r**. To abort the save operation, press the Return key.

If you wish to save the worksheet under a new file name, simply begin typing the new file name to replace the old one. To save the worksheet in a new directory (in Release 2), press Esc three times and then type in a new path name. If the file name you enter has not been used before, you will not be prompted with the Cancel/Replace options. If it has, you will see these options. If you go ahead and use the Replace option, the new worksheet will replace the contents of the one originally stored under that file name.

The /File Save command is used only to save worksheets in disk files. It saves all data, formulas, display formats, global and range settings, range names, graph definitions (only the latest graph if more than one graph has been defined and each graph has not been named), and the cell pointer position.

To save your data in an ASCII file, you use the /Print File command (see Chapters 25 and 29). To save graphs in a format so that they can be printed, you use the /Graph Save command (see Chapter 24).

MACROS

ALT-S, A SAVE-AND-CONTINUE MACRO

Label	*Macro Contents*
'\s	**'/FS~R**

This macro saves edits made in a worksheet under the same file name that you originally gave to the worksheet when you first saved it. To save the worksheet the first time, you must manually enter the /File Save command and the file name you want to use. Thereafter, you can save all subsequent changes to the file simply by pressing Alt-s.

Note: If you are using Lotus 1-2-3 on a 3270 PC, you must give this macro a name different from Alt-S, perhaps Alt-F (for file).

SEE ALSO

/File Retrieve

/File Retrieve

MENUS

/File
Retrieve

KEYBOARD ENTRY

/FR

FUNCTION

This command loads the worksheet you specify into the computer's memory, allowing you to make revisions or print it.

USAGE

When you need to use a worksheet that has been saved in a disk file with the /File Save command so that you can make changes to it or print it, you use the /File Retrieve command to load it into the computer's memory. After you type **/FR**, Lotus 1-2-3 displays an alphabetical listing of all files saved in the current directory. To select the file desired, move the cursor highlight to it and press the Return key. In Release 2, you can press F3 to see a full-screen listing of the files in the current directory.

You can also type in the file name after invoking this command. If you have saved a worksheet under a file name with an extension other than .WKS or WK1 (in Release 2 only), you must type in the entire file name, including the extension, in order to retrieve it.

If the file you wish to load is not listed among the files displayed or if Lotus 1-2-3 is unable to locate the file name you entered, you may need to look for it in another directory. To obtain a listing of worksheet files in a new directory, first change the current directory with the /File Directory command and then use the /File Retrieve command again. If you wish to see a full-screen listing of all of the worksheet files in the new current directory to verify that it contains the desired file, use the /File List Worksheet command before you use the /File Retrieve command.

If the file you retrieve is not the one you wanted, use the /File Retrieve command again and select a new file. When you use /File Retrieve, any worksheet in memory is automatically cleared before another one is loaded.

SEE ALSO

/File Directory
/File List Worksheet

/File Combine

MENUS

/File
Combine
Copy Add Subtract
Entire-File Named/Specified-Range

KEYBOARD ENTRY

/FCCE /FCAE /FCSE
Name of file to combine: **<file name>**

/FCCN /FCAN /FCSN
Enter range name or coordinates: **<range name or range>**
Name of file to combine: **<file name>**

FUNCTION

This command copies either an entire worksheet file or a specific range within it into the worksheet currently loaded into memory in the location you specify.

USAGE

The /File Combine command provides the method for combining separate worksheets into one. It offers three options, Copy, Add, and Subtract, any of which will work with all of the data in a worksheet (Entire-File) or just a specific range within it (Named/Specified-Range) when performing the combine operation.

USING THE /FILE COMBINE COPY COMMAND

The Copy option makes a complete copy of all of the data in one worksheet file or in a specified range into another file. When you use this command, locate the cell pointer at the beginning of the range into which you want the data copied. Invoke the command by typing **/FCC**.

If you wish to copy all of the data from another worksheet into the current file, choose the Entire-File option by typing **e**. You will then be prompted to enter the name of the file to be combined. You can select this file name from the displayed listing of files by moving the cursor highlight to it, or you can type in the file name manually. After you press the Return key, the program copies all the data from the specified file into the worksheet currently in memory. This data is copied into the range beginning at the cell pointer's current position; any existing data in this range is overwritten.

If you wish to copy only a particular range from the file, choose the Named/Specified-Range option after you enter the /FCC command. You will then be prompted to enter the range name or, if you have Release 2, the coordinates (cell addresses) of the range to be combined.

If you do not know the exact range address or range name, you will have to abort the command (Ctrl-Break) and obtain this information before completing the /File Combine Copy operation. To do this, use the /File Retrieve command to load the worksheet that contains the range of data to be combined. Then verify the range name by using the /Range Name Create command or determine the cell addresses by taking the cell pointer to the range.

After noting the information, reload the original worksheet into which you want to copy this range, locate the pointer at the beginning of the area where you want the data to appear, and reenter the command. After you give the range name or its coordinates, you will be prompted for the name of the file. When you enter the file name and press Return, the range will be copied into the worksheet currently in memory, beginning at the pointer's current position. Just as when using the Entire-File option, you must take care that no existing data is located in this range; it will be wiped out by the copy operation.

USING THE /FILE COMBINE ADD COMMAND

The Add option copies values contained in one worksheet file and adds them to corresponding cells in another worksheet that also contain values or are empty. This type of /File Combine operation is used when you need to consolidate the values in two or more worksheets, as when preparing a consolidated income statement by using the figures contained in several separate income statements. For such a consolidation to operate properly, the spreadsheets must share a common layout and the ranges must be overlaid correctly during the /File Combine Add operation.

To combine the values of an entire worksheet with those in another, locate the cell pointer at the beginning of the spreadsheet where you want the consolidation to occur, type **/FCAE** (for /File Combine Add Entire), and enter the name of the worksheet file whose values you want to include. After Lotus 1-2-3 has finished combining the worksheets, all values whose cells exactly correspond in the two worksheets will be summed in the original worksheet.

Any cells containing values in the second worksheet that correspond to empty cells in the first will now contain the values added from the second (this is because an empty cell carries a value of zero). Any cells that contain values or labels in the original worksheet corresponding to cells that contain labels in the second worksheet will continue to contain their original values or labels (i.e., no combining takes place). These various conditions are illustrated in Figures 9.3 to 9.4 in the Examples section.

When you save the resulting consolidated worksheet, give it a new file name unless you no longer want to maintain a copy of the unconsolidated data in the original worksheet.

To combine the values of a specific range in one worksheet with those in another worksheet file, locate the cell pointer at the beginning of the range to be summed in the original worksheet file and then use the /File Combine Add command with the Named/Specified-Range option. You must supply the range name (or range coordinates, if you have Release 2) as well as the file name in which the range you want to add is stored.

USING THE /FILE COMBINE SUBTRACT COMMAND

The Subtract option works much like the Add option in that it copies only values contained in one worksheet file, which in this case are then subtracted from corresponding cells in the other worksheet that also contain values or are empty. This type of /File Combine operation is used most often when you need to remove the values in one worksheet or range that have already been combined during a previous consolidation that used the Add option.

When using this command, you have the option of subtracting the values of the entire worksheet file or a specified range (by address or range name) just as when you use the /File Combine Copy or Add commands.

To subtract the values of an entire worksheet, locate the cell pointer at the beginning of the worksheet from which you want the values subtracted and type the command **/FCSE**. Enter the file name of the worksheet whose values are to be subtracted or select it with the highlight; then press the Return key. Lotus 1-2-3 consolidates the worksheets, subtracting all values in corresponding locations. Where a cell is empty in the currently loaded worksheet but contains a value in the worksheet you are subtracting, the opposite of its value will appear in the combined worksheet (negative if the value was positive and positive if the value was negative).

To combine the values of a specific range in one worksheet with those in another worksheet, locate the cell pointer at the beginning of the range from which you want values to be subtracted and then use the /File Combine Subtract command with the Named/Specified-Range option. You must supply the range name (or range coordinates, if you have Release 2) as well as the file name in which the range to be subtracted is stored.

EXAMPLES

Figures 9.3 and 9.4 illustrate how the /File Combine commands work. In Figure 9.3 you can compare the contents of two ranges, A2..C3, in two worksheet files that are about to be consolidated. The range in the first file contains four numbers, the label Text, and an empty cell. In the second file, CONSOLID.WK1, the range consists of five numbers and the label New Text.

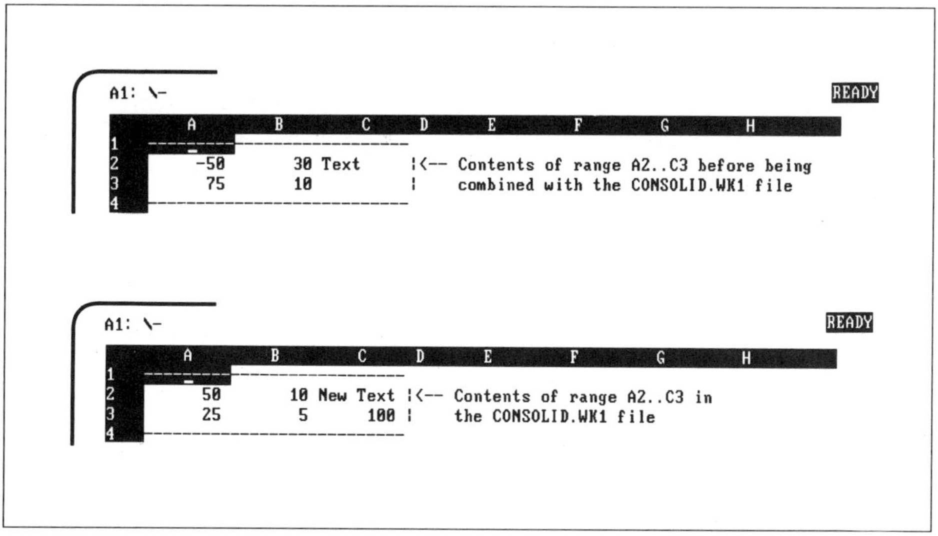

FIGURE 9.3: Two worksheets that are about to be combined by using the various /File Combine command options. The contents of the second file, called CONSOLID.WK1, are consolidated with those of the original file (shown above it) by using the /File Combine Add, Subtract, and Copy options. The results of these operations are shown in Figure 9.4.

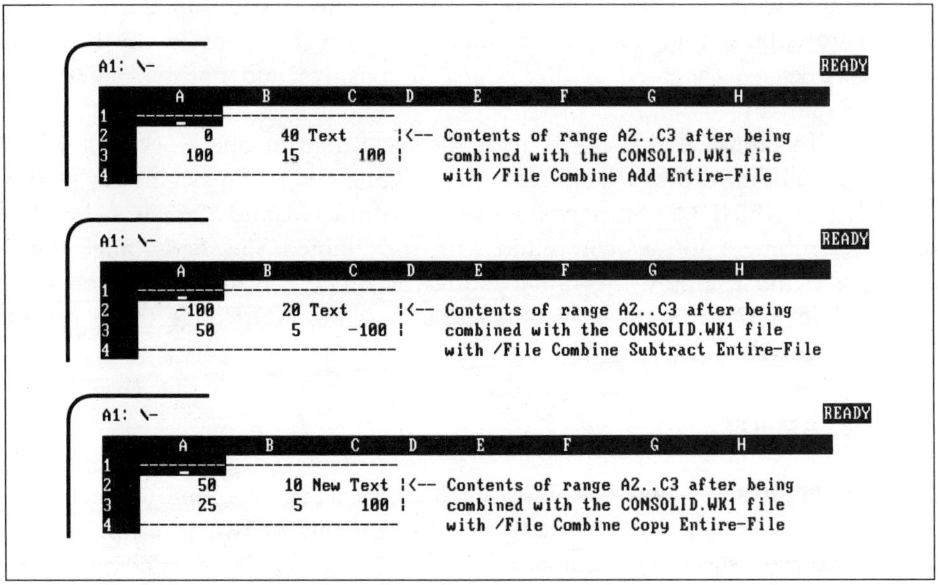

FIGURE 9.4: The result of combining the two files with the various /File Combine commands. In the top part of this figure, the values shown in the range A2..C3 are totals of the original values shown in these same cells in Figure 9.3 and those shown below in the same range in the CONSOLID.WK1 file. Notice that what was previously the empty cell C3 in Figure 9.3 now contains the value 100, added from C3 in the CONSOLID.WK1 file, while the label Text has not been affected by the operation. The result of combining the two ranges by using the /File Combine Subtract command is shown in the middle part of the figure. Notice that the effect of using this option is very similar, except that all of the values have been subtracted. The lower part of this figure illustrates the result of repeating this operation by using the /File Combine Copy command. In this case, the contents of the CONSOLID.WK1 file completely overwrote those of the original worksheet.

Figure 9.4 shows the different results obtained when the various /File Combine commands are used. In each case, the cell pointer was located in cell A1 before giving the appropriate /File Combine command.

In the top part of Figure 9.4, where the effect of using the Add option is demonstrated, all of the cells in the original worksheet that contained values as well as the one empty cell were summed. In the case of the empty cell (which carries a value of zero) the result is 100, the same value that was in that cell in the incoming worksheet file. Notice that the cell containing the label Text was unaffected by this operation. Only values in the same locations are affected when you use the /File Combine Add command.

In the middle part of Figure 9.4, where the Subtract option was used, similar results were obtained. This time, the values in the incoming

CONSOLID.WK1 file were subtracted from the values in the original worksheet. The new value in A2 is −100 because the original value of −50 was combined with the opposite of 50, the incoming value (−50 − 50 = −100). Notice that cell C3, which was originally empty, now has the value of −100, the opposite of its value in the CONSOLID.WK1 file. Just as in the case of using the /File Combine Add command, this operation had no effect on the cell containing the label Text.

The lower part of Figure 9.4 shows the results of using the /File Combine Copy command on the same range. Unlike the other two examples, this operation produced a duplicate of the CONSOLID.WK1 file. All of the original values, the label, and the empty cell were overwritten. This demonstrates why you should locate the cell pointer in new areas of the worksheet if you wish to protect your existing data from being destroyed.

SEE ALSO

/File Xtract

/File Xtract

MENUS

/File
Xtract
Formulas   Values

KEYBOARD ENTRY

/FXF   /FXV
Enter xtract file name: **<file name>**
Enter xtract range: **<range>**

FUNCTION

This command copies the range specified in a worksheet into a separate worksheet file by saving it under the file name you supply.

USAGE

The /File Xtract command offers you two options, Formulas and Values, for copying specified ranges within a worksheet to separate files. When you use the Formulas option, all formulas used in the specified range are copied to the new file, and their cell references are automatically adjusted to reflect their new location. When you choose the Values option, only the values currently calculated are transferred to the new file.

Using this option provides an effective way to convert formulas to their current values if you are using Release 1A. (Release 2 users can use the /Range Value command to do the same thing.) If you wish, you can then copy the range back into the original worksheet by using the /File Combine Copy command.

To copy a cell range to a new file, move the cell pointer to the beginning of that range and issue the /File Xtract command by typing **/FX**. You will then be prompted to choose between the Formulas and Values options. The Formulas option transfers literal values and formulas to the new spreadsheet. The Values option transfers values only. After typing either **f** or **v**, you will be prompted to enter a file name for the file you are about to create. When you enter the file name, you will be prompted for the range of cells to copy. You can indicate the location of the range by pointing, by entering the appropriate cell addresses, or by entering the range name if you have assigned one to it. After you press the Return key, Lotus 1-2-3 saves the range, starting at cell A1 in the new worksheet file.

When you use the Formulas option with this command, you may find when you retrieve the new worksheet that the cell references in your formulas have become corrupted during the transfer. Cells that are referenced in the original spreadsheet may not have been extracted into the new spreadsheet (see the examples that follow). In such cases, you may be required to edit key formulas and then copy them throughout the range or add key input cells to correct these errors.

EXAMPLES

The /File Xtract procedure is easy to perform, as is demonstrated in Figure 9.5. All you have to do is choose between the Formulas and Values options, designate a new file name, and then designate the range to be copied. In this particular figure, the new file is called SUBSET.WK1, and the

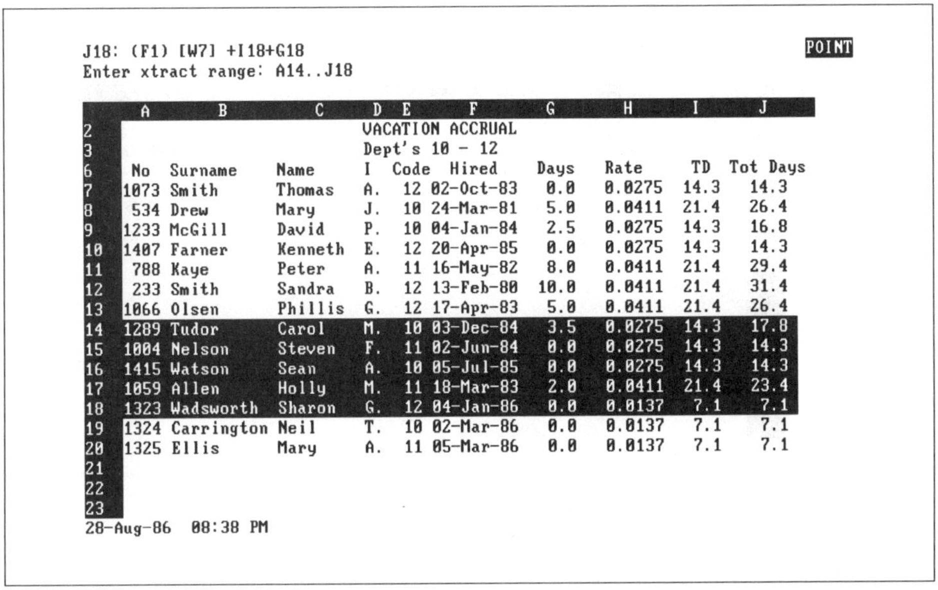

J18: (F1) [W7] +I18+G18 POINT

Enter xtract range: A14..J18

	A	B	C	D	E	F	G	H	I	J
2				VACATION ACCRUAL						
3				Dept's 10 - 12						
6	No	Surname	Name	I	Code	Hired	Days	Rate	TD	Tot Days
7	1073	Smith	Thomas	A.	12	02-Oct-83	0.0	0.0275	14.3	14.3
8	534	Drew	Mary	J.	10	24-Mar-81	5.0	0.0411	21.4	26.4
9	1233	McGill	David	P.	10	04-Jan-84	2.5	0.0275	14.3	16.8
10	1407	Farner	Kenneth	E.	12	20-Apr-85	0.0	0.0275	14.3	14.3
11	788	Kaye	Peter	A.	11	16-May-82	8.0	0.0411	21.4	29.4
12	233	Smith	Sandra	B.	12	13-Feb-80	10.0	0.0411	21.4	31.4
13	1066	Olsen	Phillis	G.	12	17-Apr-83	5.0	0.0411	21.4	26.4
14	1289	Tudor	Carol	M.	10	03-Dec-84	3.5	0.0275	14.3	17.8
15	1004	Nelson	Steven	F.	11	02-Jun-84	0.0	0.0275	14.3	14.3
16	1415	Watson	Sean	A.	10	05-Jul-85	0.0	0.0275	14.3	14.3
17	1059	Allen	Holly	M.	11	18-Mar-83	2.0	0.0411	21.4	23.4
18	1323	Wadsworth	Sharon	G.	12	04-Jan-86	0.0	0.0137	7.1	7.1
19	1324	Carrington	Neil	T.	10	02-Mar-86	0.0	0.0137	7.1	7.1
20	1325	Ellis	Mary	A.	11	05-Mar-86	0.0	0.0137	7.1	7.1
21										
22										
23										

28-Aug-86 08:38 PM

FIGURE 9.5: Using the /File Xtract command with the Formulas option to copy a range of cells to a new file named SUBSET.WK1. In this example, the range A14..J18 has been indicated as the extract range. Because the Formulas option was chosen, not only the values in this range but also their formulas will be stored in the new SUBSET.WK1 file when the Return key is pressed.

range is indicated as A14..J18. As soon as you press the Return key, Lotus 1-2-3 stores all of this data in the new file.

Figure 9.6 shows the resulting SUBSET worksheet that has been retrieved with the /File Retrieve command. Whenever a cell range is extracted, it is always copied to a range beginning at cell A1 in the new file. In this example, the formulas transferred to SUBSET.WK1 have become corrupted because a cell on which most of the formulas depend was not copied during the /File Xtract operation. This must now be corrected manually.

SEE ALSO

/File Combine

```
A1: [W5] 1289                                                 READY

     A    B          C       D  E  F          G      H       I       J
1  1289 Tudor      Carol    M.  10 03-Dec-84  3.5    0.0137 ******-431.9
2  1004 Nelson     Steven   F.  11 02-Jun-84  0.0    0.0137 ******-435.4
3  1415 Watson     Sean     A.  10 05-Jul-85  0.0    0.0137 ******-435.4
4  1059 Allen      Holly    M.  11 18-Mar-83  2.0    0.0137 ******-433.4
5  1323 Wadsworth  Sharon   G.  12 04-Jan-86  0.0    0.0137 ******-435.4
6
7
8
9
10
11
12
13
14
15
16
17
```

FIGURE 9.6: The contents of the new SUBSET.WK1 file. Notice that the range extracted from the larger worksheet in Figure 9.5 is automatically located in the range beginning with cell A1 in the new worksheet. Also, because the cell containing the current date was not copied into SUBSET.WK1 and all of the formulas in column H depend on this value, the formulas in this worksheet are not functioning correctly. This must now be corrected by adding the value and reentering the formula in cell H1, which will then be copied down the rest of the column.

/File Erase

MENUS

Release 1A	*Release 2*
/File	/File
Erase	Erase
Worksheet Print Graph	Worksheet Print Graph Other

KEYBOARD ENTRY

/FEW **/FEP** **/FEG** **/FEO** (Release 2 only)
Enter name of file to erase: **<file name>**

FUNCTION

This command deletes Lotus 1-2-3 files from the current directory.

USAGE

The /File Erase command allows you to delete files without having to use the DOS DEL or ERASE commands at the operating system level. It automatically subdivides files according to type—thus the options Worksheet, Print, Graph, and (in Release 2) Other.

To delete a specific worksheet file, you use the /File Erase Worksheet command (/FEW). The program displays an alphabetical list of all worksheet files stored in the current directory, just as it does when you use the /File Retrieve, Save, or List commands. You can indicate the name of the file to be deleted either by typing in its name or by moving the highlight to its display and then pressing the Return key. In Release 2, press F3 to see a full-screen file listing. Release 2 also automatically displays worksheet files created in either version of the program (i.e., those carrying both the .WKS and .WK1 extensions). You are then prompted to enter **Y** to carry out the deletion. As No is the default, you can abort this command by pressing the Return key.

Deleting ASCII text files or graphs involves a similar procedure. To erase ASCII files given the extension .PRN by Lotus 1-2-3, type **/FEP** and indicate the name of the file. To erase graph files given the extension .PIC (when saved with the /Graph Save command), type **/FEG** and indicate the file name.

If the file you wish to delete does not carry the .WKS, .WK1, .PRN, or .PIC extension, you can still use any of these commands to delete it, but you must type in the exact file name, including the extension. Because Release 2 allows you to save worksheet files with file name extensions other than .WK1, you can use the /File Erase Other command to list and delete any data file, regardless of its extension.

These commands allow you to erase only a single data file at a time, so you must use them many times to delete a group of unwanted files. In such cases, it is often more efficient to use the DOS DEL or ERASE commands with the DOS wildcard characters to delete a group of files with related file names in one operation.

Note: Do not confuse the function of this command with that of the /Worksheet Erase command, which only deletes the worksheet currently on the screen from the computer's memory, leaving any previously saved file untouched on the disk. The /File Erase command deletes the file from the disk on which you store your Lotus 1-2-3 data files. To retrieve files deleted with the /File Erase commands, you must use a stand-alone utility program or possess a thorough knowledge of the workings of DOS and its commands. You cannot do this from within the Lotus 1-2-3 program.

SEE ALSO

/File Directory

/File List

MENUS

Release 1A	*Release 2*
/File	/File
List	List
Worksheet Print Graph	Worksheet Print Graph Other

KEYBOARD ENTRY

/FLW **/FLP** **/FLG** **/FLO** (Release 2 only)

FUNCTION

This command obtains a directory listing of Lotus 1-2-3 files from the current directory.

USAGE

The /File List commands allow you to list the data files in the current directory without having to use the DOS DIR command at the operating system level. It automatically subdivides files according to type—thus the options Worksheet, Print, Graph, and (in Release 2) Other.

To obtain a listing of all your worksheet files, you use the /File List Worksheet command (/FLW). The program displays a full-screen alphabetical listing of all worksheet files stored in the current directory. In Release 1A, this listing does not include the file name extension, and the program gives the amount of available disk space in bytes at the top of the screen. If no worksheet files are found there, the program goes into EDIT mode to allow you to revise the directory.

The Release 2 directory screen displays both the file name and its extension (.WKS or .WK1). Instead of giving you the amount of free space left on the disk, it displays the complete file name, the date and time of creation, and the file size in bytes of the currently highlighted file name. You can move the highlight to obtain these statistics on the various files listed. To move from left to right across the listing, press the space bar or use the → key. Pressing the End key takes the highlight to the last file; pressing the Home key takes it directly to the first file in the listing.

With either version of the program, after you use any of the /File List command options, you press the Return key to return to the worksheet. In Release 2, you can also press the Esc key to return to the current directory prompt. To view a listing of files in another directory, you can press the Esc key twice more and type in the full path name followed by a *.WK? to display all of the worksheet files stored there. (You can also substitute the patterns *.PRN to see the ASCII text files, *.PIC to see the graph files, and *.* to see all of the files.)

Listing ASCII text files or graphs involves a similar procedure. To list all ASCII files given the extension .PRN by Lotus 1-2-3, type **/FLP**. If the ASCII text files do not have this extension, they will not be included in the directory listing (see the Other option if you are using Release 2). To list all graph files given the extension .PIC (when saved with the /Graph Save command), type **/FLG**.

Because Release 2 allows you to save worksheet files with file name extensions other than .WK1, you can use the /File List Other command (/FLO) to list all data files, regardless of their file name extensions. This makes it possible to get a complete listing of all data files stored in the current directory, regardless of whether they were created in Lotus 1-2-3.

SEE ALSO

/File Directory

/File Directory

MENUS

/File
Directory

KEYBOARD ENTRY

/FD
Enter current directory: **<path name>**

FUNCTION

This command allows you to view or change the current directory, which Lotus 1-2-3 uses when saving, retrieving, listing, and erasing files with the associated /File commands.

USAGE

When you use the /File Directory command, Lotus 1-2-3 displays the directory that has been set as the default by using the /Worksheet Global Default Directory command. To change the directory for the current work session, type in the new directory path name you wish to use. If this directory is located on a new physical drive, be sure to preface the directory path name with the appropriate drive letter.

You can specify any directory that has been set up on a hard disk by giving its full path name. (You can also specify a different hard disk drive such as D:\ if you have more than one physical device or have set up partitions called C and D within a single hard disk.)

After you issue the command by typing **/FD**, type in the name of the current directory, including the drive letter and full path name. Then press the Return key. You will be returned to the worksheet, and Lotus 1-2-3 will use this directory for saving, retrieving, and listing data files until you change it again by using the same command. When you exit Lotus 1-2-3 and start the program again, the program will once again use the default directory set with the /Worksheet Global Default Directory command.

SEE ALSO

/Worksheet Global Default Directory

The /System Command (Release 2 Only)

The /System command allows you to exit temporarily to DOS, where you can use the DOS commands for working with directories and manipulating files, for example.

/System

MENUS

/System

KEYBOARD ENTRY

/S

FUNCTION

This command temporarily suspends a Lotus 1-2-3 session and exits directly to DOS.

USAGE

The /System command allows you to exit temporarily to the operating system and use any DOS commands (such as CD, MD, RD, DIR, FORMAT, CHKDSK, and DEL) that do not terminate and stay resident (you cannot use the so-called TSR DOS commands such as PRINT, GRAPHICS, and MODE). After you type **/s**, you are immediately placed in the DOS directory containing the Lotus 1-2-3 program files (A:\ on a two-drive system and C:\LOTUS, C:\123, etc., on a hard disk system). The program also displays the message

(Type EXIT and press [RETURN] to return to 1-2-3)

If you are using Lotus 1-2-3 on a two-drive system and have not copied the COMMAND.COM file onto your Lotus System Disk, you will receive the error message "Cannot invoke DOS." In such a case, replace your Lotus System Disk with a copy of your DOS disk and then press the Esc key to complete the command. To return to the Lotus 1-2-3 worksheet and continue your work, type **exit** and press the Return key (you can do this from any DOS directory).

The warning about not using TSR DOS commands also extends to starting up any other programs that terminate and stay resident, such as SideKick or SuperKey. The only programs that you can safely load are those like WordPerfect or dBASE III, which are terminated from memory when you exit them. In addition, using these programs is possible only if your computer has sufficient memory to hold Lotus 1-2-3, the worksheet you were working on before using the /System command, and the new program files.

Unlike other programs that provide a DOS shell command (like WordPerfect, which continues to display its Type Exit message after every DOS command you use), Lotus 1-2-3 will not continue to display this message to remind you that have exited to DOS. You may forget that you have exited to DOS and try to load a TSR program or use a TSR command. You may even forget that you need to type **exit** to return to Lotus 1-2-3. It is up to you to remember that you have made a temporary exit from the program.

As a precaution against losing data, always save the worksheet currently loaded in memory before you use the /System command. For more information on applications for the /System command, refer back to the section, "Using the DOS Shell Command (/System) in Release 2."

SEE ALSO

/Quit

THE /QUIT COMMAND

The /Quit command terminates your session with Lotus 1-2-3. It allows you to leave Lotus 1-2-3 and enter either the Lotus Access System Menu, where you can use the File-Manager and Disk-Manager options with your files, or DOS, where you can use any of the DOS commands.

/Quit

MENUS

/Quit
No Yes

KEYBOARD ENTRY

/QY

FUNCTION

This command is used to quit Lotus 1-2-3 or to return to the Lotus Access System (if you entered **lotus** as the startup command) and from there to DOS. It returns you directly to DOS if you entered **123** as the startup command.

USAGE

The /Quit command terminates your work session in Lotus 1-2-3. After you type **/Q**, you are presented with Yes/No options. No is the default. If you entered the /Quit command by mistake or realize that you are exiting the program without having first saved the worksheet currently in memory, press the Return key to return immediately to the worksheet. To go ahead and exit Lotus 1-2-3, type **y**; you will be returned to DOS. If you entered **lotus** as the startup command, you will be returned to the Lotus Access System Menu.

Unlike the /System command, once you have reentered DOS with the /Quit command, you are free to start up other programs and use the DOS commands that terminate and stay resident (see the /System entry).

Note: If you have already saved your work, you can power down your computer without using the /Quit Yes command and not cause damage to either the program or your data. However, this is not the preferred method for terminating a work session, because the habit of turning off the power without bothering to use the /Quit command can lead you to use this method with other programs that do require an exit to prevent data corruption (as do most stand-alone database management programs).

SEE ALSO

/System

SUMMARY

This chapter has covered all the Lotus 1-2-3 commands on the /File menu, with the exception of the /File Import command. It has also covered the methods offered by the program for combining worksheet files and for creating new files from parts of existing worksheets. The following reference guide will help you locate other information related to these topics.

For information on setting the default directory:

- Chapter 2, "Installing and Customizing Lotus 1-2-3"

For information on defining and naming cell ranges:

- Chapter 8, "Working with Cell Ranges"

For information on storing graph files in Lotus 1-2-3:

- Chapter 24, "Creating and Using Graphs"

For information on using the /File Import command and storing Lotus 1-2-3 files as ASCII text files:

- Chapter 29, "Importing and Exporting ASCII Files"

For information on how to take files created with other programs into Lotus 1-2-3:

- Chapter 30, "The Translate Utility"

PART 3

SPREADSHEET FORMULAS AND FUNCTIONS

The real power of a Lotus 1-2-3 spreadsheet lies in the formulas it contains. The formulas are the means by which it automatically performs all the mathematical calculations you require of it. Part 3 examines formulas and each group of built-in @ functions that can be used in Lotus 1-2-3. To make it easier for you to locate the information you need about a particular type of function, each group of functions is presented in separate chapters.

Chapter 10 contains an overview on how to create and use simple as well as complex formulas in a worksheet. It also discusses the use of the /Copy command specifically as this command relates to formulas. Here you will find information on when to use relative, mixed, and absolute cell addressing. This chapter also discusses how to use @ functions in formulas as a prelude to specific information about each type of function in the next eight chapters.

Chapters 11 through 18 discuss the usage of specific groups of @ functions in Lotus 1-2-3. Release 2 of the program has added a number of important functions that are absent from Release 1A. These functions are labeled as "Release 2 only." Also, note that all of the functions covered in Chapter 17, "The String Functions," exist only in Release 2.

Chapter 19 ends this part of the handbook by discussing the three interrelated subjects: creating spreadsheet models, avoiding and trapping errors, and using methods for recalculating formulas. In this context, you will find a discussion of circular references: when they represent errors that must be eliminated and when and how they can be intentionally used in models. At the end of this chapter you will find reference entries for the /Worksheet Global Recalculation command.

CHAPTER 10

WORKING WITH FORMULAS AND FUNCTIONS

WORKING WITH FORMULAS AND FUNCTIONS

This chapter covers the construction and general use of formulas in Lotus 1-2-3 spreadsheets. As such, it also serves as an introduction to the various specialized Lotus 1-2-3 functions, which are arranged by group and examined individually in the next eight chapters (Chapters 11–18). In this chapter you will also find a discussion of the use of relative, mixed, and absolute cell addressing in constructing formulas that are to be copied into new locations in the worksheet.

CREATING FORMULAS

A formula is a cell entry that performs some kind of calculation in a Lotus 1-2-3 spreadsheet. In Release 1A, this calculation must be mathematical, so the components of a formula must contain or refer to entries in the spreadsheet that are considered to be values by the program. In Release 2, the scope of formula calculation has been expanded to include label entries by the addition of special string functions and a concatenation operator (&).

The following discussions on constructing and copying formulas focus on formulas that perform mathematical calculations (i.e., they consist only of values) and can be used with either version of the program. For specific discussions and examples of calculations involving character strings, see Chapter 15, "Logical Functions," and Chapter 17, "String Functions."

Rules for Constructing Formulas

A formula entry can consist of up to 240 characters (the maximum number of characters that can be entered into any single cell of the worksheet). No spaces are allowed between the elements of a formula, the punctuation marks, or the operators. Lotus 1-2-3 will perform the calculations called for in a formula on constants (literal values such as 1, 1.5, 0.05, and so forth), on cell references containing values (either constants or calculated values), or on a mixture of constants and cell references. References to cell ranges are restricted to those Lotus 1-2-3 functions whose arguments require cell ranges.

Beginning a Formula

When you begin constructing a formula, Lotus 1-2-3 must be in VALUE mode. If your formula starts with a constant, the program automatically goes into VALUE mode. If your formula starts with a cell reference, you must preface it with a character that forces Lotus 1-2-3 to go into VALUE mode. Table 10.1 summarizes all such beginning characters and their usage. Most often, the plus sign (+) is the appropriate choice because its use does not alter the calculated results. The other characters also cause the program to go into VALUE mode, but they alter the formula's meaning in some way.

CHARACTER	USAGE	EXAMPLE
+	Used when the formula begins with a cell reference.	+A2*.75 +A4/A5
–	Used when the formula begins with a negative constant or when the opposite of the value referenced by the cell address is to be used.	–50*B5 –B6/B6
0–9	Used when the formula begins with a constant beginning with zero or an integer between 1 and 9.	1.5*D2 9+(D1/D2)
.	Used when the formula begins with a decimal value.	.5*E3 .125*57
(	Used when the beginning part of the formula's natural order of calculation must be altered through the use of a pair of parentheses. The calculation contained in the parentheses can consist of constants, cell references, or a mixture of the two.	(G1–G2)/G3 (G5+10)*G6
@	Used when the formula begins with a Lotus 1-2-3 function.	@ABS(H3)+2 @SUM(H4..H9)

TABLE 10.1: Characters Used to Begin Formula Construction

CHARACTER	USAGE	EXAMPLE
$	Used when the formula begins with an absolute or mixed cell address in which the column must be kept absolute when the formula is copied elsewhere in the worksheet. (This symbol is **not** used to denote that the formula begins with a currency value such as $125.00.)	$J$1/J2 $J3*($J4 – 10)
#	Used in the rare case in which the formula begins with the Boolean operator #NOT#. Ordinarily, #NOT# is included as part of the argument of an @IF function, in which case another symbol is used to begin the formula. In the example shown, a value of true (1) will be returned if the value of K1 is less than or equal to that of K2. A value of false (0) will be returned if K1 is greater than that of K2.	#NOT#K1 >K2

TABLE 10.1: Characters Used to Begin Formula Construction (continued)

USING MATHEMATICAL, LOGICAL, AND BOOLEAN OPERATORS

A Lotus 1-2-3 formula must include operators that determine the calculated results between the constants, cell references, or mixture of the two entered into it. There are three groups of operators; their symbols and meanings are summarized in Table 10.2.

Mathematical operators are used to calculate results in simple formulas or in more complex formulas involving the Lotus 1-2-3 functions, while the logical and Boolean operators are almost always used in those formulas that employ the @IF function.

THE ORDER OF CALCULATION IN FORMULAS

When you construct formulas in the worksheet, it is important that you know the order in which Lotus 1-2-3 conducts calculations according to the operators specified, because the order of calculation affects the result. Lotus 1-2-3 uses the algebraic order of precedence (described in Table 10.3), meaning that formulas are evaluated from left to right, with precedence given to calculations according to the type of operators used.

	SYMBOL	MEANING
Mathematical operators	+	Addition between elements of the formula, such as +A1+B1.
	−	Subtraction between elements of the formula, such as +A1−B1. When this symbol is also used to denote the opposite of the value of a constant or cell reference, it should be enclosed in parentheses, such as A1−(−B1).
	*	Multiplication between elements of the formula, such as +A1*B2 or −A1*−B1.
	/	Division between elements of the formula, such as +A1/B1 or −A1/−B1.
	^	Exponentiation of one or more of the elements of the formula, such as 3^2 (three squared) or +A1^3 (the value of A1 cubed).
Logical operators	=	A condition in which one or more elements of the formula are stated to be equal in value to one or more other elements, such as @IF(A1=B1,1.5*A1,A1).
	<	A condition in which one or more elements of the formula are stated to be less than the value of one or more other elements, such as @IF(A1<B1,1.5*A1,A1).
	>	A condition in which one or more elements of the formula are stated to be greater than the value of one or more other elements, such as @IF(A1>B1,1.5*A1,A1).
	<>	A condition in which one or more elements of the formula are stated to be not equal to the value of one or more other elements, such as @IF(A1<>B1,1.5*A1,A1).
	<=	A condition in which one or more elements of the formula are stated to be less than or equal to the value of one or more other elements, such as @IF(A1<=B1,1.5*A1,A1).

TABLE 10.2: The Mathematical, Logical, and Boolean Operators

	SYMBOL	MEANING
Logical operators	>=	A condition in which one or more elements of the formula are stated to be greater than or equal to the value of one or more other elements, such as @IF(A1>=B1, 1.5*A1,A1).
Boolean operators	#AND#	A condition in which both elements of the formula must be true for the calculation to be performed, such as @IF(A1=C1#AND#B1=C1, 1.5*A1,0).
	#OR#	A condition in which the calculation is performed if either of the elements of the formula is true, such as @IF(A1=C1#OR#B1=C1, 1.5*A1,0).
	#NOT#	A condition in which the elements of the formula must not be true for the stated calculation to be performed, such as @IF(#NOT#A1=B1, 1.5*A1,0).

TABLE 10.2: The Mathematical, Logical, and Boolean Operators (continued)

OPERATOR	PRECEDENCE WITHIN A LOTUS 1-2-3 FORMULA
^	Exponents in a formula are calculated first. If more than one is called for, they are calculated in order of occurrence from left to right.
* and /	Multiplication and division are calculated next. Neither of these two mathematical operations has precedence over the other. If both are called for, or if more than one multiplication or division operation is called for, calculations proceed in order of occurrence from left to right.

TABLE 10.3: Natural Order of Calculation in a Formula

OPERATOR	**PRECEDENCE WITHIN A LOTUS 1-2-3 FORMULA**
+ and −	Addition and subtraction are calculated next. Neither of these two mathematical operations has precedence over the other. If both are called for, or if more than one addition or subtraction operation is called for, calculations proceed in order of occurrence from left to right. **Note:** When the minus sign is used to denote the negative (or opposite) of a value rather than to denote subtraction, the operation changing its value follows exponentiation but precedes all other mathematical and logical operations called for in the formula.
= and <>	The logical evaluations of equality and inequality in the sense of equal or not-equal conditions between elements are performed next. Neither of these two logical evaluations has precedence over the other. When they both occur in a formula, they are evaluated in order of occurrence from left to right.
< and >	The logical evaluations of inequality in the sense of less-than and greater-than conditions between elements are performed next. Neither of these two logical evaluations has precedence over the other. When they both occur in a formula, they are evaluated in order of occurrence from left to right.
<= and >=	The logical evaluations of equality or inequality in the sense of less-than-or-equal or greater-than-or-equal conditions between elements are performed next. Neither of these two logical evaluations has precedence over the other. When they both occur in a formula, they are evaluated in the order of occurrence from left to right.
#NOT#	Inequality between components of a formula in the sense that a stated condition "is not true" is evaluated next. If the formula contains more than one #NOT# operator, they are evaluated in order of occurrence from left to right.
#AND# and #OR#	Equality between components of a formula in the sense that a stated condition "is true in both this case and that" or "is true in either this case or that" is evaluated next. Neither of these operators has precedence over the other. If they both exist in a formula, or if more than one of either exist, the truth of these conditions is evaluated in order of occurrence from left to right.
&	Concatenation between strings in the formula is performed after all other mathematical operations in the formula. If concatenation of multiple string elements is called for in a formula, the strings are combined in order of occurrence from left to right (Release 2 only).

TABLE 10.3: Natural Order of Calculation in a Formula (continued)

You can alter this natural order by using pairs of parentheses. When the formula contains nested pairs of parentheses, the elements within the inmost parentheses are calculated first, regardless of the operators specified, and subsequent calculations in the formula then use this result.

To illustrate how the use of parentheses alters the natural order of calculation and how this works in formulas that require nested parentheses, consider the examples shown in Figure 10.1.

THE SYNTAX OF FUNCTIONS

Lotus 1-2-3 functions share a common syntax, though they differ considerably in particulars. The following points should be noted when using functions in formulas:

- All functions begin with @ (the at symbol) followed immediately by the function name.

```
H1:                                                                    READY

        A         B         C         D         E         F         G         H
1      -5
2      10
3       5
4
5      75 <-- +A1^2+A2*A3 = (-5)(-5) + (10)(5) = 25 + 50 = 75
6
7     175 <-- (A1^2+A2)*A3 = ((-5)(-5) + 10) X 5 = (25 + 10) X 5 = 175
8
9      -3 <-- +A1+A2/A3 = -5 + 10/5 = -5 + 2 = -3
10
11      1 <-- (A1+A2)/A3 = ((-5) + 10)/5 = 5/5 = 1
12
13   -2.5 <-- +A1/A2*A3 = -5/10 X 5 =  -2 X 5 = -2.5
14
15   -0.1 <-- +A1/(A2*A3) = -5/(10 X 5) = -5/50 = -0.1
16
17 EQUAL     <-- @IF(A1^2=A2*2+A3,"EQUAL","NOT EQUAL")
18
19 NOT EQUAL<-- @IF(A1^2=A2*(2+A3),"EQUAL","NOT EQUAL")
20
12-Aug-86  05:39 PM
```

FIGURE 10.1: Sample formulas illustrating the order of calculation and how to alter it with parentheses. This figure contains four pairs of formulas that are identical except for the use of parentheses that change the natural order of calculation. In the first example, the program begins by calculating the square of A1. It then calculates the product of A2 times A3 and adds these results, producing 75 as the answer. In the second formula in that pair, adding parentheses significantly changes the order in which this formula is evaluated. The value in A1 is still squared first, but this time its product is added to that in A2 before multiplying the result by A3, which produces 175 as the answer. The other examples illustrate similar effects.

- All function names must be entered exactly as Lotus 1-2-3 expects them, though they can be entered without regard to case. The convention of showing all function names in uppercase is followed consistently in this handbook even though you can enter them in lowercase—in other words, the sum function is shown as @SUM(), even though you can enter it into a cell as **@sum()**.
- Most functions require arguments, which must always be set off by a pair of parentheses. A limited number of functions do not take arguments but merely require the @ symbol and function name, such as @TODAY, @NOW, @RAND, @PI, @TRUE, @FALSE, @ERR, and @NA.
- Many functions require multiple arguments. When a function requires more than one argument, each argument must be separated by a comma [or whichever other delimiter character (. or ;) is in effect if the /Worksheet Global Default Other International command has been used to change the delimiter from the comma].
- Some functions require single values, while others will accept cell ranges or lists comprised of a combination of ranges or values. Those that require values will accept constants (literal values) or references to cells that contain constants or values calculated by other formulas. Those that require ranges will accept the range name or cell addresses of the range containing the values (see the section "Using Cell Ranges in Formulas" for more information).
- While most functions calculate new values according to the arguments given, some merely evaluate the current contents of the cells referred to in the arguments. Some examples of this type are the @IS functions, such as @ISERR(x) or @ISNA(x), and the string functions, such as @CELL(attribute,range) and @CELLPOINTER(attribute).

Note: This handbook uses the same conventions as the Release 2 documentation in stating the type of arguments required by Lotus 1-2-3 functions.

Figure 10.2 illustrates the typical components of a formula that consists of a Lotus 1-2-3 function.

Using Cell Ranges in Formulas

For those functions that allow ranges as arguments, you can enter the range to be used as you would any other Lotus 1-2-3 cell range: by

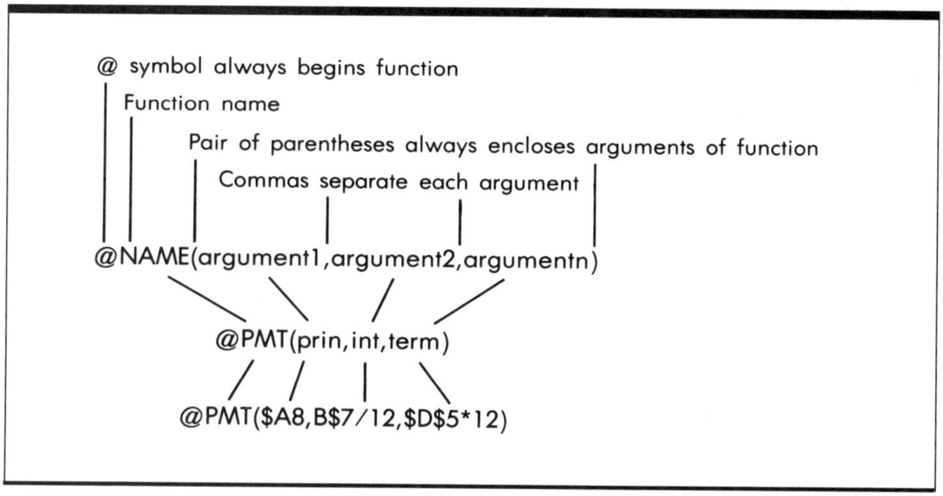

FIGURE 10.2: The typical components of a Lotus 1-2-3 function. As the illustration shows, a Lotus 1-2-3 function is always prefaced with the @ symbol, followed by the name of the function. In most cases, Lotus 1-2-3 functions also require arguments that are always enclosed in a pair of parentheses, though their type and number differ according to the function used. If more than a single argument is required, the arguments are separated by commas. The @PMT(prin,int,term) example in the figure shows the transition from the general paradigm to one in which the actual function name and abbreviations for the arguments required are substituted. The example below it shows the transition to an actual formula in which the cell references holding these arguments are given.

pointing or by typing in the cell addresses. (See Chapter 8, "Working with Cell Ranges," for more detailed information about designating cell ranges in the worksheet.)

If you have given the cell range a range name with either the /Range Name Create or the /Range Name Labels command, you can enter the range name as the argument of the function instead of designating its location by pointing or entering cell addresses.

The only restriction caused by using range names instead of the cell addresses of the range is that you cannot designate mixed references within the range if you are going to copy the formula. You can, however, designate range names as absolute references by prefacing them with the dollar sign (such as $SALES for a range of figures named SALES) or leave them relative by merely entering their name as the argument. (For more information on relative, mixed, and absolute cell references, see the following section, "Copying Formulas in the Worksheet.")

If you delete a range name from the worksheet, it will be replaced by cell addresses in all functions in which it has been used.

COPYING FORMULAS IN THE WORKSHEET

While the mechanics of using the /Copy command for copying parts of a spreadsheet are covered in Chapter 7, "Formatting Worksheets," the discussion of the use of relative, mixed, and absolute cell references when copying formulas is more relevant to the topic of constructing formulas. It is important to note that these different kinds of cell references are required only when you intend to copy a formula to new areas of the worksheet. Because such formula copying is called for in almost all spreadsheet applications, you should understand thoroughly how and when these references are used.

How Lotus 1-2-3 Adjusts the Cell References When a Formula Is Copied

When you copy a formula from one part of the worksheet to another, Lotus 1-2-3 follows the direction of the copy and the location of the source of the copy, adjusting the cell references in the destination range accordingly. For instance, when you make a one-to-many copy of a formula across a row from left to right, the references to cells in the column of the source cell are adjusted one column right in each of the copies in the destination range. For example, if a formula to be copied were located in cell A5 and contained the function @SUM(A1..A3), the copies of the formulas in the destination range B5..C5 would contain functions @SUM(B1..B3) and @SUM(C1..C3), respectively.

When you make a one-to-many copy of a formula down a column, the references to cells in the row of the source cell are adjusted one row down in each of the copies in the destination range. For example, if a formula to be copied were located in cell E1 and contained the function @SUM(A1..D1), the copies of the formulas in the range E2..E3 would contain the functions @SUM(A2..D2) and @SUM(A3..D3), respectively.

Similar cell reference adjustments are made when making one-to-many copies in two dimensions (both down and over) as well as when making many-to-many copies of formulas.

This kind of cell-reference adjustment according to relative position (so many rows over or so many rows down) in the direction the copy is being made works fine in most instances, which is why it is the program's natural way of handling formula copying. However, sometimes you may not want such adjustments. If you do not prevent them by using mixed or absolute cell references in your formula before you copy it, you will get errors in the worksheet.

If a value referenced in a formula by cell address must remain constant when the formula is copied, you must countermand the automatic adjustment of the cell reference in each copy. This usually occurs when the value or range of values represents a constant in each formula, as in a lookup table. In such cases, change the relative cell reference to an absolute cell reference to ensure that each copy uses the same value.

You may sometimes want the cell references in copied formulas to be adjusted in one direction but not in the other. Such cell references are referred to as *mixed references*. There are two types of mixed references: relative in regard to column but absolute in regard to row, and relative in regard to row but absolute in regard to column. In the first type, copied formulas have the same column reference as that in the original formula, but their row references are adjusted accordingly. In the second type, the copied formulas have the same row reference as that in the original formula, but their column references are adjusted. For an example of a copy using all three types of nonrelative cell references, see the section "Using Mixed and Absolute Cell References" later in this chapter.

Indicating Mixed and Absolute Cell References

To designate a part of a cell address as absolute (a mixed reference) or both parts as absolute (an absolute reference), place a $ symbol before each component of the cell address (the column letter, row number, or both) to indicate its absolute (fixed) status. The following examples illustrate the various combinations that are possible:

- $A$1 denotes an absolute cell reference in which both the column (A) and the row (1) are absolute when the formula is copied.
- A$1 denotes a mixed cell reference in which the column (A) is relative and the row (1) is absolute when the formula is copied.
- $A1 denotes a mixed cell reference in which the column (A) is absolute and the row (1) is relative when the formula is copied.

You can enter the $ sign before each component of the cell address when you are typing the formula or function argument, or you can use the Absolute function key (F4) to have the program automatically add the $ sign to the cell reference. This key can be used in either POINT or EDIT modes. When using it in EDIT mode, place the cursor anywhere within the cell address and press F4. Lotus 1-2-3 will cycle through all the possible combinations outlined in Table 10.4.

CYCLE	DESCRIPTION OF RESULT	EXAMPLE
1st time pressed	Changes from a completely relative reference to a completely absolute cell reference (i.e., from A1 to $A$1).	$A$1
2nd time pressed	Changes to a mixed reference with relative column, absolute row.	A$1
3rd time pressed	Changes to a mixed reference with absolute column, relative row.	$A1
4th time pressed	Changes back to the original, completely relative cell reference.	A1

TABLE 10.4: Using the ABS (Absolute) Function Key to Change Cell References

Using Mixed and Absolute Cell References

Figures 10.3 and 10.4 show an example using the @PMT function, which requires both kinds of mixed cell references as well as an absolute cell reference in order to generate a payment schedule. The formula that is constructed consists entirely of the @PMT function. It requires three arguments: the amount of the principal, the interest rate, and the term of the loan.

In this particular table, the three cells that supply these arguments are located in D3, D4, and D5. Cell D3 contains the input for the beginning principal, D4 that of the beginning yearly interest rate, and D5 that of the term specified in years. To create a table that shows monthly payments for various loan amounts at various interest rates, the values in the first two input cells are brought forward to cells A8 and B7, respectively. Regular intervals are set up both for the principals in column A and for the interest rates in row 7.

This is accomplished by first creating the formula +A8+500 in cell A9. It is then copied down the range A10..A17 to create various principal amounts increasing by $500.00 intervals. A similar formula, +B7+.0025, is then entered in cell C7. It is copied across the row to the range D7..G7 to create various interest rates increasing by a quarter of a percent.

Notice that in each case the cell references in the formulas were left as relative references. This is because the cell references in both situations needed to be adjusted in the direction of the copy. In the first copy, that of the formula in A9 down the cell range A10..A17, each succeeding copy refers to the cell immediately above it, thus increasing the principal. In the

```
B8: (F2) @PMT($A8,B$7/12,$D$5*12)                                      READY

     A          B          C          D          E          F          G          H
1               Payment Schedule for Simple Interest Loans
2
3  Beginning Principal          $100,000
4  Beginning Interest Rate        10.00%
5  Term (in years)                    30
6
7                  10.00%     10.25%     10.50%     10.75%     11.00%     11.25%
8     100,000      872.57
9     100,500
10    101,000
11    101,500
12    102,000
13    102,500
14    103,000
15    103,500
16    104,000
17    104,500
18
19
20
12-Aug-86  05:39 PM
```

FIGURE 10.3: Constructing the @PMT formula with mixed and absolute references. The @PMT formula is shown on the first line of the Control Panel. Because it will be copied to the range B8..G17 to complete the schedule in one copy operation, the types of cell references need to be taken into consideration. The first argument contains the mixed cell reference $A8 to ensure that each copy uses only the principal values in column A. The second argument contains the other type of mixed reference (B$7) to ensure that each copy uses only the interest rate values in row 7. The third argument contains the absolute cell reference $D$5 to ensure that each copy uses the same value for the term input there.

second, that of the formula in C7 across the range D7..G7, each succeeding copy refers to the cell to its left, thus increasing the interest rate.

After making these copies, the formula containing the @PMT function was constructed in cell B8. Once this formula was created, it was copied both down rows 8 to 17 in column B and across columns C through G. Figure 10.3 shows the completed formula on the first line of the Control Panel. The two-dimensional copy of the original formula to the range B8..G17 required the two types of mixed references ($A8 and B$7) as well as the use of an absolute reference ($D$5).

For the first argument of the @PMT function, the principal in A8 was referenced. To ensure that every copy of the formula across columns B through G used only the principal amounts in column A, it was made absolute ($A). However, to ensure that each new principal amount was used in every copy of the formula down rows 8 through 17, the row reference had to be kept relative (8).

B8: (F2) @PMT($A8,B$7/12,$D$5*12) READY

	A	B	C	D	E	F	G	H
1		Payment Schedule for Simple Interest Loans						
2								
3	Beginning Principal			$100,000				
4	Beginning Interest Rate			10.00%				
5	Term (in years)			30				
6								
7		10.00%	10.25%	10.50%	10.75%	11.00%	11.25%	
8	100,000	872.57	896.10	914.74	933.48	952.32	971.26	
9	100,500	881.96	900.58	919.31	938.15	957.09	976.12	
10	101,000	886.35	905.06	923.89	942.82	961.85	980.97	
11	101,500	890.74	909.54	928.46	947.48	966.61	985.83	
12	102,000	895.12	914.02	933.03	952.15	971.37	990.69	
13	102,500	899.51	918.50	937.61	956.82	976.13	995.54	
14	103,000	903.90	922.98	942.18	961.49	980.89	1000.40	
15	103,500	908.29	927.46	946.76	966.15	985.65	1005.26	
16	104,000	912.67	931.95	951.33	970.82	990.42	1010.11	
17	104,500	917.06	936.43	955.90	975.49	995.18	1014.97	
18								
19								
20								

12-Aug-86 05:40 PM

FIGURE 10.4: The completed payment schedule table after copying the @PMT formula down and across the range. The one-to-many copy of the formula in B8 was made in two dimensions: down rows 8 to 17 in column B and then over to column G. To ensure that the formulas copied to this range contain the appropriate cell references, the combination of mixed and absolute cell references seen in the formula were required.

For the second argument of the @PMT function, the interest rate in cell B7 was referenced. To ensure that every copy of the formula down rows 8 through 17 used only the interest rates in row 7, it was made absolute ($7). But to make sure that every copy of the formula across columns B through G used each new interest rate, the column reference was left relative (B). The amount provided by this cell is divided by 12 because it represents an annual interest rate, and the function requires the monthly interest rate to calculate the monthly payment correctly (B$7/12 converts the annual rate into a monthly figure).

For the third argument of the @PMT function, that of the term, the input cell D5 was referenced. It represents a constant in the table because all of the resulting payments at various principals and interest rates are for 30-year mortgages. To ensure that each copy of formula uses the same term, this cell reference is made entirely absolute ($D$5). Each copied formula supplies the third argument of the function from the value in this cell.

The value is multiplied by 12 because the term input into D5 is the number of years the mortgage is held. The @PMT function requires the total number of monthly payments to calculate monthly payments correctly ($D$5*12 converts the term in years to the term in months).

Figure 10.4 shows the completed schedule after the formula entered into B7 was copied to the range B7..G17. Because the proper mixed and absolute cell references were used when the original formula was created, the finished schedule could be completed in one copy operation.

The model can now be easily subjected to what-if analysis. Changing the input values of any or all of the three input values in cells D3, D4, and D5 allows you to look at the effects that changing principals, interest rates, and terms have on the resulting monthly payments required. Because of the way the model was constructed, trying any number of new combinations requires no changes in the underlying formulas.

SUMMARY

The information in this chapter has provided a general introduction to using the Lotus 1-2-3 functions, which are discussed individually in the next eight chapters. Each of these chapters examines a particular group of related functions. You can use the following reference to locate particular functions you are interested in. References related to topics discussed in this chapter are also listed.

- Chapter 11, "Mathematical, Scientific, and Engineering Functions," covers @ABS, @INT, @MOD, @RAND, @ROUND, @SQRT, @EXP, @LN, @LOG, @PI, @SIN, @COS, @TAN, @ASIN, @ACOS, @ATAN, and @ATAN2.
- Chapter 12, "Statistical Functions," covers @SUM, @AVG, @COUNT, @MAX, @MIN, @STD, and @VAR.
- Chapter 13, "Financial Functions," covers @PMT, @NPV, @PV, @RATE, @TERM, @CTERM, @IRR, @SLN, @DDB, and @SYD.
- Chapter 14, "Date and Time Functions," covers @TODAY, @NOW, @DATE, @DAY, @MONTH, @YEAR, @DATEVALUE, @TIME, @HOUR, @MINUTE, @SECOND, and @TIMEVALUE.
- Chapter 15, "Logical Functions," covers @IF, @TRUE, @FALSE, @ISERR, @ISNA, @ISNUMBER, and @ISSTRING.

- Chapter 16, "Database Statistical Functions," covers @DSUM, @DAVG, @DCOUNT, @DMAX, @DMIN, @DSTD, and @DVAR.
- Chapter 17, "String Functions," covers @CHAR, @CODE, @EXACT, @FIND, @LEFT, @LENGTH, @LOWER, @MID, @N, @PROPER, @REPEAT, @REPLACE, @RIGHT, @S, @STRING, @TRIM, @UPPER, and @VALUE.
- Chapter 18, "Special Functions," covers @HLOOKUP, @VLOOKUP, @INDEX, @CHOOSE, @ERR, @NA, @@, @CELL, @CELLPOINTER, @COLS, and @ROWS.

For information on the mechanics of using the /Copy command:

- Chapter 7, "Formatting Worksheets"

For information on trapping errors in formulas and on formula recalculation:

- Chapter 19, "Spreadsheet Models, Error Trapping, and Recalculation"

For more information on using strings in formulas in Release 2:

- Chapter 15, "Logical Functions"
- Chapter 17, "String Functions"

CHAPTER 11

Mathematical, Scientific, and Engineering Functions

Mathematical, Scientific, and Engineering Functions

This chapter examines the Lotus 1-2-3 mathematical and scientific functions. The program contains a number of specialized mathematical functions that can be used to refine spreadsheet models of all types. It also offers a substantial number of more specialized trigonometric functions that are generally used in scientific and engineering applications.

Mathematical Functions

The mathematical functions include two types: those that calculate new values—such as @MOD, @RAND, and @SQRT—and those that alter the way Lotus 1-2-3 stores values already calculated—such as @ABS, @INT, and @ROUND.

When you use the latter, remember that unlike the /Range Format commands, which alter only the display of values but not their precision, these functions return new values of a precision that you specify as a part of the function's arguments. When you use @INT and @ROUND, you are actually changing the precision of the values brought forward and used in subsequent formulas.

@ABS

The @ABS function returns the absolute value of an expression; that is, its value without regard to a positive or negative sign.

SYNTAX

@ABS(x)

where x is a value input into a cell, a cell reference to a value, or a value derived by formula calculation.

USAGE

This function is most often used to ensure that the value returned is not negative, because the absolute value of any number is equivalent to its positive value. For instance, entering either **@ABS(45)** or **@ABS(−45)** returns a value of 45 in the cell in which this function was entered.

The @ABS function in Lotus 1-2-3 can be used only with single values. It will not accept a cell range as its argument. For example, entering the function **@ABS(D3..D8)** would not be accepted, whereas **@ABS(@AVG(D3..D8))** would be. Therefore, if you need to use only the absolute value of cells in a range extending from D3 to D8 in a worksheet, you have to enter the @ABS function for each of the six cells in that range. You can do this quickly by entering the function in the first cell and copying it down the column or across the row as required. See Figure 11.1 for an illustration of this situation.

The @ABS function is often used with the @SQRT function to ensure that the value whose square root is to be returned is not negative, because the @SQRT function returns an ERR value if a negative value is specified as its argument (see the @SQRT entry at the end of this section).

EXAMPLES

Figure 11.1 illustrates how the @ABS function can be used. The differences between various beginning and ending temperatures are calculated in the range D3..D8. By using a formula containing the @ABS function, the difference between this value and zero degrees is calculated as an unsigned number. Because the difference can sometimes be a negative value, the @ABS function is used if the value is less than 0; otherwise, the value itself is used in the accompanying expression.

At the end of the column range, the average of the differences has been calculated by using the @AVG function in cell D10. To return the absolute value of this average, the formula **@ABS(@AVG(D3..D8))** was used in cell D12.

@INT

The @INT function returns the integer part of a value by stripping away any values following the decimal point.

```
F3: [W9] @IF(D3<0,"<- Down from 0 by "&@STRING(@ABS(D3),1)&" degrees","<- UREADY

      A         B        C          D     E    F          G          H
1              Start    End
2              Temp     Temp     Difference
3   Run 1        100    -567.0     -467.0     <- Down from 0 by 467.0 degrees
4   Run 2         45     -10.5       34.5     <- Up from 0 by 34.5 degrees
5   Run 3          0      -4.6       -4.6     <- Down from 0 by 4.6 degrees
6   Run 4         15     -23.4       -8.4     <- Down from 0 by 8.4 degrees
7   Run 5        450     -34.6      415.4     <- Up from 0 by 415.4 degrees
8   Run 6          0     -25.7      -25.7     <- Down from 0 by 25.7 degrees
9
10  @AVG(D3..D8) ---------->          -9.3
11
12  @ABS(@AVG(D3..D8)) ---->           9.3
13
14
15
16
17
```

FIGURE 11.1: Examples of the @ABS function. In this figure, a range of differences between various starting and ending temperatures is calculated in the range D3..D8. The average difference (−9.3) has been calculated in D10. The formula for deriving the absolute value of the average is shown in cell A12. The @ABS function was also used to print the messages to the right of the values, indicating the number of degrees above or below zero (see the formula in the entry line).

SYNTAX

@INT(x)

where x is a value input into a cell, a cell reference to a value, or a value derived by formula calculation.

USAGE

The @INT function truncates numbers so that only the integer portion of the value is used in further calculations. The value can be positive or negative. This function does not round the value; it merely truncates it by removing all decimal values.

EXAMPLES

Table 11.1 illustrates the operation of @INT in the worksheet.

CELL LOCATION	ORIGINAL VALUE	@INT FUNCTION	VALUE RETURNED
	3.1415926536	@INT(@PI)	3
A3	−34.56	@INT(−34.56)	−34
A4	0.5056179775	@INT(A4)	0

TABLE 11.1: Examples of the @INT Function

@MOD

The @MOD function returns the remainder after division of two numbers specified as the arguments of the function. This remainder is referred to in mathematics as the *modulus,* thus the name @MOD.

SYNTAX

@MOD(x,y)

where x is the dividend and y is the divisor. In using @MOD, x and y can be values input into cells or values derived by formula calculation.

USAGE

This function takes two arguments, the first of which, x, is divided by the second, y. It can be used to test whether a cell contains an even or odd value (see the examples for this formula below) as well as in any situation that calls for using the remainder in calculations.

EXAMPLES

Figure 11.2 illustrates the workings of the @MOD function as well as an application for it. In this figure, the values in the range C2..C7 are tested for evenness or oddness by the formulas in the range D2..D7. These formulas use the @MOD function to perform this test, because a value that can be divided by 2 with no remainder is by definition even.

By combining this function with @IF, one of two messages is displayed, determined by whether or not a remainder of zero is returned from @MOD. If @MOD returns a value of zero after dividing the

```
D2: @IF(@MOD(C2,2)=0,"<--- This value is even","<--- This value is odd")   READY

      A       B        C        D      E       F        G        H
 1
 2                          45 <---_This value is odd
 3                          90 <--- This value is even
 4                         2.1 <--- This value is odd
 5                       34.55 <--- This value is odd
 6                          48 <--- This value is even
 7                           5 <--- This value is odd
 8
 9            24                              2
10          ------                          ------
11        2 ¦ 48.0    <--- This value is   2 ¦ 5.0    <--- This value is
12            4            EVEN                4           ODD
13            --                               --
14            08                               1      <--- @MOD(5,2)
15             8
16            --
17             0      <--- @MOD(48,2)
```

FIGURE 11.2: Using the @MOD function to test a value for evenness or oddness. The formula calls for dividing each value by 2 with the @MOD function. If the remainder is 0, the number is even and the message "This value is even" is displayed. If not, the message "This value is odd" is displayed. The illustrations at the bottom of this figure show how @MOD works. The value given for y is divided into the value given for x, as in the case of 5 divided by 2. The remainder of 1 indicates that this value is odd.

value by 2, the message "This value is even" is displayed. Otherwise, the message "This value is odd" appears.

How the @MOD function works is illustrated at the bottom of the figure for the last two values, 48 and 5. When you divide 48 by 2, the @MOD function returns a value of zero as the remainder, therefore displaying the even message. When you divide 5 by 2, the remainder is 1, showing that this is an odd number. As soon as the @MOD function returns the value 1, the @IF function returns the odd message.

@RAND

The @RAND function generates a random number between 0 and 1.

SYNTAX

@RAND

The @RAND function takes no argument. It is merely entered into a cell or combined within another Lotus 1-2-3 function.

USAGE

The @RAND function returns a value between 0 and 1 with a precision of 15 decimal places. The value it returns is recalculated each time the spreadsheet is recalculated, either when you press the Calc key (F9) if the program is in manual recalculation mode or when you enter a new value if the spreadsheet is in automatic mode.

To prevent @RAND from recalculating a new number, you must convert the value returned by @RAND to a constant value by using the /Range Value command (see Chapter 8) if you are using Release 2. In this case, specify the same range containing the @RAND value or values for the FROM range as you do for the TO range. (If you are using Release 1A, you have to use /File Xtract Values and copy the range to a separate file to accomplish this—see Chapter 9.)

EXAMPLES

Table 11.2 shows how to control the range of random numbers generated by the @RAND function. If you use @RAND by itself, the value will be a decimal number between 0 and 1. To generate numbers within a specific range, multiply the @RAND function by the difference

	RANGE	@RAND FUNCTION	EXAMPLE
Random Numbers with Decimals	0–1	@RAND	0.704890
	1–10	@RAND*9+1	9.278552
	10–100	@RAND*90+10	59.01583
	100–1000	@RAND*900+100	697.1504
Rounded Random Numbers	0–1	@ROUND(@RAND,0)	1
	1–10	@ROUND(@RAND*9+1,0)	3
	10–100	@ROUND(@RAND*90+10,0)	62
	100–1000	@ROUND(@RAND*900+100,0)	110
Truncated Random Numbers	0–1	@INT(@RAND)	0
	1–10	@INT(@RAND*9+1)	2
	10–100	@INT(@RAND*90+10)	91
	100–1000	@INT(@RAND*900+100)	437

TABLE 11.2: Examples of the @RAND Function

between the upper and lower limits and add the number of the lower limit to the result.

To obtain a whole random number, you can use either the @ROUND function or the @INT function. The difference between them is illustrated in Table 11.2 in the first range, 0–1. In the case of combining @ROUND with @RAND, the decimal value was rounded up to 1. When @INT was combined with @RAND, the decimal part of the value was truncated, returning the value 0.

@ROUND

The @ROUND function rounds a value to the place value specified in the arguments.

SYNTAX

@ROUND(x,n)

where x is a value input into a cell, a cell reference to a value, or a value derived by formula calculation, and n is the number of digits to be rounded.

USAGE

With the @ROUND function, the n argument can be a number between −15 and 15, specifying the amount and placement of digits to be affected. If the n argument is a negative number, the program rounds to the left of the x value's decimal point to the number of digits specified. If the n argument is a positive number, the program rounds to the right of the x value's decimal point to the number of digits specified. If the n argument is zero, the program rounds the x value to the nearest integer.

EXAMPLES

Table 11.3 illustrates the amount of control the @ROUND function gives you over the values in a worksheet. It shows the effect of using various n arguments. In the first example, with 0 as n, the value is rounded to the nearest integer. With positive n arguments, the decimal

FUNCTION ENTERED	VALUE RETURNED	COMMENTS
@ROUND(15675.3456,0)	15675	Value is rounded to nearest integer
@ROUND(15675.3456,1)	15675.3	.34 is rounded to .3
@ROUND(15675.3456,2)	15675.35	.345 is rounded to .35
@ROUND(15675.3456,3)	15675.346	.3456 is rounded to .346
@ROUND(15675.3456, −1)	15680	75 is rounded to 80
@ROUND(15675.3456, −2)	15700	675 is rounded to 700
@ROUND(15675.3456, −3)	16000	5675 is rounded to 6000

TABLE 11.3: Examples of the @ROUND Function

portion of the value is affected. In the second example with the n argument as 1, the tenths place is affected, so it is rounded to .3 (if the decimal was .35 or higher, it would have been rounded up to .4). In the third example with n as 2, the hundredths place is affected, so .345 is rounded to .35. In the fourth example with n as 3, the thousandths place is affected, so .3456 is rounded to .346.

With negative n arguments, the whole-number portion of the value is affected. In the fifth example with n as −1, the tens place is rounded, so 75 becomes 80 (if the value were 74, it would have been rounded to 70). In the sixth example with −2 as n, the hundreds place is affected, so 675 is rounded to 700. In the last example with −3 as n, the thousands place is affected, so 5675 is rounded to 6000.

@SQRT

The @SQRT function returns the square root of a positive value.

SYNTAX

@SQRT(x)

where x is a positive value input into a cell, a cell reference to a value, or a value derived by formula calculation. Lotus 1-2-3 returns an ERR value if the value is negative.

USAGE

The @SQRT function can find the square root only of positive values in the spreadsheet. Because it will return an ERR value if the value is negative, you can combine it with the @ABS function if you know that the value will be negative or if you are not sure and want to guard against error values. To do this, use the following paradigm:

@SQRT(@ABS(x))

EXAMPLES

Figure 11.3 illustrates the use of the @SQRT function in the worksheet. As you can see from this figure, the argument of the @SQRT function can be a value input as the argument, as in the first example in C7 where the perfect square 1600 was used. It can also be a cell reference to another value in the spreadsheet, as in the second example where C4 was used. In the third example, the argument includes a calculation between two cell references—in this case, the difference between C4 and D4.

The fourth example illustrates what happens when you try to obtain the square root of a negative value in the spreadsheet. Notice that you can avoid the ERR value that was returned for the square root of −789 by using the @ABS function, as was done in the fifth example.

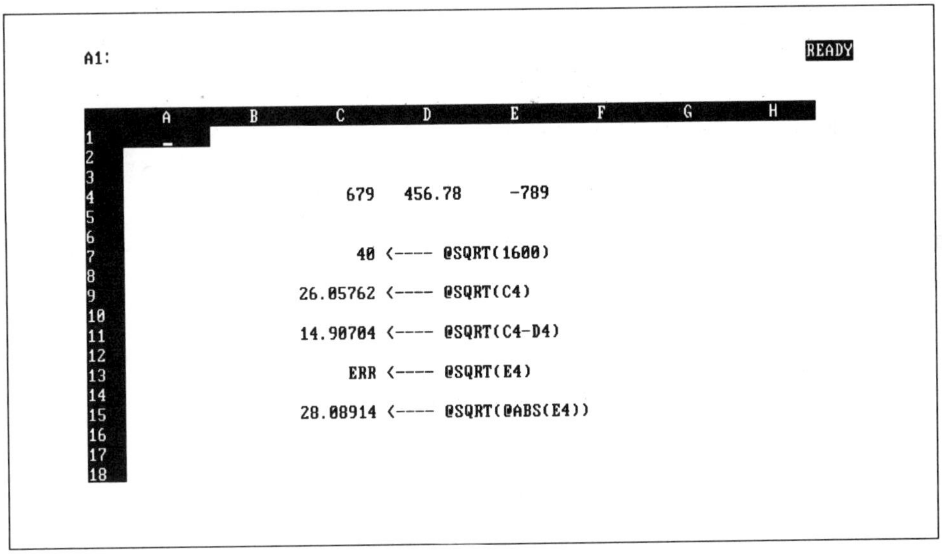

FIGURE 11.3: Examples of the @SQRT function. In this figure, the square roots of various values are found by using the @SQRT function. In the first example in C7, the perfect square 1600 was entered as the argument of the @SQRT function. In the second, the argument refers to a value input into cell C4. In the third, it refers to the result of a formula calculation between C4 and D4. In the fourth example, the argument refers to a negative value input in E4, thus the ERR value. This has been rectified by adding the @ABS function in the fifth example.

Scientific and Engineering Functions

Lotus 1-2-3 includes a number of powerful functions that are most often required in scientific and engineering worksheet applications. The program supports logarithmic functions in two bases: the natural logarithm in base e with @LN and its inverse, @EXP, as well as logarithms in base 10 with @LOG. In either of these bases, it is easy to create a formula to convert to some other base. This is illustrated in both the @LN and @LOG entries that follow.

In addition to logarithms, Lotus 1-2-3 has a variety of trigonometric functions. These include @PI to return the value of π, as well as the three basic trig functions of @SIN to return the sine of the angle, @COS to return its cosine, and @TAN to return its tangent. These latter three functions can be used to include their reciprocal functions, cosecant, secant, and cotangent. Lotus 1-2-3 also includes the inverse functions of sine, cosine, and tangent in @ASIN for arc sine, @ACOS for arc cosine, and @ATAN for arc tangent. Release 2 has added a new trigonometric function, @ATAN2, that allows you to derive the arc tangent in a four-quadrant system.

In the case of all trigonometric functions with the exception of @PI, Lotus 1-2-3 works in radian measure instead of degrees. Formulas for converting from radians to degrees and vice versa are included with each reference entry.

@EXP

The @EXP function returns the value of the constant e raised to the power specified as the argument of the function. It represents the inverse of the Lotus 1-2-3 function @LN.

SYNTAX

@EXP(x)

where x is a value input into a cell, a cell reference to such a value, or a value calculated by formula.

USAGE

The @EXP function uses the constant e, which is approximately equal to 2.7182818. This represents the constant of base e used in natural logarithms.

The x argument that you supply in the function represents the exponent or power by which the constant e is raised in calculation.

EXAMPLES

The @EXP function is useful in scientific calculations that require exponential functions. In applying this formula to a given formula, you must understand how to translate the parts of the formula into forms accepted by the Lotus 1-2-3 function.

For instance, radioactive materials are known to decay spontaneously at a rate that depends on the amount of material present at any given time. The amount decreases exponentially depending on the half-life of the material. In the case of strontium 90, you can calculate the approximate amount of remaining material by the following formula:

$$M = Ge^{-.0248t}$$

where M is the amount of strontium 90 remaining, G is the number of grams of material you start with, and t is the number of years. To find the amount of strontium 90 remaining after 80 years when you start with 10 grams, you would enter the formula as follows:

@EXP(−0.0248*80)*10 = 1.375180

As you can see from this example, you supply the exponent of e as the argument of the function within the parentheses. In this case, it is the calculated value of −0.0248*80, which is then multiplied by the number of grams you started with. Lotus 1-2-3 then tells you that approximately 1.38 grams of the original 10 grams of strontium 90 remain after 80 years have passed.

If you need to use the constant e in other formulas, you can also use the @EXP function to generate its value. In this case, using the number 1 as the argument results in the value of e as follows:

@EXP(1) = 2.7182818285

@LN

The @LN function returns the natural logarithm of its argument. It solves for the logarithm of the argument to base e (the mathematical constant approximately equal to 2.7182818285).

SYNTAX

@LN(x)

where x is a value input into a cell, a cell reference to such a value, or a value calculated by formula. If the value is negative or equal to zero, the program returns an ERR value.

USAGE

The @LN function is the inverse of @EXP, so the value of @LN (2.7182818285) is 1. When you use it in Lotus 1-2-3, the argument supplied as x must not be equal to zero or a negative value.

EXAMPLES

The @LN function has many uses in solving scientific formulas. The following example illustrates how it can be applied.

The formula for determining the approximate number in years of the age of plant or animal remains with carbon 14 dating is shown below:

$$t = \frac{\ln P}{-0.00012}$$

where t is the answer in years and ln is the natural logarithm of P, the percent of radioactive carbon 14 retained by the remains. To find the age in years of an animal's jawbone that retains 31 percent of its carbon 14, you would enter the formula as follows:

@LN(0.31)/−0.00012 = 9759.85817

The jawbone in question is almost 10,000 years old.

To find logarithms in other bases with the @LN function, divide the number whose logarithm you wish to find by the base, as in the following example:

@LN(25)/@LN(10) = 1.3979400087

In this example, Lotus 1-2-3 returns the value 1.3979400087, the logarithm of 25 in base 10. To check that it works, you can find the logarithm of 25 with the @LOG function as follows:

@LOG(25) = 1.3979400087

@LOG

The @LOG function returns the logarithm of its argument. It solves for the logarithm of the argument to the base 10.

SYNTAX

@LOG(x)

where x is a value input into a cell, a cell reference to such a value, or a value calculated by formula. If the value is negative or equal to zero, the program will return an ERR value.

USAGE

The @LOG function is the reciprocal of base-10 exponentiation, or scientific notation. When you use it in Lotus 1-2-3, the argument supplied as x must not be zero or a negative value.

EXAMPLES

The @LOG function has many uses in solving scientific formulas. The following example illustrates how it can be applied.

The decibel rating of an event can be calculated by the following formula:

$$L = 10 \log_{10} \frac{I}{I_0}$$

where L is the decibel rating, I is the sound intensity, and I_0 is the threshold intensity of human hearing. To find the decibel rating of a jet plane on takeoff if its sound intensity is rated as $10^{12}I_0$, you would enter the formula as follows:

@LOG(10^12)*10 = 120

showing that the sound intensity is 120 decibels at takeoff.

To find logarithms in other bases with the @LOG function, divide the number whose logarithm you wish to find by the base, as in the following example:

@LOG(25)/@LOG(@EXP(1)) = 3.2188758249

which gives you the logarithm of 25 in base e. To prove that this method works, you can check the answer by using the @LN function to determine the logarithm of 25 in base e as follows:

@LN(25) = 3.2188758249

@PI

The @PI function returns the value of the constant π, using the value 3.1415926536.

SYNTAX

@PI

The @PI function requires no argument.

USAGE

The @PI function returns the approximate value of the mathematical constant π, which represents the ratio of a circle's diameter to its circumference. This function is used in a variety of mathematical formulas, especially with the other Lotus 1-2-3 trigonometric functions (see the examples below).

EXAMPLES

You can use the @PI function to determine the area of a circle by plugging it into the standard formula πr^2, as in the following example:

@PI*14^2

where 14 inches is the radius of the circle.

The Lotus 1-2-3 trigonometric functions @SIN, @COS, and @TAN all require arguments expressed in radians rather than in degrees. Their inverses, @ASIN, @ACOS, and @ATAN (and @ATAN2 in Release 2) return the calculated angles measured in radians rather than degrees. You can use the @PI function to convert degrees to radians and vice versa when you are working with these functions.

To convert degrees to radians, use the following formula:

x*@PI/180

where x is the number of degrees. For example, if you have an angle of 33.5 degrees, use this formula in Lotus 1-2-3 to convert it to radians:

33.5*@PI/180 = 0.584685

To convert radians to degrees, use this formula:

x^r*180/@PI

where x^r is the number of radians. For instance, if you have an angle of .78539816^r, the following formula would convert it from radians to degrees:

.78539816*180/@PI = 44.99999

@SIN

The @SIN function returns the sine of the angle specified as its argument expressed in radians.

SYNTAX

@SIN(x)

where x is a measurement of the angle expressed in radians.

USAGE

The @SIN function solves the sine of a specified angle. The answer is given in radians and lies between −1 and 1. This function is used in a wide variety of scientific and engineering formulas. To convert an angle measured in degrees into radians for use with this function, multiply the number of degrees by @PI/180, as illustrated in the following examples.

EXAMPLES

To find the index of refraction according to Snell's law for a light ray as it passes from air to another medium, you would use the following formula:

$$n = \frac{\sin \theta_i}{\sin \theta_r}$$

where n is the index of refraction for the given medium and θ_i and θ_r are the incident and refracted rays, respectively. To apply this formula to water, which has a θ_i of 43.2 degrees and a θ_r of 31.0 degrees and find its index of refraction, you would enter the formula as

@SIN(43.2*@PI/180)/@SIN(31*@PI/180) = 1.329119

To use the cosecant function in your formulas, use the reciprocal of the @SIN function in Lotus 1-2-3. Divide 1 by the value of the sine, as illustrated by the definition of the cosecant:

$$\csc\theta = \frac{1}{\sin\theta}$$

@COS

The @COS function returns the cosine of the angle specified as its argument expressed in radians.

SYNTAX

@COS(x)

where x is a measurement of the angle expressed in radians.

USAGE

The @COS function is most useful in scientific and engineering formulas that involve right triangles and their various relationships. To convert an angle measured in degrees into radians for use with this function, multiply the number of degrees by @PI/180.

EXAMPLES

The values returned by this function vary between −1 and 1, which is suggested by the following relationship:

- If $\theta = 0^r$ (0°) then $\cos\theta = 1$
- If $\theta = \pi^r/2$ (90°) then $\cos\theta = 0$

In Lotus 1-2-3, you can verify this by entering the following formulas:

@COS(0) = 1
@COS(@PI/2) = 3.4E−19 (approximating 0)

To use the secant function in your formulas, use the reciprocal of the @COS function in Lotus 1-2-3. Divide 1 by the value of the cosine, as illustrated by the definition of the secant:

$$\sec \theta = \frac{1}{\cos \theta}$$

@TAN

The @TAN function returns the tangent of the angle specified as its argument expressed in radians.

SYNTAX

@TAN(x)

where x is a measurement of the angle expressed in radians.

USAGE

The @TAN function has various types of applications in both scientific and engineering formulas. To convert an angle measured in degrees into radians for use with this function, multiply the number of degrees by @PI/180.

EXAMPLES

The range of the values of the tangent is the set of all real numbers, as reflected in the following relationships:

$$\tan \theta \rightarrow +\infty \text{ as } \frac{\pi}{2}$$

$$\tan \theta \rightarrow -\infty \text{ as } -\frac{\pi}{2}$$

Lotus 1-2-3 returns the value of $\pm 90°$ as follows:

@TAN(@PI/2) = 2.9E + 18
@TAN(− @PI/2) = − 2.9E + 18

As an example of an engineering application for the @TAN function, consider the following problem, where the velocity at which a vehicle can safely travel on a roadway banked at a particular angle can be measured by the following formula:

$$v = \frac{1800R \tan \theta}{121}$$

where v is the velocity and R is the radius of curvature in feet of the roadway banked at the angle θ. If the angle θ is 6.4 degrees and the radius of curvature is 1460 feet, we can find the velocity with Lotus 1-2-3's @TAN function by constructing the following formula:

@SQRT(1800*1460*@TAN(6.4*@PI/180)/121) = 49.39651

In this particular example, a vehicle could therefore safely travel at 49 mph on this roadway under normal driving conditions.

To use the cotangent function in your formulas, use the reciprocal of the @TAN function in Lotus 1-2-3. Divide 1 by the value of the tangent, as illustrated by the definition of the cotangent:

$$\cot \theta = \frac{1}{\tan \theta}$$

@ASIN

The @ASIN function returns the arc sine, an angle measured in radians, from the sine specified as its argument.

SYNTAX

@ASIN(x)

where x is the sine of the angle to be solved for. The x argument can be a value input in the function, referenced by cell address, or calculated by formula.

USAGE

The @ASIN function returns the arc sine, or the angle whose sine is specified as the x value. The x argument must be between -1 and 1; otherwise, the program will return an ERR value. This angle is measured in radians. To convert from radians to degrees, multiply the value returned by 180/@PI.

EXAMPLES

The @ASIN function is the inverse of the @SIN function in Lotus 1-2-3. You can demonstrate this by first entering a formula to derive the sine:

@SIN(45 * @PI/180) = 0.707106781

Then use the @ASIN function to return the angle of the value calculated above:

@ASIN(0.707106781) * 180/@PI = 45

The @ASIN function is often useful in solving right triangles when you need to determine the angle and know only the length of some of the sides. For instance, in a right triangle where you know that the opposite side of the right triangle measures 5 feet and the hypotenuse measures 13 feet, you can determine angle θ by using the @ASIN function as follows:

@ASIN(5/13) * 180/@PI = 26.61986

The angle is approximately 26.62 degrees.

@ACOS

The @ACOS function returns the arc cosine, an angle measured in radians, from the cosine specified as its argument.

SYNTAX

@ACOS(x)

where x is the cosine of the angle to be solved for. The x argument can be a value input in the function, referenced by cell address, or calculated by formula.

USAGE

The @ACOS function returns the arc cosine, or the angle whose cosine is specified as the x value. The x argument must be between −1 and 1; otherwise, the program will return an ERR value. This angle is measured in radians. To convert from radians to degrees, multiply the value returned by 180/@PI.

EXAMPLES

The @ACOS function is the inverse of the @COS function in Lotus 1-2-3. You can demonstrate this by first entering a formula to derive the cosine:

@COS(90*@PI/180) = 3.4061E−19

Then use the @ACOS function to return the angle of the value calculated above:

@ACOS(3.4061E−19)*180/@PI = 90

The @ACOS function is often useful in solving right triangles when you need to determine the angle and know only the length of some of the sides. For instance, in a right triangle where you know that the adjacent side of the right triangle measures 12 feet and the hypotenuse measures 13 feet, you can determine angle θ by using the @ACOS function as follows:

@ACOS(12/13)*180/@PI = 26.61986

The angle is approximately 26.62 degrees.

@ATAN

The @ATAN function returns the arc tangent, an angle measured in radians, from the tangent specified as its argument.

SYNTAX

@ATAN(x)

where x is the tangent of the angle to be solved for. The x argument can be a value input in the function, referenced by cell address, or calculated by formula.

USAGE

The @ATAN function returns the arc tangent, or the angle whose tangent is specified as the x value. This angle is measured in radians. To convert from radians to degrees, multiply the value returned by 180/@PI.

EXAMPLES

The @ATAN function is the inverse of the @TAN function in Lotus 1-2-3. You can demonstrate this by first entering a formula to derive the tangent:

@TAN(60*@PI/180) = 1.732050807

Then use the @ATAN function to return the angle of the value calculated above:

@ATAN(A5)*180/@PI = 60

The @ATAN function is often useful in solving right triangles when you need to determine the angle and know only the length of some of the sides. For instance, in a right triangle where you know that the opposite side of the right triangle measures 5 feet and the adjacent side measures 12 feet, you can determine angle θ by using the @ATAN function as follows:

@ATAN(5/12)*180/@PI = 26.61986

The angle is approximately 26.62 degrees.

@ATAN2 (Release 2 Only)

The @ATAN2 function returns the four-quadrant arc tangent, an angle measured in radians, from the values for x and y specified as its arguments.

SYNTAX

@ATAN2(x,y)

where x and y are numeric values input into the function, referenced by cell address, or calculated by formula.

USAGE

The @ATAN2 function allows you to calculate the value of the arc tangent (that is, the angle in radians) by specifying the x and y coordinates in a four-quadrant system instead of using the value of the tangent, as with @ATAN. The result returned by the program will be between $-\pi$ and π. If you specify both x and y as 0, Lotus 1-2-3 returns an ERR value.

The formula for deriving the arc tangent is y/x, where x is not equal to 0. To derive the arc tangent, you specify the values of x and y separated by a comma as arguments of the function. The range of values that will be returned by the function depends on the sign (and thus, the quadrant) of x and y, as can be seen in Table 11.4.

EXAMPLES

The relationship between quadrants and the values of x and y in the four-quadrant system is illustrated in Figure 11.4. You can see that if x and y are greater than zero (positive), the angle lies somewhere in quadrant I. If x is negative and y is positive, the angle lies somewhere in quadrant II. If both x and y are negative, the angle is in quadrant III, and if x is positive and y is negative, it is in quadrant IV. Therefore, as defined by the formula tan $\theta = y/x$, angles in quadrants I and III are positive and angles in quadrants II and IV are negative.

In the examples shown in this figure, you can see how this new Lotus 1-2-3 function is used to calculate specific angles. Compare the arc tangent values returned in these four cases (range A16..A19) with the expected range of values in Table 11.4. Also notice the relationship between the tangent values returned by using the @TAN function to the arc tangent values returned by @ATAN2 and the rule given above.

SIGN OF x	SIGN OF y	RANGE OF RESULTS
Positive	Positive	0 to $\pi/2$
Positive	Negative	$\pi/2$ to π
Negative	Negative	$-\pi$ to $-\pi/2$
Negative	Positive	$-\pi/2$ to 0

TABLE 11.4: The Relationship between the Signs of x and y Values and the Results Returned by @ATAN2

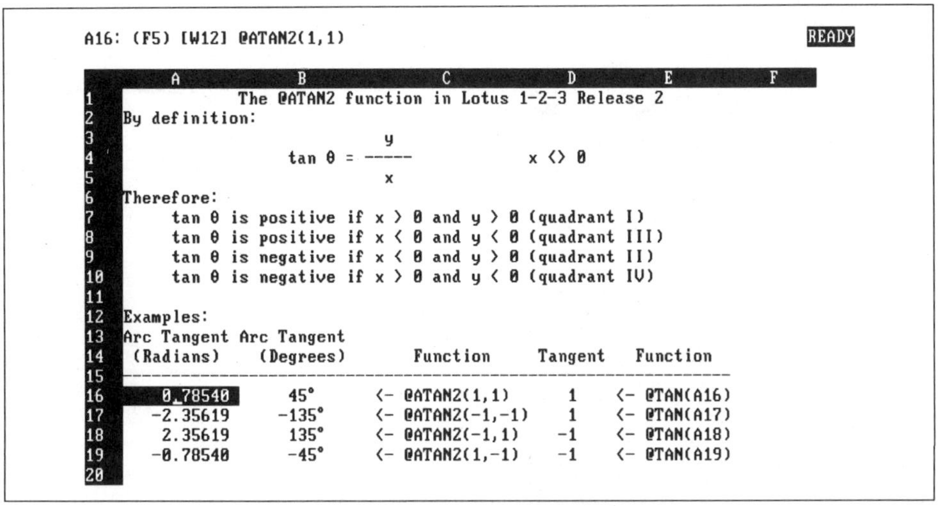

FIGURE 11.4: The @ATAN2 function in Release 2. The tangent of an angle can be defined by the formula y/x, where x is not equal to zero. The examples in this figure illustrate the relationship between this and the four-quadrant system used by Lotus 1-2-3's @ATAN2 function.

SUMMARY

In this chapter, we have looked at a specialized group of functions generally referred to as mathematical and trigonometric functions. In many cases they are not used alone but are combined with other Lotus 1-2-3 functions, especially logical functions, in actual worksheet applications. The following references give you some suggestions on where to locate information that will help you combine these functions efficiently in your applications.

For general information on creating formulas using Lotus 1-2-3 functions:

- Chapter 10, "Working with Formulas and Functions"

For information about the Lotus 1-2-3 logical functions:

- Chapter 15, "Logical Functions"

For information about how to avoid errors when using these and related functions in your applications:

- Chapter 19, "Spreadsheet Models, Error Trapping, and Recalculation"

For information on how to create graphs with the data returned by mathematical and scientific functions:

- Chapter 24, "Creating and Using Graphs"

CHAPTER 12

Statistical Functions

STATISTICAL FUNCTIONS

This chapter examines the group of seven functions called statistical functions: @SUM, @AVG, @COUNT, @MAX, @MIN, @STD, and @VAR. Their basic purpose is to give you specific measurements computed from a quantity of values in your spreadsheet.

Despite what the name implies, with the exception of the specialized @STD (standard deviation) and @VAR (variance) functions, this group of Lotus 1-2-3 functions is employed in a wider variety of applications in the worksheet than those normally considered to be "statistical" in the sense that this term is narrowly understood and used within the field of statistics.

In fact, the @SUM function is one of the most frequently needed of all of the Lotus 1-2-3 @ functions used by spreadsheet designers. It is used in preference to creating formulas consisting of anything more than simple cell addition (+A1 +B1) wherever totaling is required in the spreadsheet. Very few financial applications that you design with Lotus 1-2-3 will not use this function.

For those of you who build applications requiring statistical analysis of any type of sample populations of data, you will find that these functions represent only part of the tools that Lotus 1-2-3 offers for sophisticated statistical modeling. You will also want to become familiar with the information on the /Data Distribution, Matrix, and Regression commands in Chapter 22.

Reference entries for each of the seven statistical functions follow a discussion of the functions and the arguments they require. The functions are listed in the order @SUM, @AVG, @COUNT, @MAX, @MIN, @STD, and @VAR. This arrangement roughly represents a ranking from the most general purpose to the most specialized of these functions. Using this system allows the @STD and @VAR functions, which are functionally related to one another and whose use is most often required in the same spreadsheet, to be grouped together.

ARGUMENTS OF THE STATISTICAL FUNCTIONS

All of the functions in this group accept a list of values as their arguments. Here *list* means a listing of constants or cell references, separated by commas. These cell references can consist of single cell values, ranges of values, or a combination of the two. When you use a cell range that has been assigned a range name, you can enter the range name in the argument list instead of giving the cell addresses of the range. When you enter the cell addresses of a range, you can indicate them either by typing in the addresses or by pointing to them.

Because their arguments accept lists, you can use any of these functions to obtain statistics about discontinuous cells and cell ranges. This makes it possible to use a function like @AVG to find the average of the values in two cell ranges located in different parts of the worksheet by constructing a single formula. For example, if you need to know the average value in the cell ranges B5..B25 and AA40..AA60, you could construct the formula @AVG(B5..B25,AA40..AA60).

Labels and Values in Argument Lists

Strings (cell entries made in LABEL mode) carry the equivalent of a zero value as far as all of the statistical functions (with the exception of @COUNT) are concerned. This means that when a label is included in the argument list when using the @SUM function, its presence does not increase the calculated total. If a label is included when using the @MAX function, any value in the list will be considered higher than it, so the correct maximum value will always be returned. However, if a label is included when using the @MIN function, it will be returned as the minimum value if no other zero value has been entered or calculated in the list. This means that the presence of a label entry in the @MIN argument list can skew the correct minimum value.

LABELS AND VALUES IN THE @COUNT ARGUMENT LIST

The @COUNT function computes the number of nonblank cell entries in the argument list. By definition, this means that it uses the label entries as well as the values in the argument list to calculate its result. Because of this, you should avoid including cells that contain underscores when you need a count of the number of values in columns of figures.

Three other statistical functions—@AVG, @STD, and @VAR—use the @COUNT function in their calculations. Their results are also affected if a label entry is included in their argument lists. Figure 12.1 illustrates this by contrasting the results obtained by using the various statistical functions on a range consisting of three values and a blank cell with those obtained on a range consisting of the same three values and a repeating label.

Blank Cells and Values in Argument Lists

Blank cells in the spreadsheet carry the numeric value of zero. When they are included with values in the argument lists of the statistical functions, they do not affect the calculated results. However, if the argument list consists of a blank cell alone, you will receive ERR values when using all

```
A1:                                                                  READY

        A         B         C         D         E         F         G         H
1     _    :
2         3 :<- Range A1..A4                   3 :<- Range E2..E5
3         4 :   includes one blank             4 :   includes 1 label
4         5 :   cell & 3 values                5 :   & 3 values
5                                     ---------:
6
7        12 <---- @SUM(A1..A4)                12 <---- @SUM(E2..E5)
8         4 <---- @AVG(A1..A4)                 3 <---- @AVG(E2..E5)
9         3 <-- @COUNT(A1..A4)                 4 <-- @COUNT(E2..E5)
10        5 <---- @MAX(A1..A4)                 5 <---- @MAX(E2..E5)
11        3 <---- @MIN(A1..A4)                 0 <---- @MIN(E2..E5)
12 0.816496 <---- @STD(A1..A4)          1.870828 <---- @STD(E2..E5)
13 0.666666 <---- @VAR(A1..A4)               3.5 <---- @VAR(E2..E5)
14
15
16
17
18
19
20
20-Aug-86  05:59 PM
```

FIGURE 12.1: In this figure, the results obtained from the statistical functions when their arguments are a range that includes a label and values are contrasted to the results obtained when their arguments are a range that includes a blank cell and the same values. In column A, the cell range A1..A4, given as the argument for all seven statistical functions, includes a blank cell and three values. In column E, the cell range E2..E5, given as the argument for the same functions, includes the same three values and a repeating label. Notice that the @COUNT result in column E is 4 because the label is counted with the numbers, while in column A it is 3 because the blank cell is not counted. Accordingly, the @AVG, @STD, and @VAR results in column E do not match those returned in column A. Also, the @MIN result in this column is 0 (the value of the repeating underscores in cell E5) instead of 3, the lowest value returned in the comparable function in column A.

of the statistical functions except for @SUM and @COUNT. These two functions return a value of zero when their argument lists contain only empty cells.

Blank Cells in the @COUNT Argument List

There is one anomaly you should be aware of: when the argument list of the @COUNT function contains cell references or cell ranges that consist of a single blank cell, Lotus 1-2-3 returns a count of one even though it returns the expected zero count when the ranges consist of multiple blank cells.

Figure 12.2 illustrates this by showing three examples of using the @COUNT function with references to empty cells in the argument list. In the first example in cell A4, the argument of the @COUNT function is the

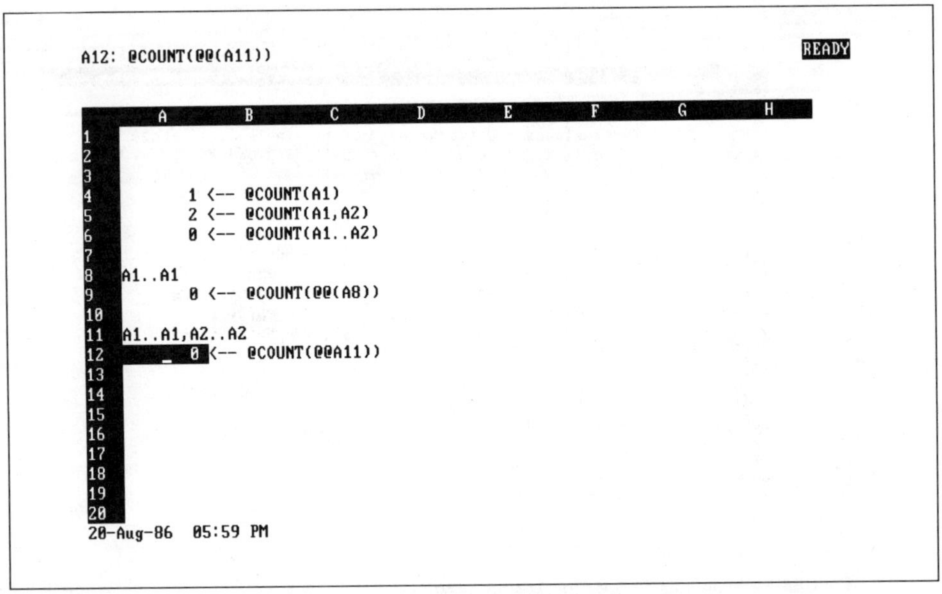

FIGURE 12.2: Results obtained when different blank cell entries are used as the arguments of the @COUNT function. In the first example, supplying the single blank cell A1 as the argument returns a result of 1. In the second example, entering two single references to the blank cells A1 and A2 causes the count to increase to 2. However, when the same two blank cells are referred to in a single multiple-cell range, as in the third example, the count becomes 0. The two examples below this show how you can force the @COUNT function to return a zero count of the same cell references as in the first two examples by using the @@ function (see text for explanation of how this works).

single blank cell A1, which returns a count of 1. (You cannot counteract this result by entering the argument as A1..A1, because Lotus 1-2-3 immediately converts it to the single cell reference A1). In the second example in cell A5, the argument list has been expanded to include a listing of two blank cells, A1 and A2, which increases the count to 2. However, if these two cell references are entered as the range A1..A2, as in the third example in cell A6, the count returned is 0.

The last two examples in cells A9 and A12 show you how to counteract this idiosyncracy of the @COUNT function. This is done by using the @@ function (available only in Release 2), which in the first example in A9 directs the @COUNT function to use the range reference entered as a label in cell A8 (A1..A1) as its argument. This is entered as @COUNT (@@(A8)). Providing the indirect reference to the blank cell, A1, causes the @COUNT function to return the expected count of zero.

The same thing is done in the second example in A12, only this time the cell reference label entered in A11 contains two single cell ranges separated by a comma (A1..A1,A2..A2). The argument A11 of the @@ function points to this cell range label, causing the @COUNT function to use single cell ranges instead of single cell references and thus to return the expected result of zero.

THE @COUNT FUNCTION IN MACROS

It is a common practice to place the condition

/XI@COUNT(range) = 0~/XQ

(or a variation of it) in a macro to cause it to stop after processing an entire range of data when the cell pointer reaches a blank row (indicating the end of the data). Because the @COUNT function will never equal zero if the range consists of only a single blank cell (as demonstrated above), you must make sure that the range you designate for the @COUNT function consists of at least two cells in order to have the technique work properly.

Figure 12.3 offers a good illustration of this point. It shows the same macro listed and discussed in Chapter 7 in the section "Using /Range Justify to Parse Labels in Release 1A." The macro commands shown in this figure automatically parse each of the full names that were originally contained in single cells in column A so that each part of the name is contained in three separate cells in columns A, B, and C. All that is required to have the macro automatically process an entire column of such

```
E27: 'Tudor                                                    SST POINT
Enter range to erase: E27..E27

     A      B    C            D        E      F         G        H
24  Full Name
25  Steven  W.   Smith                 CarCarol  L.        Tudor
26  Barry   L.   Johnson               L.
27  Doris   M.   Olsen                 Tudor
28  David   P.   McGill
29  Carol L. Tudor
30  Peter A. Kaye
31
32
33  \P           /RNCplace~{RIGHT}~
34               /XI@COUNT(place)=0~/RNDplace~/REF25..H25~/XQ
35               {GOTO}E25~/Cplace~~
36               /RJ~
37               /C~{RIGHT}~
38               {DOWN}/C~{RIGHT}{RIGHT}{UP}~
39               {DOWN}/C~{RIGHT}{RIGHT}{RIGHT}{UP}{UP}~
40               /REE25..E27~
41               {GOTO}place~/CF25..H25~~
42               {DOWN}/RNDplace~
43               /XG\P~
                                        STEP
```

FIGURE 12.3: Using the @COUNT function with the macro IF condition (/XI) to stop a macro after it has finished processing data. The purpose of this macro is to parse the long label entered into column A by copying it into a very narrow cell, E25, where the /Range Justify command breaks up the label into the three adjacent cells, E25..E27, whose contents are then copied to cells F25, G25, and H25, respectively. This range is then copied to the appropriate row in column A, and the macro moves the pointer down and begins parsing the next name. The macro has already parsed the first four names in column A and is operating on the fifth, Carol L. Tudor. It will continue to process the rest of these names until it reaches row 31, which was left blank. When the cell pointer moves down to A31, it will create a new range named "place", consisting of cells A31..B31, which are both blank. When the macro processes the second command line, the condition @COUNT=0 will be found TRUE, causing it to delete the range name "place", delete Peter A. Kaye's name in cells F25..H25, and process the Quit command (/XQ).

names is that you position the cell pointer in the cell containing the first name and press Alt-P. As long as there is a blank row after the last name in the column list, the macro will terminate after parsing the last name. (For a discussion of macros and how to write and use them, see Chapters 27–28.)

The key is the second command statement in row 34 of Figure 12.3:

/XI @COUNT(place) = 0 ~ /RNDplace ~ /REF25..H25 ~ /XQ

This command says that if the count of the range named "place" equals zero, delete the range name "place", erase the contents of the range F25..H25 (which still contains parts of the last name processed), and then quit CMD mode and return to READY mode.

The first command line of this macro is the one that creates the range called "place" and designates its extent. The line contains this statement:

/RNCplace~{RIGHT}~

Notice that after giving the command to create a new range name (/RNC) and supplying the name as "place" (some users prefer to call this range "count"), not only the current cell (~) but also the cell to the right ({RIGHT}~) are included in this range.

If it were not for the fact that the @COUNT function returns 1 when its argument is a single blank cell, there would be no reason to extend the "place" range beyond the current cell. This is done only to ensure that the condition in the second command line will be met (@COUNT = 0) when the cell pointer reaches the blank line at the end of the data.

If the first command line designated only the current cell as the "place" range, the macro would not stop when the cell pointer reached the blank row because the result of @COUNT(place) would be 1 instead of 0. The macro would continue to work its way down all the rows of the worksheet (whether or not there were any labels to parse in column A) until it reached the end of the worksheet or until you manually entered the Break command. If you use this kind of technique in your processing macros, be sure that the range supplied as the @COUNT function argument is made up of more than one cell.

The Statistical Functions

The first five of the Lotus 1-2-3 statistical functions—@SUM, @AVG, @COUNT, @MAX, and @MIN—provide you with powerful ways to obtain quantitative data about values in your worksheets. They have wide applications in all types of spreadsheet designs. In fact, no other Lotus 1-2-3 function is required as often as the @SUM function; it is used over and over again to obtain totals in almost every spreadsheet application.

The last two functions in the group, @STD and @VAR, are closely related to each other. They have more specialized applications for calculating frequency distributions. Both standard deviation (@STD) and variance (@VAR) use the measurement of the mean (the technically correct term in statistics for the average returned by @AVG) to compute how much each individual value in a sample deviates from it. The smaller the values returned by either of these functions, the closer each value is to the mean and, therefore, the less the deviation.

@SUM

The @SUM function adds all of the values contained in the list given as its argument. It returns this total in the cell where the function is entered.

SYNTAX

@SUM(list)

where list consists of single cells, cell ranges, or a combination of the two, separated by commas. The cells in the list can represent literal values, cell references, or range names. The cell ranges in the list can represent cell references or range names.

If the list contains some blank cells or cells that contain labels (which carry a value of zero), this has no effect on the total. If the list consists of all blank cells, the total returned will be 0.

USAGE

The @SUM function calculates totals of any values entered or calculated in the worksheet. To use the @SUM function, locate the pointer in the cell where you want the total to appear, type in **@SUM(**, and then enter the list of cells and/or cell ranges to be summed either by typing their addresses or by using the pointing method. If you are summing a number of discontinuous cells or cell ranges, type a comma after entering each of them. After you have completed entering the list of arguments, type) and press the Return key. If you forget to enter the right parenthesis, Lotus 1-2-3 will beep at you and go into EDIT mode when you press the Return key.

While @SUM is the equivalent of constructing a formula that adds a series of cells using cell addresses separated by the addition operator (+), it is used in preference to creating such a formula because it allows you to change the argument list without editing the formula.

For instance, if you need to know the total of the three cells B1, B2, and B3, you could enter the formula

+ B1 + B2 + B3

in cell B5. However, if you enter the formula with the @SUM function as

@SUM(B1..B3)

you have more latitude when making certain revisions to this range. For example, if you add a row at the current row 2 with the /Worksheet Insert Row command and then enter a value in the blank cell in B2, the value will automatically be included in a new updated total in B5 if B5 contained the @SUM function, whereas the new value would not be picked up in the addition formula.

To see why, contrast the effect that inserting a new row in row 2 has on each of the formulas. The addition formula becomes

+ B1 + B3 + B4

after the cell references are adjusted to accommodate the new blank row. In contrast, the @SUM formula becomes

@SUM(B1..B4)

so that a new value entered into cell B2 is automatically included in the argument range and is therefore included as part of the total. You would have to edit the first formula to reflect this change.

To maintain even greater flexibility in totals returned by the @SUM function, it is a common practice to include one extra cell at the end of the cell range as part of the argument list. This cell is often left blank or includes repeating underscores to separate the values to be summed from the cell containing their totals. This technique allows you to add new values later at the end of the range and have them automatically included in the total without editing the original @SUM formula.

You make room for these new values (by using the /Move command or inserting new columns or rows) by changing the position of the last cell in the argument list. You would enter the original @SUM example listed previously as @SUM(B1..B3) as @SUM(B1..B4) instead. Because cell B4, like all empty cells, carries a zero value, its inclusion in the range has no effect on the resulting total. (The same would be true if B4 contained a label, such as a repeating underscore.)

If more values were then to be added to this column of figures, cells B4 and B5 would be moved down an appropriate number of rows to allow for the new entries. As entries are made in the new blank cells above, the total is recalculated (assuming that the automatic recalculation default is still in effect).

While the @SUM function is more frequently used to independently total ranges of data in columns or across rows, it can also be used to sum all of the data in a table by giving the beginning and ending cell addresses of the table as the function's argument. Because @SUM accepts a list as its argument, you can also set up one formula to sum discontinuous cell entries or ranges in the spreadsheet (see Figure 12.4).

EXAMPLES

Figure 12.4 illustrates how the @SUM function can be used to total different ranges of values, and Figure 12.5 demonstrates how you can add values to ranges without revising the original @SUM formula.

@AVG

The @AVG function calculates the average (i.e., the mean or $\overline{X}$) of the values contained in the list given as its argument. It returns this average in the cell where the function is entered.

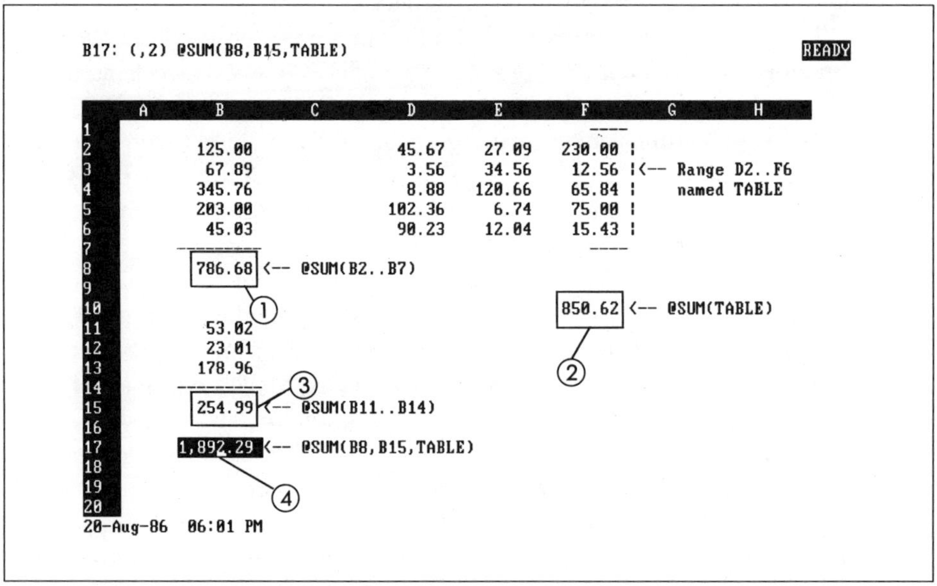

FIGURE 12.4: Examples using the @SUM function. Total 1 in column B sums the range B2..B7, which includes the repeating underscore label to allow for later addition to the values. Total 2 sums a table of values that have been given the range name TABLE. As you can see, this range name has been entered as the argument of the function. Total 4 demonstrates how you can sum separate cells and cell ranges with a single formula.

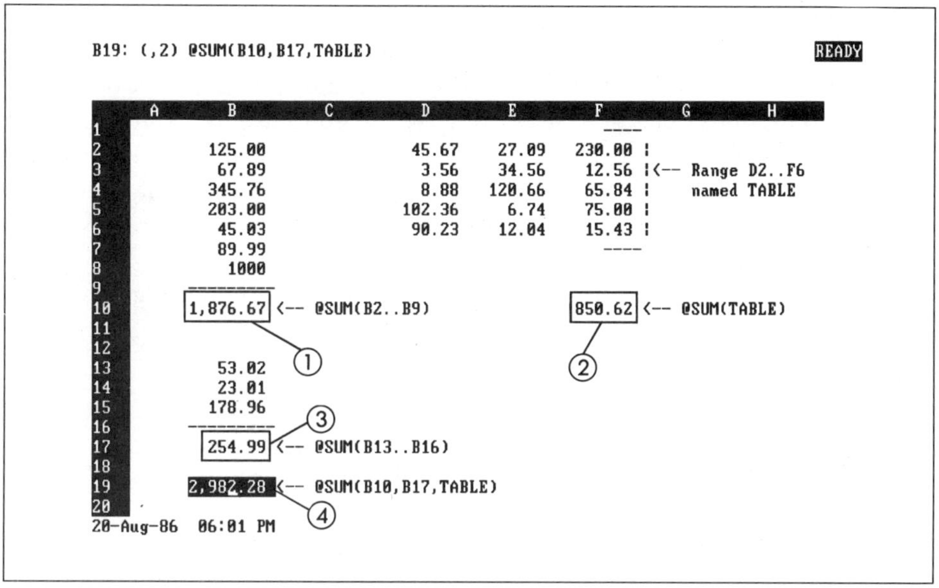

FIGURE 12.5: Adding new values to ranges totaled with the @SUM function without having to revise the original argument. In this figure, two new values in cells B7 and B8 have been added to the range summed in Total 1. This was done by moving the repeating underscores, the @SUM formula, and the rest of the entries in column B down two cells. As soon as the new values were entered in the new blank cells in B7 and B8, the sums in Total 1 and Total 4 were automatically updated to reflect their addition.

SYNTAX

@AVG(list)

where list consists of single cells, cell ranges, or a combination of the two, separated by commas. The cells in the list can represent literal values, cell references, or range names. The cell ranges in the list can represent cell references or range names.

If the list contains blank cells as well as values, these empty cells have no adverse effect on the correct average of the values. If the list contains labels as well as values, the labels will be counted, thus skewing the average returned. If the list consists of blank cells, the average returned will be ERR.

USAGE

The @AVG function calculates the mean ($\overline{X}$) of individual values in a spreadsheet. To use @AVG, locate the pointer in the cell where you want the average to appear, type in **@AVG(**, and enter the list of cells and/or cell ranges to be averaged either by typing their addresses or by using the pointing method. If you are finding the average of a number of discontinuous cells or cell ranges, type a comma after entering each of them. After you have completed entering the list of arguments, type **)** and press the Return key. If you forget to enter the right parenthesis, Lotus 1-2-3 will beep at you and go into EDIT mode when you press the Return key.

In statistics, the mean, popularly referred to as the average, is defined as

$$\overline{X} = \frac{\Sigma X}{N}$$

where ΣX is the sum of all the raw scores in the sample and N is the number of scores. In Lotus 1-2-3, this formula could be represented by the following:

@AVG(list) = @SUM(list)/@COUNT(list)

It is important to understand the practical ramifications of how Lotus 1-2-3 defines and calculates the average. While the @SUM function argument can contain labels whose zero values do not affect the resulting total, their presence in the @COUNT argument affects the resulting number because @COUNT calculates the number of nonblank cells. This means that if the list you use as the argument of an @AVG function contains labels, the result obtained will be skewed by their presence (see Figure 12.6 for an example). You must be careful that cells containing values in an @AVG list do not become converted to labels.

EXAMPLES

Figure 12.6 illustrates several examples using the @AVG function.

@COUNT

The @COUNT function counts the nonblank cells contained in the list given as its argument. It returns this number in the cell where the function is entered.

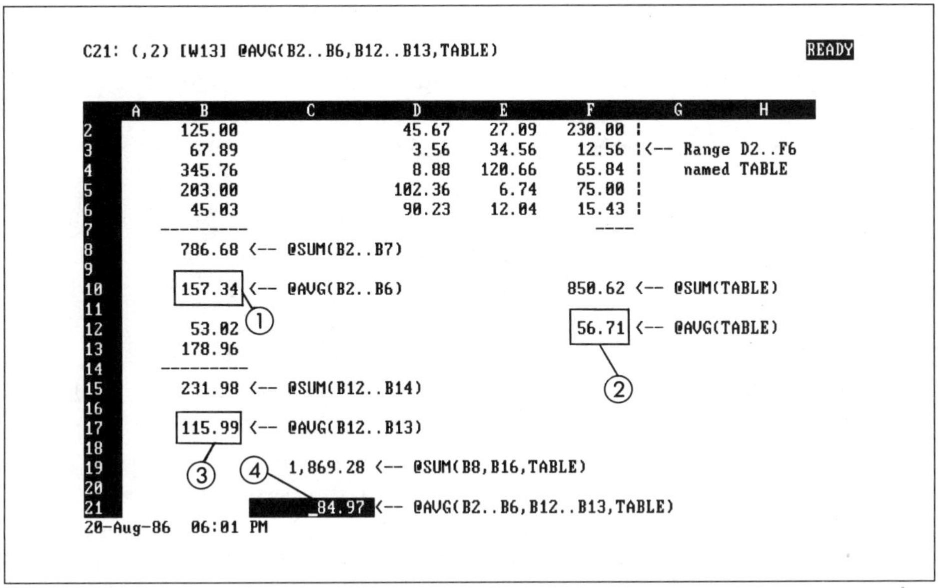

FIGURE 12.6: Examples using the @AVG function. In this figure, the totals used in Figures 12.4 and 12.5 have had formulas added to determine the average value in each range. In Averages 1 and 3, the argument of the @AVG function has been modified so that it includes only the range of values, because including the cell with the repeating label would return an incorrect average value. Average 2 illustrates calculating an average on a table of values. Notice that the @AVG formula in Average 4 gives the entire range either by cell addresses or range name for all of the values that are to be used.

SYNTAX

@COUNT(list)

where list consists of single cells, cell ranges, or a combination of the two, separated by commas. If the list contains blank cells as well as values, the empty cells have no adverse effect on the correct count of the nonblank cells. If the list contains labels as well as values, the labels will be counted along with all values in the number returned. If the list consists of a range of blank cells, the count returned will be 0. If the list consists of a single blank cell, the count returned will be 1.

USAGE

The @COUNT function is most often used to obtain a count of the number of individual entries contained in the given listing. It is important to remember that if you want to know the number of values within the list, you must make sure that no label entries are included within it. This means that you must be careful to avoid including labels like repeating underscores in the ranges specified in the argument list.

To use @COUNT, locate the pointer in the cell where you want the number to appear, type in **@COUNT(**, and enter the list of cells and/or cell ranges to be averaged either by typing their addresses or by pointing to them. If you are finding the count of a number of discontinuous cells or cell ranges, type a comma after entering each of them. After you have completed entering the list of arguments, type) and press the Return key. If you forget to enter the right parenthesis, Lotus 1-2-3 will beep at you and go into EDIT mode when you press the Return key.

The @COUNT function exhibits an inconsistency when dealing with argument lists that consist of only blank cells. If the list specified contains a range of multiple blank cells, the result obtained from using the @COUNT function is zero. However, if the range consists of a single blank cell, the result obtained will be 1. (For more information on this and its effect on using the @COUNT function to terminate macros, refer back to the section "The @COUNT Function in Macros.")

EXAMPLES

Figure 12.7 illustrates several examples using the @COUNT function.

```
B15: (G) @COUNT(B1..B6,B8,TABLE)                                      READY

     A      B           C         D        E        F        G        H
1                                                 ----
2        125.00                 45.67    27.09   230.00 ¦
3         67.89                  3.56    34.56    12.56 ¦<-- Range D2..F6
4        345.76                  8.88   120.66    65.84 ¦    named TABLE
5        203.00                102.36     6.74    75.00 ¦
6         45.03                 90.23    12.04    15.43 ¦
7      ---------                                  ----
8        786.68 <-- @SUM(B2..B7)
9
10            6 <-- @COUNT(B2..B7)            15 <-- @COUNT(TABLE)
11
12            5 <-- @COUNT(B2..B6)
13
14
15         _ 21 <-- @COUNT(B1..B6,B8,TABLE)
```

FIGURE 12.7: Examples of using the @COUNT function. In this figure, the @COUNT function is used in four examples to show how it counts nonblank cells in its argument list. Notice the difference between the count when the range includes the repeating label (B7) and when it doesn't. There are six nonblank cells above the total, but only five values are being totaled. Any time you want to know the number of values in a list, you must be sure that the list does not include label entries.

@MAX

The @MAX function determines the highest (i.e., the maximum) of the values contained in the list given as its argument. It returns this value in the cell where the function is entered.

SYNTAX

@MAX(list)

where list consists of single cells, cell ranges, or a combination of the two, separated by commas. If the list contains blank cells or labels as well as values, the empty cells or labels have no adverse effect on the correct highest value. If the list consists of blank cells, the value returned will be ERR.

USAGE

The @MAX function finds the maximum of the individual values in the cells or cell ranges specified as its argument by comparing all of the values in the list to one another and then returning the highest value. If the cell where the @MAX function is entered has not been changed to the same display format as the cells and cell ranges in the argument list, the display of the maximum value returned will not match that of the maximum value in the list.

To use @MAX, locate the pointer in the cell where you want the maximum to appear, type in **@MAX(**, and enter the list of cells and/or cell ranges to be compared either by typing their addresses or by using the pointing method. If you are finding the maximum number among discontinuous cells or cell ranges, type a comma after entering each of them. After you have completed entering the list of arguments, type) and press the Return key. If you forget to enter the right parenthesis, Lotus 1-2-3 will beep at you and go into EDIT mode when you press the Return key.

EXAMPLES

Figure 12.8 illustrates several examples using the @MAX function.

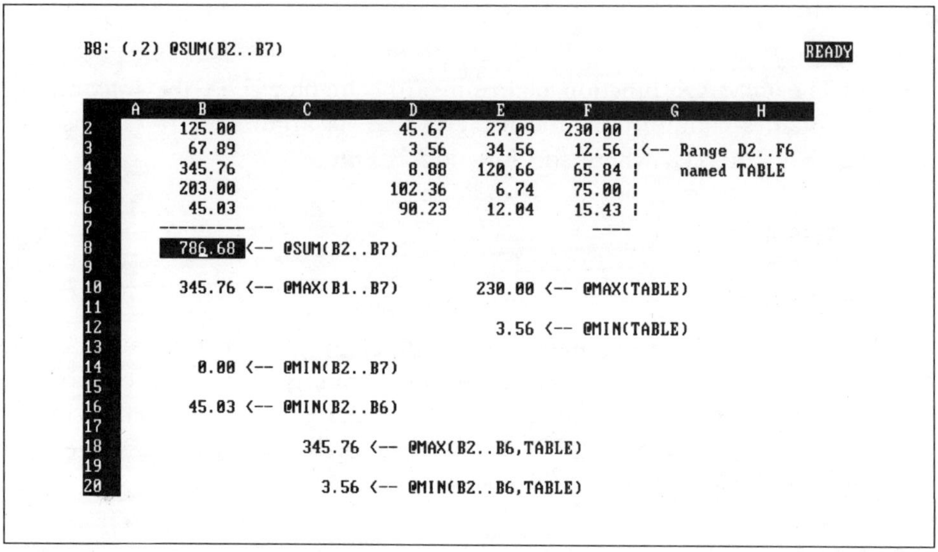

FIGURE 12.8: Examples of using the @MAX and @MIN functions. This figure contains several @MAX and @MIN functions that return the highest and lowest values in the range or list of values given as their arguments. It also demonstrates that the @MIN function can be skewed if the list includes blank cells or cells that contain labels. In either case, zero will be returned as the minimum value. In these examples, including the label in cell B7 has skewed the results in B14; 45.03 (in B16) is the correct minimum value for the range.

@MIN

The @MIN function determines the lowest (i.e., the minimum) of the values contained in the list given as its argument. It returns this value in the cell where the function is entered.

SYNTAX

@MIN(list)

where list consists of single cells, cell ranges, or a combination of the two, separated by commas. If the list contains blank cells or labels as well as values, zero will be returned as the minimum value.

USAGE

The @MIN function finds the minimum of the individual values in the cells or cell ranges specified as its argument by comparing all of the values in the list to one another and then returning the lowest value. If the cell where the @MIN function is entered has not been changed to the same display format as the cells and cell ranges in the argument list, the display of the minimum value returned will not match that of the minimum value in the list.

To use @MIN, locate the pointer in the cell where you want the minimum value to appear, type in **@MIN(**, and enter the list of cells and/or cell ranges to be compared either by typing their addresses or by using the pointing method. If you are finding the minimum number among discontinuous cells or cell ranges, type a comma after entering each of them. Be careful not to include blank cells or labels in the list of arguments, or @MIN will return zero regardless of the other values in the list. After you have completed entering the list of arguments, type **)** and press the Return key. If you forget to enter the right parenthesis, Lotus 1-2-3 will beep at you and go into EDIT mode when you press the Return key.

EXAMPLES

For examples of how to use the @MIN function, refer to Figure 12.8.

@STD

The @STD function calculates the standard deviation (i.e., *S*) of the values contained in the list given as its argument. It returns this value in the cell where the function is entered.

SYNTAX

@STD(list)

where list consists of single cells, cell ranges, or a combination of the two, separated by commas. If the list contains blank cells as well as values, the empty cells have no adverse effect on the correct standard deviation of the values. If the list contains labels as well as values, the labels will be counted, thus skewing the standard deviation. If the list consists of blank cells, the standard deviation returned will be ERR.

USAGE

Standard deviation measures the degree to which each individual score in a sample varies from the mean of the scores in the sample. As a fairly stable measurement of variability within a random sample of a population, it represents a frequently used statistic.

To use @STD, locate the pointer in the cell where you want the standard deviation to appear, type in **@STD(**, and enter the list of cells and/or cell ranges that represents values to be used either by typing their addresses or by pointing to them. If you are finding the standard deviation among values in discontinuous cells or cell ranges, type a comma after entering each of them. After you have completed entering the list of arguments, type) and press the Return key. If you forget to enter the right parenthesis, Lotus 1-2-3 will beep at you and go into EDIT mode when you press the Return key.

The standard formula for finding the standard deviation is

$$S = \sqrt{\frac{\Sigma x^2}{N}}$$

where x is the deviation score or the difference between X (the raw score) and $\overline{X}$ (the mean score), Σx^2 is the sum of individual deviation scores, and N is the number of raw scores.

Note: The formula for determining variance is identical to this one except that it does not use the radical. Variance is equal to the square of the standard deviation, so @VAR(list) = @STD(list)^2. This means that once you have found the standard deviation within a sample with the @STD function, you can then determine the variance by squaring the value of the standard deviation.

In Lotus 1-2-3, the @STD function can be represented by the following equation:

$$@STD = \sqrt{\frac{\Sigma(V_n - AVG)^2}{N}}$$

where V_n represents the nth value in the list, AVG is the mean of the values in the list returned by the @AVG function, and N is the number of values in the list.

Many statisticians use the quantity $N - 1$ rather than N when computing sample variance; $N - 1$ gives the number of degrees of freedom (the number of scores that are free to vary) in the calculation of the standard deviation. To do this in Lotus 1-2-3, you enter the following formula using the @VAR function:

@SQRT(@COUNT(list)/(@COUNT(list) – 1)* @VAR(list))

Remember when using the @STD function that labels in the cells and cell ranges in the argument list will skew the variance. When using the formula above to obtain an unbiased estimate of the population parameter, single empty cells or labels in the list will skew the result.

EXAMPLES

Figure 12.9 illustrates several examples using the @STD function.

```
H19: (F3) @COUNT(PUBF)/(@COUNT(PUBF)-1)*@VAR(PUBF)                    READY

     A        B          C          D          E          F          G          H
1             PUBLICATION CIRCULATION BY SELECTED SIC CATEGORIES
2
3           Total                 Primary SIC's                Primary SIC Ratings
4    Pub.   Circ.          34         35         36         34         35         36
5    ========================================================================
6     A       45,200     15,150      6,000      3,201        12          8         11
7     B       62,300     12,300      8,654      4,655        10         12         10
8     C       22,560      6,300      2,205      1,754         7          4          5
9     D        7,450      2,175      1,305        680         0          0          0
10    E       19,200      4,476      2,740      1,250         4          9          3
11    F       36,820      8,672      8,530      6,450         8         10          2
12
13                        Pub A      Pub B      Pub C      Pub D      Pub E      Pub F
14            X̄     =    10.333     10.667      5.333      0.000      5.333      6.667
15            S     =     1.700      0.943      1.247      0.000      2.625      3.399
16            S^2   =     2.889      0.889      1.556      0.000      6.889     11.556
17
18   S (unbiased)   =     2.082      1.155      1.528      0.000      3.215      4.163
19   S^2 (unbiased) =     4.333      1.333      2.333      0.000     10.333     17.333
20
20-Aug-86  06:02 PM
```

FIGURE 12.9: Examples of using the @STD and @VAR functions. In this figure, primary SIC ratings for codes 34, 35, and 36 for six publications (A–F) are subjected to frequency distribution analysis using the @AVG, @STD, and @VAR functions (both biased and unbiased). First, the mean score for each publication is found with the @AVG function, followed by the standard deviation with @STD and variance with @VAR. Below these results, the formulas for obtaining an unbiased standard deviation and variance are used to obtain slightly different deviation scores (the one for unbiased variance is shown in the Control Panel). Notice that even though publications C and E have the same mean score, publication C's ratings vary much less from this mean.

@VAR

The @VAR function calculates the variance (i.e., S^2) of the values contained in the list given as its argument. It returns this value in the cell where the function is entered.

SYNTAX

@VAR(list)

where list consists of single cells, cell ranges, or a combination of the two, separated by commas. If the list contains blank cells as well as values, the empty cells have no adverse effect on the correct variance. If the list contains labels as well as values, the labels will be counted, thus skewing the variance returned. If the list consists of blank cells, the variance returned will be ERR.

USAGE

Variance, like standard deviation, measures the degree to which each individual score in a sample varies from the mean of the scores in the sample. Variance is often used in analysis of variance (ANOVA), which requires multimean comparisons such as the F test comparing the ratio of one variance to another.

To use @VAR, locate the pointer in the cell where you want the variance to appear, type in **@VAR(**, and enter the list of cells and/or cell ranges that contain all of values to be used either by typing their addresses or by pointing to them. If you are finding the standard deviation among values in discontinuous cells or cell ranges, type a comma after entering each of them. After you have completed entering the list of arguments, type **)** and press the Return key. If you forget to enter the right parenthesis, Lotus 1-2-3 will beep at you and go into EDIT mode when you press the Return key.

The standard formula for finding the variance is

$$S^2 = \frac{\Sigma x^2}{N}$$

where x is the deviation score or the difference between X (the raw score) and $\overline{X}$ (the mean score), Σx^2 is the sum of the individual deviation scores, and N is the number of raw scores.

Note: The formula for determining standard deviation is identical to this one, except that the entire formula is placed under a radical. Standard deviation is equivalent to the square root of the variance, so @STD(list) =

@SQRT(@VAR(list)). This means that once you have found the variance within a sample with the @VAR function, you can determine the standard deviation by finding its square root with the @SQRT function.

In Lotus 1-2-3, the @VAR function can be represented by the following equation:

$$@VAR = \frac{\Sigma(V_n - AVG)^2}{N}$$

where V_n represents the nth value in the list, AVG is the mean of the values in the list returned by the @AVG function, and N is the number of values in the list.

Many statisticians use the quantity $N - 1$ instead of N when computing sample variance; $N - 1$ gives the number of degrees of freedom (the number of scores that are free to vary) in the calculation of the variance. To do this in Lotus 1-2-3, you would enter the following formula using the @VAR function:

@COUNT(list)/(@COUNT(list) – 1)* @VAR(list))

Remember when using the @VAR function that labels in the cells and cell ranges in the argument list will skew the variance. When using the formula above to obtain an unbiased estimate of the population parameter, single empty cells or labels in the list will skew the result.

EXAMPLES

For examples using the @VAR function to determine the degree of variability in a random sample of raw scores, refer to Figure 12.9.

SUMMARY

This chapter has discussed the use of and applications for the seven statistical functions included in the Lotus 1-2-3 program. The following references give you some suggestions on where to locate related information on statistics in this handbook.

For information on using these same types of statistical functions in a Lotus 1-2-3 database:

- Chapter 16, "Database Statistical Functions"

For information on the Lotus 1-2-3 database statistical commands:

- Chapter 22, "Data Distribution, Matrix, and Regression Commands"

CHAPTER 13

FINANCIAL FUNCTIONS

Financial Functions

This chapter covers the financial functions offered in Lotus 1-2-3. These sophisticated functions are used in a multitude of spreadsheet applications that call for financial analysis concerning cash flows, annuities, and loans.

To the original financial functions of @NPV, @IRR, @PV, @FV, and @PMT offered in the first version of Lotus 1-2-3, Release 2 has added six more: three for analyzing investments—@RATE, @TERM, and @CTERM—and three for determining depreciation—@SLN (the straight-line method), @SYD (the sum-of-the-years'-digits method) and @DDB (the double-declining balance method).

Following the general introduction to the financial functions, you will find individual reference entries for each one. These are presented in this order: @NPV, @IRR, @PV, @FV, @PMT (the financial functions common to both versions of Lotus 1-2-3), followed by @RATE, @TERM, @CTERM, @SLN, @SYD, and @DDB (all of which are found only in Release 2).

Using the Financial Functions

When you use Lotus 1-2-3's financial functions to perform investment calculations, it is important to remember the following points:

- The Lotus 1-2-3 financial functions assume that investments are ordinary annuities—in other words, that a series of equal payments are made and that each payment is made at the end of the period.
- You can enter interest and discount rates in two forms: as a percentage, as in 10.5%, or in the equivalent decimal form, as in .105. The program automatically converts a percentage entered into a cell into its corresponding decimal form. You must therefore use the /Range Format Percent command to display the rates as percentages in the spreadsheet.

- You must express the interest or discount rate and the term in the same periods of time to obtain the correct result. To convert a yearly interest rate into monthly equivalents, divide the rate by 12. To convert a term expressed in years to the corresponding number of months, multiply it by 12.

FINANCIAL FUNCTIONS IN RELEASE 1A

Release 2 has added new financial functions that calculate the compound growth rate required for an investment to grow to a specified value (@RATE) and the term required to realize future value from a single initial investment (@CTERM) or from a series of equal deposits (@TERM), as well as those that determine depreciation allowances by the three most popular methods: straight line with @SLN, double-declining balance with @DDB, and sum-of-the-years'-digits with @SYD. The latter two methods are ways to determine accelerated depreciation that are generally used (and, at times, required) in computing income tax liability. To use these functions, all you have to do is supply the original cost of the asset (cost), its salvage or residual value (salvage), its estimated useful life (life), and the period for which the depreciation is calculated (period). If you are using Release 1A, you can perform these calculations even without the benefit of the new built-in functions.

To find the formula you must use to calculate each of these, refer to the appropriate reference entry at the end of the chapter. In addition to an explanation of how these functions are used in Release 2, you will find the formulas that Lotus 1-2-3 uses to calculate them. By using these formulas in your spreadsheets, you can obtain accurate results. Methods for determining depreciation expense in Release 1A are explained in the following sections.

Determining Depreciation in Release 1A

If you are still using Release 1A of Lotus 1-2-3, you can set up the appropriate formulas to determine depreciation by any of the three most popular methods. Figure 13.1 shows a template for determining depreciation by straight line, sum-of-the-years'-digits, and double-declining balance for any fixed assest with a useful life of five years.

A20: PR READY

	A	B	C	D	E	F	G	H
1	Original cost		10000		Life		5	
2	Salvage value		500		Depreciable base		9500	
3								
4	Years			1	2	3	4	5
5		Straight-line method						
6	Depreciation percent			0.20	0.20	0.20	0.20	0.20
7	Depreciation			1900.00	1900.00	1900.00	1900.00	1900.00
8	Year-end balance		9500	7600.00	5700.00	3800.00	1900.00	0.00
9								
10		Sum-of-the-years'-digit method						
11	Depreciation percent			0.33	0.27	0.20	0.13	0.07
12	Depreciation			3166.67	2533.33	1900.00	1266.67	663.33
13	Year-end balance		9500	6333.33	3800.00	1900.00	633.33	0.00
14								
15		Double-declining balance method						
16	Depreciation percent			0.40	0.40	0.40	0.40	0.40
17	Declining balance			10000.00	6000.00	3600.00	2160.00	1296.00
18	Depreciation			4000.00	2400.00	1440.00	864.00	796.00
19	Book value			6000.00	3600.00	2160.00	1296.00	500.00
20								

FIGURE 13.1: A spreadsheet template for determining depreciation by the three most common methods: straight line, sum-of-the-years'-digits, and double-declining balance. This template will calculate the depreciation allowance by all three methods for any fixed asset with a useful life of five years. All that is required to reuse it is to change the values for the original cost (C1) and salvage value (C2). See the text for an explanation of the formulas.

THE STRAIGHT-LINE METHOD

The first set of formulas determines the depreciation by the straight-line method, in which the cost less the salvage value (the depreciable base) is multiplied by the fraction of the useful life to determine the depreciation allowance for each year. In this figure, the formula for the depreciable base in G2 is +C1−C2. This figure is brought down to C8 by the formula +G2. The fraction is determined by dividing the useful life by 1 so that the formula in D6 is 1/$G$1, which is copied to range E6..H6.

The formula for calculating the amount of depreciation in D7 is entered as +$C$8*$D$6 and copied to the range E7..H7. The formula for determining the year-end balance in D8 is entered as +C8−D7, which is copied to the range E8..H8.

THE SUM-OF-THE-YEARS'-DIGITS METHOD

The second set of formulas determines depreciation by using the sum-of-the-years'-digits method. In this method, the digits of the useful life period, which in this case is five years, are summed together as @SUM(D4..H4). The depreciation for the first year is then determined by entering the formula 5/@SUM(D4..H4) in D11; the second year's by 4/@SUM(D4..H4) in E11; the third year's by 3/@SUM(D4..H4) in F11; the fourth year's by 2/@SUM(D4..H4) in G11; and the fifth year's by 1/@SUM(D4..H4) in H11.

Then a similar formula for determining the amount of depreciation allowance each year is entered in row 12. In cell D12, the formula +$C$13*D11 is entered and copied to the range E12..H12. Finally, the formula +C13−D12 is entered in D13 and copied to the range E13..H13.

The Double-Declining Balance Method

The last set of formulas in this template uses the double-declining balance method. This method differs from the other two in that it uses the original cost instead of the depreciable base in the first year and must show the salvage value as the book value in the fifth year. It uses a depreciation percent that is double the amount taken when using the straight-line method.

To accomplish this, the formula 2*$D$6 is entered in cell D16 and copied to the range E16..H16. The original cost value in cell C1 is brought forward to cell D17 with the formula +C1. Then the formula for determining the depreciation allowance is entered in D18 as +D16*D17 and copied to the range E18..G18 (notice that it is not copied to H18, which must contain a different formula in order for the book value to equal the salvage value in that year). The book value formula in year 1 is entered in D19 as +D17−D18, and this is copied to the range E19..G19.

Then the formula to bring forward the book value of the previous year is entered into cell E17 as +D19 and is copied to the range F17..H17. Finally, the value for book value in year 5 is entered into H19 as +C2 and the formula for determining the fifth year is entered into H18 as +H17−H19.

This template can then be reused to look at the difference in depreciation allowances for any fixed asset that has a useful life of five years. To do this, all you have to do is input new values for the original cost in C1 and its salvage value in C2. You can also use the underlying formulas illustrated in this five-year example to create templates for assets with various useful life periods, such as 10 and 20 years.

The Financial Functions

The Lotus 1-2-3 financial functions greatly simplify financial analysis by taking sophisticated formulas for performing calculations concerning present value analysis, investment evaluations, and depreciation and presenting them as rather straightforward functions. To make use of them, all that is required is that you understand their underlying assumptions and the individual arguments that each takes.

The following reference entries for each financial function give you this information as well as examples to show how the functions can be applied in your own spreadsheets.

@NPV

This function calculates the net present value of a series of future cash flows according to the discount rate specified.

SYNTAX

@NPV(int,range)

where int is the discount rate and range is the range of values or cells containing values that represent the future cash flows.

USAGE

The @NPV function evaluates a series of future values by adjusting them to determine their present value equivalents. This process is referred to as "discounting to present value." This function is very useful when you are evaluating various investment opportunities to determine the best one.

To use this function, position the cell pointer where you want the NPV value to appear, type in **@NPV(**, and enter the interest rate either by cell reference or as a literal value. If you use a cell reference, you can indicate it by typing in the cell address or range name or by pointing to it. After you indicate the interest rate, type a comma and indicate the range of cells containing the stream of cash flows. When indicating this range, you can again type in the cell addresses or range name or use the pointing method. Type a **)** to complete the function; press Return to have the program calculate the result.

When you use this function, the period of the discount rate (usually annual) must agree with those of the cash flows. Also, to obtain the correct net present value, make sure that the period intervals between the cash flows are constant.

EXAMPLES

For examples of how you can use the @NPV function to evaluate various investment opportunities, see Figure 13.2.

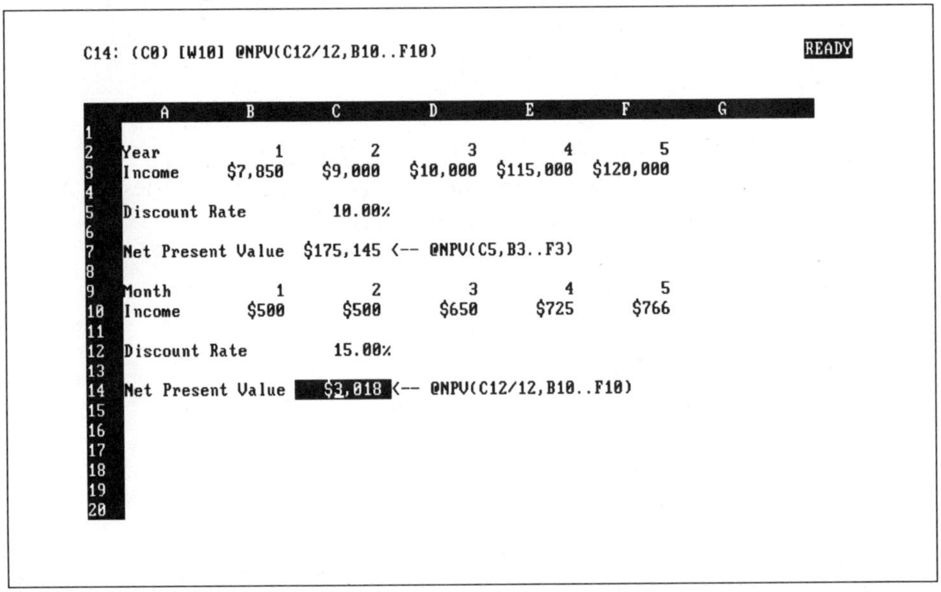

FIGURE 13.2: Calculating the net present value for two series of cash flows by using the @NPV function. In the first example in C7, the term is expressed in years, so the discount rate in C5 (representing the annual periodic interest rate) is entered as the first argument of the function. In the second example in C14, the term is expressed in months, so the annual discount rate in C12 must be divided by 12 as the first argument of the function.

@IRR

This function calculates the internal rate of return or the discount rate at which the present value of an investment outlay is equal to the present value of annual inflows, or a net present value of zero.

SYNTAX

@IRR(guess,range)

where guess is an estimated value between 0 and 1 and range is the range of values representing the cash flows resulting from the investment.

USAGE

The internal rate of return is used to determine the rate of return on a given investment and thus its desirability. The anticipated cash flows from the investment can be even or uneven, but it is assumed that they are received at regular intervals. The first value in the range must be negative.

The internal rate of return can give inconsistent or even misleading indications of the desirability of an investment, especially when the cash flows fluctuate in a series of negative values (as outlays or negative operating inflows other than the initial value in the range) as well as positive values (inflows). Also, remember that the @IRR function assumes that income from the investment is reinvested at the rate of return. When this is not the case, the actual internal rate of return will be less than that indicated by the function.

To arrive at the internal rate of return, you are required to supply a guess value that represents an estimate of the return rate that you expect to realize. It can be anywhere from 0 (0 percent) to 1 (100 percent). However, you should supply a value that is as realistic as possible (in some cases, you can receive a different IRR as the result of supplying a different guess value).

Lotus 1-2-3 calculates the internal rate of return by an iterative method. Using the initial guess value you enter, it refines the approximation by recalculating the formula until the answer converges within .0000001 of the desired result. If the program is unable to do this within 20 iterations (recalculations), you will receive an ERR value as the internal rate of return. In such a case, you may have to supply another initial estimate of the IRR and try again.

To use the @IRR function, move the cell pointer to the cell where you want the internal rate of return to appear in the spreadsheet, type **@IRR(**, and indicate the guess value, which can be entered as a constant or referenced by a cell address. Then type a comma and indicate the range of cells containing the cash flows in the spreadsheet. You can use pointing, type in the cell addresses, or enter a range name if one has been assigned. After indicating the range of cash flows, type) and press the Return key to have the program calculate the value.

EXAMPLES

For an example of using the @IRR function to calculate the internal rate of return for a potential investment opportunity, see Figure 13.3.

```
B7: (P2) [W10] @IRR(B5,B3..G3)                                          READY

          A          B         C         D         E          F         G
1
2  Year                1         2         3         4          5         6
3  Cash flows     ($9,500)   $2,450    $2,670    $1,500     $2,300    $2,750
4
5  Guess value       0.075
6
7  Rate of Return    7.24% <--- @IRR(B5,B3..G3)
8
```

FIGURE 13.3: Calculating the internal rate of return for a series of cash flows by using the @IRR function. This figure demonstrates how to use this function to determine the rate of return on a potential investment that will yield the cash flows held in the range B3..G3. An initial guess rate of 0.075 (7.50 percent) is entered in cell B5. It is then entered as the first argument of the @IRR function in B7. Notice that this estimate was just a bit higher than the actual internal rate of return calculated by the program as 7.24 percent.

@PV

This function calculates the present value of an annuity, given the payment per period and the discount rate over the period of payments specified as the term.

SYNTAX

@PV(pmt,int,term)

where pmt is the payment per period, int is the discount rate, and term is the number of payment periods.

USAGE

The @PV function is used much like @NPV to determine the current value of future payments. However, unlike when using @NPV, the cash flows (specified as the pmt argument) must be equal—thus the difference in the arguments required by the function. Like @NPV, this function is useful in evaluating various investment opportunities to determine the best one in terms of today's dollars.

To use @PV, position the cell pointer where you want the PV value to appear, type in **@PV(**, and enter the payment per period either by cell reference or as a literal value. If you use a cell reference, you can indicate it by typing in the cell address or range name or by pointing to it. After you indicate the payment, type a comma and indicate the cell containing the discount rate or enter the rate as a literal value. Finally, indicate the cell containing the term or enter it as a literal value and then type a) to complete the function. Press Return to have the program calculate the result.

The formula used by the @PV function is

@PV = +pmt*((1 − (1 + int)^term)/int)

where pmt equals the payment per period, term equals the number of payments, and int equals the periodic interest rate.

When you use this function, the period of the interest rate must agree with that of the term. Also, remember that this function assumes that payments are made at the end of each period in the term specified.

EXAMPLES

For an example of using @PV to determine the wisdom of various investments, see Figure 13.4.

```
D9: (C2) [W13] @PV(A9,B9/12,C9)                                    READY

      A        B         C          D           E        F        G
1
2                      Term      Present
3  Payment Interest  (Months)    Value               Formula
4  ---------------------------------------------------------------
5  $218.46     9.75%       36   $6,795.00 <-- @PV(A5,B5/12,C5)
6
7  $225.00    10.00%       38   $7,302.68 <-- @PV(A7,B7/12,C7)
8
9  $233.66    12.00%       40   $7,672.15 <-- @PV(A9,B9/9,C9)
```

FIGURE 13.4: Using @PV to calculate the present value of money when considering different loan alternatives. In this figure the @PV function is used to compare the amount (in today's dollars) required by three different loan alternatives. In each case, the payment, interest rate (expressed as APR), and term in months are placed in the order that they are required as arguments of the @PV function. Because the term is months, the cell reference to the interest rate is divided by 12. As anticipated, the first alternative offers the best deal.

@FV

This function calculates the future value of an annuity, given the payment per period and the discount rate over the period of payments specified as the term.

SYNTAX

@FV(pmt,int,term)

where pmt is the payment per period, int is the discount rate, and term is the number of payment periods.

USAGE

The @FV function is used to determine the future value, which is the value of an investment at a future date, given a series of payments discounted at a periodic interest rate. It is useful in evaluating whether a particular investment will be adequate to meet a future obligation.

To use this function, position the cell pointer where you want the FV value to appear, type in **@FV(**, and enter the payment per period either by cell reference or as a literal value. If you use a cell reference, you can indicate it by typing in the cell address or range name or by pointing to it. After you indicate the payment, type a comma and indicate the cell containing the discount rate or enter the rate as a literal value. Finally, indicate the cell containing the term or enter it as a literal value and then type a) to complete the function. Press Return to have the program calculate the result.

The formula used by the @FV function is

@FV = +pmt*((((1 + int)^term) − 1)/int)

where pmt equals the payment per period, term equals the number of payments, and int equals the periodic interest rate.

When you use this function, the period of the interest rate must agree with that of the term. Also, remember that this function assumes that payments are made at the end of each period in the term specified. To determine an annuity due in which payments are made at the beginning of the period, use this formula:

@FV(pmt,int,term)*(1 + int)

EXAMPLES

For an example comparing the future value of an ordinary annuity to that of an annuity due, see Figure 13.5.

```
D10: (C2) [W12] @FV(A10,B10,C10)*(1+B10)                              READY

        A          B          C          D           E          F          G
 1                           Term    Future value of an
 2   Payment   Interest    (Years) ordinary annuity        Formula
 3   ---------------------------------------------------------------------
 4    $785.67     12.50%        10  $14,125.22 <-- @FV(A4,B4,C4)
 5
 6
 7                           Term    Future value of
 8   Payment   Interest    (Years) an annuity due          Formula
 9   ---------------------------------------------------------------------
10    $785.67     12.50%        10  $15,890.87 <-- @FV(A10,B10,C10)*(1+B10)
11
```

FIGURE 13.5: Comparing the future value of an ordinary annuity to an annuity due by using the @FV function. This figure compares investing in an ordinary annuity, in which payments are made at the end of each period, with investing in an annuity due, in which the deposits are made at the beginning of each period. In both cases the amount of the deposit, the interest rate, and the term are constant. In the case of the ordinary annuity, the @FV function is used alone to calculate the future value. In the case of the annuity due, the @FV function is used in a formula that multiplies the future value by 1 plus the amount of interest (shown in the Control Panel). As expected, the annuity due offers a substantially larger return.

@PMT

This function calculates the payment required to amortize a loan amount, given the beginning amount of the principal, the interest rate, and the number of payment periods.

SYNTAX

@PMT(prin,int,term)

where prin is the amount of the loan (i.e., the beginning principal), int is the periodic interest rate, and term is the number of payment periods of the loan.

USAGE

The @PMT function provides an extremely easy method for determining the loan payment required to borrow specific amounts at a fixed rate of interest. It can be used to set up a table comparing the difference in payments depending on the interest rate charged. Using this function and the @PV function, you can generate an amortization schedule showing the interest paid and balance of a loan for each period in the term of the loan.

To use the @PMT function, position the cell pointer where you want the payment amount to appear, type in **@PMT(**, and enter the principal of the loan either by cell reference or as a literal value. If you use a cell reference, you can indicate it by typing in the cell address or range name or by pointing to it. After indicating the payment, type a comma and indicate the cell containing the interest rate or enter the rate as a literal value. Finally, indicate the cell containing the term or enter it as a literal value and then type a) to complete the function. Press Return to have the program calculate the result.

The formula used to calculate @PMT is

@PMT = +prin*(int/(1−(1+int)^−term))

where prin is the amount of the beginning principal, int is the interest rate, and term is the number of payment periods it takes to amortize the loan.

When you use this function, the period of the interest rate must agree with that of the term. To convert an annual interest rate to its monthly equivalent, divide it by 12. To convert the term expressed in years into the number of monthly payments, multiply it by 12.

EXAMPLES

For an example of setting up an amortization schedule using the @PMT and @PV functions, see Figure 13.6.

@RATE (Release 2 Only)

The @RATE function calculates the compound growth rate for an initial investment, given its present and future values.

SYNTAX

@RATE(fv,pv,term)

where fv is the future value of an initial investment, pv is its present value, and term is the number of compounding periods.

```
C4: (,2) [W11] @PMT(C1,C2/12,C3*12)                                      READY

       A         B           C           D            E           F
 1          Principal   100,000.00               Total Paid  192,054.76
 2          Interest         9.88%
 3          Term (years)        15
 4          Payment       1,066.97 <-- @PMT(C1,C2/12,C3*12)
 5
 6           Beginning   Principal    Interest       Total      Ending
 7   Month     balance        paid        Paid        Paid     Balance
 8   ---------------------------------------------------------------------
 9       1  100,000.00      244.05      822.92    1,066.97   99,755.95
10       2   99,755.95      490.12    1,643.82    2,133.94   99,509.88
11       3   99,509.88      738.20    2,462.71    3,200.91   99,261.80
12       4   99,261.80      988.33    3,279.55    4,267.88   99,011.67
13       5   99,011.67    1,240.52    4,094.33    5,334.85   98,759.48
14       6   98,759.48    1,494.78    4,907.04    6,401.83   98,505.22
15       7   98,505.22    1,751.14    5,717.66    7,468.80   98,248.86
16       8   98,248.86    2,009.60    6,526.16    8,535.77   97,990.40
17       9   97,990.40    2,270.19    7,332.54    9,602.74   97,729.81
18      10   97,729.81    2,532.93    8,136.78   10,669.71   97,467.07
19      11   97,467.07    2,797.83    8,938.85   11,736.68   97,202.17
20      12   97,202.17    3,064.91    9,738.74   12,803.65   96,935.09
                                                      CALC
```

FIGURE 13.6: Using the @PMT and @PV functions to create an amortization schedule. This figure shows the payment required to borrow $100,000.00 at 9.875% interest (APR) for a term of 15 years. This is calculated with the @PMT function in cell C4. It also shows the effect the first 12 payments have on the balance of the loan. The ending balance is determined by using the @PV function. In cell F9, the formula reads @PV(C4,C2/12,(C3*12–A9)). This determines the present value after reducing the term (in months) by 1, the value in A9. Subtracting the ending balance from the beginning balance gives you the principal paid, and subtracting the principal paid from the payment gives you the interest paid.

USAGE

This function is used to determine the periodic interest rate at which a present value investment will grow into a future value. The number of compounding periods in the term argument are assumed to occur at regular intervals throughout the term.

To use the @RATE function, position the cell pointer where you want the periodic rate to appear, type in **@RATE(**, and enter the future value of the investment either by cell reference or as a literal value. If you use a cell reference, you can indicate it by typing in the cell address or range name or by pointing to it. After you indicate the future value, type a comma and indicate the cell containing the present value or enter it as a literal value. Finally, indicate the cell containing the term or enter it as a literal value and then type a **)** to complete the function. Press Return to have the program calculate the result.

The formula used by the @RATE function is

@RATE = (fv/pv)^(1/term) − 1

where fv is the future value, pv is the present value, and term is the number of compounding periods. If the term is expressed in years and you need to determine the rate for a monthly compounded rate, multiply the term by 12.

EXAMPLES

For an example of using the @RATE function to determine the periodic rate for an investment, see Figure 13.7.

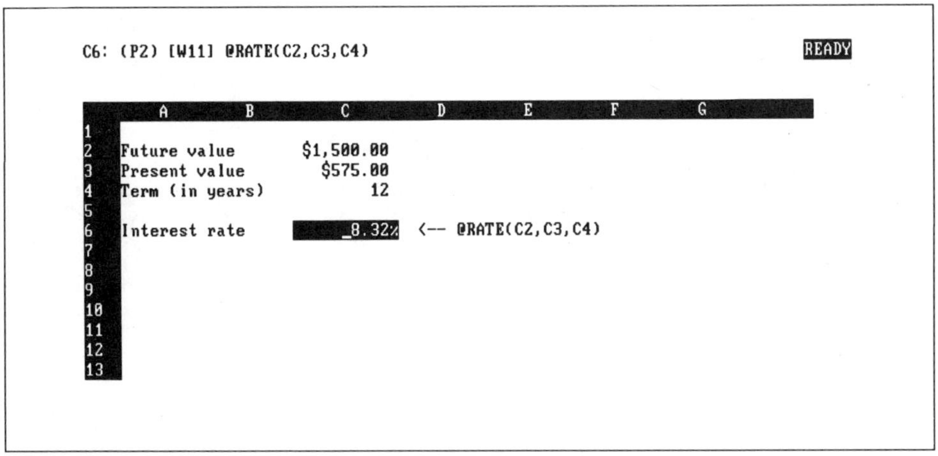

FIGURE 13.7: Calculating the periodic interest rate with the @RATE function. In this figure, @RATE was used to determine the interest rate required to make an investment of $575.00 grow into $1,500.00 in 12 years. The function was entered in C6 using the references to the values in the three cells above listed in the order they are required as arguments of the function. As you can see, the implied interest rate is 8.32 percent.

@TERM (Release 2 Only)

The @TERM function calculates the number of periods (i.e., the term) required to realize a particular future value from an investment in which equal payments are made at the end of each period at a fixed periodic interest rate.

SYNTAX

@TERM(pmt,int,fv)

where pmt is the payment per period, int is the periodic interest rate, and fv is the future value.

USAGE

This function is useful whenever you need to determine the term required to reach a specific future value of an investment when a series of deposits are made over the term.

The @TERM function uses the following formula:

@TERM = @LN(1 + (fv * int/pmt))/@LN(1 + int)

where @LN is the function to calculate the natural logarithm, fv is the future value, int is the periodic interest rate, and pmt is the payment per period.

When you use this function, the period of the interest rate must agree with that of the term. Like the other Lotus 1-2-3 financial functions, the @TERM function assumes that payments are made at the end of each period. If you wish to determine the number of periods in which payments are made at the beginning of each period, use the following formula:

@TERM(pmt,int,fv/(1 + int))

where pmt is the payment per period, int is the periodic interest rate, and fv is the future value of the investment.

EXAMPLES

For an example of how to use the @TERM function to determine the number of months required to realize a particular future value, see Figure 13.8.

@CTERM (Release 2 Only)

The @CTERM function calculates the number of periods (i.e., the term) required to realize a particular future value from making an initial investment at a fixed periodic interest rate.

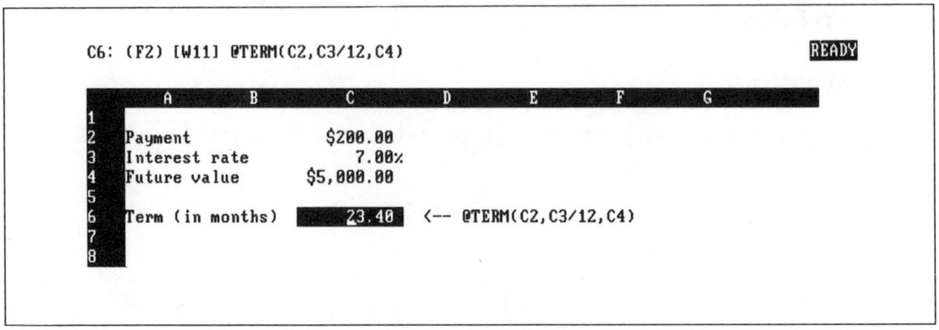

FIGURE 13.8: Using @TERM to calculate the term required to realize a future value of $5000.00 at 7 percent interest when depositing $200.00 a month. In this figure, the @TERM function was used to determine the number of months required. Notice that because the term was to be expressed in months, the cell reference to the interest rate in C3 was divided by 12. Otherwise the program would have calculated the term in years.

SYNTAX

@CTERM(int,fv,pv)

where int is the periodic interest rate, fv is the future value of the investment, and pv is the present value or initial investment made.

USAGE

The @CTERM function is similar to the @TERM function, except that it determines the number of periods required to achieve a specific future value when you make a single initial deposit or investment instead of a series of payments—thus the difference in arguments between the two functions.

To use this function, position the cell pointer where you want the number of periods to appear, type in **@CTERM(**, and enter the interest rate either by cell reference or as a literal value. If you use a cell reference, you can indicate it by typing in the cell address or range name or by pointing to it. After you indicate the rate, type a comma and indicate the cell containing the future value or enter it as a literal value. Finally, indicate the cell containing the present value or enter it as a literal value and then type a) to complete the function. Press Return to have the program calculate the result.

The formula used by the @CTERM function is

@CTERM = @LN(fv/pv)/@LN(1 + int)

where @LN is the function to determine the natural logarithm, fv is the future value, pv is the present value, and int is the periodic interest rate.

If the interest rate is given as an annual figure, divide it by 12 if it is compounded monthly. To convert the number of periods from months to years, divide the result by 12 also.

EXAMPLES

For an example of using @CTERM to calculate the number of years required to realize a specific future value on an initial investment, see Figure 13.9.

```
C7: (F2) [W11] @CTERM(C2/12,C3,C4)                                READY

        A         B         C         D     E      F       G        H
1
2   Interest rate          10.50%
3   Future value       $24,000.00
4   Present value      $12,000.00
5
6   Compound term
7     (in months)           79.56  <-- @CTERM(C2/12,C3,C4)
8
9      Compound term =          6 Years   7.6  Months
10
```

FIGURE 13.9: Calculating the term for doubling an initial investment with the @CTERM function. In this figure, @CTERM is used to determine how long it will take to double an initial investment of $12,000.00. The compound term expressed in months and calculated in cell C7 was then converted to the corresponding number of years and months by adding two more formulas: in cell C9 the formula is @INT(C7) and in cell E9 the formula is @MOD(C7,12).

@SLN (Release 2 Only)

The @SLN function calculates the depreciation of an asset by using the straight-line method. It assumes equal depreciation in each period over the useful life of the asset.

SYNTAX

@SLN(cost,salvage,life)

where cost is the original cost of the asset, salvage is the salvage or residual value, and life is the asset's useful life.

USAGE

The straight-line method of depreciation is useful for calculating depreciation of a fixed asset when one of the accelerated methods is not required (as when preparing income tax returns). It assumes that the amount depreciated is constant during each period of the useful life. Under this method, the depreciable base (the original cost minus the salvage value) is depreciated to zero.

To use the @SLN function, position the cell pointer in the cell where you want the depreciation calculated, type in **@SLN(**, and enter the original cost either by cell reference or as a literal value. If you use a cell reference, you can indicate it by typing in the cell address or range name or by pointing to it. After you indicate the cost, type a comma and indicate the cell containing the salvage value or enter it as a literal value. Finally, indicate the cell containing the useful life of the asset or enter it as a literal value and then type a **)** to complete the function. Press Return to have the program calculate the result.

If you are creating a schedule showing the year-end balance as well as the depreciation, copy the function entered for the first period to the rest of the cells containing the remaining periods.

EXAMPLES

For an example illustrating straight-line depreciation by using the @SLN function, see Figure 13.10.

```
D7: (F2) @SLN($C$1,$C$2,$G$1)                                    READY

     A        B          C        D        E        F        G        H
1  Original cost       10000             Life                      5
2  Salvage value         500             Depreciable base       9500
3
4  Years                          1        2        3        4        5
5            Straight-line  method
6  Depreciation percent        0.20     0.20     0.20     0.20     0.20
7  Depreciation             1900.00  1900.00  1900.00  1900.00  1900.00
8  Year-end balance     9500 7600.00  5700.00  3800.00  1900.00     0.00
9
```

FIGURE 13.10: Calculating straight-line depreciation with the @SLN function. In this schedule, the depreciation allowance was calculated first in cell D7 by entering the formula shown in the Control Panel. Notice that the cell references to the cells containing the cost, salvage, and life values used as arguments to this function were all made absolute so that this formula could then be copied to the range E7..H7.

@SYD (Release 2 Only)

The @SYD function calculates the depreciation of an asset using the sum-of-the-years'-digits method for determining accelerated depreciation.

SYNTAX

@SYD(cost,salvage,life,period)

where cost is the original cost of the asset, salvage is the salvage or residual value, life is the useful life of the asset, and period is the year in which the depreciation is being calculated.

USAGE

The sum-of-the-years'-digits method determines accelerated depreciation in which the digits of the period of the useful life are summed and this total is used to fix the depreciation percent for each period. This method is often used when preparing income tax returns, because it provides a higher depreciation expense in the earlier years and a lower expense in the later years of the useful life. Under this method, the depreciable base (the original cost minus the salvage value) is depreciated to zero.

To use the @SYD function, position the cell pointer in the cell where you want the depreciation calculated, type in **@SYD(**, and enter the original cost either by cell reference or as a literal value. If you use a cell reference, you can indicate it by typing in the cell address or range name or by pointing to it.

After you indicate the cost, type a comma and indicate the cell containing the salvage value or enter it as a literal value. Then type a comma and indicate the cell containing the useful life in the same way. Finally, type another comma, indicate the cell containing the useful life of the asset or enter it as a literal value, and type a) to complete the function. Press Return to have the program calculate the result.

If you are creating a schedule showing the year-end balance as well as the depreciation, copy the function entered for the first period to the rest of the cells containing the remaining periods.

EXAMPLES

For an example illustrating sum-of-the-years'-digits depreciation by using the @SYD function, see the schedule shown in Figure 13.11.

```
L7: (F2) @SYD($K$1,$K$2,$O$1,L4)                                          READY

     I        J        K         L         M         N         O         P
1  Original cost      10000               Life                  5
2  Salvage value        500               Depreciable base   9500
3
4  Years                           1         2         3         4         5
5           Sum-of-the-years'-digit method
6  Depreciation percent         0.33      0.27      0.20      0.13      0.07
7  Depreciation              3166.67   2533.33   1900.00   1266.67    633.33
8  Year-end balance     9500 6333.33   3800.00   1900.00    633.33      0.00
9
10
11
```

FIGURE 13.11: Calculating sum-of-the-years'-digits depreciation with the @SYD function. In this figure, the @SYD function was entered in cell L7 as shown in the Control Panel. Notice that the cell references to the cells containing the cost, salvage, and life values were all made absolute. However, the cell reference to the period in L4 was left relative. This is because only the first three arguments should be constant when this formula is copied to the range M7..P7. The period must be adjusted in cells M4 to P4 to calculate correctly the accelerated depreciation associated with this method.

@DDB (Release 2 Only)

The @DDB function calculates the depreciation of an asset using the double-declining balance method for determining accelerated depreciation.

SYNTAX

@DDB(cost,salvage,life,period)

where cost is the original cost of the asset, salvage is the salvage or residual value, life is the useful life of the asset, and period is the year in which the depreciation is being calculated.

USAGE

Double-declining balance offers a method of determining accelerated depreciation whereby the depreciation percent used in each period is twice the amount. Like the sum-of-the-years'-digits method, it is often used when preparing income tax returns because it provides a higher depreciation expense in the earlier years and a lower expense in the later years of the useful life. However, unlike the sum-of-the-years'-digits method, the double-declining balance method starts with the original cost (rather than the depreciable base), and the final book value of the asset is equal to the salvage value.

To use the @DDB function, position the cell pointer in the cell where you want the depreciation calculated, type in **@DDB(**, and enter the original cost either by cell reference or as a literal value. If you use a cell reference, you can indicate it by typing in the cell address or range name or by pointing to it.

After you indicate the cost, type a comma and indicate the cell containing the salvage value or enter it as a literal value. Then type a comma and indicate the cell containing the useful life in the same way. Finally, type another comma, indicate the cell containing the useful life of the asset or enter it as a literal value, and type a) to complete the function. Press Return to have the program calculate the result.

If you are creating a schedule showing the year-end balance as well as the depreciation, copy the function entered for the first period to the rest of the cells containing the remaining periods.

EXAMPLES

For an example illustrating double-declining depreciation by using the @DDB function, see the schedule shown in Figure 13.12.

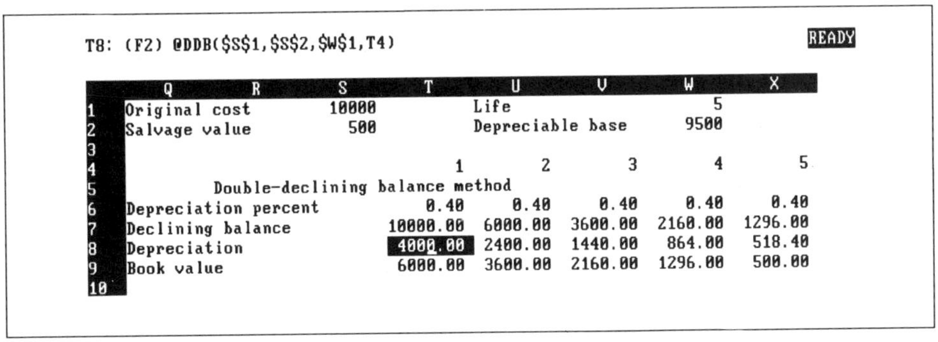

FIGURE 13.12: Calculating double-declining depreciation with the @DDB function. In this figure, the @DDB function was first entered in cell T8 as shown in the Control Panel. Notice that the cell references to the cells containing the cost, salvage, and life values were all made absolute. However, the cell reference to the period in T4 was left relative. This is because only the first three arguments should be constant when this formula is copied to the range U8..X8. The period must be adjusted in cells U4 to X4 to calculate correctly the accelerated depreciation associated with this method. Notice that the final book value for year 5 is calculated as 500.00. When using the double-declining method, the final book value must always be equal to or greater than the salvage value.

Summary

This chapter has covered the financial functions offered by Lotus 1-2-3. These functions are generally used by themselves rather than being combined in more complex formulas or with other specialized Lotus 1-2-3 functions. The references below give you suggestions on where to locate general information on using functions in spreadsheets as well as where to obtain more information on using formulas in constructing worksheets.

For general information on using Lotus 1-2-3 functions:

- Chapter 10, "Working with Formulas and Functions"

For general information on using Lotus 1-2-3 functions in building spreadsheet models:

- Chapter 19, "Spreadsheet Models, Error Trapping, and Recalculation"

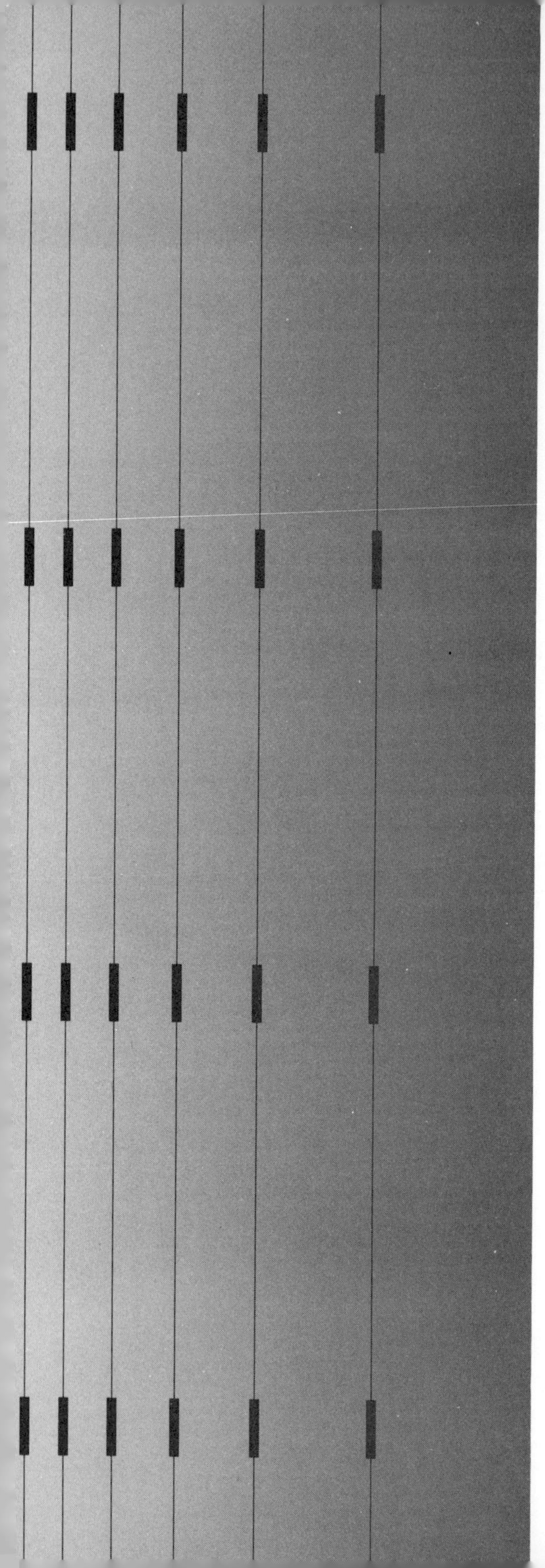

CHAPTER 14

Date and Time Functions

Date and Time Functions

This chapter examines the date and time functions offered by Lotus 1-2-3. Release 2 has added to this group substantially by including a number of time functions along with the specialized @DATE-VALUE and @TIMEVALUE functions. Experienced users of the original version of the program should note that the @TODAY function has been renamed and updated as @INT(@NOW) in Release 2. Nevertheless, you can still enter the function for returning the current date (and time) in your worksheet as @TODAY and Lotus 1-2-3 will update the function automatically to @NOW. This makes it unnecessary to revise 1A worksheets that contain formulas dependent on this function.

Following the discussions on using the date and time functions, you will find individual reference entries for each function. These are presented in two groups: one listing the date functions and the other listing the time functions. The date functions are presented in this order: @TODAY, @NOW, @DATE, @YEAR, @MONTH, @DAY, and @DATEVALUE (Release 2 only). The time functions are presented in the order @TIME, @HOUR, @MINUTE, @SECOND, and @TIMEVALUE (all of these being Release 2 functions).

Using the Date Functions

Lotus 1-2-3 date functions return a serial number assigned to each date between January 1, 1900 (0) and December 31, 2099 (73050). Using such a system enables you to perform these tasks:

- Simple arithmetic calculations between dates. For example, you can subtract two dates from one another to determine the number of days that have elapsed.
- Sort dates within a spreadsheet from earliest to most recent or most recent to earliest.
- Set up logical comparisons in spreadsheet formulas or database search criteria. For example, you can find all records in which the date entered is on or before a particular date.

Formatting the Date Display

Because the date functions calculate and return a serial number when you enter them in a spreadsheet, the program provides a number of display formats as part of the /Range Format command options to allow you to represent dates in recognizable forms. For example, if you enter **February 15, 1949** with the Lotus 1-2-3 @DATE function as shown below, it returns a serial number:

@DATE(49,2,15) = **17944**

You must then format the number 17944 by using one of the date formats. Using the /Range Format Date 1 command (DD-MMM-YY) changes the serial number to this display:

15-Feb-49

Note: The Date 1 format, which is one of the most common date formats because it uses a letter abbreviation for the name of the month and shows the year as well, requires 10 spaces to be displayed in a cell. This means that you must widen the column from the default of 9 to at least 10 in order to have Date 1 formats display properly. All of the other date formats can be displayed within the default column width of 9 spaces.

Table 14.1 shows the various date display formats available. In Release 2, two new formats, 4 (Long Intn'l) and 5 (Short Intn'l), have been added to

/RANGE FORMAT	PATTERN	EXAMPLE
Date 1	DD-MMM-YY	21-Jul-87
Date 2	DD-MMM	21-Jul
Date 3	MMM-YY	Jul-87
Date 4*	MM/DD/YY	07/21/87
Date 5**	MM/DD	07/21

*Date 4 (Long Intn'l) is a Release 2 option. It can be modified from the A default option shown in this example to B (DD/MM/YY), C (DD.MM.YY), or D (YY-MM-DD) by using the /Worksheet Global Default Other International Date command (/WGDOID).

**Date 5 (Short Intn'l) is also a Release 2 option. It can be modified from the A default shown in this example to B (DD/MM), C (DD.MM), or D (YY-MM) by using the same command (/WGDOID).

TABLE 14.1: The Date Display Formats

the original three. The Time option is also new and is discussed in the section "Formatting the Time Display."

Entering Dates in the Spreadsheet

Using the @DATE function, you can enter dates that fall between January 1, 1900 and December 31, 2099. To enter a twenty-first century date, you must enter three digits for the year as the first argument, as in @DATE(101,1,14) for the date January 14, 2001 (2001 = 101). If you enter only the first two digits of the year, Lotus 1-2-3 assumes that you mean a twentieth-century date.

Using the @TODAY function or its Release 2 equivalent, @NOW, in the spreadsheet is the method for entering the current date when you want it to remain dynamic in the spreadsheet (in other words, reflecting today's date). Both of these functions take their arguments from the system date, so all you have to enter is the @ symbol followed by the function name.

Note: If the date returned by @TODAY or @NOW is not correct, either the system date was not updated or you entered it incorrectly. In Release 2, you will notice this because the date displayed in the on-screen clock will not be correct. To correct the date, use the /System command and enter the DATE command in DOS before exiting back to Lotus 1-2-3.

All dates that you enter with the @DATE function or convert from date strings with the @DATEVALUE function (in Release 2) are static (in other words, they do not change). To change them, you must reenter the function with revised arguments.

Making Date Entry Easier

Date entry is a tedious task: it requires you to enter the function and its arguments each time you enter a date. To make entering a number of dates easier, you can use the /Copy function to copy the original date function to all other cells that require date entries. You can then edit each copy of the original date function by revising the year, month, and day arguments as required (for a full discussion of using this method, see "Methods for Inputting Dates in the Worksheet" in Chapter 5).

ALT-D, A DATE ENTRY MACRO

You can also use a date macro that automatically enters the function and then pauses at each argument to allow you to enter the appropriate year, month, and day. This macro can be entered as follows:

Label	*Macro Contents*
'\d	**'@DATE({?},{?},{?})~**

To use this macro, all you have to do is position the cell pointer where you need the date, press Alt-D, enter the year, and press Return. Then enter the month and press Return, and, finally, enter the day and press Return.

You can embellish this macro by adding the desired /Range Format Date command option. For example, if you wanted to use the Date 1 format, modify the macro as follows:

Label	*Macro Contents*
'\d	**'@DATE({?},{?},{?})~**
	'/RFD1~~

When using this particular date display format, you could also add the command to widen the column to 10 characters (/WCS10~) to automatically take care of the overflow display that appears when the column is set to the program's original global default. (Because this command is only required the first time you enter a group of dates in the same column, you may want to omit it and perform this one-time operation manually.)

Making Date Entries with the @DATEVALUE Function (Release 2 Only)

If you find it easier to enter dates in the numerical format in which each part of the date is separated by slashes (as in 11/15/88), you can use the @DATEVALUE function to create a comparable list of dates converted from strings (labels) into bona fide date entries. To do this, you must enter each date as a label by prefacing its first number with one of the label prefixes (otherwise Lotus 1-2-3 will divide each two-digit number by the succeeding two-digit number).

You then enter the @DATEVALUE function using the cell reference that contains the string value of each date you entered in the worksheet—for example, A1 if it contains the label '11/15/88. You can even automate this process by creating the following macro:

Label	*Macro Contents*
'\v	**'@DATEVALUE({?})~**
	'/RFD1~

To use this macro, position the cell pointer in the cell where you want the date entry to appear, press Alt-V (for date value), use the cursor keys to point to the cell that contains the date string (i.e., a date that has been entered as a label by using the numerical equivalents for the day, month, and year, all separated by /), and press Return. All of the dates converted with this macro can be used in date arithmetic calculations, unlike their string counterparts.

Note: This method for converting date strings to date entries in a Lotus 1-2-3 spreadsheet is particularly useful in a situation in which the data has been imported from another application program (especially from a word processor) in which all of the dates were entered in the standard number format DD/MM/YY.

Making Calculations on Dates

The real value of Lotus 1-2-3 date entries (i.e., dates entered with the @DATE function) is that the program allows you to use dates in formulas that perform arithmetic calculations or logical comparisons.

A secondary benefit is that Lotus 1-2-3 provides built-in error checking in that it will not accept outrageous arguments as the month and day arguments in the function. For example, if you enter **@DATE(88,14,14)** you will receive ERR as the result because there is no fourteenth month. Likewise, the entry **@DATE(88,11,35)** will produce an ERR value, as there is no thirty-fifth day in November.

When you subtract dates from each other, Lotus 1-2-3 returns the result in days. For instance, the following formula gives the answer in days:

@DATE(88,7,31) – @DATE(87,5,2) = 456

To convert the answer of 456 from days to years, you divide the result by 365.

It is important to understand how date arithmetic works in Lotus 1-2-3, so that you do not try to set up calculations that return absurd answers. Remember that the program uses serial numbers, which are equivalent to the number of days that have elapsed between the date function's arguments and the date January 1, 1900. This means that in the previous formula, Lotus 1-2-3 is really performing this simple arithmetic calculation:

32355 – 31899 = 456

Because the program uses serial numbers such as these, it can add two date entries together, multiply them by each other, or even divide them by each other. However, the results obtained by these calculations have no immediate meaning until they are converted to corresponding date display formats.

Most date calculations therefore involve subtracting the fixed date entered with the @DATE function from the current date entered with the @TODAY or @NOW functions. The result of such a calculation is dynamic in that the current date is updated from the system date each time the worksheet is recalculated, thus producing a new calculated result whenever the current date changes.

Making Logical Comparisons between Date Entries

Because Lotus 1-2-3 stores a serial number for each date entry, date entries can be used in logical comparisons—for example, they can be included in the condition of an @IF function, in a spreadsheet sorting operation, or as part of a search criterion for a /Data Query Find or Extract operation.

In each of these examples, the serial numbers of the dates are compared to one another according to the logical operators used. For instance, when setting up the condition for an @IF function that compares two dates, such as

@IF(@DATE(88,7,31)>@DATE(87,5,2),@TRUE,@FALSE)

Lotus 1-2-3 is really comparing the values 32355 and 31899 to determine whether the first is larger than the second (which, of course, produces a result of 1, the @TRUE value).

This is the same method that makes it so easy to sort by date in a Lotus 1-2-3 database. When you set up an ascending sort using a date column (field), Lotus 1-2-3 is really sorting the rows (records) by performing a numerical sort from smaller to larger serial numbers (0–9).

Using the Time Functions (Release 2 Only)

The time functions are new functions added to Release 2 that make it easy to enter times into a spreadsheet. You can also calculate differences between times you enter with these functions (often as elapsed time). Times are also useful in creating daily, weekly, or monthly appointment schedules in which they can be combined with the appropriate date functions.

You can see the current time value by using the @NOW function and formatting the resulting serial number in one of the time display formats.

When you need to enter a specific time, use the @TIME function. This function requires three arguments: the number of the hour followed by the number of minutes and the number of seconds. If the hour argument is larger than 23 or if the minutes and seconds are larger than 59, you will receive an ERR value. A value calculated from valid arguments is a decimal number equivalent to the fractional part of the day between 0.000 (midnight) and 0.9999 (11:59:59 PM).

In addition, you can use the @HOUR, @MINUTE, or @SECOND function for just the portion of the time value controlled by the function. If the time is entered as a string (i.e., as a label), you can convert it into its equivalent time value by using the @TIMEVALUE function.

Formatting the Time Display

When you use the @NOW and @TIME functions, you can convert their calculated decimal values into one of the four possible time display formats available as options of the /Range Format Date Time command. Table 14.2 shows you these formats with examples of how they display the time. Notice that the first two time formats add the AM/PM convention to differentiate times before and after noon, while the other two formats use the 24-hour clock convention.

/RANGE FORMAT DATE	PATTERN	EXAMPLE
Time 1	HH:MM:SS AM/PM	10:05:00 PM
Time 2	HH:MM AM/PM	10:05 PM
Time 3*	HH:MM:SS	22:05:00
Time 4**	HH:MM	22:05

*Time 3 (Long Intn'l) can be modified from the A default shown in this example to either B (HH.MM.SS), C (HH,MM,SS), or D (HHhMMmSSs) by using the /Worksheet Global Default Other International Time command (/WGDOIT). However, this merely changes the delimiting character used, as the long international format is always displayed according to a 24-hour clock.

**Time 4 (Short Intn'l) can also be modified from the A default shown in this example to B (HH.MM), C (HH,MM), or D (HHhMMm) by using the same command (/WGDOID). It, too, is always displayed according to a 24-hour clock.

TABLE 14.2: The Time Display Formats

THE DATE FUNCTIONS

The reference entries for the date functions that follow are presented in the order @TODAY, @NOW, @DATE, @YEAR, @MONTH, @DAY, and @DATEVALUE.

The @TODAY function is only of interest if you are using Release 1A; otherwise, you would use its new equivalent, @NOW. If you are using Release 1A worksheets that contain @TODAY functions, these functions will be converted automatically to @INT(@NOW) when the spreadsheet containing them is retrieved in Release 2. If, on the other hand, you are preparing to translate a Release 2 spreadsheet to Release 1A, you will want to change the @NOW functions to @TODAY before using the Translate utility.

All of the other date functions (with the exception of @DATEVALUE) are common to both versions of the program and work in exactly the same manner.

@TODAY (Release 1A)

This function enters into a cell the current date supplied by the system as a serial number.

SYNTAX

@TODAY

This function takes no arguments.

USAGE

The @TODAY function takes the current date as entered in response to the DOS DATE command and converts it into a serial number. You can then format this serial number into one of three date formats:

- Date 1 uses the pattern DD-MMM-YY. This format displays a three-letter abbreviation of the name of the month, along with the number of the day and the last two digits of the year.
- Date 2 uses the pattern DD-MMM. This format displays the date like date format 1, except that it omits the last two digits of the year.

- Date 3 uses the pattern MMM-YY. This format displays a three-letter abbreviation of the name of the month, along with the last two digits of the year.

To use @TODAY, move the cell pointer to the cell where you want the current date to appear, type **@TODAY**, and press the Return key. To format the resulting serial number to one of the date display formats, type **/RFD** and the appropriate number of the format you wish to use. If you choose date format 1 and the column width is set to 9 characters, you will have to widen the column to at least 10 characters in order to see this display.

You can use this function in formulas to perform date arithmetic that depends on the current date. It can also be combined with the other Lotus 1-2-3 date functions—@YEAR, @MONTH, and @DAY—to return just the part of the current date controlled by the function.

When you enter the date into a cell by using the @TODAY function, it is automatically updated whenever the worksheet is recalculated. This means that the date will be made current when the spreadsheet is retrieved as long as automatic recalculation was in effect when the file was saved.

This feature provides a convenient method for using formulas that depend on keeping the date current in the worksheet without requiring any manual updating. This is useful in such applications as personnel spreadsheets, where vacation accrual is calculated by using a rate determined by the length of the time the employee has been with the company. The elapsed time can be calculated easily by subtracting the date hired from the current date.

If you ever wish to freeze the current date entered with the @TODAY function, you can do so by moving the cell pointer to the cell that contains the function and pressing the Edit function key (F2) followed by the Calc key (F9). This converts the date function to the currently calculated serial number.

EXAMPLES

Figure 14.1 shows a spreadsheet in which the @TODAY function was entered in four example cells in column A (on August 24, 1986). In the first cell, A2, it was left as the serial number calculated by the program. In the next three cells, A4, A6, and A8, the three different date formats were used to illustrate the different display options offered by Lotus 1-2-3.

The last three examples illustrate how you can combine the date functions @YEAR, @MONTH, and @DAY with the @TODAY function when you need to use just a particular part of the date.

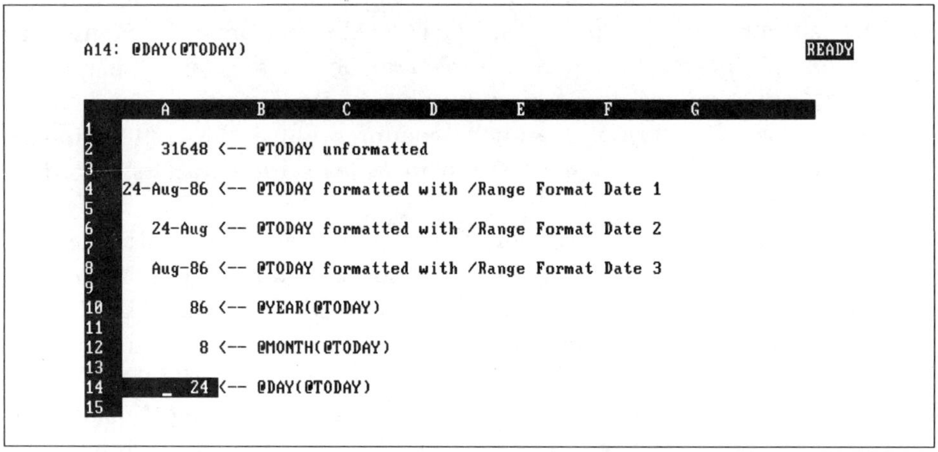

FIGURE 14.1: Using the @TODAY function in a Release 1A worksheet on August 24, 1986. The first time this function was entered (A2), the serial number calculated by the program was left unformatted. In the three following cells where it was entered, the three different date formats available were used to convert the serial number seen in A2 into more meaningful displays. In the last three examples, the @TODAY function was used as the argument for the date functions @YEAR, @MONTH, and @DAY. In each case, the function returned only the part of the date it controls. Notice that unlike the three date formats, the month returned by the formula in A12 is in number form.

@NOW (Release 2)

This function enters into a cell the current date and time supplied by the system as a serial number.

SYNTAX

@NOW

This function takes no arguments.

USAGE

The @NOW function takes the current date and time as entered in response to the DOS DATE and TIME commands and converts them into a serial number. Unlike the @TODAY function in Release 1A, the serial number calculated by @NOW includes a decimal value representing the time of day as well as digits representing the date. You can then format this serial number into one of five date formats or four time formats:

- Date 1 uses the pattern DD-MMM-YY. This format displays a three-letter abbreviation of the name of the month, along with the number of the day and the last two digits of the year.
- Date 2 uses the pattern DD-MMM. This format displays the date like date format 1, except that it omits the last two digits of the year.
- Date 3 uses the pattern MMM-YY. This format displays a three-letter abbreviation of the name of the month, along with the last two digits of the year.
- Date 4, the long international format, uses the pattern MM/DD/YY as its default. This format displays the date in a completely numerical format. It uses the forward slash with the number of the month appearing first unless you change it to another international format with the /Worksheet Global Default Other International Date command (see Chapter 2).
- Date 5, the short international format, uses the pattern MM/DD as its default. This format is the same as Date 4, except that it does not show the digits for the year. It can also be changed by using the /Worksheet Global Default Other International Date command.
- Time 1 uses the pattern HH:MM:SS AM/PM. This format displays the hours, minutes, and seconds as well as the designation AM or PM. It is shown as (D6) in the literal contents of the cell.
- Time 2 uses the pattern HH:MM AM/PM. This format is a shortened form of the Time 1 display that omits the display of the seconds. It is shown as (D7) in the literal contents of the cell.
- Time 3, the long international format, uses the pattern HH:MM:SS on a 24-hour clock (it does not include the AM/PM designation) as its default. This format is shown as (D8) in the literal contents of the cell. You can change it from this default (A), which uses colons as the delimiter, by using the /Worksheet Global Default Other International Time command and choosing any of the other three formats available (B, C, or D).
- Time 4, the short international format, uses the pattern HH:MM on a 24-hour clock as its default. This is the same as the long

international format, except that it omits the display of the seconds. It too can be changed from the default, which uses the colon delimiter, by using the /Worksheet Global Default Other International Time command.

To use @NOW, move the cell pointer to the cell where you want the current date to appear, type **@NOW**, and press the Return key. To format the resulting serial number to one of the date display formats, type **/RFD** and the appropriate number of the format you wish to use. If you choose date format 1 or any of the time formats (by typing /RFDT) and the column width is set to 9 characters, you will have to widen the column to see the display.

You can also use this function in formulas to perform date or time arithmetic that depends on the current date. It can also be combined with the other Lotus 1-2-3 date and time functions—@YEAR, @MONTH, @DAY, @HOUR, @MINUTE, and @SECOND—to return just the part of the current date or time controlled by the function.

When you enter the date and time into a cell by using the @NOW function, they are automatically updated whenever the worksheet is recalculated. This means that the date and time will be made current when the spreadsheet is retrieved as long as automatic recalculation was in effect when the file was saved. (If automatic recalculation was not in effect, simply press F9 to recalculate the worksheet and provide the current date and time.)

This feature provides a convenient method for using formulas that depend on keeping the date current in the worksheet without requiring any manual updating. This is useful in such applications as personnel spreadsheets, where vacation accrual is calculated by using a rate determined by the length of the time the employee has been with the company. The elapsed time can be calculated easily by subtracting the date hired from the current date.

If you ever wish to freeze the current date and time entered with the @NOW function, you can do so by moving the cell pointer to the cell that contains the function and pressing the Edit function key (F2) followed by the Calc key (F9). This converts the function to the currently calculated serial number representing the date and time.

EXAMPLES

Figure 14.2 shows examples of using the @NOW function with various date and time display formats (when the current date was August 24,1986).

```
A18: [W12] @SECOND(@NOW)                                          READY

     A         B         C         D         E         F         G
1
2  31648.45461 <-- @NOW unformatted
3
4    24-Aug-86 <-- @NOW formatted with /Range Format Date 1
5
6  10:54:39 AM <-- @NOW formatted with /Range Format Date Time 1
7
8           86 <-- @YEAR(@NOW)
9
10           8 <-- @MONTH(@NOW)
11
12          24 <-- @DAY(@NOW)
13
14          10 <-- @HOUR(@NOW)
15
16          54 <-- @MINUTE(@NOW)
17
18          39 <-- @SECOND(@NOW)
19
```

FIGURE 14.2: Using the @NOW function in a Release 2 worksheet on August 24, 1986. The first time this function was entered (A2), the serial number calculated by the program was left unformatted. In A4, the @NOW serial number was converted to a common date display format, while in the next example in A6 it was converted to a time display. In the next three examples, the @NOW function was used as the argument for the date functions @YEAR, @MONTH, and @DAY. In each case, it returned only the part of the date it controls. Notice that unlike the three date formats, the month returned by the formula in A12 is in number form. In the last three examples, the @NOW function was used as the argument for the time functions @HOUR, @MINUTE, and @SECOND. Here it returned the part of the current time that each controls.

In the first example in A2, the serial number calculated by the @NOW function was left unformatted. Notice that it includes not only the five-digit serial number for the date but also a decimal value that represents the fractional equivalent of the current time when this function was entered (where 0.000 is midnight and 0.9999 is 11:59:59 PM).

Though the @NOW function is most often formatted with a date display, the third example (in cell A6) demonstrates that it is possible to display only the current time. The examples below this show the effect of returning a specific portion of the date or time by using the appropriate date and time function that controls it.

@DATE

This function enters a specific date, either alone or as part of a formula, into a cell of the spreadsheet.

SYNTAX

@DATE(yr,month,day)

where yr is the last two digits of the year if the date is in the twentieth century or the last three digits of the year if the date is in the twenty-first century (100 for the year 2000), month is the number of the month, and day is the number of the day of the month.

USAGE

The @DATE function enters dates in a spreadsheet or Lotus 1-2-3 database that can be used whenever date arithmetic, sorting by date, or setting up formula search criteria using dates is required. Unlike the @NOW or @TODAY functions, the date entered with this function is static and does not change when the worksheet is recalculated.

To use the @DATE function, move the cell pointer to the cell where you want the date to appear; then type **@DATE(** and the digits of the year (only the last two are required if the date is in the twentieth century) followed by a comma, the digits of the month followed by a comma, and the digits of the day of the month followed by a).

When you press the Return key, Lotus 1-2-3 enters a serial number for the arguments that is equivalent to the number of days that have elapsed between the date specified and January 1, 1900.

To format the serial number to one of the program's date display formats, use the /Range Format Date command followed by the number of the display format you wish to use. The date display formats include the following:

- Date 1 uses the pattern DD-MMM-YY. This format displays a three-letter abbreviation of the name of the month, along with the number of the day and the last two digits of the year.
- Date 2 uses the pattern DD-MMM. This format displays the date like date format 1, except that it omits the last two digits of the year.
- Date 3 uses the pattern MMM-YY. This format displays a three-letter abbreviation of the name of the month, along with the last two digits of the year.
- Date 4, the long international format, uses the pattern MM/DD/YY as its default. This format displays the date in a completely numerical format. It uses the forward slash with the number of the month

appearing first unless you change it to another international format with the /Worksheet Global Default Other International Date command (see Chapter 2).

- Date 5, the short international format, uses the pattern MM/DD as its default. This format is the same as Date 4, except that it does not show the digits for the year. It can also be changed by using the /Worksheet Global Default Other International Date command.

Only the first three of these formats are available if you are using Release 1A of the program. If you specify date format 1 and the column width of the cell in which the function is entered is still the 9-character default, you will have to widen the column to 10 characters to view this display.

While the @DATE function is commonly used to enter particular dates into a spreadsheet or database, it can also be combined in formulas to evaluate conditions and to calculate new values. For instance, you could enter the following formula to evaluate the contents of cell A1, which contains an @DATE function, as follows:

@IF(A1>=@DATE(86,5,3),1.05*C18,C18)

The total due in cell C18 is increased by 5 percent if the condition is found to be true or left as is if it is found to be false.

You could also set up a calculation between two date values, as illustrated in the following formula:

@IF(A1-@DATE(86,11,1)>=30,"Past Due","Current")

The date entered into A1 with the @DATE function is subtracted from November 1, 1986. If the result is greater than or equal to 30 (days), the message Past Due is entered into the cell; otherwise the message Current is entered.

EXAMPLES

Figure 14.3 shows a sample application using the @NOW and @DATE functions in a personnel database to determine the length of service with the company and to determine which employees are due for a salary review. The years with the company are calculated in E6 by the formula

(@NOW-D6)/365

which subtracts the employee's date of hire from the current date and then converts the number of days returned to year equivalents by dividing

```
G6: @IF(@NOW-F6>=360," Yes"," No")                                      READY

     A            B          C          D        E         F          G
1  Accounting Department Personnel
2  Length of Service and Review Schedule
3
4  Employee     Last       First      Date     Yrs w/    Date of
5  Number       Name       Name       Hired    Company   Last Review Review?
6  451-23-4567  Harris     Parry      Jun-84     2.21    12/04/85    No_
7  345-78-0987  Smith      Janet      May-83     3.25    02/18/86    No
8  231-09-7854  Reyes      Philip     Feb-82     4.53    05/04/85    Yes
9  176-23-4598  Davis      Margaret   Aug-80     6.01    06/01/85    Yes
10 450-87-6543  Svenson    Paul       Nov-84     1.80    01/15/86    No
11 432-32-9983  Jacobs     Sandra     Mar-79     7.46    03/22/85    Yes
12 502-37-1543  Robinson   Thomas     Jan-80     6.57    09/27/85    No
13
14
15
16
```

FIGURE 14.3: A personnel database using the @DATE function to enter the date hired and date of last review for each employee. The length of service in column E is calculated by subtracting the date hired entered in column D from the current date entered by using the @NOW function in the formula. Because the result returned is in days, this value is also divided by 365 to convert it into years. The formula for determining whether an employee is due for a salary review is shown in the Control Panel. If the date of the last review is about a year or more ago (360 days), the Yes message is displayed. Because the @NOW function is used in both formulas, these values and messages will change whenever the file is retrieved later.

the result by 365. Each date of hire in the database was entered in column D, using the @DATE function to make this calculation possible. The column was then formatted with the /Range Format Date command using date format 3, which displays the three-letter abbreviation for the month and the last two digits of the year.

This formula was then copied down column E to determine the length of service for all of the other employees listed.

The formula for evaluating whether the employee is due for a salary review was first entered in cell G6 as

@IF(@NOW – F6> = 360," Yes"," No")

It subtracts the current date from the date of last review entered in F6. This review date as well as all of the others in column F were entered by using the @DATE function to make this calculation possible. These dates were then formatted with the /Range Format Date command using date format 4, the long international date display.

If the result of this subtraction is equal to or greater than 360 (days, approximating the number of days in a year), then the formula enters the message Yes in the cell; otherwise, it indicates No. This formula was then copied down column G for each of the employees listed.

Note: If you are using Release 1A, you cannot use character strings as arguments of the @IF condition (see Chapter 15); therefore, you cannot have messages like Yes and No entered in column G. Instead, you could use the @TRUE and @FALSE functions, which would return 0 if the employee were not yet due for a review and 1 if he or she were due. You must also use the @TODAY function, so the first formula would read @IF(@TODAY – F6> =360,@TRUE,@FALSE).

@YEAR

This function returns the number of the year represented by the digits of the date serial number given as the argument.

SYNTAX

@YEAR(date number)

where date number is a serial number between 0 (which returns 0 for 1900) and 73050 (which returns 199 for 2099). Most of the time, the date number is supplied by using another of the date functions to calculate it, although it can be entered manually.

USAGE

This function calculates the number of the year by supplying the date serial number as the argument. The date number used as the argument can consist of a manual entry, a date function that calculates the number, or a cell reference that contains the date number, which has been either manually entered or calculated by the date functions @NOW or @DATE. This function is useful whenever you need to work with only the year rather than the entire date.

To use @YEAR, move the cell pointer to the cell where you want the year to appear, type **@YEAR(**, and indicate the date number either by referencing another cell, entering the date function @NOW or @DATE (yr,month,day), or typing in the digits of the serial number. Then type a **)** and press the Return key.

EXAMPLES

To find the year represented by the serial number calculated by entering @DATE(86,11,15) in cell A1, you would enter the following in the cell where you want the year to appear:

@YEAR(A1)

Lotus 1-2-3 returns the value 86.

To return only the year portion of @DATE(86,11,15), which has not yet been entered into another cell of the worksheet, enter the following in the cell where you want the year to appear:

@YEAR(@DATE(86,11,15))

Lotus 1-2-3 returns the value 86.

You can also use @YEAR to enter the year in a logical statement that uses the @IF function. The following example checks to see whether the year represented by the serial number calculated in cell A1 is greater than or equal to 31778 (the serial number for January 1, 1987) and then returns the appropriate message in the cell:

**@IF(@YEAR(A1)> = 87,"Projected Budget Figures",
"Budget Figures")**

You can also return the digits of the current year in a cell by using the @NOW (or @TODAY function) as the argument of the @YEAR function. Enter it as follows:

@YEAR(@NOW)

If you wanted to use only the year portion of the date November 15, 1986 and you knew that the digits of its serial number were 31731, you could enter the following:

@YEAR(31731)

Lotus 1-2-3 returns the value 86.

@MONTH

This function returns the number of the month represented by the digits of the date serial number given as the argument.

SYNTAX

@MONTH(date number)

where date number is a serial number between 0 (which returns 1 for January) and 73050 (which returns 12 for December). Most of the time, the date number is supplied by using another of the date functions to calculate it, although it can be entered manually.

USAGE

This function calculates the number of the month by supplying the date serial number as the argument. The date number used as the argument can consist of a manual entry, a date function that calculates the number, or a cell reference that contains the date number which has been either entered manually or calculated by the date functions @NOW or @DATE. This function is useful whenever you need to work only with the month rather than the entire date.

To use @MONTH, move the cell pointer to the cell where you want the month to appear, type **@MONTH(**, and indicate the date number either by referencing another cell, entering the date function @NOW or @DATE(yr,month,day), or typing in the digits of the serial number. Then type a) and press the Return key.

EXAMPLES

To find the month represented by the serial number calculated by entering @DATE(86,11,15) in cell A1, enter the following in the cell where you want the month to appear:

@MONTH(A1)

Lotus 1-2-3 returns the value 11.

To return only the month portion of @DATE(86,11,15), which has not yet been entered into another cell of the worksheet, enter the following in the cell where you want the month to appear:

@MONTH(@DATE(86,11,15))

Lotus 1-2-3 returns the value 11.

You can also use @MONTH to enter a month in a logical statement that uses the @IF function. The following example checks whether the month represented by the serial number calculated in cell A1 is greater than or equal to 6 (June or later) and then returns the appropriate message in the cell:

@IF(@MONTH(A1)> =6,"3rd and 4th Qtr Figures", "1st and 2nd Qtr Figures")

If you wanted to use only the month portion of the date November 15, 1986 and you knew that the digits of its serial number were 31731, you could enter the following:

@MONTH(31731)

Lotus 1-2-3 returns the value 11.

@DAY

This function returns the number of the day represented by the digits of the date serial number given as the argument.

SYNTAX

@DAY(date number)

where date number is a serial number between 1 (which returns 1 for January 1, 1900) and 73050 (which returns 31 for December 31, 2099). Most of the time, the date number is supplied by using another of the date functions to calculate it, although it can be entered manually.

USAGE

This function calculates the number of the day by supplying the date serial number as the argument. The date number used as the argument can consist of a manual entry, a date function that calculates the number, or a cell reference that contains the date number, which has been either entered manually or calculated by the date functions @NOW or @DATE. This function is useful whenever you need to work with only the day of the month rather than the entire date.

To use @DAY, move the cell pointer to the cell where you want the day to appear, type **@DAY(**, and indicate the date number either by referencing another cell, entering the date function @NOW or @DATE (yr,month,day), or typing in the digits of the serial number. Then type a) and press the Return key.

EXAMPLES

To find the day of the month represented by the serial number calculated by entering @DATE(86,11,15) in cell A1, enter the following in the cell where you want the day to appear:

@DAY(A1)

Lotus 1-2-3 returns the value 15.

To return only the day portion of @DATE(86,11,15), which has not yet been entered into another cell of the worksheet, enter the following in the cell where you want the day to appear:

@DAY(@DATE(86,11,15))

Lotus 1-2-3 returns the value 15.

You can also use @DAY to enter the day in a logical statement that uses the @IF function. The following example checks whether the day of the month represented by the serial number calculated in cell A1 is less than or equal to 15 and then returns the appropriate message in the cell:

@IF(@DAY(A1)< = 15,"1st Pay Period","2nd Pay Period")

If you wanted to use only the month portion of the date November 15, 1986 and you knew that the digits of its serial number were 31731, you could enter the following:

@DAY(31731)

Lotus 1-2-3 returns the value 15.

@DATEVALUE (Release 2 Only)

This function returns the correct date serial number for a date entered as a string (a label entry).

SYNTAX

@DATEVALUE(date string)

where date string is a date entered as a label that conforms to one of Lotus 1-2-3's date formats. If it does not, this function will return an ERR value in the cell where it is entered. You will also receive an ERR value if the month exceeds 12, the number of days exceeds the normal number of days contained in the given month, or the year exceeds 199 (i.e., is not between 1900 and 2099).

The date string argument can consist of a cell reference to a cell that contains the date string or can be the date string itself enclosed in a pair of quotation marks.

USAGE

The @DATEVALUE function converts a date entered as a label in a spreadsheet to a Lotus 1-2-3 date serial number. You can then use it with other dates entered with the @NOW or @DATE functions to perform date arithmetic, sort dates, or perform searches on date columns (fields) in a Lotus 1-2-3 database. @DATEVALUE is most useful when the dates in a spreadsheet have been imported from another application in which they had to be entered as date strings, usually in the long international format of MM/DD/YY.

To use this function, move the cell pointer to the cell where you want the serial number to appear, type **@DATEVALUE(**, and indicate the cell reference that contains the date string or enter the date string enclosed in a pair of quotation marks. Then type a) and press the Return key.

You can then format the serial number calculated by this function to one of the Lotus 1-2-3 date display formats by using the /Range Format Date command and choosing the number of the format you wish to use.

EXAMPLES

The examples shown in Figure 14.4 illustrate the types of date strings that can be used successfully with the @DATEVALUE function. The date string examples in column A of this spreadsheet that begin with a number all had to be prefaced with an apostrophe to force the program into LABEL mode.

Certain date strings cannot be converted; they return ERR values in the spreadsheet. This is because these strings do not conform to Lotus 1-2-3 date display formats. The entry in cell A7 could have been converted successfully if the date had been entered as 87-10-03 and the long international display format had been changed with the /Worksheet Global Default Other International Date D command. This is the only display format that allows hyphens between date numbers, though the pattern it requires is always YY-MM-DD. If this default were in effect, the date string entered in B11 could have been converted successfully if it were changed to "87-10", which would then conform to the short international version of this format.

```
B11: [W15] @DATEVALUE("10-87")                                    READY

         A              B              C         D         E         F
1                   Serial Number  @DATEVALUE
2   Date String     Returned       Function Entered
3   ------------------------------------------------------------------
4   10/03/87                32053 <-- @DATEVALUE(A4)
5   03-Oct-87               32053 <-- @DATEVALUE(A5)
6   October 3, 1987           ERR <-- @DATEVALUE(A6)
7   10-03-87                  ERR <-- @DATEVALUE(A7)
8   Oct-87                  32051 <-- @DATEVALUE(A8)
9                           32053 <-- @DATEVALUE("03-Oct-87")
10                          32051 <-- @DATEVALUE("Oct-87")
11                            ERR <-- @DATEVALUE("10-87")
12
13
```

FIGURE 14.4: Examples using the @DATEVALUE function to attempt to convert various date strings into equivalent date serial numbers. Notice that the argument for this function can be supplied either by cell reference to a date string in another cell or by actually entering the date string enclosed in quotes. Some of the date strings entered in this figure do not conform to date display formats supported by Lotus 1-2-3; ERR values have been returned in these cases.

Also note that when only the month and year are specified in the date strings Oct-87 and "Oct-87", the @DATEVALUE function returns the serial number equivalent to the first day of the month (32051 = 01-Oct-87). Entering the date in the format in which the month is completely spelled out followed by the day, a comma, and the four digits of the year (in cell A6) cannot be accommodated with the @DATEVALUE function.

The Time Functions (Release 2 Only)

The time function reference entries are presented in the order @TIME, @HOUR, @MINUTE, @SECOND, and @TIMEVALUE. In addition to these specific time functions, the @NOW function can return the current time when it is used with one of the possible time display formats (refer to the @NOW reference entry in the previous section for details on this usage).

@TIME

This function returns the decimal equivalent of the time of day according to the values entered as arguments for the function.

SYNTAX

@TIME(hr,min,sec)

where hr is the number of the hour between 0 (for midnight) and 23 (for 11:00 PM), min is the number of minutes between 0 and 59, and sec is the number of seconds between 0 and 59. If the argument values are larger than 23 hours, 59 minutes, and 59 seconds, respectively, the function will return an ERR value. The arguments can be literal values or references to cells that contain such literal or calculated values, entered either by cell address or range name.

USAGE

The @TIME function can be used to enter a specific time of day into a cell or formula in the spreadsheet. When @TIME is used to enter times into cells, the program can perform arithmetic calculations that determine the difference between times. This is useful in applications in which you need to keep track of elapsed times, such as in time-and-billing calculations or logging differences between start and stop times.

To enter the time into a cell of the spreadsheet by using the @TIME function, move the cell pointer to the cell where you want the specific time to be displayed; type **@TIME(** and then enter the number of the hour of the day or indicate the cell reference that contains it, followed by a comma. Then indicate the number of minutes followed by another comma. Finally, indicate the number of seconds in the same way, type a), and press the Return key.

Lotus 1-2-3 returns the decimal equivalent of the time of day in the cell. You can then format the display by using the /Range Format Date Time command and choosing one of the following time display formats:

- Time 1 uses the pattern HH:MM:SS AM/PM. This format displays the hours, minutes, and seconds as well as the designation AM or PM. It is shown as (D6) in the literal contents of the cell.
- Time 2 uses the pattern HH:MM AM/PM. This format omits the display of the seconds, making it a shortened form of the Time 1 display. It is shown as (D7) in the literal contents of the cell.
- Time 3, the long international format, uses the pattern HH:MM:SS on a 24-hour clock (it does not include the AM/PM designation) as its default. This format is shown as (D8) in the literal contents of the cell. You can change it from this default (A), which uses colons as the

delimiter, by using the /Worksheet Global Default Other International Time command and choosing any of the other three formats available (B, C, or D).

- Time 4, the short international format, uses the pattern HH:MM on a 24-hour clock as its default. This format is shown as (D9). It is the same as the long international format, except that it omits the display of the seconds. It too can be changed from the default, which uses the colon delimiter, by using the /Worksheet Global Default Other International Time command.

In addition to using the @TIME function to calculate the time of day, you can use it in formulas that evaluate and calculate new values. For instance, you could enter the following formula:

@IF(@NOW = @TIME(11,12,0),"Meeting Time!"," ")

which enters the message Meeting Time! in the cell where the formula is entered as soon as the time portion of the @NOW function is equal to 11:12 AM.

You can also use the @TIME function in a formula that calculates elapsed time, as illustrated in the following formula:

(@TIME(13,0,0) – @TIME(9,15,0))*95*24

This formula calculates the amount due to a consultant on a given day by subtracting the stop time from the start time and then multiplying the result by an hourly rate of $95.00. Note that because time in Lotus 1-2-3 is measured as a decimal fraction of a day, you must multiply that fraction by 24 to convert the time into hours.

EXAMPLES

Figure 14.5 shows a spreadsheet that keeps a log of elapsed times for a battery of product tests. Column C contains the start times and column D the stop times. The elapsed time of each test is then calculated in column E by subtracting the stop time in column D from the start time in column C.

Notice that two different time display formats are used in this log. The start and stop times are formatted with time format 1, which includes the hours, minutes, and seconds with the AM/PM designation. The elapsed times are formatted with the long international time display, Time 3 [shown as (D8) in the Control Panel]. This long international format was changed from the default pattern of HH:MM:SS to HHhMMmSSs

```
E6: (D8) [W11] +D6-C6                                                READY

       A         B          C              D             E          F
1  Date:     11/05/86
2  Test Log for Product A0567
3  Tests 1234 - 1240
4
5  Test No.  Product      Start:          Stop:        Elapsed:
6  1234      A0567     09:17:45 AM   10:05:06 AM   00h47m21s
7  1235      A0567     10:12:05 AM   01:01:06 PM   02h49m01s
8  1236      A0567     09:25:17 AM   11:15:02 AM   01h49m45s
9  1237      A0567     01:02:50 PM   01:55:30 PM   00h52m40s
10 1238      A0567     02:01:00 PM   02:20:40 PM   00h19m40s
11 1240      A0567     03:10:01 PM   03:23:30 PM   00h13m29s
12
```

FIGURE 14.5: A product testing log using the @TIME function to enter start and stop times and to calculate elapsed time during testing. In this figure, the starting times in column C and the ending times in column D were entered with the @TIME function. These columns were then formatted with /RFDT1. The elapsed time figures in column E were calculated by subtracting the stop time from the start time as shown in the first formula in the Control Panel. These figures were then formatted with /RFDT3. This long international format was altered to the display seen in this column using /WGDOITD.

shown in the figure by using the /Worksheet Global Default Other International Time command with the D option.

@HOUR

This function returns the number of the hour between 0 (for 12:00 AM or midnight) and 23 (for 11:00 PM) represented in the time serial number entered as the argument.

SYNTAX

@HOUR(time number)

where time number is a value between 0.000, which returns the hour 0 for midnight, and 0.9999, which returns the hour of 11:00 PM. If the argument is a mixed number, only the decimal part of the value is used to determine the hour. If the argument is an integer, the function uses 0.000 as the time value and returns the hour of midnight (0).

The time number argument can be another time function, such as @NOW, @TIME, or @TIMEVALUE, a fractional serial number, or a calculation that results in such a number.

USAGE

This function returns the number of the hour from a fractional serial number. It is often used to return only the hour portion of a time value entered with the @TIME or @NOW functions. It can also be used to return the hour of the day from a decimal value representing the fractional serial number that is entered manually or calculated by a formula that does not use the @TIME function. @HOUR is useful whenever your work requires using only the hour portion of the time.

To use the @HOUR function to enter the number of the hour in a cell of the spreadsheet, move the cell pointer to the cell where you want the number of the hour to appear, type **@HOUR(**, and indicate the time value either by cell reference or by entering it manually. Then type **)** and press the Return key.

Besides using the @HOUR function to enter the hour of the day in a cell, you can combine it in formulas. For instance, you could use it in a conditional statement, as in the following formula:

@IF(@HOUR(@NOW)>17,"You are on overtime!"," ")

which displays the overtime message as soon as the hour in the current time passes 5:00 PM.

@HOUR can also be used in formulas that calculate new values, as in this example:

@HOUR(A1) – @HOUR(A3)

This formula returns the difference between the hours calculated by the @TIME function in A1 and that in A3.

EXAMPLES

The argument of the @HOUR function can be entered in a variety of ways. To determine the hour of the day when you enter the decimal equivalent of the time of day, enter the formula in the following way:

@HOUR(0.8567)

It returns a value of 20 or 8:00 PM.

To determine the hour of the day when entering a calculation as the argument, enter the formula like this:

@HOUR(6.5/12.75)

It returns a value of 12 or 12:00 PM.

You can also combine the @HOUR function with the @TIME or @NOW function. For example, if you enter the function @TIME (7,45,15) in cell A1 and then enter the formula

@HOUR(A1)

Lotus 1-2-3 returns the value 7 in the cell where this function is entered.

If the argument of the @HOUR function is an integer, it returns a value of zero: entering the formula

@HOUR(32501)

returns the value of 0, equivalent to midnight.

@MINUTE

This function returns the number of the minute between 0 and 59 represented in the time serial number entered as the argument.

SYNTAX

@MINUTE(time number)

where time number is a value between 0.000 and 0.9999. If the argument is a mixed number, only the decimal part of the value is used to determine the minute. If the argument is an integer, the function uses 0.000 as the time value and returns the minute 0.

The time number argument can be another time function, such as @NOW, @TIME, or @TIMEVALUE, a fractional serial number, or a calculation that results in such a number.

USAGE

This function extracts the number of minutes represented by the time serial number used as its argument. It is useful whenever you need to work with only the minute portion of the time either in data entry in the spreadsheet or when using formulas to calculate new time values. Like the @HOUR function, @MINUTE can be used with the time functions @NOW, @TIME, and @TIMEVALUE to return only the number of minutes from their calculated time numbers.

To use the @MINUTE function to enter a minute value in a cell, move the cell pointer to where you want the value to appear, type

@MINUTE(, and indicate the time value either by cell reference or by entering it manually. Then type) and press the Return key.

The @MINUTE function can be combined in formulas, as in the following example:

@IF(@MINUTE(A1)> = 45,@HOUR(A1) + 1,@MINUTE(A1))

This example adds an additional hour to the number of hours represented in the time number in cell A1 if the number of minutes is over 45; otherwise, it returns the number of minutes in this number into the cell where the formula is entered.

EXAMPLES

The argument of the @MINUTE function can be entered in a variety of ways. To determine the minute when you enter the decimal equivalent of the time of day, enter the formula as follows:

@MINUTE(0.8567)

It returns a value of 33 minutes.

To determine the minute of the hour when entering a calculation as the argument, enter the formula like this:

@MINUTE(6.5/12.75)

It returns a value of 14 minutes.

You can also combine the @MINUTE function with the @TIME or @NOW functions. For example, if you enter the function @TIME(7,45,15) in cell A1 and then enter the formula

@MINUTE(A1)

Lotus 1-2-3 returns the value 45 in the cell where this function is entered.

If the argument of the @MINUTE function is an integer, it returns a value of zero: entering the formula

@MINUTE(32501)

returns the value of 0 minutes.

@SECOND

This function returns the number of seconds between 0 and 59 represented in the time serial number entered as the argument.

SYNTAX

@SECOND(time number)

where time number is a value between 0.000 and 0.9999. If the argument is a mixed number, only the decimal part of the value is used to determine the seconds. If the argument is an integer, the function uses 0.000 as the time value and returns a seconds value of 0.

The time number argument can be another time function, such as @NOW, @TIME, or @TIMEVALUE, a fractional serial number, or a calculation that results in such a number.

USAGE

This function extracts the number of seconds represented by the time serial number used as its argument. It is useful whenever you need to work with only the seconds portion of the time either in data entry in the spreadsheet or when using formulas to calculate new time values. Like the @HOUR function, @SECOND can be used with the time functions @NOW, @TIME, and @TIMEVALUE to return only the number of seconds from their calculated time numbers.

To use the @SECOND function to enter a minute value in a cell, move the cell pointer to where you want the value to appear, type **@SECOND(**, and indicate the time value either by cell reference or by entering it manually. Then type) and press the Return key.

The @SECOND function can be combined in formulas, as in the following example:

@IF(@SECOND(A1)> = 45,@MINUTE(A1) + 1,@SECOND(A1))

This example adds an additional minute to the time number in cell A1 if the number of seconds is over 45; otherwise, it returns the number of seconds unchanged into the cell where the formula is entered.

EXAMPLES

The argument of the @SECOND function can be entered in a variety of ways. To determine the minute when you enter the decimal equivalent of the time of day, enter the formula as follows:

@SECOND(0.8567)

It returns a value of 39 seconds.

To determine the number of seconds when entering a calculation as the argument, enter the formula like this:

@SECOND(6.5/12.75)

It returns a value of 7 seconds.

You can also combine the @SECOND function with the @TIME or @NOW function. For example, if you enter the function @TIME(7,45,15) in cell A1 and then enter the formula

@SECOND(A1)

Lotus 1-2-3 returns the value 15 in the cell where this function is entered.

If the argument of the @SECOND function is an integer, it returns a value of zero. Entering the formula

@SECOND(32501)

returns the value of 0 seconds.

@TIMEVALUE

This function returns the correct time serial number for the time entered as a string (a label entry).

SYNTAX

@TIMEVALUE(time string)

where time string is a time entered as a label that conforms to one of Lotus 1-2-3's time formats. If it does not, this function will return an ERR value in the cell where it is entered. You will also receive an ERR value if the hour exceeds 23 or if the minutes or seconds exceed 59.

The time string argument can consist of a cell reference to a cell that contains the time string, or it can be the time string itself enclosed in a pair of quotation marks.

USAGE

The @TIMEVALUE function converts a time entered as a label in a spreadsheet to a Lotus 1-2-3 fractional serial number. You can then use it with other times entered with the @NOW or @TIME functions to perform arithmetic operations between times or set up calculated criteria using times to perform searches in a Lotus 1-2-3 database. @TIMEVALUE is most useful when the times in a spreadsheet have been imported from another application in which they had to be entered as time strings, usually in the format of HH:MM:SS AM/PM.

To use this function, move the cell pointer to the cell where you want the fractional serial number to appear, type **@TIMEVALUE(**, and indicate the cell reference that contains the time string or enter the time string enclosed in a pair of quotation marks. Then type a) and press the Return key.

You can then format the fractional serial number calculated by this function to one of the Lotus 1-2-3 time display formats by using the /Range Format Date Time command and choosing the number of the format you wish to use.

EXAMPLES

The examples shown in Figure 14.6 illustrate the types of time strings that can be used successfully with the @TIMEVALUE function. The time string examples in column A of this spreadsheet all had to be prefaced with an apostrophe to force the program into LABEL mode.

The program assumes that hours between 1 and 11 are AM times unless the label contains the PM designation. In the example in A7, the time string is entered as 23:59:59 to avoid this ambiguity.

Also notice that entering the number of minutes as 60 in cell A8 caused the function to return an ERR value in B8 where the @TIME-VALUE function was entered, because the minutes cannot exceed 59 without adding an additional hour to the time.

```
B10: [W15] @TIMEVALUE("11:59 PM")                                    READY

          A              B               C          D        E        F
1                  Serial Number   @TIMEVALUE
2    Time String   Returned        Function Entered
3   ------------------------------------------------------------
4    11:59:59 AM     0.4999884259 <-- @TIMEVALUE(A4)
5    11:59:59        0.4999884259 <-- @TIMEVALUE(A5)
6    11:59:59 PM     0.9999884259 <-- @TIMEVALUE(A6)
7    23:59:59        0.9999884259 <-- @TIMEVALUE(A7)
8    11:60                    ERR <-- @TIMEVALUE(A8)
9                    0.4993055556 <-- @TIMEVALUE("11:59")
10                   0.9993055556 <-- @TIMEVALUE("11:59 PM")
11
```

FIGURE 14.6: Examples using the @TIMEVALUE function to convert various time strings into equivalent fractional serial numbers. Notice that the argument for this function can be supplied either by cell reference to a date string in another cell or by actually entering the time string enclosed in quotes. The function entered in B8 returned an ERR value because the number of minutes cannot exceed 59. Also notice that the program assumed that all times with 11 as the hour were AM times unless the PM notation was attached.

SUMMARY

This chapter has covered the date and time functions offered by Lotus 1-2-3. These functions convert dates and times into special serial numbers that can be used in arithmetic calculations and applications that call for comparison. Because the serial numbers returned by these functions are generally unintelligible to the user, Lotus 1-2-3 provides a variety of display formats for both dates and times; they are accessed by using the /Range Format command.

The date functions have numerous applications in Lotus 1-2-3 spreadsheets, especially those involved with accounting, job scheduling, and personnel record keeping in which dates are used to age accounts, to calculate vacation accrual, to keep track of shipping dates, order dates, project start and stop dates, hire dates, and so on. The time functions can be used in time and billing applications as well as to create meeting schedules and keep time logs.

The references below give you suggestions on where to locate general information on the use of functions in the spreadsheet.

For general information on using Lotus 1-2-3 functions:

- Chapter 10, "Working with Formulas and Functions"

For information on using the logical functions, especially @IF, with which the date and time functions are often combined:

- Chapter 15, "Logical Functions"

For general information on using Lotus 1-2-3 functions in building spreadsheet models:

- Chapter 19, "Spreadsheet Models, Error Trapping, and Recalculation"

CHAPTER 15

LOGICAL FUNCTIONS

Logical Functions

This chapter examines the group of Lotus 1-2-3 functions known as the logical functions. In addition to the basic core of five logical functions offered in Release 1A (the functions @IF, @TRUE, @FALSE, @ISNA, and @ISERR), Release 2 has added two additional functions, @ISNUMBER and @ISSTRING, in keeping with this version's ability to process character strings as special string values.

Following the opening discussions on the general use of the logical functions and the use of strings in the @IF function in Release 2, you will find a reference entry and examples for each of these seven functions in the order they are listed above.

How the Logical Functions Operate

The logical functions assign the value 1 as the logical value carrying the meaning of true and, conversely, 0 as the logical value carrying the meaning of false. They all evaluate the contents of a specific cell in the spreadsheet and return a value of either 1 or 0, depending on whether a particular condition exists.

The simple logical functions @ISNA and @ISERR and the two new functions @ISNUMBER and @ISSTRING require only a single cell reference as their argument. They work alike in that they examine the contents of the cell specified in the argument to determine whether it contains the kind of entry they are designed to test for. If it does, they return the value 1; if it does not, they return the value 0.

The @TRUE and @FALSE functions take no arguments and so work somewhat differently from this group. Whenever you enter @TRUE in a cell in the spreadsheet, it always returns 1 in that cell. As expected, entering @FALSE in any given cell always returns 0 in that cell. This would be of limited usefulness were it not for the fact that @TRUE and @FALSE can be combined with the most versatile of the logical functions, the @IF function.

Using the @IF Function

Like all of the other logical functions, the @IF function tests the contents of a cell and returns the logical value of 1 for true and 0 for false. However, unlike the others, it allows you to set up alternative values that are to be used, depending on the outcome of the test.

These alternative values are supplied as arguments of the function following the conditional statement that you create. The format for entering the @IF function is often given as follows:

@IF(condition,true value,false value)

The condition to be used is always the first argument in the @IF function; it is followed by the value that is to be used if the condition proves to be true (referred to as the x argument), and then the value to be used if the condition proves to be false (referred to as the y argument).

When you set up a condition that contains an equation, you can use one or more of the logical operators. If you need to set up a complex condition that requires more than a single logical operator, you join the logical operators by using one of the Boolean operators. The logical and Boolean operators and their functions are summarized in Table 15.1. Additional examples of the applications that follow are also given in the reference section.

	SYMBOL	DEFINITION	EXAMPLE
Logical operators	=	Equal to	A1=10
	<>	Not equal to	A1<>10
	>	Greater than	A>10
	>=	Greater than or equal to	A1>=10
	<	Less than	A1<10
	<=	Less than or equal to	A1<=10
Boolean operators	#AND#	Both cond1 and cond2	A1>10#AND#A1<20
	#AND##NOT#	Both cond1 and not cond2	A1>10#AND##NOT#A1=20
	#OR#	Either cond1 or cond2	A1=10#OR#A1=20
	#OR##NOT#	Either cond1 or not cond2	A1=10#OR##NOT#A1>20
	#NOT#	Not cond1	#NOT#A1=10

TABLE 15.1: The Logical and Boolean Operators

USING THE @IF FUNCTION TO DOCUMENT THE CONDITION

At the most basic level, you can use the @IF function to evaluate and document whether the stated condition exists. To do this, you can use the @TRUE and @FALSE functions as the true and false values as follows:

@IF(B45 = 500,@TRUE,@FALSE)

As long as the value in B45 is 500, this formula will return 1, the value calculated by the @TRUE function. Should the value ever become anything other than 500, the formula will return 0, the value calculated by the @FALSE function.

USING THE @IF FUNCTION FOR ALTERNATE CALCULATIONS

Beyond the level of just documenting whether a condition exists, you can also use the @IF function to perform calculations or supply new values, depending on the outcome of testing the condition. For instance, to have the spreadsheet calculate a bonus of 2 percent whenever a salesperson's total monthly sales equal or exceed $5,000.00, you could use the @IF function and the logical operator > = (greater than or equal to) to state the condition. Assuming that the total sales figure is contained in cell C35, you enter the following formula:

@IF(C35> = 5000,C35*.02,0)

In this case, Lotus 1-2-3 calculates the 2 percent bonus only if the sales figure is found to be at least $5,000.00. If it is not, the value of zero is entered in the cell where this formula is input.

USING OTHER LOGICAL FUNCTIONS IN @IF CONDITIONS

You can also use one of the other logical functions (other than @TRUE and @FALSE) offered by Lotus 1-2-3 in constructing the @IF condition. This provides an effective method for identifying and trapping potential errors that could spread to other formulas whose values depend on the content of the cell in question.

For instance, you can set up an @IF formula that checks whether a particular cell contains an ERR value. If it does, the @IF function returns a value of zero, which is carried forward to the dependent formulas in place of the ERR value. If the cell doesn't contain an ERR value, the original value in the test cell is allowed to be carried forward. The following example demonstrates this:

@IF(@ISERR(D125),0,D125)

The value in D125 is returned in the cell where this @IF function is entered only if D125 does not contain an ERR value. (For more information on the @ISERR function, see its reference entry at the end of this chapter.)

You can do similar types of error trapping by using the @ISNA function and Release 2's @ISNUMBER and ISSTRING functions. These functions are especially effective when combined in macros that test keyboard input to prevent a certain type of illegal entry that would result in an ERR value (such as a label in a cell which is used in calculations).

Using Nested @IF Functions

Used alone, the @IF function can supply you with only two alternative values to be used, depending on the result of testing your condition (it uses either the x or y value). When you have more than two alternatives that need to be covered, you can nest @IF functions within the original @IF formula to increase the possible outcomes.

You do this by entering another @IF function either as the true value (x argument) or as the false value (y argument). For an example, consider the following @IF formula that evaluates the three possible outcomes of the condition:

@IF(T5>500,@IF(T5 = 2*T4,1000,800),400)

This formula works by evaluating the value in cell T5 to see if it is greater than 500. If it is, it evaluates the second @IF function used as the true value. If it is not, it simply enters the value 400 in the cell where this formula is entered.

Assuming that the value is found to be more than 500 and the nested @IF function is therefore evaluated, the program tests the value of T5 against that of twice the value in cell T4. If that equation is true, 1000 is entered. If it is not, 800 is entered.

You could also use a second @IF function as the false value instead of the true value. Consider this example:

@IF(T5> = 250,.75*T5,@IF(T5 – T4>0,.5*T5,T5))

The program returns 75 percent of the value in T5 if the value in T5 is found to be greater than or equal to 250. If it is less, the program compares the value returned when the value in T4 is subtracted from that in T5. If this remainder is greater than zero, it returns 50 percent of the value of T5. If this remainder is 0 or less, it returns the current value of T5.

You are not restricted to a particular number of nested @IF functions that can be used in either the x or y arguments of an original @IF function. However, the formula must not contain over 240 characters, the maximum for any Lotus 1-2-3 formula, or 32 sets of nested parentheses.

@IF formulas can easily become quite complex (and consequently difficult to decipher) as the result of adding all of the nested @IF functions required to cover all possible outcomes. When you construct an elaborate @IF formula, you must be careful not to omit the final parenthesis for any of the @IF functions used. This is an easy thing to overlook when you are entering a really long formula with several nested @IF functions.

You must also make sure that the logic you set up by the order and number of the nested @IF functions used results in all of the outcomes you desire. The flow of the logic is from the most general case to the most specific, with each nested @IF function tightening the parameters whenever the test passes or fails the condition of the @IF function surrounding it.

It is usually a good idea to write out the formula on paper before trying to enter it into the spreadsheet. This allows you to mark each @IF function as an x or y argument of the preceding @IF function, check the overall logic, and make sure that all of the arguments of all of the @IF functions used have been closed off with their own right parenthesis. For each left parenthesis, there must be a balancing right parenthesis. You can check this by counting each type to make sure you haven't omitted one.

Finally, after you have entered the @IF formula successfully, you must ascertain that it is performing as planned. This may not be at all obvious from the result you obtain from your original entry of the formula. Sometimes it is helpful to substitute @TRUE and @FALSE functions for the @IF functions used as arguments of another @IF function. You can then determine from the values obtained from this substitution that all is working properly at each stage of the nesting. You can also set up several test values that should return each possible outcome you anticipate in the spreadsheet to make sure the formula is performing correctly.

USING STRINGS IN THE @IF FUNCTION (RELEASE 2 ONLY)

Release 2 allows you to use character strings in the arguments of an @IF function, as long as they are enclosed in pairs of quotation marks. For instance, the following formula is valid in Release 2:

@IF(A1 = "Balance Sheet",@TRUE,@FALSE)

where the true value of 1 is returned if cell A1 contains the label Balance Sheet, and 0 is returned if it contains any other label. If, however, A1 contains some sort of value, an ERR value will be returned, indicating a type mismatch.

More often, you will use the ability of an @IF function to accept character strings to insert different messages, depending on the outcome of evaluating the conditional argument. For instance, you could enter the following to alert you to the presence of an exceedingly high credit balance due:

@IF(B55>10000,"OVER LIMIT","")

In this example, the message OVER LIMIT would appear in the cell where this formula is entered whenever the credit balance contained in B55 is greater than $10,000.00.

Using the @IF Function to Concatenate Strings

Because you can use string values in an @IF function, you can also use the & operator to join labels together. To prevent an error that would occur if you tried to join a label and a value with the & operator, you can use the @ISSTRING function in the condition to check that each cell to be joined does indeed contain a label.

For instance, you could use such a formula to automatically create a full-name column in column C of a database, using the last name entered in column A joined with the first name entered in column B. If you do this under the control of an @IF function using the @ISSTRING function in the condition to check that each name has been entered as a label, you can prevent ERR values in the new column as well as have an easy method for locating any values that have crept into the first or last name columns. Such a formula would look something like this:

**@IF(@ISSTRING(A3)#AND#@ISSTRING(B3),B3&" "&A3,
"TYPE MISMATCH")**

If you use such a formula, it will be easy to go back and locate any names that were not joined successfully. To do this, you would simply enter TYPE MISMATCH as the search criterion under the full-name column in the criterion range and then issue the /Data Query Find command. If Lotus 1-2-3 finds any rows where this message was entered instead of a full name, you can then edit whichever entry in the first or last name field contains the value so that the concatenation can take place.

The Logical Functions

The individual reference entries for the logical functions common to both versions of Lotus 1-2-3 are listed first in the following order: @IF, @TRUE, @FALSE, @ISNA, and @ISERR. These are then followed by the entries for the two new Release 2 logical functions @ISNUMBER and @ISSTRING.

@IF

The @IF function evaluates the condition that makes up its first argument. If the condition is true, it returns the value entered as the second argument (the x value). If the condition is false, it returns the value given as the third argument (the y value).

SYNTAX

@IF(cond,x,y)

where cond is a conditional statement in the form of an equation or inequality, x is the value returned if the conditional statement is found to be true, and y is the value returned if the conditional statement is found to be false.

The conditional statement can contain a literal or calculated value or a cell reference to such values in the logical formula. The logical formula is separated by one or more of the logical and Boolean operators (see Table 15.1) and can also contain mathematical operators if a calculation is called for within the statement to be evaluated.

The x and y arguments, sometimes referred to as the "true and false" values, can contain literal values or cell references to literal values, calculations of some sort, or other Lotus 1-2-3 functions, including more @IF functions.

In Release 2 of the program, the arguments can also contain string values, as long as they are enclosed in a pair of quotation marks (refer back to the section "Using Strings in the @IF Function" in this chapter).

USAGE

The @IF function provides a powerful means not only for evaluating whether a particular condition exists in the spreadsheet but also for having the program take a particular action, depending on the outcome of the evaluation. This capability can be put to good use in a multitude of spreadsheet designs involving diverse applications.

In part, the @IF function is versatile because you can combine the other logical functions within it, thus allowing you to incorporate the particular type of testing each function is designed to do in the condition you develop. For instance, combining the @ISERR or @ISNA functions within an @IF condition allows you to do basic error trapping for either kind of value. In Release 2, you can incorporate the @ISNUMBER or @ISSTRING functions in the same way to test for the presence of a particular type of entry. This method is especially effective in macros that screen user input before processing it, as in adding new rows to a Lotus 1-2-3 database.

The @IF function is also quite versatile because it allows you to build complex conditions using the Boolean operators AND, OR, and NOT in addition to the full group of logical operators. Other @IF functions can also be nested within the basic @IF function, providing you with multiple branches off the original condition to cover all possible conditions that can arise and must be accounted for. When you create complex conditions or use nested @IF functions, you must be aware of the way Lotus 1-2-3 processes the finished formula so that your formula takes care of all of the potential conditions you wish to include (refer back to the section "Using Nested @IF Functions" for more information on this).

To use the @IF function, move the cell pointer to the cell where you want the result to appear and type **@IF(**. To create the condition, refer to the cell that is to be evaluated either by typing in its address or by pointing to it. After you indicate the cell to be used and whether it is to be used in some sort of calculation, type in the appropriate logical operator, followed by the value it is to be evaluated against. This value can be a literal value, another cell reference, or some sort of calculation.

When you use another logical function as the condition rather than a formula, type in its name, preceded by the @ symbol and followed by the cell reference it is to evaluate. Remember that each of these functions requires its own pair of parentheses.

If the condition involves more than one cell or if the same cell is to be evaluated in various ways, use the appropriate Boolean operator after you indicate the first cell. Remember that you must repeat the cell reference after each Boolean operator. For instance, the following complex condition will not be accepted by Lotus 1-2-3 because it does not repeat the cell reference:

@IF(A2>100#AND#<500,A2*.5,A2)

Instead, it must read

@IF(A2>100#AND#A2<500,A2*.5,A2)

After you indicate the condition, type a comma. Then begin to construct the formula or enter the value to be used if the condition is true. This formula or value can include literal values, cell references, or both, or it can even consist of another @IF function (or series of @IF functions) complete with its own condition and true and false values.

After you enter the x argument in one of these ways, type another comma and indicate the formula or value to be used if the condition is false. This is done in the same way that you indicate the true value. The y argument can also be a simple literal value, a calculated value involving literal values, cell references, or both, or it can be another series of @IF functions. After you have finished entering the y argument, type) and press the Return key to process the formula.

EXAMPLES

The @IF function has a great many uses in constructing spreadsheet formulas. At the most basic level, it can be used to choose between two alternate calculations that should take place, depending on the value of a particular cell:

@IF(K12<30000,K12*1.33,K12*1.5)

In this formula, the value in K12 is increased by 1.33 only when its value is below $30,000.00; otherwise, its value is increased 1.5 times. Using the @IF function in this way, you can have the program automatically calculate markups, commission rates, bonuses, and the like, whenever they are based on clear-cut break points.

Many times, the possible alternatives are not limited to two as in the preceding example. In such situations, you expand the basic @IF function to accommodate all of the possibilities by combining @IF conditions, as in the following example:

@IF(R2> =50000,@IF(R2< =75000,R2*.04,R2*.10),R2*.02)

In this example, you are testing for three possibilities: first, that the value in R2 will be below $50,000.00; second, that it will be greater than or equal to $50,000.00 but still be below $75,000.00; or, third, that it will be above $75,000.00.

Nesting is not limited to the above example, which evaluates three potential conditions in the spreadsheet. In fact, nesting can continue until the formula reaches 240 characters, the maximum allowed in any one formula.

The following example contains two @IF formulas within a basic @IF function. In this case, four conditions are evaluated and acted on accordingly:

@IF(A22< = 10000,@IF(B22< = 1,@VLOOKUP(A22,TBL1,1), @VLOOKUP(A22,TBL1,2)),@IF(B22< = 1,@VLOOKUP (A22,TBL2,1),@VLOOKUP(A22,TBL2,2)))

In this example, the basic problem is that you use two different lookup tables to determine the amount of the discount given on any customer sale. The factor determining which table is to be used is whether the total sale exceeds the amount of $10,000.00. Within each table, there is a further breakdown to be considered: preferred customers who have done volume business with the company in the past are given slightly larger discounts for the same dollar amount than are first-time or nonpreferred customers. The lower discount rates for first-time purchasers are listed in the first column to the right of the index column (offset 1), and the slightly higher rates are listed in the second column to the right (offset 2).

The formula automates this decision making, assuring you that the proper discount is given as long as the total sale in A22 and the code number (1 or blank for first-time buyers and 2 for preferred customers) in B22 is correctly entered. It works by first instructing the program to check the value in cell A22. If it is less than or equal to $10,000.00, the first nested @IF function is evaluated. If it is more, the second nested @IF function is evaluated. This condition provides the basic method for having the program choose between using either the discount lookup table 1 (called TBL1) or the discount lookup table 2 (called TBL2).

Then the program evaluates a code number in cell B22. If this code is less than or equal to 1, the lower discount percentage in offset 1 is returned; otherwise, the higher percentage listed in offset 2 is used. In both cases, you are assured that Lotus 1-2-3 is looking in the correct table because of the basic logic of the original @IF function.

@TRUE

The @TRUE function returns the logical value of 1.

SYNTAX

@TRUE

This function takes no arguments.

USAGE

When used alone, the @TRUE function returns the value of 1 in the cell where the function is entered. It is particularly useful when combined with the @IF function (as the x argument), where it offers a convenient method for validating and documenting the existence of the condition stated as the conditional argument. If the condition exists, the value of 1 is entered into the cell where the @IF function is used. Usually in such applications, the @FALSE function is used as the y argument so that the logical value of 1 for true is counterbalanced by the logical value of 0 for false. This provides a convenient method for visually checking the existence of a condition elsewhere in the spreadsheet that may not be at all obvious when just scanning the data.

This method of validating a true condition in the spreadsheet is especially important to Release 1A users who do not have the ability to place a text message such as "Yes", "True", or "Exists" as the x argument of the @IF function. When you use the @TRUE function in this way, it is also sometimes advantageous to format the results with the /Range Format +/− display, which converts the number 1 to a plus sign and 0 to a period.

When you use the @TRUE function, you merely type **@TRUE** and press the Return key.

EXAMPLES

The example below illustrates the use of the @TRUE function as an argument of an @IF function to validate the existence of a particular condition in the spreadsheet:

@IF(@NOW−A4>=45,@TRUE,@FALSE)

Cell A4 holds the invoice date. In this condition, the @IF function tests whether the invoice has aged 45 or more days by subtracting the invoice date from the current date. If it has, the function places a 1 in the cell where this function is entered. To make the use of the @TRUE function clear in the spreadsheet, you would probably want to enter this formula in the cell directly below a column heading of Overdue.

You could take this a step further by building another @IF condition in another cell to the right that then evaluates the results of this evaluation. For instance, say that the Overdue column is located in column G and the formula shown above was originally entered in G4. In cell H4, you could then construct this formula:

@IF(G4 = 1,E4*1.05,E4)

It evaluates the results of the @TRUE and @FALSE functions used as the arguments of the first @IF function in G4. If the account is found to be overdue (indicated by the value 1 in G4), a 5 percent late charge is added to the current account balance held in cell E4 before it is brought forward to cell H4 (used as the balance due cell); otherwise, the current balance is entered here unchanged.

@FALSE

The @FALSE function returns the logical value of 0.

SYNTAX

@FALSE

This function takes no arguments.

USAGE

When used alone, the @FALSE function always returns a value of 0 in the cell where it is entered. Like the @TRUE function, @FALSE is often combined with the @IF function so that its calculation of a zero value is used only when the condition stated does not exist in the spreadsheet. This makes it useful in situations where you need to validate and document whether a particular condition exists in another part of the worksheet.

In such an application, the @FALSE function is used as the y argument or the false value of the @IF condition (the @TRUE function is most often the x argument or true value). This allows you to determine quickly which cells fail the condition.

For users of Release 1A, using the zero returned by the @FALSE function to mark a false condition is the only avenue open because this version will not accept string values such as "No", "False", and "Does not exist" as the y argument, as is possible with Release 2.

When you use the @FALSE function, you merely type **@FALSE** and press the Return key.

EXAMPLES

The example below illustrates the use of the @FALSE function as an argument of an @IF function to validate the failure of a particular condition in the spreadsheet:

@IF(@AVG(C5..C8)<75000,@TRUE,@FALSE)

Zero is returned in the cell where this formula is entered if the average of the figures in the range of cells indicated as the argument of the @AVG function is above 75,000. If these figures represent weekly sales totals of a particular salesperson, the result of 1 indicates that his or her average monthly sales have fallen below the quota figure of a monthly average of $75,000.00 in sales.

When this formula was copied for all of the other salespeople in the store, you would have a reference table that would tell you immediately which of your sales force did not make the par for a given month.

@ISNA

The @ISNA function evaluates the x value given as its argument and returns the logical value of 1 (true) when the value is NA. It returns the logical value of 0 (false) if the cell contains any other numeric value or a string.

SYNTAX

@ISNA(x)

where x is a single cell reference that contains a label, value, or formula.

USAGE

This function is most often used with the @IF function to evaluate whether a particular cell contains the special numeric value NA, entered with the @NA function (see Chapter 18). If the cell is found to contain such a value, the spread of this NA value to all other formulas that depend on the value in this cell can be checked.

This is usually accomplished by specifying zero as the x argument of the @IF function, meaning that zero instead of NA will be used in all of the dependent formulas. If the cell does not contain the NA value, the calculation specifies its formula as the y argument of the @IF function (see the examples that follow).

EXAMPLES

The @ISNA function can be used alone to test for the presence of the NA value in a specific cell. Assume that you enter the following formula in cell B40:

@ISNA(B5)

The result is 1 in B40 if B5 contains NA and 0 if B5 contains any other value or a label. Cell B5 would contain an NA value either if the @NA function had been entered into it or if it were dependent on some other formula in which the @NA function was entered.

To prevent the proliferation of NA values into cells in other parts of the spreadsheet (assuming that they contain formulas dependent on the value calculated in B40), this formula could be combined with an @IF function:

@IF(@ISNA(B5),0,B11/B5)

In this example, zero is returned in B40 if B5 contains the NA value. Only when B5 does not contain NA will the program attempt to divide the value in B11 by B5. This prevents the ERR value being calculated in B40, which would result from attempting to divide a numeric value in B11 by an NA value in B5.

@ISERR

The @ISERR function evaluates the x value given as its argument and returns the logical value of 1 (true) when the value is ERR. It returns the logical value of 0 (false) if the cell contains any other numeric value or a string.

SYNTAX

@ISERR(x)

where x is a single cell reference that contains a literal value or one calculated by formula.

USAGE

The @ISERR function, like the @ISNA function, is most often used in the condition of an @IF function to evaluate whether a particular cell in the spreadsheet contains an ERR value. The purpose is to stop the spread of ERR values from this cell to all others whose formulas depend on it.

When used in this way, the value zero is often specified as the x argument of the @IF function so that it will be used in the dependent formulas in place of the ERR value. This means that dependent formulas can be calculated and the spreadsheet will not be littered with ERR values in the rest of the dependent formulas. The y argument is then the cell reference itself, allowing its value to be used in all dependencies whenever it is not ERR (see the examples that follow).

Note: Using zero as the x argument of an @IF condition containing an @ISERR function works only when the cell reference supplied as the argument of the @ISERR function is not used as a denominator in division in any of the dependent formulas, because division by zero is one of the major causes of ERR values in spreadsheets. (See Chapter 19 for more information about using this error-trapping technique.)

EXAMPLES

The @ISERR function can be used alone to check for the existence of an ERR value in a particular cell. Assume in the following example that the @ISERR function is entered into cell AB50 in the spreadsheet:

@ISERR(F50)

If cell F50 contains an ERR value, cell AB50 will contain a 1 to indicate this. If cell F50 contains any other kind of value or a label, AB50 will contain 0, indicating that the ERR value is not present there.

To prevent the proliferation of ERR values in a spreadsheet with formulas that depend on a specific value, the @ISERR function is often combined in an @IF function as follows:

@IF(@ISERR(X10),0,@IF(X10<15000,X10*1.5,X10))

In this example, the value 0 is returned in the cell where this formula is entered if the presence of an ERR value is detected in cell X10. Only if X10 does not contain an ERR value will Lotus 1-2-3 go ahead and evaluate the second @IF condition, and, depending on the value it contains, either multiply that value by 1.5 or use it as is.

@ISNUMBER (Release 2 Only)

The @ISNUMBER function evaluates the x value given as its argument and returns the logical value of 1 (true) when x is found to contain any type of numerical value (including ERR and NA values). It returns the logical value of 0 (false) if the cell contains a string.

SYNTAX

@ISNUMBER(x)

where x is a single cell reference that contains a literal value or one calculated by formula.

USAGE

This function is most useful when you need to ascertain that a particular cell in the spreadsheet contains a numeric value rather than a string value, which would result in an ERR value if it were used in another dependent formula calculation.

While the @ISNUMBER function can be used by itself to test whether a specific cell contains a value or string, it is most often used with the @IF function so that you can control what happens when the test fails (indicating that the cell does contain some sort of label).

Because both NA and ERR are special values in Lotus 1-2-3 that you will want to exclude from further calculation, you can set up a complex condition by using the @IF function to test both for the presence of a value and that this value is neither NA nor ERR. This usage is illustrated in the examples section that follows.

The @ISNUMBER function is also useful in macros where you need to validate that a user has entered a numeric value in a particular cell before the macro continues processing. This provides an error-checking routine to prevent label entries from causing ERR values in calculations. Inadvertent label entries can occur by pressing the lowercase letter l instead of the number 1 in a value that begins with 1.

EXAMPLES

To make a simple test for the presence of a value in a cell, you could enter the @ISNUMBER function as follows:

@ISNUMBER(D25)

This formula returns a 1 if D25 contains a value and 0 if it contains some sort of label (string).

More often, you will want to combine the @ISNUMBER function with the @IF function as part of the stated condition:

@IF(@ISNUMBER(D25),D25*1.5,"LABEL")

The condition checks for the presence of a value in cell D25 before multiplying it by 1.5. If D25 does not contain a value, the message LABEL will appear instead to alert you that D25 must be edited.

If you were concerned that the contents of cell D25 might contain either a label or ERR, which could proliferate ERR values in dependent formulas, you could then create a complex condition using the @ISNUMBER and @ISERR functions together as follows:

@IF(@ISSNUMBER(D25)#AND##NOT#@ISERR(D25),D25*1.5,0)

In this @IF formula, Lotus 1-2-3 checks whether D25 holds either a label or an ERR value. If neither of these conditions is true, it multiplies the value in D25 by 1.5; otherwise, it enters a zero value in D25. In this case, zero was used as the y argument because the message LABEL would cause ERR values in other cell dependencies that try to use the string as part of their calculations.

Note: You can do the same thing to guard against the presence of an NA value in the cell. You can also use this same complex condition with the @ISSTRING and @ISERR functions without having to use the #AND# and #NOT# operators (see the @ISSTRING function that follows).

@ISSTRING (Release 2 Only)

The @ISSTRING function evaluates the x value given as its argument and returns the logical value of 1 (true) when x is found to contain a string value (label). It returns the logical value of 0 (false) when the cell contains any kind of numerical value.

SYNTAX

@ISSTRING(x)

where x is a single cell reference that contains a literal value or one calculated by formula.

USAGE

This function is the logical counterpart of the @ISNUMBER function. It is used when you need to ascertain that a particular cell in the spreadsheet contains a label rather than a value. For instance, @ISSTRING could be used in a macro to prevent the user from entering a numeric zip code into a database column that already contains other zip codes entered as labels.

While the @ISSTRING function can be used by itself to test whether a specific cell contains a string or value, it is most often used with the @IF function so that you can control what happens when the test fails (indicating that the cell does contain some sort of value).

Like the @ISNUMBER function, @ISSTRING is also useful in macros, but it is used when you need to validate that a user has entered a label rather than a value in a particular cell before the macro continues processing. This provides an error-checking routine to prevent value entries that could cause ERR values, such as trying to join two labels together with the concatenation operator (&) when one contains a value and the other contains a label.

Such an application allows you to prevent simple mistakes like forgetting to preface an entry that begins with a number with one of the label prefixes. These kinds of mistakes can cause processing problems or inconsistencies in the data.

EXAMPLES

To make a simple test for the presence of a label in a cell, you could enter the @ISSTRING function as follows:

@ISSTRING(C10)

This formula returns a 1 if C10 contains a string value (i.e., was entered as a label) and 0 if C10 contains some sort of numerical value.

More often, you will want to combine the @ISSTRING function with the @IF function as part of a stated condition:

@IF(@ISSTRING(C10)#AND#@ISSTRING(D10),
C10&" "&D10,"VALUE")

This condition checks for the presence of labels in cells C10 and D10 before attempting to combine their contents in the cell where this formula is entered. If either C10 or D10 does not contain a string, the message VALUE appears instead to alert you that one of these cells must be edited before the concatenation can take place.

The @ISSTRING function can also be used in situations where you need to ensure that a cell contains neither a label nor the values NA or ERR, but only numeric content. To set up such a complex condition, you could enter a formula similar to this one:

@IF(@ISSTRING(A20)#OR#@ISNA(A20)#OR#
@ISERR(A20),0,A20/A17)

Here, the IF condition will return a value of zero in cell A20 if A20 contains anything other than a numeric value. This prevents an ERR value (from dividing A20 by A17 when A20 contains a nonnumeric value or a label) from being calculated in the cell where this formula is entered.

SUMMARY

Because the logical functions covered in this chapter, especially the @IF function, are often used with other Lotus 1-2-3 functions, you can learn more about them and how they can be used by referring to other related sections of this handbook as outlined in the following reference guide.

To obtain general information about Lotus 1-2-3 formulas:

- Chapter 10, "Working with Formulas and Functions"

To obtain more specific information about using character strings in formulas:

- Chapter 17, "String Functions"

For information about using the NA value in a cell:

- Chapter 18, "Special Functions"

For more information about using the @ISNA and @ISERR functions to perform error trapping in the spreadsheet:

- Chapter 19, "Spreadsheet Models, Error Trapping, and Recalculation"

CHAPTER 16

DATABASE STATISTICAL FUNCTIONS

Database Statistical Functions

The database statistical functions include the same functions as the group known as the statistical functions. Both sets of functions share the same names; the database statistical functions are prefaced with a D to mark them from their counterparts. This group includes @DSUM, @DAVG, @DCOUNT, @DMAX, @DMIN, @DSTD, and @DVAR.

These functions give you an easy way to collect specific statistics that describe the large pool of data you track and maintain in your database. They make it easy to analyze and report on data relationships that may not be at all obvious. Because these functions can work within the criteria you set up for the database, they give you greater control: you can restrict their use to the specific conditions you set up.

Following a general discussion of the arguments required by the database statistical functions and their use, you will find individual reference entries for each of the functions. These follow the order @DSUM, @DAVG, @DCOUNT, @DMAX, @DMIN, @DSTD, and @DVAR.

Arguments of the Database Statistical Functions

The database statistical functions perform the same calculations on a column (field) in a Lotus 1-2-3 database as the regular statistical functions perform on a list of cells in a spreadsheet (see Chapter 12). But because these functions work with a database, they require quite different arguments. The arguments required are the same for each and can be summarized as follows:

@Dfunction name(input,offset,criterion)

The first argument, called input, is synonymous with the input range of the database—that is, the cell range that includes a single row of unique column descriptions (field names) as the first row, followed by all the columns and rows of data in the entire table. The input argument required by the database statistical functions is exactly the same as the one you define as the input range for the database with the /Data Query Input command. (If you are unsure how to set up a Lotus 1-2-3 database, see Chapter 20.)

The second argument, called offset, refers to the numbering of the columns in the input range. The leftmost column has an offset number of 0, with each column to the right given the next whole number. The last offset number is always one less than the total number of columns in the database, because the numbering begins with zero.

The third argument, called criterion, is the cell range that contains the same column description (field name) as that entered in the first row of the database; the criteria to be used are entered into the cell directly below it. You can set up as many criterion ranges as you wish, but you must make sure that the column description is identical both in the input range and in the first cell of the criterion range.

The criterion range used as the function argument can be the same as the criterion range defined for the database with the /Data Query Criterion command, though it need not be. To specify an OR condition, you use a vertical placement, setting up the criteria in the same column beneath the column description. To specify an AND condition that includes several columns, you use a horizontal arrangement and set up the column names and criteria next to one another, thus creating a single range of cells. If the cells beneath the column descriptions (field names) are blank, the database statistical function will apply to all of the data in the database.

Figure 16.1 illustrates the cell ranges used as the input argument and possible criterion arguments when using the database statistical functions with a typical personnel database. It also shows the numbering of the offset for each column in the database that you must supply when you apply the function to that particular column of data in the database.

The offset number directs the program to the appropriate column when calculating the statistic governed by the particular function used. For instance, if you wanted to obtain the total of the salaries in the database, you would enter **7** as the offset argument in the @DSUM function. If you wanted to know how many of the employees are female, you would enter **3** as the offset argument in the @DCOUNT function.

USING THE DATABASE STATISTICAL FUNCTIONS

It is important to realize that despite the name *database statistical functions,* you can apply this group of functions to any table of worksheet data as long as the arguments that the functions require are satisfied. All this means is that the columns of data must have unique column headings, and

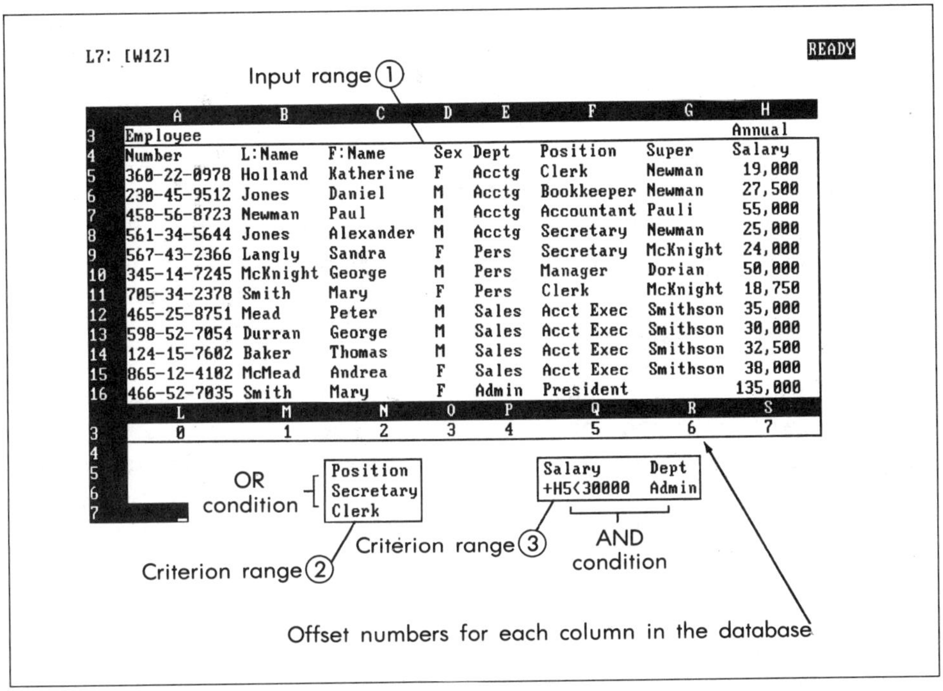

	A	B	C	D	E	F	G	H
3	Employee							Annual
4	Number	L:Name	F:Name	Sex	Dept	Position	Super	Salary
5	360-22-0978	Holland	Katherine	F	Acctg	Clerk	Newman	19,000
6	230-45-9512	Jones	Daniel	M	Acctg	Bookkeeper	Newman	27,500
7	450-56-8723	Newman	Paul	M	Acctg	Accountant	Pauli	55,000
8	561-34-5644	Jones	Alexander	M	Acctg	Secretary	Newman	25,000
9	567-43-2366	Langly	Sandra	F	Pers	Secretary	McKnight	24,000
10	345-14-7245	McKnight	George	M	Pers	Manager	Dorian	50,000
11	705-34-2370	Smith	Mary	F	Pers	Clerk	McKnight	18,750
12	465-25-8751	Mead	Peter	M	Sales	Acct Exec	Smithson	35,000
13	590-52-7054	Durran	George	M	Sales	Acct Exec	Smithson	30,000
14	124-15-7602	Baker	Thomas	M	Sales	Acct Exec	Smithson	32,500
15	865-12-4102	McMead	Andrea	F	Sales	Acct Exec	Smithson	38,000
16	466-52-7035	Smith	Mary	F	Admin	President		135,000

FIGURE 16.1: Components of a database are often used as arguments in the database statistical functions. Range 1 is the input range of the database; it would be supplied as the input argument of a database statistical function. Notice that it includes a single row of column descriptions, each of which is unique, above the rows of data. (You cannot use multiple-line headings.) These unique headings are duplicated in the criterion range. Ranges 2 and 3 are possible criterion ranges that could be supplied as the criterion arguments in various functions. Row 3 in the lower window shows the offset number of each column in the database that would be supplied as the offset argument, depending on which column's data is to be analyzed by the function.

that when you apply one of the functions to a particular column, you must copy its description to a new part of the spreadsheet that acts as the beginning of the criterion range.

Database Statistical Functions versus Standard Statistical Functions

One difference between the database statistical functions and their standard statistical counterparts is that with the ordinary statistical functions, you can specify disjointed (multiple) ranges and noncontiguous cells as arguments. In database functions, only contiguous cell ranges are accepted.

However, the database functions operate on selective cells by using the criterion range. In fact, the database statistical functions are more versatile than the regular statistical functions in that they can easily be applied to specific criteria. To illustrate this difference, consider the personnel database shown in Figure 16.1. You could obtain the average salary earned easily enough by using the regular statistical function @AVG. To calculate this average, you enter the list of salary figures contained in the Annual Salary column (extending from H4 all the way to H23). This formula would be entered as

@AVG(H5..H23)

However, if you must also determine the average salary earned by only the women in the company, it is much easier to switch to the @DAVG function. If you use the @AVG function to obtain this statistic, you must manually pick out each salary where the sex is marked F in the entire database and add it to the list argument of the @AVG function.

To use the @DAVG function, you only have to enter (or copy) the column description Sex, enter an F in the cell below the one containing Sex (as shown in the range L4..M5 in Figure 16.2), and then use the following formula:

@DAVG(A4..H23,7,L4..M5)

Note: Entering arguments of database statistical functions is even easier if you name the input range by using the /Range Name Create command. For instance, the formula to determine the average salary made by women in the company was actually entered as @DAVG(TABLE,7,L4..M5) after giving the cell range A4..H23 the name TABLE.

If you also need to know the average salary earned by women in each department, the same @DAVG function becomes an even more efficient way to obtain these statistics. You simply add the individual department names to the criterion range that already contains the F (to restrict the search to female employees) and change the criterion argument in each @DAVG formula you use.

In Figure 16.2, this was done by first copying the criterion range L4..M5, which contains the Sex and Dept column descriptions, the F as the criterion in the cell below Sex, and the empty cell beneath Dept, down the range L6..M15.

The criteria were then narrowed to obtain the average for each department by entering each department name beneath each cell containing the Dept description. The formulas using the @DAVG function in column Q

```
Q7: (,2) [W11] @DAVG(TABLE,7,L4..M5)                                    READY

     A            B        C          D   E     F          G         H
 4   Number       L:Name   F:Name     Sex Dept  Position   Super     Salary
 5   360-22-0978  Holland  Katherine  F   Acctg Clerk      Newman    19,000
 6   230-45-9512  Jones    Daniel     M   Acctg Bookkeeper Newman    27,500
 7   458-56-8723  Newman   Paul       M   Acctg Accountant Pauli     55,000
 8   561-34-5644  Jones    Alexander  M   Acctg Secretary  Newman    25,000
 9   567-43-2366  Langly   Sandra     F   Pers  Secretary  McKnight  24,000
     L            M        N          O     P       Q          R         S
 3   0            1        2          3     4       5          6         7
 4   Sex          Dept
 5   F                     Average Salaries Earned by Women
 6   Sex          Dept
 7   F            Acctg    Company wide      47,664.29
 8   Sex          Dept     Accounting        19,000.00
 9   F            Admin    Administration   102,500.00
10   Sex          Dept     Marketing         28,900.00
11   F            Mktg     Personnel         21,375.00
12   Sex          Dept     Sales             38,000.00
13   F            Pers
14   Sex          Dept
15   F            Sales
```

FIGURE 16.2: Determining the average salaries for women within different departments of the company. In this figure, the @DAVG function was used with various criterion ranges, including both the Dept and Sex fields of the database. To obtain the overall average of salaries earned by women, the Dept criterion cell in the criterion range L4..M5 was left blank. To obtain the averages for each department, each department name as it appears in the database was entered into a similar criterion range. Each @DAVG formula in cells Q7 to Q12 has the same input and offset arguments. Only the criterion argument was changed in each to match the correct criterion range in columns L and M.

are all the same except for the criterion argument entered. Whereas the criterion in the @DAVG formula that determines the company-wide average for women was entered as the cell range L4..M5 in cell Q7, the one in cell Q8 for determining the average in the accounting department was entered as L6..M7.

Entering Formulas in the Criterion Range

When you use the database statistical functions, you can set up conditions in the criterion range by entering formulas just as you can when setting up search criteria for use with the /Data Query Find or Extract commands. If you are using Release 2, these formulas can contain search strings (labels) as well as values, as long as you remember to enclose the strings in pairs of quotation marks.

Figure 16.3 shows an example in which a formula has been entered in the criterion range using a string and numeric formula to determine the

```
AC27: (C2) [W13] @DAVG(TABLE,7,AA30..AA31)                                READY

       B        C         D   E      F          G          H      I
 4  L:Name   F:Name     Sex Dept   Position   Super      Salary  Hired
 5  Holland  Katherine  F   Acctg  Clerk      Newman     19,000 04/03/80
 6  Jones    Daniel     M   Acctg  Bookkeeper Newman     27,500 02/06/84
 7  Newman   Paul       M   Acctg  Accountant Pauli      55,000 10/23/78
 8  Jones    Alexander  M   Acctg  Secretary  Newman     25,000 03/15/83
 9  Langly   Sandra     F   Pers   Secretary  McKnight   24,000 01/20/85
10  McKnight George     M   Pers   Manager    Dorian     50,000 04/10/79
11  Smith    Mary       F   Pers   Clerk      McKnight   18,750 11/01/85
12  Mead     Peter      M   Sales  Acct Exec  Smithson   35,000 06/07/82
13  Durran   George     M   Sales  Acct Exec  Smithson   30,000 02/20/84
              AA                      AB        AC          AD        AE
24    The Number of Men Hired after 12/31/83 with Average Salaries
25
26  @DCOUNT(TABLE,8,AA30..AA31) ---------->             4
27    @DAVG(TABLE,7,AA30..AA31) ---------->    $27,500.00
28
29  Criterion:
30  Sex
31  +D5="M"#AND#I5>@DATE(83,12,31)
32
```

FIGURE 16.3: Using a formula to enter criteria to calculate the number of men hired after December 31, 1983 and their average salaries. In cell AA31 in the lower window in this figure, you can see the formula that sets up the criteria used in the @DCOUNT and @DAVG functions entered in cells AC26 and AC27, respectively. Notice that in each part of this compound formula, the cell address refers to the appropriate column (D contains the gender data, while I contains the date-hired data) and the first row of the database that contains data (row 5 in this case, because row 4 contains the column names). Also notice that the offsets used in the two formulas differ; though each uses the same criteria, they perform their calculations on different columns in the database.

number of males hired after December 31, 1983 and the average of the salaries they are currently earning. The formula entered in the criterion range is shown in cell AA31 in the lower window. Notice that the M in the first formula is enclosed in a pair of quotation marks. This is the only way you can mix strings and values in formulas that evaluate both.

Notice that using a compound formula in the criterion range with the #AND# logical operator makes it unnecessary to set up a range with both the Sex and Hired column descriptions in a block of separate cells with the appropriate criteria beneath them. If you are using Release 1A, you will have to set up the traditional four-cell range, arranged horizontally, with the column designators above the criteria listing the sex side by side that of the date hired. You can set up such criterion formulas using the other logical or Boolean operators as well. This allows you to set up OR conditions without having to place the various criteria in separate cells below the name of the column.

When you use a formula, the name of the column under which it is placed does not have to match any of the columns referred to in the criterion formula to work properly, though it must be an exact match of one of the column names in the input range. For instance, in the formula shown in Figure 16.3, the column description in cell AA30 could just as well have been given as Salary or Dept. However, the test cell referred to at the beginning of the formula does have to contain the proper cell address; it must refer to the correct column, and the row number must be that of the first row of data in the table.

The Database Statistical Functions

The database statistical functions all require the same three types of arguments: an input range, an offset number, and a criterion range. Their use is often combined to obtain meaningful statistics describing the data contained in the database.

To illustrate this relationship, two example figures are used in the following reference section:

- Figure 16.4 uses the functions @DSUM, @DAVG, @DCOUNT, @DMAX, and @DMIN to obtain descriptive statistics about specific groups and their salaries in the same personnel database used in the earlier examples (Figures 16.1 through 16.3).
- Figure 16.5 contains an example in which the functions @DAVG, @DSTD, and @DVAR are used with several different criteria to obtain more predictive statistics about the ages, salaries, and genders of the employees in the same database.

@DSUM

This function calculates the total of the values in a specific column of the data table given as the offset argument, according to the criteria set up in the criterion range.

SYNTAX

@DSUM(input,offset,criterion)

where input is the input range containing both a single row of unique column designations (field names) and all of the rows of data in the table; offset is the number of the column to be summed, starting with 0 as the leftmost column; and criterion is the criterion range that includes duplicates of the column designations with the criteria entered in the cells directly beneath each.

The input and criterion arguments can be designated by the cell addresses of the range or by range name if one has been previously assigned. The offset argument is usually entered as a literal value, although it can also be a cell reference to such a value.

USAGE

The @DSUM function obtains totals of specific values in a database. If no criterion is entered beneath the column designator in the criterion range, all of the data in the column specified by the offset number is summed.

To use the @DSUM function, move the cell pointer to the cell where you want the total to appear in the worksheet, type **@DSUM(**, and designate the input argument either by typing in the cell addresses of the range, by entering the range name assigned to it, or by pointing to the cells. Then type a comma and enter the number of the offset as a literal value or as a cell reference to such a value. After you indicate the offset number that determines which column is to be totaled, type a comma and indicate the criterion range as you did for the input argument. Then type a) to close off the arguments. When you press the Return key, Lotus 1-2-3 calculates the total.

If you wish to obtain the total for only part of the values in a column of the database, set up a criterion formula that limits the range of values to be included. For example, if the column containing the values you want totaled is column D, if it is offset 3 of the database, and if you want the total of values only between 10000 and 50000, you would enter a formula similar to

+D5>10000#AND#D5<50000

in the criterion cell. Assuming that this formula is in cell P10 of the worksheet and the column heading Sales is directly above it, you would enter an @DSUM formula similar to the following to obtain your total:

@DSUM(TABLE,3,P9..P10)

EXAMPLES

Figure 16.4 illustrates the use of @DSUM along with the @DAVG, @DMAX, @DMIN, and @DCOUNT functions to analyze the distribution of salaries in the company on two lines: those making under $50,000 and those making $50,000 or more, and, within each of these groups, the distribution according to the gender of the employee.

In order to find these results, four criterion ranges are set up, extending from AA1 to AE2. Four different criterion formulas are needed to cover all of the conditions:

- +H5<50000#AND#D5 = "M" in cell AA2
- +H5<50000#AND#D5 = "F" in cell AB2
- +H5>=50000#AND#D5 = "M" in cell AD2
- +H5>=50000#AND#D5 = "F" in cell AE2

```
AB8: (C2) [W13] @DSUM(TABLE,7,AA1..AA2)                                      READY

         H                   AA          AB         AC     AD              AE
 4  Salary           1  Salary    Salary               Salary         Salary
 5   19,000          2                0           1              0                0
 6   27,500          3            Those earning                   Those earning
 7   55,000          4            below $50,000                   $50,000 or more
 8   25,000          5
 9   24,000          6  Profile for Male Employees
10   50,000          7
11   18,750          8  Total       $202,500.00        Total       $314,500.00
12   35,000          9  Average       28,928.57        Average       62,900.00
13   30,000         10  Maximum       35,000.00        Maximum       82,500.00
14   32,500         11  Minimum       25,000.00        Minimum       50,000.00
15   38,000         12  Count                 7        Count                 5
16  135,000         13
17   62,000         14  Profile for Female Employees
18   70,000         15
19   82,500         16  Total       $128,650.00        Total       $205,000.00
20   65,000         17  Average       25,730.00        Average      102,500.00
21   28,900         18  Maximum       38,000.00        Maximum      135,000.00
22   27,500         19  Minimum       18,750.00        Minimum       70,000.00
23   25,000         20  Count                 5        Count                 2
```

FIGURE 16.4: Using the database statistical functions to profile salary distribution in a company. In this figure, two criteria are used when calculating the statistics—the amount earned and the gender of the wage earner. The two major groups are divided according to the criterion of Salary (H5) less than 50000 or Salary greater than or equal to 50000. When combined with the gender designation in the Sex column (D5) set equal to either F or M, the four criterion ranges are established by formulas using the #AND# operator in row 1 of the second window. In the Control Panel, you can see the criterion argument used in all the functions in cells AB8 down to AB12. The formulas in these cells all contain the arguments (TABLE,7,AA1..AA2).

The values of 0 and 1 shown in these cells in Figure 16.4 indicate only whether the condition set up by this formula is true in the test cell H5. Because the salary in H5 is below 50000 and the label in D5 (not visible in this figure) contains an F, only cell AB2 displays a 1 (for true), showing that its criteria have been met.

Note: To set up the same criteria using Release 1A of Lotus 1-2-3, you would need to extend each of these criterion ranges to include cells containing the Sex column designator and the value of either F or M beneath it. For instance, the first criteria of salary less than $50,000 and sex equal to male would be represented by placing the column name Sex in cell AB1 and the value M in cell AB2. Then the functions in AB9 through AB12 of Figure 16.4 would all be given the criterion range AA1..AB2 as their third argument.

The formulas using the database statistical functions in column AB for those who earn below $50,000 a year are very similar to each other, except that those formulas for the male employees in cell AB8 to AB12 all use the range AA1..AA2 as the criterion argument of their various functions, while those formulas for the female employees in cells AB16 to AB20 use the range AB1..AB2.

The database statistical functions entered for each group (such as for the men who make less than $50,000 a year) all have identical arguments because they use the same criterion range. The same is true for each of the other three groups in this figure. All that varies is the name of the function, such as @DSUM, @DAVG, and so on. To make this first profile for the men, the first @DSUM formula was entered with absolute references as

@DSUM($TABLE,7,$AA$1..$AA$2)

This formula was then copied down to the cell range AB9..AB12. Each function name in AB9 to AB12 was then individually edited to reflect the correct statistical function. The same method was followed to create the formulas for the remaining groups that are profiled.

@DAVG

This function calculates the average or mean of the values in a specific column of the data table given as the offset argument, according to the criteria set up in the criterion range. For specific information on how this function calculates the average, refer back to the @AVG function reference in Chapter 12.

SYNTAX

@DAVG(input,offset,criterion)

where input is the input range containing both a single row of unique column designations (field names) and all of the rows of data in the table; offset is the number of the column to be averaged, starting with 0 as the leftmost column; and criterion is the criterion range that includes duplicates of the column designations with the criteria entered in the cells directly beneath each.

The input and criterion arguments can be designated by the cell addresses of the range or by range name if one has been previously assigned. The offset argument is usually entered as a literal value, although it can also be a cell reference to such a value.

USAGE

The @DAVG function obtains average value in a range of specific values in a database. If no criterion is entered beneath the column designator in the criterion range, all of the data in the column specified by the offset argument is used in determining the average.

To use the @DAVG function, move the cell pointer to the cell where you want the average to appear in the worksheet, type **@DAVG(**, and designate the input argument either by typing in the cell addresses of the range, by entering the range name assigned to it, or by pointing to the cells. Then type a comma and enter the number of the offset as a literal value or as a cell reference to such a value. After you indicate the offset number that determines which column is to be totaled, type a comma and indicate the criterion range as you did the input argument. Type a) to close off the arguments. When you press the Return key, Lotus 1-2-3 calculates the average for the values within the criterion used.

Because the @DAVG function calculates the average by calculating the sum and dividing it by the count, it is possible to obtained skewed results if the criterion range allows zero values and the column contains labels (in which case @DAVG returns ERR). When calculating the sum, labels (which carry zero values) do not affect the total; however, as nonblank cells they do increase the count. Blank cells within a column do not affect the @DAVG function.

If you are concerned that some of the cells in a column of values could contain some misplaced label entries, you can perform a /Date

Query Find or Extract operation using the @ISSTRING function as the criterion (Release 2 only). The argument of this function should be the address of the test cell with the letter of the column in question.

EXAMPLES

For examples illustrating the use of the @DAVG function, refer to Figures 16.2, 16.3, and 16.4. For an example of using the @DAVG function with the @DSTD and @DVAR functions, see Figure 16.5 in the @DSTD entry.

@DCOUNT

This function returns the number of nonblank cells in a specific column of the data table given as the offset argument, according to the criteria set up in the criterion range. For specific information on how this function calculates the count, refer to the @COUNT function reference in Chapter 12.

SYNTAX

@DCOUNT(input,offset,criterion)

where input is the input range containing both a single row of unique column designations (field names) and all of the rows of data in the table; offset is the number of the column to be counted, starting with 0 as the leftmost column; and criterion is the criterion range that includes duplicates of the column designations with the criteria entered in the cells directly beneath each.

The input and criterion arguments can be designated by the cell addresses of the range or by range name if one has been previously assigned. The offset argument is usually entered as a literal value, although it can also be a cell reference to such a value.

USAGE

The @DCOUNT function obtains the number of nonblank cells in a range of entries in a particular column of database. If no criterion is entered beneath the column designator in the criterion range, all of the data in the column specified by the offset argument is used in determining the count.

To use the @DCOUNT function, move the cell pointer to the cell where you want the count number to appear in the worksheet, type **@DCOUNT(**, and designate the input argument either by typing in the cell addresses of the range, by entering the range name assigned to it, or by pointing to the cells. Then type a comma and enter the number of the offset as a literal value or as a cell reference to such a value. After you indicate the offset number that determines which column is to be counted, type a comma and indicate the criterion range as you did the input argument. Type a) to close off the arguments. When you press the Return key, Lotus 1-2-3 calculates the number of nonblank cells.

Because the @DCOUNT function includes only nonblank cells in the column (blank cells do not affect it, however), you may want to check that all of the cells in a given column of the database have entries by comparing the results obtained by using the @DCOUNT function on two different columns of data. If possible, enter one of the @DCOUNT functions using as the offset a column that you are reasonably sure has no empty fields. Compare the tally obtained by this formula to that received from the column in question. If the number is equal, chances are that no blank cells have been left in either column.

EXAMPLES

For examples using the @DCOUNT function, refer to Figures 16.3 and 16.4.

@DMAX

The @DMAX function returns the maximum value in a specific column of the data table given as the offset argument, according to the criteria set up in the criterion range.

SYNTAX

@DMAX(input,offset,criterion)

where input is the input range containing both a single row of unique column designations (field names) and all of the rows of data in the table; offset is the number of the column to be evaluated, starting with 0 as the leftmost column; and criterion is the criterion range that includes duplicates of the column designations with the criteria entered in the cells directly beneath each.

The input and criterion arguments can be designated by the cell addresses of the range or by range name if one has been previously assigned. The offset argument is usually entered as a literal value, although it can also be a cell reference to such a value.

USAGE

The @DMAX function obtains the highest value in a range of values in a particular column of a database. If no criterion is entered beneath the column designator in the criterion range, all of the data in the column specified by the offset argument is evaluated when determining the maximum value.

To use the @DMAX function, move the cell pointer to the cell where you want the maximum value to appear in the worksheet, type **@DMAX(**, and designate the input argument either by typing in the cell addresses of the range, by entering the range name assigned to it, or by pointing to the cells. Then type a comma and enter the number of the offset as a literal value or as a cell reference to such a value. After you indicate the offset number that determines which column is to be used, type a comma and indicate the criterion range as you did the input argument. Type a) to close off the arguments. When you press the Return key, Lotus 1-2-3 returns the value that is the highest within the range of values meeting the criteria specified.

When this function is used in a column of the database that contains date values (entered with the @DATE function), it returns the most recent date as the maximum value.

EXAMPLES

For an example of how to use the @DMAX function to find the highest value in a database, refer to Figures 16.4 and 16.5.

@DMIN

This function returns the minimum value in a specific column of the database given as the offset argument, according to the criteria set up in the criterion range.

SYNTAX

@DMIN(input,offset,criterion)

where input is the input range containing both a single row of unique column designations (field names) and all of the rows of data in the table; offset is the number of the column to be evaluated, starting with 0 as the leftmost column; and criterion is the criterion range that includes duplicates of the column designations with the criteria entered in the cells directly beneath each.

The input and criterion arguments can be designated by the cell addresses of the range or by range name if one has been previously assigned. The offset argument is usually entered as a literal value, although it can also be a cell reference to such a value.

USAGE

The @DMIN function is used to obtain the lowest value in a range of values in a particular column of the database. If no criterion is entered beneath the column designator in the criterion range, all of the data in the column specified by the offset argument is evaluated when determining the minimum value.

To use the @DMIN function, move the cell pointer to the cell where you want the minimum value to appear in the worksheet, type **@DMIN(**, and designate the input argument either by typing in the cell addresses of the range, by entering the range name assigned to it, or by pointing to the cells. Then type a comma and enter the number of the offset as a literal value or a cell reference to such a value. After you indicate the offset number that determines which column is to be used, type a comma and indicate the criterion range as you did the input argument. Type a **)** to close off the arguments. When you press the Return key, Lotus 1-2-3 returns the highest value within the range of values meeting the criteria specified.

When this function is used in a column of the database that contains date values (entered with the @DATE function), it returns the oldest date as the minimum value, because dates are converted to serial numbers and older dates have smaller serial numbers.

EXAMPLES

For an example of how to use the @DMIN function to find the lowest value in a database, refer to Figures 16.4 and 16.5.

@DSTD

This function returns the standard deviation (i.e., *S*) of the values in a specific column of the database given as the offset argument, according to the criteria set up in the criterion range. For specific information on how Lotus 1-2-3 calculates the standard deviation and its uses, refer to the reference entry for the @STD function in Chapter 12.

SYNTAX

@DSTD(input,offset,criterion)

where input is the input range containing both a single row of unique column designations (field names) and all of the rows of data in the table; offset is the number of the column to be evaluated, starting with 0 as the leftmost column; and criterion is the criterion range that includes duplicates of the column designations with the criteria entered in the cells directly beneath each.

The input and criterion arguments can be designated by the cell addresses of the range or by range name if one has been previously assigned. The offset argument is usually entered as a literal value, although it can also be a cell reference to such a value.

USAGE

The @DSTD function calculates the standard deviation, which is a statistical measurement of the degree to which an individual score in a range of values in a particular column of the database varies from its mean score. If no criterion is entered beneath the column designator in the criterion range, all of the data in the column specified by the offset argument is evaluated when determining the standard deviation.

To use the @DSTD function, move the cell pointer to the cell where you want the standard deviation to appear in the worksheet, type **@DSTD(**, and designate the input argument either by typing in the cell addresses of the range, by entering the range name assigned to it, or by pointing to the cells. Then type a comma and enter the number of the offset as a literal value or as a cell reference to such a value. After you indicate the offset number that determines which column of data is to be used, type a comma and indicate the criterion range as you did the input argument. Type a) to close off the arguments. When you press the

Return key, Lotus 1-2-3 returns the value representing the standard deviation from the mean of those values meeting the criteria specified.

Remember that when using the @DSTD function, misplaced label entries in the column can skew the result of the mean value and consequently that of the standard deviation if the criteria allow zero values in the criterion range.

EXAMPLES

Figure 16.5 illustrates the use of the @DSTD function, along with @DAVG, @DMAX, @DMIN, and @DVAR, to compute age statistics describing the distribution of ages for the company overall as well as for the male and female employees.

AC19: (F1) @DSTD(TABLE,11,AC1..AD2) READY

	I	J	K	L
3	Date	Yrs w/	Date of	
4	Hired	Company	Birth	Age
5	04/03/80	6.6	03/15/48	38
6	02/06/84	2.7	06/07/44	42
7	10/23/78	8.1	02/03/60	26
8	03/15/83	3.6	12/12/40	46
9	01/20/85	1.7	07/09/65	21
10	04/10/79	7.6	10/02/54	32
11	11/01/85	0.9	07/09/56	30
12	06/07/82	4.4	03/25/61	25
13	02/20/84	2.7	01/17/58	28
14	09/12/82	4.1	08/09/42	44
15	08/28/81	5.2	08/16/66	20
16	10/01/78	8.1	02/15/49	37
17	04/16/83	3.5	08/26/45	41
18	06/10/79	7.4	02/07/58	28
19	12/03/82	3.9	06/16/60	26
20	07/18/83	3.3	04/08/51	35
21	05/01/79	7.5	03/05/50	36
22	10/15/84	2.0	11/04/63	23

	AA	AB	AC	AD
1	Age	Sex	Age	Sex
2		M		F
3		All Employees		
4	Average Age		31.6	
5	Oldest		46.0	
6	Youngest		20.0	
7	Standard deviation		8.0	
8	Variance		63.5	
9		Male Employees		
10	Average Age		32.5	
11	Oldest		46.0	
12	Youngest		22.0	
13	Standard deviation		8.4	
14	Variance		70.4	
15		Female Employees		
16	Average Age		30.0	
17	Oldest		38.0	
18	Youngest		20.0	
19	Standard deviation		6.9	
20	Variance		47.7	

FIGURE 16.5: Using the database statistical functions to profile the distribution of ages throughout a company. In this figure, the highest, lowest, and average ages of the employees are calculated along with the standard deviation and variance. Three groups of age statistics are calculated: the distribution for all of the employees, that for the male employees, and that for the female employees. To determine the age statistics for the company as a whole, no criterion was entered below cell AA1 containing the column name. Giving the range AA1..AA2 as the criterion argument for the first group of statistical functions ensured that all of the ages listed in column L of the database were included. To restrict the data to only the male and female employees, the criterion ranges were changed to include either the M or F values.

To compute the statistics for each group, the various database statistical functions all share the same criteria and, therefore, the same criterion ranges. To determine the average age for all of the employees, the criterion argument was entered as AA1..AA2. As AA2 contains no criterion, all of the ages in the database are used.

Because all of the statistics for the employees use the same arguments, you could enter the first formula in AC4 with absolute references and then copy it down to the range AC5..AC8. You could then edit the function name to return the maximum, minimum, standard deviation, and variance for the entire group of employees.

When setting up the criteria for the second group of statistics that describe the ages of only the male employees, a different criterion range had to be used. In this figure, it is the cell range AA1..AB2. This includes the previous criterion range that does not restrict the age values but does restrict the Sex to M. Again, because the input, offset, and criterion arguments are the same for all of the database statistical functions used for this second group, the first function, @DAVG in cell AC10, was entered with absolute cell references. It was then copied down the column, and the function names were individually edited.

The last group of ages for the females in the company allows for the same entry technique, although a new criterion range was added in cells AC1..AD2. This criterion range is very similar to that for the men but has an entry of F in AD2 for the criterion beneath the column designation Sex.

In looking at the results, it is easy to see that this is a very young company overall and that, although the age distribution is greater among the males than the females, all are very close to the company's mean age of just under 32 years.

@DVAR

This function returns the variance (i.e., S^2) of the values in a specific column of the database given as the offset argument, according to the criteria set up in the criterion range. For specific information on how Lotus 1-2-3 calculates the variance and its uses, refer to the reference entry for the @VAR function in Chapter 12.

SYNTAX

@DVAR(input,offset,criterion)

where input is the input range containing both a single row of unique column designations (field names) and all of the rows of data in the table; offset is the number of the column to be evaluated, starting with 0 as the leftmost column; and criterion is the criterion range that includes duplicates of the column designations with the criteria entered in the cells directly beneath each.

The input and criterion arguments can be designated by the cell addresses of the range or by range name if one has been previously assigned. The offset argument is usually entered as a literal value, although it can also be a cell reference to such a value.

USAGE

The @DVAR function calculates the variance, which is a statistical measurement of the degree to which an individual score in a range of values in a particular column of a database varies from its mean score. This statistic is equal to the square of the standard deviation. If no criterion is entered beneath the column designator in the criterion range, all of the data in the column specified by the offset argument is evaluated when calculating the variance.

To use the @DVAR function, move the cell pointer to the cell where you want the variance to appear in the worksheet, type **@DVAR(**, and designate the input argument either by typing in the cell addresses of the range, by entering the range name assigned to it, or by pointing to the cells. Then type a comma and enter the number of the offset as a literal value or as a cell reference to such a value. After you indicate the offset number that determines which column of data is to be used, type a comma and indicate the criterion range as you did the input argument. Type a) to close off the arguments. When you press the Return key, Lotus 1-2-3 returns the value representing the variance from the mean of those values meeting the criteria specified.

Remember when you use the @DVAR function that, just as with the @DSTD function, misplaced label entries in the column can skew the result of the mean value and consequently that of the variance if the criteria allow zero values in the criterion range.

EXAMPLES

For examples of how to use the @DVAR function, refer to Figure 16.5.

SUMMARY

This chapter has examined the database statistical functions that perform the same type of statistical calculations as the parallel group of regular statistical functions. They differ primarily in that the database functions allow you to set up criteria that determine which values are used in the calculations rather than requiring you to enter the values as specific references in an argument list. This gives you greater flexibility in analyzing relationships among your raw data.

These functions have a great many applications, especially in areas of marketing and advertising, where they can be applied to tables that contain survey figures, market research, data, direct mail responses, and so on.

Because these functions are so closely related to the regular statistical functions offered by Lotus 1-2-3, you may want to refer to the information about the statistical functions in Chapter 12. You may also want to refer ahead to Chapters 22 and 23 to obtain more information on Lotus 1-2-3's statistical analysis capabilities and see how these functions can be combined with the /Data Table commands.

CHAPTER 17

STRING FUNCTIONS

String Functions

The string functions perform a wide variety of tasks on character strings (labels) used in a worksheet. All of these functions are new to Release 2 of Lotus 1-2-3. If you are familiar with Symphony by Lotus Development Corporation, you will find that the string functions in Lotus 1-2-3 work in an identical manner.

While the string functions can sometimes be useful when you are developing a spreadsheet or database application manually, they are more often used in macros that process data containing character strings. This chapter contains specific information on what each string function does with examples illustrating how each one works. You can find more information on applications for string functions in Chapter 28, which covers the macro command language.

After the opening discussion of the string functions and how they are used, you will find individual reference entries for each of the string functions. These reference entries are arranged in alphabetical order from @CHAR to @VALUE.

Using the String Functions

The string functions expand your ability to perform operations that manipulate strings in the worksheet. Strings can be defined as any characters in the cells of a worksheet that contain one of the three label prefixes: ' signifying a left-aligned label, ^ signifying a centered label, and " signifying a right-aligned label. Another way of defining a string is to say that a string is any entry made in LABEL mode.

The functions that manipulate such strings perform a variety of tasks and thus require slightly different types of arguments. Nevertheless, you need to be familiar with some generalizations about the use of string functions:

- When you enter a string as an argument in a function, you can indicate it either by cell reference or as a manual entry. If you enter the string manually, you must enclose it in a pair of quotation marks just as you would when using a string as an argument of another Lotus 1-2-3 function such as @IF or @CHOOSE.

- Release 2 uses a special character set referred to as LICS (the Lotus International Character Set) that contains codes from 0 to 255. Code numbers from 0 to 127 correspond to ASCII codes, while those from 128 to 255 do not correspond to the IBM extended character set. Their character assignments are unique to Lotus Development products. The @CHAR and @CODE string functions work with these codes.
- Each character of a string has a particular LICS code value. For instance, the Greek letter π is LICS code 173. A cell that contains only one of the three label prefixes and no other character is referred to as an *empty string.* It has a length of 0 as well as an LICS code of 0. This is not the same as a blank cell (though they appear the same in a worksheet), which contains no entry of any kind. A blank cell is not given an LICS code number.
- Many of the string functions that work with substrings use position numbers to locate the characters in the string that are to be manipulated in some way. The first character position always starts with the position number 0, and the count increases by 1 for each character to the right. For example, in the string "New rate", the N is position 0, e is 1, w is 2, the space is 3, and so on.
- When you indicate the position number in a string function that requires it, use a positive integer value. Entering a negative value like −1 will cause the program to return an ERR value. If you enter a mixed number like 2.66, the program will use only the integer portion. For example, if you enter the value 2.66 as the start position argument in an @MID function using the string "New rate", the function begins extracting characters from position 2, i.e., the w in New.

Working with String Functions

Many of the string functions work only with portions of the string in question (substrings). These functions require that you specify position, paying attention to the fact that the first position is counted as 0. To locate the starting position of a particular string, you can use the @FIND function. This function locates the first exact match to the substring you enter as its first argument within the string you designate as its second argument.

The @FIND function is often combined with other substring functions such as @MID when you don't already know the starting position of a substring. To illustrate the use of position, consider the following @FIND example in which the label Actual versus Budgeted is entered in cell A1. If the function is entered in A5 as

@FIND("Budgeted",A1,0)

Lotus 1-2-3 returns the value 14 in A5. Beginning with the start position of 0 (the A in Actual—the apostrophe as the label prefix is never counted as a position by Lotus 1-2-3), the B in Budgeted occupies position 14 in the string. Notice that the string Budgeted was entered in the formula with an uppercase B, exactly as it appears in the title in A1. This is because the substring functions are case sensitive, unlike many other Lotus 1-2-3 functions. (If you had entered "budgeted" rather than "Budgeted" in this formula, the function would have returned an ERR value, indicating that no match was found.)

SUBSTRINGING

The @FIND function is often combined with the @MID function when you don't already know the starting position of a substring. The @MID function extracts a part of the overall string, an operation referred to as *substringing.* It requires that you enter the string to be used as the first argument, followed by the start position of the substring to be extracted, followed by the number of characters to be extracted.

Assume that you wanted to extract and enter the label Budgeted in cell C6. You could use @MID to extract it for you. This substring is contained in the title Actual versus Budgeted in cell A1 from the previous example. Now that you know that the start position of Budgeted is 14, you could enter the @MID function in C6 as

@MID(A1,14,8)

to have it enter Budgeted into the cell. If, however, you had not performed the earlier operation with the @FIND function to locate the starting position of Budgeted in the title, you could do so by entering the @FIND function as the second argument of the @MID function in C6:

@MID(A1,@FIND("Budgeted",A1,0),30)

Because the @FIND function returns the start position 14 required as the second argument of an @MID function, it works just as well as entering the literal value.

Notice that the length was not specified as eight characters here, which is all you really wanted to extract. This demonstrates that the @MID length argument does not have to be the same as the length of the substring you are extracting. However, if the title had contained any more characters after Budgeted, they would also have been entered into C6. This technique of entering a sufficiently high number to extract all of the characters after a certain point in the string relieves you of having to count the exact number wanted.

In addition to @MID, two simpler string functions, @LEFT and @RIGHT, extract the number of characters desired starting either from the beginning (left) or end (right) of the string. In this case, the name of the function sets the character position, so all you have to enter is the string to be used and the number of characters to be extracted.

To enter the first part of the title Actual versus Budgeted as a label into cell D6, you could use the @LEFT function as

@LEFT(A1,6)

Conversely, to extract Budgeted and enter it into cell C6, you could use the following @RIGHT function instead of the more complex @MID function illustrated earlier. Using this method requires that you enter only

@RIGHT(A1,8)

You can use the @LENGTH function to have Lotus 1-2-3 find the length of a string for you. If this function were applied to our title in A1 of Actual versus Budgeted as

@LENGTH(A1)

it would return the value 22, indicating that the string is made up of 22 characters (one more than the final position number of this title, which is 21 because position begins with 0).

Another versatile function in substringing is the @REPLACE function. It allows you to replace the original string with another string. This function requires the most arguments of any of the string functions: the original string; the starting position, indicating where the replacement substring is to go; the length, indicating the number of characters in the original string to be replaced; and, finally, the characters of the replacement substring itself.

As an example of how @REPLACE is used, assume that you want to use the title entered into A1 in a slightly modified form elsewhere in the spreadsheet. Instead of Actual versus Budgeted, you want to enter **Actual versus Projected Expenses**. To have this new heading entered into cell

A45, you could use the @REPLACE function

@REPLACE(A1,14,8,"Projected Expenses")

in A45 to have the program enter the label Actual versus Projected Expenses. If you did not remember that 14 was the start position for Budgeted, which is to be replaced with Projected Expenses, you could replace that argument with the @FIND("Budgeted",A1,0) function to have Lotus 1-2-3 determine the position for you.

When you use the @REPLACE function, you can replace part of the string with a new substring, leaving most of the string intact. For instance, assume that the modified title in A45 is to be **Actual compared to Budgeted.** This requires replacing the string "versus" with the longer string "compared to". Using the @REPLACE function, you would enter

@REPLACE(A1,@FIND("versus",A1,0),6,"compared to")

You allow the program to determine the start position of the substring "versus" with the @FIND function. Because you have called for the replacement of only six characters (the length of the word "versus") from this start position, Lotus 1-2-3 leaves the Budgeted part of the title alone and inserts the "compared to" replacement string between Actual and Budgeted so that the label in A45 reads Actual compared to Budgeted.

Case Conversion

The string functions include three very useful functions that automatically convert strings to all uppercase (@UPPER), all lowercase (@LOWER), or capitalize the first letter of each word in the string (@PROPER). When you use the @PROPER function, the program recognizes the end of a word and the beginning of the next by the space entered between them.

These functions make it extremely easy to ensure that groups of similar labels all share the same case. This is very important in databases, where case differences can affect the sorted order. For instance, if you sort a database by the state abbreviation in ascending order and you have entered the abbreviation for Colorado as co in some cases instead of CO, the rows containing co will be out of sequence: they will be placed at the very beginning of the database separated from those entries in which CO was used.

The case conversion string functions require only the string to be converted or a cell reference to it as their argument. For instance, to convert to uppercase letters a state abbreviation entered in cell L5 as ga for

Georgia, you would enter the @UPPER function as

@UPPER(L5)

Lotus 1-2-3 would enter GA in the cell where this formula was entered.

The @PROPER function can also be applied to database column entries, especially those in a client database where you may use the name and address columns to prepare mailing labels. In this way you can ensure that all entries begin with a capital letter.

For example, assume that you noticed that street addresses entered into column E of your client database contained inconsistent capitalization for the first letter of the street name and street designation (St., Rd., Ave., etc.). To ensure that they were all properly capitalized, you would use the @PROPER function.

If row 5 contains the first row of data, you could move to an empty column, say column AE, and in AE5 enter the @PROPER function to convert the street address in E5:

@PROPER(E5)

If the entry in E5 were '1234 pine view rd., the entry in AE5 would be '1234 Pine View Rd. This function could be copied down column AE as far as required to process all of the entries in column E of the database. After processing, you could move the contents of column AE to column E to replace the inconsistent street addresses.

The @PROPER function can also be used when your entries are all in uppercase and you want to convert them to first-letter capitalization. For instance, you may have purchased an ASCII mailing list in which all of the entries are in uppercase letters. After parsing the data into separate columns of a database, you would then need to convert it into proper upper- and lowercase letters before printing the mailing labels.

To process the ASCII data, you would use the @PROPER function so that each word begins with a capital letter. Figure 17.1 illustrates such a situation. Notice, however, that last names like McKnight, which require dual capitalization, are not correctly converted because there are no spaces between the parts of the last name. Such entries would have to be edited manually.

When working with case conversions among strings, you may also need to use @EXACT to verify and document that two strings are exactly the same. This function is case sensitive, so it requires not only a match in letters but also in their case.

Figure 17.2 demonstrates the difference between using the @EXACT function in a formula that determines whether two strings are the same, as

```
C10: @PROPER(A10)                                                          READY

       A        B        C        D        E        F        G        H
1   Name list           Name list after
2   imported from       conversion with
3   ASCII file          @PROPER function
4
5   HOLLAND             Holland  <--------- @PROPER(A5)
6   JONES               Jones
7   NEWMAN              Newman
8   JONES               Jones
9   LANGLY              Langly
10  MCKNIGHT            Mcknight
11  SMITH               Smith
12  MEAD                Mead
13  DURRAN              Durran
14  BAKER               Baker
15  MCMEAD              Mcmead
16  SMITH               Smith
17  DORIAN              Dorian
18  SMITHSON            Smithson
19  PAULI               Pauli
20  BAKER               Baker
```

FIGURE 17.1: Using the @PROPER function to convert a list of names all in uppercase to the appropriate capital-and-lowercase combination. The list of surnames in column A was transferred into the spreadsheet from an ASCII file. To convert the names to their proper form, the first @PROPER function shown was entered in C5 and then copied down column C to the last row in the name list. Notice that the names McKnight and McMead are not correct as a result of this conversion, for the @PROPER function capitalizes only the first letter of each word separated with a space. After manually editing these entries, the new name list in column C will be moved to column A to replace the original uppercase entries.

```
A6: [W10] @IF(@EXACT(A1,A2),"Exact match","Different")                     READY

       A        B        C        D        E        F        G
1   Account Receivables
2   Account receivables
3
4   Same      <---- @IF(A1=A2,"Same","Different")
5
6   Different <---- @IF(@EXACT(A1,A2),"Exact match","Different")
7
8
```

FIGURE 17.2: Testing whether two strings have the same value by using two slightly different @IF formulas, one using a simple equality, the other the @EXACT function. In this figure cells A1 and A2 contain two nearly identical strings. When a comparison is made using an @IF function in A4 to test whether A1 equals A2, they are found to be the same because the case difference is discounted. Only when they are compared using the @EXACT function in A6 are they found to be different, because the case of each letter does not match.

opposed to using a formula that determines whether they are simply equal. The first formula in A4 determines that A1 and A2 are the same because they contain the same characters, while the @EXACT function in A6 determines that they are different because of a single case difference.

Converting Strings to Values and Values to Strings

The @VALUE function allows you to convert strings quickly into numeric values and use them in calculations. This function makes it unnecessary to use a macro that strips away the label prefix or to remove the prefix manually, as in Release 1A.

The @VALUE function offers an additional benefit over these methods in that it can deal effectively with trailing spaces between numbers when they are expressed as mixed numbers with fractions. For instance, suppose that you had imported a list of stock quotations as labels into a spreadsheet and, in keeping with Wall Street practice, the stock quotations were all entered as mixed numbers in the form of 34 1/4, 158 1/2, and so on.

To use these prices as values and perform mathematical calculations on them, you cannot simply delete their label prefixes, because Lotus 1-2-3 will not accept the space between the integer and its fraction. However, the @VALUE function is able not only to trim the space but also to convert the number correctly. If cell B23 contains the label '158 1/2 and you enter

@VALUE(B23)

Lotus 1-2-3 returns the value 158.50 in the cell where this formula is entered. You can then use this newly created right-justified value in any calculation and format it with any of the /Range Format options.

The opposite of the @VALUE function is the @STRING function, which converts a value to a string. This command also allows you to specify the number of decimal places to be used in the display of the newly created label. The number is entered as the second argument of the @STRING function.

For example, say that cell D5 contains the calculated value of 4.5678, which you wish to use as a label elsewhere in the spreadsheet. However, you also want this label to display only two decimal places. If you move the cell pointer to the cell where you want the label and enter

@STRING(D5,2)

Lotus 1-2-3 returns 4.57 as the new label. As when using the /Range Format Fixed command, Lotus 1-2-3 automatically rounds the value to the specified number of decimal places.

If you wanted this new label to contain a preceding dollar sign, you would have to alter the formula by using the concatenation operator & to add the dollar sign to the new label as follows:

+"$"&@STRING(D5,2)

This would produce $4.57, left justified in the cell where this formula was entered. Remember, though, that because this label was entered by formula, you cannot change its alignment in the cell to centered or right justified by using the /Range Label command options. These options work only on labels that contain the apostrophe label prefix, either entered manually or with a macro.

Returning the Values of Strings and Numbers

The string functions @N and @S complement the other error-trapping functions included in Release 2 of Lotus 1-2-3 (for information on the others, see Chapter 15, "Logical Functions"). They allow you to prevent potential errors in formulas that try to mix values and labels. You will often find it convenient to combine these functions with the logical functions @ISSTRING and @ISSNUMBER in @IF formulas.

These two functions are the only string functions that require ranges as their arguments. When evaluating a range of values or labels, however, they use only the first cell of the range (the one in the upper-left corner). When you use them with a single cell, you can add a preceding exclamation point as the notation for a single-cell range (!A1), or you can have Lotus 1-2-3 automatically convert the single cell address into a cell range for you (that is, it will convert A1 to A1..A1).

@N returns the value of the upper-left cell in the range. As an example of using the @N function, consider this formula:

@N(!B3) + @N(!C3)

If either of the cells contains a label, the value returned by the @N function for that cell is 0, so that the total is not increased. If both cells contain labels, both are given zero values and the sum is 0. The inclusion of the @N functions ensures that under no circumstances will the addition of these two cells produce an ERR value that could propagate throughout the spreadsheet.

The @S function provides the opposite kind of insurance against ERR values in the spreadsheet. For instance, when you attempt to concatenate two labels in a new cell, you might enter this formula:

@S(!B3)&" "&@S(!C3)

In this case, the @S functions prevent an ERR value in the cell where this formula is entered, because any value found in either B3 or C3 will be converted to a null string value. In this example, if B3 contains a value and C3 a label, the resulting label contains only the contents of C3 preceded by a space. If, however, B3 contains a label and C3 contains a value, only the contents of B3 are displayed left justified in the cell. Should both cells contain values, the cell will be empty. Without the @S value conversions ERR values would be displayed under any of these three conditions.

ASCII/LICS Code Functions

The Lotus International Character Set, abbreviated as LICS, gives you the ability to add and use a number of special Greek, math, and foreign-language symbols in your spreadsheets. To enter one of these symbols into a spreadsheet, you press the Compose key combination (Alt-F1) and type the two-letter compose sequence. (These compose sequences and the symbols they produce are listed in Appendix B of this handbook.)

If you find yourself using particular LICS characters like the Greek letter π or the pound sterling currency symbol, you may wish to store the compose sequence in a keystroke macro rather than enter it manually each time. In this case you cannot use {COMPOSE} followed by the keys used in the compose sequence; although {COMPOSE} signifies pressing the Alt-F1 keys, it is not recognized as a valid macro keyword. To create such macros, you must use the @CHAR function with the LICS code number as its argument. Examples illustrating how you might set up such macros with the @CHAR function are shown in Table 17.1.

LABEL	MACRO CONTENTS	DESCRIPTION
'\p	@CHAR(173){CALC}~	Press Alt-P to enter π
'\l	@CHAR(163){CALC}~	Press Alt-L to enter the pound symbol

TABLE 17.1: Sample Macros for Entering LICS Symbols in a Spreadsheet

Note: Using the @CHAR function with Alt-P or Alt-L enters these symbols by themselves in a cell of the spreadsheet. To enter the symbol as part of a label, such as π = 3.1415926535, edit the cell containing the π symbol already entered with the Alt-P macro and enter the rest of the label. You can also enter this label by entering the symbol manually (using the Compose key, then the compose key sequence) and following it with the rest of the text.

To use LICS characters as part of a label, you can set up formulas using the @CHAR function and the & operator. For example, if you wished to enter the label "Angle within ± ½°" in the spreadsheet, you could enter

+"Angle within"&" "&@CHAR(177)&" "&@CHAR(189)
&@CHAR(176)

in the cell where you want the label to appear.

Be aware when using LICS characters in spreadsheets that your printer may not be able to interpret and print the characters correctly. For instance, if you printed a spreadsheet containing the label in the previous formula by using an IBM Graphics printer and the /Printer Print command, the plus-or-minus sign and degree symbol would not print correctly, though the entire label can be printed correctly by using the Shift-PrtSc key combination.

Another string function, the @REPEAT function, can often be used to good advantage with the @CHAR function when you want to repeat a symbol in a cell a specific number of times. The @REPEAT function provides a variation on the repeating-label function of typing \ followed by the character to be repeated.

With the @REPEAT function, you must state in the second argument the number of times that the program is to repeat the character or characters specified in the first argument. If the resulting label overflows the cell width, it will still be displayed, provided that the cell or cells to the right required to display all of it are blank. Remember that when the \ is used to enter a repeating label, the repeated characters never overflow the cell width display. Figure 17.3 shows you some of the results you can obtain when combining the @REPEAT and @CHAR functions in a spreadsheet.

The opposite of the @CHAR function is the @CODE function, which returns the LICS code number for the first character in the string entered as its argument. Because you can enter only ASCII characters into strings in the spreadsheet from the keyboard, the numbers returned by using the @CODE function will always be below LICS code 128.

For instance, if you look in your printer manual and find out that the escape sequence to turn on enhanced, enlarged, and doublestrike print is

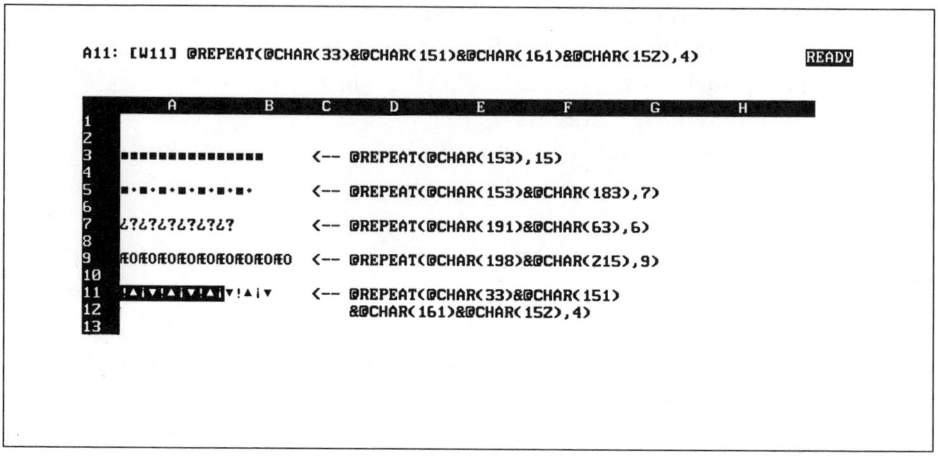

FIGURE 17.3: Using the @REPEAT and @CHAR functions with various LICS graphics and foreign-language symbols to produce repetitive designs. In the first example in row 3, the LICS character 153, which produces a solid square, is repeated 15 times, starting in cell A3 where this function was entered. In the second example, code 183 (which produces a dot) is interspersed with the same code. Notice that this pair of symbols is repeated seven times, producing 14 characters. All of the examples in this figure spill over into column B because the @REPEAT function was used and column B was empty. However, if \@CHAR(153) had been used in A3, the squares would fill only the width of that cell.

Esc ! 8, you could then use the @CODE function to find out what codes should be entered in the spreadsheet to print the title of the spreadsheet using these three attributes.

To find out their codes, you would enter these two formulas in separate cells:

@CODE("!")
@CODE("8")

The first formula would return the value 33 for the exclamation point and 56 for the number 8. To add the escape sequence for turning on this triple attribute in the spreadsheet, you would enter

¦¦\027\033\056

in the row above the title. (For detailed information on how to use special print attributes in reports, refer to Chapter 25).

THE TRIM AND CLEAN FUNCTIONS

Two more functions, the @TRIM and @CLEAN functions, are included in the group of string functions. While @TRIM has more general applications than @CLEAN, you may find both of them useful when working with data imported from other sources rather than generated in Lotus 1-2-3.

The @TRIM function strips out any preceding or trailing spaces and compresses any multiple embedded spaces between words down to a single space in the string referred to in its argument. It can be used whenever a label contains any kind of extraneous spaces. It is often applied to ASCII text that was indented with hard spaces so that the resulting labels are all left justified in their cells. It can also be used to copy titles in the spreadsheet that contain extra spaces to spread them out.

For instance, suppose that two spaces precede every label in a list that was generated in a word processor and was then taken into a Lotus 1-2-3 spreadsheet. If the list begins in A3, you could enter the following formula using the @TRIM function in B3 to strip out these spaces:

@TRIM(A3)

This formula is then copied down column B as far as required to generate a new column with all of the labels left justified in column B.

The @CLEAN function is used to strip out any nonprintable ASCII characters (codes below 32) from strings. These codes are sometimes imported into a spreadsheet along with the text of a file, especially if it was saved via a modem transmission. The codes can include format codes, special print attributes, and the like.

You can combine the @CLEAN and @TRIM functions to make sure that not only all extraneous spaces but also all nonprintable codes are removed from each label. For instance, to perform both functions with one formula, the example cited earlier using just the @TRIM function could easily be modified to

@CLEAN(@TRIM(A3))

THE STRING FUNCTIONS

The arguments required by the string functions are diverse, but a few generalizations can be made about them:

- Most of these functions require a string argument. The argument can contain a cell reference to a label in the spreadsheet, or it can be a manual entry of the string to be evaluated. When you enter the string argument, you must enclose it in a pair of quotation marks.

- Some string functions require a start number that marks the position of the first character to be evaluated. Position numbers are counted from 0; do not count the label prefix, but do count any spaces used.
- Certain string functions require an argument that counts the length in characters of the string to be evaluated. This number is counted from 1, including any spaces.
- The @N and @S functions are the only string functions that require ranges as their arguments. Even when specifying a range of values or labels to be used, only the value of the first cell of the range (that in the upper-left corner) is used. When you designate a single cell as the range, you can enter only the cell reference. You can precede the cell reference by an exclamation point as in @N(!G15) to indicate a single-cell range.

The reference entries for the string functions are listed in alphabetical order.

@CHAR

The @CHAR function returns the appropriate LICS character for the code supplied as its argument.

SYNTAX

@CHAR(x)

where x is a value between 0 and 255 representing one of the 256 LICS codes. The x argument can be entered as a value or as a cell reference to such a value. If the value is not between 0 and 255, the function will return an ERR value. If the value is below 32, the character will not print on your screen. (Note that 32, the code for a space, is also not a visible character.)

USAGE

The @CHAR code can be used to enter one of the printable LICS characters in the spreadsheet. It is especially useful for entering special foreign-language and math symbols in the worksheet and for entering characters not available on the keyboard. It must be used instead of the Compose key and compose character sequence when creating a macro to enter such codes (the {COMPOSE} symbol is not recognized as a macro keyword). The LICS characters and code numbers are shown in Appendix B of this handbook.

To use the @CHAR function, move the cell pointer to the place in the spreadsheet where you want the character to appear and type **@CHAR(**. Then either type in the code number or indicate by cell reference a cell that contains this value. Enter **)** and press the Return key. Lotus 1-2-3 returns the LICS character in the cell, and the literal contents of the cell contain the formula. To convert this formula to the LICS character, press the Edit (F2) and Calc (F9) keys to replace it with its literal string or numeric value.

EXAMPLES

You can use the @CHAR function as part of string formulas to enter labels that require vowels with special accent marks in your spreadsheet. For example, if you needed to enter the various addresses on the Champs-Élysées in Paris into a database, you could make your job easier by entering the first street address by formula and then copying it and editing in all the other cells. You could enter the first address at number 119 as follows:

+"119 Av. des Champs-"&@CHAR(201)&"lys"&@CHAR(233)&"es"

@CHAR(201) enters the capital E with the acute accent, while @CHAR-(233) enters the lowercase e with the acute accent.

@CLEAN

The @CLEAN function removes any nonprintable ASCII characters contained in the string supplied as its argument.

SYNTAX

@CLEAN(string)

where string is any character string entered between a pair of quotation marks or is a reference to a cell that contains a label entry.

USAGE

The @CLEAN function is required only when you import data that contains (or is suspected to contain) nonprintable ASCII codes generated in another program. These codes can be special formatting characters or indentations, or they can print attributes such as those used to print boldface type.

To use @CLEAN, you simply enter **@CLEAN(** and then indicate the cell reference containing the string you wish to strip of codes. You can type in the cell address, enter its range name, or point to it. After you type) and press the Return key, the program displays the string in the cell where you entered the function. Because nonprintable characters are not visible on the screen, the strings will appear identical, even though the strings returned from the @CLEAN function will no longer contain any nonprintable codes.

EXAMPLES

To ensure that a particular label imported into cell A2 contains no nonprintable ASCII characters, move the cell pointer to B2 and enter

@CLEAN(A2)

If you had an entire column of such labels, you could then copy the formula in column B down the rows.

You can also combine this function with the @TRIM function to remove all extraneous spaces as well as nonprinting codes in one operation. To do this, you could enter

@CLEAN(@TRIM(A2))

in cell B2. See the @TRIM reference entry for more information on this function.

@CODE

This function returns the ASCII/LICS code of the first character of the string supplied as its argument.

SYNTAX

@CODE(string)

where string is any character string entered between a pair of quotation marks or is a reference to a cell that contains a label entry.

USAGE

The @CODE function is useful whenever you need to know the ASCII code for a particular printable symbol or letter and do not have access to the LICS or ASCII code chart.

To use it, enter **@CODE(** and then enter the character enclosed in quotation marks or enter a cell reference to a cell that contains a string. If you are using a cell reference, you can type in the cell address or range name or point to it. After you type) and press the Return key, Lotus 1-2-3 calculates the appropriate code number. If the cell referenced in the argument contains more than a single character, only the code of the initial character will be returned. These code numbers are not prefaced by 0, so you will have to add it when using the code in embedded printing commands.

EXAMPLES

To find the ASCII/LICS code for the capital letter A, enter

@CODE("A")

The program returns the value 65 in the cell where this formula was entered. To obtain the ASCII code for a lowercase "a" in the label "after tax" in cell C10, enter

@CODE(C10)

The program returns the value 97, which is the value of the first letter, lowercase "a", in "after tax". (Note that the ASCII codes for the same letter in different cases do not have the same value.)

@EXACT

This function compares the two strings supplied as its arguments and returns the logical value 1 for true if they match exactly and the logical value 0 if they are different.

SYNTAX

@EXACT(string1,string2)

where string1 and string2 are character strings entered between a pair of quotation marks or are references to cells that contain the label entries to be compared to one another.

USAGE

The @EXACT function compares two strings to determine not only whether they match each other in terms of the characters they contain but also whether their capitalization matches. This function is most often used to document that a particular cell entry matches a required string entry. As such, it can be used in macros to check user input against a required entry before continuing processing. The @EXACT function can also be used to locate nonstandard entries in a particular column of a database by documenting those entries that do not conform to the required entry.

To use the @EXACT function, position the cell pointer in the cell where you want the true or false value to appear and type **@EXACT(**. Then either type in the first string enclosed in quotation marks or indicate by cell reference a cell that contains this string. Type a comma and indicate the second string that is to be compared to the first. Then type) and press the Return key. The program returns the value of 1 if the two strings are an exact match; otherwise, it returns the value of 0.

EXAMPLES

To use the @EXACT function to compare the label in cell A5 in the spreadsheet against the string "Closing costs", enter

@EXACT(A5,"Closing costs")

in the cell where you want the result to appear. If, for instance, A5 contains the label Closing Costs, this function returns the value 0, showing that there was no exact match.

You can also incorporate the @EXACT function as the condition in an @IF formula to have the program process different alternatives, depending on the outcome of the string comparison, as in

@IF(@EXACT(A6,"Posted"),A25,@NA)

In this formula, the value in A25 is brought forward and entered in the cell where this formula is entered only if the label in A6 contains the word Posted. If it does not, the value NA is entered in the cell instead.

@FIND

The @FIND function returns the value of the position of a substring contained in another string. It starts its search for the substring from the position indicated as the start number argument.

SYNTAX

@FIND(search string,string,start number)

where search string is the substring to be located, string is the overall string that contains the search string, and start number marks the position in the string where the search is to begin.

The search string or string arguments can be supplied by entering the string enclosed in quotation marks or by cell reference to cells containing these strings. The start number can be entered as a value or as a reference to a cell containing such a value. The start number is computed from 0, marking the position of the first character, and is increased by one for every character to the right.

USAGE

This command performs a search for the string given as its first argument in the string supplied as its second argument. The search is for an exact match not only between characters but also between their capitalization (just as when using the @EXACT function). Lotus 1-2-3 begins the search from the position entered as its third argument.

If no match for the substring is located in the string or if the start number specified is greater than the number of positions in the string, the function returns an ERR value. When the function locates its first match for the search string, it returns the position of the first character in that search string.

@FIND is quite useful when you need to determine the position of a particular character or group of characters in labels in the spreadsheet. It is often combined with the @MID or @REPLACE functions to locate a particular string position and then have the program extract or replace the string as required. @FIND can be used in macros to locate particular substrings that require some sort of processing.

To use the @FIND function, position the cell pointer in the cell where you want the value of the beginning of the search string to appear and type **@FIND(**. Then either type in the search string enclosed in quotation marks or indicate by cell reference a cell that contains this string. Type a comma and indicate the overall string to be searched for. Then type a comma and enter the start number marking the position where the program is to begin the search. Finally, type) and press the Return key.

If Lotus 1-2-3 locates the search string, it returns the value of its starting position in the overall string. Remember that position is counted from 0, not 1, so this value is always one less than the number of characters that precede the first character of the search string.

EXAMPLES

To determine the position of the first occurrence of the string "value" in the label "Market value/Book value ratio" entered in cell A23, enter the formula

@FIND("value",A23,0)

it calculates 7 as the position of the v in the first occurrence of the substring "value". If you then want to test this same string in A3 to determine whether it contains another occurrence of "value" and where it is located, enter

@FIND("value",A23,8)

it returns 18 as the position of the v in the second occurrence of the word. The start number in this formula was given as 8 because the first formula returned the value of 7. By adding one more to this number, you ensure that the program will bypass the first occurrence and evaluate only any subsequent appearances of the search string.

If you want to locate the occurrence of a particular character in a label, you can also use the @FIND function. In the following formula, the @FIND function locates the first occurrence of a hyphen in a date entered as a label in cell E14 in the format 07-04-87:

@FIND("-",E14,0)

This formula returns the value 2, marking the position of the first hyphen in the date. If this formula were entered in cell E25, you could then locate the second occurrence of a hyphen by entering the following formula below it in cell E26:

@FIND("-",E14,E25 + 1)

This gives the start position for the search for the second hyphen by calculating it as one more than the position of its first occurrence.

Note: You can also use the @FIND function with the @MID or @REPLACE functions. For instance, you could use it with @MID to extract the day or year in this date label or use it with @REPLACE to have Lotus 1-2-3 replace the hyphen with the forward slash. For illustrations combining @FIND with these functions, see the Examples sections of the @MID and @REPLACE reference entries.

@LEFT

The @LEFT function extracts the number of characters designated as its n argument from the beginning of the string specified as its first argument.

SYNTAX

@LEFT(string,n)

where string is any character string entered between a pair of quotation marks or is a reference to a cell that contains a label entry, and n is the number of characters to be extracted from the beginning of the string.

USAGE

The @LEFT function is useful whenever you need to copy only part of a particular label into a new cell, starting with characters that occur at the very beginning of the string. Because the function name establishes the beginning search position, you need only specify the string and the number of characters to be extracted.

To use this function, position the cell pointer in the cell where you want the extracted characters to appear, type **@LEFT(**, and either type in the complete string enclosed in quotation marks or indicate by cell reference a cell that contains this string. Type a comma and indicate the number of characters to be extracted. Then type **)** and press the Return key.

The program will copy the number of characters starting from the beginning of the string into the cell, and they will be left justified in the cell, like any label. However, the literal contents of the cell will be the formula @LEFT(string,n). To convert this formula to a label entry, press the Edit key (F2) followed by the Calc key (F9) and then press the Return key. This converts the cell entry to a true label, allowing you to format it with the /Range Label command options—unless the resulting string happens to be composed of only numeric values. In that case, pressing Edit, Calc, and Return converts the formula to a true value that is right justified and can be used in other formula calculations.

EXAMPLES

The @LEFT function can be used to copy only a portion of the first part of label entries in a particular column or row of the spreadsheet or database without requiring any manual entry. For instance, assume that you have a column in the database that contains a three-part identification number (like a part number or a customer or employee ID number), and you need to enter only the first three digits of the number in a new column in the database. As long as the identification numbers have been entered as labels, you can use the @LEFT function to do the task.

If the first cell containing the number is F5 and you are building the new field in column P, move the cell pointer to P5 and enter the @LEFT formula. If the number is formatted like 101-AH-04567 and you need only the first three digits in the new field, enter this formula in the cell:

@LEFT(F5,3)

The function returns 101 in P5. You could then copy this formula down the entire length of column P for as many rows as you have in the identification number column.

If you needed to copy only the first two parts of this number (101-AH) to the new column, you would enter this @LEFT function:

@LEFT(F5,6)

@LENGTH

The @LENGTH function returns the number of characters contained in the string specified as its argument.

SYNTAX

@LENGTH(string)

where string is any character string entered between a pair of quotation marks or is a reference to a cell that contains a label entry.

USAGE

This function is useful whenever you need to determine the length of a particular string in the worksheet. It is often incorporated into macros where the length of the string is not to exceed a particular value. @LENGTH can also be used to determine automatically the required spacing for displaying or positioning labels.

To use the @LENGTH function, position the cell pointer in the cell where you want the number of characters to appear and type **@LENGTH(**. Either type in the complete string enclosed in quotation marks or indicate by cell reference a cell that contains this string. Then type) and press the Return key. The program returns the total number of characters in the string, including spaces between words.

You can use the & operator to concatenate cells so that the @LENGTH function returns the combined length of more than a single string. These strings can be literal (enclosed in quotes), cell references, or range names assigned to single-cell ranges.

EXAMPLES

To determine the length of a label in cell A12, simply enter

@LENGTH(A12)

If cell A12 contained the label Human Resources, the program would return the value 15, indicating that there are 15 characters in this title, including the space between the words.

To determine the combined length of this label and one in B12, enter

@LENGTH(A12&B12)

If the label in B12 contains the label Accounting, the result of this calculation is 25.

If you want to know the length of a new label created by concatenating these labels with the word "and" in a new cell, enter

@LENGTH(A12&" and "&B12)

This results in the value 30, indicating that such a label is 30 characters long. If this label were entered in a cell where there were data or labels in the cell to its right, you would have to set the cell width to 30 in order for the label to be displayed completely.

@LOWER

The @LOWER function converts all of the letters in the string specified as its argument to lowercase.

SYNTAX

@LOWER(string)

where string is any character string entered between a pair of quotation marks or is a reference to a cell that contains a label entry.

USAGE

The @LOWER function is very useful when you need to convert all letters in a particular label to lowercase. To use the @LOWER function, position the cell pointer in the cell where you want the string converted to lowercase letters to appear, type **@LOWER(**, and then either type in the complete string enclosed in quotation marks or indicate by cell reference a cell that contains this string. Then type **)** and press the Return key. The program will copy the string all in lowercase letters, regardless of how it was entered.

EXAMPLES

To convert a label entry in G29, which contains the string Cost Plus 40%, to lowercase letters, move the pointer to the cell where you want the converted label to appear and enter

@LOWER(G29)

The function returns the label "cost plus 40%".

You can also use the & operator to have the program convert to lowercase and join more than a single label. If C14 contains the label PRICE, you could join it to the label in G29 with this formula:

@LOWER(C14&" equals "&G29)

The label "price equals cost plus 40%" would appear in the cell where the function is entered.

@MID

The @MID function searches a string from a specified position within that string and extracts the number of characters desired from within it.

SYNTAX

@MID(string,start number,n)

where string is the overall string that contains the characters to be extracted (the substring), start number marks the position in the string where the search is to begin, and n is the number of characters in the substring to be extracted.

The string argument can be supplied by entering the string enclosed in quotation marks or by entering a cell reference to the cell containing the string. The start number and n arguments can be entered as values or as references to cells containing such values. The start number is computed from 0, marking the position of the first character, and increased by one for every character to the right.

USAGE

The @MID function complements the @LEFT and @RIGHT functions. It allows you to extract (copy) a substring from a string by specifying the beginning position and the number of characters to be extracted. It is used whenever the substring characters to be reused are not located at the beginning of the string (where the @LEFT function is used) or the end of the string (where the @RIGHT function is used).

Because @MID requires the starting position, which is often unknown, as one of its arguments, you can effectively combine @MID with @FIND, which calculates the start position for you (see the examples that follow).

If the start number specified is a negative number or is greater than the number of positions in the string (equal to one less than the number of characters in the string), the function returns an ERR value. If the start number is entered as a mixed number, Lotus 1-2-3 uses only the integer portion of the number.

To use the @MID function, position the cell pointer in the cell where you want the extracted substring characters to appear and type **@MID(**. Then either type in the search string enclosed in quotation marks or indicate by cell reference a cell that contains this string. Type a comma and indicate the number marking the position where the program is to begin the search. Then type a comma and the number of characters to be extracted. Finally, type a) and press the Return key. Lotus 1-2-3 returns the specified number of characters from the overall string as a left-justified label.

EXAMPLES

To extract only a portion of a date entered as a label in the format MM-DD-YY, such as 11-23-87, you can use the @MID function. For instance, if you want only the day portion of such a date entered in cell

S34, enter the following:

@MID(S34,3,2)

where 3 is the start position of the day value and 2 is the number of characters to be extracted.

However, if you are extracting days from this type of date label and some of them were entered with single digits for the month (as in 2-13-90), specifying a start number of 3 will return the wrong characters. You can construct a formula that locates the day regardless of whether the month was entered with one or two digits:

@MID(S34,@FIND("-",S34,0) + 1,2)

This formula locates the position of the first hyphen and then uses this value plus one to locate the day and extract it.

The formula works fine only as long as the day consists of two digits, as in 2-13-90. It will not work correctly if the date were 2-3-90. In such a case, you could use an @IF formula with the @RIGHT function to return only the single digit for the day of the month:

@IF(@RIGHT(@MID(S34,@FIND("-",S34,0) + 1,2),1) = "-",
@MID(S34,@FIND("-",S34,0) + 1,1),
@MID(S34,@FIND("-",S34,0) + 1,2))

This formula evaluates the substring located by the @MID formula to determine whether the last character (@RIGHT,1) is a hyphen. If it is, a similar @MID formula is used to extract the substring, except that the n argument is adjusted to 1 to take only the single digit of the day of the month. If the last character is not a hyphen, the original @MID formula is used to return the two digits for the day.

@N

The @N function returns the value of the first cell of the range specified as its argument.

SYNTAX

@N(range)

where range is a cell range designated by cell address or range name. This function returns only the value of the first cell (the one in the upper-left corner) of a range composed of multiple cells. A single-cell range can also be specified. If the range consists of only a single cell, you can enter the address of that cell and Lotus 1-2-3 will automatically convert it into a cell range for you (e.g., it will convert A3 to A3..A3).

USAGE

The @N function returns a value of 0 for the first cell in a cell range if the cell contains a string. It is used in error-trapping routines to prevent ERR values that would otherwise occur if calculations between strings and values were attempted.

To use the @N function, enter **@N(** and indicate the cell range to be used. Indicate the cell range as you would any other cell range in Lotus 1-2-3—by typing in its addresses, entering its range name, or pointing to it. If it is a single-cell range, you can enter the cell address or point to it. After you enter the range, be sure to enter) before continuing to build your formula.

EXAMPLES

To convert the contents of cells C3 and C4 to their numerical values and ensure that no ERR value could occur when they are added together, enter

@N(C3) + @N(C4)

in the cell where you want their sum. If C3 contains the label Price and C4 contains 105.45, the result would be 105.45 instead of the ERR value that would have been returned if you had not used the @N function. Because the value in C3 was returned as 0 by the @N function, no ERR value was calculated.

@PROPER

The @PROPER function converts to uppercase only the initial letters of words separated by spaces in the string specified as its argument.

SYNTAX

@PROPER(string)

where string is any character string entered between a pair of quotation marks or is a reference to a cell that contains a label entry.

USAGE

The @PROPER function is very useful when you need to convert initial letters of words in a particular label to uppercase letters. @PROPER capitalizes initial letters of alphabetic strings and any letters separated by nonalphabetic characters.

To use the @PROPER function, position the cell pointer in the cell where you want the converted string to appear, type **@PROPER(**, and then either type in the complete string enclosed in quotation marks or indicate by cell reference a cell that contains this string. Then type) and press the Return key. The program will copy the string, converting initial letters in each word to uppercase, regardless of the capitalization used when the original string was entered.

EXAMPLES

@PROPER regards nonalphabetic characters (numbers and symbols) as delimiters between words. For example, @PROPER converts

123-x

to

123-X

It converts

intro 12a

to

Intro 12A

To use @PROPER to convert a label entry in B12 containing the string "california consolidated", move the pointer to the cell where you want the converted label to appear and enter

@PROPER(B12)

It returns the label California Consolidated.

You can also use the & operator to have the program do this kind of conversion and join more than a single label. If B12 contains the label FIXED ASSETS, you can join it to the label in D12 with this formula:

@PROPER(B12&" - "&D12)

The formula produces the label California Consolidated - Fixed Assets.

@REPEAT

The @REPEAT function repeats the specified string the number of times indicated as its n argument.

SYNTAX

@REPEAT(string,n)

where string is any character string entered between a pair of quotation marks or is a reference to a cell that contains a label entry, and n is the number of times those characters are to be repeated.

USAGE

The use of this function differs from that of a repeating label. When you use a repeating label, the characters are repeated until they fill the entire width of the cell. When you use the @REPEAT function, the characters are repeated as many times as indicated by the value supplied as the n argument. The characters may spill into the cells on the right if those cells are empty.

The @REPEAT function can be used to repeat any printable character, including special mathematical, graphics, or foreign-language symbols included in the LICS codes. To repeat one or more of these special characters, you use the @CHAR function as the string argument of the @REPEAT function.

To use @REPEAT, position the pointer in the cell where you want the repeating characters to start, type **@REPEAT(**, and then indicate the characters to be repeated. You can enter the characters in the string enclosed in quotation marks or use a reference to a cell that contains the string. Then type a comma and indicate the number of times the string is to be repeated. You can either enter a value or reference a cell that contains such a value. Then type) and press the Return key.

EXAMPLES

To repeat the characters - and * five times in cell A15 using the @REPEAT function, enter

@REPEAT("-"&"*",5)

This produces the following string of symbols:

-*-*-*-*-*

If the column width of column A were 9, one of these characters would be displayed in cell B15 if it were blank.

@REPLACE

The @REPLACE function locates a specific position in a string and replaces the desired number of characters with the new string specified as its last argument.

SYNTAX

@REPLACE(original string,start number,n,new string)

where original string is enclosed in quotation marks or is a reference to the cell that contains the string to be replaced. The start number is the value that marks the first position where the replacement is to be made. It is counted from 0 as the leftmost character in the original string. The n argument marks the number of characters to be replaced. The new string argument contains the replacement characters or a reference to the cell that contains the characters.

USAGE

The @REPLACE function adds a new substring to an original string, creating a new label. It can be used to replace part of a label and add new text to it. Only the number of characters indicated as the n argument will actually be deleted, even though all characters in the new string argument will be added at the position indicated by the value of the start number.

Because this function requires the starting position, which is often unknown, as one of its arguments, you can effectively combine @REPLACE with @FIND, which calculates this start position for you (see the examples that follow).

If the start number specified is a negative number or is greater than the number of positions in the string (equal to one less than the number of characters in the string), the function returns an ERR value. If the start number is entered as a mixed number, Lotus 1-2-3 uses only the integer portion of the number.

To use the @REPLACE function, position the cell pointer in the cell where you want the new string to appear, type **@REPLACE(**, and then either type in the original string enclosed in quotation marks or indicate by cell reference a cell that contains this string. Type a comma and indicate the start number marking the position where the program is to begin the search. Then type another comma and indicate the number of characters to be replaced. Next, indicate the characters in the new string that will be added to the original string either by typing them enclosed in quotation marks or by referencing a cell that contains this string. Finally, type) and press the Return key. Lotus 1-2-3 returns the new string in the cell where you entered this function.

EXAMPLES

To use @REPLACE to amend a label in cell A5 that contains the text Profits so that it reads After-Tax Profits, enter

@REPLACE(A5,0,0,"After-Tax")

The following @REPLACE function locates the position of the first hyphen in a date entered as a label in the format MM-DD in cell E20 and replaces it with the forward slash:

@REPLACE(E20,@FIND("-",E20,0),1,"/")

If the label in E20 contains the date 4-24, it will be converted to 4/24 in the cell where this function is entered. The @FIND function automatically locates the position of the hyphen in E20, which is then the only character replaced in the string.

The date could also be simultaneously converted with the @DATEVALUE function to a serial date number that could be used in calculations calling for date arithmetic:

@DATEVALUE(@REPLACE(E20,@FIND("-",E20,0),1,"/"))

The resulting serial number will represent April 24 of the current year supplied by the @NOW function. It can then be formatted to the long international date format by using the /Range Format Date 4 command.

@RIGHT

The @RIGHT function extracts the number of characters designated as its n argument from the end of the string specified as its first argument.

SYNTAX

@RIGHT(string,n)

where string is any character string entered between a pair of quotation marks or is a reference to a cell that contains a label entry, and n is the number of characters to be extracted from the end of the string.

USAGE

The @RIGHT function is useful whenever you need to copy part of a particular label into a new cell, starting with characters that occur at the end of the string. The number of characters extracted is counted from right to left from the end of the string, according to the value supplied as the n argument.

To use this function, position the cell pointer in the cell where you want the extracted characters to appear, type **@RIGHT(**, and then either type in the complete string enclosed in quotation marks or indicate by cell reference a cell that contains this string. Type a comma and indicate the number of characters to be extracted. Then type) and press the Return key.

The program will copy the specified number of characters starting from the end of the string into the cell; they will be left justified in the cell, like any label. However, the literal contents of the cell will be the formula @RIGHT(string,n). To convert this formula to a label entry, press the Edit (F2) key, followed by the Calc (F9) and Return keys. This converts the cell entry to a true label that you can format with the /Range Label command options, unless the resulting string happens to be composed of only numeric values. In that case, pressing Edit, Calc, and Return converts the formula to a true, right-justified value that can be used in other formula calculations.

EXAMPLES

To extract only the last three characters from cell T8 containing the label "+2.4%", use the @RIGHT function as follows:

@RIGHT(T8,3)

It produces the label ".4%" in the cell where this function was entered.

@S

The @S function returns the value of the first cell of the range specified as its argument as a string value.

SYNTAX

@S(range)

where range is a cell range designated by cell address or range name. This function returns the value of only the first cell, (the one in the upper-left corner) of a range composed of multiple cells. A single-cell range can also be specified. If the range consists of a single cell, you can enter only the address of that cell; Lotus 1-2-3 automatically converts it into a cell range for you (e.g., it converts A3 to A3..A3).

USAGE

The @S function returns a null string value for the first cell in a cell range if the cell contains a value. It is used in error-trapping routines to prevent ERR values that would otherwise occur if calculations between values and strings were attempted.

To use the @S function, enter **@S(** and indicate the cell range to be used. Indicate the cell range as you would any other cell range in Lotus 1-2-3—by typing in its addresses, entering its range name, or pointing to it. If it is a single-cell range, you can enter the single cell address or point to the cell. After you enter the range, be sure to enter) before continuing to build your formula.

EXAMPLES

To ensure that a concatenation between the strings in cells H7 and H8 could not result in an ERR value regardless of their contents, enter the formula

@S(H7)&" "&@S(H8)

in the cell where you want the labels joined. If cell H7 contains the label After-Tax and cell H8 contains the value 0.33, the result will simply be the label After-Tax. If cell H7 contains the value 5.67 and H8 contains the label Profits, the result will be Profits preceded by a single space. If cell

H7 and H8 both contain values, the cell will appear blank, even though it contains a single space. Under no conditions will the result be an ERR value, as could easily be the case if the @S function were not used.

@STRING

The @STRING function converts the numerical value specified as its x argument into a string.

SYNTAX

@STRING(x,n)

where x is the value or the cell reference to the value to be converted into a string, and n is the number of decimal places to be displayed. The @STRING function uses the Fixed format when converting a value to a string. The original value is rounded in the resulting string if the value of the n argument is less than the number of decimal places it contains.

USAGE

The @STRING function can be used any time you want to convert a value into a string. To use it, position the cell pointer where you want the string to appear and enter **@STRING(**. Then indicate the value to be converted either by entering it or by referencing the cell that contains it. Type a comma and indicate the number of decimal places to be displayed in the resulting string. You can type in the number or reference a cell that contains the appropriate number. Then type **)** and press the Return key.

Lotus 1-2-3 returns a left-justified label containing the numeric string. If you want the label justified in some other way, you must add the appropriate number of spaces by concatenating them. (You cannot use the Edit and Calc keys, because they will convert the string back into a value.)

EXAMPLES

To convert the value 3.456 in cell K26 to a string value displaying only one decimal place, enter

@STRING(K26,1)

Lotus 1-2-3 returns the label "3.5" in the cell where you enter this function.

To convert the same value in cell K26 to a string displaying a percent sign, amend this formula to

@STRING(K26,1)&"%"

which produces the label "3.5%".

@TRIM

This function trims all preceding, trailing, and extra spaces from the specified string. The resulting string will still contain single spaces between words.

SYNTAX

@TRIM(string)

where string is any character string entered between a pair of quotation marks or is a reference to a cell that contains a label entry.

USAGE

This function can be used whenever you need to remove extraneous spaces from a label in the worksheet. It is especially useful in those situations where your data is imported with preceding spaces that must be removed. It relieves you of the tedious task of manually editing each label to delete the preceding spaces. @TRIM can also be used to copy a spreadsheet title that has been purposely spaced out by adding extra spaces between each word.

To use the @TRIM function, position the cell pointer in the cell where you want the copied string to appear, type **@TRIM(**, and then either type in the complete string enclosed in quotation marks or indicate by cell reference a cell that contains this string. Type) and press the Return key. The resulting string will contain only one space between any words within the string that were separated by one or more spaces in the original string, and all preceding and trailing spaces will be removed.

EXAMPLES

To remove the extraneous spaces from cell B2, which contains the string

Consumer   Deposits   and   Loans

enter this @TRIM function:

@TRIM(B2)

It returns the label Consumer Deposits and Loans.

You could also use this function to remove spaces used to indent a column of labels when these labels are to be reused elsewhere in the spreadsheet without any indentation. If the first label occurs in cell E17, move the pointer to the first cell where you want the copy and enter

@TRIM(E17)

This formula would then be copied down as far as necessary to remove all of the spaces used to indent the rest of the labels.

ALT-T, A MACRO TO TRIM STRINGS

You can also create a simple keystroke macro to trim the spaces and then convert the resulting formula to a true label (or value if the label contains only numeric characters):

Label	*Macro Contents*
'\t	**'@TRIM({?})~{EDIT}{CALC}~**

To use this macro, position the pointer where you want the trimmed label to appear, press Alt-t, and then indicate the string. You can either type in the address of the cell containing the original string or point to it. When you press the Return key, the trimmed string is entered. If the trimmed string contains only numeric values, the result will be a right-justified value entry; otherwise, it will be a left-justified label.

@UPPER

The @UPPER function converts all letters in the string specified as its argument to uppercase.

SYNTAX

@UPPER(string)

where string is any character string entered between a pair of quotation marks or is a reference to a cell that contains a label entry.

USAGE

The @UPPER function is useful whenever you need to convert a label to all uppercase letters. A good example of this is in an address database that contains a column for the state. You probably always want the two-letter state abbreviations to be in all uppercase letters so that the database can be sorted properly. Using the @UPPER function in the area used to enter new records will ensure that all new state entries are consistent. This function can also be used to convert existing entries to the required format.

The @UPPER function comes in handy in macros that evaluate characters input by the user in order to branch to different subroutines. Using the @UPPER function allows the user the choice of using either upper- or lowercase letters.

To use the @UPPER function, position the cell pointer in the cell where you want the string converted to uppercase letters to appear, type **@UPPER(**, and then either type in the complete string enclosed in quotation marks or indicate by cell reference a cell that contains this string. Type **)** and press the Return key. The program will copy the string all in uppercase letters, regardless of how the original string was entered.

EXAMPLES

To convert an entry made in all lowercase letters in cell G145 to uppercase, enter

@UPPER(G145)

If cell G145 contained the label "ny", the label in the cell where this function was entered would be NY. To convert the formula to a true label, you could then press the Edit key (F2), the Calc key (F9), and the Return key.

You can then use the /Move command to move the uppercase label to the location containing the original label and replace it with the correct form. You can use the macro that follows to save time when you have to process a number of labels in a column or row.

You can also use the @UPPER function with the @EXACT function to locate those entries in a database that are not in all uppercase letters. Using the /Data Query Find command, you can then locate the improper entries and manually edit each one. For instance, suppose that you wish to locate and edit any states that have not been entered in all uppercase letters before you sort the database by state and zip code. If the first cell containing a state entry is G5, you could use the following formula in the criterion range to find all improper entries:

#NOT#@EXACT(G5,@UPPER(G5))

Then, when you perform a find operation with /Data Query Find, Lotus 1-2-3 will stop at all states that have been entered either in all lowercase letters or in a mix of capital and lowercase letters. Then you can edit each improper entry as it is found.

ALT-U, A MACRO TO CONVERT A LABEL TO UPPERCASE

You can automate the procedure of converting a column or row of labels to uppercase by entering the following keystroke macro:

Label	*Macro Contents*
'\u	**'@UPPER({?})~{EDIT}{CALC}~**

To use this macro, position the pointer where you want the uppercase label to appear, press Alt-u, and then indicate the string. You can type in the address of the cell containing the original string or point to it. When you press the Return key, the string is entered as a left-justified uppercase label.

@VALUE

The @VALUE function converts the string specified as its x argument into a value that can be included in calculations.

SYNTAX

@VALUE(string)

where string is a numerical string enclosed in quotes or is a cell reference to such a string.

USAGE

The @VALUE function can be used any time you want to convert a string containing numeric values into values that can be used in mathematical calculations. To use @VALUE, position the cell pointer where you want the value to appear and enter **@VALUE(**. Indicate the string to be converted either by entering it or by referencing the cell that contains it. Then type) and press the Return key.

Lotus 1-2-3 returns a value as long as the string indicated as its argument is expressed in one of the following formats:

- A label made up of all integers, such as 1345
- A label made up of decimal values, such as 17.678
- A label made up of fractions, such as 3 7/8
- A label using scientific notation, such as 1.24E3

The program returns an ERR value if the string contains comma delimiters, dollar signs, percent signs, or other such characters. You must add these by using the /Range Format command and the appropriate format.

EXAMPLES

To convert the label in cell R30 containing 5 7/16 to a value that can be used in calculation, enter

@VALUE(R30)

Lotus 1-2-3 returns the value 5.4375 in the cell where the function is entered.

To add two strings, one entered as 12.5 in R2 and the other entered as 3/8 in D2, enter

@VALUE(R2) + @VALUE(D2)

The program enters the calculated result 12.875 in the cell where this formula is entered.

SUMMARY

This chapter has examined the wide variety of string functions now offered by Lotus 1-2-3. Because a great many of these functions are often used in macros, you may also want to refer to Chapter 28, which covers the macro command language. By examining the commands listed there and looking at examples of how they are used, you can get a better idea of the practical possibilities for many of these functions.

CHAPTER 18

SPECIAL FUNCTIONS

Special Functions

This chapter examines the group of functions called special functions by the Lotus 1-2-3 documentation. The types of functions in this group are mixed, but they can be classified into three subgroups:

1. Lookup functions—@HLOOKUP, @VLOOKUP, @CHOOSE, and the new Release 2 functions, @INDEX and @@
2. Release 2 functions that return specific information about the cells in question—@CELL, @CELLPOINTER, @COLS, and @ROWS
3. The @NA (Not Available) and @ERR functions, which produce special numeric cell entries

The discussions that open this chapter examine the first two groups, the lookup functions and those that return specific attributes describing the current cell contents. If you need information about using @NA or the meaning of the @ERR function, proceed directly to those particular reference entries near the end of the chapter.

The reference entries for the group of special functions are found after these general discussions, listed in alphabetical order from @@ to @VLOOKUP.

Using the Lookup Functions

The lookup functions provide a variety of ways to retrieve specific data that is to be used in the spreadsheet. Some of the lookup functions, such as @HLOOKUP, @VLOOKUP, and @INDEX, retrieve the data from lookup tables located somewhere in the same spreadsheet. Others, such as the @CHOOSE and @@ (At At) functions, do not require the use of data in a two-dimensional table. The data the @CHOOSE function works with is listed as part of the arguments the function takes, while the @@ function uses the data contained in another cell in the spreadsheet whose cell reference is the function's argument.

However the lookup functions retrieve the data, they all serve as a powerful means for automating the selection among different data. Their use helps standardize the data supplied to key formulas in a model's design, which keeps discrepancies to a minimum and makes updating and maintaining the correct data much easier.

The Functions That Use Lookup Tables

Lookup functions that work with data tables match the values referenced or entered as part of its arguments against those contained in a particular cell range. This cell range contains the data of the lookup table. When an appropriate match is found based either on position in the table or on values, that data is returned to the cell that contains the lookup function.

To the two basic lookup-table functions of @VLOOKUP and @HLOOKUP found in Release 1A, Release 2 has added a third, @INDEX. Figures 18.1, 18.2, and 18.3 illustrate how these three functions work on a data table to return appropriate values.

The @VLOOKUP Function

In Figure 18.1, notice that when using the @VLOOKUP function the column is scanned for a match to the selector value given as its first argument. The function works in a vertical direction, starting with the first cell of the range defined as the second argument. It then works down the first column, referred to as the *index column,* in an attempt to find an exact match for the selector value.

In this particular example, there is no exact match for the number 9 in the table. The program therefore continues down the index column until it locates the first value higher than the selector value, which in this case is the value 10, entered in cell A7. Notice, however, that because this is not an exact match, it then moves up one row, which contains the next lower value, before moving across the row to retrieve the lookup value.

It is the last argument, containing the column offset, that determines how many columns to the right the program will look to find the actual value it returns in cell A1. Like Lotus 1-2-3 databases, data tables use offsets that begin with 0. The index column of a vertical lookup table always has an offset of zero, with the offset number increasing by one for each column to its right.

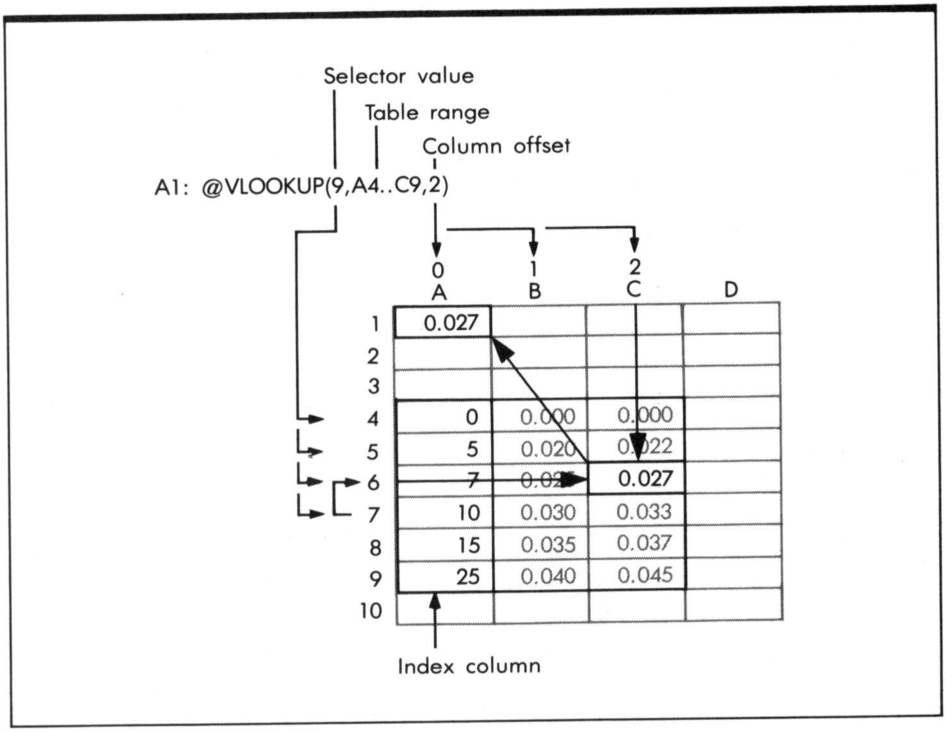

FIGURE 18.1: How the @VLOOKUP function finds a match for the selector value and chooses the appropriate value. First, the function locates the selector value (which in this figure was entered as a literal value). Next, it locates the first cell of the lookup table by using the cell addresses of the table range argument. In this case, this first cell is A4. Because the vertical lookup function was used, it then moves down the index column (the column with offset 0) until it locates a match. Because there is no match for the number 9, it stops at the row containing the next highest value (10) and then moves up a row. Finally, it uses the column number (offset) argument to locate the value to be retrieved and copies it into the cell where the function is entered.

For @VLOOKUP to work properly, the index values in the lookup column must be in ascending order. If the values are out of order, @VLOOKUP will return an incorrect value. For example, if the lookup range A4..C8 were

0
5
9
7
20

and you executed @VLOOKUP as

@VLOOKUP (15, A4..C8, 2)

the function would move to 20, go up one line to 7, and then report the value corresponding to this line.

Many lookup tables that contain numerical data (such as price lists and tax tables) are set up in this manner, where each value represents a step in often uneven ranges of values. Notice that in selecting the value 0.027 in Figure 18.1, Lotus 1-2-3 has responded correctly to the implicit meaning of the way this table was set up.

If we assume that the table represents a discount table and that the index column holds the number of items that must be purchased to get a particular discount percentage, we can see that purchases involving seven, eight, or nine items entitle the customer to a discount of 2.5 percent or 2.7 percent. It is only when a customer orders between 10 and 14 items that this discount is increased to 3.0 percent or 3.3 percent.

The @HLOOKUP Function

The @HLOOKUP function works much like the @VLOOKUP function. The major difference is in its orientation. In the @HLOOKUP function (Figure 18.2), the index column becomes an index row, beginning with the first row in the cell range containing the lookup table. Accordingly, the function scans across this row, starting with the first cell in the range, until it makes the appropriate match to the selector value (again given as the first function argument).

Just as before, offsets are counted from 0 and are taken from the value given as the last argument of the function. Once a match has been made (again the next lower value in the index row is used because there is no exact match to the selector value), the program looks down the column and uses the value it finds at the appropriate offset.

The @INDEX Function (Release 2 Only)

Release 2 includes a new function, @INDEX, that also uses a lookup table to select the appropriate value. It differs from the @VLOOKUP and @HLOOKUP functions in that it does not select a value in the table by matching a selector value against a value in the index column or row. When using this function, you must specify both the column and row offset values as part of its arguments.

Like @VLOOKUP and @HLOOKUP, @INDEX counts these offsets from 0. The first cell of the cell range specified as the first argument has a

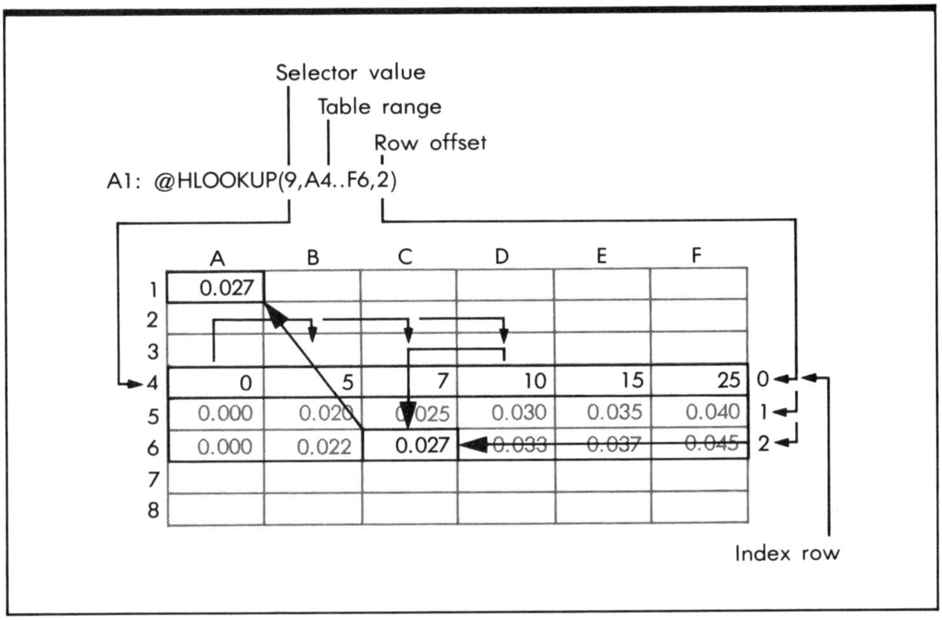

FIGURE 18.2: How the @HLOOKUP function finds a match for the selector value and chooses the appropriate value. First, the function locates the selector value (which in this figure was entered as a literal value). Next, it locates the first cell of the lookup table by using the cell addresses of the table range argument. In this case, this first cell is A4. Because the horizontal lookup function was used, it then moves across the index row (the row with offset 0) until it locates a match. Because there is no match for the number 9, it stops at the column containing the next highest value (10) and then moves back one column. Finally, it uses the row number (offset) argument to locate the value to be retrieved and copies it into the cell where the function is entered.

column and row offset of 0. In Figure 18.3, the value of 0.027 is selected because it has a column offset of 2 and a row offset of 2.

The @INDEX function is used only when you know the appropriate offsets (that is, when you already know where the appropriate value is located in the lookup table).

Using Labels in Lookup Tables

In Release 1A, you cannot use the @VLOOKUP and @HLOOKUP functions in tables that contain labels. The lookup tables used with these functions must contain values, such as the ones in Figures 18.1, 18.2, and 18.3. However, Release 2 does allow you to retrieve data from a table that contains labels.

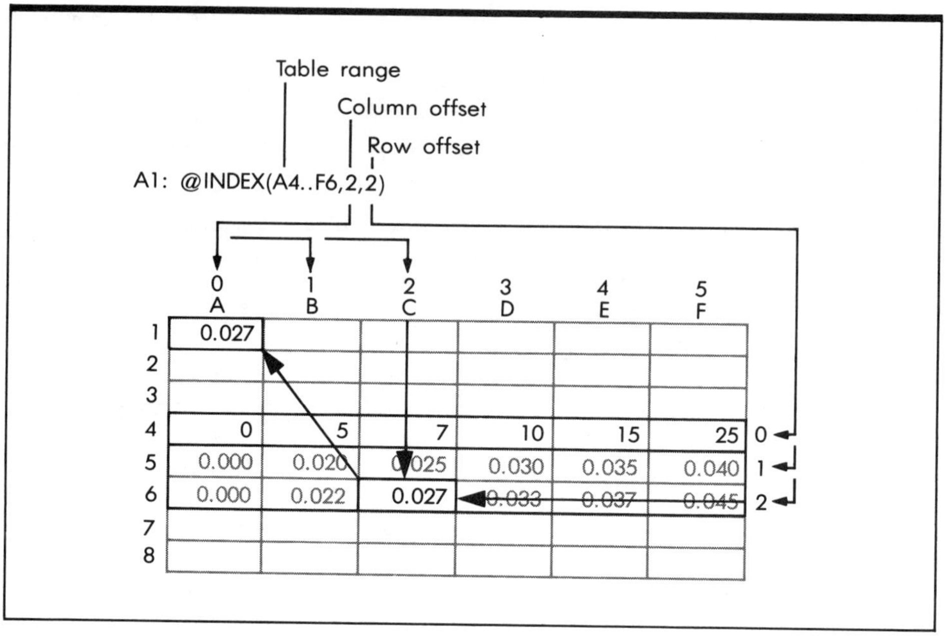

FIGURE 18.3: How the @INDEX function selects the appropriate value by using the column and row offset numbers. First, the function locates the first cell in the range containing the lookup values by using the cell addresses of the table range argument. It then moves across the columns of the table and stops at the column whose offset value matches that of the column number argument. Next, it moves down that column and stops at the row whose offset value matches that of the row number argument. The value in the cell located at this junction is the one returned to the cell that contains the @INDEX function.

Figure 18.4 illustrates a sample application for the @INDEX function whose lookup table contains labels. In this figure, a simple table contains the first-quarter sales figures for five salespeople. The cell range that actually contains the data (cells A4 to D8) has been given the range name SALES_TABL and has been used as the lookup table cell range in the formulas using the @INDEX function in E11, E12, and E13.

The @INDEX formulas in the figure (E11..E13) bring forward the appropriate sales figures from the table, depending on the offset values supplied in B13 and in cells B16 to B18. The figures retrieved by these formulas are then totaled by a simple @SUM formula in cell E15.

The column offset for each @INDEX formula is supplied from the column offset numbers entered in cells B16, B17, and B18, while the row offset is determined by a formula calculation in B13. This cell contains the formula @VLOOKUP(B11,SALES_TABL,0). It returns the value of the column lookup, depending on the name of the salesperson entered into cell

```
E11: [W10] @INDEX($SALES_TABL,$B16,$B$13)                                  READY

        A            B          C          D          E          F
 1
 2
 3    Salesperson        Jan        Feb        Mar
 4        Jenkins     34,675     30,568     34,567
 5          Grill     23,689     32,456     31,250
 6         Farner     42,678     28,945     35,600
 7          Davis     32,680     45,230     44,219
 8          Smith     23,599     27,455     31,876
 9
10
11 Salesperson    Davis                  Jan             32680
12                                       Feb             45230
13 Row offset               3            Mar             44219
14                                                  ----------
15 Column offset                         Qtr Total    $122,129
16             Jan          1
17             Feb          2
18             Mar          3
19
20
```

FIGURE 18.4: Using the @INDEX function to retrieve quarterly sales figures from a sales table. In this figure, three formulas use @INDEX to copy the appropriate sales figures for each salesperson into cells E11 to E13. To obtain a new total for another salesperson only requires entering his or her name in cell B11. An @VLOOKUP function in cell B13 uses the name entered there to return the appropriate row offset used by the three @INDEX formulas. These formulas obtain the column offset from the values entered in cells B16 through B18.

B11. Because offset 0 is specified, this vertical lookup function returns the row offset number for the match made between the label entered in B11 and a label in column A of the range SALES_TABL.

To obtain the quarterly total for another salesperson, all that is required is to type a new name in cell B11. The @VLOOKUP function will then calculate the appropriate row offset number, which will be used in the three @INDEX functions in cells E11 to E13.

Choosing Items from a List

The @CHOOSE function is very useful when you do not want to set up a two-dimensional lookup table in the spreadsheet. Figure 18.5 compares the use of an @CHOOSE function to an @VLOOKUP function, both of which return the name of the month by entering its numerical value. The @CHOOSE function also uses an offset entered as the first argument to decide which value to use in the list. Just as with the @VLOOKUP and @HLOOKUP functions, the first offset for the value in the list is zero.

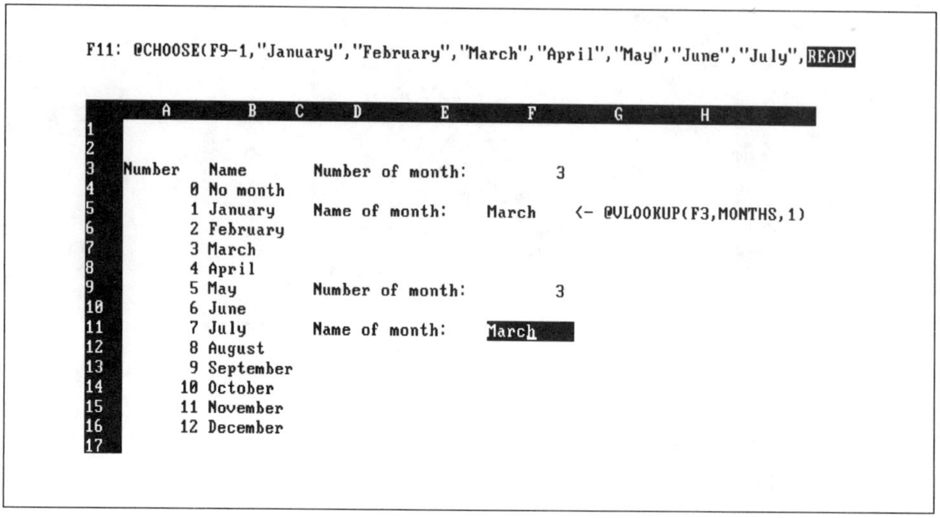

FIGURE 18.5: Converting the numbers of the months into their equivalent names with @VLOOKUP and @CHOOSE. This figure contrasts two methods for obtaining the correct month name from the equivalent number for the month. The @VLOOKUP formula in cell F5 requires the use of a lookup table that positions the names of the months next to their numbers. The @CHOOSE formula in F11 does the same thing by choosing the appropriate month name from the list of names entered as its value arguments. It chooses the name by taking the number of the month entered in F9 and subtracting it from 1 to obtain the correct offset value for the list of month names.

In Figure 18.5, the @CHOOSE function entered in cell F11 is used to return the appropriate name of the month from the number between 1 and 12 entered in cell F9. To do this, the twelve month names are entered in order as value arguments of the function.

Because the first value, "January", has an offset of 0, the value entered in cell F9 (which supplies the selector argument used as the offset) must be one less in order to choose the correct month name. Though January is the first month of the year and would be indicated by entering the number 1 in F9, its offset in the @CHOOSE function is 0, thus the F9 − 1 argument.

Notice that the @VLOOKUP function accomplishes the same conversion by using a simple month-number-to-month-name lookup table. It also uses the same kind of offset numbers down the index column (A4..A16). It contains a label of "No month" for month number 0. Unlike the @CHOOSE function, a dummy entry for offset 0 must exist in the lookup table so that the actual month names are arranged in the correct offset position in the table.

Note: If you are using Release 1A, you cannot mix labels and values when using lookup functions. You cannot therefore use the @CHOOSE or @VLOOKUP functions as illustrated in Figure 18.5. This release of the product restricts you to processing values in lookup tables and @CHOOSE value lists.

The @CHOOSE function can replace a series of @IF statements in macro commands that require a decision in the worksheet. The first argument can take the input made by the user and return a corresponding value that would otherwise require a complex set of nested @IF functions.

Obtaining Data by Indirect Referencing

The @CHOOSE function is not the only lookup function that does not require a lookup table in order to retrieve data. The @@ function retrieves a value or label entered into another cell through an indirect reference. To use it, you simply enter a reference to a cell that itself contains the cell reference to the one containing the data you want to use.

This a very different process from using the direct method of entering + and the cell address to bring forward a value in the spreadsheet. For instance, to bring forward the calculated value of 125.5 in cell X200 to cell F10 in the spreadsheet, you could enter +X200 in F10.

To use the @@ function to do the same thing, you need an intermediary reference to the cell address X200. Assuming that you enter the label X200 into cell F11, you could bring forward the value of 125.5 to cell F9 by entering @@(F11) in F9. This instructs the program to look at the cell reference in F11 (which contains the reference X200) and then look up and retrieve the data contained there.

The first formula says, "bring forward the value (125.5) contained in X200," while the second with the @@ function says, "go to F11 to obtain another location (X200) and return the data (125.5) contained in that location."

This kind of indirect referencing with the @@ function is quite useful when it is combined with the use of range names. Figure 18.6 illustrates a situation where the quarterly sales figures for each salesperson are spread throughout the worksheet. (For convenience of viewing, the data in this figure has been kept in the same local area of the spreadsheet. But this could well represent a situation in which these figures were spread out over widely separated areas in a worksheet.)

To avoid having to copy the names and sales figures to create a new two-dimensional lookup table, the @@ function is used to return the total sales made for an individual salesperson. Each salesperson's name was given as the range name for his or her sales by using the /Range Name

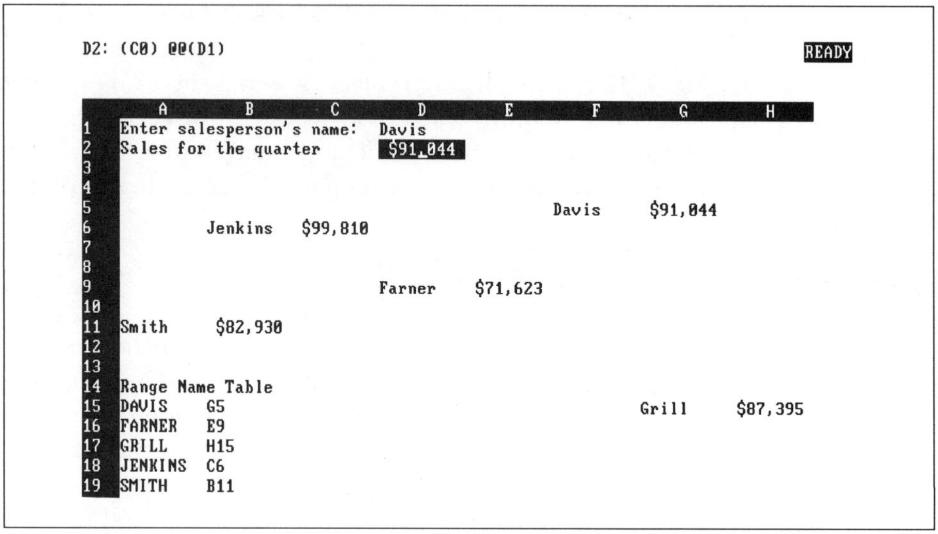

FIGURE 18.6: Using the @@ function to return the quarterly sales figures for an individual salesperson. This figure represents a situation in which totaled sales figures are scattered throughout the worksheet. To obtain the totals without having to copy this information to a lookup table, the @@ function is used. Each of the quarterly sales figures is given the range name associated with the salesperson responsible (done with /Range Name Labels Right). The @@ formula entered in D2 obtains the cell reference from the salesperson's name entered in the cell above (D1). It then retrieves the appropriate sales figures from the cell with the corresponding range name. The range name table indicating the cell addresses of each named range is included to help illustrate how the indirect reference to D1 as the @@ argument works. In the case of Davis now shown in D1, the function is really reading the cell address G5. This tells it where to go to retrieve the quarterly total.

Labels Right command. The @@ function in cell D2 looks for the range name in cell D1 and then retrieves the appropriate figure associated by range name.

In order to view any salesperson's total, all that is required is to type in that person's name. The @@ function looks at the name as indicating a new range name and then returns the value in the cell that carries that range name. Again, it works as a two-step process, indirectly retrieving the desired value.

Determining the Attributes of a Cell

Release 2 includes a new group of functions that can give you certain types of information about any given cell or cell range in the worksheet. These functions are most useful in a wide range of macros that automatically processes data in cells, depending on the cell's position, contents, or both.

The information these functions return is referred to as an *attribute* of the cell. Attributes describe the following:

- The number of columns and rows in a particular cell range
- The column letter and row number of a specific cell
- The type of data in an individual cell (that is, whether it contains a value or label)
- The display format (if a cell contains a value) or its label prefix (if it contains a label)
- The current width of the column in which a particular cell is located
- The actual (or literal) contents of a specific cell

Determining the Number of Columns and Rows in a Cell Range

The @COLS and @ROWS functions are specialized. They return the number of columns or rows contained in a cell range. This is very useful information when you are creating a macro that sequentially processes data in a cell range until it reaches the last column or row in the range.

Determining Specific Information about a Single Cell

The @CELL or @CELLPOINTER functions have more widespread uses, because they allow you to enter attribute arguments that specify the kind of information you want about the cell. These functions are often used in macros when a particular attribute of a cell determines the appropriate subroutine to be used. For instance, the macro would automatically use a numeric subroutine if the cell were found to contain a value, as opposed to branching to a string-processing subroutine if the cell contained a label.

The @CELL function requires a cell range in the argument, although, much like the @N and @S string functions, it works on only the first cell in the range. With @CELL, you obtain information on the attribute in question only for the first cell in that range (that is, the one in the upper-left corner of the range). The @CELLPOINTER function does not require any range argument, because it returns information for the attribute specified only for the cell containing the cell pointer.

Table 18.1 shows the attribute arguments that can be used in either of these functions and the kind of information each attribute will give you. If you enter the attribute in the argument rather than refer to it as a label in

<table>
<tr><th>ATTRIBUTE ARGUMENT</th><th>INFORMATION RETURNED AND MEANING</th></tr>
<tr><td>"address"</td><td>Current cell address</td></tr>
<tr><td>"row"</td><td>Current row number between 1 and 8192</td></tr>
<tr><td>"col"</td><td>Current column number between 1 and 256</td></tr>
<tr><td>"contents"</td><td>Current cell contents</td></tr>
<tr><td>"type"</td><td>The type of data in the current cell:
b (blank) if cell has no contents
v (value) if cell has a number or formula
l (label) if cell has a string</td></tr>
<tr><td>"prefix"</td><td>The label prefix of the current cell:
' for a left-justified label
^ for a centered label
" for a right-justified label
\ for a repeating label
| for an embedded printer command such as a page break or specific escape code</td></tr>
<tr><td>"protect"</td><td>The protection status of the current cell:
1 for cell protection on
0 for cell protection off</td></tr>
<tr><td>"width"</td><td>Width of current cell's column between 1 and 240</td></tr>
<tr><td>"format"</td><td>The numeric format of the current cell: F0–F15 for Fixed and the number of decimal places
S0–S15 for Scientific and the number of decimal places
C0–C15 for Currency and the number of decimal places
G for General format
+ for the +/− graphic format
P0–P15 for Percent and the number of decimal places
D1 for Date 1 format with the pattern DD-MMM-YY
D2 for Date 2 format with the pattern DD-MMM
D3 for Date 3 format with the pattern MMM-YY
D4 for Date 4 or Long International format with the default pattern MM/DD/YY. This default can be modified to DD/MM/YY, DD.MM.YY, or YY-DD-MM.
D5 for Date 5 or Short International format with the default pattern MM/DD. This default can be modified to DD/MM, DD.MM, or YY-MM.
D6 for Time 1 format with the pattern HH:MM:SS AM/PM
D7 for Time 2 format with the pattern HH:MM AM/PM
D8 for Time 3 or Long International format with the default pattern HH:MM:SS. This default can be modified to HH.MM.SS, HH,MM,SS, or HHhMMmSSs.
D9 for Time 4 or Short International format with the default pattern HH:MM. This default can be modified to HH.MM, HH,MM, or HHhMMm.
T for Text format, which displays the literal contents of the cells (any formulas used)
H for Hidden format
Blank if the cell contains an empty string (only a label prefix)</td></tr>
</table>

TABLE 18.1: Attributes Used by the @CELL and @CELLPOINTER Functions

a particular cell, you must always enclose its name in quotation marks, as shown in this table.

When you enter an @CELLPOINTER function, it returns information about the cell in which the @CELLPOINTER formula is entered. This self-referencing does not, however, result in a circular reference. For instance, if you use the function with the attribute argument "type", it will initially return a v for value because it contains the @CELLPOINTER function. However, as soon as you move the cell pointer to a different cell and recalculate the worksheet, the type will change to reflect the contents of the new current cell. If you have entered the @CELLPOINTER function and you move the pointer to a cell that contains a spreadsheet title and press the Calc function key (F9), the type will change from v to l for label.

When you use the "address" attribute argument, Lotus 1-2-3 gives you the cell address in absolute form. For instance, if you enter the @CELL function

@CELL("address",IN_FLOWS)

where IN_FLOWS is the cell range located in cells B15..D27, the program will return $B$15 for the cell address of the first cell in this range.

When you use the "col" attribute in an @CELL or @CELLPOINTER function, the program returns a number between 1 and 256 rather than the letter or letters of the column. Column letters between A and Z can be returned if you also use the @CHAR function. For example, consider the following:

@CHAR(@CELL("col",A1) + 64)

This returns A as the column letter for cell A1 by adding the column number of 1 returned by the @CELL function to 64, which produces 65, the ASCII code for capital letter A. The @CHAR function then converts this code number to the letter A. This same formula can be used for any column letter up to Z.

When the column designation consists of a double-letter combination, converting its column number to the appropriate letters is more complicated. Because there are 26 letters in the alphabet, you must divide the number returned as the "col" attribute by 26, add 64 to the result, and then use the @CHAR function on the integer portion returned to obtain the first letter. To return the second letter, you must obtain the remainder of dividing the column number by 26 with the @MOD function and add 64 to that. The following formula shows how you would obtain the column letters for the column number of cell AD1:

@CHAR(@INT(@CELL("col",AD1)/26) + 64)&@CHAR(@INT (@MOD(@CELL("col",AD1),26) + 64))

This works fine unless the double-letter column ends in Z, such as cell AZ or BZ. Because Z is the twenty-sixth letter of the alphabet, its remainder is 0 when it is divided by 26. In these circumstances, you must alter the formula. Below is a formula that uses the column number obtained for column AZ to return the A portion and concatenates the letter Z to it:

@CHAR(@INT(@CELL("col",AZ)/26) + 63)&"Z"

You can combine these to create a formula that uses the appropriate way to return the column letter or letters, depending on the value of the column returned by the @CELL function:

@IF(@CELL("col",range)< = 26,@CHAR(@CELL("col",range) + 64), @IF(@MOD(@CELL("col",range),26) = 0,@CHAR(@INT (@CELL("col",range)/26) + 63)&"Z",@CHAR(@INT(@CELL ("col",range)/26) + 64)&@CHAR(@INT(@MOD(@CELL ("col",range),26) + 64))))

By supplying a range name for the range argument in this formula, you can convert any column number returned by the @CELL function to the appropriate column letter or double-letter combination.

Beyond the position of the beginning of a particular cell range or cell in the worksheet, these functions can give you information on the type of data contained there or the contents of the cells. When you use "type" as the attribute argument, Lotus 1-2-3 will return an abbreviation indicating whether it is blank, a value, or a label.

The "type" attribute gives you an alternative method to using the @ISNUMBER or @ISSTRING functions to test the contents of a cell. For instance, you could test whether a cell contains a value as follows:

@IF(@CELL("type",X1..Z5) = "v",@S(X1),X1)

Perhaps even more useful is the ability to test whether a cell is currently blank. Division using a blank cell or one with a value of 0 as the divisor will result in an ERR value. If you test for "type" equal to blank, you can prevent such values, as in this example:

@IF(@CELL("type",B5) = "b"#OR#B5 = 0,0,C5/B5)

If the cell contains a blank or zero value, no division will be attempted that would result in an ERR value, which would then spread to all of the formulas that reference the cell where this is entered.

Beyond testing a cell for the type of data, you can have the program let you know the kind of prefix that has been used if the type is a label, or the kind of display format that has been used if the type is a value. This is the purpose of the "prefix" and "format" attribute arguments.

The prefixes returned include not only the apostrophe for left-justified, circumflex for centered, and quotation mark for right-justified label prefixes, but also the backslash for the repeating label prefix and the vertical bar (¦) for page breaks or special printer escape codes.

Formats used on values either with the /Range Format options or the /Worksheet Global Format options are given codes indicating the type and, if called for, the number of decimal places used. These are the same codes that are displayed in parentheses on the first line of the Control Panel after the cell address whenever the current cell has been formatted with one of the /Range Format commands.

The Special Functions

The special functions represent a diverse group of built-in functions. However, rather than being a catch-all classification, these functions fall into three main subgroups:

- Lookup functions. These functions include @VLOOKUP, @HLOOKUP, and @INDEX, which retrieve values from lookup tables, and the @CHOOSE and @@ functions, which do not.
- Attribute functions. These include the @COLS and @ROWS functions, which return the number of columns and rows in a particular cell range, and the @CELL and @CELLPOINTER functions, which give you information about specific attributes of a cell, such as its position, contents, display format, label prefix, and so on.
- @NA and @ERR. These allow you to input the special values of NA for not available and ERR for error.

The following reference entries are listed in alphabetical order from @@ to @VLOOKUP.

@@ (Release 2 Only)

The @@ function allows you to use the contents of a cell by indirect reference. Its argument contains a cell reference from which the program extracts the entry.

SYNTAX

@@(cell address)

where cell address is entered as a cell address or range name given to a single-cell range. The cell reference used as the argument must itself contain a single-cell range name, a cell address entered as a label, or a string formula that results in a cell address or single-cell range name, or the @@ function will return an ERR value.

USAGE

The @@ function allows you to use data from other cells by indirect reference in the spreadsheet. The argument of the @@ function contains another cell reference entered either as a range name or cell address. The @@ function uses this cell reference as its lookup value and retrieves its contents in the cell where the @@ function is used.

This is most useful when you want to look up various information scattered throughout a worksheet. By referencing an input cell where you want the lookup value to be copied, you can look up various data. All that is required is that you enter a new cell address or range name in this input cell. The @@ function's argument can be either the literal label name of another cell, such as 'X200, a range name, or a string formula whose result is a cell address or range name. To look up another item of data, you simply change the range name label or cell address label in the input cell.

To use the @@ function, locate the cell pointer in the cell where you want the retrieved data to appear and type @@(, followed by the cell address or range name that contains the cell address label or range name where the data is actually entered. Terminate the function by typing); press the Return key, and the program will return the desired entry. If the cell referenced in the argument does not contain a valid cell address or range name entered as a label, you will receive an ERR value.

EXAMPLES

The following @@ function returns the value 110, which is stored in cell AA20, by using the cell reference entered as the label AA20 in cell A5:

@@(A5)

This @@ function returns the label After-tax Income, stored in cell AB105, by using the cell reference entered as the label AB105 in cell A10:

@@(A10)

This @@ function returns the calculated value 1256.45, contained in a single-cell range named SUBTOTAL, whose range name has been entered into cell C12:

@@(C12)

The range name was given to this cell containing the value 1256.45 by using the /Range Name Labels Right command with the heading Subtotal in the cell directly to its left. In cell C12, the label Subtotal was entered. The @@ function uses the range name entered in C12 as its reference to the cell containing the value 1256.45, which it copies to the cell where this @@ function is entered.

@CELL (Release 2 Only)

The @CELL function returns specific information about one particular attribute of the first cell in a cell range. Depending on the attribute specified, you can obtain information about the cell's contents, location, protection status, or width.

SYNTAX

@CELL(attribute,range)

where attribute is either "address", "row", "col", "contents", "type", "prefix", "protect", "width", or "format" or a cell reference to a cell containing one of these labels, and range is a cell range. The range argument can be specified by entering the cell addresses or range name or by the pointing method.

If a single-cell range is used, you can simply enter the cell address; Lotus 1-2-3 will automatically convert the cell address into a single-cell range. If a multiple-cell range is used, the function will return information about the attribute argument specified only for the cell in the upper-left corner of the range.

USAGE

The @CELL function is used to return a specific item of information about a particular cell in the spreadsheet, referred to as an *attribute.* It is most often used to check a user's input in a processing macro to guard against certain types of entry. It can also be used to check whether a particular key cell contains data. The outcome of such tests can then be used to determine which subroutine is to be used by the macro.

The @CELL function can check a cell for several individual attributes. When you use the function, you first supply the type of attribute you wish the function to check for, followed by the cell range that contains the cell you want checked. You can indicate the type argument by entering the name of the type as a string (enclosed in quotation marks, as in "contents") or by cell reference to a cell that contains the type as a label entry.

Although the @CELL function uses cell ranges for its second argument, in a multiple-cell range it uses only the cell in the upper-left corner position. You can use the @CELL function with a single-cell range. When doing this, you can preface the cell address by an exclamation point that indicates it as a single-cell range (Lotus 1-2-3 will also accept the input of a single-cell address and automatically convert it to a single-cell range).

When you make a change to the cell or to its contents that affects the type of attribute information returned by the @CELL function, the formula results are not always automatically updated. (However, when "contents" is the attribute and you make a new entry in the cell, the formula results are immediately updated.) To have the @CELL formula reflect the change you have made, you must press the Calc function key (F9).

EXAMPLES

If cell A10 contains the label Income, right justified in the cell, and if the cell width has been widened to 12 characters, any of the following could be used as arguments of the @CELL function:

@CELL("address",A10)

would return $A$10.

@CELL("contents",A10)

would return Income.

@CELL("type",A10)

would return 1 for label.

@CELL("width",A10)

would return 12.

@CELL("prefix",A10)

would return " for right justified.

If cell B10 contains the value 1500 and the cell width has been formatted with the Currency format showing two decimal places, any of the following could be used as arguments of the @CELL function:

@CELL("contents",B10)

would return 1500.

@CELL("format",B10)

would return C2 for Currency format with two decimal places.

@CELL("type",B10)

would return v for value.

@CELLPOINTER (Release 2 Only)

The @CELLPOINTER function returns specific information about one particular attribute of the current cell. Depending on the attribute specified, you can obtain information about the cell's contents, location, protection status, or width.

SYNTAX

@CELLPOINTER(attribute)

where attribute is either "address", "row", "col", "contents", "type", "prefix", "protect", "width", or "format", or a cell reference to a cell containing one of these labels.

USAGE

The @CELLPOINTER function is similar to the @CELL function, except that it returns attribute information only about the cell currently holding the cell pointer. Because the function deals only with the current cell, it requires the entry of a single argument, that of the type of attribute to be described.

When you first enter the @CELLPOINTER function in a cell of the worksheet, it describes the type of attribute for the cell that contains the @CELLPOINTER function. As the cell pointer is moved to different cells in the spreadsheet, the cell containing the @CELLPOINTER function is updated only when a new entry is made in the spreadsheet. To update the attribute information when the cell pointer is located in a cell that already contains data, you must press the Calc function key (F9). When you are using the @CELLPOINTER function in macro commands, you may have to include the commands {CALC}, {RECALC}, or {RECALCCOL} when you need to have the function return new information about a particular attribute of a new current cell.

To use the @CELLPOINTER function, move the cell pointer to the cell where you want to store the attribute information and enter **@CELLPOINTER(**. Then enter the type of attribute to be used, enclosed in quotation marks, or enter a cell reference that contains the desired attribute type entered as a label. Type) and press the Return key.

The @CELLPOINTER function will describe the type of attribute used as the argument for the cell where @CELLPOINTER is entered. As you move the cell pointer to different cells in the worksheet, you can update this information by pressing the Calc function key (F9).

EXAMPLES

When you enter **@CELLPOINTER("contents")** in a cell, the function returns the value 0 in the cell where this function is entered. If you then move the cell pointer to a new cell that contains the value 675 and press the Calc function key (F9), the program returns the value 675 in the cell that holds this function.

When you enter **@CELLPOINTER("type")** in a cell, the function returns v (for value) in the cell where the function is entered. If you move the cell pointer to a cell that contains the label Payment and press the Calc function key (F9), the program returns l (for label).

@CHOOSE

The @CHOOSE function returns the value (or label if you are using Release 2) in the list of arguments that coincides with the offset value given as its first, or x, argument.

SYNTAX

@CHOOSE(x,v0,v1,...,vn)

where x is the number of the offset of the value to be returned and v0,v1,...,vn form the list of possible values.

The x argument can be entered as a value or as a cell reference to a value that corresponds to the offset of the value to be used. If the x argument exceeds the value of the last offset or is a negative number, the function returns an ERR value. If the x argument contains a mixed number, the function uses only the integer portion as the offset (that is, an x argument of 0.5 uses the offset value of 0, 2.5 uses 2, and so on).

The value arguments can contain a list of entries or cell references (by cell address or range name). If you are using Release 2, these arguments can consist of either strings or values. All strings must be enclosed in quotation marks when they are entered in the list of value arguments. (If you are using Release 1A, these arguments must all contain values.)

USAGE

The @CHOOSE function allows you to enter a list of lookup values without requiring that you set up a separate lookup table in the worksheet. The lookup values are listed as arguments of the function. The offset value given as the first argument determines which of these lookup values is returned in the cell where the function is entered.

To use this function, locate the cell pointer in the cell where you want the selected value to appear, type **@CHOOSE(**, and enter the offset value to be used either as a literal value or as a reference to a cell that contains such a value. Then type a comma, followed by the list of values that can be selected. Each value must be separated by a comma. When you have finished entering this list, type **)** and press the Return key to have the program return the appropriate value.

EXAMPLES

You can use the @CHOOSE function to return the weekday. In the following example, the day of the week is entered in cell A2 and the @CHOOSE function uses it to return the correct weekday:

@CHOOSE(A2 – 1,"Monday","Tuesday","Wednesday",
"Thursday","Friday","Saturday","Sunday")

To obtain Sunday, you would enter 7 in cell A2. Because the offset of Sunday in the list of arguments is 6, the function subtracts 1 from the value entered in cell A2.

The listing of the weekdays with Monday as the first day and Sunday as the seventh makes it possible to use the @DAY function with this @CHOOSE function to return the proper weekday for any date entered with the @DATE or @NOW functions.

To do this, the @DAY function would be entered in cell A2. Assume that the @DATE (or @NOW) function is entered in cell C2. The @DAY function in A2 would be

@MOD(@DAY(C2),7)

The @MOD function returns the remainder from dividing the number of the day in the @DATE function entered in C2 by 7. This value is then converted into the appropriate offset value in the @CHOOSE function and the correct weekday is returned in the cell where the @CHOOSE function is used.

@COLS (Release 2 Only)

The @COLS function returns the number of columns contained in the range of cells specified as its argument.

SYNTAX

@COLS(range)

where range is a cell range defined by cell addresses or range name. The range argument can be specified by typing in the cell addresses or by pointing to it.

USAGE

The @COLS function can help you indirectly determine the width of a particular cell range. By knowing the number of columns in the range, you can approximate the width in characters by estimating the average column width in the cell (often with the @CELL function using the "width" attribute) and multiplying that value by the number of columns returned by the @COLS function.

Calculating this information can help you set up the appropriate margins when printing a report. This is especially useful because it is not easy to count columns referred to by letter combinations. It can also help when referring to ranges by their range name, where the cell addresses are not used at all. Such calculations are often included in macros that automatically set up the appropriate parameters for printing a particular range of cells in the spreadsheet.

EXAMPLES

If you have a cell range named DATA and you want to estimate its width for printing, you could enter the following formula to estimate its width in characters:

@COLS(DATA)* @CELL("width",DATA)

If the range named DATA extends from cells X12..AF90 and the cell width of X12 is 13, this formula would return the value 117 in the cell where it is entered. You would therefore be advised to use the setup string to turn on condensed mode before printing this range on an 80-column printer.

@ERR

The @ERR function returns the ERR value, indicating the presence of an error in the cell where it is entered.

SYNTAX

@ERR

This function takes no argument.

USAGE

The @ERR function is seldom used to introduce an ERR value into a particular cell. More often, it is included as part of an @IF formula to introduce an ERR value only under particular conditions. For instance, if a calculated value is not to fall below a certain amount, you could set up a condition that evaluates the result and uses the @ERR function to enter an ERR value into the cell if that result is less than you will allow. Otherwise, you would have the @IF condition go ahead and perform the calculation (for a specific example, see the Examples section that follows).

Like the NA value entered with the @NA function, an ERR value introduced into a cell will cause all cells containing dependent formulas to show an ERR value. Most often, you will want to prevent the proliferation of such an ERR value to all of the dependent formulas. To trap the ERR value, you can use the @ISERR function in the dependent formulas so that a value like zero is returned whenever ERR is brought forward (for more information on trapping the ERR value with @ISERR, see Chapter 15, "Logical Functions").

Note: Lotus 1-2-3 will also automatically enter an ERR value into a cell whose calculation is not allowed under the program's rules of calculation. Most often, the cause of ERR values entered by the program is a calculation that calls for division by zero or the deletion of a necessary cell reference or range name. This ERR value introduced automatically by the program is identical to the ERR value entered with the @ERR function.

EXAMPLES

To alert yourself to the fact that a particular cell has a calculated value that you deem unacceptable, you can use the @ERR function as part of an @IF formula. In the following formula, the program enters an ERR value if the calculated result in cell C50 ever falls below $10,000.00. Otherwise, it goes ahead and uses its value in the intended division by the value in D50:

@IF(C50<10000,@ERR,C50/D50)

If this formula were entered in cell C52 and its result were used in another formula in C53, you could use the @ISSERR function there to restrict the potential ERR value to cell C52:

@IF(@ISERR(C52),0,C52*.5)

@HLOOKUP

The @HLOOKUP function matches the value specified as its x argument against values listed in the first row of a lookup table whose extent is indicated in the range argument. It then returns the value listed in the row indicated by the row number argument in the column holding the matching value.

SYNTAX

@HLOOKUP(x,range,row number)

where x is the selector value that is to be matched in the first row of the lookup table, range is the range of cells that contains all of the values in the lookup table, and row number indicates the row offset used to return the value.

The x or range argument can be indicated by cell addresses or range name. Row offsets are counted from 0 from the first row of the range. The row offset argument is usually entered as a value, although it can also be a reference to a cell that contains the appropriate row offset number.

USAGE

The @HLOOKUP table is used to automatically retrieve values from a horizontal lookup table located in the same spreadsheet. This lookup function is data dependent in that it uses a selector value to locate the appropriate value to be retrieved.

In the horizontal arrangement, the index column against which the selector value is matched is the first row of the lookup table. The program matches this value against values listed in this row, moving from the first cell of the range to the right.

When an exact match is located, the value in the column that corresponds to the row offset number is entered in the cell that holds the function. If no exact match is located in the table, the program stops at the column holding the next higher value and then moves back to the previous column. Once this column is located, the row offset is used to select the appropriate value.

To use this function, enter **@HLOOKUP(** and indicate the value that is to be looked up in the index column (the first row) of the table. This value can be indicated by cell address or range name. Then type a comma and indicate the range of cells containing all of the lookup values. Type another comma and indicate the offset number. When you enter the offset number argument, remember that row offsets are counted from zero from the first row down the lookup table. Then type **)** and press the Return key. The @HLOOKUP function returns the appropriate value from the table.

In Release 2, the selector value and values in the lookup table can contain strings (labels) as well as numeric values. If you are using Release 1A, both the selector value and all the values in the lookup table must consist of numeric values.

EXAMPLES

Figure 18.7 illustrates the use of the @HLOOKUP function to return the ASCII codes for using different print enhancements for various types

```
E6: @HLOOKUP(E1,PRINT_TABLE,@VLOOKUP(E4,TYPE,1))                                READY

        A          B              C              D          E          F
 1      Type of printer (Epson, IBM, or Laserjet):          Laserjet
 2
 3     Print (Condensed [17 cpi], Elite [12 cpi],
 4            Pica [10 cpi], or Expanded [5 cpi]):          Condensed
 5
 6                           Use setup string:              \27&k2s
 7
 8
 9  Print                    Printer type
10             Epson         IBM              Laserjet
11  Condensed  \015          \015             \27&k2s
12  Elite      \027M         \027\077         NA
13  Pica       \027P         \018             \027&k0S
14  Expanded   \027W1        NA               NA
15
16
17                           Condensed                1
18                           Elite                    2
19                           Pica                     3
20                           Expanded                 4
```

FIGURE 18.7: Using the @HLOOKUP function to retrieve the appropriate setup codes required by several different types of printers for various special printing effects. The horizontal lookup formula entered in E6 uses the type of printer entered in cell E1 to locate the column holding the appropriate setup codes in the PRINT_TABLE range (A10..D14). Notice that it also uses an @VLOOKUP function as its argument for obtaining the appropriate row number. The @VLOOKUP function uses the type of print entered in E4 to look up the appropriate row offset listed as the second column of the TYPE lookup table (C17..D20).

of printers. Once the required setup code is known, it can be used selectively or globally in printing the worksheet (see Chapter 25, "Printing Reports," for more information on using print enhancements in reports).

The @HLOOKUP function matches the type of printer entered in E1 against those listed in the first row of the lookup table (in cells A10..D14). The row number (given as the row offset) is returned by using the @VLOOKUP function entered as the last @HLOOKUP argument. It uses the lookup table located in the cell range C17..D20. The second column of this table contains the row offset values corresponding to the type of print enhancement entered in cell E5.

@INDEX (Release 2 Only)

The @INDEX function returns the value from the lookup table indicated by the range argument. The value is specified by the column and row offsets included as the function's column and row arguments.

SYNTAX

@INDEX(range,column,row)

where range is the range of cells containing all of the lookup values, column is the column offset number, and row is the row offset number.

The range can be indicated by cell addresses or range name. Column and row offsets are counted from zero from the first cell of the range (the one in the upper-left corner of the range), so that this cell has a column and row offset of 0.

If the values for the column or row offsets are negative or exceed the total number of offsets, the function returns an ERR value. If a mixed number is used as either offset value, the program uses only the integer portion.

USAGE

The @INDEX function retrieves a particular value from a lookup table located in the same spreadsheet. Unlike the @HLOOKUP and @VLOOKUP functions, the @INDEX function retrieves the appropriate value by its position in the table alone. Therefore, it requires that you enter both the column and row offsets as arguments.

This function is used in situations in which the appropriate value can be selected by supplying two known values corresponding to the column and row offset positions in the lookup table itself.

To use it, type **@INDEX(** and indicate the cell range that contains the lookup values either by cell addresses or range name. Type a comma and enter the column offset; type a second comma and enter the row offset value. These arguments can be indicated by entering the appropriate values or by referencing the cells that contain them by cell address or range name. Type) and press the Return key to have Lotus 1-2-3 retrieve the value in the lookup table located at the junction of the column and row offset values.

EXAMPLES

For an example of how the @INDEX function can be used to retrieve data from a lookup table, refer back to Figures 18.3 and 18.4.

@NA

The @NA function returns the NA value, indicating that a value is not available in the cell where it is entered.

SYNTAX

@NA

This function takes no argument.

USAGE

The @NA function is used to introduce the notation NA (for not available) in any cell that requires data which you do not yet have. When you use @NA, it enters this notation as a special value that is then brought forward to any other cell that contains a formula whose calculation depends on its value. As soon as you replace the NA value with a value and recalculate the spreadsheet, all NA values in those cells will be replaced by their correctly calculated values.

The @NA function is useful because it immediately signals that a particular value is still required to complete all of the necessary calculations in a particular spreadsheet. To use @NA, you simply move the cell pointer to the cell that requires data, type **@NA**, and press the Return key.

You may sometimes want to use the @NA function to indicate that particular input cells still require values, while preventing the proliferation of this NA value to the dependent formulas. To trap the NA value, you can use the @ISNA function in the dependent formulas to return a value such as 0 whenever NA is brought forward (for more information on trapping the NA value with @ISNA, see Chapter 15, "Logical Functions").

EXAMPLES

Figure 18.8 illustrates how the @NA function works. In this income statement, the General Overhead figure for the first quarter is not yet available. To indicate this fact so that the statement will not be printed as a final report until this figure has been entered, the NA value was entered in cell B14.

Entering this single NA value caused the rest of the NA values to appear in the income statement. All of the formulas below and to the right of this cell depend in some way on this value. They will remain NA values until the General Overhead figure is entered into cell B14.

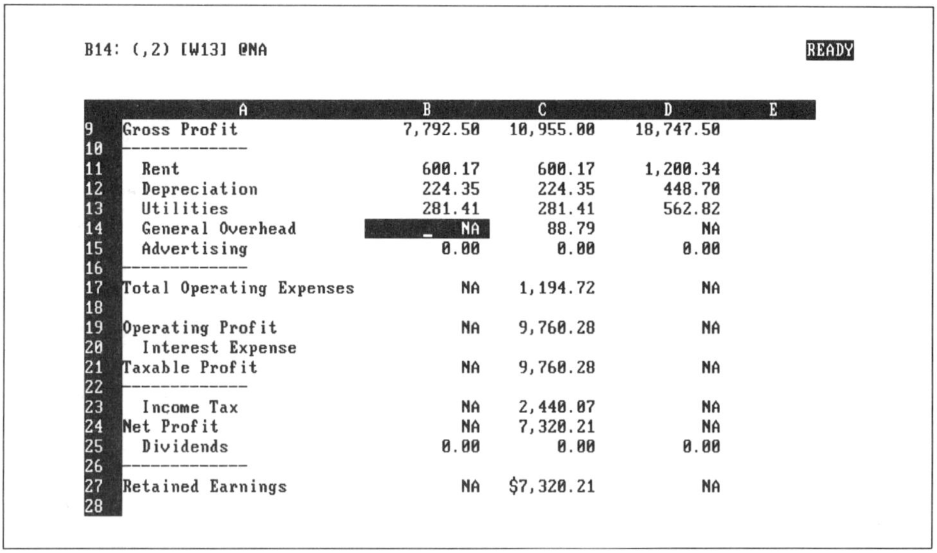

FIGURE 18.8: Entering the NA value into an income statement with @NA to indicate missing overhead expense figures for the first quarter. In this example, when @NA was entered in cell B14, it immediately spread to other cells in columns B and D that contain formulas whose calculations depend on B14. As soon as the overhead expense becomes available and is entered into B14, all of the NA values displayed in this income statement will be replaced by the correctly calculated values.

@ROWS (Release 2 Only)

The @ROWS function returns the number of rows contained in the range of cells specified as its argument.

SYNTAX

@ROWS(range)

where range is a cell range defined by cell addresses or range name. The range argument can be specified by typing the cell addresses or by pointing.

USAGE

The @ROWS function is similar to that of the @COLS function; they are often used together to determine the overall size of a particular cell range in a spreadsheet. Because rows cannot be widened or narrowed, the value returned by the @ROWS function always tells you the exact line length of the range.

This function can be used to find out the length of the range to help you set up printing parameters, especially to determine where to place page breaks in a report by using the /Worksheet Page command. It is also used in macros that process data row by row in a range.

To use the @ROWS function, position the cell pointer in the cell where you want the number of rows in the selected range to appear and type **@ROWS(**. Then indicate the range either by cell addresses or by range name, type), and press the Return key.

To determine the number of cells in a particular range, you multiply the number of columns by the number of rows as follows:

@COLS(range)* @ROWS(range)

where the range is entered by cell addresses or range name.

EXAMPLES

Figure 18.9 illustrates a macro that uses the @ROWS function to evaluate the length of a cell range named PrintBlock. The first row of this data range contains a row of column headings; it is given the range name Headings.

The number of rows returned by @ROWS(PrintBlock) is stored in the range named Length. If the number of rows exceeds 45, the macro branches to the range named Page. There the cell pointer moves down 45 rows and inserts a new page character by using the /Worksheet Page command (/WP). It then inserts a new row where the column headings for the print range are copied.

The macro then clears the currently set print range and redefines it as PrintBlock. Because the newly inserted page break command and copied column headings are within the print range, the range PrintBlock does not need to be redefined.

If the length determined by the @ROWS function is less than 45, the macro goes ahead and prints the PrintBlock range without inserting the page break. Using a macro like this allows you to specify a particular number of rows to be printed together without having to change the page length setting.

```
A169: [W7]                                                          READY

     A              B                         C        D        E
150
151 Name   Macro commands               Description
152 -----------------------------------------------------------------
153 \K     {LET Length,@ROWS(PrintBlock)} Find number of rows in print range
154        {IF Length>45}{BRANCH Page}    If rows > 45, goto Page routine,
155        {BRANCH Print}                 otherwise goto Print routine
156
157 Page   {GOTO}PrintBlock~              Cell pointer to beginning of range
158        {DOWN 45}~                     Cell pointer down 44 lines
159        /WP                            Insert page break
160        /WIR~                          Insert new row for column headings
161        /CHeadings~~                   Copy column headings
162 Print  /PPCRRPrintBlock~AGPQ          Print range
163
164 Length                                Store number of rows in
165                                       print range
166
```

FIGURE 18.9: This figure contains a macro called Alt-K (for keep together) that evaluates the length of a print range and prints only the first 45 rows of its data before beginning a new page. This allows you to print less than a full page without changing the page length parameter. If the print range contains more than 45 rows, the macro positions the cell pointer in the 45th row, inserts a page break character, copies down the column headings (from the first line of the range), and then prints the entire range on two pages. If the print range contains less than 45 rows, the macro prints it on a single page.

@VLOOKUP

The @VLOOKUP function matches the value specified as its x argument against values listed in the first column of a lookup table whose extent is indicated in the range argument. It then returns the value listed in the column indicated by the column number argument in the row holding the matching value.

SYNTAX

@VLOOKUP(x,range,column number)

where x is the value that is to be matched in the first column of the lookup table, range is the range of cells that contains all of the values in the lookup table, and column number indicates the column offset used to return the value.

The range argument can be indicated by cell addresses or range name. Column offsets are counted from 0 from the first column of the range.

USAGE

The @VLOOKUP function is used to retrieve values from a vertical lookup table located in the same spreadsheet. This lookup function is data dependent in that it uses a selector value to locate the appropriate value to be retrieved.

In the vertical arrangement, the index column against which a particular value is matched is the first column of the lookup table. The program matches this value against values listed in this column, moving from the first cell of the range down.

When an exact match is located, the value in the row that corresponds to the column offset number is entered in the cell where the function is entered. If no exact match is located in the table, the program stops at the row holding the next higher value and then moves up to the previous row. Once this row is located, the column offset is used to select the appropriate value.

To use this function, enter **@VLOOKUP(** and indicate the value that is to be looked up in the index column (the first column) of the table. This value can be indicated by cell address or range name. Then type a comma and indicate the range of cells containing all of the lookup values. Type another comma and indicate the column number. When you enter the column number argument, remember that column offsets are counted from 0 from the first column down the lookup table. Then type **)** and press the Return key; the @VLOOKUP function returns the appropriate value from the table.

In Release 2, the selector value and values in the lookup table can contain strings (labels) as well as numeric values. If you are using Release 1A, both the selector value and all values in the lookup table must be numeric values.

EXAMPLES

Figure 18.10 illustrates the use of the @VLOOKUP function to return either the price or cost of a particular item. All that is required is that the user enter the appropriate item code in cell D3, followed by either the label Cost or Price in cell D4. The formula in D5 then uses this information to return the appropriate value in cell D5.

To make this work, two @VLOOKUP functions using two different lookup tables are used. The second @VLOOKUP function is nested

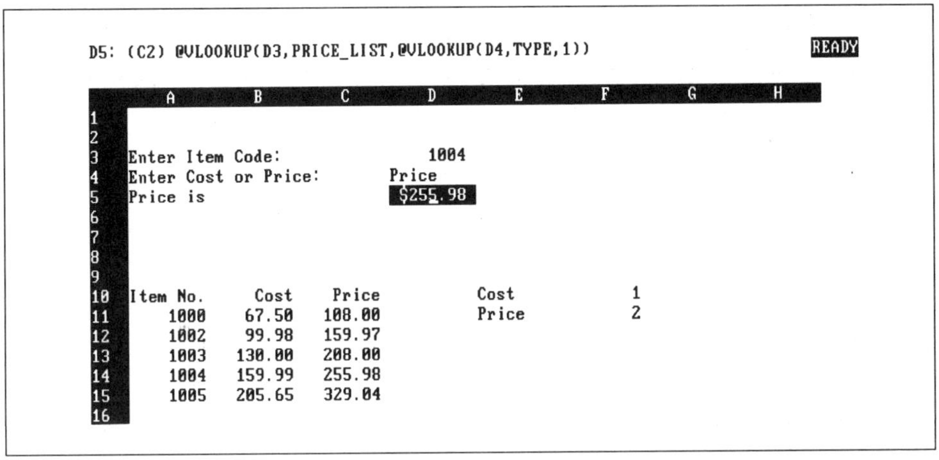

FIGURE 18.10: Using the @VLOOKUP function to look up either the cost or price of a particular item by entering its item code number. To do this requires the use of two @VLOOKUP functions, one nested inside the other. The first one compares the item code entered in D3 to those listed in the index column of the PRICE_LIST lookup table. To obtain the appropriate column offset, the second @VLOOKUP function is used as the column number argument of the first. It returns the correct column offset by comparing the entry made in cell D4 with the index column of its own lookup table (E10..F11). Once it locates a match, it returns the corresponding offset number listed in its second column.

within the first to return the appropriate column offset value by matching the Cost or Price label in D4 against the index column of its lookup table. The first @VLOOKUP function uses the item number to locate the appropriate row. Together they make it possible to obtain the desired information easily.

SUMMARY

This chapter has examined the last group of Lotus 1-2-3 functions, known collectively as the special functions. While many of these functions, especially the lookup functions, are used alone in spreadsheets or databases, the majority of them are of most value when used in macro command statements. For this reason, you may want to refer to the discussions and reference entries for the macro commands in Chapter 28, "The Macro Command Language."

Because the @NA and @ERR functions are often used with their own error-trapping functions @ISNA and @ISERR, you may want to obtain more information on their use; if so, see Chapter 15, "Logical Functions."

CHAPTER 19

Spreadsheet Models, Error Trapping, and Recalculation

Spreadsheet Models, Error Trapping, and Recalculation

This chapter completes Part 3, Spreadsheet Formulas and Functions, by discussing techniques commonly used in building complex spreadsheet models. The first set of discussions covers techniques for avoiding as well as trapping errors when designing and working with models.

As part of the general discussion on avoiding errors, you will find the topic of using circular references within a spreadsheet. Although in many cases circular references are entered as the result of errors in constructing formulas, they can sometimes be put to good use when used with the Iteration option of the /Worksheet Global Recalculation command.

The final group of discussions centers around using the global recalculation options to control both when and how the formulas in your model are recalculated. At the end of the chapter you will find a complete reference entry for the /Worksheet Global Recalculation command.

Building Spreadsheet Models

Few of the applications that you build with Lotus 1-2-3 represent spreadsheets that are used only once to document and calculate one unique set of data. More often, spreadsheets depict conditions in your business that must be continuously documented in the same, or a very similar, manner. When designing a new spreadsheet, it is important that you consider whether the application you are about to build represents a model of the way you do business that can and should be reused.

Spreadsheet models have two distinct uses. The first is simply to document some aspect of the operation of your business. Examples of this type include financial statements such as income statements, balance sheets, and tax forms. The second is to analyze, plan, and forecast the future operations of your business. Examples of this type include projected financial statements such as sales forecasts, working budgets, breakeven analysis, long-term financing, and the like.

Many times, the same spreadsheet template can be used for both types of applications. For instance, it is common practice to prepare an income statement that historically documents revenue and expense transactions that occurred during the fiscal year as well as projects income for the coming year. In such cases, you may find that the same (or a very similar) Lotus 1-2-3 spreadsheet template can be used to prepare both portions of the statement, even though the models the portions represent are quite different (historical versus optative). To promote consistency, save time, and reduce potential errors, it is in your best interest to design as few spreadsheet templates as possible to perform all the necessary data-keeping tasks required in your work.

The term *template* is used in the sense of the organizational layout both of data items and of the required formulas for calculating results. You can think of a template as a form that is to be filled in. As such, a spreadsheet template contains all of the category headings, underlying formulas, and formatting necessary to produce a complete financial model once live data is available and is entered into the appropriate cells. In short, it includes everything but the data it takes to make a unique financial model. It makes no difference whether the resulting model represents real or projected conditions.

Input versus Result Cells in the Model

When you develop a particular template that can be reused to produce numerous spreadsheets of a single type, you must take great care in two areas:

- Economy in terms of data input
- Avoidance of calculation errors

In fact, the first area—minimizing the input cells in a template—is related to the second, because it provides the initial step for avoiding errors in the final spreadsheet.

Input cells in a template are those in which the user must enter specific data as constant values (sometimes referred to as *literal values*). In the income statement example, these would include the revenue figures, cost of goods sold, and individual categories of operating expenses as broken out in the template.

The values entered into the input cells are most often fed to the formulas entered in the result cells of the template (or output cells). In the formulas contained in these cells, the input constants become their data variables (because the calculated result varies, depending on what values are entered). In the income statement, the result cells include such items as the gross profit, total operating expenses, operating profit, taxable profit, income tax, net profit, and retained earnings.

Of course, some of the result cells in a template can themselves include constant values that are used with other calculated variables to produce the resulting value. For example, the cell that calculates the amount of income tax owed in an income statement includes a constant in the form of a percentage representing the corporation's appropriate tax bracket. This value is then multiplied by the variable returned in the cell that calculates the taxable profit figure.

When planning any type of spreadsheet template, it is wise to begin by identifying and clarifying which of the cells will be input cells and which will be result cells. Much of this work can be carried on while working out the formulas that will be required to calculate each of the result cells.

Avoiding Design Errors in the Template

As you build the necessary formulas, you should be aware of two types of design errors that frequently occur:

- Formulas that correctly calculate the results as planned in a model whose underlying assumptions are ill-conceived or unreliable
- Formulas that incorrectly calculate the results as planned in a model whose underlying assumptions are dependable

Of course, a worst-case scenario is one in which the template contains a mix of both incorrectly defined formulas and unreliable underlying assumptions.

The first type of error (prevalent in models that project business outcomes) is potentially much more dangerous because no ERR values or calculated results that you can recognize as wildly absurd will appear to alert you to the errors. In some ways, Lotus 1-2-3 contributes to this problem by making it easy to construct financial models and to subject them to continued what-if analysis.

The only way to ground yourself against such shocks is to subject the whole model to a little nonelectronic what-if analysis. Although the spreadsheet numbers say that a particular new venture can't lose, ask yourself what would happen if the new product or service fails to take off in the market as planned, or, even more down-to-earth, what effect would it have on the business if the underlying assumptions are incorrect. (After all, the calculated spreadsheet already tells you what to expect if the assumptions are right.)

The second type of error, though often vexing, is somewhat more manageable. This type is usually the result of a mistake in the logic or operation of the formulas, incorrect cell references in the formulas (especially those caused when copying formulas throughout the template), or incorrect data entry when loading data into the template as you construct an individual model.

When you construct the template, you need to be on the lookout for errors in formula operation and cell references. They can be difficult to spot because the template does not yet contain data for any of the input cells. Unless the incorrect formulas happen to produce an unexpected ERR value, the zeros throughout your template can do little to alert you to the existence of the problem formulas in the result cells. These often become obvious only when the input cells are loaded with test or real data.

Trapping and Eliminating Formula Errors

Typos (incorrect entries) account for many formula errors. It is easy to type the wrong operating symbol. One way to trap such errors is to obtain a printout containing only the formulas in the completed template by using the /Print Printer Options Other Cell-Formulas command and then check the results. Often this task is made easier by saving the template and then loading test data (preferably with simple values that are easy to spot-check). Then, if you locate a result that seems suspect, you can check the formula that derived it.

Probably the best way to cut down on errors that result from using the wrong cell references when constructing formulas is to use the pointing method instead of typing in cell addresses. Because Lotus 1-2-3 supplies the cell addresses, you have to worry only about pointing to the correct cell. This method also allows you to check the meaning and purpose of the formula as you build it. Instead of concentrating on the formula in terms of cell addresses, such as +G18/G5, you can be thinking of the formula in terms of its function, such as return on sales equals total net income divided by total sales.

Consistently using this method as you construct the template also gives you a feel for the type of dependencies you are building into it. This is important, because Lotus 1-2-3 gives you no way to highlight and therefore easily identify and locate cell dependencies in the final template or completed spreadsheet model. This too must be done by documenting a printout containing the template's formulas or results. One way to make the task of identifying cell dependencies easier is to replace individual input cells with an NA value by using the @NA function. All cells containing dependent formulas will then be recalculated to NA, revealing the result cells tied to the particular input cell.

Another prevalent cell reference error that finds its way into spreadsheet templates comes from copying formulas that were not constructed with the necessary absolute or mixed references. To prevent this type of problem, as you are entering each formula, focus on where and under what conditions it will need to be copied. As you design, you want to minimize the amount of original formula construction to cut down on possible incorrect cell addresses in new formulas that perform the same type of calculation as well as reduce the amount of work involved in completing the template.

When you realize that a formula you are about to enter should be copied, you should consider the extent and direction of the copy to determine which, if any, of the cell references should be changed from relative to mixed or absolute references. Keep in mind the function of the formulas you are about to create through copying. If each formula depends on the same cell, that particular cell must be entered as an absolute reference, such as $F$25. If each one depends on cells in the same column, and an adjustment must be made in each succeeding row reference, then a mixed address with an absolute column and relative row reference must be used, such as $F25. If the opposite is true, the mixed address will consist of a relative column and absolute row reference, such as F$25.

If, when you complete the template and load test data into it, you find that a formula you copied throughout the spreadsheet does not have the correct type of references, you can edit that formula by using the Abs function key (F4) to change the cell references and then recopy the edited formula.

Using Error-Trapping Functions

As discussed in Chapter 15, Lotus 1-2-3 contains the @ISERR and @ISNA logical functions, which allow you to trap ERR or NA values in particular cells and arrest the spread of all these values in dependent formulas. In addition, the @ISNUMBER and @ISSTRING functions can prevent formulas from returning ERR values under certain conditions.

When constructing a template, you should be able to isolate quite easily those formulas that require the @ISERR function. Because the template contains only zero values or empty cells, those formulas that require division by one of the values in these cells will display the ERR value.

For example, any cells that perform ratio analysis in a financial statement will contain ERR values as soon as you define the required division in their formulas. You can then edit these formulas by using the @ISERR function to prevent the ERR values from being displayed. For instance, if an income statement contains a formula that calculates return on sales, which is defined by dividing the total sales by the total net income, the cell that contains the formula will display an ERR value. Assuming that you prefer this to remain a zero value until the values are entered, you would amend the formula so that it contained an @ISERR function within an @IF formula.

If the original formula that defines this division was entered into cell G20 as

+G18/G5

its contents would then be changed to

@IF(@ISERR(G18/G5),0,G18/G5)

That way, 0 would be displayed until the data was entered into the input cells.

It is more difficult to predict when and under what conditions you will need to trap NA values or use the @ISSTRING or @ISNUMBER functions when constructing a template. The need for these functions usually becomes apparent only in a particular model that is being constructed from the original template.

Circular References

Circular references introduced into formulas can be another source of errors in a spreadsheet template. A formula containing a circular reference is one that contains a reference to the cell in which it is entered, either directly or indirectly. The clearest example of a circular reference in a formula is one in which the cell reference used to calculate the result is the same as the cell where the formula is entered, as in

+A1+1

entered in cell A1. Lotus 1-2-3 cannot calculate the proper result the way the formula is defined because the formula depends on its own value, which is not yet available. (It solves this by supplying 0 as the original value and adding 0 to the constant 1, thus returning 1 as the answer the first time the formula is calculated.)

Another way that circular references can be introduced into a spreadsheet is when two formulas depend on the results returned by each in order to calculate their results. For example, if cell A1 contains the formula

+A2+1

and cell A2 contains the formula

+A1+1

a circular reference has been set up.

Lotus 1-2-3 indicates that a circular reference has been introduced into the worksheet by displaying the CIRC status indicator in the middle of the bottom line of the display screen (as long as the order of calculation is still the default setting of Natural calculation—see "Controlling the Order of Recalculation" later in this chapter). Release 2 will also indicate the last location of a circular reference by cell address when you issue the /Worksheet Status command.

Most of the time, circular references are introduced by mistake. They often occur because the cell addresses used in the formula were typed in erroneously (which is another reason for using the pointing method to define formulas). Once you locate the cell containing the circular reference, it is usually not too difficult to isolate the self-referencing cell reference and correct it.

There are also times when circular references are purposely introduced and, indeed, are unavoidable if you are to obtain the desired results in the template. The classic example is calculating the amount to be set aside in a bonus pool whose amount is based on a certain percentage of net profit for any given quarter. Defining the formula for determining the bonuses does not in itself cause a circular reference (it is simply a constant percentage multiplied by the net profit calculated). But as soon as the bonus figure is tied in as an expense that affects the amount of operating profit and ultimately the amount of net profit, a circular reference occurs. This situation is exemplified in Figures 19.1 and 19.2.

Fortunately, this particular circular reference can be resolved. There is a balance point where the effect of calculating the bonus amount as an expense (indirectly determining the net profit) on the net profit cancels itself out. However, Lotus 1-2-3 is not able to resolve this difference and find this balance point the first time the income statement is calculated.

To speed this process along, you can change the iteration control from its default setting. When automatic recalculation is in effect, the default is one recalculation of all formulas each time a new entry is made into the spreadsheet or each time the Calc function key (F9) is depressed. You can use the

```
B11: (,0) [W12] +B18*0.1                                          READY

     A                B           C           D           E           F
1  Data 2000 Corporation
2  Income Statement
3  January 1  - December 31, 1986
4
5                    1st Qtr     2nd Qtr     3rd Qtr     4th Qtr       Total
6  Revenues          425,000     487,500     527,000     501,200   1,940,700
7    COGS            195,000     189,500     175,600     180,300     740,400
8  Gross Profit      230,000     298,000     351,400     320,900   1,200,300
9  ------------
10 Operating Expense  85,000     100,000      97,500      98,500     381,000
11   Bonus Pool        7,812      10,742      13,970      12,078      44,603
12 ------------
13 Operating Profit  137,188     187,258     239,930     210,322     774,697
14   Interest Exp     17,000      22,000      25,000      24,500      88,500
15 Taxable Profit    120,188     165,258     214,930     185,822     686,197
16 ------------
17   Income Tax       42,066      57,840      75,225      65,038     240,169
18 Net Profit         78,122     107,418     139,704     120,784     446,028
19
20
                                            CIRC
```

FIGURE 19.1: Using a converging circular reference to calculate the amount to be set aside in bonuses equal to 10 percent of the net profit figure for any quarter. Because the bonus figure is itself an operating cost that must be used to calculate the amount of net profit, circular references are set up in cells B11 to E11. By setting the number of iterations to 5 and pressing the Calc function key (F9), these circular references were resolved so that their final amounts do indeed reflect 10 percent of the after-tax profit.

/Worksheet Global Recalculation Iteration command to set the number of iterations (that is, the number of times the formulas are recalculated at one time) from 1 to 50. Resolving this particular example of a circular reference does not require any more than a few iterations.

A circular reference such as the one in the bonus example that can be resolved by further recalculation is called a *converging circular reference.* You can always tell a converging circular reference from its opposite, a *diverging circular reference,* because each time the formulas involved in converging circular references are recalculated, their results are closer to the so-called true solutions—the balance point where the differences cancel each other out. In practical terms, this means that the differences between the current values calculated and those returned by the prior calculation become less and less with each successive iteration.

Sometimes Lotus 1-2-3 cannot resolve converging circular references within the number of iterations you have set with the /Worksheet Global Recalculation Iteration command. In such a case, you can either press the

```
                                                              STAT

Available Memory:
  Conventional..... 416043 of 419056 Bytes (99%)
  Expanded......... (None)

Math Co-processor:  (None)

Recalculation:
  Method........... Automatic
  Order............ Natural
  Iterations....... 5

Circular Reference: E11

Cell Display:
  Format........... (G)
  Label-Prefix..... '
  Column-Width..... 9
  Zero Suppression. Off

Global Protection:  Off
                                          CIRC
```

FIGURE 19.2: The worksheet status screen showing the recalculation method, order, iterations, and location of a circular reference in the spreadsheet shown in Figure 19.1. Notice that in the information on recalculation, you see not only the method and order of recalculation but also the current iteration count (which was set to 5 to resolve the circular references set up in the worksheet). The screen shows the location of the last circular reference entered into the spreadsheet in E11 because this was the cell where the copy of the formula containing the original circular reference in B1 was made. The Release 1A status information does not include information on the number of iterations or the location of circular references, although it does give you the method and order of recalculation currently in use.

Calc function key (F9) to have it recalculate the formulas again or use the /WGRI command to increase the number of iterations still further.

Not all circular references converge in such a manner. Diverging circular references exhibit just the opposite effect. Each time their formulas are recalculated, the gulf between them and their previously calculated results grows wider.

Creating Models from Templates

Once you have completed the template and checked it thoroughly for design errors, it can be used to build a model. If someone else is to do the necessary data input, you may want to enable global protection and then unprotect only the input cells before turning over a copy of the template.

Remember, you can also use the /Range Input command to restrict data entry to these cells after setting up the appropriate protection status throughout.

When creating a unique model, you may need to construct new formulas that calculate required input values. Harkening back to the income statement example, these would include schedules that total the revenues and expenses for each category elsewhere in the same spreadsheet. Once these figures were calculated, they would be fed into the appropriate input cells of the income tax template itself.

If the model you are working on represents a variation of the basic template, you may also have to construct new categories and their required formulas or make alterations to existing ones.

Avoiding Errors in the Model

When you create and update a spreadsheet model, you have to stay on the lookout for new types of potential errors. By far the most prevalent are those caused by deleting mistakenly entered or no-longer-wanted entries by using the space bar. Unfortunately, this practice has become common because it appears to offer a much quicker and easier alternative to using the somewhat awkward /Range Erase Return combination.

Although it *appears* that using the space bar erases a cell entry (in the spreadsheet display at least), it actually enters a space character into the cell. This space character can introduce errors into the results calculated by the spreadsheet and database formulas that use certain Lotus 1-2-3 functions. For instance, although the space character will not affect an @SUM function, it will affect functions that use the count of nonblank cells, such as @AVG, @COUNT, @STD, and @VAR, as well as their database statistical counterparts.

Figure 19.3 illustrates this point. The formulas for obtaining the sum, average, standard deviation, and count in column A were copied to columns C and E in this sample worksheet. The second input cell in column C was then blanked out by using the space bar, while its counterpart in column E was deleted with the /Range Erase command. Notice the differences in the results returned in rows 9 through 11 for those formulas in these two columns. Only the results in column E are correct. The presence of a space in C5 (indicated by the ' in the literal contents shown on the first line of the Control Panel) throws off the results because this cell is not really empty. All functions that depend on the equivalent of the @COUNT function count nonblank entries in the list argument.

```
C5: '                                                        READY

      A        B        C        D        E        F        G         H        I
 1
 2
 3
 4        45                45                45
 5        45                _
 6        45                45                45
 7   ---------        ---------       ---------
 8       135                90                90       <--- @SUM
 9        45                30                45       <--- @AVG
10         0                21                 0       <--- @STD
11         3                 3                 2       <--- @COUNT
12
13
14
```

FIGURE 19.3: The difference between blanking out an entry using the space bar and using the /Range Erase command. Here, the formulas for obtaining the sum, average, standard deviation, and count in column A were copied to columns C and E. The second value in the range C4..C6 was then blanked out by using the space bar. The values in the range E4..E6 were deleted with the /Range Erase command. Notice that the calculated values in column C for the average, standard deviation, and count have been skewed by the presence of the space character in C5. Pressing the space bar and Return only appears to delete the intended entry. Only the values in corresponding cells in column E contain the values expected after deleting a single entry from the range.

The use of the space bar to blank out criteria in a database criterion range also affects the outcome of any /Data Query Find or Extract operation. In this case, the program attempts to match a blank space character in the column where this technique was used as well as any visible criteria you enter.

Many other types of input errors that occur are reflected in the spreadsheet as soon as they are made. For instance, if you attempt to enter a label into a cell that contains a formula, you receive an ERR value, indicating that the calculation cannot be carried out.

However, you cannot count on ERR values to alert you to all of the problems that can be caused by making necessary editing changes. Sometimes values can still be calculated, although the results no longer reflect the desired results accurately. Great care must be taken when revising a complex model, especially if it represents a variation on the original template.

CHANGING THE METHOD OF RECALCULATION

When working with a reasonably large and complex spreadsheet model, you will experience fairly noticeable waiting periods between the time a new value or formula entry is entered and the time it takes for Lotus 1-2-3 to return to READY mode. Each time a new entry is made, all of the formulas in the spreadsheet are recalculated. Depending on the amount of formulas and their complexity, these wait states can considerably slow down your progress in completing data entry.

For this reason, most users prefer to change the method of recalculation from the default of automatic to manual recalculation by issuing the /Worksheet Global Recalculation Manual command. After you change the recalculation method to manual, you can complete all of your entries and formula construction without having to wait for the program to recalculate all of the formulas.

While the global recalculation is set to manual, new formulas will be calculated as they are entered, but any dependent formulas will not be updated. Lotus 1-2-3 displays the CALC status indicator at the bottom of the screen to let you know that new entries have been made while in manual recalculation mode and that you need to press the Calc function key (F9) to have the entire model updated.

As soon as you have finished all data input and any editing changes and you press the Calc function key, the CALC status indicator disappears to let you know that all of the formulas are currently updated. This does not mean, however, that the program is no longer in manual recalculation method. The only way to change the recalculation method back to automatic is to issue the /Worksheet Global Recalculation Automatic command. If you save your spreadsheet with the method set to manual, this setting will be saved with the updated file.

If you are working with a spreadsheet model created by someone else and are not sure what method of recalculation is currently the default, you can check it by using the /Worksheet Status command. If the recalculation method is still set to the program's original default of automatic and you have a lot of data entry to do, you may want to set it to manual to make your job easier. When you are finished with all of your entries and modifications, be sure to press the Calc function key to update the model before you save it or print a report.

THE WORKSHEET GLOBAL RECALCULATION COMMAND

This command is used either to change how Lotus 1-2-3 goes about recalculating formulas in a spreadsheet or to change when or how many times the formulas are recalculated.

/Worksheet Global Recalculation

MENUS

/Worksheet
Global
Recalculation
Natural Columnwise Rowwise Automatic Manual Iteration

KEYBOARD ENTRY

/WGRN /WGRC /WGRR /WGRA /WGRM /WGRI

FUNCTION

The /Worksheet Global Recalculation function allows you to set the method of recalculation to manual or back to automatic, change the number of iterations used each time the worksheet is recalculated, or change the order of recalculation to columnwise, rowwise, or back to natural.

The first three options on the Recalculation Menu—Natural, Columnwise, and Rowwise—control the way Lotus 1-2-3 proceeds when calculating the formulas in the worksheet. This is referred to as the order of recalculation. Natural, which is the default, is seldom changed. (See "Controlling the Order of Recalculation" later in this chapter.)

The first two of the second three options—Automatic and Manual—control when the formulas in the spreadsheet are recalculated. When the default setting of Automatic is changed to Manual, formulas are recalculated only when you press the Calc function key (F9). The last of this last group of options, Iteration, controls how many times the formulas in the spreadsheet are recalculated. You can increase the number of iterations from the default of 1 up to 50.

USAGE

The /Worksheet Global Recalculation command is used to control three separate aspects of the way Lotus 1-2-3 recalculates the worksheet you are currently working on: the order, method, or number of iterations. The default settings of the program are Natural order, the Automatic method of recalculation, and a single iteration (recalculation) of the formulas.

Controlling the Method of Recalculation

The /Worksheet Global Recalculation command is most often used to change the method of recalculating the spreadsheet from the default of Automatic to Manual. This is often necessary as the number of formulas in the spreadsheet grows, because it takes longer to recalculate the entire worksheet after each new value or formula entry is made. This slows down the pace at which you can change and update the spreadsheet.

Changing this setting to Manual becomes very important when you do what-if analysis in a spreadsheet, especially if you are not using the /Data Table commands. It allows you to change the values of input variables without having to wait for the entire model to be recalculated after each change.

To set the method to Manual, you merely type **/WGRM** from anywhere in the worksheet. To set it back to Automatic, type **/WGRA**.

Controlling the Order of Recalculation

The /Worksheet Global Recalculation command also controls the order of recalculation used by the program. The default setting is Natural. Under natural recalculation, all of the cell dependencies between formulas are calculated without regard to their location in the worksheet. That is, before Lotus 1-2-3 calculates a formula, it first updates the values of all the cells referenced in that formula. Because the order of recalculation is not tied to a linear progression across the columns and down the rows (or vice versa) but rather to the way in which the cell dependencies in the formulas advance, you can be sure that all of your formulas have been properly recalculated when the program is left in natural mode.

Older spreadsheet programs, like the original VisiCalc, did not provide this type of natural recalculation order. Lotus 1-2-3 allows you to change this method to either Columnwise or Rowwise. In columnwise order, the program begins recalculating each formula from cell A1 down the entire column before progressing to the next column and down across the entire worksheet. In rowwise order, the program begins recalculating each formula from cell A1 to the end of the row before moving down to the beginning of the next row and so on down the entire worksheet.

Although using these other modes instead of the Natural default can sometimes decrease recalculation time, if you use these other modes, make sure your spreadsheet contains no forward references. A forward reference is created when a formula's calculated value depends on the results returned by some other formula or group of formulas located in cells located down or to the right of its position.

For example, assume that a formula in cell A1 contains a reference to cell A10 (as in +A10+48). If the order of recalculation is columnwise, Lotus 1-2-3 will attempt to evaluate the formula in cell A1 before updating the value in cell A10, on which the formula in cell A1 depends.

Formulas that contain such forward references will not be properly updated if the mode of recalculation has been set to Columnwise or Rowwise. Therefore, use these mode changes with care. The majority of the time, it is best to leave the mode set to Natural; then change to manual recalculation and wait to have your formulas updated when you press the Calc function key.

While the /Worksheet Global Columnwise and Rowwise commands affect the way all formulas in the worksheet are updated, in Release 2 you can use the macro keywords {RECALC} and {RECALCCOL} to control the recalculation of a portion of the formulas in the worksheet. The {RECALC} keyword works in the same way as the Rowwise option, and {RECALCCOL} works in the same way as the Columnwise option. (Refer to the references for these two keywords in Chapter 28 for more information about their use.)

Changing the Number of Iterations

The /Worksheet Global Recalculation Iteration option controls how many times the formulas in a worksheet are recalculated, regardless of the mode or method used. It is set to a single iteration as the default but can be increased up to 50.

As discussed earlier in the section on circular references, this option is used most often to speed the process of resolving converging circular references introduced into the spreadsheet by design. By increasing the number of times Lotus 1-2-3 recalculates the formulas, you can resolve such circular references much quicker than by continually pressing the Calc function key.

To change the number of iterations, type **/WGRI** and then type in the number of times you wish to set it to. Then press the Return key. When you want to reset the number of iterations back to 1, reissue the command and enter **1** before pressing the Return key.

EXAMPLES

For an example of changing the number of iterations with the /Worksheet Global Recalculation Iteration command, refer to Figure 19.1. For an example of the status screen that lets you know the current recalculation settings, see Figure 19.2.

SEE ALSO

/Worksheet Status

SUMMARY

This chapter has examined the topics of using templates to create complex models, avoiding and trapping errors when creating and working with such models, and using recalculation methods to maintain models. Much of this information is related to specific topics found elsewhere in this handbook. You can use the reference guide that follows to look up related information that may be of interest.

For more information on designing the basic worksheet, using global protection, unprotecting cell ranges, using range input, and using the /Worksheet Status command:

- Chapter 5, "Creating Worksheets"

For more information on safely editing the contents of a spreadsheet:

- Chapter 6, "Editing Worksheets"

For more information on how to use the various error-trapping functions:

- Chapter 15, "Logical Functions"

For specific information on using the @NA and @ERR functions in spreadsheets:

- Chapter 18, "Special Functions"

For more information on using the Release 2 macro keywords {RECALC} and {RECALCCOL}:

- Chapter 28, "The Macro Command Language"

PART 4

LOTUS 1-2-3 DATA MANAGEMENT

Data management in Lotus 1-2-3 means two things: organizing data in a structured database and using commands that work on groups of data in a spreadsheet or database. Part 4 divides these functions as follows: Chapters 20 and 21 discuss the formal structure and use of the Lotus 1-2-3 database; Chapter 22 covers the /Data Distribution, Matrix, and Regression commands (the latter two are in Release 2 only); and Chapter 23 discusses the use of the /Data Table commands.

The Lotus 1-2-3 database uses the worksheet environment in a special way to set up data in a table of fields and records much as is done in stand-alone database management programs. Chapter 20 discusses how to set up such a database and enter and edit the data within it. (You will also find references on using the /Data Fill and /Data Sort commands in this chapter.) Chapter 21 covers the various database operations, including searching and extracting data according to search criteria you set up. It therefore concentrates on the use of the commands attached to the /Data Query menu.

Chapter 22 takes up the subject of the types of data analysis that are possible with Lotus 1-2-3. It begins by discussing frequency distribution performed with the /Data Distribution command. In addition, Release 2 has added two very powerful analytical tools, one for performing matrix algebra and another for performing simple and multiple linear regression analysis. How and when these can be used to solve typical business problems are discussed in the techniques sections as well as in separate reference entries.

Chapter 23 examines the /Data Table commands. These commands make it possible to perform extended what-if analysis on data either in a spreadsheet or in a database format. The program supports two kinds of data tables: a one-input or a two-input data table. The use of both types is related to spreadsheet and database applications in the technique discussions and in their separate reference entries.

CHAPTER 20

Creating a Lotus 1-2-3 Database

Creating a Lotus 1-2-3 Database

This chapter introduces the Lotus 1-2-3 database by covering the basics of its creation and uses. It begins with information on how to set up your database and do data entry within it. It continues with an illustration of how to create a data input form using a macro. This example input form is intended to give you ideas on how you might use Lotus 1-2-3's macro facilities to create data input forms for your own databases.

Following this section, you will find a technique for using the /Data Fill command to give record numbers to the individual entries in the database and, after that, a full discussion on using the /Data Sort command to sort the records into the appropriate order.

Following these introductory sections, you will find the reference entries for the /Data Fill and /Data Sort commands.

Components of a Database

A Lotus 1-2-3 database consists of three basic components:

1. A single row of unique column descriptions for each of the items tracked in the database. These are referred to as the *field names* of the database. These are simply short, one-cell descriptions of the type of data contained in each column of the database.
2. The columns that contain the individual items of data entered into the database. These column entries are referred to as the *fields* of the database. Each field tracks a single type of data item, such as company name or address.
3. The rows that contain all of the individual data items relate to one another in some way. Each row of the database is considered a single *record,* and each record completely describes the object of the database. For instance, if the object of the database is client transactions, all of the data items in each row of the database relate to one customer transaction.

Figure 20.1 illustrates these components in a Lotus 1-2-3 personnel database. The column descriptions, or field names, run across the columns in row 4. Even though the column description for column A is Employee Number, only Number (the part of the label entered into cell A4) is the field name for that column of the database. In a Lotus 1-2-3 database, the field names must be contained in a single row of the database, and this row must be the first one in the database.

Therefore, the field names for columns B and C are differentiated as L:Name and F:Name. While it would have been more convenient to have entered the label Last in B3 and Name in B4, and the label First in C3 and Name in C4, this would have resulted in both columns having the field name Name, and all field names in the database must be unique because field names are restricted to a single row.

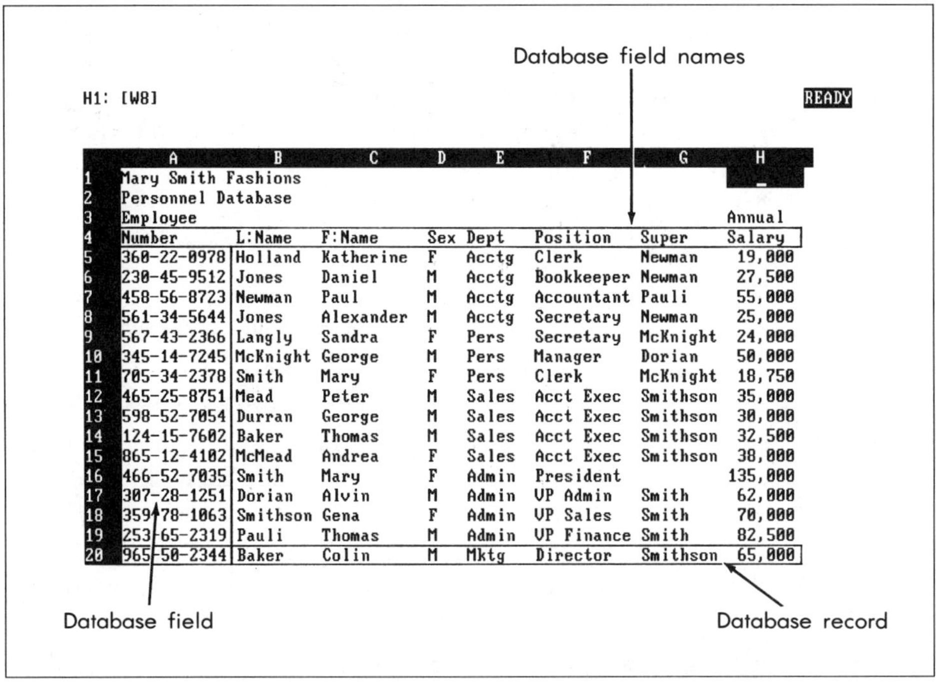

	A	B	C	D	E	F	G	H
1	Mary Smith Fashions							
2	Personnel Database							
3	Employee							Annual
4	Number	L:Name	F:Name	Sex	Dept	Position	Super	Salary
5	360-22-0978	Holland	Katherine	F	Acctg	Clerk	Newman	19,000
6	230-45-9512	Jones	Daniel	M	Acctg	Bookkeeper	Newman	27,500
7	458-56-8723	Newman	Paul	M	Acctg	Accountant	Pauli	55,000
8	561-34-5644	Jones	Alexander	M	Acctg	Secretary	Newman	25,000
9	567-43-2366	Langly	Sandra	F	Pers	Secretary	McKnight	24,000
10	345-14-7245	McKnight	George	M	Pers	Manager	Dorian	50,000
11	705-34-2378	Smith	Mary	F	Pers	Clerk	McKnight	18,750
12	465-25-8751	Mead	Peter	M	Sales	Acct Exec	Smithson	35,000
13	598-52-7054	Durran	George	M	Sales	Acct Exec	Smithson	30,000
14	124-15-7602	Baker	Thomas	M	Sales	Acct Exec	Smithson	32,500
15	865-12-4102	McMead	Andrea	F	Sales	Acct Exec	Smithson	38,000
16	466-52-7035	Smith	Mary	F	Admin	President		135,000
17	307-28-1251	Dorian	Alvin	M	Admin	VP Admin	Smith	62,000
18	359-78-1063	Smithson	Gena	F	Admin	VP Sales	Smith	70,000
19	253-65-2319	Pauli	Thomas	M	Admin	VP Finance	Smith	82,500
20	965-50-2344	Baker	Colin	M	Mktg	Director	Smithson	65,000

FIGURE 20.1: The three basic components of a Lotus 1-2-3 database are illustrated in the sample personnel database in this figure. The first component consists of the field names, a single row of unique field descriptions located in row 4 of this database. The fields, or individual items of the same type, make up the second component in the database. This figure points out the first field, which contains the employee number for each staff member. There are eight fields shown in this figure, each one occupying a single column of the worksheet. The third component is the record, which occupies a single row of the database and includes an entry for each of the fields it contains.

Usually, you will find it convenient to keep these column descriptions brief so that you do not have to widen any column of the database more than is required to display its longest entry. This is the reason Employee Number was not entered as a single entry in column A. To do so would have required widening the column more than required by the 11-character Social Security number.

Notice in the database in Figure 20.1 that there is no blank row or row containing dashed lines separating the field names from the actual data in the database. When you set up a database, you must never enter any type of separation row between the column descriptions and the data contained in each column. Having such a row would throw off your data query operations.

In Figure 20.1, notice that each column, or field, contains exactly the same type of information on each employee in the database—only Social Security numbers are found in column A (the employee number field), only last names are in column B (the last name field), and so on. Also notice that each field in the database (actually there are more fields in this database than can be shown in the figure) contains only a part of the information that we wish to keep on each employee. Looking at row 20, you can see that each data item in that row relates and belongs to Colin Baker, the particular subject of this record. In turn, Colin Baker's record is one entry in the database, whose object is to track all personnel in the company.

DESIGNING A LOTUS 1-2-3 DATABASE

When designing your own databases, you must first decide which information you need to track and maintain. This process requires you to look carefully at the overall purpose of the database and then decide what constitutes a complete record within it.

After deciding these aspects, you must then determine the best way to split up the information into separate fields in each record. For instance, in a client or personnel database there are different ways in which you can organize names. You could keep each full name in its own field or split each part of the name into two or more separate fields, such as last name, first name, and middle initial. Doing the former may make it more difficult to rearrange the data and use it in other applications, such as printing mailing labels or form letters, while doing the latter will require you to use more columns.

In making these types of decisions, it helps to try to think of all of the types of reports you will have to produce from the database. Often, a particular requirement of a report determines what items must be kept in individual columns.

The last design step is to come up with column headings that describe the data items to be kept in each column. Remember, each item description (field name) must be unique and must fit within a single cell in the first row of the database.

Creating the Database

Once you have decided on the design elements of your database, you must decide where to locate the database in the spreadsheet. To maximize the number of records the database can contain, you should always begin in the first few rows of the worksheet. The larger question is which column to use for the first field of the database.

If you are planning to do all of the data entry manually or via a menu macro that directs you to the location of the data entry form, you may want to begin in column A (much like the layout of the database in Figure 20.1). However, if you are planning to construct a data entry form that is not controlled from a menu macro, you may want to place it (and other forms for defining search criteria, extract operations, and report printing) in the first several columns of the worksheet and then locate the actual database in columns to the right (this kind of arrangement is illustrated in Figure 20.3 in the next section, "Creating a Data Input Form").

Remember that you can move the database left and right as well as insert new columns at any time. However, as your database grows, moving it can be rather time consuming. Wherever you decide to locate the database, you should leave all of the rows down to the very end of the worksheet empty of any other kind of data except for new records. Always construct your criterion and output ranges and macros to the right (or left) of the database itself. You can use the window function to align the criterion range and the beginning of the output range beneath the beginning of the database without actually placing them in the columns reserved for each part of the records.

Because the database is created and maintained within the Lotus 1-2-3 worksheet itself, you can construct any type of valid spreadsheet formula using any of its available functions. This allows you to set up calculated fields that perform their calculations based on data in other fields of the same record, use lookup tables located in the same worksheet, or use a combination of the two. In Figure 20.2, which shows the rest of the fields

L5: [W4] @YEAR(@NOW)-@YEAR(K5) READY

	D	E	F	G	H	I	J	K	L
1									
2									
3					Annual	Date	Yrs w/	Date of	
4	Sex	Dept	Position	Super	Salary	Hired	Company	Birth	Age
5	F	Acctg	Clerk	Newman	19,000	04/03/80	6.6	03/15/48	38
6	M	Acctg	Bookkeeper	Newman	27,500	02/06/84	2.7	06/07/44	42
7	M	Acctg	Accountant	Pauli	55,000	10/23/78	8.1	02/03/60	26
8	M	Acctg	Secretary	Newman	25,000	03/15/83	3.7	12/12/40	46
9	F	Pers	Secretary	McKnight	24,000	01/20/85	1.8	07/09/65	21
10	M	Pers	Manager	Dorian	50,000	04/10/79	7.6	10/02/54	32
11	F	Pers	Clerk	McKnight	18,750	11/01/85	1.0	07/09/56	30
12	M	Sales	Acct Exec	Smithson	35,000	06/07/82	4.4	03/25/61	25
13	M	Sales	Acct Exec	Smithson	30,000	02/20/84	2.7	01/17/58	28
14	M	Sales	Acct Exec	Smithson	32,500	09/12/82	4.2	08/09/42	44
15	F	Sales	Acct Exec	Smithson	38,000	08/20/81	5.2	08/16/66	20
16	F	Admin	President		135,000	10/01/78	8.2	02/15/49	37
17	M	Admin	VP Admin	Smith	62,000	04/16/83	3.6	08/26/45	41
18	F	Admin	VP Sales	Smith	70,000	06/10/79	7.5	02/07/58	28
19	M	Admin	VP Finance	Smith	82,500	12/03/82	3.9	06/16/60	26
20	M	Mktg	Director	Smithson	65,000	07/18/83	3.3	04/08/51	35

21-Oct-86 06:38 PM

Calculated fields in the database

FIGURE 20.2: This figure shows the rest of the fields contained in the sample personnel database introduced in Figure 20.1. The fields shown here include two calculated fields that employ standard Lotus 1-2-3 formulas. The first calculated field shown is the Yrs w/ Company field in column J. The entries in this field are calculated by the formula (@NOW – I5)/365, which was copied down this column. The second calculated field is the Age field in column L. The formula that determines these entries is shown in the Control Panel of the figure.

in the personnel database introduced in Figure 20.1, there are two such calculated fields, Yrs w/ Company and Age. The years with the company are calculated by subtracting the date hired from the current date and dividing the result by 365. Cell J5 contains this formula:

(@NOW – I5)/365

The formula for calculating each employee's age is shown in the Control Panel of Figure 20.2.

When you create calculated fields, you only have to enter the appropriate formula in each field of the first record. Then, after you have entered all of the data that is not calculated, you simply copy the formula down to the rest of the records.

Entering Data in the Database

Entering data in a database is no different from entering data into any Lotus 1-2-3 spreadsheet. As in spreadsheet applications, there is a distinction between entries made as labels and entries made as values. You can format any field containing labels with the /Range Label Format command, changing them from their left-justified default setting to either centered or right justified. Conversely, you can also format any field containing values to any of the numerical or date formats available from the /Range Format command. Also, dates used in formulas in calculated fields must be entered by using the @DATE function rather than entering them as labels.

The biggest problem in doing data entry in a Lotus 1-2-3 database is remembering when a particular field entry requires an apostrophe to force an entry that would otherwise be considered a value into a label before trying to enter it. For instance, if your database contains a street address field, many if not most of your entries in this field will require this kind of treatment because most addresses begin with a number, such as 123 Elm Street. As soon as you type the first number of the address, the program goes into VALUE mode unless you remember to force it into LABEL mode by prefacing the number with an apostrophe.

Zip code fields should also be entered as labels, even though in their five-digit form they consist entirely of numbers. Entering zip codes as labels allows you to add extended zip codes or special-delivery codes to them later. This cannot be done if you enter them as values, because the program interprets the dash between the digits as a minus, indicating subtraction.

Creating a Data Input Form

Manual data entry can be tedious because you have to remember when to preface a particular entry with an apostrophe to make it a label, and you may have to use the @DATE function several times in a single record. To make things easier, you can create a data input form controlled by a macro for your database. This reduces the tedium of entering new records and also cuts down significantly on data errors. Figure 20.3 shows a sample data input form for the personnel database illustrated previously, and Figure 20.4 illustrates the macro commands that control it.

Notice in Figure 20.3 that the data input form occupies the first screen of the spreadsheet. In this case, the database itself is located to the right in the range N4..Y23. In the input form, the field descriptions are not restricted

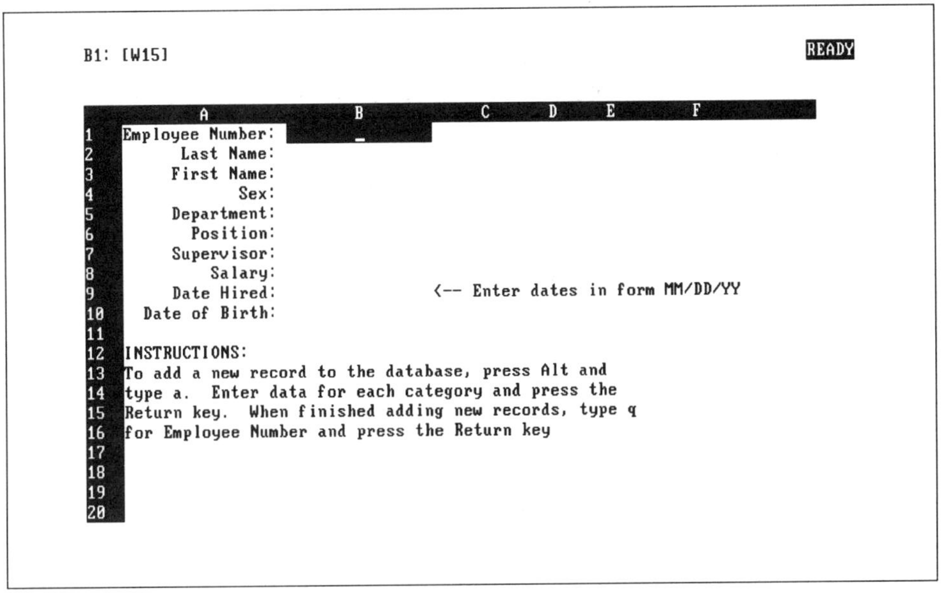

FIGURE 20.3: A data input form for adding new records to the sample personnel database. This data input form is controlled by the macro shown in Figure 20.4. To add a new record to the database, the data entry operator activates the macro by pressing Alt-A. All apostrophes required to ensure that field entries are entered as labels are automatically supplied for the operator. After the data for each field has been entered, the macro automatically advances the cell pointer to the next field entry. When all fields have been entered, the entries are automatically copied to a new row in the database and the data input form is cleared to allow the addition of another record. When the operator is finished adding new records, he signals this by typing a **q** in the first cell of the input form; the macro automatically erases this character, saves the worksheet, and returns to READY mode.

to a horizontal row listing as they are in the database. As a result, each field is listed vertically in column A with a full field name description. The order in which the field names appear matches that of the database to make it easier to transfer the data entered into the input form to a new database record.

The macro that controls the input form is called Alt-A for Add records. Once activated, it controls the entry of a single record by first positioning the cell pointer in cell B1. As soon as the entry is made for the Employee Number field and the Return key is pressed, it automatically moves the cell pointer down to the next cell, where the Last Name field entry is made. As soon as the last field entry is made (in the Date of Birth field in cell B10), the macro copies all of the data entered for each field into the last blank row of the database. (Note that this macro is designed specifically for this database; you must adapt it for use with your own database.)

The macro then clears the data input form and locates the cell pointer back in cell B1, awaiting the entry of the next record to be added. To signify that no more records are to be entered, the operator simply types a **q** for quit as the Employee Number. As soon as the Return key is pressed, the macro erases the q in B1, saves the worksheet, and terminates.

To control the data entry in the input form and transfer the record to the database, several range names have been set up. The database, including the field names and all records already entered, has been given the range name Input. The cell range containing the input form (A1..B10) has been given the range name InputForm.

Within InputForm, the blank cells in column B (B1..B10) have been given the range name Fields. Further, each cell within this range has been individually named so that B1 has the range name Field1, B2 is Field2, and so on, down to B10.

While the input form macro has been kept simple, certain features have been added to it to make data entry as easy as possible. First, a command has

```
\a          {GOTO}InputForm~
            {RIGHT}
Entry       {IF @CELLPOINTER("row")=1#or#@CELLPOINTER("row")>8#and#@CELLPOINTER("type")="b"}'
            {?}{DOWN}
            {IF Field1="q"}{BRANCH End}
            {IF @CELLPOINTER("row")>10}{Transfer}
            {BRANCH Entry}

Transfer    {GOTO}Input~
            {END}{DOWN}{DOWN}
            /rtB1..B8~~
            {RIGHT 7}/rf,0~~
            {RIGHT}@DATEVALUE(Field9)~/rfd4~/rv~~
            {RIGHT}/c{UP}~~
            {RIGHT}@DATEVALUE(Field10)~/rfd4~/rv~~
            {RIGHT}/c{UP}~~
            /reFields~
            {BRANCH \a}

End         {GOTO}Field1~/re~{HOME}/fs~r{QUIT}
```

FIGURE 20.4: Text of the Alt-A macro that controls data entry in the data input form. This macro is meant for the sample database. It is composed of three subroutines, Entry, Transfer, and End, which control various phases of the data input process using the data input form shown in Figure 20.3. The Entry routine checks the row position of the cell pointer to determine when to add an apostrophe to force the program into LABEL mode as well as when the entry has been completed in the form. As soon as data entry is complete, it branches to the Transfer routine, which copies each entry into the appropriate fields of a new row of the database. It erases the data input form and prepares to process another record. If the operator enters a q in the first field of the form, it branches to the End routine, which removes the q from the form before saving the worksheet and returning to READY mode. (See the accompanying text for more specific information on how this macro operates.)

been entered that automatically enters an apostrophe into Field1 (B1) so that the Social Security number is not taken as a value entry by the program.

To make the two date entries in the Date Hired and Date of Birth fields (Field9 and Field10) as easy as possible, the @DATE function is not used at all. Instead, apostrophes are automatically added to each field so that when the operator enters a date such as 6/7/87 in the form, it is accepted as a label entry. When the entries in these fields are transferred to their appropriate database fields, the macro converts them to date serial numbers with the @DATEVALUE function and the /Range Value command and formats them in the Long International date format used for all of the other date entries.

The macro also copies the formulas for calculating the number of years an employee has been with the company as well as his or her age during the data transfer process. Notice that these two calculated fields are not represented in the data input form itself.

Figure 20.4 shows the text of the macro that controls this data input form. The macro is meant for the sample database. It contains four range names: \a, which names and locates the macro; Entry, which evaluates and controls the data entry into the form; Transfer, which controls the copying of the information in the input form to the database itself; and End, which clears the data input form before saving the worksheet and returning to READY mode.

Note: The Alt-A macro can be adapted and used in this form only if you are using Release 2 of the program. A similar, though less sophisticated, version of this macro can be created and used in Release 1A. However, because Release 1A does not include the /Range Transpose command, the basic input form should mirror the horizontal layout of the fields in the database. Then the /Copy command can be used to transfer all of the field entries to a new row of the database. Also, because Release 1A does not support the @CELLPOINTER and @DATEVALUE functions, these techniques cannot be used to make data entry easier.

In looking at the text of the macro, notice that after positioning the cell pointer in B1 with {GOTO}InputForm~ (which takes it to the beginning of the form, or A1) and {RIGHT} (which moves it one cell to the right, to B1), the macro encounters a long IF statement at the beginning of the Entry routine. This IF statement evaluates the row number of the cell pointer. If it is in either row 1 or any row greater than 8 (covering rows 9 and 10) and the cell is blank, the macro enters the apostrophe required to make each of these three field entries label entries.

Then the macro encounters the {?}{DOWN} statement, where it waits for the field entry and moves the cell pointer down to the next cell of the input form when the Return key is pressed to resume the macro execution. The next line asks it to evaluate the contents of the first field entry. If the cell contains the letter q, indicating that no more records are to be entered, the macro branches to the End routine. This is followed by another IF statement that evaluates the row position of the cell pointer. If it is below row 10, signaling the completion of the record entry, the macro goes to the Transfer routine to copy the data into the database. (When you construct a similar data input macro for your own databases, you must, of course, adjust these IF statements to reflect the row numbers of the fields where you want apostrophes to be entered automatically as well as the cell that signals the end of the data entry for a single record.)

As long as neither IF condition is true, the macro loops back to the beginning of the Entry subroutine, continuing to position the cell pointer in a new field entry cell. Once all of the fields are entered, the macro procedes to the Transfer routine. The first two command lines there position the cell pointer in the first cell of the database (named Input) and then reach the last record (with the {END}{DOWN} command). The cell pointer is correctly positioned in the first field of the new record by the addition of the second {DOWN} command.

The next statement uses the /Range Transpose command to copy the first eight field entries in the cell range B1..B8 to the first eight fields of the new record. After doing that, the {RIGHT} command moves the cell pointer to the Salary field and the /Range Format command formats the salary entry, using the comma format with zero decimal places.

Because the two date field entries are made as labels, they are copied into position by using the @DATEVALUE function as part of the /Range Transpose procedure. As soon as this function has converted each date string into a serial number with /rv~~, the /rfd4~ statement formats the new field entry to the Long International format used throughout the database. In between the two @DATEVALUE statements, the macro copies the formula for determining the number of years with the company from this field in the record directly above. The same command is used after the second date string for the Date of Birth field has been copied and converted to copy the formula for calculating the employee's age.

As soon as these steps are carried out, the macro erases all of the data entries in the input form (given the range name Fields) and branches back up to the very beginning of the macro. When the operator is finished adding records and enters a **q** in B1 (named Field1) in the input form, the macro branches to the End routine. This routine begins by erasing the q label entry in Field1; it then saves the worksheet, terminates CMD mode, and returns to READY mode.

There are many more features that could easily be added to this basic macro. For one thing, you could keep all but the cells containing the input fields globally protected. This allows you to use the /Range Input command to restrict the cell pointer movement to the first 11 cells in column B. It also prevents access to all of the menu commands, so that a stray initial forward slash character would not disturb the data entry operator. When the data input form is completed, the global protection could be lifted so that the field entries could be successfully copied to the new record of the database.

Also, instead of using the /Range Transpose command to copy the first eight fields into the new row of the database in one operation, you could transfer them by using other string functions such as @PROPER and @UPPER. This allows you to prevent inconsistent field entries from getting into the database. The tradeoff in using this piecemeal method is that it significantly slows down the time it takes to add a single record to the database. Even using the @DATEVALUE and copy commands in the macro to transfer the last four fields in the record slows down processing speed.

Finally, this data input macro could be added to a menu macro under a menu option for adding a new record. This menu macro would also include menu options for performing other necessary database operations, such as defining search criteria, doing find and extract operations, and printing specific reports. You could save this menu macro under \0 so that it would automatically control use of the database any time the file was retrieved.

NUMBERING DATABASE RECORDS

Unlike some stand-alone database management software, Lotus 1-2-3 does not automatically assign a record number to each record as it is added to the database. To add such record numbers to a database, you can enter all of the records and then use the /Data Fill command to give each one a record number. Often, record numbers are not added to the database until all of the initial data has been entered and the database has been sorted to the most favored arrangement (such as last name, first name alphabetical order).

Using record numbers gives you a very easy way to return the database to its original entry order after you sort it in different ways. In some databases that lack any unique identifying number (unlike the use of Social Security numbers in the personnel database), using record numbers also gives you another method for quickly locating a particular record for updating or deletion. With Release 2, you can keep the record number from being printed in a final report by using the /Worksheet Column Hide command on it.

Figure 20.5 shows the addition of record numbers to the example personnel database by using the /Data Fill command. First, a new column was inserted at column A by using the /Worksheet Insert Column command. Then the column was narrowed to five characters, the cell pointer was positioned in cell A5, and the /Data Fill command was issued. The range for the data fill was extended down to the last row in the database by using the

```
A5: [W5] 1                                                          READY

      A    B             C        D          E   F      G          H
2          Personnel Database
3          Employee
4     Rec  Number        L:Name   F:Name     Sex Dept   Position   Super
5       1  360-22-0978   Holland  Katherine  F   Acctg  Clerk      Newman
6       2  230-45-9512   Jones    Daniel     M   Acctg  Bookkeeper Newman
7       3  450-56-8723   Newman   Paul       M   Acctg  Accountant Pauli
8       4  561-34-5644   Jones    Alexander  M   Acctg  Secretary  Newman
9       5  567-43-2366   Langly   Sandra     F   Pers   Secretary  McKnight
10      6  345-14-7245   McKnight George     M   Pers   Manager    Dorian
11      7  705-34-2378   Smith    Mary       F   Pers   Clerk      McKnight
12      8  465-25-8751   Mead     Peter      M   Sales  Acct Exec  Smithson
13      9  598-52-7054   Durran   George     M   Sales  Acct Exec  Smithson
14     10  124-15-7602   Baker    Thomas     M   Sales  Acct Exec  Smithson
15     11  865-12-4102   McMead   Andrea     F   Sales  Acct Exec  Smithson
16     12  466-52-7035   Smith    Mary       F   Admin  President
17     13  307-28-1251   Dorian   Alvin      M   Admin  VP Admin   Smith
18     14  359-78-1063   Smithson Gena       F   Admin  VP Sales   Smith
19     15  253-65-2319   Pauli    Thomas     M   Admin  VP Finance Smith
20     16  965-50-2344   Baker    Colin      M   Mktg   Director   Smithson
21     17  625-86-5139   Jones    Sylvia     F   Mktg   Secretary  Baker
```

FIGURE 20.5: Adding a record number field to the personnel database with the /Data Fill command. Before using the /Data Fill command to number the records, a new column was added to the database by using the /Worksheet Insert Column command in column A. The new column was then narrowed to five characters with the /Worksheet Column Set-Width command. The cell pointer was then positioned in cell A5 and the /Data Fill command was issued. The fill range was set by anchoring the range at A5 and then using the ↓ key to highlight all of the rows used in the database. The start number was given as 1, and the step and stop number defaults were used without modification. The record numbers added with /Data Fill can be used as a primary sort key to return the records to the original entry order after sorting the database on some other key. They can also be used in the criterion range to locate a specific record by record number. Using the /Worksheet Column Hide command will hide this record number field when printing database reports.

↓ key, the start number was made 1, and the step and stop number defaults were accepted by pressing the Return key.

Once a database has been numbered in this way, the titles can be moved back to column A with the /Move command. The record numbers assigned can then be used in search criteria or in sorting to return the records to their original order.

Sorting the Database

Once the database has been set up and all of its initial data has been entered, you may find that you want to sort it in an order that differs from the way the records were originally entered. To do this, you use the /Data Sort command. This command contains several options that you use to set up the sort order before giving the command to perform the sort. As with all Lotus 1-2-3 menus that allow you to cycle through several options without returning you to READY mode each time, this command contains a Quit option that you use to return to the spreadsheet (pressing the Esc key several times will also return you to READY mode).

The /Data Sort command allows you to sort data on two fields (columns) of the database. The first field is defined by using the Primary-Key option, and the second is defined with the Secondary-Key option. Either sorting key can be specified in either ascending (0 to 9 and A to Z) or descending (9 to 0 and Z to A) order. Remember that in Release 2 sorting can be altered by changing the Collating option (see "Changing the Sort Order in the Spreadsheet" in Chapter 2).

You need to define a secondary key column only when the primary key that you define allows for duplicates that need to be arranged in an order different from that in which they were originally entered. The most common example of this is when sorting the database alphabetically by last name. Those people with the same last names will be arranged together in the order their records were entered. If you need to refine this sort, you would choose a secondary key such as the first name field and perform the sort on both last and first name fields in ascending order. In this way, all records for people with the same last names would be arranged alphabetically by their first name, regardless of the order in which the records were originally entered.

When you need to sort data on more than two key columns, you must perform a sequence of sort operations with the /Data Sort command to arrive at the final desired order. For instance, to sort the example personnel database alphabetically first by department, then by position, and finally by last name requires two sorting operations using different keys. (The reason for sorting on a third key is to arrange the people in the Sales department, because they all have the position title of Account Executive.)

The first time the database is sorted, the Position field (cell G5) is defined as the primary key and the L:Name field (C5) as the secondary key. Then the Go option is used to perform this first sort. The /Data Fill command is then used in column A to renumber the records now ordered alphabetically by position and then last name. Then the /Data Sort command is used a second time, this time defining the record number (A1) as the primary key and the department (F5) as the secondary key. The record number is used to maintain the arrangement created by the first sort operation. In this procedure, the secondary columns of position and last name are arranged before doing the final sort by department. This brings up an important rule to use when setting up sorts: *sort from inside out.* For example, if you have three keys on which to sort, sort on the second and third keys first and then sort on the first and second keys. Otherwise your results will not be accurate.

While sorting is normally associated with arranging records in a database, it can also be used to rearrange data in a spreadsheet. Just be sure that the data range you specify does not include any headings, or these will be sorted into the resulting arrangement. Also, remember to save a copy of the worksheet in its original order before performing any sorting. This allows you to retrieve a copy of the worksheet in its previous order if you specify the wrong data range or columns.

Database Commands Used When Creating a Database

The /Data Fill and /Data Sort commands are often used to create a new database as well as to maintain it later. The /Data Fill command quickly enters sequential numbers in any column or row of the worksheet. It can also be used to number the records in a database, creating either a permanent record number field or a temporary field used in complex sorting routines.

The /Data Sort command is most often used to rearrange the records in a database according to particular fields within the records. While the command can be applied to the database itself, you will probably find it more convenient to use /Data Sort to sort subsets of the database that have been extracted according to particular criteria. As the central database grows in size and the order in which new records are added becomes haphazard, it becomes less and less practical to sort all the records each time you use the database.

/Data Fill

The /Data Fill command automatically enters a sequence of numbers in either ascending or descending order in a specified range of cells. When you use the command, you set the starting number, the value by which each succeeding number is increased or decreased in the sequence, and the number at which to stop.

MENUS

/Data
Fill

KEYBOARD ENTRY

/DF

FUNCTION

The /Data Fill command makes it easy to enter a sequence of numbers in a spreadsheet or database application. It can be used to have the program generate a series of values that increase or decrease from a specific value. It is often used to produce number progressions for use with the other /Data commands such as /Data Table 1 or 2 or for defining the bin range for the /Data Distribution command. As discussed previously, /Data Fill is also useful in generating record numbers for database records and can be used in complex sorting routines involving more than the two keys supported by the /Data Sort command.

You can use Lotus 1-2-3's built-in functions to calculate the first value in the number sequence. For instance, you could use the /Data Fill command to generate a sequence of dates or times using the @NOW, @DATE, or @TIME functions. When you use such functions, remember to set the stop value (which determines the last value generated) high enough to accommodate current serial dates, which run in the 30,000s.

USAGE

When you use the /Data Fill command, you must specify four values:

1. The cell range where the values are to be entered. It can be specified by cell addresses or range name. Though this range most often consists of cells in a single column or row of the worksheet, it need not be. The /Data Fill command will work with two-dimensional cell ranges. When entering values in such a range, Lotus 1-2-3 always numbers down each column instead of across each row.
2. The start value, which is the number entered in the first cell of the specified range. The program supplies the default value of 0. To specify a new value, you merely type it in. Start, step, and stop values need not be integers or literal numbers. You can enter formulas, mathematical expressions, and functions that return numbers.
3. The step value, which determines by how much each value in the sequence is increased or decreased. To create a series of numbers that decrease, you specify the step value as a negative number.
4. The stop value, which determines the highest value entered in the sequence. The program supplies the default 8191 (or 2047 in Release 1A). Most of the time you can just accept this default value when specifying ascending number progressions by pressing the Return key: the cell range used will control the highest (or lowest) number generated in the sequence. You would specify a lower value if you want the /Data Fill command to stop after reaching a particular value that might occur before the cell range is entirely filled. When generating a decreasing number list, you must enter a stop number that is as low or lower than the last value that will be generated in the specified range.

To use the /Data Fill command, position the cell pointer in the cell where you want the number sequence to begin and type **/DF**. Indicate the extent of the range by typing in the cell addresses or by pointing to the cells; then press the Return key. Type in a new start value if you do not wish to use 0 as the start value; then press the Return key. Type in a new step value if you do not wish to increase each value by 1; then press the Return key. Finally, type in a stop value if you wish the sequence to stop with a particular value that it might reach before the entire cell range specified is filled. If you have specified a negative step value, enter a new stop value low enough to allow the program to enter all of the numbers in the range. Otherwise, press the Return key to accept the default stop value and have the program generate the number list.

Once you use the /Data Fill command in a worksheet, Lotus 1-2-3 remembers all of the values used. When using the /Data Fill command to create subsequent number lists, you must press the Esc key to unanchor the previously defined cell range if you wish to use the pointing method to define a new fill range. You will also have to enter new start, step, and stop values if these no longer suit the new sequence. You can undo the current entry for the start, step, and stop values by pressing Esc.

EXAMPLES

Figure 20.6 shows four example number sequences generated with the /Data Fill command. Range 1 was generated by giving the fill range as

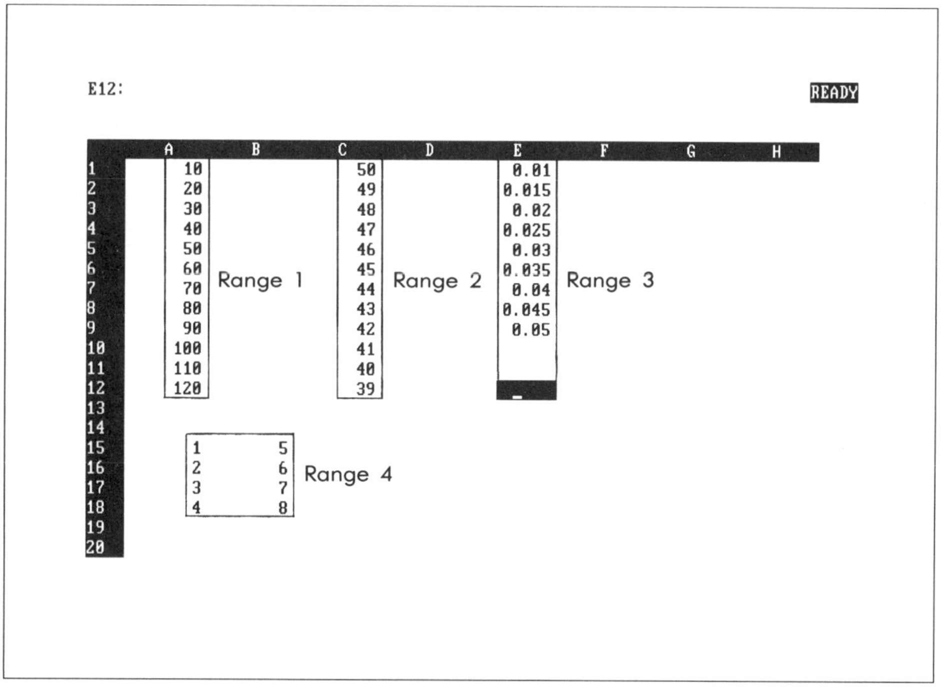

FIGURE 20.6: This figure shows four examples of the kinds of number sequences that can be generated with the /Data Fill command. Range 1 was created by giving the fill range as A1..A12, the start number as 10, the step number as 10, and accepting the stop number default of 8191. Range 2 was created by giving the fill range as C1..C12, the start number as 50, the step number as −1, and the stop number as 1. Range 3 was created by giving the fill range as E1..E12, the start number as 1%, the step number as .5%, and the stop number as 5%. Notice that the entire range of percentages appears in the fill range because the program reached the stop number before it reached the last cell of the range. Range 4 was generated by giving the fill range as A15..B18, the start number as 1, the step number as 1, and the stop number as 10. Notice that when specifying a two-dimensional fill range, Lotus 1-2-3 enters the number sequence down each column. It never enters the progression across columns, no matter how the fill range is specified.

A1..A12, setting the start value at 10, setting the step value at 10, and accepting the stop value of 8191. Range 2 was generated by giving the fill range as C1..C12, the start value as 50, the step value as −1, and the stop value as 1. Range 3 was generated by giving the fill range as E1..E12, the start value as 1%, the step value as .5%, and the stop value as 5%. Range 4 was generated by giving the fill range as A15..B18, the start value as 1, the step value as 1, and the stop value as 10.

SEE ALSO

/Data Table
/Data Distribution

/Data Sort

The /Data Sort command is used to rearrange the data in a specific range of a spreadsheet or database.

MENUS

/Data
Sort
Data-Range   Primary-Key   Secondary-Key   Reset   Go   Quit

KEYBOARD ENTRY

/DS

FUNCTION

The /Data Sort command allows you to sort data in the worksheet in either ascending or descending order according to a specific field or column in the range of values. It is most often used to arrange records in a database by a particular field, such as sorting the records alphabetically by last name or from most recent to oldest by order date.

The column (or field) that controls the order in which the records are arranged is referred to as a *key*. The Lotus 1-2-3 /Data Sort command allows you to specify up to two keys that determine the final sorted order. Using more than a single (primary) key is required only when duplicate entries are found in the primary key column. In such a case, the secondary key acts as a tie breaker, determining the sequencing of all records that contain duplicate primary key values.

When sorting data in a spreadsheet or database, you must be careful when the range to be used contains cells referenced by formulas outside that range. All cell references are adjusted within the data range that is sorted, while cell references in dependent formulas outside the specified range are not affected. As a result, formulas outside the sorted data range may no longer refer to the correct value because it has been moved to a new cell position.

Data sorting is most often used to arrange records in an order different from the one in which they were originally entered. It is also frequently used to sort subsets of database records obtained through extract operations into an order required by a particular printed report. When you use /Data Sort to sort database records, be sure that the data range you specify does not include the row of field names (which must be included when defining the /Data Query input range). If you make the /Data Sort data range the same as the /Data Query input range, the row of field names will be sorted with the actual records of the database.

The sorting command is not limited to database applications. It can be used to sort single columns or rows of data into a new ascending or descending order. It is often useful when you need to arrange index columns or rows of lookup tables in ascending order so that they can be used with the @VLOOKUP or @HLOOKUP functions. It can even be applied to financial worksheets to sequence particular values that were entered in a random order.

Whenever you use the /Data Sort command, be sure that you have saved a copy of the current worksheet before you perform the sort operation. It is all too easy to define the sort order incorrectly, only to find that there is no way to return the records or data to their original order, short of reentering them manually. For this reason, many people use the /Data Fill command to add record numbers to the database before sorting on other fields. That way, the new record number field can be used as the primary key to return the database to its original order (refer back to "Numbering Database Records" in this chapter for more information on this technique).

Release 2 of the program allows you to change the sorting order used by the /Data Sort command by using the Install program. It now supports three different collating sequences:

1. Numbers last, which produces this kind of sequence:

   Freelance
   Lotus 1-2-3
   Symphony
   1-2-3 Report Writer

2. Numbers first (the program default), which alters the previous order to

   1-2-3 Report Writer
   Freelance
   Lotus 1-2-3
   Symphony

3. ASCII, which places numbers before uppercase letters, with lowercase letters following all uppercase letters. If the product name Freelance were not capitalized, the following order would be produced:

   1-2-3 Report Writer
   Lotus 1-2-3
   Symphony
   freelance

To change to a different collating order, you must use the Advanced Options on the Install Menu (see "Changing the Sort Order in the Spreadsheet" in Chapter 2).

USAGE

When you access the /Data Sort command by typing **/DS**, the program provides a menu containing six options. To perform your first sorting operation, you must use at least the Data-Range and Primary-Key options before using the Go option to have the program perform the sort. Each of these menu options is described below.

DEFINING THE DATA RANGE

The Data-Range option defines the location of the data to be sorted. The range should include only the actual values and/or labels to be sorted, not the field names (in a database) or column or row headings (in a spreadsheet).

To define the data range, position the cell pointer in the first cell of the range, type **d**, and indicate the extent of the range. You can indicate this range by typing in the cell addresses or by pointing. If you use pointing, anchor the range by typing a period before using the arrow keys. Press the Return key as soon as you have indicated the full extent of the range. You will be returned to the /Data Sort menu options, where you can go on to define the keys to be used.

Because Lotus 1-2-3 remembers the range defined with this option, you can perform various sorts on the same range by chaining the primary and secondary keys without redefining the range. When you save the worksheet, the last-defined data range is saved as part of the file.

The Data-Range option defines only the data to be repositioned. It does not in any way determine the order by which this range is sorted. This can be done only by using the Primary-Key and Secondary-Key options.

Defining the Primary Key

The Primary-Key option indicates the field or column that is to be used first in determining the new order of the records or data specified with the Data-Range option. To define the primary key, type **p** and then indicate the column that contains the data by which the sort is to be performed. You can indicate the column by pointing or by typing in an appropriate cell address. This can be a cell address in any row of this column (even outside the rows in the data range). The primary key can include more than a single column as the Primary-Key range, although indicating two fields as the primary key would not have the same effect as defining one field as the primary key and the other as the secondary key; only the data in the first field of the Primary-Key range will determine the final order.

After you press the Return key, you will be prompted to indicate the type of sort: either A for ascending order or D for descending order. The first time you define a primary key, Lotus 1-2-3 will supply D as the default sort order. After that, it will use whatever sort order was specified previously.

After you type A or D and press the Return key, you will be returned to the /Data Sort menu options, where you can either indicate a secondary key with the Secondary-Key option or have the program perform the sorting operation by using the Go option. If you perform the sort and later find that your primary key contains duplicates that must also be sorted, you can add a secondary sort key after performing the sort without having to redefine the primary key (the program remembers the field defined as the primary key).

DEFINING THE SECONDARY KEY

The Secondary-Key option defines a second field or column of data to be used in determining the arrangement of records that contain duplicate entries in the primary key field. It is defined in exactly the same way as the primary key.

When you define a secondary key, you can use a different sort order than that used in the primary key. For instance, if you want to sort a database by ascending part numbers and then by descending order amounts, you would indicate A as the sort type when designating the part number field as the primary key and D as the sort type when indicating the order amount field as the secondary key.

THE RESET OPTION

The Reset option clears the ranges set with the Data-Range, Primary-Key, and Secondary-Key options. Because Lotus 1-2-3 remembers all of these ranges throughout a work session, the Reset option is often used when you are about to sort a completely different data range on totally new keys. This makes defining all new parameters easier, especially in POINT mode, because the program does not keep referring to the previously used ranges as you define the new sort conditions.

THE GO OPTION

The Go option tells the program to go ahead and perform the sort according to the definitions set up with the Data-Range, Primary-Key, and Secondary-Key options. Once you type **g** for Go, the program begins rearranging the data or records in the data range. To abort a sort operation before the program has finished sorting, type **q** for Quit (or press Ctrl-Scroll Lock, also called the Break key combination).

THE QUIT OPTION

The Quit option is used to return to READY mode. It provides a faster alternative for bailing out of a sort operation than pressing the

Break key combination. It is also an easier method of exiting the /Data Sort menu than pressing the Esc key several times.

EXAMPLES

Figure 20.7 shows the sample personnel database used throughout this chapter sorted alphabetically first by last name and then by first name. The L:Name field was designated as the primary key and the type of sort was designated as ascending. Because the L:Name field includes duplicate Bakers, Joneses, and Smiths, the F:Name field was used as the secondary key to determine the order in which the records for these employees would be arranged. The type of sort used for this secondary key was also ascending.

A5: [W5] 16 READY

	A	B	C	D	E	F	G	H
2	Personnel Database							
3	Employee							
4	Rec	Number	L:Name	F:Name	Sex	Dept	Position	Super
5	16	965-50-2344	Baker	Colin	M	Mktg	Director	Smithson
6	10	124-15-7602	Baker	Thomas	M	Sales	Acct Exec	Smithson
7	19	306-73-2176	Clarkson	Sean	M	Mktg	Artist	Baker
8	13	307-20-1251	Dorian	Alvin	M	Admin	VP Admin	Smith
9	9	598-52-7054	Durran	George	M	Sales	Acct Exec	Smithson
10	1	360-22-0978	Holland	Katherine	F	Acctg	Clerk	Newman
11	4	561-34-5644	Jones	Alexander	M	Acctg	Secretary	Newman
12	2	230-45-9512	Jones	Daniel	M	Acctg	Bookkeeper	Newman
13	17	625-86-5139	Jones	Sylvia	F	Mktg	Secretary	Baker
14	5	567-43-2366	Langly	Sandra	F	Pers	Secretary	McKnight
15	18	465-10-2450	Lawson	Mark	M	Mktg	Assistant	Baker
16	6	345-14-7245	McKnight	George	M	Pers	Manager	Dorian
17	11	865-12-4102	McMead	Andrea	F	Sales	Acct Exec	Smithson
18	8	465-25-8751	Mead	Peter	M	Sales	Acct Exec	Smithson
19	3	458-56-8723	Newman	Paul	M	Acctg	Accountant	Pauli
20	15	253-65-2319	Pauli	Thomas	M	Admin	VP Finance	Smith
21	12	466-52-7035	Smith	Mary	F	Admin	President	

FIGURE 20.7: The sample personnel database sorted alphabetically first by last name and then by first name. The L:Name field in column C was designated as the primary key and the type was designated as ascending. Because there are many duplicate last names in this field, the F:Name field was designated as the secondary key, again in ascending order. Because the /Data Fill command was used to add record numbers to the rows of the database, these records could easily be returned to their original order by performing another sort using the Rec field as the primary key.

SEE ALSO

/Data Fill

SUMMARY

This chapter has introduced the basics of creating and entering data into a Lotus 1-2-3 database. To learn how to locate and extract data from an existing database, see Chapter 21, which covers all database operations using the /Data Query commands. There you will find techniques for setting up search criteria, locating specific records for editing, extracting subsets of the database for reports, eliminating duplicate records, and deleting unwanted records.

As part of this chapter on setting up a database, the /Data Fill and /Data Sort commands were introduced. The /Data Fill command is used not only when working with databases but also when creating number sequences with other /Data management commands, such as the /Data Table 1 and 2 and /Data Distribution commands. For more information on the /Data Distribution command, see Chapter 22. For more information on the two /Data Table commands, see Chapter 23.

As mentioned in regard to the /Data Sort command, if you are using Release 2, you can alter the underlying sorting order used by the program by changing the collating order in the Install program. For specific information on how to do this, refer back to the section entitled "Changing the Sort Order in the Spreadsheet" in Chapter 2.

CHAPTER 21

DATABASE OPERATIONS

Database Operations

This chapter examines the various database operations that can be performed on a Lotus 1-2-3 database by using the /Data Query command options. The discussion sections include explanations of how to use the /Data Query Input, Criterion, and Output options to define the cell ranges required to perform various query operations; presentations of the various methods for setting search criteria that determine which records are selected when using such Query options as Find, Extract, Unique, or Delete; and discussions of when to use the Find, Extract, Delete, and Unique options. After these general discussions, you will find a complete reference entry for the /Data Query command, covering all of its options.

Defining the Database Input, Criterion, and Output Ranges

To perform various operations on a database, such as locating specific records for editing, extracting subsets of the database, or deleting records, you must use the /Data Query command to define three different ranges in the database worksheet:

1. The input range, which includes the field names and all of the records in the database. This range tells Lotus 1-2-3 where to go to find the records that meet the search criteria you set up.
2. The criterion range, which includes some or all of the field names used in the database as well as at least one row of cells located below these field names, where you enter the search criteria to be used. If you decide to keep this row blank, no search criteria are used and all records are matched. The field names you enter into the criterion range must match those used to define the fields in the database (however, differences in capitalization do not matter).
3. The output range, which includes copies of the field names used in the database that determine which fields are to be copied from each record meeting the search criteria when using the /Data Query Extract or Unique command. In Lotus 1-2-3, the output range can

consist of a single row containing only these field names. In such a case, Lotus 1-2-3 copies all of the data from records matching the criteria in as many blank rows as required below these field names. You can also restrict the output range by specifying the number of blank rows to be included below the one containing the field names. If the extract or unique operation includes more records than will fit in this restricted output range, Lotus 1-2-3 will copy as many as it can, beep, go into ERROR mode, and display the error message "Too many records for Output range".

Figure 21.1 illustrates these three ranges defined for a sample personnel database used in the figures in this chapter.

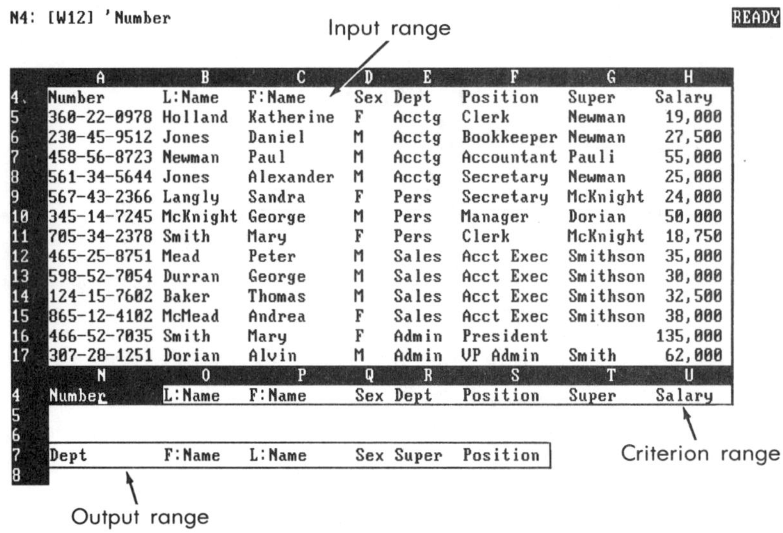

FIGURE 21.1: The input, criterion, and output ranges defined for the sample personnel database. The input range consists of the first row of field names plus all of the records in the database. It is used in /Data Query commands to locate the fields used in search criteria and to locate all matching records. The criterion range consists of duplicates of the field names used in the database as well as cells in which the various search criteria are entered. In this example, the criterion range includes all of the field names, with a single empty cell below each one. This is the minimum criterion range required for performing any of the /Data Query operations. The output range consists of the field names that designate which field entries are to be copied from all matching records during /Data Query Extract or Unique operations. The program places this information from all qualifying records in the empty columns beneath the field names, according to the order in which the field names occur.

You define an output range in a worksheet only when you want to use the Extract or Unique option to copy specific records from the database, thus creating a subset of the database defined by the criteria set up in the criterion range. If you use only the Find or Delete commands, you need to define only the input and criterion ranges.

As with other Lotus 1-2-3 /Data commands, the program remembers the previously defined input, criterion, and output ranges during a work session and saves them as part of the worksheet file. The /Data Query command menu also works like the other /Data commands, such as /Data Sort, /Data Regression, and /Data Parse, in that it allows you to choose different options without returning you to READY mode each time you select an option. The menu therefore includes a Quit option that returns you to the spreadsheet. Because the criteria are set up in the worksheet itself, you must often use the Quit option to exit the menu and redefine the search criteria.

Using the Query Function Key

To help reduce the amount of shuttling back and forth between the /Data Query menu and the criterion range in the worksheet, you can use the Query function key (F7). Pressing this key invokes the last-used query command. In other words, if the last query operation performed from the menu was a find operation, pressing the Query function key initiates another find operation. The Query function key continues to perform in this way until you use another /Data Query command. If you then use the command menu to do an extract operation, the Query function key changes its function to extract (the same thing occurs after you issue a /Data Query Unique or Delete command). This allows you to change the criteria in the criterion range and then perform the same operation without retyping the command keystrokes.

Formulating Search Criteria and Defining the Criterion Range

When you set up a criterion range, you will often find it convenient to copy the field names from the database to a new range in the worksheet. Usually, you will want to copy this row of field names to a range to the right of the database rather than to blank rows beneath. That way, you will not have to keep moving the established criterion range as you add new records to the database.

Copying the field names with the /Copy command also ensures that no typographical errors will occur that could affect the outcome of your query operations. Remember that the field names entered in the criterion range must be spelled exactly as they are in the input range, but they need not be copied in the same order. You don't have to copy all field names into the criterion range. If you use a shorter criterion range, you simply limit the kinds of criteria you can specify in query operations. After copying the field names, you can define the criterion range, including the cells holding these field names and at least one row of cells directly beneath them.

Because Lotus 1-2-3 uses a spatial relationship to represent AND and OR relationships in search criteria, you will sometimes have to expand the criterion range by including more than a single row of cells to hold the search criteria. To set up an AND condition, you set up single match criteria beneath each field name to be included in the condition, so that the criteria extend horizontally across one row in the criterion range.

To set up an OR condition, you enter each OR condition in its appropriate field in a separate row of the criterion range. You are not limited to the criteria stacked in a single field. This would give you only OR conditions such as "look for this last name OR that last name." You can set up more sophisticated OR conditions such as "find all records that have this last name OR that department OR that sex OR . . . ." Of course, AND and OR conditions can also be mixed. In any case, the criterion range must include all cells that contain search criteria as well as the field names listed above them.

Figure 21.2 demonstrates the different criterion ranges that must be used when setting up an AND condition as opposed to an OR condition. If the criterion range includes the cell range Q4..S5, the search condition means "find all records where the sex is F and the position is Accountant." If the criterion range includes the cell range S4..S7, the search condition is changed to "find all records where the position is either Accountant, Clerk, or Director." In such a case, it does not matter which sex is entered in the Sex field.

If the criterion range were then enlarged to include the cell range Q4..S7, the condition would be changed to "find all records where the sex is F AND the position is Accountant OR all the records where the position is Clerk OR Director." Because the AND condition applies only to the criteria entered in row 5, the program would include records in which the position is Clerk or Director, regardless of which gender was entered in the

Sex field. The F criterion pertains only to the Accountant position. Similarly, to restrict the condition to females in the Clerk or Director positions, Fs would also have to entered in the criterion cells Q6 and Q7.

When you set up OR criteria in a vertical arrangement below a particular field name, you must also be sure that the criterion range includes these cells as part of its range. Conversely, if you erase previously used OR criteria and set up new criteria in only the first empty row of the criterion range, you must remember to restrict the criterion range so that it no longer includes these now-blank cells before you use one of the /Data Query commands. If you do not, Lotus 1-2-3 will find that *all records in the database match the search condition.* This occurs because an empty cell in the criterion range sets the criterion equal to any field entry made. Because it is so easy to forget to reset the criterion range after erasing criteria, you should develop the habit of always checking the criterion range whenever you change from an OR to an AND condition or vice versa.

```
N4: [W12] 'Number                                                     READY

       A          B        C         D   E     F          G        H
4  Number      L:Name   F:Name     Sex Dept  Position   Super    Salary
5  360-22-0978 Holland  Katherine  F   Acctg Clerk      Newman    19,000
6  230-45-9512 Jones    Daniel     M   Acctg Bookkeeper Newman    27,500
7  458-56-8723 Newman   Paul       M   Acctg Accountant Pauli     55,000
8  561-34-5644 Jones    Alexander  M   Acctg Secretary  Newman    25,000
9  567-43-2366 Langly   Sandra     F   Pers  Secretary  McKnight  24,000
10 345-14-7245 McKnight George     M   Pers  Manager    Dorian    50,000
11 705-34-2378 Smith    Mary       F   Pers  Clerk      McKnight  18,750
12 465-25-8751 Mead     Peter      M   Sales Acct Exec  Smithson  35,000
13 598-52-7054 Durran   George     M   Sales Acct Exec  Smithson  30,000
14 124-15-7602 Baker    Thomas     M   Sales Acct Exec  Smithson  32,500
15 865-12-4102 McMead   Andrea     F   Sales Acct Exec  Smithson  38,000
16 466-52-7035 Smith    Mary       F   Admin President           135,000
17 307-28-1251 Dorian   Alvin      M   Admin VP Admin   Smith     62,000
       N          O        P         Q   R     S          T        U
4  Number      L:Name   F:Name     Sex Dept  Position   Super    Salary
5                                  F         Accountant
6                                            Clerk
7                                            Director
8
```

FIGURE 21.2: The placement of search criteria as well as the definition of the cells included in the criterion range can be used to designate AND and OR conditions for qualifying the records selected by various /Data Query commands. In this figure, if the criterion range is defined as cell range Q4..S5, the criterion is Sex = F AND Position = Accountant. If the range is modified to S4..S7, it becomes Position = Accountant OR Clerk OR Director. If it were set to Q4..S7, it would be Sex = F AND Position = Accountant OR Position = Clerk OR Director. Implicit in these last criteria is that the gender of the employee is a qualifier only in the case in which the position is Accountant. Gender is not taken into consideration with the other two positions.

Using Exact-Match Criteria

To locate records that contain exact matches to particular field entries, you merely enter the value or label that is to be matched beneath the appropriate field name in the criterion range. In Release 2, when you specify matches for fields that contain label entries, the criterion does not have to match the case of the field entry in the records. Lotus 1-2-3 matches any record whose field contains the same letters in the same sequence as entered in the criterion range (for techniques for obtaining only exact case matches, see the section entitled "Using Formulas to Set Up Search Criteria" that follows). In Release 1A, case does matter here. Entries in the criterion range must match letter for letter, including case, with entries in the input range.

USING WILDCARD CHARACTERS

Often you may not remember exactly how a particular entry was made in the database, or you may need to expand the criteria slightly to include more than exact matches. In such cases, you can use certain wildcard characters recognized by Lotus 1-2-3. With the exception of the tilde, these characters are the same as the DOS wildcard characters and are used in the same way. Table 21.1 shows you these wildcard characters and illustrates how they are used.

CHARACTER	MEANING	EXAMPLES
*	The asterisk represents global replacement; it matches any characters of any length at and after the asterisk's position.	J* matches all names that begin with J regardless of length: Jim, Jane, John, Johnston, etc.
?	The question mark represents a single character replacement; it matches any single character in the question mark's position.	Jo??? matches all five-letter names that begin with Jo: Jones, JoAnn, Johns, etc.
~	The tilde represents exceptions to the characters that follow it; it matches any characters other than those after the tilde.	~CA matches all states other than California.

TABLE 21.1: Wildcard Characters Used in Search Criteria

For example, to isolate and extract only the records in which the last names begin with the letter S, you would enter **S*** as the criterion under the L:Name field name in the criterion range. To extract only the records in which the last name begins with Sm and contains five letters, you would enter **Sm???** in its place. Such a criterion would return records in which the last name was Smith or Smyth, excluding those with last names like Smiths and Smithson.

The tilde before a criterion entry matches every entry except the one entered in the criterion range. This is often a good method for excluding extremely large numbers of records. For example, in a national sales database in which most of your customers are in California and New York, you could exclude these records by entering **~CA** and **~NY** beneath the State field name in the criterion range. If you then did an extract operation, Lotus 1-2-3 would copy all of the records in which the states were not entered as CA or NY.

Using Formulas to Set Up Search Criteria

While exact-match criteria are adequate for locating records where specific fields do or do not contain particular entries, they are not adequate when you need to locate records in which specific field entries fall between certain ranges of values. For instance, while you could enter 25000 as the search criterion under the Salary field name to find all employees who make $25,000 a year, this method does not enable you to locate those who make between $25,000 and $35,000 a year.

To set up and use such criteria, you can construct a formula in the criterion cell. In addition to allowing you to formulate target ranges, using formulas to determine the search criteria offers other benefits:

- When you use a formula that determines the search criteria, you can use the #AND# and #OR# operators to create AND and OR conditions without arranging the criteria spatially in the criterion range or redefining the criterion range.
- Criterion formulas can be entered beneath any valid field name in the criterion range. Because the formulas contain cell references to the appropriate fields in the database, they do not rely on the field names in the criterion range to find the column in which to locate matching entries.

- You can include calculated values in a criterion formula against which field entries can be matched. For instance, you could set up a criterion that returns only those records in which the Salary entry was greater than the average Salary entry.
- You can include certain Lotus 1-2-3 functions in a criterion formula. For instance, you could set up a criterion formula with the @EXACT function to ensure that matches are made only for those entries that correspond to the label you specify, in case as well as in characters used. The database statistical functions are the functions that are most often used in criterion formulas.

Guidelines for Constructing Criterion Formulas

When you create a criterion formula, you must include a cell reference that tells Lotus 1-2-3 where to begin the search. This cell reference marks not only the correct column (field) to be used but also the row (record) where the search is to begin. This cell reference must be the first field entry directly beneath the correct field name if you want all of the records in the entire database to be included in the search.

To make criterion formulas more descriptive and thus easier to formulate, many people use the /Range Name Labels Down command to give each field entry in the first record its own field name as a range name. This is a single, simple operation. You just locate the cell pointer in the cell containing the first field name, type **/RNLD**, and then press the End key, the → key, and the Return key.

After that, you need not refer to the first field by cell address in your formulas. For instance, if you wanted to locate all records in which the salary was between $25,000 and $35,000 a year, you could specify the criterion formula as

+Salary>=25000#AND#Salary<=35000

instead of

+H5>=25000#AND#H5<=35000

Not only is the first criterion formula more descriptive than the second, but you can also create it without having to refer to the database itself to check the cell address of the first Salary field entry.

Whenever you enter a valid criterion formula in the criterion range, the program returns either a 0 or 1 value in the cell where it was entered. It returns a 0 if the first field entry does not match the criterion set up by the formula (fails the condition) and a 1 if it does match the criterion (passes the condition).

You can test the condition on the first field against the result returned by your criterion formula to check that the formula is working as planned. If you check the first entry and the result obtained does not match the result you expected, you know that you must reformulate the criterion formula before going ahead with the planned query operation. When you issue the desired /Data Query command, Lotus 1-2-3 will search all of the field entries in all of the records and will match each against the criterion formula. As long as the cell references in the formula represent the entries in the first record, you can rest assured that Lotus 1-2-3 will search through the entire database and that no matching records will be omitted from the query operation.

You can use any of the logical and Boolean operators in criterion formulas in the same way you use them in constructing regular spreadsheet formulas. In fact, you can think of criterion formulas as @IF formulas that do not require the @IF function. For instance, you can think of the criterion formula

+ Hired> @DATE(83,12,31)#AND#Hired< @DATE(85,1,1)

as meaning "find or extract a record if the date hired is after December 31, 1983 and before January 1, 1985" (that is, if it falls between January 1 and December 31, 1984). (To review the meanings and uses for the logical and Boolean operators, refer back to Table 10.2 in Chapter 10, "Working with Formulas and Functions.")

If you are using Release 2, you can include character strings in your criterion formulas as well as use string functions to develop the search criteria. However, when you use search strings in formulas, unlike using them as exact-match criteria, you must remember to enclose the strings in quotation marks.

For example, to find all records in which the last name falls in the first half of the alphabet (between A and M), you could enter the criterion formula

+ L:Name<"N"

remembering to enclose the letter N in quotes. Similarly, if you wanted to locate any missing (blank) field entries in the Dept field of a database, you could use the @CELL function

@CELL("type",Dept) = "b"

to test for the type attribute equal to b as long as the b were enclosed in quotation marks.

Locating and Extracting Records

Lotus 1-2-3 provides two query operations that locate all records matching the criteria entered in the criterion range: the /Data Find command and the /Data Extract command. As mentioned earlier, you only need to define an output range in the worksheet when you use the /Data Extract command. To use either of these commands, you first enter the search criteria in the appropriate cells of the criterion range and then give the appropriate /Data Query command.

Performing Data Query Find Operations

The /Data Query Find command highlights each record in the database that matches the stated criteria. It indicates a match by displaying the entire record in inverse video. When you use this command, Lotus 1-2-3 goes into FIND mode. To locate records beyond the one currently highlighted that meet your criteria, you press the ↓ key. If you press this key and Lotus 1-2-3 beeps at you, there are no more records that meet the specified criteria. You can use the ↑ key to return to the previously highlighted record at any time while in FIND mode. To exit FIND mode and return to READY mode during the find operation, you press the Return key.

The /Data Query Find command is often used to locate records that must be edited in some way. Release 2, unlike Release 1A, allows you to edit a highlighted record while still in FIND mode. To change a particular field in the record, you can use the ← or → key to move the flashing cursor to the appropriate entry and then enter the new data or use the Edit function key (F2) to make the necessary changes. Lotus 1-2-3 will not return to READY mode when you press the Return key unless no editing changes have been made to the record.

If you are using Release 1A, you must exit FIND mode and manually relocate the particular record that needs to be edited while in READY mode. To make this easier, you should note the cell address of the record before leaving FIND mode. That way, you can use the Goto function key (F5) to take the cell pointer directly to the record to be edited.

To repeat a find operation using new criteria, exit FIND mode, enter the new criteria in the criterion range, erasing any old criteria that are no longer used, and press the Query function key (F7). Remember to adjust the criterion range if the new criteria no longer require the same cell range (as when switching from an OR condition using exact-match criteria to an AND condition or vice versa) before reissuing the /Data Query Find command with the Query function key. Also, always use the /Range Erase command to delete criteria that are no longer needed. You cannot erase a criterion by using the space bar and pressing the Return key, because that would enter a space and create a new search criterion for field entries that contain a space character.

Performing Data Query Extract Operations

The /Data Query Extract command actually copies those records that meet the stated criteria into a new area of the worksheet you have defined with the /Data Query Output command. It is most often used to create reports that contain only a specific group of records that meet your search criteria. When you use the Extract command, remember to check your criterion range very carefully. If you have defined the output range only by the field names to be used and the criterion range contains only empty cells below its field names, Lotus 1-2-3 will copy all of the records in the database into the output range. If the output range was restricted to a limited number of blank rows during its definition, records would be copied only until they filled the range. If this happens, you can clear the output range by entering an impossible criterion in the criterion range and then performing the /Data Query Extract operation again.

When you set up the output range for an extract operation, enter only the field names of the fields that you want to be included in the report. This can be all fields or just selected fields, and they can be arranged in any order you desire as long as the field names used in the output range match those used in the input range.

You can also do extract operations based on criteria for fields not to be included in the output range. For instance, you could create a report from a personnel database based on the number of years of service with the company but not include this information in the extracted report. In such a case, you would enter the appropriate criterion beneath the field name that marked the column in which this data was stored in the criterion range while omitting the field name in the output range.

Each time you do an extract operation after changing the criteria but without redefining the output range, Lotus 1-2-3 clears the output range of all records copied during the previous extract operation before copying those that meet the new criteria. If you wish to save a copy of this subset of records without defining a new output range, you can use the /File Xtract command to save them in a new file.

Note: Whenever Lotus 1-2-3 does an extract operation, it copies only values from calculated fields, not the formulas that derived them. Because of this, it is not possible to copy formulas to the new file by using the /File Xtract Formulas command from an output range.

Once you have copied the records to a new file, you can perform another extract operation using the same output range. Later, you can retrieve the new file, sort it as required, define any print enhancements to be used, and then print it directly from this file instead of from the database worksheet.

Deleting Records

You can delete records from the database by setting appropriate criteria in the criterion range and then using the /Data Query Delete command. Before giving this command, you should save a copy of the database, for Lotus 1-2-3 provides no undelete feature. Once you give the go-ahead by typing **D** at the Cancel/Delete prompt, there is no way to retrieve the deleted records except from a backup copy of the database. If the criteria you entered prior to deleting the records are broad, you can lose many records and will have to reenter them manually if you have no backup copy to use.

When Lotus 1-2-3 deletes records from a database with the /Data Query Delete command, it does not leave blank rows where records have been eliminated. If you have given the database a range name, its cell addresses will be adjusted automatically to reflect its more limited size.

You can always delete records from a database manually by using the /Range Erase command, although doing so will leave a blank row that must be eliminated by using the /Move command to repack the database.

On the whole, using the /Data Query Delete command is a superior alternative to using /Range Erase as long as you are careful and make sure that you have a complete backup of the database before using it.

Deleting Duplicate Records

To locate and delete any unwanted duplicate records in a database, you can use the /Data Query Unique command. This works just like an extract operation except that only unique records are copied to the output range. To eliminate duplicate records from a report you are creating, leave all of the criterion cells in the criterion range blank and use the /Data Query Unique command (/DQU). Lotus 1-2-3 will copy all records except those in which every field entry in the entire record is the same in one or more of the other records in the database. It does not consider a record to be a duplicate if even one of the field entries is slightly different.

If your database is not too large and you need to ensure that it contains no duplicate records, you can use the /Data Query Unique command to eliminate duplicates in the output range and then copy the contents of the output range to the input range in the same worksheet. You can also use the /File Xtract command to create a new file that holds a copy of the database containing only unique records.

Using the Unique Option to Determine Unique Entries in a Specific Field

In addition to using /Data Query Unique to eliminate duplicate records from the database or from a report you are creating, you can use it to create a list of all of the unique entries in a specific field. For instance, if you were working with a sales database and wanted to know how many different cities your salespeople were currently servicing as well as what those cities were, you could use the /Data Query Unique command to find out this information quickly.

To do this, you would redefine the output range to include just the City field name. Then you would erase any criteria entered in the criterion range before issuing the /Data Query Unique command. Lotus 1-2-3 would then extract all unique city entries into the output range. The Unique option used in this way ensures that no matter how many times a particular city is entered into records in the database, it occurs only once in the output range and that each unique city entry is represented in the extracted list.

The /Data Query Command

The /Data Query command provides the means for locating and retrieving specific data from a Lotus 1-2-3 database. The menu attached to this command gives you four different query options: Find, Extract,

Unique, and Delete. To use the Find and Delete operations, you must first define an input range and a criterion range by using the /Data Query Input and Criterion options. To use the Extract and Unique operations, you must define a third range, the output range, by using the /Data Query Output option.

/Data Query

MENUS

/Data
Query
Input Criterion Output Find Extract Unique Delete Reset Quit

KEYBOARD ENTRY

/DQ

FUNCTION

The /Data Query commands are used to locate all records in the database that match the criteria you set up. These search criteria are entered into cells of the same worksheet as that containing the database. From the /Data Query menu, you can perform a find operation that highlights all records that meet your criteria, an extract operation that copies all of these records into a new area of the worksheet, or a delete operation that eliminates such records from the database. The last query operation using the Unique menu option works just like an extract operation except that it copies only unique records, eliminating any complete duplicates.

USAGE

The /Data Query command is attached to a menu containing nine different options that are used either to define the cell ranges required to perform particular query operations or to perform the operations themselves. Like other /Data command menus, after using a particular option you are returned to the /Data Query menu rather than to READY mode. Therefore, to make it easier to return to READY mode, the menu includes a Quit command as one of its options.

To enter this menu, type **/DQ**. Then type the initial letter of the command option you wish to use. If you attempt to perform a particular query operation before you have defined all of the necessary ranges, Lotus 1-2-3 will beep to indicate that it cannot perform the desired operation. It will not, however, display an error message to inform you of the particular range or ranges that must be defined.

Defining the Input Range

The input range defined with the Input option consists of the cell range containing the field names as well as all cells containing records in the database. It must be defined before any data query operation can be performed.

To define the input range, type **/DQI**, or just type **I** if you are already in the /Data Query menu. You can indicate the range containing the database field names and records by typing in the cell addresses or range name or by using the pointing method. The Input command does not automatically anchor the range at the current cell, so when using pointing to define the input range, be sure to type a period after locating the cell pointer in the first cell of the database.

Lotus 1-2-3 will remember the input range defined during a work session and will save it as part of the file when you use the /File Save command. To define a new input range, you can use the Reset option (though this clears the currently defined criterion and output ranges as well) and indicate a new cell range or just replace the cell range suggested by the program. To do this by pointing, you will have to use the Esc key to unanchor the cell pointer so that you can move it to the beginning of the new input range.

Defining the Criterion Range

The criterion range must contain at least one of the field names found in the first row of the database and at least a single cell located directly beneath it. The cell beneath the field name is where you enter the criterion that the program uses to locate matching records.

To define the criterion range, type **c** from the /Data Query menu and indicate the cells containing the field names and criterion input cells by typing the cell addresses or range name or by pointing to them. Lotus 1-2-3 remembers the currently defined criterion range during a work session and saves it as part of the worksheet.

The criterion range should be positioned in an area of the worksheet where it cannot overlap either the input or output ranges, preferably to one side or the other of the database and above the output range. While the criterion range can use just one field of the database, it is often more convenient to set up the criterion range initially so that it includes all the field names used in the database and the single row of cells beneath each of them. Defining the criterion range in this way allows you to change your search criteria without redefining the criterion range: you simply enter new values below the appropriate field names. To ensure that the field names match those in the database, you can use the /Copy command to copy all of the field names from the first row of the input range to the location where you are setting up the criterion range.

To set up AND conditions using exact-match criteria, you merely enter the values or labels to be matched under the appropriate field names in the criterion range. To set up OR conditions using exact-match criteria, you must enter the values or labels to be matched in separate rows below the appropriate field names. When you set up such OR conditions, you must also make sure that these entries are included as part of the criterion range. To check that the conditions are part of the criterion range, enter **/dqc** and see whether the range highlight includes the new conditions.

You can also set up criterion formulas with search criteria that contain ranges of values between which matching records must fall. These formulas can contain logical and Boolean operators, as well as Lotus 1-2-3 functions.

When you set up such formulas, you enter cell references that correspond to the appropriate field in the first record of the database where the criterion is to apply. This cell reference tells the progam which field to search (rather than using the field name to locate it) and ensures that all records in the database will be included in the search. If the condition set up in the criterion formula is true in the case of this first field entry, the program returns a 1 in the cell where the formula was entered. If it is not, the program returns 0 in this cell.

For more specific information on how to construct exact-match criteria and criterion formulas, see the section "Formulating Search Criteria and Defining the Criterion Range" earlier in this chapter.

Defining the Output Range

The output range tells the program where to copy records that meet the search criteria defined in the criterion range when either a /Data

Query Extract or Unique command is issued. At a minimum, the output range can consist of the row of field names copied from the database that indicates which fields of the matching records are to be copied into the output range. If the output range consists of the single row of cells containing these field names, Lotus 1-2-3 will use all rows it requires directly below them to copy the records that meet the search criteria.

You can also restrict the output range to a cell range including a specific number of blank rows below the field names as well as each of the field names to be used. If more records match the search criteria in an extract operation than will fit in this limited number of rows, Lotus 1-2-3 will copy as many as it can, then beep, go into ERROR mode, and display the error message "Too many records for Output range." In such a situation, you will have to redefine the extent of the output range and then perform your extract operation a second time.

When you enter the field names to be included in the output range, you can include only the names of those fields you want to be displayed in the extracted report, and you can arrange them in any order you want, even if this does not match their order in the database. The only restriction on setting up field names in the output range is that they must be spelled as they are in the input range (though there may be case differences).

After you enter all the field names you want to use, type **/DQO** and indicate their cell addresses by typing them in or pointing to them. Just as with the input and criterion ranges, the program remembers the output range that you define during a current work session and stores it as part of the saved worksheet file.

Using the Find Option

The /Data Query Find command, which is issued by typing **/DQF**, highlights all records that meet the search criteria entered into the criterion range. Lotus 1-2-3 highlights all fields in the first record that meets the criteria. To see whether other records in the database have been located, you press the ↓ key. You can continue to view all of the matches in this way. When you press ↓ once Lotus 1-2-3 has reached the last matching record, the program beeps to indicate that it has highlighted the last match.

When you perform a find operation with this command, the program enters FIND mode to let you know that the search is currently under way. When in this mode, you can press the ↑ key to return to the previously highlighted record. If you are using Release 2, you can stop and edit a record's contents while in FIND mode. To edit a field entry, use the ← and → keys to move the blinking cursor to it. You can make your editing change by typing new data and pressing the Return key or by using the Edit function key (F2).

If you make an editing change to a field used in the criteria that located the record, you will not be able to return to that record by pressing the ↑ key, because it will no longer match the current search criteria. To exit FIND mode and return to READY mode, press the Return key (if you have just made an editing change to a field entry, you will have to press the Return key twice: once to enter the change and a second time to return to the worksheet).

If you have just finished performing a find operation and you make changes to the search criteria, you can perform another find operation by pressing the Query function key (F7) instead of issuing the command from the menu by typing **/DQF**.

Using the Extract Option

The extract operation copies the contents of the fields in records that match the search criteria in the criterion range below the appropriate field names included in the output range. You cannot issue this command without having first defined an output range in addition to an input and criterion range. After you enter the criteria on which the records are to be extracted, type **/DQE** to have the matching records copied into the output range.

The Extract option is often used to generate reports made up of a subset of the database records based on the criteria specified. Extract is also used to prepare reports that include only specific fields in the database but contain information from all of the records in it. An example of this kind of report is a phone list generated from a personnel database that uses only the name, department, and telephone-number fields out of all the fields in the database but extracts these items of information for every employee listed in the database. To generate such reports, you list only those field names in the output range and leave all criterion input cells in the criterion range blank.

Once a subset of the records has been copied to the output range, you can save these records to a new file by using the /File Xtract command.

In the new file they can be sorted, if need be, and printed according to the print specifications you set up for the file. Although you can also do this while the records are in the output range of the main database worksheet, creating a new file for the records often makes these procedures easier to perform, especially if the database is very large.

If the last query operation you performed was an extract operation, you can perform another by changing the criteria in the criterion range and then pressing the Query function key (F7). Lotus 1-2-3 will clear the output range of any data placed there during the last extract operation before copying all records that meet the new criteria. For this reason, if you want to save the results of a previous query operation before performing further extract operations, you must either move the data in the output range to a new location in the worksheet, save it in a new file, or define a new output range in order to prevent the data from being overwritten by the next extraction.

USING THE UNIQUE OPTION

The /Data Query Unique command works like the Extract command except that it copies only unique records that meet the specified criteria to the output range. As when using the /Data Query Extract command, you must have an output range defined in the worksheet prior to using the /Data Query Unique command.

Because duplicate records are eliminated, you can use this command to purge a database of any identical records you may have added by mistake. To do this, you specify no criteria in the criterion range, so that all records will be used, and then use the Unique option instead of the Extract option. Any identical records will not be copied to the output range. The records copied there can then be saved in a new file or copied over the input range of the same worksheet.

For two records to qualify as duplicates, all entries in each of their fields must be the same. For instance, if you have two customer records in the database with the same company name and address but with different contact names, these records would not be considered duplicates; both would be copied into the output range if they met the specified criteria.

Note, however, that this technique may not be feasible if your database is very large and the amount of memory in your computer is limited to the conventional RAM. Database operations are extremely memory intensive, and it is not uncommon to receive memory-full error messages when attempting such operations. If such is the case when you use no criteria in the criterion range, you will have to modify the technique by specifying criteria that extract smaller groups of records to the output range.

The /Data Query Unique command can also be used to view the unique entries in a particular field of the database. For example, if you wanted to know how many different job titles were represented in your database, you could use this command to find out. In this case, you would restrict the output range to include only the Position field name, clear the criterion range of all criteria, and issue the /Data Query Unique command. Each job title used in this field of the database would be represented in the output range only once, regardless of how many or few times it is entered into individual records.

Using the Delete Option

The /Data Query Delete command is used to delete records in the database that match the search criteria set up in the criterion range at the time the command is issued. After typing **/DQD**, you are presented with two additional options, Cancel or Delete. To have Lotus 1-2-3 go ahead and delete all matching records, you must then type **D**. If you wish to abort the Delete command, especially if you realize at that point that you have not yet saved a copy of the current database, type **C**.

Using the Delete command allows you to purge the database of unneeded records without having to use the more cumbersome /Range Erase command (which leaves a blank row in the database that must be eliminated) or the more all-inclusive /Worksheet Delete Row command. The /Data Query Delete command works much like the /Worksheet Delete Row command, except that it affects only the part of the row within the input range. It also provides the advantage of being able to delete many records of a type in one operation, regardless of where they are located in the database.

Because the Delete command is so powerful, you must be careful that the criteria you have specified are correct, or you could delete many records that are still required. As a precaution against this, always make sure that you have a current copy of the entire database on file before using the /Data Query Delete command.

Using the Reset Option

The Reset option clears the currently defined input, criterion, and output ranges. This allows you to redefine each of the ranges by using the pointing method without having to unanchor the cell pointer and then move it to new areas of the spreadsheet as you redefine new input, criterion, and output ranges.

This option is also used in macros that automatically create specific reports from a database. In such cases it is used to clear the ranges before it redefines them. In this way, you are assured that all new records that have been added since the report was last run will be included in the search set up in the criterion range. (If the input range were not redefined each time the report was generated, only those records in the database at the time it was last defined would be included.) For an example of this use for the Reset command, refer to Figure 21.5 in the Macros section that follows.

To use the Reset option, you simply type **R**. All three ranges will be cleared immediately. If you save the worksheet immediately after using this command, none of these ranges will be defined when you retrieve the worksheet.

Using the Quit Option

The Quit command puts the program directly into READY mode. It can be used to abort an extract operation quickly without requiring you to press the Esc key repeatedly or use the Break key combination (Ctrl-Scroll Lock). It also allows you to return to the worksheet, where you can define new criteria to be used in further find, extract, or delete operations. If you wish to repeat the operation you last performed using the /Data Query command menu, you can press the Query function key (F7).

To use the Quit option and return immediately to READY mode, you merely type **q** from the /Data Query command menu.

EXAMPLES

Figures 21.3 and 21.4 illustrate the use of the /Data Query Find and Extract commands, respectively. During a find operation, records meeting the search criteria are individually highlighted in the database. To see the next record, if any, that qualifies, you press the ↓ key. Lotus 1-2-3 signals that it has highlighted the last record that meets your criteria by beeping when you press ↓.

When using the Extract option as illustrated in Figure 21.4, the program copies all field entries called for in the output range (by listing their field names) from all records that meet the search criteria. In this example, only six of the eight fields are used in the output range. As you can see, the order of the extracted data does not follow that used in the database. The only requirement when setting up the fields to be used in the output range is that the field names listed there consist of the same characters that were used in the database itself.

MACROS

Some of the most effective data query macros are those that automatically process and prepare a routine report. They work by defining the input, criterion, and output ranges, then enter the standard criteria and perform the extract or unique operations, sort the report data in preferred order, and, finally, print the report.

Figure 21.5 contains such a macro that automatically prepares a report from a sample personnel database listing each employee, the employee's department, position, supervisor's name, and date hired. The report is sorted by department as the primary key and position as the secondary key.

```
A8: [W12] '561-34-5644                                                    FIND

        A          B          C       D    E         F          G          H
 4 Number      L:Name     F:Name     Sex Dept   Position   Super      Salary
 5 360-22-0978 Holland    Katherine  F   Acctg  Clerk      Newman      19,000
 6 230-45-9512 Jones      Daniel     M   Acctg  Bookkeeper Newman      27,500
 7 458-56-8723 Newman     Paul       M   Acctg  Accountant Pauli       55,000
 8 561-34-5644 Jones      Alexander  M   Acctg  Secretary  Newman      25,000
 9 567-43-2366 Langly     Sandra     F   Pers   Secretary  McKnight    24,000
10 345-14-7245 McKnight   George     M   Pers   Manager    Dorian      50,000
11 705-34-2378 Smith      Mary       F   Pers   Clerk      McKnight    18,750
12 465-25-8751 Mead       Peter      M   Sales  Acct Exec  Smithson    35,000
13 598-52-7054 Durran     George     M   Sales  Acct Exec  Smithson    30,000
14 124-15-7602 Baker      Thomas     M   Sales  Acct Exec  Smithson    32,500
15 865-12-4102 McMead     Andrea     F   Sales  Acct Exec  Smithson    38,000
16 466-52-7035 Smith      Mary       F   Admin  President              135,000
        N          O          P       Q    R         S          T          U
 4 Number      L:Name     F:Name     Sex Dept   Position   Super      Salary
 5                                   M          Secretary
 6
 7
 8
 9
```

FIGURE 21.3: Using the /Data Query Find command to locate a record to be edited. The criteria for locating the records in the database are set to Sex = M AND Position = Secretary. As you can see in this figure, after issuing the /Data Query Find command, Lotus 1-2-3 highlights the first record that contains both these field entries, that of Alexander Jones in row 8. In Release 2, editing changes to specific fields in this record can be made while the program is FIND mode. To make editing changes in Release 1A, you have to mark the location of this qualifying record, exit FIND mode, and then move the cell pointer to the record.

For this macro to work, three cell ranges have already been defined and given range names. The input range corresponds to the original /Data Query input range created at the same time as the macro itself. It is used only to locate the beginning of the database, so it is not updated by the macro itself. Instead, the macro creates a new range name, Data, that ensures that all new database records are included in the report.

The criterion and output ranges named and saved with the file do not vary from report to report. The criterion range contains no qualifying criterion because all of the records in the database are to be represented in the final personnel report. The output range contains the field names representing the six fields to be used in the report (see Figure 21.6). As long as each report requires only these items of information, there is no need for the macro to update this range.

Once the macro is activated by pressing Alt-Q, the cell pointer is located at the beginning of the range named Input, which corresponds

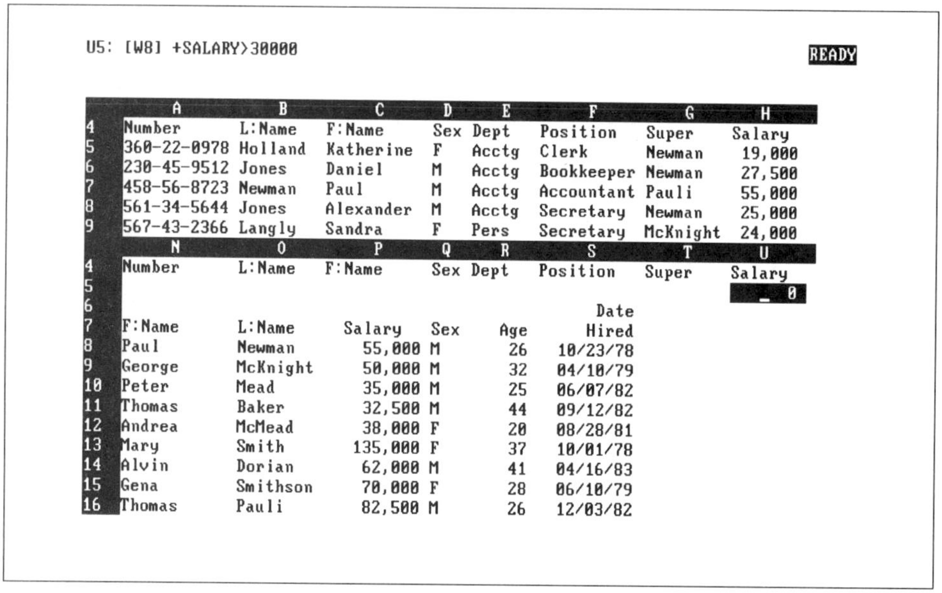

FIGURE 21.4: Using the /Data Query Extract command to create a subset of records where the Salary entry is greater than $30,000. To extract just these records into the output range (defined as N7..S7), the criterion formula shown in the Control Panel was used. Because the cell containing the first entry (H5) was given the range name of the cell above it, the formula was entered as +Salary>30000 in the criterion range. As this is not true for the entry made there, the formula returns 0 in cell U5. After the /Data Query Extract command is issued, the program copies all the field entries in which this condition is true into the output range, listed by field name. Notice that the columnwise order of the field names in this range determines the arrangement of the copied data, not the columnwise order in the database itself.

the beginning of the database. All /Data Query settings are cleared with the /DQRQ command on the next line. Notice that the final Q for the Quit option is included there so that the database can be defined and given the range name Data by using the pointing method.

After defining the range named Data, the /Data Query input, criterion, and output ranges are defined and the Extract command is used. After leaving the /Data Query command menu (using the Quit command), the cell pointer is moved to the beginning of the range named Output with the {GOTO}Output~ command.

This range contains the field names that are not to be used as the column headings for the printed report. Accordingly, the cell pointer is moved down a row and a new row is inserted by the {DOWN}/WIR~ statement. The macro then enters the new uppercase headings above each

```
NAME   MACRO                                      DESCRIPTION
\q     {GOTO}Input~                               Goto 1st field in database in input range
       /DQRQ                                      Reset all data query settings
       /RNCDatabase~{END}{DOWN}{END}{RIGHT}~      Assign range name Data
       /DQIDatabase~CCriterion~OOutput~EQ         Set input, criterion, and output ranges
       {GOTO}Output~                              Goto range named Output
       {DOWN}/WIR~                                Move down, insert new row
       DEPARTMENT{RIGHT}POSITION{RIGHT}           Enter new report headings
       FIRST NAME{RIGHT}LAST NAME{RIGHT}          for each field in new row
       SUPERVISOR{RIGHT}DATE HIRED~
       {BRANCH Sort}                              Goto Sort subroutine

Sort   /RNCReport~{END}{LEFT}{END}{DOWN}~         Name range Report
       /DSRQ{DOWN}/DSD.{END}{LEFT}{END}{DOWN}~    Reset sort, define data range
       P{END}{LEFT}~A~S{LEFT 4}~A~G               Select primary and secondary keys
       {BRANCH Print}                             Goto Print subroutine

Print  /PPCARReport~AGPQ                          Print report
       {UP}/WDR~/RNDDatabase~/RNDReport~          Delete new row and range names
       {HOME}{QUIT}                               Goto cell A1, return to READY mode
```

FIGURE 21.5: The text of a macro that automatically generates, sorts, and prints a routine report from the personnel database. In this macro, the input, criterion, and output ranges have already been established and give the range names Input, Criterion, and Output. The macro uses the location of the input range to locate the beginning of the database. However, because new records could have been added since the last report was run, the macro clears the ranges previously used by the /Data Query commands and then defines the current extent of the database, giving it the range name Data. After that, the macro establishes the necessary /Data Query ranges and performs the extract operation. Because the field names in the output range are not descriptive enough for the final report, a new row is added and new headings are entered there before sorting the database by department and position. After sorting, the report is printed, the new row containing the modified column headings and the two range names created by the macro are deleted, the cell pointer returns to A1, and the program returns to READY mode. This kind of macro can be used with any database that requires periodic reports in which the search criteria and fields used do not vary.

field in this newly created row. When it has finished, the macro branches to the Sort routine.

Before sorting the extracted data, a range named Report is defined to include the new column headings and the data beneath them. This range is used by the Print routine to locate all of the cells to be printed. After defining this range, all previously set /Data Sort parameters are cleared with the /DSRQ command. Next, the cell pointer is moved down a row before the macro defines the /Data Sort data range. This is necessary to prevent sorting the new column headings along with the extracted data.

Because the cell pointer was positioned in the last field (column) of the extracted report data when the macro entered the new report headings, the data range is defined by using the {END}{LEFT}{END}{DOWN} pointing movements. Remember that a period must be entered to anchor the data range because this command does not automatically anchor itself to the current cell.

The primary and secondary keys, the Department and Position fields, must also be defined by pointing to the left, given the current location of the cell pointer. The Department field is the first extracted field, so it is

DEPARTMENT	POSITION	FIRST NAME	LAST NAME	SUPERVISOR	DATE HIRED
Acctg	Accountant	Paul	Newman	Pauli	10/23/78
Acctg	Bookkeeper	Daniel	Jones	Newman	02/06/84
Acctg	Clerk	Katherine	Holland	Newman	04/03/80
Acctg	Secretary	Alexander	Jones	Newman	03/15/83
Admin	President	Mary	Smith		10/01/78
Admin	VP Admin	Alvin	Dorian	Smith	04/16/83
Admin	VP Finance	Thomas	Pauli	Smith	12/03/82
Admin	VP Sales	Gena	Smithson	Smith	06/10/79
Mktg	Artist	Sean	Clarkson	Baker	07/23/85
Mktg	Assistant	Mark	Lawson	Baker	10/15/84
Mktg	Director	Colin	Baker	Smithson	07/18/83
Mktg	Secretary	Sylvia	Jones	Baker	05/01/79
Pers	Clerk	Mary	Smith	McKnight	11/01/85
Pers	Manager	George	McKnight	Dorian	04/10/79
Pers	Secretary	Sandra	Langly	McKnight	01/20/85
Sales	Acct Exec	Thomas	Baker	Smithson	09/12/82
Sales	Acct Exec	Andrea	McMead	Smithson	08/28/81
Sales	Acct Exec	George	Durran	Smithson	02/20/84
Sales	Acct Exec	Peter	Mead	Smithson	06/07/82

FIGURE 21.6: The text of the report produced by the Alt-Q macro illustrated in Figure 21.5. This report uses only some of the fields in the database, although the data included here represents all of the records in the database (because no matching criterion was specified in the criterion range). Because space limitations prevented the field names from being sufficiently descriptive, they were not used as the column headings in this report. The macro substituted the uppercase headings before sorting and printing the report.

located by the {END}{LEFT} command. The Position field is immediately to its right, or four cells to the left of the current pointer location—thus the {LEFT 4} command. (If you are using Release 1A, change this to {END}{LEFT}{RIGHT}, because you cannot include the number of times the pointer is to be moved in a certain direction.) After defining the key, the macro performs the sort operation and branches to the Print subroutine.

The first command line there clears all previously used print settings, gives the range name Report as the print range, and prints the report. After paging down, the macro quits the Print menu. The cell pointer is then moved up to the inserted row containing the report column headings entered there, and this row is deleted. This ensures that no blank row is left in the database or in any other work areas in this part of the worksheet. (Of course, the macro commands themselves must be located so that this command does not introduce a blank row between the lines of the macro itself.) The two ranges, Data and Report, created by the macro are then deleted, because the macro must redefine them each time it is used (presumably, they increase each time a report is run). Finally, the cell pointer is moved to cell A1, and the macro terminates.

This example macro could, of course, be embellished in many ways, especially in the Print routine. You could, for example, insert commands to add a report header and footer, add a new row of underscore characters to separate the column headings from the data, or include embedded print commands to print the headings in boldface type. It is also advisable to add {WINDOWSOFF}{PANELOFF} and {WINDOWSON}{PANELON} statements to such fully automated macros, because the operator is not prompted for any input during processing.

Another useful macro that can be created for the /Data Query commands is one that automatically sets up a criterion range and prompts the user to enter the criteria prior to using either the Find, Extract, Unique, or Delete options. You can find examples of such macros in books dedicated to Lotus 1-2-3 macros, such as Alan Simpson's *1-2-3 Macro Library.*

SEE ALSO

/File Xtract
/Data Sort

SUMMARY

This chapter has covered the data query operations required to maintain and use data records stored in a Lotus 1-2-3 database. To use these commands, of course, you must have already created such a database. If you need information on how this is done, refer back to Chapter 20, "Creating a Lotus 1-2-3 Database." There, you will also find information on the /Data Sort command, which is often used in conjunction with the /Data Query Extract command explained in this chapter.

Because the /Data Query commands are frequently used with the database statistical functions, you may wish to refer to the information on their use in Chapter 16, "Database Statistical Functions."

If you need to perform other types of statistical analysis on the data in the database, you may want to explore the use of the /Data Distribution command, which allows you to compute frequency distributions on any of your data. This command is discussed in the next chapter, "Data Distribution, Matrix, and Regression Commands."

Finally, reference was made in the sections on using the /Data Query Extract command to using the /File Xtract command for creating a new file containing only those records copied to the output range. If you need specific information on how to use this command, you will find it back in Chapter 9, "File Operations."

CHAPTER 22

Data Distribution, Matrix, and Regression Commands

Data Distribution, Matrix, and Regression Commands

This chapter examines three /Data menu commands: Distribution, Matrix, and Regression. Of these three, only /Data Distribution is available if you are using Release 1A. The other two, /Data Matrix and /Data Regression, are newly added to Release 2. These provide more sophisticated statistical analysis techniques whose functions are discussed at length in the sections that follow.

You will find discussions concerning the use of each of these data analysis commands preceding their reference entries. Both the discussions and the reference entries are presented in the order in which these commands appear on the /Data menu: Distribution, Matrix, and Regression.

Frequency Distribution Analysis

Lotus 1-2-3 provides an easy way to classify worksheet data into categories by using its /Data Distribution command. This command enables you to quickly generate a table that shows the frequency of specific values occurring in a particular range of values.

Frequency distribution of this kind has many practical uses, chief of which is to tally the values that fall into certain intervals in order to graph the distribution. When working with large sets of data, this provides a practical way for condensing and organizing the data so that it can be presented in one of the available graphic formats.

Frequency distribution tables are created whenever tallies are made that classify numerical data by the number of times a value falls within a particular category. As a result, the /Data Distribution command has wide-ranging applications in many business areas. It is especially useful when analyzing market potential or market share for a company's products or services, because it can allow you to categorize and analyze data obtained from research records or surveys.

For an example of how the /Data Distribution command works and how it can be applied, refer to Figure 22.1. This figure shows the results of a survey that asked each of the respondents to indicate, among other things, their annual income and whether their company rented, leased, or owned the building in which they were quartered. The income indicated as well as Y or N responses to the rent, lease, or own question were then entered in a worksheet.

Once all of the responses were recorded in the worksheet, the /Data Distribution command was used to determine how many of the companies responding to the survey fell into various income brackets. Four income brackets were established: up to $100,000, between $100,000 and $500,000 (i.e., greater than 100,000 and less than or equal to 500,000), between $500,000 and $1,000,000 (i.e., greater than 500,000 and less than or equal to 1,000,000), and over $1,000,000.

After the brackets were established, they were entered into the worksheet as shown in this figure. Notice that only three actual intervals are entered,

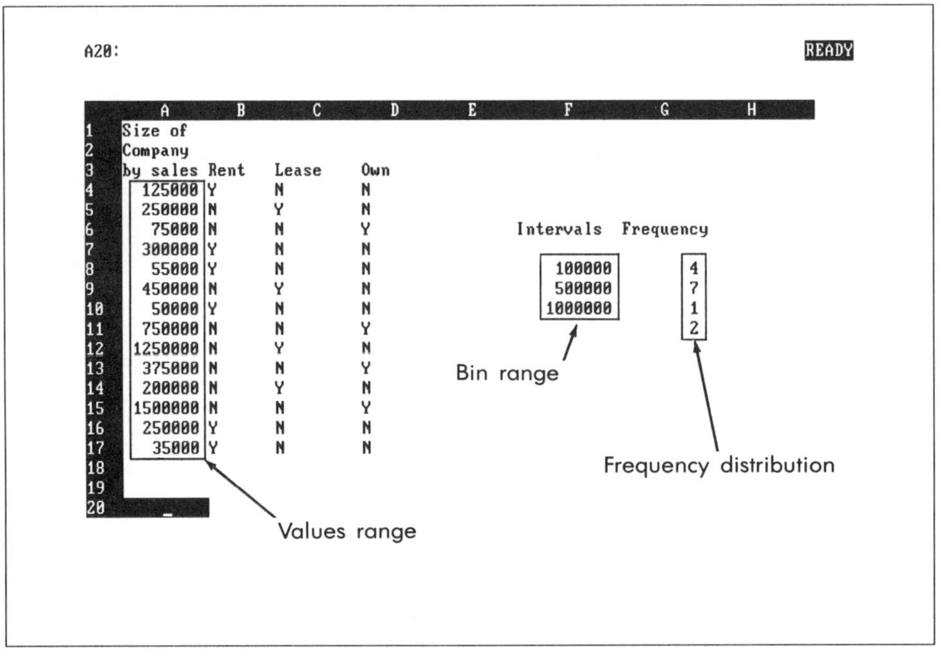

FIGURE 22.1: Using the /Data Distribution command to determine the number of companies in the survey that fall into each income bracket. In this figure, there are four income brackets—sales up to $100,000, sales between $100,000 and $500,000, sales between $500,000 and $1,000,000, and sales over $1,000,000—indicated by the three interval values in the bin range. After specifying the values range (A4..A17) and this bin range, the program produced the frequency distribution values in the cell range G8..G11. These statistics show that four companies in the data sample fall into the first range, that of sales of $100,000 or less, seven fall into the second range, one falls in the third, and two are in the last range of more than $1,000,000 in sales.

and each is established by entering its upward limit. There is no need to enter an interval for the fourth bracket, those who earn over $1,000,000. When using the /Data Distribution command, the number of all values in the data range that exceed the last interval is always automatically entered below the frequency for the last interval in the bin range (this is why the value 2 was entered in cell G11 in this figure).

When you use the /Data Distribution command, you are required to provide two pieces of information: the cell range that contains all of the values for which the frequency distribution is be prepared (the values range), and the cell range that contains the intervals by which they are tallied. This range is referred to as the bin range by Lotus 1-2-3.

In the example in Figure 22.1, the values range is the cell range A4..A17, and the bin range is the cell range F8..F10. (When you specify the bin range, you must list the values in ascending order—the lowest limit first, followed by the second lowest, the next higher, and so forth.) Regardless of where the cell pointer is located in the worksheet when the /Data Distribution command is used, the frequency values calculated by the command are always entered in the column immediately to the right of the bin range, starting with the same row occupied by the first cell of the bin range. In this particular example, the cell pointer was located in cell F4 when the /Data Distribution command was issued, giving the two cell ranges indicated in the figure. As you can see, Lotus 1-2-3 placed the frequency values in the cell range G8..G11.

Because the program always locates the results of the /Data Distribution command next to the bin range, you must be sure that these cells are empty before you use the command. Any existing cell entries located in these cells will be overwritten by the calculated frequency values.

When setting up the bin range in a worksheet, you may find it convenient to use the /Data Fill command. With it, you can generate any type of sequenced numbers as long as they are incremented in equal intervals. For example, the /Data Fill command could have been used to generate the bin range for the frequency distribution table created in this example. The fill range would have been entered as F8..F10, the start value as 100000, the step value as 500000, and the stop value as 1000000.

The /Data Fill command cannot, however, be used to generate bin ranges that do not have equal intervals throughout. For instance, if the intervals for the bin range were set as 100000, 250000, 750000, and 1000000, you would have to enter the bin range values manually.

Cross Tabulations

The Lotus 1-2-3 /Data Distribution command is not really set up to perform cross tabulations between the frequency values obtained with it. Nevertheless, by performing a few extra manipulations, it is possible to cross tabulate such data. Because this procedure is often required to analyze survey data fully, we will illustrate how it might be done with the survey responses used in the previous example.

In this survey, the respondents were asked to state not only the annual income of their companies but also whether they rented, leased, or owned their facilities. The responses given to these questions were then entered in the worksheet using Y or N to indicate the response. (The method of entering a 1 to indicate a positive response or 0 to indicate a negative response could also be used.)

If your goal were to create a frequency distribution table from this data showing how many companies in each of the income brackets (under $100,000, $100,000–500,000, $500,000–1,000,000, and over $1,000,000) rent, lease, or own their buildings, you could not use the /Data Distribution command as was done previously to determine how many of the surveyed companies fell into each income bracket. You must first relate the responses in each of these categories to income entered for each company before you can use the /Data Distribution command to determine the frequency distribution.

Figure 22.2 shows how this can be done. First, three new columns are added to the worksheet with the headings Rent, Lease, and Own in columns E, F, and G. Then an @IF formula is constructed in cell E4 that copies the sales figure given in cell A4 only if the response to the rent question is positive. The formula entered in this cell is

@IF(B4 = "Y",$A4,"")

This formula is then copied to the cell range E5..G17, which results in the figures shown in these columns in Figure 22.2. Notice that each income figure is copied into the appropriate column according to the response given for each of these questions. When the response is N, nothing is entered into the cell.

This formula would not achieve the desired goal if it inserted a zero when the response was N, because the zero value would skew the frequency distribution (all zero values would be counted in the first interval up to $100,000). Therefore, this approach cannot be used in Release 1A, in which the @IF function cannot contain string values such as "". It would not work if the formula were

@IF(B4 = "Y",$A4,0)

However, it would work if the yes/no responses were coded by 0s and 1s and the formula were

@IF(B4 = 1,$A4,"")

The values returned to these cells by the @IF formulas are now correlated with the income figure given so that they can be used as the values ranges to create three separate frequency distribution tables with the /Data Distribution command. Figure 22.3 shows these results. To produce these tables, it was necessary to copy the bin range values from column Q to columns S and U. If the bin range Q11..Q13 were used for each, the frequency distribution returned in cells R11 to R14 would be overwritten each time the command was used.

A20: READY

	A	B	C	D	E	F	G	H
1	Size of							
2	Company							
3	by sales	Rent	Lease	Own	Rent	Lease	Own	
4	125000	Y	N	N	125000			
5	250000	N	Y	N		250000		
6	75000	N	N	Y			75000	
7	300000	Y	N	N	300000			
8	55000	Y	N	N	55000			
9	450000	N	Y	N		450000		
10	50000	Y	N	N	50000			
11	750000	N	N	Y			750000	
12	1250000	N	Y	N		1250000		
13	375000	N	N	Y			375000	
14	200000	N	Y	N		200000		
15	1500000	N	N	Y			1500000	
16	250000	Y	N	N	250000			
17	35000	Y	N	N	35000			
18								
19								
20								

FIGURE 22.2: In order to obtain statistics from the survey data in this worksheet on how many companies in each income bracket rent, lease, or own their facilities, you must use formulas to cross tabulate the data. In this example, an @IF formula is used to return the annual sales figures for each company only if the response to the Rent, Lease, or Own question is Y. The frequency distribution of these figures can be determined by using the /Data Distribution command as shown in Figure 22.3.

Each time the /Data Distribution command was used, the values range and bin range had to be changed. To produce the Rent figures, the values range was given as E4..E7 and the bin range as Q11..Q13. To produce the Lease figures, these ranges were changed to F4..F17 and S11..S13, and, finally, to produce the Own figures, they were changed to G4..G17 and U11..U13.

The top of Figure 22.3 shows the final table produced using these frequency distributions. The values calculated by the /Data Distribution command were copied to the appropriate columns of this table, and a new column, Total, was added that uses the @SUM function to return the totals for each income bracket. These figures correspond to the frequency distribution of these incomes originally obtained with the /Data Distribution command (to check this, refer back to Figure 21.1).

```
V14: 1                                                          READY

        Q          R          S          T          U          V          W          X
1   Company Size in $        Rent      Lease       Own      Total
2
3        up to $100,00         3          0          1          4
4     $100,001-500,000         3          3          1          7
5   $500,001-1,000,000         0          0          1          1
6       over $1,000,000        0          1          1          2
7
8
9
10  Rent       Freq       Lease      Freq       Own        Freq
11    100000          3    100000          0    100000          1
12    500000          3    500000          3    500000          1
13   1000000          0   1000000          0   1000000          1
14                    0                    1                    1
15
16
17
18
19
20
```

FIGURE 22.3: This figure shows the frequency distribution statistics obtained for each group of cross-tabulated data created in Figure 22.2. The /Data Distribution command was used three times to obtain the statistics in the ranges R11..R14, T11..T14, and V11..V14. Each of these frequency distributions uses the same bin range values but was generated using the appropriate values range generated by cross tabulating annual sales with the responses to the Rent, Lease, and Own questions (see Figure 22.2). These values were then copied into the table above them.

Predictive Statistical Analysis

Release 2 of Lotus 1-2-3 provides two powerful statistical commands available from the /Data menu—Matrix and Regression—that can be applied to many types of business problems involving probabilities, linear regression, and correlation. The /Data Matrix command allows you to multiply or invert a matrix, while the /Data Regression command allows you to determine the correlation between a dependent variable and up to 16 independent variables in a worksheet.

Matrix multiplication and inversion make it possible to quickly solve problems that call for matrix algebra. These are tedious processes when their calculations must be performed by hand. Matrix multiplication is often used to solve problems involving probabilities. It represents a specialized method for multiplying the contents of one matrix by another.

Matrix inversion is most often used to solve simultaneous equations. It has fewer direct business uses than matrix multiplication, although it can be applied effectively to some business problems, such as those involving the allocation of resources. It involves finding the reciprocal or inverse of values in a matrix, providing a method analogous to division (division in matrix algebra is not defined). It can be performed only on a square matrix.

The best way to understand how to use these commands is to see how they can be applied to typical business problems. We will start with matrix multiplication before proceeding to matrix inversion, which often includes matrix multiplication as one of its final steps.

Using Matrix Multiplication to Determine Maximum Profits

It is common in business to have to determine the maximum daily profit that can be expected from a particular business venture. As an example, consider a florist who must determine how many dozen of each kind of flower to stock daily in order to maximize his profit. Flowers are a very transient commodity. If they are left unsold, they are worthless and must be replaced by new stock.

To help determine how many of a particular type of flower to order each day, the florist must make estimates of how many can be sold daily. These estimates are expressed as probability factors, with 0 representing the certainty of selling none of the product and 1 representing the certainty of selling all of the product. Values between these two represent less certain outcomes expressed as probability percentages.

To see how the /Data Matrix Multiply command can help the florist determine how many of a certain type of flower to order to maximize daily profits, consider the following scenario. Assume that the flowers in question are roses that must be ordered a day in advance. Roses cost $5 a dozen, and they are sold for $15 a dozen.

The florist must choose between ordering 12, 13, or 14 dozen a day. To figure out which quantity is most economical, he must determine the profit he can expect from ordering each quantity. Assume that he has determined the probability factor for each as follows:

Daily Sales (dozens)	Probability of Daily Sales
12	0.65
13	0.40
14	0.15

To determine how many dozen roses to order daily to maximize his daily profit, the florist must first construct a simple profit table and then multiply it by the probability factor associated with each quantity. Figure 22.4 shows this table below the probability factor for selling all of the roses ordered.

The formula for determining the possible profit for the first quantity of 12 dozen in cell C10 is

Profit = total revenue − total cost

which translates into

($B10*15)−(C$8*5)

This formula is then copied to the cell range C10..E12 to fill out the table. Unfortunately, the calculated values in column C for sales of 13 and 14 dozen (cells C11 and C12) and that in column D for 14 dozen (cell D12) will not be correct. You cannot sell 13 or 14 dozen if all you have to sell is 12 dozen that day. Therefore, $120 is the maximum profit that you realize when the number of dozen ordered is 12. The same problem arises in the next column where you have maximized your profit at $130 when you have sold all 13 dozen ordered that day.

The profit table must be adjusted to reflect these realities before using the /Data Matrix Multiply command to determine the profit that can be expected when ordering various quantities, given the probability of selling all the roses ordered on that day.

The profit table is a square matrix made up of three rows by three columns. Following the conventions of matrix algebra, the matrix is described first by the number of rows and then by the number of columns. Because this matrix is square, it is described as a 3 × 3 matrix. However, if the table contained only two rows of data in three columns, it would be described as a 2 × 3 matrix; the number of rows precedes the number of columns.

To multiply matrices with the /Data Matrix command, the number of columns in the first matrix must equal the number of rows in the second.

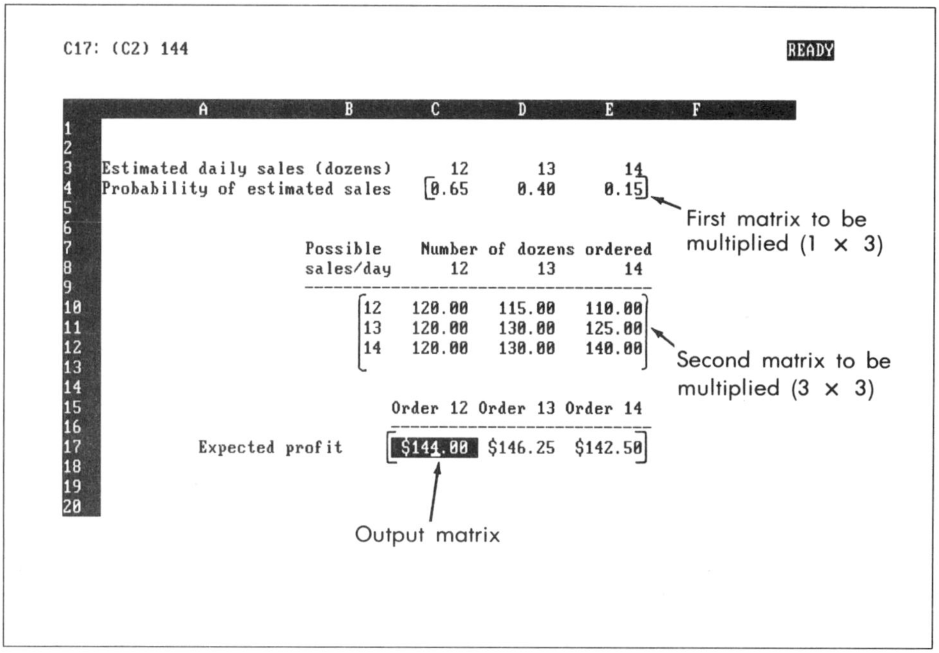

FIGURE 22.4: Using the /Data Matrix Multiply command to determine the number of dozen roses a florist should order daily to maximize his profits. To determine this, the probability factors expressing the degree of certainty of selling all of the roses ordered on a given day are entered for each quantity (C4..E4). Then a maximum profit table is constructed to determine the maximum profits that can be made if all of the roses ordered are sold (B7..E12). When these values are multiplied by the probability factors, expected profits for ordering each quantity can be determined. To do this, the /Data Matrix Multiply command is used, giving the cell range C4..E4 as the first matrix (a 1 × 3 matrix), the cell range C10..E12 as the second matrix (a 3 × 3 matrix), and cell C17 as the output range. As you can see from the results of this matrix multiplication, maximum daily profits can be expected when ordering 13 dozen roses each day.

This is why the probability of estimated sales is laid out horizontally in row 4 in the three columns C, D, and E (one row and three columns produce a 1 × 3 matrix). If you try to multiply two matrices in which the number of columns in the first does not match the number of rows in the second, you will receive the error message "Matrices incompatible for multiplication". If the probability factors had been laid out in a 3 × 1 matrix, you would have had to reverse the order of multiplication, so that the profit table matrix was multiplied by the probability factor matrix (a 3 × 3 matrix by a 3 × 1 matrix).

To use the /Data Matrix Multiply command, you must supply three ranges: the cell range of the first matrix, which is C4..E4 in this example; the cell range of the second, which is C10..E12; and the cell range of the output matrix. When defining the cell range of the output matrix, only the first cell of the range needs to be given, so it is defined as cell C17 in this example.

Figure 22.4 shows the results calculated by Lotus 1-2-3 for this example problem in cells C17 to E17. As you can see from the figure, the expected profit is maximized when ordering 13 dozen roses daily. The table below illustrates how Lotus 1-2-3 arrived at the figures you see there:

Ordering 12 Dozen	**Ordering 13 Dozen**	**Ordering 14 Dozen**
120 × 0.65 = 78	115 × 0.65 = 74.75	110 × 0.65 = 71.5
120 × 0.40 = 48	130 × 0.40 = 52	125 × 0.40 = 50
120 × 0.15 = 18	130 × 0.15 = 19.5	140 × 0.15 = 21
144	146.25	142.5

As you can see, the program multiplies every value in the profit table by the probability factor associated with the number of dozen ordered and then sums these values. These values are the products of multiplying the two matrices together.

Inverting a Matrix

Inverting a matrix involves much more complex computations than the tedious but straightforward steps required to multiply one matrix by another. Having the /Data Matrix Invert command can save you a great deal of time when your work requires this specialized process.

Many people are often puzzled as to the uses for inverting a matrix and are curious as to whether it could be used in any of their work. To illustrate some of its potential applications, we will begin by describing one of its most common applications, that of solving simultaneous linear equations, before moving on to more business-oriented examples.

SOLVING SIMULTANEOUS LINEAR EQUATIONS

Figure 22.5 presents three first-degree equations including three unknowns, x, y, and z. By organizing their coefficients into a 3 × 3 matrix and then using the /Data Matrix Invert command, it is possible to solve for these unknowns quickly. Once the coefficients of each are entered in the first, or input matrix, in the cell range C8..E10, the /Data Matrix Invert command is used to calculate their inverted values in the cell range C13..E15, the output matrix.

Then the values returned in this 3 × 3 inverted matrix are multiplied by those in the cell range G8..G10, a 1 × 3 matrix. The output range for

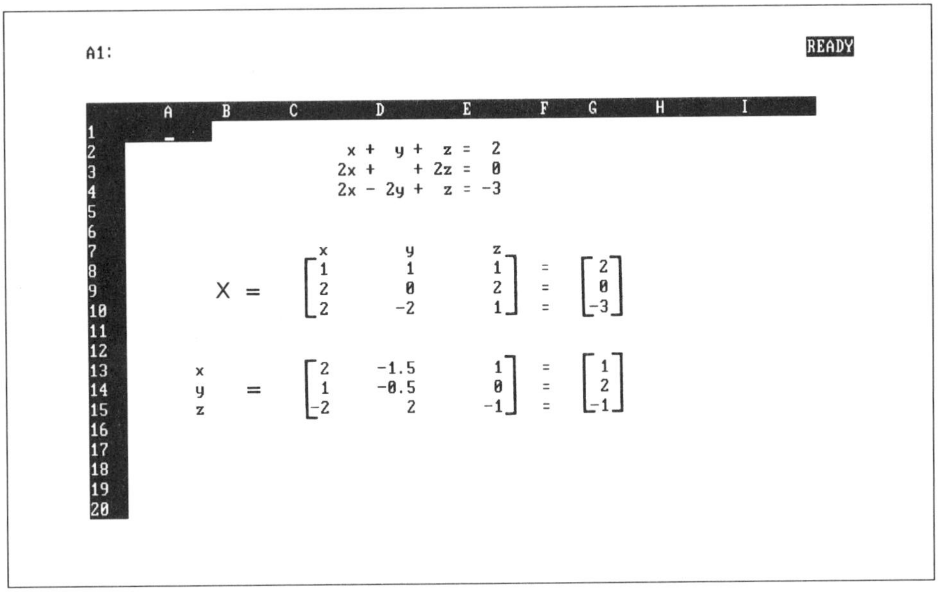

FIGURE 22.5: Using the /Data Matrix Invert command to solve simultaneous equations. To find the values for three unknowns, x, y, and z, matrix algebra is used. The first step is to express these equations in matrix form. To do this, the coefficients of each unknown are copied to the matrix in the cell range C8..E10 and their equivalents in the cell range G8..G10. Then the /Data Matrix Invert command is used to invert the coefficient matrix. The results of this inversion were entered into the cell range C13..E15. This matrix is then multiplied by the matrix in G8..G10 to obtain the solutions for x, y, and z in the cell range G13..G15 (the output range).

this matrix multiplication is given as G13, which results in the values in the range G13..G15, which are the solutions for x, y, and z in this particular example.

Resource Allocation Problems

To illustrate potential uses for inverting matrices in business, we will look at a couple of simple resource allocation problems. Figure 22.6 shows an example in which a service station owner must determine the number of mechanics and service station attendants required to staff a new full-service gas station.

During a typical eight-hour shift, the owner estimates that a mechanic should spend 3/4 of the time repairing automobiles and 1/4 of the time

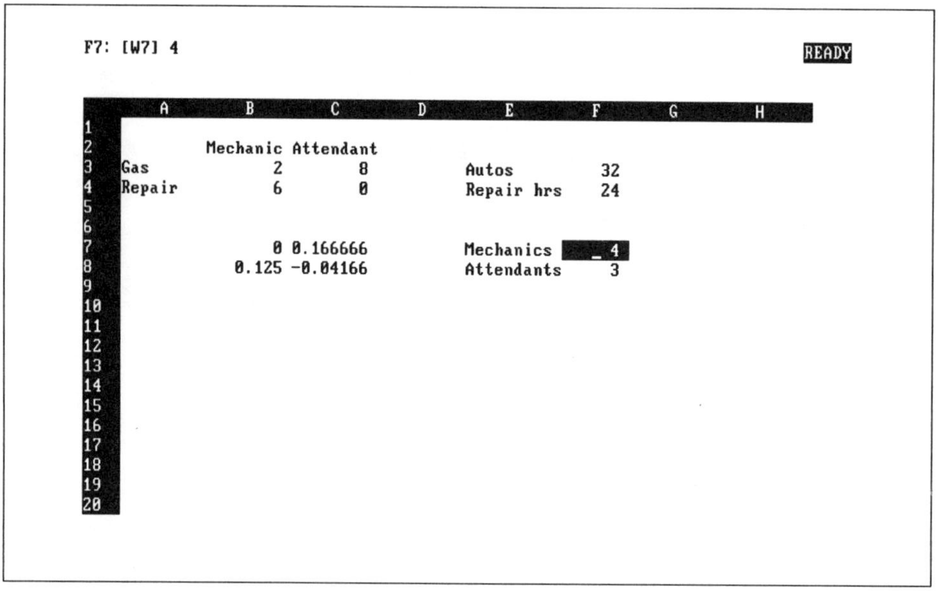

FIGURE 22.6: Using the /Data Matrix commands to estimate personnel requirements for a new filling station. To determine the number of mechanics and service attendants required to staff this station, a matrix containing the number of worker-hours to be devoted to each activity during an eight-hour shift is entered in the cell range F3..F4. Then the matrix containing the number of hours each type of worker should devote to each activity is entered in the cell range B3..C4. This matrix is inverted and its output is shown in the cell range B7..C8. To find out how many of each type of worker to hire, this matrix is multiplied by the one containing the worker-hours devoted to each activity (F3..F4). The output range is given as F7. As you can see, four mechanics and three attendants are required to meet these requirements.

pumping gas, while an attendant will spend all of his or her time pumping gas and attending to motorists' needs. The owner estimates that on the average it requires 1/10 of a worker-hour to service each automobile that comes in for gas. Further, he estimates that the new station will need to sell gas to 320 autos a day and have at least 24 worker-hours of the mechanics' time available for repair work.

To figure out how many attendants and mechanics to hire, a square matrix is set up in the cell range B3..C4 containing the time allotted for mechanics and attendants to pump gas and do repairs. A second 2 × 1 matrix containing the time for pumping gas and doing repairs is set up in the cell range F3..F4. Because 320 autos are anticipated and it is estimated that 1/10 of a worker-hour is required to service each, the first value in the matrix is entered as 320/10 or 32 worker-hours. The second value is 24 worker-hours required to do repairs during a single day's business.

The /Data Matrix Invert command is used to invert the first matrix. Its output range is B7..C8. This output matrix is then multiplied by the worker-hour matrix and its output range is given as cell F7. The output matrix tells the owner that under these conditions, he will need to hire four mechanics and three service station attendants.

The /Data Matrix commands can also be used in similar problems to estimate the number of goods that can be produced given a certain number of personnel and the time it takes to finish a particular manufactured product. Figure 22.7 illustrates an example of this type of situation. The /Data Matrix commands are used to determine how many cabinets and desks a fine furniture manufacturer can turn out during a single eight-hour work shift.

Time estimates show that it takes approximately 22 1/2 worker-hours on the shop floor and 28 1/4 worker-hours in the finishing area to produce a single desk. Studies also show that it takes 14 1/8 worker-hours on the shop floor and 37 5/8 worker-hours in the finishing area to produce a single cabinet. There are 12 people working on the shop floor, and 20 are employed in the finishing area. In order to determine how many desks and cabinets can be produced in a day, matrices similar to the service station problem are set up, and the /Data Matrix commands are used in the same manner.

In Figure 22.7, you can see that the first matrix in the cell range B3..C4 contains the worker-hour estimates for each product in each area. The second 1 × 2 matrix in the cell range E3..E4 contains the number of workers in the shop and finishing areas. The first matrix is then inverted using the /Data Matrix Invert command. The output of this operation is shown in the cell range B7..C8. This matrix is then multiplied by the second matrix containing the number of employees. Its output range is given as cell E7.

The figures returned by this calculation represent the number of pieces that can be finished in a single hour, so these results must be multiplied by eight to determine the quantities of each completed during one shift. These results are shown in cells G7 and G8. The results were rounded by using the @ROUND function. Under ideal circumstances, the workers should be able to produce three finished desks and two cabinets each day.

Performing Simple Linear Regression Analysis

The principal objective in simple linear regression analysis is to establish a quantitative relationship between two variables that can be expressed in the form of an equation. The variable that is predicted is referred to as the

```
F7: @ROUND(+E7*8,1)                                              READY

      A          B         C         D        E          F        G         H
1
2               Desk     Cabinet            Employees
3  Shop          22.5     14.125                 12
4  Finishing    28.25     37.625                 20
5
6
7            0.084072 -0.03156           0.377627          3 Desks
8            -0.06312 0.050275           0.248027          2 Cabinets
9
10
11
12
13
14
15
16
17
18
19
20
```

FIGURE 22.7: Using the /Data Matrix commands to determine maximum piece production given worker-hour and personnel estimates. In this figure, the worker-hours required in each area (shop and finishing) for each product are entered in the matrix in the cell range B3..C4. This matrix is inverted with the /Data Matrix Invert command and its output is shown in the cell range B7..C8. The values in this matrix are then multiplied by those in the matrix in the cell range E3..E4. This matrix contains the number of employees working in each area. The output range for this matrix is cell E7. The values returned represent the number of each product that can be produced in an hour. To find out how many products can be produced during an eight-hour shift, both of these values must be multiplied by eight. These numbers, 3 and 2, are shown in cells F7 and F8.

dependent variable and is designated by Y. The variable that is known is referred to as the *independent variable* and is designated by X.

To be able to establish a relationship between these two variables, you need to obtain sample data. The following table shows sample data comparing the volume of units produced to their total cost by five firms involved in the same industry. The independent variable, X, is the volume of units produced. The dependent (or predicted) variable is the total cost of producing each unit.

Y **Total Cost (thousands)**	**X** **Units Produced**
9	2
12	4
15	6
14	5
10	3

Representing the Variables Graphically

Once the sample data is obtained, the relationship between the dependent and independent variables can be determined either graphically or mathematically. Figure 22.8 shows these values represented graphically in an XY graph or scatter plot. The values for the independent variable (X) are plotted along the horizontal or X axis of the graph, while the values for the dependent variable (Y) are plotted along the vertical or Y axis of the graph.

As soon as all of the sample data is plotted, a straight line that best represents the relationship between the data is drawn. This line is labeled the estimated regression line in Figure 22.8. Using it, you can predict the value of Y for any value of X. For instance, if X is known to be 6.5 units, you can predict that the cost will be close to 17 (thousand dollars). This relationship is represented by the dotted lines in the figure.

However, there is a major drawback to what otherwise may appear to be a straightforward method—namely, how can you be sure that the estimated regression line represents the best fit between the two variables? Many times, the graphic relationship between the dependent and independent variables in the scatter plot cannot be approximated so easily. It may require estimating a regression line that is really a segment of a curve.

THE LEAST-SQUARES METHOD

To resolve such ambiguities, Lotus 1-2-3 uses the least-squares method to determine the estimated regression line that best fits the data variables in the sample. A linear relationship between two variables can be represented by the mathematical formula whose general equation is

$$Y = a + bX$$

where a is the Y intercept and b is the slope of the line. The Y intercept value tells you where the Y axis of the graph is intersected when the X-axis value is zero. The slope of the line determines the angle of the estimated regression line. The b value tells you the amount the line rises on the Y axis for each unit that it extends on the X axis of the graph. These constants, a and b, are the *regression coefficients* of the equation. This equation is referred to as the *linear regression equation.*

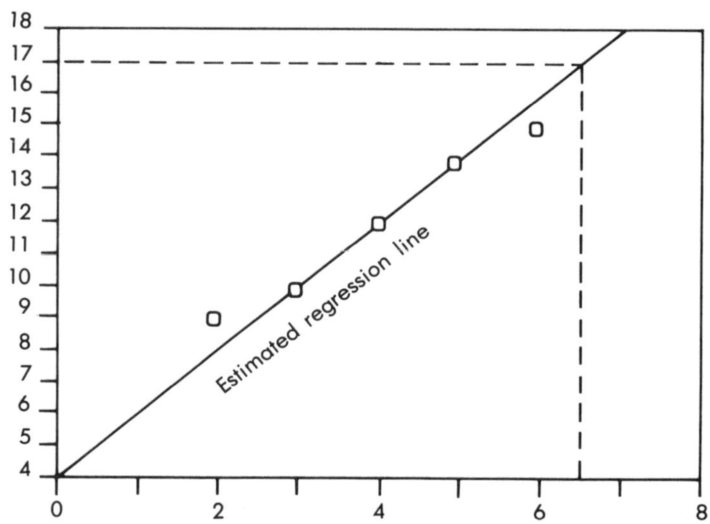

FIGURE 22.8: A scatter-plot diagram can be used to correlate sample data obtained for the independent variable, representing units produced, and the dependent variable, representing total cost. Each independent variable value is plotted on the X axis of the graph against the paired dependent variable value plotted on the Y axis. Then a straight line, labeled the *estimated regression line,* is drawn to represent a possible relationship between the X and Y variables. The one shown here connects three of the five data points. The dotted vertical and horizontal lines show how other values can be predicted by using this estimated regression line. From it, we would expect that it will cost approximately $17,000 to produce 6.5 units.

The first calculation made using the least-squares method can be summarized in the following table:

Y	X	Y^2	X^2	XY
9	2	81	4	18
12	4	144	16	48
15	6	225	36	90
14	5	196	25	70
10	3	100	9	30
$\Sigma Y = 60$	$\Sigma X = 20$	$\Sigma Y^2 = 746$	$\Sigma X^2 = 90$	$\Sigma XY = 256$

Once these values are calculated, they can be substituted into two simultaneous equations whose general forms are

$$\Sigma Y = na + b\Sigma X$$
$$\Sigma XY = a\Sigma X + b\Sigma X^2$$

where n is the number of paired observations. Substituting the values calculated from the previous table, the simultaneous equations for this example become

$$60 = 5a + 20b$$
$$256 = 20a + 90b$$

When these two equations are solved, the regression equation becomes

$$Y = 5.6 + 1.6X$$

Figure 22.9 shows that these are indeed the values for a and b that are returned by Lotus 1-2-3 using the /Data Regression command with the sample data shown there in columns A and B. The value of 5.6 for a is called the *constant* and that of 1.6 for b the *X coefficient(s).*

The program automatically generated the regression output table, including both the headings and calculated values shown in the cell range D5..G13. To obtain these values, it was necessary to define the cell range B5..B9 as the /Data Regression X-Range, the cell range A5..A9 as the /Data Regression Y-Range, and the cell D5 as the output range.

The Standard Error of the Estimate The regression equation $Y = 5.6 + 1.6X$ can be drawn on an XY graph where the sample data is plotted. Figure 22.10 shows this line and its relationship to our XY data points. A distinction is made between the observed values plotted by using the sample data values and the estimated values determined by the regression line. The average difference between the observed and estimated values is used to determine a statistic referred to as the *standard error of the estimate* (Lotus 1-2-3 refers to this as the Std Err of Y Est in the regression output table).

This statistic gives you an indication of how well the regression equation describes the relationship between the two variables. If the standard error of the estimate is small, the regression equation can be taken as a good description of the relationship.

This value is always measured in the same units as the Y variable. In this example, it is measured in thousands of dollars. In Figure 22.9 you can see that this value has been calculated as 0.365148, which in thousands of dollars equals about $365.15. If our dependent variable data were measured in hundreds of thousands of dollars instead of thousands, this standard error of estimate would be 100 times as large. Because this statistic varies according to the units Y is measured in, it is not taken as a good measure of the degree of a relationship.

```
D5:                                                                READY

        A          B       C       D        E        F        G
 1
 2       Y          X
 3 Total Cost   Units
 4 (thousands) Produced
 5           9        2           _ Regression Output:
 6          12        4           Constant                        5.6
 7          15        6           Std Err of Y Est           0.365148
 8          14        5           R Squared                  0.984615
 9          10        3           No. of Observations               5
10                                Degrees of Freedom                3
11
12                                X Coefficient(s)        1.6
13                                Std Err of Coef.   0.115470
14
15
16
17
18
19
20
```

FIGURE 22.9: Using the /Data Regression command to determine the strength of the relationship between total cost and the number of units produced. The paired sample data for the dependent variable (marked Y) and the independent variable (marked X) is entered into the cell ranges A5..A9 and B5..B9, respectively. When using the /Data Regression command, these two ranges were defined as the Y-Range and X-Range, respectively, and cell D5 was given as the output range. Lotus 1-2-3 then generated the regression output table shown in this figure. Figure 22.10 illustrates the scatter diagram that can be drawn from these calculated statistics.

The Coefficient of Determination What is used instead is a more abstract statistic that is unaffected by the change in units in which Y is measured. This is referred to as the *coefficient of determination,* or r^2 (Lotus 1-2-3 names this value R Squared in the regression output table). This statistic is calculated by dividing the total variation by the explained variation. The total variation represents the sum of the squared deviations between the actual values and the mean value of the sample, while the explained variation represents the sum of the squared deviations between the estimated values and the mean value of the sample.

The coefficient of determination expresses the proportion of the variation in Y related to the variation of X. In this example, Lotus 1-2-3 has calculated an r^2 value of 0.984615, which means that you can be approximately 98.5 percent certain that the cost of producing a particular product is related to the number of units produced.

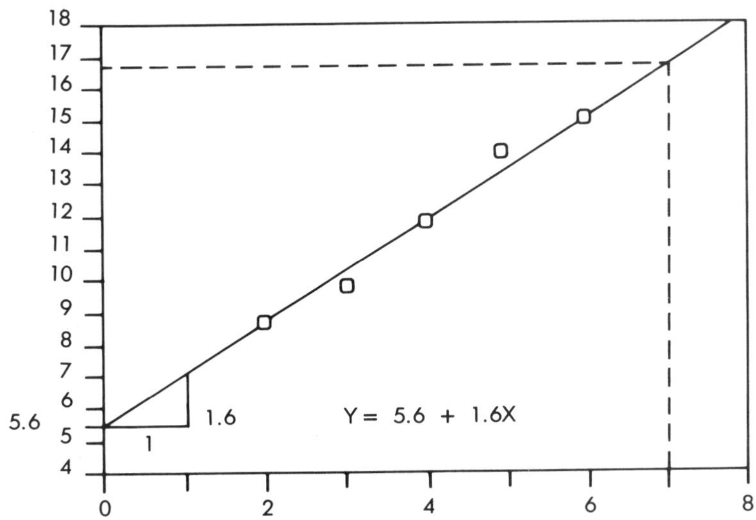

FIGURE 22.10: This figure shows an XY graph of the regression output calculated by Lotus 1-2-3 in the form of the equation Y = 5.6 + 1.6X. The constant, 5.6, is the Y intercept, the point at which the regression line intersects the Y axis when X is zero. The slope of the line is calculated by the coefficient of X, 1.6. For every single unit that X increases, Y increases 1.6 units. The regression line determined by these coordinates could be used to determine new values for Y, depending on the X value chosen. In this figure, the dotted lines show that it would take $17,000 to produce 7 units.

If the actual and estimated values of Y are identical for every observation in the sample, there is an exact relationship between X and Y. In such a case there is a one-to-one correspondence between total variation and explained variation, and the coefficient of determination will equal 1, in which case the data points will fall exactly on the line.

Therefore, $r^2 = 1$ is the highest coefficient of determination possible; it describes an exact correspondence between the dependent and independent variables. However, if the two variables are unrelated, this coefficient will equal zero ($r^2 = 0$). The higher the R-squared value returned by Lotus 1-2-3, the stronger the relationship between the dependent and independent variables.

Note: Because the coefficient of determination is a squared value, theoretically there should be no circumstances under which r^2 is returned as a negative value. Nevertheless, it is possible under peculiar circumstances that the algorithm used by Lotus 1-2-3's /Data Regression command will cause it to return a negative R-squared value. For instance, this could happen if you are using purely random variables and you set the Intercept option to zero. Any regression output with a negative R-squared value should be completely disregarded.

The Significance of Correlation Although the coefficient of determination is a leading indicator of the strength of the relationship between the dependent and independent variables, it is by no means the only one. The *coefficient of correlation,* represented by r (the square root of the coefficient of determination) is also used. Although in statistics r^2 is generally considered more reliable because it can never be a negative value (see the Note above), r is useful when you are trying to explore the broader question of how the correlation between the sample values relates to the general population.

When using linear regression, even after ascertaining that there is a strong relationship between the variables in the sample data, a larger question remains to be considered. That is, how is the sample data used in the regression analysis related to that in the general or true population? This question can be formulated using r by asking how the coefficient of correlation of the sample data is related to the coefficient of correlation for the population.

Regardless of how much data is in the sample, we cannot say that its correlation coefficient is significant, because we do not know the population correlation coefficient. Indeed, it is generally conceded that we can never know this statistic. Nevertheless, by using the r value and the degrees of freedom, it is possible to infer whether this coefficient of correlation is significant within specified risk groups.

Lotus 1-2-3 returns the degrees of freedom as part of its regression output table. It determines this value by subtracting 2 from the number of observations in the sample data (n – 2). In our example in Figure 22.9, the degrees of freedom is calculated as 3. With an R-squared value of 0.958695, we can determine r is 0.992277 (by using the @SQRT function).

To determine whether this coefficient of correlation is significant, it is necessary to consult a table (such tables are included in many statistics textbooks) that lists critical levels of r for the various degrees of freedom. Even with such few observations, such a high correlation coefficient exceeds the critical level for 3 degrees of freedom, so we can reasonably reject the null hypothesis (the hypothesis that there is no correlation between our variables in the general population) with a risk factor of no more than 1 percent. This further reassures us that this strong relationship between our variables is representative of those in the population at large.

APPLYING THE REGRESSION OUTPUT TO BUSINESS PREDICTIONS

Having established a strong relationship between the cost of producing a particular product and the number of units produced in the sample problem, you can use the statistics obtained by the regression analysis to predict estimated costs of producing various quantities of a product. For instance, assume that you wanted to use these statistics to estimate the cost of producing 10 units.

Using the values calculated in the regression output table (Figure 22.9), this is quite easy to do. As 10 represents a new X variable, the result on Y can be found by plugging it into the linear regression equation

$$Y = a + bX$$

The program has determined the value of a to be 5.6 and the value of b to be 1.6. Substituting these values into the equation, we obtain the following value for Y:

$$Y = 5.6 + 1.6(10)$$
$$Y = 21.6$$

or $21,600.

Once you have determined that there is a strong relationship between the two variables by using the /Data Regression command, you can easily use the output to set up a table in the spreadsheet that estimates any number of Y (dependent variable) values based on new X (independent variable) values.

Performing Multiple Linear Regression Analysis

The Lotus 1-2-3 /Data Regression command is not limited to linear regression analysis involving just one independent variable. In fact, you can perform multiple regression analysis with up to 16 independent variables. To demonstrate, we will examine another example, this time relating the amount of sales made for several different products to their prices and to the amounts spent on advertising each one.

Figure 22.11 shows the sample data. In this case, the amount of sales of each product in (listed in column C) represents the dependent or Y variable. The retail prices are the first independent or X_1 variable listed in

```
B11: [W8]                                                         READY

     A       B         C         D        E         F        G
1
2                    Sales              Advertising
3         Product (thousands)Price     (thousands)
4            A          850      12          50
5            B          910      11           0
6            C         1000      10         100
7            D         1020       9          50
8            E         1080       9         120
9            F         1200       9         200
10
11                 Regression Output:
12        Constant                     1465.286
13        Std Err of Y Est             32.95967
14        R Squared                    0.957564
15        No. of Observations                 6
16        Degrees of Freedom                  3
17
18        X Coefficient(s)    -53.8488 0.960032
19        Std Err of Coef.    14.73395 0.267155
20
```

FIGURE 22.11: This figure shows the regression output statistics produced when doing multiple linear regression with the /Data Regression command. In this case, the amount of sales for each product is the Y or dependent variable, and the price and amount spent on advertising are two X or independent variables. Because two X variables are used, the program returns two X Coefficient and Std Err of Coef. statistics. Those in column D relate to the independent variable of price and those in column E relate to the independent variable of advertising.

column D. In addition, the amounts spent advertising each product are the second independent or X_2 variable listed in column E.

The regression output table is shown to the right of the sample data. Notice that the statistics returned here are the same as when doing simple linear regression except for the X Coefficient and Std Err of Coef. statistics. The program returns two values, the first for the price variables and the second for the advertising variables.

Figure 22.12 shows a table using the statistics obtained from this regression output table to predict expected sales for a new product (G) depending on various potential retail prices and advertising budgets. To determine the estimated sales, the constant obtained from the regression output is added to the price times the first X coefficient plus the advertising amount times the second X coefficient. These estimated sales figures can then be used with figures obtained by doing breakeven analysis to determine the best pricing/advertising strategy for the new product.

```
L4: [W11] +$CONSTANT+I4*$COEFX+J4*$COEFZ                               READY

      H         I          J          K         L           M        N       O
1          Product G
2                      Advertising         Estimated Sales
3          Price       (thousands)         (thousands)
4                   8           50         1082.49657
5                   8           25         1058.49575
6                   8            0         1034.49493
7                   7           50         1136.34546
8                   7           25         1112.34464
9                   7            0         1088.34382
10
11
12
13
14
15
16
17
18
19
20
```

FIGURE 22.12: Using the multiple regression output statistics to predict sales for a new product. The table shown in this figure uses the statistics obtained for the multiple linear regression in Figure 22.11 to predict sales for a new product G. The general equation for finding new Y values is Y = constant + X_1(X_1 coefficient) + X_2(X_2 coefficient). The various prices in column I represent X_1 values, while the various advertising budgets in column J represent X_2 values.

THE /DATA DISTRIBUTION, MATRIX, AND REGRESSION COMMANDS

The /Data Distribution, Matrix, and Regression commands allow you to perform sophisticated statistical analysis techniques. Only /Data Distribution is available if you are using Release 1A. Reference entries for each of these commands follow.

/Data Distribution

This command provides an easy way to perform frequency distribution on a range of values in the worksheet. Before applying it to a range of data, you must set up a bin range that contains the maximum values for each interval.

MENUS

/Data
Distribution

KEYBOARD ENTRY

/DD
Enter Values range:
Enter Bin range:

FUNCTION

This command determines the frequency within which values in a range fall within specified intervals or "bins." It is most useful when you need to perform statistical analysis on research data, especially data obtained by surveys, because it can tally such results quickly. The /Data Distribution command is often used to summarize large data samples into a more condensed presentation that can be graphed using Lotus 1-2-3's graphics capabilities.

USAGE

When using the /Data Distribution command, you must specify two cell ranges: a values range containing all of the data to be classified and a bin range containing the maximum value for each classification. The values cell range should not contain any blank columns or rows within it. Such empty areas will affect the results obtained when using this command. Also, make sure that the values range does not contain any NA or ERR values within it. These are counted in the frequency statistics, as are empty cells.

When setting up a bin range in the worksheet, you must arrange your interval values in ascending order. If necessary, use the /Data Sort command to arrange them in order. If all the intervals in the range are equal, you can use the /Data Fill command to create the values.

The cells in the column immediately to the right of the bin range must be blank. This is the area Lotus 1-2-3 automatically uses as the output range into which the frequency distribution results are placed. This output range must also contain one empty cell at the bottom, in which the number of values exceeding the last interval value in the bin range is placed. Any data that exists in this range before using the /Data Distribution command will be overwritten by the data it generates.

To use the /Data Distribution command, type **/DR** and specify the cell range to be used as the values range. This can be done by entering the cell addresses or range name or by pointing to them. After you specify the extent of this range, press the Return key and then specify the bin range in a similar manner. As soon as you press the Return key to enter this range, the program will calculate the frequency distribution and return the results in the output range next to it. You do not have to specify the location of this range or position the cell pointer in any particular cell location when using this command.

EXAMPLES

For an example of how to use the /Data Distribution command to perform simple frequency distribution, refer back to Figure 22.1 in the section entitled "Frequency Distribution Analysis." For ideas on how to apply this command to cross tabulations of data, refer to Figures 22.2 and 22.3 in the section "Cross Tabulations."

/Data Matrix (Release 2 Only)

This command provides you with the means to perform matrix multiplication and inversion. To multiply two matrices, the number of columns in the first matrix must equal the number of rows in the second. To invert a matrix, the input matrix must be square.

MENUS

/Data
Matrix
Invert   Multiply

KEYBOARD ENTRY

/DMI
Range to invert:
Output Range:

/DMM
First range to multiply:
Second range to multiply:
Output Range:

FUNCTION

The /Data Matrix commands greatly simplify matrix algebra by providing you with the tools for either multiplying two matrices or inverting a matrix. Matrix algebra is most often applied to solving problems in the scientific and engineering fields. It is also commonly applied to economic modeling, especially in the area of input-output economics. Though less often applied to financial analysis and planning, it can be used to solve certain kinds of problems such as those involving resource allocation. (For examples of business applications, refer to the earlier discussion sections on using matrix multiplication and inverting a matrix.)

USAGE

To use the /Data Matrix commands effectively, you must understand how a matrix is organized and described. The spreadsheet is a natural environment for creating a matrix, for a matrix is nothing more than a rectangular array whose entries are laid out in rows and columns. However, unlike a regular cell range, which is described first by its columns and then by its rows, a matrix is always described first by the number of the rows and then by the number of columns within it.

A matrix's size is referred to as the number of rows it occupies by the number of columns. Therefore, a matrix that takes up four rows and three columns in a spreadsheet is called a 4 × 3 matrix. This is important, because matrix multiplication can take place only when the number of columns in the first matrix is equal to the number of rows in the second. For example, a 4 × 3 matrix (three columns) can be multiplied only by a second matrix that has three rows. If you tried to multiply a 4 × 3 matrix with one that was 2 × 3, Lotus 1-2-3 would go into ERROR mode and display the error message "Matrices incompatible for multiplication".

A square matrix is one in which the numbers of rows and columns it occupies are equal. You can invert only a square matrix. For example, if you tried to use the /Data Matrix Invert command on a 4 × 3 matrix, Lotus 1-2-3 would go into ERROR mode and display the error message "Not a square matrix". Obviously, two square matrices of equal size can always be successfully multiplied, because the number of rows in the first is necessarily equal to the number of columns in the second. A 90 × 90 matrix is the largest possible matrix that can be used with either /Data Matrix command.

Although the /Data Matrix commands do not include options for adding or subtracting matrices, this can be accomplished by entering one matrix in one worksheet file and the second in another file. Then you can use the /File Combine Add or Subtract commands to perform the required operation. If the matrices you wish to add together or subtract from one another are located in the same worksheet, use the /File Xtract command to copy one of them into a separate file before using the appropriate /File Combine command.

Procedure for Multiplying Matrices

After you type **/DMM** to issue the /Data Matrix Multiply command, you are prompted to specify three cell ranges in this order:

- First range to multiply, which is the location of the cells containing the first matrix

- Second range to multiply, which is the location of the cells containing the second matrix
- Output range, which marks the cell range where the program will enter the product of this operation

When specifying the output range, you do not need to indicate any more than the first cell of this range, although you should make sure that this cell is at the beginning of a sufficiently large blank range so that no existing data will be overwritten.

When specifying these three ranges, you can type in their cell addresses or range name or use the pointing method to indicate them. Lotus 1-2-3 always remembers the cell ranges used in a previously issued /Data Matrix Multiply command; it includes no Reset option, however. To multiply different matrices in the same worksheet, you must press the Esc key each time to designate the three new cell ranges when using cell pointing.

Procedure for Inverting a Matrix

After typing **/DMI** to issue the /Data Matrix Invert command, you are first prompted to indicate the cell range that contains the matrix to be inverted. You can indicate it by typing the addresses of the cells, entering a range name, or pointing out the range with the cell pointer. When you press the Return key, you will be prompted to indicate the output cell range where Lotus 1-2-3 will locate the inverted values. You can indicate the first cell of this range either by cell address or by pointing to it. Then press the Return key to have the program calculate the inverted values.

If the cell range indicated as containing the matrix to be inverted does not have an equal number of rows and columns, you will receive an error message indicating that it is not square. Lotus 1-2-3 cannot invert a matrix that is not square or that is any larger than 90 × 90.

Certain matrices are singular, meaning that their values cannot be inverted. If the values in your matrix cannot be inverted, the program will let you know by displaying the error message "Cannot invert matrix".

EXAMPLES

For examples of how to use the /Data Matrix Multiply command, refer to Figure 22.4 in the section entitled "Using Matrix Multiplication to Determine Maximum Profits." For examples of using the /Data Matrix Invert command, refer to Figures 22.5, 22.6, and 22.7 in the section "Inverting a Matrix."

/Data Regression (Release 2 Only)

This command provides you with the means to perform simple or multiple linear regression analysis. Simple linear regression involves correlating sample data for the dependent variable with data for a single independent variable. Multiple linear regression involves correlating sample data for the dependent variable with data for up to 16 independent variables.

MENUS

/Data
Regression

X-Range	Y-Range	Output-Range	Intercept	Reset	Go	Quit
			Compute			
			Zero			

KEYBOARD ENTRY

/DR

FUNCTION

The /Data Regression commands are used to obtain statistics that indicate the strength of the relationship between two or more sets of data in a worksheet. If a strong relationship, or high correlation, is shown to exist between them, these statistics can be used to predict future trends and returns. These commands can be applied to a wide range of financial problems of any type in which you have sample data and wish to examine how one sample might be related to another. The commands are also particularly useful in marketing activities where research or survey data must be correlated.

To perform regression analysis, you must have at least two paired sets of data, one representing the dependent variable and another representing the independent variable. The dependent variable contains the predicted values and is designated as the Y variable. The independent variable contains the known values and is designated as the X variable. If the data in these variables is shown to be strongly related, a change in the X variable will predict the amount of change in the Y variable.

The relationship between variables can be shown graphically by plotting them in a scatter diagram (just like a Lotus 1-2-3 XY graph). A straight line (thus the name linear regression) can be drawn in such a diagram describing the best fit between the observed data in the sample containing the actual values of the dependent and independent variables. This is called the *estimated regression line;* it can be expressed mathematically by the equation

$$Y = a + bX$$

where a is the Y intercept, or the point on the Y (vertical) axis where the regression line intersects when the value on the X (horizontal) axis is zero, and b describes the slope of the line. This b value, referred to as the *coefficient of X,* tells you how much the line rises or falls on the Y axis for an increase of one unit along the X axis.

Whenever you use the /Data Regression command, Lotus 1-2-3 returns a standard set of specific regression statistics in an area of the worksheet indicated as the output range. These statistics are listed as follows:

- Constant, which is the value of the Y intercept of the estimated regression line
- Std Err of Y Est, which is the average of the differences between the estimated values on the regression line and the observed values of the dependent variable
- R Squared, the coefficient of determination, which gives you an idea of the strength of the relationship between the variables
- No. of Observations, which is the number of values in the sample data
- Degrees of Freedom, which is 2 less than the number of observations $(N-2)$
- X Coefficient(s), which is the slope of the estimated regression line (or lines if multiple regression analysis involving several independent variables has been performed)
- Std Err of Coef., which is the average difference between the X coefficient of the estimated regression line and that of the independent variable.

Of all these statistics, the most important are the constant, R-squared, and X coefficient(s), because they can be used to predict future values and trends if you are satisfied from the results that there is a strong relationship between your dependent and independent variables.

USAGE

To use the /Data Regression command, you must specify three cell ranges: the X range, which contains the data representing the independent variable or variables; the Y range, which contains the data representing the dependent variable; and the output range, where the program places the regression output table.

The output range must be located in an area of the worksheet that contains a sufficiently large area of blank cells to accommodate this table without destroying existing data. Such a table requires nine rows of the spreadsheet and two more columns than the number of columns used to indicate the Y and X ranges. When you indicate this range, you need only indicate the cell address or point to the location of the first cell in it.

When entering your sample data, organize the dependent variable in one column of the worksheet. When using more than one independent variable, you must arrange the values in a contiguous cell range with each column containing the values for each independent variable. The number of rows in each range must be the same, because regression analysis requires the use of paired data variables.

The /Data Regression command options are arranged in a menu much like the one associated with the /Print command. On it, you can define various parameters before using the Go option to have the program perform the regression analysis. However, unlike the /Print command, the /Data Regression command does not include a Quit option to return to READY mode. Instead, you are automatically returned to READY mode as soon as the calculations are complete and Lotus 1-2-3 has created the regression output table in the worksheet.

To use the /Data Regression command, type **/DR**; then type **X** and indicate the cell range containing the independent variable values. You can indicate this cell range by typing in the cell addresses, entering a range name, or pointing to it. Then type **Y** to indicate the cell range containing the dependent variables in a similar manner.

After defining these two ranges, you can type **G** to have the program perform the necessary calculations. If you do, Lotus 1-2-3 will use the Compute default to compute the Y intercept for the estimated regression line. If you wish, you can force it to use zero as the Y intercept point by typing IZ (for Intercept Zero) before using the Go option. To reset the program to the Compute default later, type **IC**.

Lotus 1-2-3 will remember the options defined from the /Data Regression command menu during a work session and will save them in the worksheet file when you next use the /File Save command. If you wish to perform regression analysis using new data variables in the worksheet, you can use the Reset option to clear the previously used variables and settings. Using Reset makes it a lot easier to define new X and Y ranges if you are doing this by pointing.

EXAMPLES

For an example of how to perform simple linear regression analysis with the /Data Regression command, refer to Figure 22.9 in the section "Performing Simple Linear Regression Analysis." For an example of how to do multiple linear regression, refer to Figures 22.11 and 22.12 in the section "Performing Multiple Linear Regression Analysis."

SUMMARY

The /Data Distribution, Matrix, and Regression commands covered in this chapter are generally associated with spreadsheet applications that call for statistical analysis. For more information about the statistical functions included in Lotus 1-2-3, refer to Chapter 12, "Statistical Functions," and Chapter 16, "Database Statistical Functions."

When using the /Data Distribution command, you may find it convenient to use the /Data Fill command to create the data in the bin range. To locate specific information on using this command, refer to the reference section in Chapter 20, "Creating a Lotus 1-2-3 Database." There you will also find information on how to use the /Data Sort command, which is often needed to arrange data in the bin range in ascending order when using the /Data Distribution command, or to do a similar sort with data samples when you want to create an XY graph to accompany the regression analysis obtained from using the /Data Regression command.

When using matrix algebra, you may want to perform matrix addition and subtraction as well as the multiplication and inversion done with the /Data Matrix commands. To perform these operations, you use the /File Combine Add or Subtract commands and may need to use the /File Xtract command as well. To find specific information on how to use these commands, refer to Chapter 9, "File Operations."

When performing linear regression analysis with the /Data Regression commands, you may want to create scatter diagrams to accompany the mathematical calculations performed by the program. To obtain information on how to create XY graphs with Lotus 1-2-3, refer to Chapter 24, "Creating and Using Graphs."

CHAPTER 23

DATA TABLE COMMANDS

DATA TABLE COMMANDS

This chapter examines the uses of Lotus 1-2-3's /Data Table commands. These commands allow you to automate "what-if" analysis in a spreadsheet by creating a table of calculated values based on various input values with which a particular master formula is recalculated. Lotus 1-2-3 supports two types of data tables: a one-input what-if table and a two-input what-if table, referred to in the program as Data Table 1 and Data Table 2, respectively.

The uses of both types of data tables are covered at length in the following discussions. As these commands can be applied to traditional spreadsheet what-if analysis as well as to database statistical analysis, both areas of usage are examined. Following these discussions, you will find a reference entry for the /Data Table command.

OVERVIEW OF LOTUS 1-2-3 DATA TABLES

The data tables that can be created with the program's /Data Table commands utilize four components:

1. A formula in which several input variables are recalculated by the /Data Table command. This is referred to as the master formula.
2. A list that contains all the input variables or new values that are to be substituted into the master formula. The number of input variables used depends on whether you create a one-input (which substitutes one set of new values in one or more master formulas) or a two-input (which substitutes two sets of new values in a single master formula) data table.
3. An input cell into which the program substitutes the values from the input list.
4. An output area into which the program places the results of calculating the master formula with each of the values in the input list.

With the exception of the input cell, all of these components are located within a range of cells given as the table range. The layout of the master formula, input list, and output area varies according to whether you are creating a one- or two-input data table.

Figures 23.1 and 23.2 illustrate the differences in layout between these two types of data tables. In Figure 23.1, notice that when setting up a one-input data table, the first cell of the table range (that in the upper-left corner) is left blank. The master formulas are placed in the cells to its immediate right. The list of input variables is entered below this empty cell, and Lotus 1-2-3 places the results of the calculations below each master formula.

In Figure 23.2 you can see that the master formula is placed in the first cell of the table range when using the /Data Table 2 command. Because a two-input data table uses two different lists of input variables, they are arranged in the rows below and columns to the right of the master formula. The cells in the rows below it in the same column contain the input values that will be substituted in the first input cell. Those in the columns to the

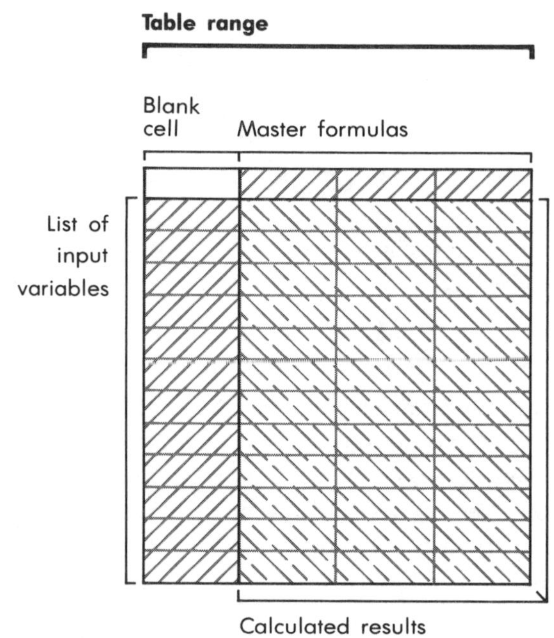

FIGURE 23.1: A diagram of the layout of a one-input data table created with the /Data Table 1 command. The list of input variables to be tested in the master formulas is entered in a single column beneath a single blank cell. The master formulas are listed in the cells to the right of this blank cell. The results calculated by the program when generating the data table are entered into the cells at the intersection of each master formula and input variable. Notice that the table range includes all of these cells. The input cell, which must also be defined to use the /Data Table 1 command, is not shown in this diagram, because it must be located outside the table range.

right of the same row contain input variables for the second input cell. The results of these calculations are then returned at the intersection of the input variables in the two lists.

Benefits of Using Data Tables

Data tables are used primarily to subject parts of a spreadsheet to what-if or sensitivity analysis without requiring that you continually change the input values in the formula or formulas in question. Under normal circumstances, to test new assumptions in a formula, you must alter one of the input values and then recalculate the worksheet. The problem is that

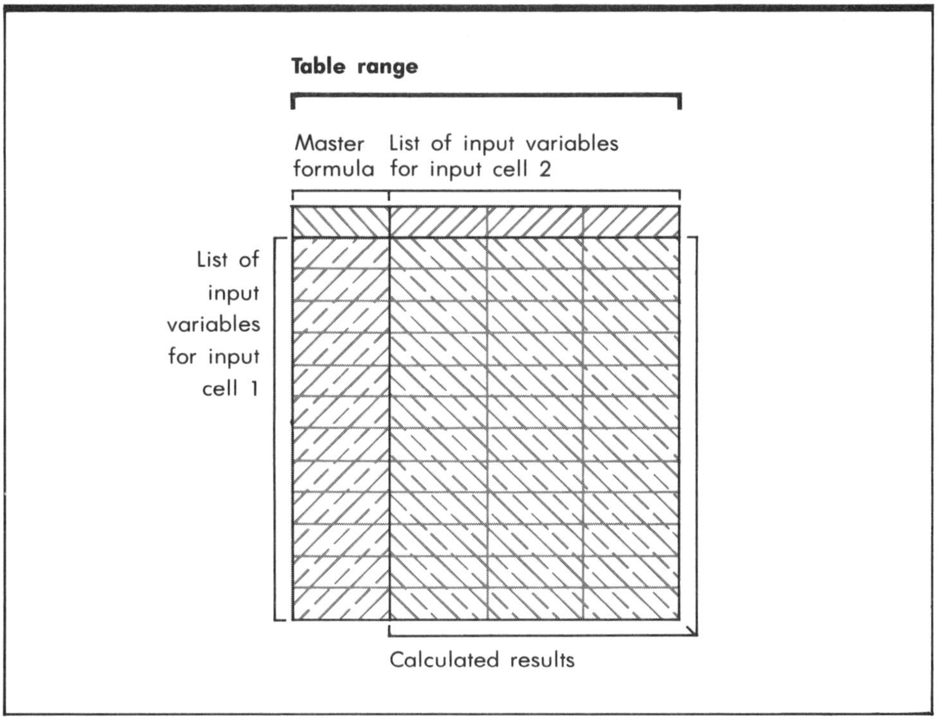

FIGURE 23.2: A diagram of the layout of a two-input data table created with the /Data Table 2 command. In this type of data table, only a single master formula can be subjected to what-if analysis. It must be entered into the first cell of the table range. The list of the first set of input variables is entered in the same column beneath this master formula. The second set of input variables must be located in the same row in the columns to its right. The results calculated from using these pairs of input variables in the formula are entered into the intersecting cells of each pair. The two input cells, Input cell 1 and Input cell 2, required to generate this type of data table are not shown, because they must always be located outside the table range.

the original input value must then be restored or the new results must be saved in a new worksheet file if you wish to keep a record of the original results. Also, when you use this method, you must keep changing the input value and recalculating the formula to subject it to further analysis using other possible values.

By creating a data table, you can keep a record of the effect of testing multiple input values without disturbing the original result or having to update the input value continually and recalculate the formula. This table is saved as part of the same worksheet, which makes it unnecessary to create multiple copies of the worksheet. Also, the /Data Table commands arrange the results in a concise table whose results can be graphed easily.

Because the results in the table are returned as actual values, they are not recalculated when new values are entered or changed elsewhere in the worksheet. If you wish to perform further what-if analysis in the same data table, you need to use a special function key, the Table key (F8), after you enter new input values to update the results in the data table.

Because the data tables created with the /Data Table commands are static and can be recalculated only by using this function key, their presence in the worksheet does not slow down recalculation as you continue to build or refine the worksheet. Also, being stored as values, they use up less memory than would be required if you copied a basic formula and used slightly different input values in each copy.

How the /Data Table Commands Work

Data tables work by taking the values listed in the input range and sequentially plugging them into the master formula. The results are then stored in the results cells in the table range. The existing values (if any) in the input cell or cells are stored before each new result is calculated using each of the values in the input list. After the table has been generated by copying the results, the original values are restored to the input cell or cells. It makes no difference whether this input cell contains a value or is left blank, although it must be a cell address outside those designated as part of the table range.

Because the program recalculates the master formula one time for each of the values in the input list, Lotus 1-2-3 may take some time to generate the complete data table. The method of recalculation does not affect the time it takes to perform all the calculations required in the data table. It makes no difference whether the global recalculation is set to Automatic or Manual unless the values in the input list are themselves calculated. In this case you will want to recalculate the spreadsheet before issuing the appropriate /Data Table command. This ensures that the values substituted in the master formula are current when the data table is generated.

Performing Sensitivity Analysis in a Spreadsheet with Data Tables

The /Data Table commands have applications both in spreadsheets and in databases created with Lotus 1-2-3. To illustrate how one-input and two-input data tables are constructed and used, we will begin by examining their uses in performing sensitivity analysis before going on to database applications that use the database statistical functions. Sensitivity analysis basically means determining the degree to which a value depends on or changes with a change in data—as when a dependent variable changes as its independent variable changes.

Using One-Input Data Tables

A one-input data table created with the /Data Table 1 command performs a one-way sensitivity analysis by calculating new values for the master formula based on changes to only one input variable. However, with a one-input data table you can test the effect of changing these input values on more than one master formula.

To see how this is done, we will look at how this type of data table can be applied to what-if analysis involving a projected income statement. The income statement is shown in Figure 23.3. The values calculated in this five-year projection are based on a particular percentage of annual growth in gross sales. In addition, the cost of goods sold and the total expenses are determined as percentages of these expected gross sales.

The values that were used to produce the results in this income statement projection can be seen in the cell range A23..B30 in Figure 23.4. This figure also contains the one-input data table created to determine the effect that changes in the assumed growth rate would have on the gross sales figure for each year charted in the income statement.

To create this data table, the /Data Fill command was used to input the various growth rate percentages in the cell range A34..A40. As you can see, the rates range from assumptions of 0 percent to 30 percent growth over the sales made in 1987. This is the range of input values that is substituted into the master formulas to determine new gross sales estimates. Although the /Data Fill command was used to create this data, the numerical order of data items does not affect the calculations themselves, only the order in which they appear in the calculated range.

The formulas that determine the sales in the income statement in cells B6 to F6 are brought forward to the first row of the data table, the cell range B33..F33. These are the master formulas that are used to calculate the gross sales for each growth rate in the cell range in column A of the data table. Each of these five cells containing the formulas was given the range name of the year it describes. This means that they could be brought forward by entering the plus sign and the number of the year rather than by referring to its cell address. These formulas were then formatted with

```
B6: +B23*(1+$B$24)                                                READY

            A                 B        C        D        E        F
1   Data 2000 Corporation
2   Five-Year Projected Income Statement
3
4   Year                    1988     1990     1991     1992      1993
5
6   Sales                 414000   496800   596160   715392  858470.4
7   COGS                  269100   322920   387504 465004.8 558005.76
8                         ---------------------------------------------
9   Gross Profit          144900   173880   208656 250387.2 300464.64
10                        =============================================
11  Total Expenses         35190    42228  50673.6 60808.32 72969.984
12                        =============================================
13  Operating Profit      109710   131652 157982.4 189578.8 227494.65
14  Interest Expense       15000    15000    15000    15000     15000
15                        ---------------------------------------------
16  Taxable Profit         94710   116652 142982.4 174578.8 212494.65
17  Income Tax           25571.7 31496.04 38605.24 47136.29 57373.557
18                        ---------------------------------------------
19  Net Income           69138.3 85155.96 104377.1 127442.5 155121.09
20                        =============================================
03-Nov-86   03:06 PM
```

FIGURE 23.3: This figure shows a projected income statement for a five-year period. The annual sales, cost of goods sold, and total expenses in this spreadsheet are calculated according to a specific percentage by which income and expenses are expected to grow. (The input cells that contain these percentages are entered in the spreadsheet below the income statement. They can be seen in Figure 23.4.) To see the effect that changes in income or COGS growth percentages would have on the sales and net income figures, you could enter new percentage values and recalculate the income statement. However, you would have to do this many times to see the effect of multiple changes, and you would have no way to either preserve these original values or save each separate what-if calculation. Using the /Data Table commands to generate data tables solves all of these problems (see Figures 23.4 and 23.5).

the /Range Format Text command so that their contents rather than their calculated values are displayed in the data table.

To generate the data table, the /Data Table 1 command was then used. The first prompt that you receive when using this command asks that you establish the table range. In this example, it was given as the cell range A33..F40. The last prompt asks that you indicate the input cell. This is cell B24, which contains the growth rate percentage used in the original income statement. The program then recalculates each of the five master formulas in B33 to F33, using each of the input values in A34..A40. Because there are seven input values in this list, Lotus 1-2-3 calculates the spreadsheet 35 times (5 × 7) to generate the results shown in the data table in the cell range B34..F40.

```
A33: [W20]                                                          READY

                 A                B        C         D         E         F
22
23  Totals Sales 1987       345000
24  Sales growth rate         20.0%
25
26  Percentage of sales
27    COGS                    65.0%
28    Total Expenses           8.5%
29
30  Interest Expense         15000
31
32  Growth Rate            Estimated Gross Sales
33                         +1988     +1990     +1991     +1992     +1993
34                    0.0% 345,000   345,000   345,000   345,000     345,000
35                    5.0% 362,250   380,363   399,381   419,350     440,317
36                   10.0% 379,500   417,450   459,195   505,115     555,626
37                   15.0% 396,750   456,263   524,702   603,407     693,918
38                   20.0% 414,000   496,800   596,160   715,392     858,470
39                   25.0% 431,250   539,063   673,828   842,285   1,052,856
40                   30.0% 448,500   583,050   757,965   985,355   1,280,961
41
03-Nov-86  03:06 PM
```

FIGURE 23.4: This figure shows a one-input data table created with the /Data Table 1 command. It tests the effect of a series of different growth rates on the estimated sales for the five years in the projected income statement. The growth rates range from 0 percent to a maximum of 30 percent (in the cell range A34..A40). These are the input variables tested in each master formula in the cell range B33..F33. These cells use range names to reference the same formulas that calculate the sales for each year in the income statement itself (shown in the cell range B6..F6 in Figure 23.3). The range names given to these formulas are the same as the years they represent. They are displayed in this figure instead of the sales figures because the cells have been formatted with the /Range Format Text command. The input cell for this data table was designated as B24, the one that currently holds the sales growth rate used in the income statement itself.

Using Two-Input Data Tables

The sensitivity analysis begun with the one-input data table on the projected income statement can easily be expanded by using a two-input data table to explore the effects on annual sales if two data variables change. Unlike a one-input data table, this type of data table cannot include more than a single master formula. To test more than one formula using the same set of input variables, you must set up separate data tables.

Figure 23.5 shows a two-input data table that calculates the projected income for 1988 based not only on changes in the percentage of sales growth but also on changes in the percentage of sales estimated as the cost of goods sold. This kind of two-way sensitivity analysis requires that you position the master formula in the first cell of the table range, which is normally left blank when creating a one-input data table.

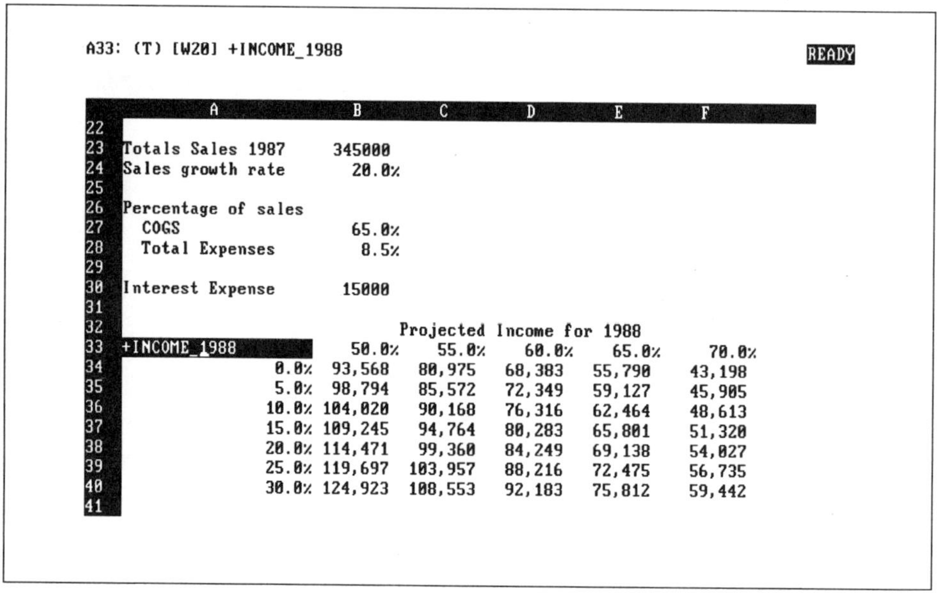

A33: (T) [W20] +INCOME_1988 READY

	A	B	C	D	E	F
22						
23	Totals Sales 1987	345000				
24	Sales growth rate	20.0%				
25						
26	Percentage of sales					
27	COGS	65.0%				
28	Total Expenses	8.5%				
29						
30	Interest Expense	15000				
31						
32			Projected Income for 1988			
33	+INCOME_1988	50.0%	55.0%	60.0%	65.0%	70.0%
34	0.0%	93,568	80,975	68,383	55,790	43,198
35	5.0%	98,794	85,572	72,349	59,127	45,905
36	10.0%	104,020	90,168	76,316	62,464	48,613
37	15.0%	109,245	94,764	80,283	65,801	51,320
38	20.0%	114,471	99,360	84,249	69,138	54,027
39	25.0%	119,697	103,957	88,216	72,475	56,735
40	30.0%	124,923	108,553	92,183	75,812	59,442
41						

FIGURE 23.5: This figure shows a two-input data table created with the /Data Table 2 command. It presents the results that changing both the sales growth rate and the cost of goods sold has on the net income for the first year in the projected income statement. Because only one master formula can be tested in this type of data table, the table represents the results for only one year. The master formula is entered into the table by direct reference using its range name, INCOME_1988. The first input variables are the various growth rates entered in the cell range A34..A40. The second input variables are the various percentages of sales required to produce the goods sold (COGS) in B33..F33. Input cell 1 was given as B24; it contains the currently used growth percentage. Input cell 2 was given as B27; it contains the currently used percentage of sales represented by COGS. Testing the effect these same variables would have on the net income for the rest of the years in this spreadsheet requires generating four other data tables in a similar way.

In this example, cell A33 displays the formula +INCOME_1988. This is the range name given to the formula in cell B19 in the original income statement (shown in Figure 23.3). In addition to the list of input values representing changes in projected growth rate in the cell range A34..A40, a second list of input variables has been added in row 33 in the cell range B33..F33. These represent changes in the projected cost of goods sold. Both of these ranges were created using the /Data Fill command and then formatted as percentages with the /Range Format Percent command.

When using a two-input data table, you must not only give the table range, which in this case is the cell range A33..F40, but also indicate the cell address of the first and second input cells. The first input values represent changes to the growth rate in annual sales, so this cell was given as B24 when using the /Data Table 2 command. The second input values exemplify changes to the percentage of sales that COGS represents, so the second input cell is designated as cell B27.

When Lotus 1-2-3 generated the final data table shown in Figure 23.5, it calculated the spreadsheet 35 times, once for each pair of new input values. If the same type of figures were required for each year of the projected income statement, four separate two-input data tables would have to be created, each one using the formula that calculates the net income for the appropriate year as its master formula. To update the data table, you would change the input values in either or both lists of input values and then press the Table function key (F8).

Performing Statistical Analysis in a Database with Data Tables

In addition to making it easy to perform extensive what-if analysis in a spreadsheet, the /Data Table commands can be used to perform statistical analyses that summarize the data in a Lotus 1-2-3 database. This is done by setting up master formulas that contain specific database statistical functions, such as the @DSUM, @DAVG, @DCOUNT, @MAX, and @DMIN functions.

Using a one-input data table allows you to generate different summary statistics with these database statistical functions. Using a two-input data table allows you to generate cross-tabulated statistics from the database using a single database function but based on two different values in two fields. In both cases, the input variables are used as successive criteria in the master formula, which contains the appropriate database statistical function.

Using One-Input Data Tables with a Database

Figure 23.6 shows a sales database that tracks the quarterly sales figures for eight account executives. It records not only the amount of sales made by each but also the quarter in which the sales were made, the region where they were made, and the type of sale, either directly to a corporate customer or to a retail outlet.

The database (the cell range A3..F21) was given the range name DB, and this range name was then used to designate the input range with the /Data Query Input command. This figure also shows the criterion range in the cell range I1..N2, which has been given the range name CRIT. This range name was used to designate the database criterion range with the /Data Query Criterion command.

Figure 23.7 shows three one-input data tables that were generated with the /Data Table 1 command to create summary statistics charting the

01: READY

	A	B	C	D	E	F	G
1	Sales Database						
2			QTRLY				
3	L:NAME	F:NAME	SALES	QTR	REGION	TYPE	
4	Jordan	Michael	145789	1	Midwest	Corporate	
5	Parker	Anthony	132760	1	West	Retail	
6	Baker	Thomas	164300	1	East	Corporate	
7	Bailey	Anna	202500	1	Midwest	Corporate	
8	West	Carol	122300	1	South	Retail	
9	Jordan	Michael	167100	1	Midwest	Retail	
10	Forrest	Brett	165900	1	East	Corporate	
11	Adams	Susan	112400	1	West	Corporate	
12	Parker	Anthony	153100	2	West	Retail	
13	Carson	James	200300	2	South	Retail	
14	West	Carol	134750	2	South	Corporate	
15	Baker	Thomas	109570	2	East	Retail	
16	Forrest	Brett	198875	2	East	Corporate	
17	Bailey	Anna	136500	2	Midwest	Corporate	

	I	J	K	L	M	N	O
1	L:NAME	F:NAME	SALES	QTR	REGION	TYPE	
2							

FIGURE 23.6: This figure shows a sales database that includes the the first and last names of each salesperson, their quarterly sales, the region where their sales were made, and the type of sales, either corporate or retail. The cell range A3..F21, which includes the entire database, has been given the range name DB and defined as the input range. The criterion range for this database, I1..N2, can be seen in the lower window of the figure; it has been given the range name CRIT. Figures 23.7 and 23.8 show examples using the /Data Table commands to summarize and cross tabulate statistics from this data.

totals, averages, and number of sales made by each salesperson, in each region, and in each quarter.

In the first data table (the cell range P1..S9), the /Data Query Unique command was used instead of retyping the names of the salespeople to enter the list of input values. Before using this command, the cell P1 containing the field name L:NAME was given as the output range with the /Data Query Output command. The names were then sorted using the /Data Sort command in ascending order.

Three master formulas containing @DSUM, @DAVG, and @DCOUNT functions were used in generating all three data tables. Their contents, instead of their calculated results, are displayed in the spreadsheet because they were formatted with the /Range Format Text command and their columns were widened until the contents of each formula was visible. Each of the formulas lists the input range argument by its range name, DB, the offset argument as

P20: READY

	P	Q	R	S	T
1	L:NAME	@DSUM(DB,2,CRIT)	@DAVG(DB,2,CRIT)	@DCOUNT(DB,2,CRIT)	
2	Adams	211,150.00	105,575.00	2	
3	Bailey	339,000.00	169,500.00	2	
4	Baker	273,870.00	136,935.00	2	
5	Carson	395,975.00	197,987.50	2	
6	Forrest	565,225.00	188,408.33	3	
7	Jordan	312,889.00	156,444.50	2	
8	Parker	430,210.00	143,403.33	3	
9	West	257,050.00	128,525.00	2	
10					
11	REGION	@DSUM(DB,2,CRIT)	@DAVG(DB,2,CRIT)	@DCOUNT(DB,2,CRIT)	
12	East	839,095.00	167,819.00	5	
13	Midwest	651,889.00	162,972.25	4	
14	South	653,025.00	163,256.25	4	
15	West	641,360.00	128,272.00	5	
16					
17	QTR	@DSUM(DB,2,CRIT)	@DAVG(DB,2,CRIT)	@DCOUNT(DB,2,CRIT)	
18	1	1,213,049.00	151,631.13	8	
19	2	1,572,320.00	157,232.00	10	
20					

FIGURE 23.7: This figure shows three one-input data tables that summarize the totals, averages, and number of sales by salesperson, region, and quarter. The master formulas for all three return sales figures according to the various input variables used as match criteria. They do this because all the database functions in the master formulas use offset 2 (referring to the third field in the database, which contains the sales). In the first table, the input variables include all of the salespeople entered into the database. The input cell for this data table was given as cell I2. In the second, the variables include the four regions serviced by the salespeople, and its input cell was given as cell M2. In the third, the variables include the two quarters included in the database; its input cell was given as cell L2.

2 (which contains the SALES field), and the criterion range argument as CRIT, the range name given to the cell range I1..N2 (shown in Figure 23.6).

When the /Data Table 1 command was used to generate the first data table, the table range was entered as P1..S9; the input cell was entered as I2. This corresponds to the input cell beneath the L:NAME field name in the criterion range (named CRIT). Lotus 1-2-3 generated the results shown in the first table by substituting each of the last names in the list of input values (the cell range P2..P9) in this criterion cell. This meant that the first total in cell Q2 was calculated using the criterion in which the last name is equal to Adams. Next, the program substituted Bailey as the criterion and calculated her total, and so on, using all of the names in this list. The same process was used to return the averages and the number of sales made by each.

The only difference between the first data table and the other two shown in Figure 23.7 is that the list of input values has been changed. This, in turn, changes the criterion used to calculate the sales totals, averages, and counts. In the second data table (in the cell range P11..S15), the four sales regions were used as the criteria. When indicating the input cell for this data table, the cell N2 below the field name REGION was entered in place of I2 for the first data table.

The third data table gives the same type of summary statistics, this time broken down by the quarter in which they were made. This required designating a new table range (P17..S19) and a new input cell (L2), the one beneath the field name QTR. Notice that in all three examples, the cells in the upper-left corners of the various table ranges were not left blank. This cell does not have to remain empty as long as the master formulas and list of input values used by the /Data Table 1 command have been laid out and indicated properly.

Using Two-Input Data Tables to Cross Tabulate Data

The foregoing examples are intended to give you a good idea of how the database statistical functions can be combined with the /Data Table command to create useful summary statistics. Beyond this type of one-way analysis, the /Data Table command can also be used to perform two-way statistical analysis. By creating a master formula that includes a database statistical function and setting up a two-input data table with the /Data Table 2 command, you can also generate cross-tabulated statistics from your Lotus 1-2-3 databases.

To illustrate this type of analysis, we can use the same sample sales database and set up a two-input data table to correlate the total sales made by each salesperson with the type of sale. Further, we can create a data table that correlates the total amount of each type of sale (either corporate or retail) with the regions in which the sales were made.

Figure 23.8 shows the two data tables that generated these valuable statistics. Notice that just as when using two-input data tables with spreadsheets, the two lists of input variables are arranged below and to the right of the single master formula. However, in these examples the input variables represent the criteria by which each result is totaled with the @DSUM function.

The first data table, in the cell range U1..W9, contains the last names of the salespeople as the first list of input variables and the two types of sales

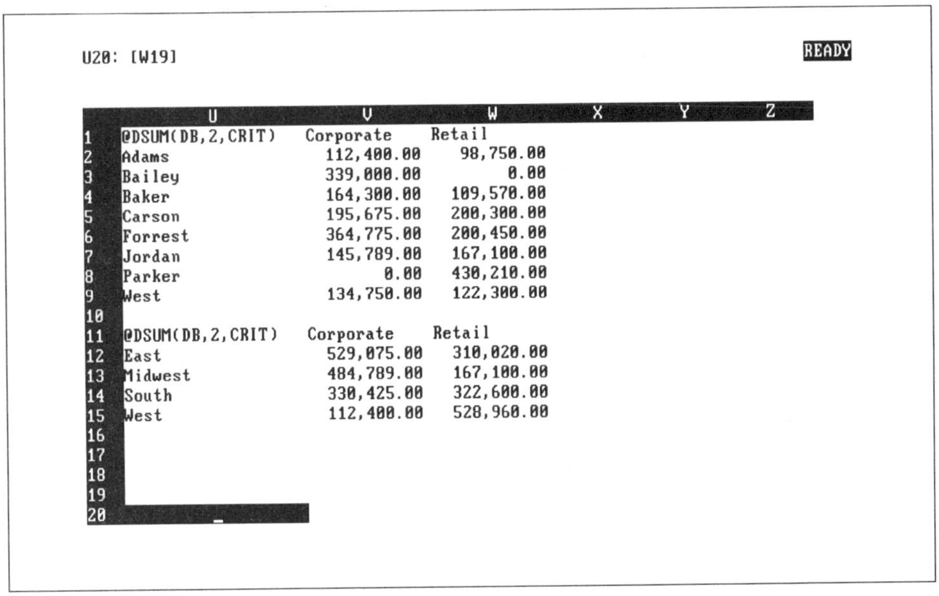

FIGURE 23.8: This figure contains a two-input data table that correlates the total sales made by each salesperson with the type of sale made and another that correlates the total sales made in each region with the type of sales. The master formula for each data table is the same, as is the second set of input variables that represents the two types of sales. The first set of input variables in the first data table includes all the salespeople represented in the L:NAME field of the database, while that for the second table includes all four regions entered in its Region field. When creating the first data table, input cell 1 was designated as I2 and input cell 2 as N2. In the second data table, input cell 1 was given as M2, while input cell 2 was given again as cell N2.

as the second input variables. The cell range named CRIT (which contains all the field names copied from the database with a single empty cell below each) is again used as the criterion range argument in the master @DSUM formula (shown at the bottom of Figure 23.6). When indicating the first input cell, the cell I2 below the field name L:NAME is given. When indicating the second input cell, the cell N2 below the field name TYPE is given.

When Lotus 1-2-3 generated this data table, it substituted each pair of values into the criterion range used by the @DSUM formula. In other words, the first total in cell V2 was generated using the criteria L:NAME equal to Adams and TYPE equal to Corporate. The second total in V3 used the criteria L:NAME equal to Bailey and TYPE equal to Corporate, and so on until totals were calculated using every pair of input values as criteria.

To generate the second data table, the first list of input values was changed to contain each of the four sales regions. Then when issuing the /Data Table 2 command, the cell range U11..W15 was designated as the table range, cell M2 was given as the first input cell, and cell N2 was given as the second input cell.

Using Criterion Formulas to Generate Data Tables

You must exercise care when using criterion formulas as the input variables in a data table that generates statistics from a database. Remember that criterion formulas return either the logical true value 1 or the logical false value 0, based on the initial evaluation of the contents of the cell address entered in the formula. This cell address indicates the location of the first entry in the field of the database that is to be tested according to the contents of the criterion formula.

If such a formula is used as one of the input cells required to build the data table or as one of the master formulas, Lotus 1-2-3 will end up searching the appropriate database field for the presence of 0 or 1 entries instead of matching the condition indicated by the formula. This happens because Lotus 1-2-3 calculates the formula (in much the same way as the Edit and Calc function keys change a formula to its calculated value) before it generates the table. For instance, if your criterion formula were set up to search for salaries in the range of $35,000 to $50,000 a year, you could enter it as

+Salary>=35000#AND#Salary<=50000

Depending on the contents of the first entry in the Salary field (given the range name Salary with the /RNLD command), the formula would return either 0 for false, indicating that the field entry was not within this range, or 1 for true, indicating that it is within the range.

If you wanted to use this formula to create a data table that counted the number of salaries that are in this range by department, you could not use a one-input data table to do so. If you tried to set up such a table with the individual department names listed as the input variables, the @DCOUNT formula as the master formula, and this criterion formula in the input cell in the criterion range, the resulting table would contain nothing but zeros. This is because the program would count only salaries that contain 0 or 1 (depending on the outcome returned by the formula) in the table. Assuming that no salaries contain such entries, no matches would be found for the criterion and subsequently tallied by the @DCOUNT formula.

In this particular example, you would fare no better by creating a two-input data table, using the criterion formula as the second input variable and leaving the input cell in the criterion range blank. The program would generate the same results as in the example above because it would find no match in a particular department where the salary was entered as either 0 or 1.

There are, however, many circumstances under which you can use criterion formulas to generate data tables successfully. Figure 23.9 illustrates a slightly different example. The function of this data table is to total salaries by department for those employees who were hired on or before January 1, 1983.

To generate this table, the criterion formula

+I5<=@DATE(83,1,1)

was entered in cell V5, beneath the field name Hired. (Because this is a formula, it could have been entered beneath any field name in this criterion range.) The cell address I5 refers to the address of the cell that contains the first field entry in the Date Hired field in the database. As you can see from this figure, the formula returned the logical value of 1 in V5, indicating that the hire date entered there is before or equal to January 1, 1983.

A one-input data table was then constructed in the cell range S10..T14. The five department names are listed as the input variables in the first column of the table. The master formula in cell T9 uses the @DSUM function. The offset argument is given as 7, the number of the offset for the Salary field in the database (corresponding offset numbers are shown in Figure 23.9 in row 3 above the criterion range in rows 4 and 5).

When using the /Data Table 1 command, the input cell was indicated as cell R5, the empty cell beneath the Dept field name in the criterion range. Because the criterion formula is not contained in this input cell (or as part of the input variables in the table range), the program correctly totals the salaries by department only for those employees hired before January 1, 1983.

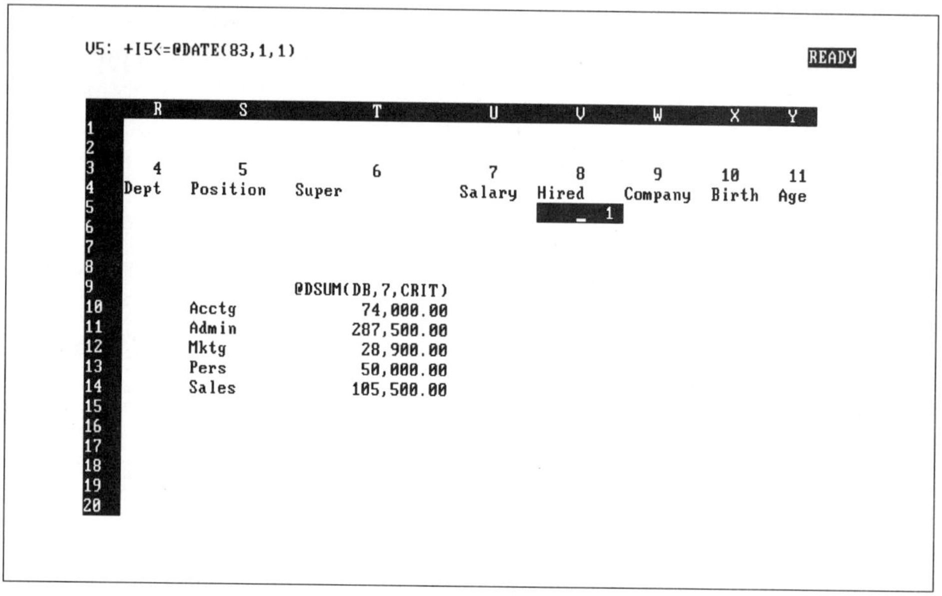

FIGURE 23.9: This figure illustrates a one-input data table that totals the salaries by department for employees hired on or before January 1, 1983. The input variables include the five departments as they are entered into the Dept field of the database. The @DSUM function in the master formula totals the salaries because the offset value, 7, is that of the Salary field in the database (offset values are shown above the field names in the criterion range in rows 4 and 5 in this figure). You can see the criterion formula in the first line of the Control Panel. It refers to cell I5 because the Date Hired field is in column I of the database and row 5 contains its first record. The logical true value of 1 in cell V5 indicates that the entry in this cell is a date on or prior to 1/1/83. The input cell for this data table was designated R5. The /Data Table 1 command would not have worked properly if this criterion formula had been entered in the same cell that was given as the input cell (see the text for an explanation).

THE /DATA TABLE COMMAND

The /Data Table command allows you to generate two types of what-if tables: a one-input data table with the /Data Table 1 command and a two-input data table with the /Data Table 2 command. A one-input data table tests a single set of input variables in one or more master formulas. A two-input data table tests two sets of input variables in a single master formula.

/Data Table

MENUS

/Data
Table
1 2 Reset

KEYBOARD ENTRY

/DT1
Enter Table range:
Enter Input cell 1:
/DT2
Enter Table range:
Enter Input cell 1:
Enter Input cell 2:

FUNCTION

The /Data Table command allows you to perform extended what-if analysis in a spreadsheet whose results are saved in tabular form. Lotus 1-2-3 creates the data table by substituting each of the various input variables listed in the table into a master formula. Because the results calculated by testing the new input variables in the formula are stored as values, the table is not subject to further recalculation in the normal way. Lotus 1-2-3 allows you to generate a new data table in the same area of the worksheet by inputting new input values and then pressing the Table function key (F8).

The benefits of using data tables to do what-if analysis are many:

- Data tables are easier to generate than copying formulas and then changing key input values.
- Data tables take up less memory and storage space in the worksheet than duplicating formulas with different input values.

- Data tables are laid out in a format that is easy to graph using the Lotus 1-2-3 graph commands.
- Data tables do not modify the formulas in the original spreadsheet. The original assumptions coexist with the results returned in the tables.

The /Data Table commands can also be used to generate statistical tables of data in a Lotus 1-2-3 database by using the database statistical functions in the master formulas. When the /Data Table commands are applied to databases, they you allow to generate quickly various types of summary statistics or even cross-tabulated results.

USAGE

The /Data Table command has three menu options: 1 to create a one-input data table, 2 to create a two-input data table, and Reset to clear all previously defined data table settings for either type 1 or type 2 tables. The Reset option is quite useful when you are generating subsequent tables from the same spreadsheet or database and you are using the pointing method to indicate the table range, input variables, or both. However, the /Data Table menu is not a "sticky" menu: you are returned to READY mode whenever you issue the Reset option. This means that you must type **/DT** before choosing the 1 or 2 options and defining the new data table range and input variables.

/Data Table 1

To generate a one-input data table with the /Data Table 1 command, you must establish a list of the input variables to be tested in the master formula in a single column of the worksheet. These values must be in a contiguous cell range, although they need not be arranged in any particular order. You can often use the /Data Fill command to have the program generate these input variables for you rather than entering the values manually.

The formula in which these values are to be tried must be entered in the column immediately to the right of the input variables and one row above the cell containing the first input variable (Figure 23.1 contains a diagram illustrating this layout).

You can often enter this master formula into the appropriate cell by direct reference (by entering + followed by the address of the cell that already contains the formula) rather than by manually reentering the formula. You can, however, enter any type of valid formula in this cell location even if it is not contained elsewhere in the spreadsheet. If you wish to have these input variables tested in more than one master formula, enter them in the cells in the columns immediately to the right of the one containing your first master formula.

After you enter the input variables and the master formula, issue the /Data Table 1 command by typing **/DT1**. You will then be asked to indicate the table range. This cell range must include all of the rows and columns that contain input variables and the master formula or formulas. This means that the first cell of the table range is an empty cell, located to the left of the cells containing your formulas and just above the list of the input variables. The last cell in this range is defined by the junction of the column of the last master formula and the row of the last input variable.

When indicating this range, you can type in the cell addresses or use pointing. Painting the range by using the cell pointer to point to its two corners is a much safer method. It gives you visual feedback so that you can make sure you have included all the cells where Lotus 1-2-3 will return the calculated results.

After you indicate the table range and press the Return key, you will be asked to designate the cell address of the input cell. This cell can be any cell located outside the table range you have just defined. You may find it convenient to indicate the address of the cell in the spreadsheet that contains the input value used in the original formula. It does not matter whether this cell contains a value; the program will restore the original value after generating the data table.

After you indicate the cell address of the input cell (by typing in its address or pointing to it), press the Return key once more to have the program calculate the results and enter them in the table. Lotus 1-2-3 will recalculate the spreadsheet one time for each of the input variables in each of the master formulas used. This may take some time if you are testing many input values in more than one formula. You do not have to be concerned whether the global recalculation default is set to Automatic or Manual.

Once the data table has been generated, it is no longer subject to further recalculation. To recalculate a data table using new input values and/or master formulas that do not require redefining the table range, make your changes and then press the Table function key (F8).

Using /Data Table 1 with Databases When you generate a one-input data table using a database, you follow much the same procedure as when using it to create a what-if table in a spreadsheet. There are, however, some differences:

- The master formula or formulas contain database statistical functions. To use these functions, you must supply valid arguments that include the input range of the database, the number of the offset column indicating the database field to be used, and the criterion range of the database. (For details on how to use each of the database statistical functions, see Chapter 16.)
- The list of input variables represents valid field entries that determine the criterion by which the database statistical functions are calculated.
- The input cell will be the cell beneath the field name in the criterion range that matches the field from which the input variables are chosen.

When using the /Data Table 1 command to produce summary statistics from a database, the program substitutes each input variable into the input cell in the criterion range and calculates the results returned by the particular database statistical function based on matches to this value in the appropriate field of the database.

/DATA TABLE 2

When you use the /Data Table 2 command, you must use a slightly different table layout from that used for /Data Table 1. Because only one master formula can be used in this type of data table, it is always located in the first cell of the table range, the one usually left blank when using the /Data Table 1 command. It can be entered in the same way as master formulas are in the first type of table, either by direct reference or literal input.

This type of table requires that you list two different sets of input variables to be tested in the formula. The first set of values are entered in the same column as the master formula, starting with the row directly below it. The second set of input variables are entered in the same row as the master formula, starting with the column immediately to its right. The table range includes all the cells included within the columns and rows used to enter these two sets of input variables. It may be possible to enter one or both of these input values by using the /Data Fill command.

After you enter the master formula and the two sets of input variables, type **/DT2** to begin the procedure to generate the data table. You will first be asked to indicate the table range. Define this range either by typing in the cell addresses or by pointing to it. Then press the Return key. You will then be asked to designate input cell 1. It must be a cell that is not part of the table range, where the program can temporarily store the first input variables listed below the master formula. After you indicate this cell address and press the Return key, you will be prompted to indicate input cell 2. This must also be a cell outside the table range and different from input cell 1. This is where the second set of input variables located to the right of the master formula can be temporarily stored.

These input cells can be empty or can contain data. If they contain values, Lotus 1-2-3 will restore the values after generating the data table. You will often find it convenient to use the cell addresses of those cells in the spreadsheet that contain the original input values used in the master formula.

After you define input cell 2 and press the Return key, the program will calculate the formula using all of the input variables listed in the table. The results of these calculations will be entered into the data table in their appropriate column and row positions.

Once the data table has been generated, it is no longer subject to further recalculation. To recalculate a data table using new input variables and/or master formulas that do not require redefining the table range, make your changes and then press the Table function key (F8).

Using /Data Table 2 with Databases When you generate a two-input data table using a database, you follow much the same procedure as when using it to create a what-if table in a spreadsheet. There are, however, some differences:

- The master formula contains database statistical functions. To use these functions, you must supply valid arguments that include the input range of the database, the number of the offset column indicating the database field to be used, and the criterion range of the database. (For details on how to use each of the database statistical functions, see Chapter 16.)
- The two sets of input variables represent valid field entries from two different fields in the database that determine the criterion by which the database statistical function is calculated.

- The first input cell will be the cell beneath the field name in the criterion range that matches the field from which the first set of input variables is chosen. The second input cell will be the cell beneath the field name in the criterion range that matches the field from which the second set of input variables is chosen.

When using the /Data Table 2 command to produce cross-tabulated statistics from a database, the program substitutes each input pair of variables into the input cells in the criterion range and calculates the results returned by the particular database statistical function based on matches to these values in their appropriate fields in the database.

EXAMPLES

For an example of using the /Data Table 1 command in a spreadsheet, refer to Figure 23.4. For an example of using this command to generate statistics from a database, see Figure 23.7. For an example of using /Data Table 2 in a spreadsheet, refer to Figure 23.5. For an example of how to use this command to create cross-tabulated results from a database, see Figure 23.8. Refer to Figure 23.9 to see an example using a criterion formula to generate summary statistics from a database.

SUMMARY

This chapter presented the /Data Table commands and illustrated how they can be used to perform both extended what-if analysis in a spreadsheet and statistical analysis in a database. These commands generate tables that return calculated results based on various input variables that you enter into the table. You can often use the /Data Fill command to make the task of generating the input variables easier. To review information on how to use this command, see Chapter 20, "Creating a Lotus 1-2-3 Database."

If you are using these commands to construct statistical tables, you will be using the Lotus 1-2-3 database statistical functions. If you need information on how to use these functions and the arguments they require, see Chapter 16, "Database Statistical Functions." Detailed information on setting up a Lotus 1-2-3 database can be found in Chapter 20, "Creating a Lotus 1-2-3 Database," which contains specifics on using /Data Fill. Information on how to set up and define input and criterion ranges can be found in Chapter 21, "Database Operations."

PART

5

LOTUS 1-2-3 GRAPHICS

Visual presentation of Lotus 1-2-3 data is becoming increasingly important in all types of business applications. Lotus 1-2-3 graphics capabilities are renowned for two things: the ease with which you can create them from worksheet data, and the fact that they remain dynamically linked to the data from which they are drawn and can, therefore, be subjected to what-if analysis.

Part 5 includes all of the information you will need about creating and using Lotus 1-2-3 graphs. It does not, however, describe how to print graphs by using the PrintGraph utility. This subject is discussed in Chapter 26 in Part 6 of this book.

Chapter 24 begins with a discussion of how to select the graph type and assign data variables to be graphed from your worksheet data. It then covers how to use the many graph options to customize the graph you are creating. You can add titles and grid lines, adjust the scaling of the graph, format the values that appear on the graph scales, and add data labels to annotate each data variable used.

Release 2 has a new feature for pie graphs that allows you to assign various fill types or explode sections of the pie. Techniques for adding these enhancements to the pie charts you create are discussed next.

As graphics have become increasingly important to the typical business user, so the requirements of presentation business graphics have become more sophisticated. This chapter discusses how Lotus 1-2-3 graphs can be enhanced and how certain of their limitations can be overcome. To provide an example of how using a compatible stand-alone graphics program can increase the quality of your 1-2-3 graphics, Chapter 24 also examines Freelance, a new graphics utility program published by Lotus Development Corporation.

After these technique and application discussions, you will find a complete reference entry for all the options on the Lotus 1-2-3 /Graph menu. Here you will find information on how to save your graphs both as part of the worksheet and as separate files that you can print and plot by using the PrintGraph program (discussed in Chapter 26).

CHAPTER 24

Creating and Using Graphs

Creating and Using Graphs

Lotus 1-2-3 graphics allow you to represent spreadsheet and database data in a variety of standard business graph formats: line graph, bar graph, stacked-bar graph, XY graph, and pie chart. Creating graphs in Lotus 1-2-3 is a straightforward process of choosing one of these graph types and assigning various data variables from existing data in the worksheet. There are a number of enhancements, including titles, legends, grids, manual scaling, and formatting, that you can also define from the /Graph Menu.

This chapter includes information on all aspects of creating and using Lotus 1-2-3 graphs. It begins with discussions of techniques and applications that outline how to set up graphs and save them, both as part of the worksheet file and in separate files that can be printed or plotted. It does not, however, contain information on how to print graphs using the Lotus 1-2-3 PrintGraph program. You will find this information in Chapter 26, "Printing and Plotting Graphs."

Following these general discussions, you will find the complete reference entry explaining all of the options found on the /Graph Menu. These options are presented in the order in which they are encountered when you use the /Graph Menu.

Lotus 1-2-3's Graphics Capabilities

The Lotus 1-2-3 graphics program allows you to define and save any number of graphs with the worksheet you create. Each graph is created by using data already entered into the worksheet itself. In order to view the graphs you create on the screen, your computer must be equipped with some type of graphics adapter. If you have a monochrome monitor, you need some sort of monochrome graphics card, such as the Hercules Graphics Card. If you have a color monitor, you need to have some type of color/graphics card. If you are using Release 2, Lotus 1-2-3 will support the use of an extended graphics adapter.

If you do not have one of these graphics adapters installed in your system, you can still define and save graphs, although you cannot preview them on the screen before you print them. It is important to understand that graphs defined with Lotus 1-2-3 are saved as part of the worksheet with the /File Save command, but they are not printable with the Print-Graph utility unless they are also saved in separate files using the Save command on the /Graph Menu. This creates a file automatically given the file name extension .PIC by the program. (For specific information on how to print graphs once they are saved in these files, refer to Chapter 26, "Printing and Plotting Graphs.")

When you define more than one graph in a single worksheet, you must give each one a separate name by using the Name option on the /Graph Menu. If only one graph has been created, it is automatically saved as part of the worksheet file when you use the /File Save command, even if you have not named it with this command. However, when you define a second graph, you must first use the Name option to preserve your first graph. The second graph changes any earlier settings, and its definition will be the only one saved as part of the file.

Lotus 1-2-3 always considers the graph most recently viewed at the time the worksheet was last saved as the current graph. (If you have defined only one graph, it is necessarily the current graph.) You can view the current graph by pressing the Graph function key (F10) whenever you retrieve a worksheet. To view another graph that you have named and saved as part of the worksheet file, you must make it current by using the Name Use command from the /Graph Menu.

Components of Graphs

Most Lotus 1-2-3 graph types create a diagram that plots the change of one variable in relation to one or more other variables on an X-Y coordinate system. The basic reference lines of the X-Y coordinates are referred to as the *axes* of the graph. The horizontal reference line is called the *X axis* of the graph. Very often, it represents the changes over time or the time element of the graph. The units of time are equal but can be any type of unit, such as weeks, months, or years. The vertical reference line is called the *Y axis* of the graph. It usually represents the changes in values of the data variables. Again, the units in which these values are represented are up to you.

This X-Y axis system is used by every Lotus 1-2-3 graph type except the pie chart. (The pie chart is a specialized graph form; it is discussed in its own separate section that follows.) Lotus 1-2-3 scales the X and Y axes of a graph automatically according to the type of graph chosen, the number of values in each data variable, and the number of data variables graphed.

The values to be graphed are assigned by their cell range or ranges in the worksheet itself. Each group of values in a single cell range represents one data variable. You can define up to six separate data variables or cell ranges for all graph types except the pie chart. Lotus 1-2-3 graphs are dynamically linked to the values in these cell ranges. If you change these values, the graph using them is automatically modified to reflect these changes the next time the graph is drawn.

There are a number of options that can be used to label and refine the graph after its type and data variables have been defined. Lotus 1-2-3 allows you to view the graph at any stage in its definition by using the View command. To return to the /Graph Menu and continue creating graphs, you can press almost any key. (If you use the /Graph Quit option to return to the spreadsheet for any reason, you can view the currently defined graph by pressing the Graph function key, F10.)

The available options let you add several types of titles to the graph, add legends for each data variable, add horizontal and/or vertical grid lines, set new upper and/or lower limits for either the X or Y axis, format the values on the X and Y axes, and display data labels in various locations in the graph.

Figure 24.1 shows the spreadsheet data used to draw the bar graph in Figure 24.2. The bar graph in Figure 24.2 contains many of the components typical of Lotus 1-2-3 graphs. It has two data variables, named A and B. These were defined by giving the cell range B7..E7 as data variable A and the cell range B9..E9 as data variable B. The X-axis labels were supplied by giving the cell range B5..E5 as the X-axis range.

Notice that the first and second titles in the graph are taken from the spreadsheet. This is done by entering **\A1** as the first title and **\A3** as the second title. This same kind of referencing was used to define the legend for the graph. The legend for data variable A was entered as **\A7**, and the legend for data variable B was entered as **\A9**. However, the X-axis and Y-axis titles were typed in; they were not taken from labels already existing in this spreadsheet. When you define titles by referring to labels stored in cells, it is often wise to assign range names to these cells so that the titles are not affected in the graph if the labels in the cells are moved to new locations in the spreadsheet.

In the graph in Figure 24.2 you can see that the Y scale was formatted (using the /Options Scale Y Scale Format command) to Currency with zero decimal places. This is why the values on the Y axis are displayed with dollar signs. Finally, the data in cell range B7..E7 was used again, this time defined as the data labels for data variable A (using the /Options Data-Labels A Above command). Data labels for data variable B were defined in a similar manner, this time specifying the cell range B9..E9.

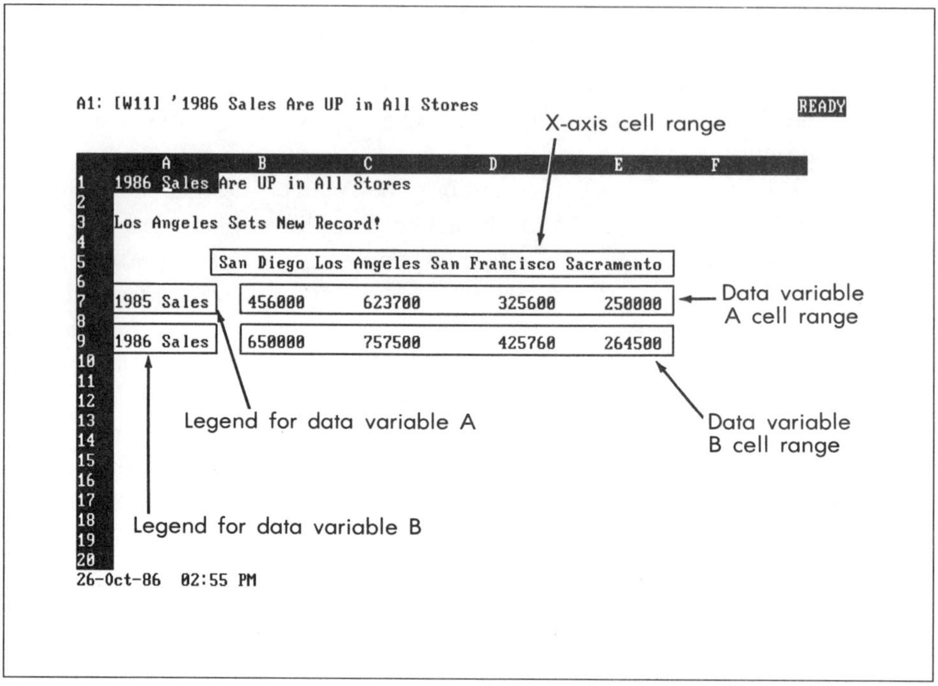

FIGURE 24.1: This figure shows the data used to generate the bar graph shown in Figure 24.2. Cell range B7..E7 contains the data for the first data variable, labeled A, in the graph. The data in the parallel cell range below it, B9..E9, supplies the data for the second data variable, labeled B. The column headings in the cell range B5..E5 were given as the X-axis range. These provide the labels along the X axis, allowing the reader to identify each group of paired values for the years 1985 and 1986. The spreadsheet titles in cells A1 and A3 are used as the first and second titles in the bar graph. The row headings identifying the years in cells A7 and A9 provide the labels for the legend in the graph.

Creating Graphs

Graphs are defined, named, and saved from the /Graph Menu (activated by typing **/G**). This menu is a "sticky" menu that allows you access to each graph component without returning you to READY mode each time. As such, it includes a Quit option that can be used to return directly to READY mode and the spreadsheet.

There are many levels to the /Graph Menu. To orient yourself to the placement of the graph commands in the menu system as they are referred to in the subsequent discussions on creating and using graphs, the /Graph Menu diagram introduced in Chapter 4 is reproduced in Figure 24.3.

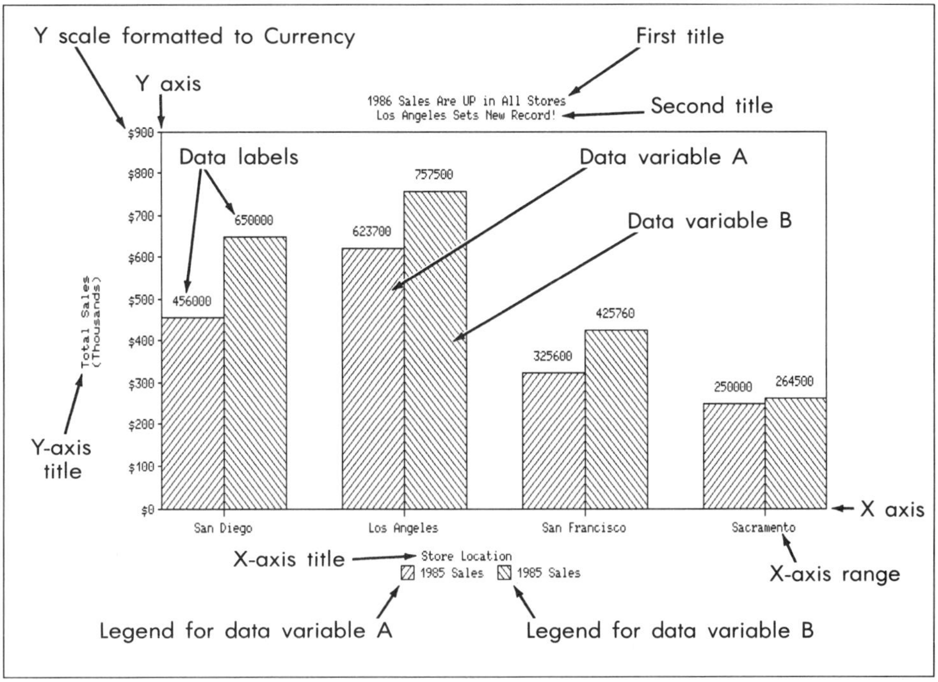

FIGURE 24.2: This figure shows the standard bar graph drawn from the data in the spreadsheet in Figure 24.1. It illustrates many components typical of Lotus 1-2-3 graphs. This graph contains two general titles above the frame, which is automatically drawn for all graphs except pie charts. It has an X-axis title drawn below the X axis, and a Y-axis title that reads up the left side of the graph above the Y axis. Because there are two groups of data (sales for 1985 and 1986), there are two data variables in the graph, labeled A and B, respectively. To identify the source of these sales, the column headings containing the stores' names are used as the X-axis range, shown centered below each pair of bars representing the sales for the two years. The Y scale has been formatted to Currency to make it clear that this axis measures dollars. The (Thousands) indicator next to the Y-axis title lets you know that each amount on this scale represents thousands of dollars. A legend has been added to make it clear what year is represented by the different types of crosshatching fill assigned to the bars.

Graph Types

As shown on the menu map, the first level of menu options begins with the Type command. It is used to choose the type of graph you wish to use. Its default setting is Line, so Lotus 1-2-3 will represent the data variables you define in a line graph if you do not choose one of the other four types with the Type command. You can always change the type of graph after defining the data variables. This allows you to view the graph in several

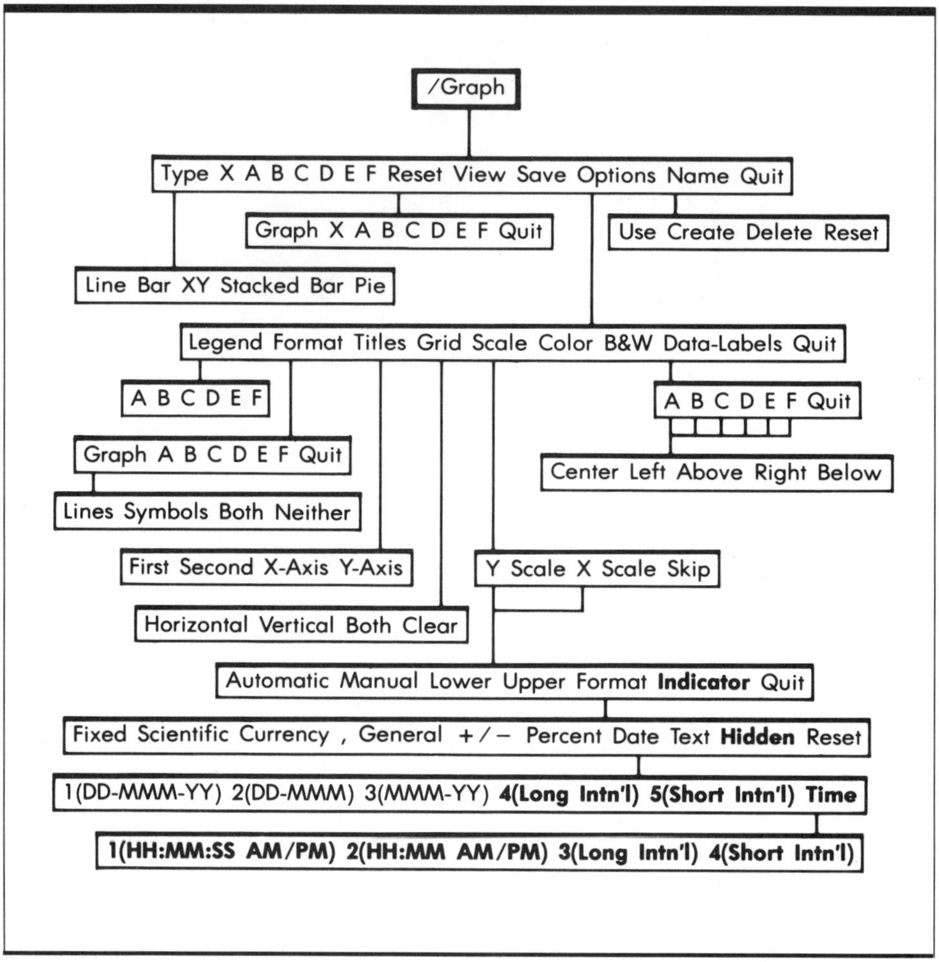

FIGURE 24.3: The Lotus 1-2-3 /Graph Menu is used to generate and save all the graphs you create from your spreadsheet and database data. There are five graph types. All graphs except pie charts can use up to six data variables (A to F) defined by range in the worksheet. You can save multiple graph settings, although each must be named with the /Graph Name Create command and saved with the worksheet. To be able to print a graph, it must also be saved with the /Graph Save command. Lotus 1-2-3 gives all of these graph files the extension .PIC (for picture file).

different formats to determine the most appropriate type before naming and saving the graph as part of the worksheet or in a separate printable file.

There are five graph types to choose from (although strictly speaking, the Pie type is not a graph because it does not plot data on an X-Y coordinate system). The features of each type of graph are summarized in Table 24.1.

TYPE	DESCRIPTION
Line	Plots the magnitude of each data variable as a data point. A different symbol is used for each data variable defined. The symbols are assigned according to the letter of the data variable: A □ D △ B + E × C ◊ F ▽ Each data point for each data variable can be connected by lines (the default), represented by its symbols (by typing **OFGS**), represented by lines (by typing **OFGL**), or suppressed (by typing **OFGN**). The actual values of the data points can be displayed in a line graph by using the Data-Labels option and then choosing the appropriate letter of the data variable. You locate the data variable by choosing among the Center, Left, Above, Right, and Below options.
Bar	Plots the magnitude of each data variable as a (vertically oriented) bar on the X axis. Each data variable defined is represented by its own bar. When using color, each data variable is assigned its own color according to the letter of the data variable: A White D White B Red E Red C Blue F Blue In black and white, the fill pattern is chosen according to the letter of the data variable: A Wide forward slash pattern B Wide backslash pattern C Narrow forward slash pattern D Narrow backslash pattern E Diamond crisscross pattern F Crisscross pattern Neither the colors used nor the fill pattern can be changed. There is no option to change the orientation of the bars from vertical to horizontal.
XY	Plots each data value of the data variable as a data point on two numerical axes in the order in which they are entered in the cell range. No correlation in time is assumed when using this graph type. The same display options and symbols are used with this graph type as are used with the line graph (see the description above). This type of graph is often referred to as a **scatter plot** or **scatter diagram**.

TABLE 24.1: The Types of Lotus 1-2-3 Graphs

TYPE	DESCRIPTION
Stacked Bar	This format is similar to the bar type except that the value for each data variable is accumulated to determine the magnitude of each bar on the Y axis. There are as many stacks within a single bar as there are data variables defined. It uses the same fill types or colors for each data variable as does the bar graph (see the description above). This is sometimes referred to as a **cake graph**.
Pie	Plots each value of a single data variable as a segment of a circle, representing it as a percentage of the total of the values. The absolute value of negative values in the data variable range is plotted. Segments of the pie chart are not given fill types. In Release 2, you can assign fill types by defining code numbers between 0 and 7 to represent different fill types as a B data variable. Individual segments can also be exploded by adding 100 to to the value of the basic code number to be used.

TABLE 24.1: The Types of Lotus 1-2-3 Graphs (continued)

To view specific examples of each type of graph, see Figures 24.10 through 24.14 in the /Graph command reference entry under the section entitled "Selecting the Kind of Graph with the Type Command."

Assigning Data Variables

The data variables plotted in a graph are defined by referring to the cell range in the worksheet that contains the values to be used. Each data variable is assigned a single letter option between A and F. You assign the cell ranges containing the values to be graphed as you would any cell range in Lotus 1-2-3, either by typing their cell addresses or range names or by pointing to them. Each data variable to be included in the graph should be assigned in order from A to F.

The X option on the /Graph Menu is used to define labels for the X axis of the graph. These, too, are defined by referencing the cell range in the worksheet that contains the appropriate labels. You can generally use the cell range that contains column headings above the cell ranges with the values that are being graphed. However, if you are creating an XY graph, the cell range defined as the X variable will not contain labels but will contain the numerical values to be used as the X axis.

Note: If you are creating a scatter diagram to accompany simple linear regression analysis done with the /Data Regression command, the cell range for the X data variable would correspond to the one defined as the X range for the independent variable when using that command.

Graph Options

You use the Options submenu on the /Graph Menu to enter the titles you wish to give your graph as well as to refine several aspects affecting the presentation of the graph. It contains these options:

Legend Format Titles Grid Scale Color B&W Data-Labels Quit

Using Legends to Label Data Variables

The Legend option is used to label the different symbols, crosshatching, or colors assigned by the program to each data variable in the graph. You can type in the text of the legend (up to 19 characters) or define it by referencing a cell that already contains the appropriate text. To reference such a cell, you precede the cell address by a backslash—for example, \A1. If you change or erase the contents of the label in this cell, it will change the legend.

Legends are always displayed at the bottom of the graph, below the X-axis line. There is no way to relocate legends to another area of the graph. The text of the legends often overlaps when you view the graph on the screen. This does not mean that your legends will appear this way when you print the graph, but if your labels are too long, or if there are too many of them, the program may not print all of them on the graph.

Because the resolution of the display monitor is much more limited than that of your printer, the graph displayed on the screen may not always exactly match the graph when printed. If you are preparing your graphs for a slide show, you will often have to abbreviate the text of your legends even more than required by the 19-character limit, because Lotus 1-2-3 often truncates legend text when it prints or plots graphs.

Changing the Display of Line and XY Graphs

When you create a line or XY graph, the data points representing each value of the data variables are automatically connected to one another by lines. To change this display so that only the symbols representing the data variables or only lines are displayed, you use the Format option. You can apply these format options to the entire graph by using the Graph option or to a specific data variable by typing its letter or letters (between A and F).

To display only the symbols at data points, you choose the Symbols option. To see only the lines created by the data values, choose the Lines option. If you wish to suppress the display of a data variable entirely, choose the Neither option. There is also a Both option that is used to reset the graph to the default of displaying both the symbols and lines connecting them.

In an XY graph, the Lines option can be used to include diagonal or straight lines that represent particular upper or lower limits between which most of the data points fall. To add such lines to a graph, you enter the range of values that delineates the line in the worksheet and assign it to a new data variable. Then choose Options Format, enter its data variable letter, and, finally, select the Lines option. For instance, if this line were assigned to data variable E, you would type **OFELQ**.

The Neither option on the Format submenu can be used to position comment lines within the borders of the graph. To locate the comments, data values are entered into a phantom data range in relation to real plotted variables and are assigned a new data variable letter. A comment line for this phantom data point is then entered and associated with the letter of the new data variable by using the Data-Labels option. The display of the symbol for this phantom data point is then suppressed by using the Neither option, leaving only the comment line in the graph. Figures 24.4 and 24.5 illustrate this technique for adding phantom data points and data labels to be used as comments displayed in the graph.

Adding Titles to a Graph

You can assign various titles to a graph by using the Titles option on the Options menu. These titles include two general headings that are automatically centered and placed above the graph (defined with the First and Second options), a title for the X axis, and one for the Y axis. The X-axis title is centered below the X-axis reference line and is placed on the line just above the legends, if they are used. The Y-axis title is rotated 90 degrees so that it reads up the left side of the graph.

Just as when assigning legends, you can enter the graph titles either by typing in the text or by referencing a cell in the worksheet that already contains the appropriate title. If you reference a cell address, preface it with the backslash, as in \A5. Be careful when using this system that you do not

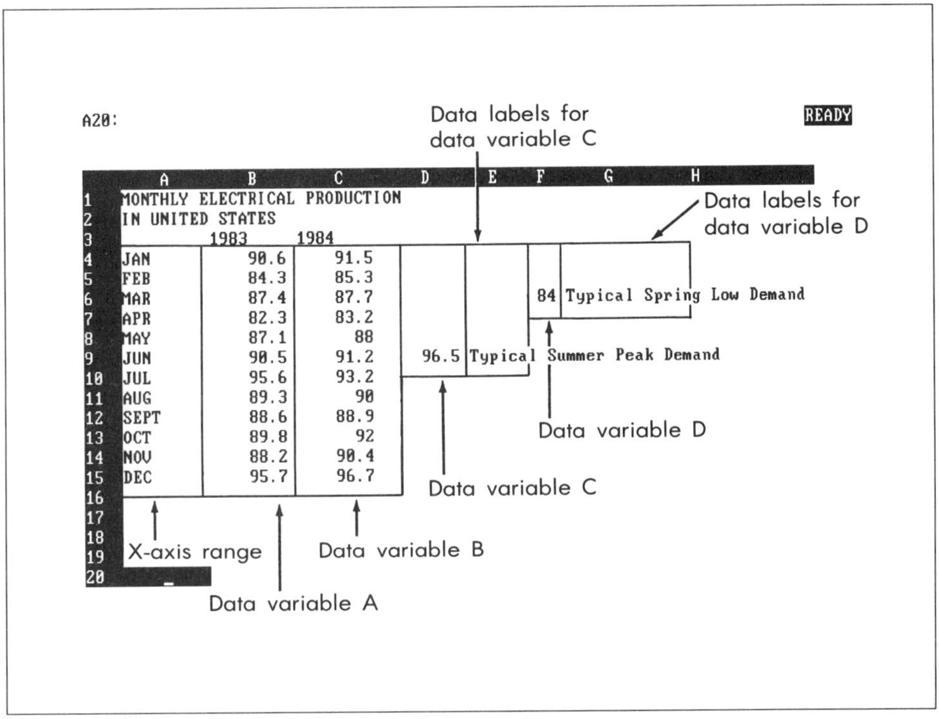

FIGURE 24.4: This figure shows the cell ranges containing the data graphed in the line graph shown in Figure 24.5. It contains four cell ranges for data variables A, B, C, and D. Only the data for data variables A and B actually shows up in the resulting graph. The single values in data variables C and D have been added only to position the data labels assigned to them (shown in cells in the columns immediately to their right). To suppress their display, the Options Format C and D commands were used along with the Neither option. Then the Data-Labels command was used to assign labels to C and D using the labels in E9 and G6, respectively. The data labels for data variables C and D were then positioned with the Right option. You can see the results of using these phantom values and data variables to position these data labels in Figure 24.5.

erase or move the contents of such a cell, or the title that uses that cell will be missing from the graph.

Adding Grid Lines to a Graph

The Grid option on the Options menu can be used to add horizontal, vertical, or both types of grid lines to a graph. The grid lines are drawn from each tick mark on the appropriate axis to the opposite border of the graph. The tick marks on the X axis represent the number of values in each data variable. The tick marks on the Y axis are determined by the scale generated by the program to accommodate the range of values included in each data variable.

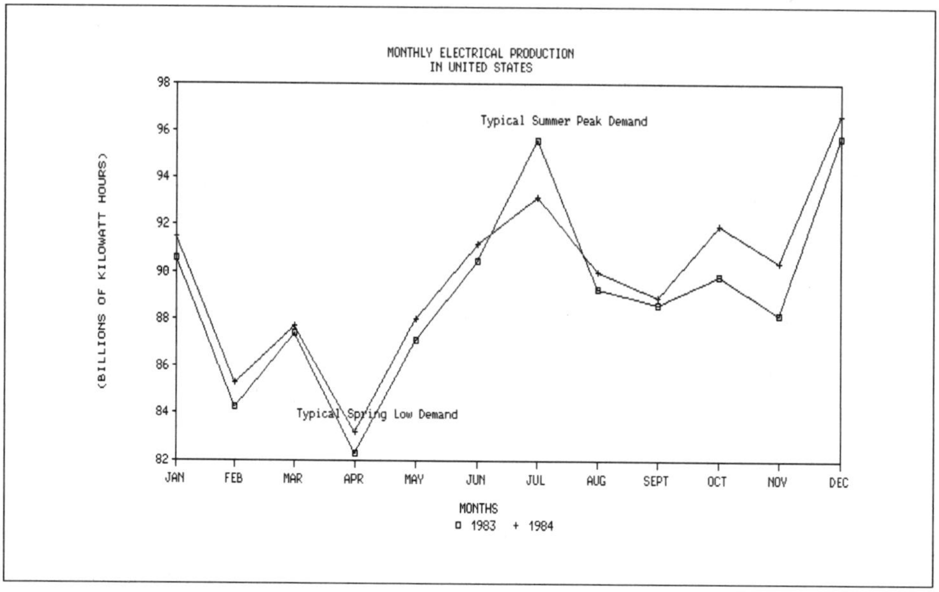

FIGURE 24.5: Screen view of the line graph created from the spreadsheet data in Figure 24.4, using phantom data variables to position data labels within its borders. The two labels identifying the low and high peak periods are positioned by two factors: the value given to the associated data point and the position of the value in its cell range. The Typical Spring Low Demand label was positioned vertically by the phantom value of 84 and horizontally by being entered as the third value in its range (the same as Mar in the graph). The Typical Summer Peak Demand label was positioned vertically by the phantom value 96.5 and horizontally by being entered as the sixth value in its range (the same as Jun in the graph). Both labels are positioned to the right of their invisible data points.

Adding grid lines can sometimes improve a graph's legibility by making it clear when individual values in the graph exceed or fall below values called out by the tick marks. However, they can also clutter a graph and possibly obscure the symbols Lotus 1-2-3 uses to represent the individual data points, especially if you are creating a line or XY graph. When the program draws grid lines, the lines go right through the graph symbols used and any data labels assigned. Instead of providing a background against which the graph is drawn, in Lotus 1-2-3 they are always in the foreground, both when viewed on the screen and when printed. Often this overpowers the graphed data and detracts from the graph's overall legibility.

Using data labels offers an alternative to using grid lines. With them, you can display the actual numerical values near the plotted data variables. Having the actual values displayed above the data variables can clear up any ambiguities about where they fall in relation to the axes of the graph.

ADJUSTING THE SCALING OF A GRAPH

When Lotus 1-2-3 scales the Y axis, it chooses the upper and lower limits for the scale based on the highest and lowest values of the data assigned to the various data variables. It then subdivides this range into equal increments and displays a tick mark with its appropriate value labeled on the Y-axis line. When it scales the X axis, it takes the number of values in each data variable and spaces them equally along the X-axis reference line. Each value represented is given its own tick mark on this horizontal line.

Although Lotus 1-2-3 handles this scaling of the X and Y axes automatically, you can also set the upper and lower limits for either axis manually. You may want to adjust the scaling of the axes when you find that the plotting of one of your data variables coincides with the top line of the graph (which is an extension of the highest value on the Y axis) or falls on the Y-axis line itself.

You may also want to adjust the scaling when you are creating a number of graphs that are to be compared with one another. It is always easier to compare graphs when they are on the same scale. If you leave it to automatic scaling, they will probably all have slightly different Y scales because of the differences in high and low values in the spreadsheet data used to create each graph.

Setting New Upper and Lower Limits for the X and Y Scale To adjust the scale, you must choose the Scale option from the Options submenu and then choose either Y Scale or X Scale, whichever is appropriate. The menu options attached to both of these commands contain a Manual option that must be accessed as well as either the Lower or Upper options to reset the scale. These commands are located on this same menu level rather than being presented as suboptions. Once you have selected Manual, choose either the Upper or Lower option, depending on which limit you need to adjust. Then type in the new value be used, making sure that it is sufficient to adjust the scale as needed.

Sometimes when you view your graph after setting a new upper limit for the Y axis, you may find that Lotus 1-2-3 has set a limit that is actually higher than the new upper value you entered. This often results when the program chooses new increments for the Y scale to accommodate the new upper limit and then has to choose an upper value that represents the next highest whole increment, which ends up being above the value you entered.

Even when this happens in an on-screen display of a graph, when you print the graph you will find that Lotus 1-2-3 uses the value you entered as the upper limit for the Y scale, again adjusting the increments used on the Y scale. This is another example of the discrepancies that can occur between the on-screen display of a graph and the hard copy you obtain from using the PrintGraph utility.

Using the Skip Option In addition to choosing new upper and lower values for the X and Y scales, you can use the Skip option to adjust the values or labels used to identify the tick marks on the X axis. You generally need to use this option when these marks overlap each other at the bottom of the graph. If you have too many values in each data variable, you will find that the values or labels cannot be displayed without overcrowding.

The Skip option allows you to use only some of the values or labels to identify the tick marks on the X axis. The number you specify after choosing this option is used as the skip factor, which tells the program how many values to skip over in the cell range specified as the X variable. For instance, if you designate a skip value of 3, every third label or value in this cell range would be displayed below its tick mark on the X axis. In this case Lotus 1-2-3 displays all of the tick marks but tags only every third one. Using the appropriate skip factor therefore eliminates the overlapping that occurs when all values or labels are displayed.

Formatting the Values Along the X or Y Axis Not only can you adjust the scaling from the submenu attached to the Scale option, but you can also format the values that appear next to the X- and Y-scale tick marks just as you would format values in the worksheet itself. To do this, you choose the Format option; it gives you a menu with options identical to those found on the /Worksheet Global Format and /Range Format menus.

Most often, you will use this command to format the values on the Y scale to give the reader an idea of what type of units are represented on this axis. For instance, you could use the Currency format option to let the reader know that graph units are measured in dollars (if the Currency default symbol is still the dollar sign and has not been set to some other symbol like the British pound symbol). When using the scaling format options, you must also designate the number of decimal places to be displayed, just as when choosing a format from the /Range Format menu.

Of course, the Format command can also be applied to the X scale if it contains values whose meanings would be clarified if they were also formatted with a particular option. This is not usually the case in graphs besides the XY type, because in those the X axis often represents a time factor that is better expressed with labels taken from spreadsheet column headings.

Using the Indicator Command (Release 2 Only) There is one more Scale option, the Indicator option (added to Release 2 of the program), which allows you to remove the (Thousands) scale label indicator automatically added by the program to the annotate the Y axis. This indicator is added only when the units in the data variables to be graphed are entered in thousands or higher. Lotus 1-2-3 automatically divides the values assigned to the Y scale by thousands and adds the (Thousands) indicator to the graph. For example, if your values are expressed in hundreds of thousands of dollars, the Y-scale increments will be displayed as hundreds with the (Thousands) indicator comment added.

This system works fine as long as you have entered the values in the spreadsheet without applying any scaling factor of your own. For instance, if you enter a range of values in millions abbreviated to thousands (like 3000 for 3,000,000), the scale label indicator added to the graph will be incorrect.

In Release 1A, you have no way to remove this indicator, even if it does not correctly represent your values. In Release 2, you can suppress this indicator label, but you cannot add a new scale indicator label of your own (although you could add this kind of comment as a Y-axis title, as is done in Figure 24.5). To suppress this indicator, choose the Indicator option and select the No option from the Yes/No menu options displayed.

Having Your Graphs Displayed in Color

By default, Lotus 1-2-3 graphs are displayed on the screen in black and white. If you have a color monitor, you can use the Color command on the Options menu to display the bars or lines of a graph in different colors. The program does not, however, allow you to choose the individual colors that represent each data variable. This is preprogrammed according to the letter designation of the data variable. The following color sequence is used:

A	White	D	White
B	Red	E	Red
C	Blue	F	Blue

Data variables D, E, and F are the same colors as A, B, and C. It can be somewhat confusing to have two different data variables represented by the same color line or bar.

Changing the display from the black-and-white default to color with the Color command does not affect the printing of the graph with the Print-Graph program. You can still use this command to see your graphs in color on the screen even if you do not have a color printer or plotter.

However, if your printer is capable of printing only black-and-white graphs, you will want to use the B&W option before you use the /Graph Save command to save graphs in separate printable files. This assures that the PrintGraph program will supply the appropriate crosshatching fill for each data variable (this is really only crucial when the graph type is bar or stacked bar). Otherwise, it will print all of the bars representing different data variables in solid black.

If you have a monochrome monitor but are using a color printer, you will want to do just the opposite. When you view graphs on the screen, you will want to leave the B&W default operative, but before you save the graph in a .PIC file with the /Graph Save command, you will want to use the Options Color option. That way, the PrintGraph program will print the bars in solid fill using different colors according to the capabilities of your color printer (see Chapter 26 for specific information on printing graphs in color). After saving the graph, you can then use the B&W option to have it displayed again with different crosshatching.

Using Data Labels to Annotate Your Graph

The last option on the Options menu before the Quit option (used to return to the main /Graph Menu options) is the Data-Labels option. It allows you to place the actual data values that have been graphed or the labels contained in a range of cells in the spreadsheet near the data variable within the confines of the graph itself.

When you use this option, you must specify the letter of the data variable to which these data labels are to be applied, the cell range in the spreadsheet that contains your data labels, and, finally, where the labels are to be positioned in relation to the data points or bars used to represent the data in the graph. There are five positioning options from which you can choose: Center, Left, Above, Right, and Below.

If your graph is a bar or stacked-bar type, Lotus 1-2-3 will automatically locate the data labels above all bars representing positive values and beneath all bars representing negative values. You cannot assign data labels to a pie chart (assigning a cell range for the X range is equivalent to assigning data labels for this kind of graph).

This means that these positioning options really apply only to line and XY graphs. Depending on the number of data variables graphed and their display, you may need to locate data labels for different data variables in different positions to avoid overlapping and to keep the graph legible. You will often have to experiment by choosing a particular positioning option and then viewing the graph. If you find that your data labels conflict with other elements, you will have to select Options Data-Labels again, using the same data variable but this time choosing another positioning option. Often, because of the limited resolution of your monitor, you will find that data labels appearing very close to particular data points in an on-screen view are not located that close in the printed copy of the graph.

When you set up a cell range that holds the data labels, you do not have to enter labels for each graphed value. However, to associate the data label with the appropriate graphed value, you should enter it in the same relative position in its cell range as the value holds in the cell range containing the values. You can leave blank all cells in this range that do not require data labels.

You can also enter data labels for phantom values associated with a new data variable letter. This technique makes it possible to enter special titles inside a graph that are properly positioned with the positioning options. For more information on using this technique, refer back to the section entitled "Changing the Display of Line and XY Graphs" in this chapter.

Creating Pie Charts

Pie charts represent a special type of graph that does not use the X-Y coordinate system. Instead, they relate the various values in a single data variable as a percentage of their total. Visually, each value is drawn as a segment of a circle that represents the sum of all of the values. Each segment, or slice of the pie, is scaled according to the percentage it represents.

Because this type of graph is not drawn against an X-Y coordinate system, it does not use any of the options on the Options menu except the Titles option. When you use the Titles option with a pie chart, you use only the First and Second options to give the entire graph its general headings, as there are no X or Y axes to assign titles to.

To create a pie chart, you select the Pie option from the Type menu and define the cell range in the spreadsheet that contains the values for the First, or A, data variable. To label the segments of the pie chart, you designate the cell range in the spreadsheet that contains the appropriate labels as the X-axis range. Lotus 1-2-3 automatically calculates and displays the percentage that each segment (or value in the data variable range) represents. You cannot, however, use any type of data labels to display the actual values as well (unless they are part of the labels assigned to the X-axis range).

If there are any negative values in the range designated as the A data variable, Lotus 1-2-3 will use their absolute values and represent them in the pie as though they were entered as positive values. (There is no way to represent values less than zero without a coordinate system.) Although Lotus 1-2-3 can generate a pie chart containing negative values, be aware that their segments in the pie do not carry the appropriate meaning and another type of graph should really be used to get this point across.

When you view the pie chart you have created with the View option (or by pressing the Graph function key, F10, if you are no longer in the /Graph Menu), the pie will not appear as a perfect circle. Because most monitors have limited resolution, curves of any kind (which are drawn by short straight-line segments) appear rough and not perfectly rounded. On monitors with greater resolution, the pie may not appear as rough but may appear instead as an ellipse rather than as a perfect circle.

There is another annoying distortion that is also quite common when displaying pie charts. The labels for the segments at the widest part of the circle on the left and right side of the pie are not always entirely visible on the screen. Very often on the right side, part of the percentage value and the right parenthesis at the end of the caption is wrapped around to the left edge of the screen. Also, the caption on the left side of the graph can sometimes be truncated so that you do not see all of the segment's label on that side.

Fortunately, many printers and all plotters can do a better job of creating more rounded and more nearly perfect circles than monitors can display them on the screen. Also, because a pie chart is printed much smaller in proportion to the text of its labels when printed, none of the labels are ever split from their segments in the printed version.

Assigning Fill Types and Exploding Sections of a Pie (Release 2 Only)

Release 2 of the program has added two new features to pie charts. You can now assign your own fill types, represented by different types of cross-hatching, to individual segments of the pie as well as explode different sections. Normally, when Lotus 1-2-3 draws a pie chart, it does not use any fill for each segment but leaves each section blank. Exploding a segment of a pie chart means that the program will draw its segment slightly separated from the rest of the pie. This technique is very effective for emphasizing a particular value represented by this segment in the graph.

Both of these enhancements are accomplished by adding code numbers to a new cell range in the spreadsheet and then assigning this range as a B data variable for the pie chart you are creating. There are seven different code numbers, each representing a different type of crosshatching. Figure 24.6 shows the code numbers and the fill type associated with each one. Notice that no fill is indicated as zero. Actually, you do not need to enter this code into a cell in the B data variable range. Leaving the cell blank accomplishes the same thing.

To explode a segment of a pie graph, you add 100 to the code number representing the fill type you want to assign to it. Figure 24.8 shows an example of a pie chart in which the second segment has been exploded. To accomplish this, the code number 102 was used (this segment uses the crosshatching assigned by code 2). All of the code numbers used in this pie chart (shown in Figure 24.7) were entered into the cell range D6..D9. This cell range was then defined as data variable B of the graph.

You can explode as many segments of your pie graph as you want; this feature is not limited to only one segment. To explode a segment and leave it blank, you merely enter the number 100 in the appropriate cell of the cell range defined as data variable B.

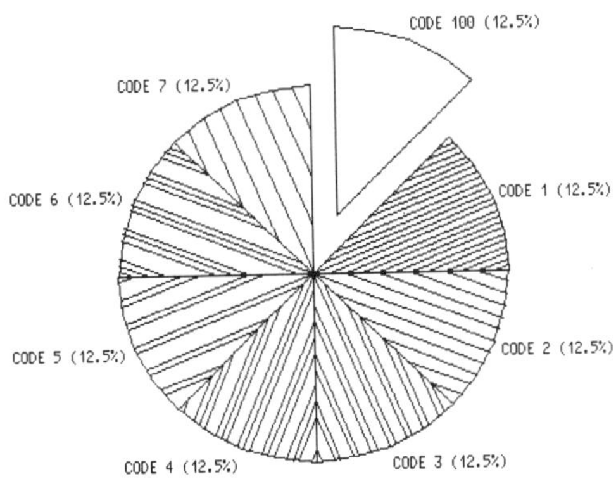

FIGURE 24.6: The seven different fill types that can be used in a pie chart are shown here associated with their code numbers. The first code number, 0, has been exploded by entering it as 100 (when you wish to have a segment remain blank and not explode it, you do not need to enter any code number for it). The other fill types can also be used in exploded segments of the pie graph by adding 100 to each of their code numbers. Figures 24.7 and 24.8 illustrate how these numbers are entered into a spreadsheet and how they affect the resulting pie graph.

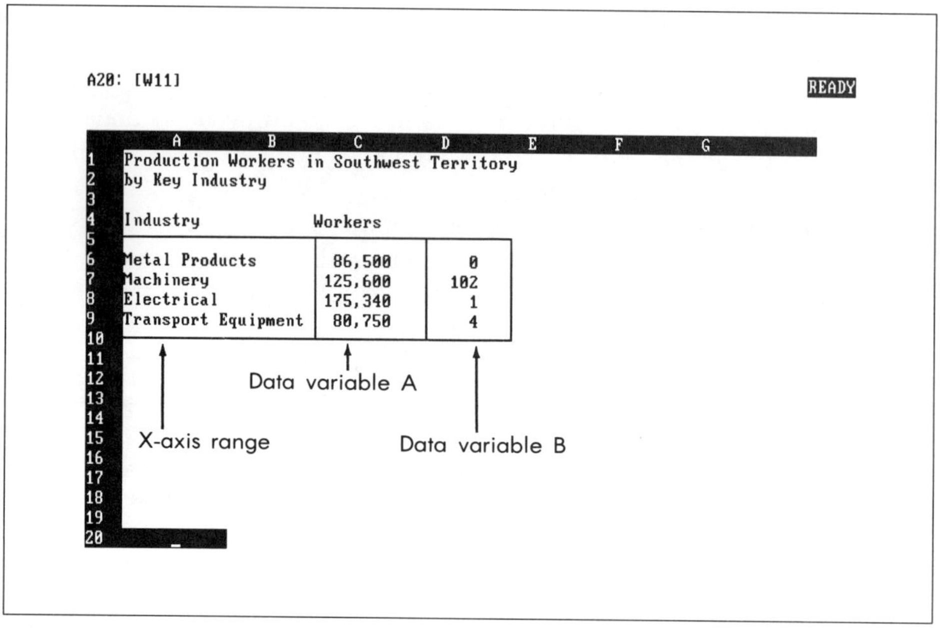

FIGURE 24.7: This figure shows the spreadsheet data used to produce the exploded pie chart in Figure 24.8. The cell range C6..C9, which contains the data on the number of workers in each industry, is defined as data variable A. Its values determine the size of the segments and the percentages displayed next to each. The cell range A6..A9 containing the industry labels is defined as the X-axis range. To assign different fill types and to explode the second segment of the pie (showing the percentage of workers in machinery), the values in cell range D6..D9, representing the fill codes, were added. This range is defined as data variable B (which is normally not used by pie graphs). You can see the result of adding these code numbers in Figure 24.8.

You will often find it convenient to enter the code numbers for assigning fill types, exploding pie segments, or both, in a cell range directly below or to the right of the range of cells containing the graphed values. You can then use the /Range Format Hidden command to hide their display in the spreadsheet itself because their values are extraneous to the worksheet but must remain there to control the graph. You can also use the Hidden format to suppress the display of other graph titles and phantom values that control other types of graphs but add nothing to your spreadsheets.

Enhancing Lotus 1-2-3 Graphs

While almost all users are impressed by the ease with which Lotus 1-2-3 can generate graphs from spreadsheet data, many are somewhat disappointed with

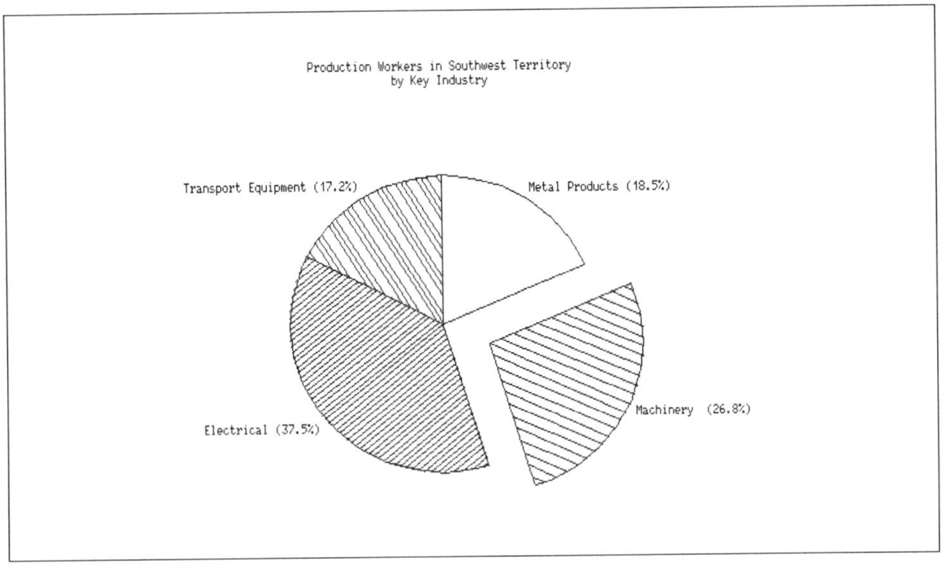

FIGURE 24.8: This figure shows the pie chart produced from the spreadsheet in Figure 24.7. The first segment, representing the percentage of metal workers in the territory, is left blank because the first cell of the range assigned to data variable B contains a 0 (the same result would occur if the cell had been left empty). The second segment, for machinery workers, uses the second fill type and is exploded, because the second cell of this cell range contains the value 102 (100 for exploding and 2 for the fill type). The third segment, for electrical workers, uses the first fill type (code number 1), and the fourth segment, for transportation workers, uses the fourth fill type (code number 4).

the results, especially when more sophisticated graphics capabilities are required than the program currently offers. This is particularly true when the graphs produced from worksheet data are to be captured by some sort of photographic process and turned into slides or transparencies. In most cases, the slides produced from Lotus 1-2-3 graphs are not of sufficiently high quality for use in formal business presentations.

Even in situations where the graphs are not going to be used in media presentations but instead are going to be included in formal written reports, there are many times when the limited selection of graph types and inflexibility with regard to graph layout make it impossible to use Lotus 1-2-3 graphs without modification.

For instance, many users who regularly use bar charts would like to be able to have the bars run horizontally from left to right across the graph plane instead of vertically from bottom to top (the only way supported by the program). Even when the basic graph presentation fits the bill, some fixed style choices made by Lotus 1-2-3 can cause problems.

A good example of this is the way Lotus 1-2-3 handles graph legends, automatically placing them at the bottom of the graph beneath the X-axis title. Traditionally, legends are placed on the right side of the graph plane, usually running vertically down this side, balancing the Y axis and its titles on the left side. Placed at the bottom of the graph as Lotus 1-2-3 does, they have quite a bit less impact. Also, the program does not leave sufficient room between the X-axis title and the legend (it doesn't even skip one line between them). As a result, when you use a long X-axis title and have a complicated legend containing many different elements, this area becomes overcrowded and hard to read.

Using Add-On Graphics Products to Enhance Lotus 1-2-3 Graphs

One way around these limitations is to use an add-on graphics product that allows you to enhance the basic graph created by Lotus 1-2-3 without requiring you to redraw it. Many such products are available. If you work a great deal in graph production from Lotus 1-2-3 spreadsheets, you may find it advantageous to invest in one of these products, especially if you find yourself having to make manual changes to graphs after they are printed.

One of these products, called Freelance, is put out by Lotus Development Corporation. As you might expect, this product is compatible with all Lotus 1-2-3 graphs and can directly read all files that carry the .PIC file extension. In fact, it contains two import options, PIC and RAW PIC. The PIC option is most often used to convert a Lotus 1-2-3 graph directly into the Freelance format (see Figure 24.9 for an example). If the program is not able to convert your graph into its format, you use the RAW PIC format. This draws the Lotus 1-2-3 graph exactly as it appears in the program as line segments in Freelance. However, using this method makes editing a slower process, because you do not have the benefit of having the graph converted into various Freelance shapes (rectangles, pie segments, and the like) that can be rearranged easily.

Another benefit Freelance offers is that its menu system is very similar to Lotus 1-2-3's, and it works in the same way as in Lotus 1-2-3. In Freelance, you can type the first letter of the command word or use the cursor keys to highlight it and then press the Return key to access any command. For example, Freelance contains a very similar File menu: you save your graphs with File Save, load them with File Retrieve, and bring

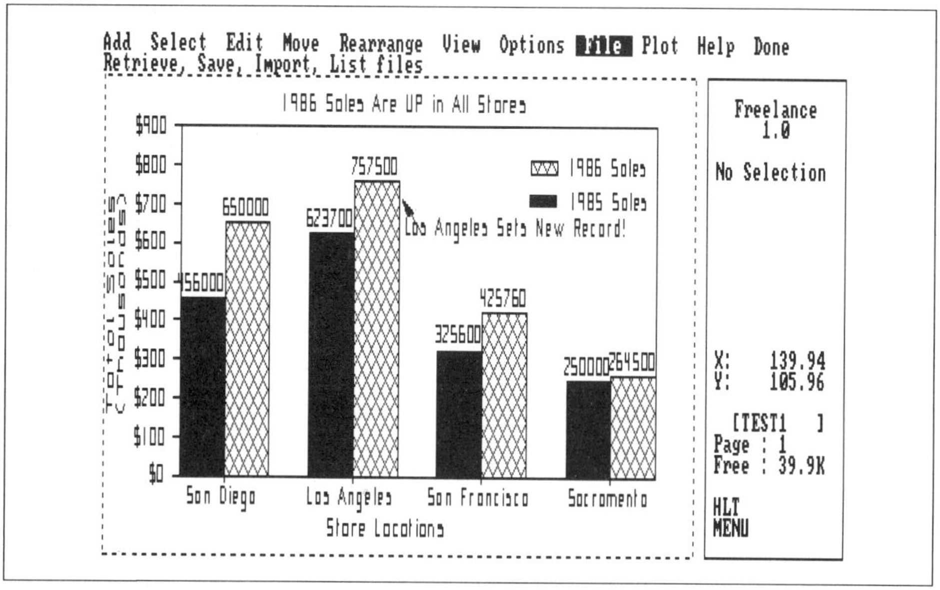

FIGURE 24.9: This figure shows the Freelance menu system and a copy of the bar graph shown in Figure 24.2, which was imported directly into Freelance and enhanced. The screen is divided into three areas: a Menu area, which works like the Lotus 1-2-3 menu system; an Information Panel, which gives you information about the graphics elements selected; and a View area, which currently contains the bar graph created in Lotus 1-2-3. Notice that the fill types assigned by Freelance to the bars in this graph are not the same as those assigned by Lotus 1-2-3 (see Figure 24.2). A few changes have already been made to the graph to improve its legibility, most noteworthy of which is the relocation of the graph legend from the bottom of the graph to the right corner of the graph (see the accompanying text for a description of others).

in Lotus 1-2-3 graph files with File Import. These can be accessed by just typing FS, FR, and FI (none of the Freelance commands requires typing the /, as in Lotus 1-2-3, because the Freelance command menu always remains visible on the screen). Of course, Freelance also contains many unfamiliar commands and menus because of its specialized application as a presentation graphics program.

To get an idea of how such a product can help you enhance a typical Lotus 1-2-3 graph, refer to Figure 24.9. This is the same bar graph illustrated earlier in this chapter in Figure 24.2. In fact, an exact copy of the graph file used to produce this figure was imported into Freelance by using the File Import PIC command. When Freelance converted this bar graph into its own format and drew it on the screen, it automatically changed the fill types used for the bars. This change from wide left and right crosshatching in the Lotus 1-2-3 graph to solid and the crisscrossed pattern seen in Figure 24.9 was not done by using Freelance's editing features.

There are, however, some changes to this graph that were accomplished by using the editing features of Freelance. First, the legends for data variables A and B were moved from below the X axis, where Lotus 1-2-3 always places them, to the upper-right corner of the graph. Also, the original X-axis title, Store Location, was deleted and then reentered in Freelance. This was done to enlarge the title so that it would print as large as the first title of the graph (Lotus 1-2-3 always puts the second, X-axis, and Y-axis titles in a smaller font than the first title).

Then the second title was moved from the line beneath the first title to its present position just below the repositioned graph legend. An arrow was then drawn from this title to point out the bar to which it refers. Finally, the first title was repositioned so that it would be printed closer to the top border of the graph.

While many more changes and additions could still be made to this graph, it is important to point out that these modifications took just a few minutes, because each title and legend box was already converted into a discrete Freelance graph element. This made it extremely easy to select each one and move it into its new position. (However, these changes are not nearly so quick and easy in cases when the .PIC file has to be imported into the program by using the RAW PIC option.)

Freelance has many capabilities whose descriptions are beyond the scope of this book, and it is not the only presentation graphics program that can be used to enhance Lotus 1-2-3.

THE /GRAPH COMMAND MENU

The /Graph Menu controls all aspects of creating graphs from existing spreadsheets. You also use it to view graphed results on the screen, name individual graphs that are to be saved as part of the worksheet file, and save graphs in separate graph files. You cannot, however, print graphs from this menu. All graph printing is controlled from a separate PrintGraph program that can be accessed from the Lotus Access System Menu or directly from the DOS operating system (for information on printing graphs, see Chapter 26).

Many of the menu options available from the /Graph main menu are tied to suboptions. The most complex is the Options menu, whose many options are used to refine the basic graph. Many of the menus attached to the /Graph command have Quit options, allowing you to select various command options from them by typing only the initial letter of the command word. Each of the menus and their individual options is explained in the Usage section that follows. They are presented in the order in which they occur on their menus.

MENUS

/Graph
Type X A B C D E F Reset View Save Options Name Quit

KEYBOARD ENTRY

/G
T X A B C D E F R V S O N Q

FUNCTION

The /Graph command gives you access to all of the command options needed to create graphs from data already entered into a Lotus 1-2-3 spreadsheet or database application. The program gives you a choice of five basic graph types: line, bar, XY, stacked bar, and pie.

When creating a graph, you can use the View command to view its current state if your computer is equipped with some sort of graphics card. Lotus 1-2-3 switches the full-screen view from the spreadsheet to the graph. To return to the /Graph Menu and the spreadsheet from the graph display, you can press any key. If you use the Quit option on the /Graph Menu to return to READY mode to make some changes to the worksheet, you can view the graph currently defined by pressing the Graph function key (F10). Again, pressing any key will then return you to the spreadsheet view.

USAGE

To create a Lotus 1-2-3 graph, you specify only two elements from the /Graph Menu: the type of graph by using the Type command (Line graph is the default supplied if you do not use this option) and the cell range or ranges containing the values to be graphed. You define each cell range as a specific data variable by designating it as an alphabetical letter between A and F. If you are using a graph type other than the pie graph, you can designate the labels or values that identify the X axis by using the X option to define the appropriate cell range in the worksheet.

After defining the basic graph in this way, you can add many types of enhancements before saving the graph as part of the worksheet file or in a separate, printable graph file. This is done by using the commands available from the Options menu. From there, you can add titles, legends, or grid lines to your graph, change the scaling of its X or Y axis, format its values, set the graph to display in color (if you have a color monitor), and specify labels to identify the data points for each data variable.

The use of all the /Graph Menu options, with the exception of the Quit commands attached to various submenus, is discussed in the individual sections that follow. The Quit commands on these menus all work just like pressing the Esc key: they back you up to the previous menu level. For instance, if you manually change the upper limit of the Y scale (by typing **OSYMU** and entering its new value) and then want to view its effect on the graph, you would use the Quit command twice to back up to the /Graph Menu and then use the View command to display the graph (by typing **QQV**). You can also return to the View command by pressing the Esc key twice.

Selecting the Kind of Graph with the Type Command

The first option on the /Graph Menu is Type; it is used to assign one of the five graph types to the graph you are building. The default graph type is Line. The Type menu options appear as follows:

Line Bar XY Stacked-Bar Pie

To choose a new graph type, type the first letter of the graph name.

You can use the Type command to change the graph type at any time after defining it. This allows you to view the information graphed in another format. Often, experimenting with different graph types helps you decide which one displays the data most clearly.

If you wish to save your data in more than one type of graph, you first access the Type command, select the appropriate type, and then use the Name Create command to give it a unique name. You would then use the Type command a second time, this time selecting a new graph type, which you would give another name by using the Name Create command. When the worksheet was saved with the /File Save command, you would then have the same information presented in two different graph formats that could be viewed or saved in separate graph files for printing.

The Line Graph Option A line graph represents your data as individual data points connected by lines. Each data point represents the magnitude of the value in that data variable compared against the Y scale of the graph. Each data variable used in the graph is defined by assigning a range of values in the spreadsheet to a particular data variable letter from A to F.

The values in each data variable are given different symbols to differentiate them in the graph. These are assigned according to the letter of the data variable used. They can be seen in Table 24.1 earlier in this chapter.

If you wish to change the way a line graph is displayed to show just the symbols or lines, you use the Format option attached to the Options menu. You can use the Legend option on the Options menu to create a legend that labels each of the symbols used. This helps the reader quickly identify what each data variable represents. (See "The Options Command Menu" section for information on using this command.)

Figure 24.10 shows an example of a typical line graph drawn by Lotus

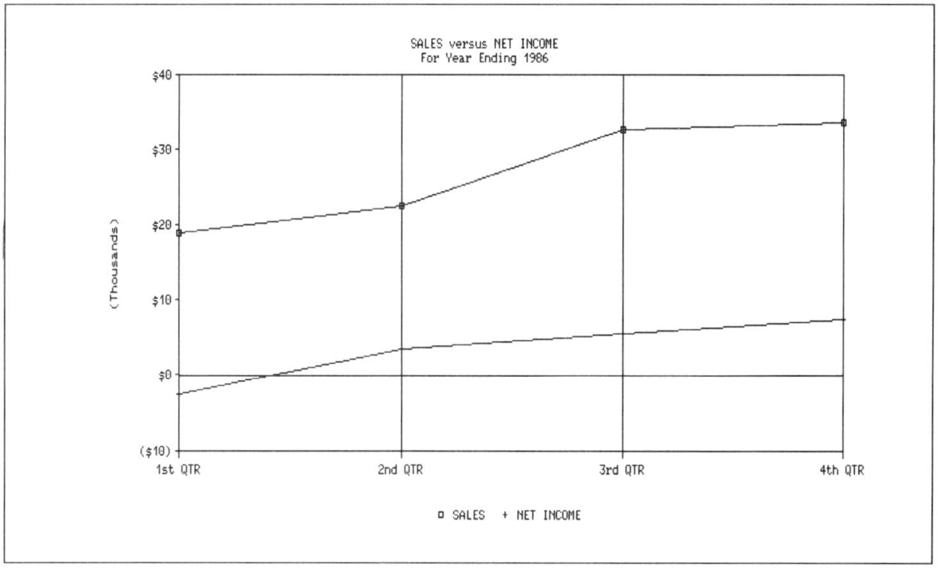

FIGURE 24.10: This figure shows a typical line graph using the program's default display, whereby the symbols for the data points are displayed along with interconnecting lines. Vertical grid lines were added to this graph by using the Options Grid Vertical command sequence; their presence obscures the cross symbol used to represent the Net Income figures, making it appear as though only the Lines Format option were used for this data variable. Notice that the negative value entered for the first-quarter Net Income figure has caused Lotus 1-2-3 to add a zero baseline. The Y scale was formatted using the Currency format with zero decimal places (using the command sequence Options Scale Y Scale Format Currency 0).

1-2-3. This line graph contains two data variables (A and B) comparing gross sales to the net profit figures for four quarters. Notice how it highlights the negative value for the first-quarter loss by automatically drawing a horizontal base line representing zero in the graph.

The Bar Graph Option A bar graph represents data as individual vertical bars, each one showing the magnitude of the value compared to the Y scale of the graph. Each data variable used in the graph is defined by assigning a range of values in the spreadsheet to a particular data variable letter from A to F.

The bars representing individual data values in each data variable are given different crosshatching fill patterns or colors to differentiate them from one another in the graph. These are assigned according to the letter of the data variable used. If you have a color monitor, you can have the bars of the graph displayed in different colors by using the Color option on the Options menu. For a listing of the fill patterns and colors assigned, refer to Table 24.1.

You can use the Legend option on the Options menu to create a legend that labels each of the fill types or colors used. This helps the reader quickly identify what each data variable represents (see "The Options Command Menu" section for information on using this command).

Figure 24.11 contains the same information graphed as a line graph in Figure 24.10, this time shown as a bar graph. The bar graph contains thc samc two data variables (A and B). Notice how this type of graph emphasizes the negative value for the first-quarter Net Income figure not only by drawing a zero baseline but also by drawing the bar down from this line.

The XY Graph Option The XY graph, also known as a scatter plot or scatter diagram, differs significantly from the other types of Lotus 1-2-3 graphs, even though its format resembles that of the line graph. An XY graph uses numerical values for both the X and Y axes of the graph. Each data point in the graph is plotted according to pairs of values, one set for the X axis and another for the Y axis. This kind of graph can be used to illustrate simple linear regression analysis done with the /Data Regression command.

Typically, an XY graph illustrates only one data variable, with the symbols representing the data points shown without any connecting lines

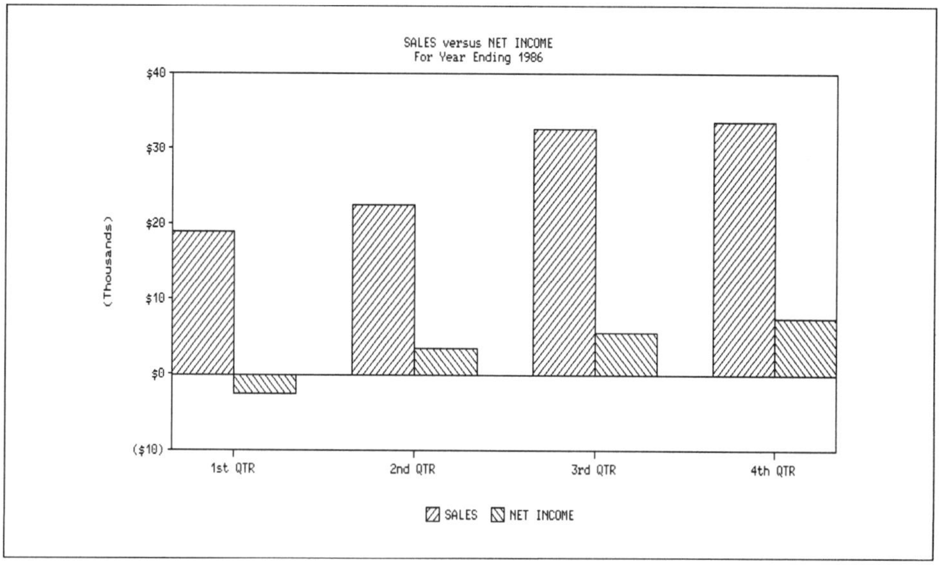

FIGURE 24.11: The graph in this figure represents the same data shown in Figure 24.10, this time as a bar graph. In fact, it was created from the line graph in that figure by using the Type Bar and the Options Grid Clear command sequences. This time, the negative value for the first-quarter Net Income is handled a little differently. Lotus 1-2-3 not only draws a zero baseline but also draws the bar down from this baseline, emphasizing the loss even more.

between them. The magnitude of the data points on the Y scale is plotted by using the values in a cell range defined as the first variable with the A command on the /Graph Menu. The magnitude of the data points on the X axis is plotted by using the values in a cell range defined as the X-axis range with the X command on the /Graph Menu. It often improves the legibility of an XY graph to use the /Data Sort command to arrange the A data variable values in ascending order before creating the graph.

To display an XY graph showing only the symbols, you use the Format option attached to the Options menu (see "The Options Command Menu" section for information on using this command). Because only one data variable is represented by the pairs of values in the spreadsheet, only the first type of symbol is used and a legend is not required.

Figure 24.12 shows a typical XY graph drawn with Lotus 1-2-3. This graph illustrates the relationship between income and consumption from a data sample taken from six families at random. In keeping with common practice for drawing scatter diagrams, the default display showing both data point symbols and the line connecting them was changed to symbols only.

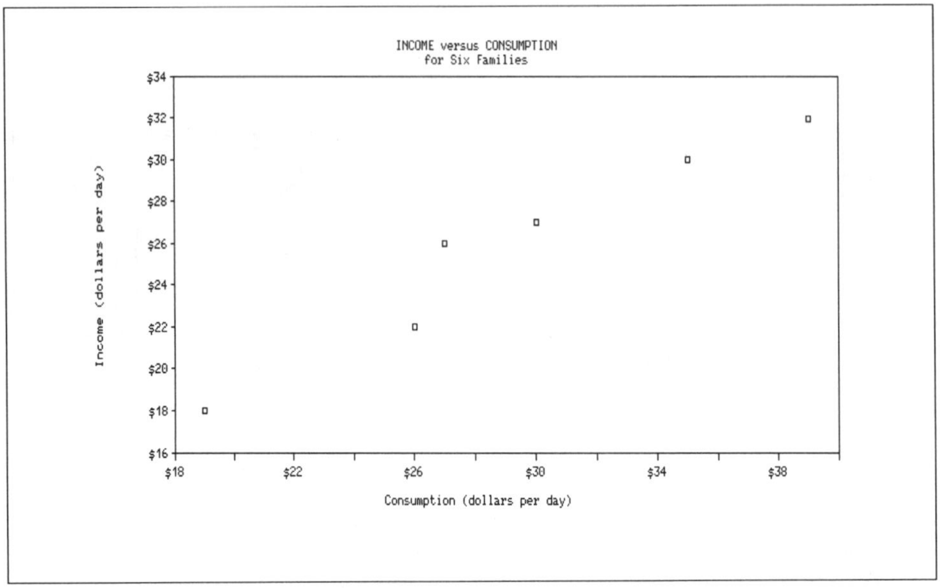

FIGURE 24.12: This figure shows an XY graph plotting income versus consumption for six families chosen at random. The income figures (in dollars per day) were entered into one range of the spreadsheet and assigned to data variable A. The consumption figures (again, in dollars per day) were entered into a second range assigned to the X-axis range. The Options Format Graph Symbols command sequence was used to display only the data points, as is common practice when creating a scatter diagram. Notice that both the Y axis and the X axis were formatted to the Currency format.

The Stacked-Bar Graph Option A stacked-bar graph is a special type of vertical bar graph in which the value for each data variable is accumulated to determine the magnitude of the bar on the Y axis. There are as many stacks in a single vertical bar as there are data variables defined. Each stack is given its own fill pattern or color to differentiate it within each bar. The relative size of the stack represents the percentage of each value to the total of all values. This type of graph is useful for comparing each value to the total for each time period as well as for comparing these totals to each other across the time periods.

The position of the stack in each bar and the type of fill pattern or color used is determined by the order in which the data variables are defined using the letter commands A to F on the /Graph Menu. You can use the Legend option on the Options menu to create a legend that labels each of the fill types or colors used. This helps the reader quickly identify what type of data is represented by each data variable (see "The Options Command Menu" section for information on using this command).

Figure 24.13 shows the same information that was graphed as a line graph in Figure 24.10 and as a bar graph in Figure 24.11. Here it is shown as a stacked-bar graph using the same two data variables (A and B). Instead of being displayed by two bars, these are now shown as stacks in the same bar, with net income above the sales figures. The loss in the first quarter is represented by the crisscross fill pattern, which is not used in the rest of the top stacks representing net income.

The Pie Graph Option The Pie option on the Type menu is used to represent data as a pie chart. This type of graph uses only one data variable, assigned with the A command on the /Graph Menu, for a single range of values in the spreadsheet. Each value in the data variable is compared as a percentage of the total of all values used. This percentage is represented by an individual segment of a circle representing the total, or 100 percent. This type of graph is very good for comparing the parts as they relate to the whole.

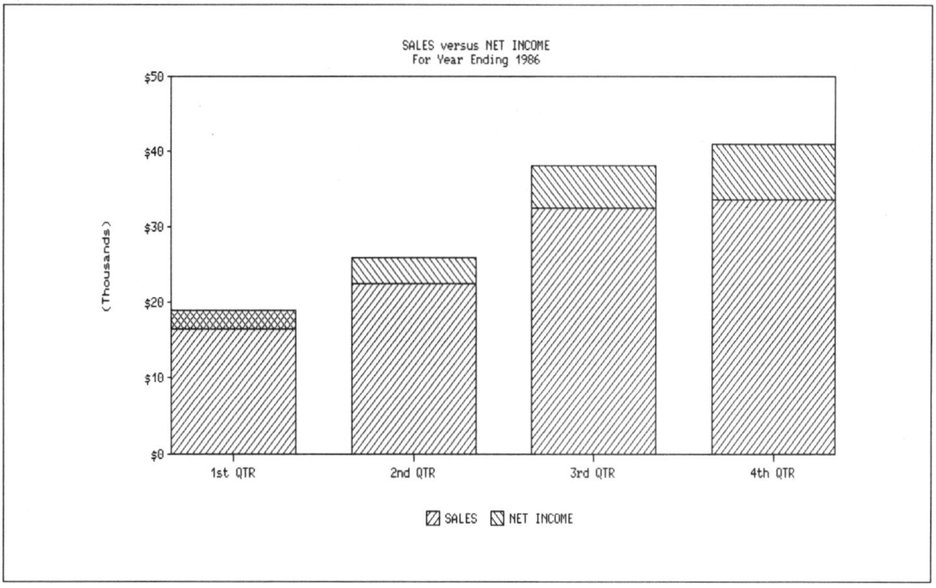

FIGURE 24.13: This figure uses the same data shown in a line graph in Figure 24.10 and in a bar graph in Figure 24.11 to produce a stacked-bar graph. In this type of graph, the values are stacked on top of each other rather than being represented by two bars, side by side. The negative value for the first-quarter loss is highlighted by the crisscross fill in the top stack of the first bar, not shared by the other stacks shown for the other three quarters. The absolute value of this loss figure has been used so that the graph can show its relative size compared to the sales figures for this quarter. As a result, the negative value no longer appears below a baseline. This graph could easily be misinterpreted.

Lotus 1-2-3 automatically displays the percentage it calculates for each segment. To add labels to identify what type of data each segment represents, you use the X-axis range (the X command on the /Graph Menu) to assign these labels from a cell range in the spreadsheet. Negative values in the range are graphed as though they were entered as positive values, displaying their segments incorrectly as positive percentages.

No fill type or special color is assigned to each segment. If you are using Release 2, you can assign different fill patterns to each segment of the pie as well as explode specific segments to emphasize them in the graph. For information on how to use these features, refer to the section "Assigning Fill Types and Exploding Sections of a Pie."

Figure 24.14 shows a typical pie chart comparing the percentages of different types of expenses for the year ending 1986—G&A, Operating, Marketing, and a miscellaneous category called Other. This graph was prepared with Release 2 to illustrate the use of different shading patterns and exploding a section for emphasis.

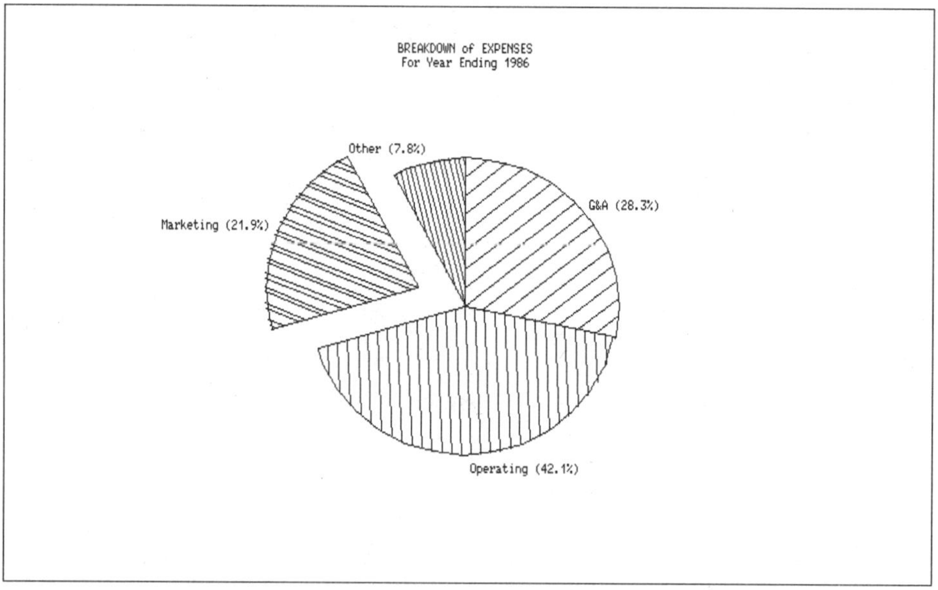

FIGURE 24.14: This figure shows a pie graph that compares expenses broken down by category for a single fiscal year. Each figure entered by category in the spreadsheet is transformed into a percentage of the total expenses in this format. The size of each slice of pie representing one type of expense is determined by its percentage. To enhance this graph, fill types have been assigned to each segment of the pie. The share of marketing expenses has been emphasized by exploding its slice.

Defining Data Variables with the X A B C D E F Commands

The group of commands represented by alphabetical letters is used to assign the values in your spreadsheet that are to be included in the graph you are creating.

Defining the X-Axis Range The first command in this group, X, is used to designate the X-axis range. The use for this command varies according to the type of graph you are creating:

- In line, bar, and stacked-bar graphs, the X-axis range designates a cell range containing labels that are to be displayed along the X axis of the graph. Each label is associated with a specific tick mark and identifies the data in each data variable graphed.
- In an XY graph, the X-axis range designates a cell range that contains one set of the pairs of values that determine the placement of the data points along the X axis.
- In a pie chart, the X-axis range designates a cell range containing the labels used to identify each section of the pie. If you specify an X-axis range, these labels are placed immediately before the percentages displayed by the program, next to the appropriate segment.

When you define the cell range for each X-axis range, you indicate its extent just as you would any other Lotus 1-2-3 cell range—that is, by typing in the cell addresses or range name or by pointing. If you are using this option to define a range of values for an XY graph, the values contained in the range are placed below each tick mark and can be formatted with the Scale Format option.

Defining Data Variables A through F The commands A B C D E and F are used to designate the cell ranges in the worksheet that contain the various values to be graphed. You can specify up to six different ranges, each representing a letter variable from A to F. You define each cell range containing values to be graphed by first typing the letter of the data variable and then indicating the range of cells that contains the values to be used. When you define the cell range for each variable, you indicate the extent of the range just as you would any other Lotus 1-2-3 cell range—that is, by typing in the cell addresses or range name or by pointing. When you use pointing, you must type a period to anchor the range before using the appropriate arrow key to indicate its extent.

You specify only as many data variables as you have sets of values to be graphed in the worksheet. The letter of the data variable determines its order in the graph, with A being the first data variable and F being the sixth data variable.

When Lotus 1-2-3 creates the graph, it plots the value in each data variable against the scale of the Y axis, using the symbols appropriate to the type of graph selected. The exception to this occurs when creating a pie chart. This type of graph has no X-Y axes and requires only an A data variable to be assigned.

When you assign cell ranges to data variable letters, it is often wise to arrange your data ranges so that they can be assigned in alphabetical order. The program remembers the cell range assigned to each data variable letter. To reassign a cell range by using pointing, you must press the Esc key to unanchor the cell range and then move the pointer to the beginning of the new range.

THE RESET COMMAND

The Reset command has the following menu options:

Graph X A B C D E F Quit

Selecting the Graph option clears all previously defined graph options, returning all values to their default settings. You need to use this option only when the graph you are creating is so different from the previous one that very few or none of the previous settings apply to it.

More often, you will use the individual letter options from A to F to clear the cell range containing the values assigned to a specific data variable. This allows you to assign new values while retaining some of the common settings such as legends and titles. Resetting individual data variables makes it easier to use the pointing method to indicate new ranges of values to be used, because the screen view is not shifted to the location of the previous range. Also, you do not have to press the Esc key to unanchor the range before moving the cell pointer.

THE VIEW COMMAND

The View command on the /Graph Menu allows you to see the graph on the screen at various stages during its creation. Whenever you type **V** from the /Graph Menu, the menu and spreadsheet display is replaced by a new screen showing only the current graph. To return to the /Graph Menu, you can press any key.

Using the Graph Function Key to View the Current Graph If you have used the Quit command from the /Graph Menu to return to the spreadsheet, you need not type **/GV** to view the current graph. Instead, you can press the Graph function key (F10) to display the graph. This function key allows you to change various values represented in the graph and then see their effects without having to use the /Graph View command.

Whenever you retrieve a worksheet file, you can use the F10 function key to view the current graph. The current graph is the one that was last used when the file was last saved. To view another graph that has been saved in the same file, you must use the Name command on the /Graph Menu, select the Use option, and then type in the name of the graph. As soon as you press the Return key to enter the name, Lotus 1-2-3 automatically draws the graph on the screen. After that, you can use the Graph function key to display the graph on the screen whenever you like.

THE SAVE COMMAND

The Save command on the /Graph Menu is used to save the current graph in a separate file under the file name you assign to it. This file name is automatically appended with the file name extension .PIC. This marks it as a special file that can be printed using the PrintGraph program. If you do not use this Save command on a graph, you will not be able to print it. The graph will, however, be saved as part of the worksheet file if you use the /File Save command before exiting the program.

When assigning names to your graph files, you must obey the same file-naming conventions as when saving a regular worksheet file. Again, you can use only eight characters for the file name, and you must not use any spaces. When you issue the /Graph Save command, the program displays a line listing of all the graph file names currently in use. To give your graph a new name, type it in. The graph will be saved in whatever directory is currently set as the default.

If you wish to obtain a directory listing of only the graph files on your disk or in the current directory, you can enter the command /File List Graph (by typing **/FLG**). To delete a graph file, you must use the /File Erase command. For information on how to use the PrintGraph program to print the graph you have saved, see Chapter 26.

THE OPTIONS COMMAND MENU

The Options command provides the most complex menu hierarchy on the /Graph Menu. The commands that you access through it control all aspects of graph definition beyond selecting the graph type and the data to be graphed, naming graphs, and saving graphs. When you select Options, you are presented with the following menu:

Legend Format Titles Grid Color B&W Data-Labels Quit

As you can see, these menu options include a Quit command that allows you to choose among the various options you wish to assign to the graph you are creating without having to preface each command with O for Options. To view your graph at any stage in its development, you would type **QV** after returning to this menu.

The Legend Option The Legend option assigns labels that identify each of the graph elements used to represent the data variables in your graph. When assigning a legend, you can type in the descriptive label (up to 19 characters long) or reference a cell in the spreadsheet that contains the appropriate label. To use a label existing in a cell, preface the cell address with a backslash followed by the cell address (as in **\D10**).

The command is attached to a simple menu listing of the possible data variables from A to F. To assign a legend for each of your data variables, you must type its letter and then give the description you wish to assign to it. After you assign a legend to a particular data variable by letter, you are returned immediately to the Options menu. To assign the next legend, you must retype L before you type its letter.

The Format Option The Format command allows you to change the way Lotus 1-2-3 represents the data in line and XY graphs. It is attached to the following menu options:

Graph X A B C D E F Quit

This menu is used to designate how much of the graph is to be affected by the changes made to the way the graph elements are displayed. To change all of the data variables, select the Graph option. To change only a specific data variable in a line or XY graph, select the appropriate letter for the data variable. Using the Quit option returns you immediately to the Options menu.

After choosing the appropriate command from this menu, you are presented with the following menu options:

Lines Symbols Both Neither

If you do not want lines connecting each data point in a data variable, you can change the format of the data variable by selecting the Symbols option. To suppress the use of the symbols and show only the line for each data variable, select the Lines option.

To return a data variable to its default of displaying both symbols and the connecting lines, use the Both option. The last option, Neither, suppresses the display of the data points in the graph. You use this option to add data labels to the graph that are positioned by the values in the data variable (for an explanation and example of how this is done, refer to the section entitled "Changing the Display of Line and XY Graphs").

The Titles Option The Titles option allows you to add four different types of titles to your graph: two general titles (First and Second), a title for the X axis, and one for the Y axis. The Titles option contains these suboptions:

First Second X-Axis Y-Axis

You use the First option to enter a general title for the graph that appears on the very first line. When prompted for the title, you can type it in or reference a cell in the spreadsheet that already contains the appropriate text by typing \ and the cell address (such as **\A2**). The first title of the graph is printed in a larger font than is used to print the graph (although this is not evident when viewing a graph on the screen) to make it stand out.

If you want, you can add a second graph title by using the Second option. This title is automatically placed below the first title with a blank line left between them. Both the first and second titles are centered over the entire graph and can contain a maximum of 36 characters. This title can be entered in the same manner as the first title.

The X-Axis option lets you add a title summarizing the content of the labels or values assigned as the X-axis range. This title is centered on its own line below the tick mark labels and above the line containing the graph legend, if any has been defined. It is entered in the same way that you enter the first and second titles.

The last type of title you can define with the Title opton is a Y-axis title. This title summarizes the content of the values on the Y axis of the graph. It is rotated 90 degrees so that it reads up the left side of the graph. This title is centered between the X-axis reference line and the top border line of the graph. You can enter this title by typing in the text or by referencing a cell that already contains a suitable label, just as you enter the other types of titles.

The Grid Option The Grid option on the Options menu is used to add grid lines that form a background on the screen similar to that of graph paper. However, unlike graph paper, when Lotus 1-2-3 displays grid lines, they cut through the data points and data labels in the graph instead of appearing as a background against which the graph is drawn. The Grid option has the following suboptions attached to it:

Horizontal Vertical Both Clear

Use the Horizontal option to have the program add grid lines that run horizontally across the graph, extending from each tick mark on the Y axis to the opposite border line. Use the Vertical option to have the program add grid lines that run vertically up from each tick mark on the X axis to the top border line of the graph. Use the Both option to add both types of grid lines to the graph. Use the Clear option if you want to remove any grid lines that you previously defined for the graph with these other options.

The Scale Option The Scale option on the Options menu has several uses:

- You can use its Manual, Upper, and Lower options to set new upper and lower values for either the X or Y scale of the graph.
- You can use its Format option to format the values on the X or Y axis, using the same types of formats used to change the display of the values in the spreadsheet (with either the /Worksheet Global Format or the /Range Format command).
- If you are using Release 2, you can use its Indicator option to suppress the display of the (Thousands) label indicator or any other scale notation Lotus 1-2-3 uses when values along an axis are best represented in other units, such as (Millions) or, above a million, (Times 10E9).
- You can use its Skip option to have the program display some of the labels or values in the X-axis range at an interval that you set by number, such as displaying the label for every third tick mark on the X axis.

When you select the Scale option, you receive the following menu options:

Y Scale X Scale Skip

Choose the Y Scale or X Scale options when you want to change the upper or lower value displayed for either axis or when you want to format the values of one of these axes. If you wish to use the Indicator option, you must choose the Y Scale option first, as the Indicator option affects only the Y axis.

If you wish to restrict the display of the labels or values in the cell range defined as the X-axis range, choose the Skip command. You will then be prompted to enter a value between 1 and 8192 to be used as the skip factor. For instance, if you enter 5, the program will display only every fifth label or value in the cell range below the appropriate tick mark on the X axis. All of the other tick marks will still be displayed at the bottom of the graph, although they will no longer be labeled. This command is used to avoid the overlapping of X-axis labels that sometimes occurs when you are graphing many values.

After you choose either the Y Scale or X Scale options, the following menu of options is displayed:

Automatic Manual Lower Upper Format Indicator Quit

To set new values for the axis, choose either the Lower or Upper options, whichever applies. In either case, you will be prompted to enter the new value. After doing so and pressing the Return key, you will be returned to this menu. When you change the scale values, you must choose the Manual option before leaving this menu to have the program use your new scaling values. If you do not, you will find that the scale has not been changed when you next view the graph. You can also choose the Manual option before using the Lower and/or Upper options. To return the scale to the values automatically set up when Lotus 1-2-3 generated the graph, select the Automatic option.

To add one of the formats used by the program to the values on one of the graph scales, use the Format option. You are presented with a menu of format options identical in form and use to that found on the /Range Format menu (for detailed information on the use of each format, see the /Range Format reference entry in Chapter 5). When using formats like Currency and Fixed, you will be required to enter the number of decimal places to be displayed. However, after you choose the format and indicate the number of decimal places (if applicable), you are not required to specify the cell range to which it applies. It is automatically applied to the scale you specified before accessing the Format option.

If you are using Release 2, this menu will contain the Indicator option. Choose it to remove the (Thousands) or some other indicator label that

Lotus 1-2-3 automatically adds when it scales the Y axis and graphs values that contain thousands or larger values. When you use this command, you are presented with Yes and No options. Choose No to suppress the display of the indicator label. You can later restore it to the graph by accessing the Indicator option again, this time choosing the Yes option.

The Color and B&W Options The Color option changes the display of graphs from black and white (the program's default) to color. If you have a color monitor and some type of color/graphics card, you will want to use this option to enhance the on-screen display of your graphs. However, if you do not have a color printer, you will want to use the B&W option to change the setting back to black and white before saving your bar and stacked-bar graphs with the /Graph Save command. Otherwise, the bars will be printed solid black instead of with different crosshatching patterns.

If you have a monochrome monitor and a color printer, you will want to do just the opposite. Keep the default set to black and white until you are ready to save the graphs in their own files. Then select the Color option before using the /Graph Save command. You can then use the B&W option to restore the black-and-white setting for viewing your graphs on the screen.

The Data-Labels Option The Data-Labels option on the Options menu allows you to select a range of cells in the spreadsheet that contains labels you wish to be displayed in the graph next to their graphic representation. In line and XY graphs, the labels are displayed near the individual data points represented by various symbols. In bar and stacked-bar graphs, they are displayed over or below (when the values are negative) the vertical bars. Data labels are not used with pie charts.

When you choose the Data-Labels option from the Options menu, you are presented with the following menu options:

A B C D E F Quit

From this menu, you type the letter of the data variable to which your data labels are to be applied. After you select the data variable by letter, you are prompted to indicate the cell range in the spreadsheet that contains the labels. You can define this range by typing its cell addresses, using a range name, or pointing. If you use pointing, you must anchor the cell pointer by typing a period before using the arrow keys to define the limits of the range.

After defining the range, you will receive a new menu of options used to tell the program where to position the data labels in relation to the data points (data labels used in bar and stacked-bar graphs are automatically placed above the bar when the value is positive and below the bar when the value is negative). This menu contains the following positioning options:

Center Left Above Right Below

To have the data labels positioned above the data points, choose the Above option. If you do not specify any other placement, Lotus 1-2-3 will center the label above each data point. The same is true if you use the Below option to have the labels displayed underneath the data points (this would be done only if you used the Format Symbols command for the data variable). The Left and Right options place the data label immediately to either side of the data point.

Once you have finished defining data labels for all the data variables that you wish and have specified their relative positions, use the Quit command to return to the Options menu (to view the graph directly, you would type **QQV**).

The Name Command

The Name command on the /Graph Menu is used to name different graphs that you have created in a single worksheet, to make a new graph current, or to delete graphs that have already been defined and named from the worksheet. When you use this command, you are presented with the following menu options:

Use Create Delete Reset

The Use Option The Use option is used to make a new graph current. When you access it, you are prompted for the name of the graph to be made current. The program shows a list of graph names in use. To select the one you wish to make current, use the arrow keys to highlight it and then press the Return key. After you make a graph current, you can make changes to it by using the other /Graph Menu options. That graph will be the one that is displayed whenever you use the View command on the /Graph Menu or press the Graph function key from within the spreadsheet.

The Create Option The Create option is used to assign a name to the graph that you have created. The name you assign can have up to 15 characters and can contain spaces just like a range name. In fact, graph names are saved as part of the worksheet file, just as range names are saved when you use the /File Save command (if you assign names with the Create option but do not save the file with /FS, your graph settings will not be saved).

When you assign graph names, be careful not to unintentionally reuse a name already given to another graph. Unlike when you inadvertently save a worksheet file under a file name that is in use, Lotus 1-2-3 will not prompt you before going ahead and overwriting the settings for the original graph with those you have just defined.

You do not have to name a graph to save its settings in a worksheet if it is the only graph you have created. It is automatically considered to be the current graph, and its settings will be saved even without a name as long as you use the /File Save command before exiting the program. However, you must name a graph to save its definition if you are going to define other graphs from the same worksheet.

The Delete Option The Delete option on this menu is used to remove a graph definition from a worksheet file. This can be done whenever a particular graph is no longer needed or when you must free up memory to continue constructing the spreadsheet. When you access the Delete command, you are prompted for the name of the graph to delete. The program shows you a listing of the graph names in use. To delete a particular graph, use the arrow keys to highlight it and then press the Return key. Lotus 1-2-3 will not prompt you for confirmation but will go ahead and erase the settings for the graph as soon as you press Return. However, if the named graph was previously saved on disk with the /File Save command, the graph will still exist there until you use the /File Save command again. If need be, it could be recalled by retrieving the worksheet with the /File Retrieve command.

The Reset Option The final Name option, Reset, erases the graph definitions for all named graphs. When you use Reset, all graph names are removed without any confirmation. Use this option with care, because there are no prompts that give you a chance to reconsider. As soon as you type R for Reset, all graphs are immediately deleted.

EXAMPLES

For examples of the various graph types that can be created with the Lotus 1-2-3 /Graph command, refer to the figures shown earlier in the individual sections explaining each graph type. Figure 24.10 illustrates a line graph, Figure 24.11 a bar graph, Figure 24.12 an XY graph, Figure 24.13 a stacked-bar graph, and Figure 24.14 a pie chart.

MACROS

Two types of graphics macros are commonly used:

- Slide-show macros that automatically select and display a series of graphs already named and saved in a spreadsheet
- Macros that automatically generate a particular type of graph using predefined ranges of values in your worksheets

(It is not possible to create a macro that will automatically print your graphs, because graphs are not printed directly from the worksheet but require the separate PrintGraph program.) You can find many examples and suggestions of how to generate such graphics macros in books dedicated to creating libraries of Lotus 1-2-3 macros.

SUMMARY

To find out how to print graphs created with these commands, see Chapter 26, "Printing and Plotting Graphs." This chapter contains all of the information you need to use the PrintGraph program. Remember that only PrintGraph can print graphs that have been saved with the /Graph Save command.

To use the PrintGraph program, you must already have configured the Lotus 1-2-3 program to use your hardware (see Chapter 2).

Also, if your job requires you to use the Lotus 1-2-3 /Graph commands to create scatter diagrams (XY graphs) for doing linear regression analysis, you may want to become familiar with the uses of the /Data Regression command added to Release 2, if you have not already done so. Detailed information on its use can be found in Chapter 22 in the section entitled "Performing Simple Linear Regression Analysis."

PART 6

LOTUS 1-2-3 PRINTING CAPABILITIES

Printing reports from the worksheets you create and the graphs that are created as part of them is among the most important functions in Lotus 1-2-3. Part 6 begins in Chapter 25 with a complete discussion of how to produce written reports from worksheets, including those containing spreadsheet as well as database applications. Chapter 26 examines the PrintGraph program that you use whenever you wish to print and plot any of the graphs you have created.

Chapter 25 looks at reports from two perspectives: defining and printing reports from spreadsheet applications and defining and printing database reports. It covers all aspects of obtaining printouts from your spreadsheet data: defining the print range; laying out the report on the page; adding headers and footers; changing margin settings; adding borders to the report; and using setup codes for various print enhancements, the most important of which is compressed printing. Release 2 users will also find valuable information here on enhancing their reports by specifying page breaks and inserting formatting and print enhancement codes within the print range.

Next, Chapter 25 discusses the creation of database reports, including generating and printing mailing labels. It also includes a sample macro that illustrates how you can automate the generation of a routine report and its printing. Finally, it introduces the use of 1-2-3 Report Writer, a new standalone utility produced by Lotus Development Corporation that is designed to make it easier to produce all types of sophisticated reports from Lotus 1-2-3 worksheets.

Chapter 26 concentrates on the techniques for using the PrintGraph utility program to print or plot your graphs. Its discussions include how to configure your hardware to work with PrintGraph, how to select the graphs for printing, how to assign colors and type fonts, and how to size and orient your graphs on the paper.

CHAPTER 25

PRINTING REPORTS

Printing Reports

To print data in a Lotus 1-2-3 spreadsheet or database, you use the /Print Menu commands. This menu offers two initial options: Printer and File. When you choose the Printer option, the program sends the data in the cell range specified to your text printer using the print settings you have defined, and the program prints out a hard copy of your report.

In order to have your report printed properly, you must have already configured your printer during the Lotus 1-2-3 installation procedure. If you have not already configured your printer, refer to Chapter 2 before returning to this chapter to find out how to print reports. If you are using Release 1A, you will find the information in the section "Configuring the Default Printer and Drive (Release 1A)." If you are using Release 2, see the section "Configuring the Default Printer(s) (Release 2)."

If you choose the File option from the /Print Menu, Lotus 1-2-3 copies the data in the cell range specified to a new disk file. This disk file is saved in a format different from the one that is used to save spreadsheet data in a .WKS or .WK1 file. As a result, it is automatically given the file name extension .PRN to mark it as a special print file. Creating this type of file by using the /Print commands is useful when you want to send the data you have created in Lotus 1-2-3 to another application program.

This chapter primarily covers information on obtaining printed reports using the Printer option. You will find information on the use of .PRN files created with the File option in Chapter 29, "Importing and Exporting ASCII Files." However, if you need information on how to define the settings for a .PRN file, you should use the reference section in this chapter to look up the appropriate menu options listed in the /Print reference entry. Most of the time, you will be concerned with the Range, Margins, and Other Unformatted commands when creating such print files.

After a discussion of general principles and techniques for setting up and printing reports, you will find a complete reference entry covering the /Print Menu and all of its options. This reference entry covers each of the menu options in the order in which they are found on the /Print Menu.

Printing Spreadsheets

In order to print data from your spreadsheet the first time, you must tell Lotus 1-2-3 the range of cells to be printed. This range can consist of all cells used in the worksheet or only a portion of them. Regardless of its extent, you must use the /Print Printer Range command and define the range as you would any other cell range in the worksheet. Once this is done, you can print your worksheet by using the Align and Go commands (by typing **AG**).

Always type A for Align (although nothing will appear to have happened), because this tells Lotus 1-2-3 that the current position of the printhead is the top of form (of course, you should check to make sure that the printhead is at the top of the page before printing). The G for Go actually sends the print range to the printer and begins the printing.

If you need to stop the printer, press the Ctrl-Num Lock key combination. This acts as a printer pause. The WAIT indicator continues to flash and the printer waits until you press any key. If you wish to abort the printing of a report before it is finished, press the Ctrl-Scroll Lock (or Break) key combination. The program returns to the /Print Menu and MENU mode.

Lotus 1-2-3 will stop printing the report as soon as it reaches the last row in the print range. This usually occurs before the printhead has advanced to the bottom of the page. To advance to the beginning of the next page, type **P** to activate the Page command. This will also cause the program to print any footer that you may have specified for that short page before advancing to the top of the next page. If you forget to type **A** to activate the Align command before typing **G** for Go, you will find that the Page command will not advance the printhead to the top of the next page (it will advance it 66 lines from wherever the printing stopped on the page).

The Printing Defaults

Lotus 1-2-3 already contains many default settings for handling the page width and length as well as the left, right, top, and bottom margins. It prints your report without the column and row borders. These are the default settings used:

- A page size of $8^1/_2 \times 11$ inches. This translates into 85 characters by 66 lines of text.

- A pitch of 10 characters per inch (pica type) and single spacing (6 lines per inch).
- A nominal left margin of 4 characters and a right margin of 76 characters (that is, 76 characters from the left edge of the paper) leaves a line 72 characters wide for your spreadsheet data. This translates into approximately 5/8 of an inch on each side with a maximum line length of 7 1/8 inches.
- A top margin and bottom margin of 5 lines each (just under an inch). This leaves 56 lines to a page.
- A top margin and bottom margin for headers and footers of 2 lines from the top and the bottom of the page (approximately 3/8 inch on top and 1/4 inch from the bottom). These settings can be changed with the Options Margins Top and Bottom options.

These default settings are shown diagrammatically in Figure 25.1.

If these default settings do not fit your requirements, you can set up new defaults that the program will use whenever you retrieve a worksheet and print a report from it. For instance, if you habitually use 14-inch wide paper, you would want to set up a new default right margin setting of 136. Information on how to set up new global printing defaults can be found in Chapter 2 of this handbook, in the section entitled "Customizing the Text Printer and Interface."

However, you can also change these settings temporarily to fit your printing needs at the time. This is done by selecting the Options Margins or Options Pg-Length options after choosing the /Print Printer command (by typing **/PP**). Any setting changes made will be saved as part of the worksheet file the next time you use the /File Save command. However, they will not override the global printer defaults, which remain in effect when you start up Lotus 1-2-3 again to create a new worksheet.

Printing Worksheets Wider than 80 Columns

Lotus 1-2-3 is set up to print eight 9-character-wide columns (the global column default width) of the spreadsheet across a standard $8\frac{1}{2} \times 11$-inch sheet of paper. This translates to a line length of 72 characters at the default pitch of 10 characters per inch. If you have changed the column widths, you may be able to print more or fewer spreadsheet columns on a single page, depending on whether you have made the columns wider or narrower.

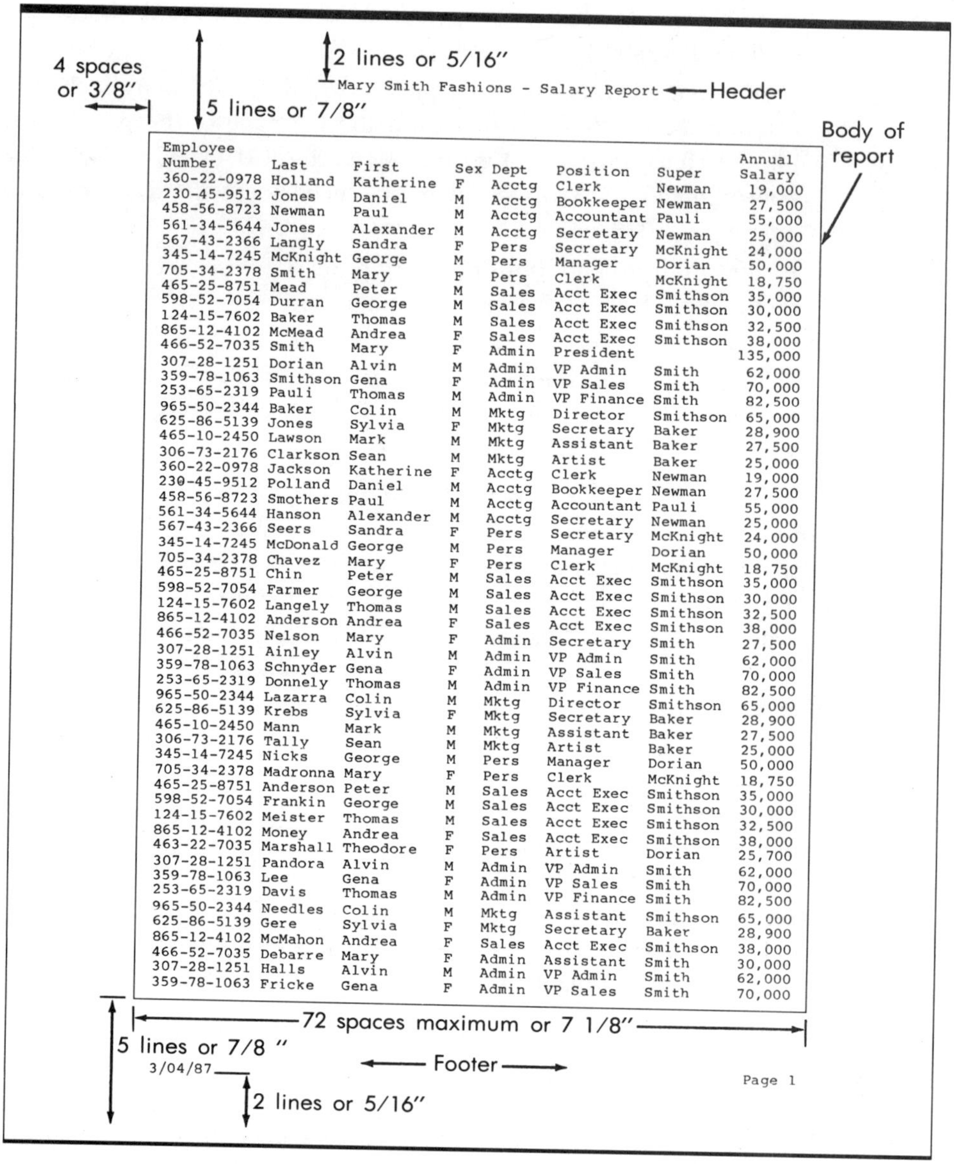

Mary Smith Fashions - Salary Report

Employee Number	Last	First	Sex	Dept	Position	Super	Annual Salary
360-22-0978	Holland	Katherine	F	Acctg	Clerk	Newman	19,000
230-45-9512	Jones	Daniel	M	Acctg	Bookkeeper	Newman	27,500
458-56-8723	Newman	Paul	M	Acctg	Accountant	Pauli	55,000
561-34-5644	Jones	Alexander	M	Acctg	Secretary	Newman	25,000
567-43-2366	Langly	Sandra	F	Pers	Secretary	McKnight	24,000
345-14-7245	McKnight	George	M	Pers	Manager	Dorian	50,000
705-34-2378	Smith	Mary	F	Pers	Clerk	McKnight	18,750
465-25-8751	Mead	Peter	M	Sales	Acct Exec	Smithson	35,000
598-52-7054	Durran	George	M	Sales	Acct Exec	Smithson	30,000
124-15-7602	Baker	Thomas	M	Sales	Acct Exec	Smithson	32,500
865-12-4102	McMead	Andrea	F	Sales	Acct Exec	Smithson	38,000
466-52-7035	Smith	Mary	F	Admin	President		135,000
307-28-1251	Dorian	Alvin	M	Admin	VP Admin	Smith	62,000
359-78-1063	Smithson	Gena	F	Admin	VP Sales	Smith	70,000
253-65-2319	Pauli	Thomas	M	Admin	VP Finance	Smith	82,500
965-50-2344	Baker	Colin	M	Mktg	Director	Smithson	65,000
625-86-5139	Jones	Sylvia	F	Mktg	Secretary	Baker	28,900
465-10-2450	Lawson	Mark	M	Mktg	Assistant	Baker	27,500
306-73-2176	Clarkson	Sean	M	Mktg	Artist	Baker	25,000
360-22-0978	Jackson	Katherine	F	Acctg	Clerk	Newman	19,000
230-45-9512	Polland	Daniel	M	Acctg	Bookkeeper	Newman	27,500
458-56-8723	Smothers	Paul	M	Acctg	Accountant	Pauli	55,000
561-34-5644	Hanson	Alexander	M	Acctg	Secretary	Newman	25,000
567-43-2366	Seers	Sandra	F	Pers	Secretary	McKnight	24,000
345-14-7245	McDonald	George	M	Pers	Manager	Dorian	50,000
705-34-2378	Chavez	Mary	F	Pers	Clerk	McKnight	18,750
465-25-8751	Chin	Peter	M	Sales	Acct Exec	Smithson	35,000
598-52-7054	Farmer	George	M	Sales	Acct Exec	Smithson	30,000
124-15-7602	Langely	Thomas	M	Sales	Acct Exec	Smithson	32,500
865-12-4102	Anderson	Andrea	F	Sales	Acct Exec	Smithson	38,000
466-52-7035	Nelson	Mary	F	Admin	Secretary	Smith	27,500
307-28-1251	Ainley	Alvin	M	Admin	VP Admin	Smith	62,000
359-78-1063	Schnyder	Gena	F	Admin	VP Sales	Smith	70,000
253-65-2319	Donnely	Thomas	M	Admin	VP Finance	Smith	82,500
965-50-2344	Lazarra	Colin	M	Mktg	Director	Smithson	65,000
625-86-5139	Krebs	Sylvia	F	Mktg	Secretary	Baker	28,900
465-10-2450	Mann	Mark	M	Mktg	Assistant	Baker	27,500
306-73-2176	Tally	Sean	M	Mktg	Artist	Baker	25,000
345-14-7245	Nicks	George	M	Pers	Manager	Dorian	50,000
705-34-2378	Madronna	Mary	F	Pers	Clerk	McKnight	18,750
465-25-8751	Anderson	Peter	M	Sales	Acct Exec	Smithson	35,000
598-52-7054	Frankin	George	M	Sales	Acct Exec	Smithson	30,000
124-15-7602	Meister	Thomas	M	Sales	Acct Exec	Smithson	32,500
865-12-4102	Money	Andrea	F	Sales	Acct Exec	Smithson	38,000
463-22-7035	Marshall	Theodore	F	Pers	Artist	Dorian	25,700
307-28-1251	Pandora	Alvin	M	Admin	VP Admin	Smith	62,000
359-78-1063	Lee	Gena	F	Admin	VP Sales	Smith	70,000
253-65-2319	Davis	Thomas	M	Admin	VP Finance	Smith	82,500
965-50-2344	Needles	Colin	M	Mktg	Assistant	Smithson	65,000
625-86-5139	Gere	Sylvia	F	Mktg	Secretary	Baker	28,900
865-12-4102	McMahon	Andrea	F	Sales	Acct Exec	Smithson	38,000
466-52-7035	Debarre	Mary	F	Admin	Assistant	Smith	30,000
307-28-1251	Halls	Alvin	M	Admin	VP Admin	Smith	62,000
359-78-1063	Fricke	Gena	F	Admin	VP Sales	Smith	70,000

3/04/87 Page 1

FIGURE 25.1: The printing defaults for Lotus 1-2-3 at startup, showing the left, right, top, and bottom margins in lines and characters per inch as well as approximate inch equivalents. The top and bottom margins to the first and last line of the body of the report are 5 lines each, or about 1 inch from the edge of the paper. Within these margins, the header is placed 2 lines above the first line and 2 lines below the last line. The left margin of 4 and right margin of 76 leaves a line length of 72 characters. With a pica pitch setting (10 cpi), this makes a maximum line length of approximately 7 1/8 inches.

When you leave the characters per inch and right margin setting defaults in effect and specify a range of cells that takes up more than 72 characters, Lotus 1-2-3 resorts to an automatic paging scheme to print all of your data. If the number of rows does not exceed 56, it prints all of the columns that will fit within the first right margin of 76 on the first page (it will not print a partial column on a page) and then prints the next set of columns on a second page.

If your report contains more rows than the 56 that will fit on a page, Lotus 1-2-3 prints the second group of rows using the first group of columns on the second page, then prints the second group of columns using the first group of rows on the third page, and so on.

To fit all of the columns of data in a print range wider than 72 characters, you have two alternatives:

- If you have a wide-carriage printer that accommodates 14-inch-wide paper, you can change the right margin to 136.
- If you have a regular 80-column printer, you can use a setup code that turns on compressed type (either to 15 cpi or 17 cpi, depending on the type of printer). You must still increase the right margin setting, or Lotus 1-2-3 will print your report using only those columns that fit within the first 72 characters.

Note: Refer to the section "Using Setup Codes to Turn on Compressed Print" if you want information on using setup codes and the codes to turn on and off compressed type for the most common printers used with Lotus 1-2-3.

For wide reports that cannot be accommodated even by using 14-inch paper and compressed type, you have a third alternative: you can invest in a stand-alone utility program like Sideways put out by Funk Software, Inc. This type of program allows you to print your spreadsheets on their side (rotated 90 degrees on the page). It also prints the columns specified in the print range continuously, even across page breaks. The result is a report that spans several pages, showing each column of data in the same relation as it was entered in the spreadsheet. With such a program, it is possible to create a report from a file with data in columns A to IV exactly as they were entered (which would be read continuously from left to right over many pages). This type of program is ideal for printing spreadsheets that are very wide but also very short (56 rows or less).

Be aware that such products work only if your printer is able to accept continuous-feed paper (the fan-folded kind with perforations between each sheet). They will not work if you are using a printer such as the HP LaserJet, which uses only single sheets of paper.

Adding Headers and Footers to Reports

You can add a one-line header, footer, or both, to your reports by using the Options Header and Footer commands. A header is text that is printed on each page of the report in the top margin. It is placed two lines down from the top of the page unless you change the default setting by using the Margins Top command from the Options menu. A footer is text that is printed on each page of the report in the bottom margin. It is placed two lines up from the bottom of the page unless you change the default setting by using the Margins Bottom command from the Options menu. To enter the text for the header or footer line, you use the command Options Header or Footer and then type the text exactly as you want it to appear in the printout.

Note: If you must add multiple-line headers and footers to your report, you will have to use an add-on product that works with Lotus 1-2-3 worksheet files. This new product, 1-2-3 Report Writer by Lotus Development Corporation, is designed to allow multiple-line headers and footers in a report. For information about this product and its capabilities, see the section entitled "Using 1-2-3 Report Writer" in this chapter.

Positioning the Text in the Header or Footer

You can use codes to specify the placement of text in a header or footer. You can also add special codes that will enter the current date or automatically number the pages of the report for you.

To center the text of a header or footer, you enter a vertical bar (¦) character before typing in the text. The vertical bar character is entered by holding down the Shift key and then pressing the backslash key (\). To right-justify the text, you would enter two vertical bar characters (¦¦) with no spaces between them before typing the text to be right aligned.

If you have three elements in your header or footer and you want the first to be left justified, the second to be centered, and the third to be right justified, you would enter the first text followed by the vertical bar, then the second text followed by a vertical bar, and, finally, the third text.

To have the current date (as supplied to the DOS operating system and shown in the on-screen clock) entered in a header or footer, you enter the @ symbol. To have the program automatically number the pages of the report, you use the # symbol. In the report, Lotus 1-2-3 will substitute the number of the page wherever this symbol occurs, beginning with the number 1. You cannot begin numbering your pages from a different number.

For example, if you wanted the title of the report to appear left justified in a header with the current date right justified, you would enter the text of the header as

PERSONNEL REPORT¦¦@

If you then wanted the page numbers to appear centered at the bottom of the report with the word Page preceding each number, you would enter the text of the footer as

¦Page #

If you had three elements to be entered in the header and you wanted them to be spaced across this line, you would modify the header as follows:

PERSONNEL REPORT¦Revision 2¦@

In this header, the title PERSONNEL REPORT would be printed flush left, Revision 2 would be centered, and the date would be printed flush right. Assuming that the current date were July 20, 1987, it would appear in the header as 20-Jul-87. To change the appearance of the date, you should change the global date format by using the /Worksheet Global Format Date command before printing the report.

Printing Identifying Columns and Rows on Each Page of the Report

In addition to printing headers and footers on each page of a report, you can use the Options Borders command to specify particular columns or rows of data to be printed on each page. This feature is generally used to add column or row headings on multipage reports to help identify the data on each page.

To use this command, you merely indicate whether columns or rows are to be duplicated on each page by using either the Borders Columns or Rows option. Then indicate the range of cells containing the columns or rows. If you do this by pointing, you must type a period to anchor the cell pointer. When indicating a range of rows, you do not need to extend the cell range horizontally to include more than the current column (this command includes all of the columns in the print range for the rows that are included). The reverse is true when indicating the range of columns. You do not need to indicate the number of rows; it is determined by the number included in the print range.

If you were using the Borders command to duplicate column headings in a single row of the spreadsheet on each page of the report, you would not include this row as part of the print range. If you did, the row of columns would be printed twice on the first page of the report, once as part of the Borders Rows range and a second time as part of the print range.

Printing the Column Letters and Row Numbers in the Report

In addition to using the Borders commands to have identifying column and row labels printed on each page, you can also have the column letters and row numbers printed in the report. Lotus 1-2-3 does not include a command that automatically prints the spreadsheet column and/or row borders as part of the report. However, you can use the Borders Columns and Rows commands if you need a printout that contains these letters and numbers.

To do this, you must insert a new row at the top of the spreadsheet (with the /Worksheet Insert Row command) and manually enter the column letters as they are displayed in the spreadsheet border above. Use the /Range Label Center command to center the range of cells containing the column letters.

To include row numbers, you would then position the cell pointer in column A and insert a new column there (with the /Worksheet Insert Column command). To add the row numbers for the border area, you can move the cell pointer down one row and use the /Data Fill command instead of having to enter each one manually.

Then, after adding the new column containing the row numbers and the new row containing the column letters, you use the Options Borders Columns and Rows options to designate the new column and the new row as the borders to be printed. Before printing the report, be sure that the print range does not include the column and row used with the Borders commands. Figure 25.2 illustrates how this arrangement would appear on the screen, and Figure 25.3 shows the final printed report with column letters and row numbers.

If you need to print a copy of the report that does not display these column letters and row numbers, use the Clear Borders command before printing the report again with the Align Go commands. Normally, when printing reports with multiple pages, you would use this technique to display only the column letters or only the row numbers, whichever is appropriate for the width and length of the print range.

Using Setup Codes to Turn on Compressed Print

When you set up the printing of a report from a spreadsheet, you can use the Options Setup command to have the report printed in a different

```
A2: [W3] 1                                                        READY

     A          B             C          D          E          F          G
 1              A             B          C          D          E          F
 2    1 Data 2000 Corporation
 3    2 Income Statement
 4    3 January 1  - December 31, 1986
 5    4
 6    5                    1st Qtr    2nd Qtr    3rd Qtr    4th Qtr      Total
 7    6 Revenues           425,000    487,500    527,000    501,200  1,940,700
 8    7   COGS             195,000    189,500    175,600    180,300    740,400
 9    8 Gross Profit       230,000    298,000    351,400    320,900  1,200,300
10    9 -------------
11   10 Operating Expense   85,000    100,000     97,500     98,500    381,000
12   11   Bonus Pool         7,812     10,742     13,970     12,078     44,603
13   12 -------------
14   13 Operating Profit   137,188    187,258    239,930    210,322    774,697
15   14   Interest Exp      17,000     22,000     25,000     24,500     88,500
16   15 Taxable Profit     120,188    165,258    214,930    185,822    686,197
17   16 -------------
18   17   Income Tax        42,066     57,840     75,225     65,038    240,169
19   18 Net Profit          78,122    107,418    139,704    120,784    446,028
20
                                                 CALC
```

FIGURE 25.2: Adding column letters and row numbers to be printed as part of a report by using the Options Borders command. To add column letter and row number references to a printed report, a new row is inserted at the top of the worksheet. In this row, the column letters are entered and then centered by using the /Range Label Center command. With the cell pointer in column A, a new column is inserted and the cell pointer is moved down one cell. There, the row numbers are entered by using the /Data Fill command. Figure 25.3 shows the printed results.

```
          A                B          C          D          E          F
 1 Data 2000 Corporation
 2 Income Statement
 3 January 1  - December 31, 1986
 4
 5                    1st Qtr    2nd Qtr    3rd Qtr    4th Qtr      Total
 6 Revenues           425,000    487,500    527,000    501,200  1,940,700
 7   COGS             195,000    189,500    175,600    180,300    740,400
 8 Gross Profit       230,000    298,000    351,400    320,900  1,200,300
 9 -------------
10 Operating Expense   85,000    100,000     97,500     98,500    381,000
11   Bonus Pool         7,812     10,742     13,970     12,078     44,603
12 -------------
13 Operating Profit   137,188    187,258    239,930    210,322    774,697
14   Interest Exp      17,000     22,000     25,000     24,500     88,500
15 Taxable Profit     120,188    165,258    214,930    185,822    686,197
16 -------------
17   Income Tax        42,066     57,840     75,225     65,038    240,169
18 Net Profit          78,122    107,418    139,704    120,784    446,028
```

FIGURE 25.3: The printed report with the column letters and row numbers. In producing this printout, row 1 was designated as the borders row and column A as the borders column. The cell range B2..G19 was used as the print range. If the report required several pages, these same column letters and row numbers would be printed on each page. In such a case, the column letters would still be correct, although the row numbers would not.

pitch. This is necessary whenever you want to keep together more columns of data than can be accommodated within a line length of 72 characters. If your printer will not accept paper wider than $8^1/_2$ inches, you will have to change to compressed print to keep the columns of data on a single page. In order to turn on compressed print, you must know the setup code used by your printer and then enter it by using the Options Setup command (you must also remember to increase the right margin setting before giving the Go command).

To find out what character string is required by your printer to turn on compressed print, refer to the documentation that accompanied your printer. Your manual will list all of the codes required to change the horizontal pitch (the number of characters per inch) and the vertical pitch (the number of lines per inch), as well as to control other types of print enhancements. It will probably also list alternatives, giving you the ASCII, decimal, and hexadecimal codes. Use the decimal codes for entering setup strings in Lotus 1-2-3. You preface each string with a backslash character and preface all two-digit numbers with a zero—for example, if your manual lists the codes to use as 27 and 14, you would enter them as \027\014.

Table 25.1 shows you some of the codes for changing the print size for the most popular types of printers. Setup codes can also be used to change

	TYPE OF PRINTER AND PITCH	SETUP STRING TO USE
Epson or IBM Graphics	12 cpi (elite) on	\027\077
	12 cpi (elite) off*	\027\080
	17 cpi (compressed) on	\015
	17 cpi (compressed) off*	\018
	8 lines per inch	\027\048
	6 lines per inch (single spacing)	\027\050
HP LaserJet	Portrait 10 cpi	\027E\027&10O
	Portrait 16.6 cpi	\027E\027&10O\027&k2S
	Landscape 10 cpi	\027E\027&l10
	Landscape 16.6 cpi	\027E\027&110\027&k2S
*When you give the code to turn off these pitches, the printer returns to 10 cpi (pica type).		

TABLE 25.1: Setup Strings for IBM/Epson Dot-Matrix Printers and the HP LaserJet

print pitches and type fonts. When experimenting with these setup strings, be sure that you have used the backslash instead of the forward slash, and that you have entered the codes exactly as they are shown (using zeros rather than Os and vice versa, and using lowercase letters where shown).

If you print a report in condensed type and exit Lotus 1-2-3 to use another application program, be aware that the printer will still be set for compressed type when you return to Lotus 1-2-3. Turning it back to the default pitch of 10 characters per inch usually requires only that you turn off the printer and then turn it back on. However, this method does not work with all types of printers. If you find that your reports or documents printed from another program are not being printed properly, look up the character string that resets the printer to its default settings and send it to the printer.

Adding Special Print Enhancements to Reports in Release 2

Release 2 has two features that give you more flexibility when setting up a printed report: a new /Worksheet Page command that forces a page break at the row where the cell pointer is located when you issue the command, and the ability to add special printer control strings within the spreadsheet to change pitch and add other enhancements such as boldface or italic type.

Using the /Worksheet Page Command

When you want to make sure that a particular number of rows are printed together on a page, you can use the /Worksheet Page command. Position the cell pointer in the leftmost column of the print range, in the row directly beneath the last row of data you want to remain on a page, and type **/WP** (you do not need to press the Return key). The page break command will not work if the cell pointer is not located in the leftmost column of the designated print range when you give the command.

Lotus 1-2-3 will enter a new row containing two colons in the cell in the leftmost column (: :). This is the symbol for a page break. Any rows of data in the print range below the row containing this symbol will begin printing on a new page of the report. If you want to print a table on its own page of the report, you would enter page break symbols by using the / Worksheet Page command both in the row right before the first row of the table and in the row below the last row of the table.

To remove a page break, position the cell pointer in one of the cells in the row containing the page break symbol, issue the /Worksheet Delete Row (/WDR) command, and press the Return key.

Adding Print Enhancements to Specific Lines of the Report

In Release 2, you can enter special print enhancements that affect only a particular group of lines in the report instead of the entire report, as is the case when you add a printer control string by using the Options Setup command. This is very useful if you want to print only the title of the spreadsheet in the report in an enlarged type such as double-width (5 cpi), leaving the rest of the report in regular pica type.

To enter a particular character string in the spreadsheet itself, position the cell pointer in the leftmost column of the print range, in the row where the enhancement is to begin. Then insert a new row to contain the printer control string by using the /Worksheet Insert Row command and pressing the Return key. Enter two vertical bar characters (¦¦) followed by the setup string to use.

To produce a report title in double-width type, the setup code is 27 14 if you are using an Epson or IBM dot-matrix printer, so you would enter this string as

¦¦\027\014

In the spreadsheet, you would see only ¦\027\014 displayed. The first vertical bar character does not appear in the cell, although it must be entered for the control string to work properly.

This particular setup code instructs the printer to print only the following line in enlarged print; it automatically returns the printer to pica type after that line is printed. However, you can enter codes that not only must be turned on by entering a code but also must be turned off again in the row below. For instance, if you wanted the spreadsheet title and the column headings printed in boldface type and the rest of the report in regular single-strike type, you would have to insert two blank rows in the spreadsheet, one containing the code to turn on boldface type and another to turn it off.

For example, the control code to turn on double-strike for the Epson and IBM graphics dot-matrix printers is \027\071, and the code to turn it off is \027\072. To have only the first few rows containing the spreadsheet title and column headings printed in boldface, you would move the cell pointer to cell A1 (or the upper-leftmost cell of the print area), insert a new row, and enter the code to turn on double-strike. Then you would move the cell pointer down to the first row below the column headings (still in the leftmost column) and insert another row where you would enter the code to turn it off.

Note: When you enter new rows that contain printer control codes, make sure that the cells containing the codes are included as part of the print range. If you have already entered a print range and then insert a new row for the codes, it will not automatically be included in the print range. If your control codes are not part of the print range, Lotus 1-2-3 will ignore them. Also remember that all printer control codes must be entered in the leftmost cell of the row (usually, column A), or they will be printed as regular spreadsheet labels.

Obtaining a Printout of the Formulas in the Spreadsheet

The Lotus 1-2-3 /Print Menu contains a Cell-Formulas option accessed with the Options Other command that allows you to obtain a printout of the contents of all cells in the specified print range. This includes all labels or formulas in the cells, although the program ignores any blank cells in the print range. Each occupied cell is printed on a separate line in the final report. The listing of the cells' contents is printed from left to right across each occupied column and then down succeeding rows from left to right.

This option allows you to store a hard copy of the complete contents of all spreadsheets you create. You can sometimes locate and identify problems by examining all of the formulas in a particular area of the spreadsheet at one time.

PRINTING DATABASE REPORTS

The /Print Menu commands that have been discussed in the previous sections on printing spreadsheets all apply to printing reports from your Lotus 1-2-3 databases. However, unless your report is to be simply a listing of all fields and records in your database, you will usually need to do more preparation than merely specifying the print range and margin settings and then sending the report to the printer.

The specific layout and type of data in a database report is highly dependent on the type of database and the purpose of the report. In general, database reports differ from those printed from spreadsheets in these ways:

- A database report usually consists of a subset of all records in the database. The records in the subset may be ordered quite differently from those in the main database and may often contain only a partial listing of the fields in each record.
- A report from a database that tracks financial data often requires the inclusion of statistics such as subtotals, averages, and grand totals that are not maintained in the database itself.

As discussed in Chapters 20 and 21, the /Data Query and Sort commands are often used to extract and then order the data to be included in a written report. You can use the /Data Query commands to set up the criteria by which the subset of records for the report is selected. By using the Extract command, you can have the program copy all of the records that meet your criteria into a new area in the worksheet.

After extracting the records to be printed, you can use the /File Xtract command to copy them into a new file. This step is suggested for two reasons. First, it creates a smaller file that is much more manageable, uses less computer memory, and reduces the risks of corrupting the data in the central database. Second, it allows you to use the /Print Menu options solely for setting up your report without changing the options in effect for printing historical reports containing the complete contents of the database.

Figures 25.4 and 25.5 illustrate how this process can work. In Figure 25.4, you see the data extracted from a personnel database and then saved in a separate file with the /File Xtract command. This subset includes only a partial listing of the fields contained in each record—namely, the department, supervisor, first name, last name, position, and salary fields.

Figure 25.5 shows the final printed report produced from this data. The first step in preparing the report was to combine the first and last names into a single field listing the last name and then the first name, separated by a comma. This was done by using the concatenating function in column G. The first formula entered in cell G1 was

+D1&", "&C1

It was then copied down the column to concatenate all of the names in the report. After combining them, the /Range Value command was used to turn the concatenating formulas into labels. The results in column G were then copied over to column C, and the contents of columns D and G were erased.

Next, the field labels were reentered in uppercase letters without the use of any abbreviations, and a new row containing a line of hyphens was

A1: [W9] 'Dept READY

	A	B	C	D	E	F	G	H
1	Dept_	Super	F:Name	L:Name	Position	Salary		
2	Acctg	Newman	Katherine	Holland	Clerk	19,000		
3	Acctg	Newman	Daniel	Jones	Bookkeepe	27,500		
4	Acctg	Pauli	Paul	Newman	Accountan	55,000		
5	Acctg	Newman	Alexander	Jones	Secretary	25,000		
6	Pers	McKnight	Sandra	Langly	Secretary	24,000		
7	Pers	Dorian	George	McKnight	Manager	50,000		
8	Pers	McKnight	Mary	Smith	Clerk	18,750		
9	Sales	Smithson	Peter	Mead	Acct Exec	35,000		
10	Sales	Smithson	George	Durran	Acct Exec	30,000		
11	Sales	Smithson	Thomas	Baker	Acct Exec	32,500		
12	Sales	Smithson	Andrea	McMead	Acct Exec	38,000		
13	Admin		Mary	Smith	President	135,000		
14	Admin	Smith	Alvin	Dorian	VP Admin	62,000		
15	Admin	Smith	Gena	Smithson	VP Sales	70,000		
16	Admin	Smith	Thomas	Pauli	VP Financ	82,500		
17	Mktg	Smithson	Colin	Baker	Director	65,000		
18	Mktg	Baker	Sylvia	Jones	Secretary	28,900		
19	Mktg	Baker	Mark	Lawson	Assistant	27,500		
20	Mktg	Baker	Sean	Clarkson	Artist	25,000		

FIGURE 25.4: This figure shows a subset of the records in a personnel database that were first extracted from the database and then saved in a separate file. In this file, the records will be prepared for printing. This process includes combining the first and last name fields (listed by last name, first name) and then sorting by department and the new name field. Next, the salary figures for each department and the whole company are totaled using the @SUM function. The final printed report can be seen in Figure 25.5.

added. These two rows serve as the border rows for the report so that they are printed at the top of each page. Then the /Data Sort command was used, sorting the data first by department (primary key A1) and then by name (secondary key C1).

Once the data in the report was sorted, new rows were inserted between each group of records at each break (change) in department. A line of repeating equal signs was added and below it was added the TOTAL label and an @SUM function to total the salaries for each department. At the end of the report, another @SUM function was used to produce a grand total for all of the salaries in the company.

Finally, the /Print commands were used to add the header and footer for the report, to designate the first two rows as border rows, and to indicate the cell range including all of the records and statistics to be printed in the report. The report was then sent to the printer.

In addition to totals for salaries, this report could have been designed to include statistics on the number of employees in each department, the average salary in each, and so on. If the database had contained hundreds of

DEPARTMENT	SUPERVISOR	EMPLOYEE	POSITION	SALARY
Accounting	Newman	Holland, Katherine	Clerk	19,000
	Newman	Jones, Alexander	Secretary	25,000
	Newman	Jones, Daniel	Bookkeeper	27,500
	Pauli	Newman, Paul	Accountant	55,000
TOTAL				$126,500
Administration	Smith	Dorian, Alvin	VP Admin	62,000
	Smith	Pauli, Thomas	VP Finance	82,500
	Smith	Smithson, Gena	VP Sales	70,000
		Smith, Mary	President	135,000
TOTAL				$349,500
Marketing	Smithson	Baker, Colin	Director	65,000
	Baker	Clarkson, Sean	Artist	25,000
	Baker	Jones, Sylvia	Secretary	28,900
	Baker	Lawson, Mark	Assistant	27,500
TOTAL				$146,400
Personnel	McKnight	Langly, Sandra	Secretary	24,000
	Dorian	McKnight, George	Manager	50,000
	McKnight	Smith, Mary	Clerk	18,750
TOTAL				$92,750
Sales	Smithson	Baker, Thomas	Acct Exec	32,500
	Smithson	Durran, George	Acct Exec	30,000
	Smithson	McMead, Andrea	Acct Exec	38,000
	Smithson	Mead, Peter	Acct Exec	35,000
TOTAL				$135,500
	SALARIES TOTAL			$850,650

FIGURE 25.5: This figure shows the final printed report developed from the data shown in Figure 25.4. Notice that in addition to line separators, the field names have been set in uppercase and all abbreviations have been dropped. The department names have also been reentered at the report breaks and all repetition of these names was eliminated by deleting these labels with /Range Erase. Also, a header and footer for the report has been added.

employee records instead of the 19 shown here, preparing it manually would have been quite time consuming.

When you find yourself generating fairly complex and long database reports, you might want to design a macro that will automate the procedure as much as possible. This is especially true if the report is periodic, such as a monthly or quarterly report. For users who rely on Lotus 1-2-3's database capabilities quite heavily and generate many different types of database reports, there is an even easier way to develop them by using 1-2-3 Report Writer. This is a new add-on product from Lotus Development Corporation that is designed to work specifically for generating reports from Lotus 1-2-3 and Symphony database files. Its capabilities are described in a separate section later in this chapter.

Generating and Printing Mailing Labels

Generating mailing labels from database records that contain name and address fields is a very common need. As Lotus 1-2-3 has no built-in facility for generating mailing labels from database records, you must accomplish this by using a macro. Figure 25.6 shows a small sample client database that contains fields for the company name, contact name (broken into two separate fields), company street address, city, state, zip code, and telephone number. Beneath these is shown the macro for generating and printing mailing labels from the information stored in each record of this database.

Note: The mailing label macro is located beneath the client database records only for the convenience of illustrating the macro commands and the database it works on all in one figure. When creating such a macro for your own database files, you would not enter the macro commands here but would enter it to the side of the database records.

The macro has been named Alt-M for mailing label. It consists of two ranges: the main body of commands that prepare the labels for printing and a second range named LabLoop, which copies the data from each record and actually prints the label.

To understand how the macro goes about creating the mailing labels, we will examine each command as it is listed. The first line of the macro is

{HOME}/RT.{END}{RIGHT}~AA1~

It begins by positioning the cell pointer in cell A1. (This command should be modified to reflect the first cell in your database if the database does not begin in this cell.) Next, the command uses the /Range Transpose command to copy all the field names in the first row of the database to cell AA1. When these field names are copied, they will be entered down column AA, running from cells AA1 to AA7. The cell address AA1 was used instead of a range name because the /Range Transpose command deletes range names when it makes a copy.

```
A7: [W9]                                                              READY

        A        B        C                  D                  E       F    G
1  Last     First    Co                Address            City     St   Zip
2  Grill    Suzanne  ABC Appliances    25 E. Main Street  Evanston IL   60628
3  Schnyder Jay      Best Accounting   14 Oakdale Road    Skokie   IL   60602
4  Gordon   Barbara                    1304 States Street Chicago  IL   60633
5  Fraesir  Grace    Fraesir Toys      3507 41st Street   Chicago  IL   60633
6  Nelson   Kay      Exact Editing     2104 Elm Street    Lakeview IL   60671
7
8
9  \m       {HOME}/RT.{END}{RIGHT}~AA1~
10          {GOTO}AA1~/RNLR{END}{DOWN}~
11          {GOTO}AC1~/WCS30~
12          +First&" "&Last~{DOWN}
13          @IF(@ISERR(@VALUE(Co))=1,Co,Address)~{DOWN}
14          @IF(@ISERR(@VALUE(Co))=1,Address,City&", "&St&"  "&Zip)~{DOWN}
15          @IF(@ISERR(@VALUE(Co))=1,City&", "&St&"  "&Zip,"")~
16          {HOME}/PPRAC1.AC7~OOUQQ
17 LabLoop  {DOWN}/RNCLabel~{BS}~
18          {IF Label=0}{QUIT}
19          /RT.{RIGHT 6}~AB1~
20          /PPAGQ{BRANCH LabLoop}
```

FIGURE 25.6: Sample client database with macro for creating and printing mailing labels using its data. This macro is designed to print a three-line mailing label whenever the company name has been left blank (as in the third record for Barbara Gordon) and a four-line mailing label for all records that contain the company name. After copying the data from each record into the appropriate format (using the /Range Transpose command), this macro prints the mailing label, spacing either three or four lines between each mailing label. The macro terminates as soon as it reaches a blank line signifying the end of the data. This macro works only in Release 2. See the accompanying text for a full description of the macro commands.

The next command is

{GOTO}AA1~/RNLR{END}{DOWN}~

It positions the cell pointer in cell AA1, which now contains the first field name, Last, in it. It then uses the /Range Name Labels Right command to give the field names now listed in cells AA1..AA7 to the cells to their immediate right (AB1..AB7).

The next command line contains this command:

{GOTO}AC1~

This command takes the cell pointer to a new cell address, that of AC1. It is here that commands listed in the next four lines will be copied. These commands copy the data in the cell range AB1..AB7 by referencing them by range name (remember that these cells have already been named with the field names in the cells to their left). They also adjust the mailing label according to whether the Co (for Company) field contains an entry. If this field has been left blank, the macro generates a three-line mailing label. If it contains a company name, the macro generates a four-line mailing label.

The first of these four command lines is

+First&" "&Last~{DOWN}

This formula merely copies the contents of the First and Last name fields into the first line of the mailing label. It assumes that all records in the database will contain both first and last name entries. It then moves the cell pointer down one cell to copy the next formula there.

This formula contains an @IF function:

@IF(@ISERR(@VALUE(Co)) = 1,Co,Address)~{DOWN}

Its function is to evaluate whether the Co field has been left blank. It does this by using the @ISERR and @VALUE functions. First, the value in the cell given the range name Co is evaluated. If it contains any characters, the @VALUE function will return an ERR value in the cell. If the @VALUE function returns an ERR value, the @ISERR function will return the logical true value of 1. If this value is 1, the true value argument of the @IF function will be used. This means that the entry in the Co field will be copied to the second line of the mailing label. If no error is detected, there is no company entry, and the contents of the Address cell are copied here instead.

This same technique for evaluating whether the company field has been left blank is used in the next three formulas copied to this area of the worksheet. Again, the cell pointer is moved down a cell before copying in the next formula:

**@IF(@ISERR(@VALUE(Co)) = 1,Address,City&", "&St&" "&Zip)~
{DOWN}**

This @IF formula copies the street address to this line if the Co field contains an entry (and thus returns an ERR value, making the @ISERR function true); otherwise, it copies the city, state, and zip code into the third line of the mailing label because the company field has been left blank.

After this formula has been copied, the cell pointer is moved down one more cell before the last @IF formula is copied. This formula is

@IF(@ISERR(@VALUE(Co)) = 1,City&", "&St&" "&Zip,"")~

It uses this line to print the city, state, and zip code information; otherwise, it copies a blank into the fourth line of the mailing label if the company field contains no entry.

Note: The formula above assumes that the zip code entries have been entered as labels. If they were entered as values, the &Zip would have to be modified to @STRING(Zip,0) to prevent an error.

After copying these formulas, the macro returns the cell pointer to cell A1 and sets up the print range for the mailing label. This command line reads

{HOME}/PPRAC1.AC7~OOUQQ

After returning to the Home cell, it sets the print range to include the cell range AC1..AC7. The mailing label requires only the first three or four lines of this range. The last cells are used to advance the printhead before printing the next label. If you use this macro, you may have to increase the cell range, depending on the size of mailing labels you use. This cell range spaces the labels about half an inch to three quarters of an inch apart.

After setting the print range, the Options Other Unformatted command is used. This Unformatted option is required so that page breaks do not disrupt the spacing of the mailing labels.

Next, the macro proceeds to the subroutine named LabLoop. This subroutine contains the commands that actually copy the field entries from the database to the cell range AB1..AB7, where they are processed in the cell range AC1..AC7 according to their contents. The first command line of this subroutine is

{DOWN}/RNCLabel~{BS}~

Because the cell pointer is already located in cell A1, which holds the first field name in the database, the {DOWN} keyword moves it to the first field of the first record. Then the /Range Name Command is used to give this cell the range name Label. The {BS} keyword (for Back Space) unanchors the range after naming this cell.

The next command stops the macro as soon as it reaches the end of the database:

{IF Label=0}{QUIT}

When the cell pointer is moved down to the beginning of the blank row signifying the end of the records, the IF statement will be true (empty cells carry a zero value) and the {QUIT} command will terminate the macro and return the worksheet to READY mode.

As long as the macro has not reached the end of the database, the next command line will be executed. It contains these instructions:

/RT.{RIGHT 6}~AB1~

This command uses the /Range Transpose command to copy the field entries into the vertical range beginning with cell AB1. It must enter a period to anchor the range because of the inclusion of the earlier {BS} keyword. The {RIGHT} keyword with a count of 6 is used instead of the usual {END}{RIGHT} combination because of the possibility of a blank cell in the Co field. This number will have to be adjusted if your database contains more fields to be included in the label than are shown in this example.

As soon as these field entries are copied into the cell range AB1..AB7, they are processed according to the command statements in the cell range AC1..AC7 (shown in rows 12 to 15 of Figure 25.6). The final command in the macro prints the label as it has been copied and arranged in this cell range with this command sequence:

/PPAGQ{BRANCH LabLoop}

After the label has been printed, the macro branches back to the beginning of the LabLoop subroutine and begins generating and printing another mailing label from the next record in the database.

This type of macro for creating mailing labels would normally be applied to a group of records that had already been extracted from the main database. These records could then be saved in a separate file by using the /File Xtract command. The worksheet file containing this mailing label macro could then be retrieved and the file containing the extracted records combined into it by using the /File Combine Copy Entire-File command. These records would presumably be sorted by zip code by using the /Data Sort command before the macro was executed.

Using 1-2-3 Report Writer

1-2-3 Report Writer is a stand-alone utility program developed specifically to make it easier to generate reports from Lotus 1-2-3 databases (although it can be applied to spreadsheet data as well). If your work with Lotus 1-2-3 requires you to produce sophisticated reports from such files, you may want to investigate this program's capabilities. It certainly makes it much easier to generate reports and mailing labels than the methods outlined in the previous sections.

The program works consistently with the way you are accustomed to working in Lotus 1-2-3. It uses a very similarly arranged command menu system that works just like Lotus 1-2-3 commands (it even uses the forward slash to bring up the menu selections). It reads all worksheet files, both those created in Release 1A carrying the .WKS extension as well as those created in Release 2 carrying the .WK1 extension.

However, you cannot use 1-2-3 Report Writer to make design changes to your database or to edit or add the data entries in it. When you retrieve the worksheet file that contains your database data, 1-2-3 Report Writer does not display the actual data in the database, but instead displays a listing of all the field names above indicators showing the length of each field and the type of data it contains.

Figure 25.7 shows the list of fields from the personnel database (the same one used to generate the report shown in Figure 25.5) as they appear on the screen in 1-2-3 Report Writer. Initially, 1-2-3 Report Writer displayed all of the fields from the database. Only those needed in this specific report were retained (deleting fields from this screen does not affect the fields in the database itself). Notice that all of these fields except the salary field are text fields, which is shown by the apostrophe that precedes the squares indicating the length of the field. The salary field is a numeric field formatted with the comma (,) format to two decimal places (this is shown by the # symbols separated by a comma).

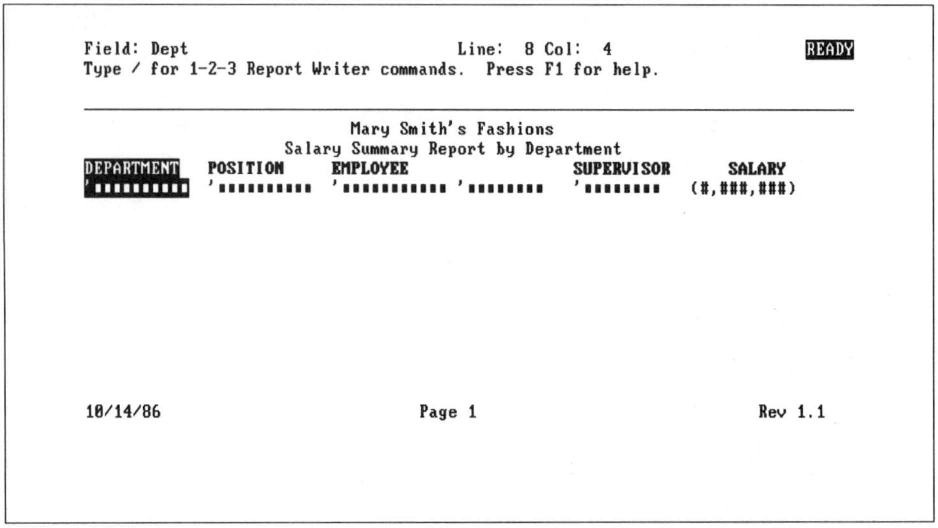

FIGURE 25.7: This figure shows the 1-2-3 Report Writer screen with the fields to be included in the report. When this Lotus 1-2-3 database worksheet file was read into 1-2-3 Report Writer, eleven fields were shown on the screen. All but the six seen here were deleted from the report (but not from the database file). Those remaining have been repositioned to reflect their placement in the printed report. Notice that 1-2-3 Report Writer shows the header and footer for this report on the screen as they will be printed. See Figure 25.8 for a screen preview of this report showing the data and the subtotals of the salaries by department.

The fields shown in this screen have been rearranged by using the /Current-Field Move command. This allows you to position each of the fields that you want to be included in the report just as you want them in the printed copy. After positioning the fields, the field names in this report were edited so that they appear in all uppercase letters and no longer use abbreviations. This figure also shows a header and footer added to this report. Notice that the header contains two lines of text, both of which are centered. Headers and footers are not limited to single lines in 1-2-3 Report Writer, as they are in Lotus 1-2-3 reports.

The text in the header and footer was positioned by using the vertical bar characters, just as they are used in Lotus 1-2-3. However, unlike when defining headers and footers from the /Print Options menu in Lotus 1-2-3, in 1-2-3 Report Writer these are displayed on the screen as they will be printed.

Figure 25.8 shows the final report displayed on the screen prior to printing. Before using the /Print Destination Display command to preview the

```
Go                                                                          MENU
Line  Screen  Restart  Quit
Proceed by one line
_____________________________________________________________________________

                          Mary Smith's Fashions
                   Salary Summary Report by Department

DEPARTMENT   POSITION     EMPLOYEE                 SUPERVISOR       SALARY
Acctg        Clerk        Katherine    Holland     Newman           19,000
             Bookkeeper   Daniel       Jones       Newman           27,500
             Secretary    Alexander    Jones       Newman           25,000
             Accountant   Paul         Newman      Pauli            55,000
-- Sum -------------------------------------------------------------------
                                                                   126,500

Admin        VP Admin     Alvin        Dorian      Smith            62,000
             VP Finance   Thomas       Pauli       Smith            82,500
             President    Mary         Smith                       135,000
             VP Sales     Gena         Smithson    Smith            70,000
-- Sum -------------------------------------------------------------------
                                                                   349,500

Mktg         Director     Colin        Baker       Smithson         65,000
```

FIGURE 25.8: The final report generated in 1-2-3 Report Writer printed to the screen with its /Print Destination Display command. This figure shows the first part of the report generated with this program. The records were sorted by department, last name (which now shows no column heading), and first name (with the column heading EMPLOYEE). The department field was then designated as the break field and the Totals Sum command was used on the salary column to print the salary totals by department (the grand total can be seen in Figure 25.9). 1-2-3 Report Writer automatically added the dashed line with the label Sum to indicate column breaks. The program was also instructed to print the department names only once after each column break. See Figure 25.9 for the complete printed report.

report, the records were sorted by the department, last name, and first name fields. When you sort records in 1-2-3 Report Writer, you can designate up to four different sorting keys (as opposed to two with the Lotus 1-2-3 /Data Sort command).

After sorting, the department field was designated as the break field. The subtotals and grand total were added to the report by designating that the salary field be totaled. This was done by pointing to the salary field and using the /Current-Field Totals Sum command. The names of the departments are not repeated in the report, because 1-2-3 Report Writer has an option that allows you to print the break field data only once. Figure 25.9 shows the final printed report produced with 1-2-3 Report Writer. (Contrast the results obtained with this product with those shown in Figure 25.5.)

1-2-3 Report Writer also includes a powerful query facility that makes it unnecessary to select records by using the /Data Query Extract command in Lotus 1-2-3. It differs from Lotus 1-2-3 /Data Query commands in that you are prompted on the screen as you construct conditions by which the records are selected.

Once you have finished defining the parameters of your report, you save it as a report file separate from the database file. If you need to, you can then use the report definition saved in the report file with another database worksheet file that shares the same or similar structure. The program also allows you to set up a command file that can generate reports from the operating system as a batch process. This allows you to compile and print a report that uses several Lotus 1-2-3 worksheet files.

Before leaving the discussion of 1-2-3 Report Writer, its handling of mailing labels must be mentioned. Unlike Lotus 1-2-3, this program is fully equipped to generate mailing labels from data in your database files. Unlike when using macros such as the one in the previous section, you are not limited to printing mailing labels one-up on the page. It is a simple process to indicate a layout in which the labels are printed two or three across, depending on the length of the entries.

With 1-2-3 Report Writer, you can preview the mailing labels on the screen as with any report. You can also use the Test Pattern option to test-print a few labels to make sure they are spaced correctly for the label size you are using. The program automatically ignores any blank fields and strips out any unnecessary spaces or lines that blank fields would cause.

Mary Smith's Fashions
Salary Summary Report by Department

DEPARTMENT	POSITION	EMPLOYEE		SUPERVISOR	SALARY
Acctg	Clerk	Katherine	Holland	Newman	19,000
	Bookkeeper	Daniel	Jones	Newman	27,500
	Secretary	Alexander	Jones	Newman	25,000
	Accountant	Paul	Newman	Pauli	55,000
-- Sum ----					**126,500**
Admin	VP Admin	Alvin	Dorian	Smith	62,000
	VP Finance	Thomas	Pauli	Smith	82,500
	President	Mary	Smith		135,000
	VP Sales	Gena	Smithson	Smith	70,000
-- Sum ----					**349,500**
Mktg	Director	Colin	Baker	Smithson	65,000
	Artist	Sean	Clarkson	Baker	25,000
	Secretary	Sylvia	Jones	Baker	28,900
	Assistant	Mark	Lawson	Baker	27,500
-- Sum ----					**146,400**
Pers	Secretary	Sandra	Langly	McKnight	24,000
	Manager	George	McKnight	Dorian	50,000
	Clerk	Mary	Smith	McKnight	18,750
-- Sum ----					**92,750**
Sales	Acct Exec	Thomas	Baker	Smithson	32,500
	Acct Exec	George	Durran	Smithson	30,000
	Acct Exec	Andrea	McMead	Smithson	38,000
	Acct Exec	Peter	Mead	Smithson	35,000
-- Sum ----					**135,500**
== Sum ====					**850,650**

11/06/86 Page 1 Rev 1.1

FIGURE 25.9: The final printed report produced with 1-2-3 Report Writer from a Lotus 1-2-3 database worksheet file. Notice that the program automatically underlined each of the column headings in this report. The Attributes command was used to print each subtotal and total in boldface type. Also, the spacing between report breaks has been increased from one line to two. Contrast the results obtained with this product to those in the printed report prepared manually in Figure 25.5. Both were produced using the same data, though the report shown here was produced directly from a database file, while the one in Figure 25.5 used a subset of the database that was extracted and saved in a separate file.

The /Worksheet Page Command (Release 2 Only)

This command is used to place a page break command at a particular row in the spreadsheet before printing it.

/Worksheet Page

MENUS

/Worksheet
Page

KEYBOARD ENTRY

/WP

FUNCTION

The /Worksheet Page command places a special page break marker in the row that contains the cell pointer. It can be used to keep data that might otherwise be printed on two pages together on a printed page. Lotus 1-2-3 begins a new page of the report whenever 56 lines have been printed. If you find that the placement of a table or range of data will cause it to be split across pages when printed, you can use the /Worksheet Page command to prevent this from happening.

USAGE

To insert a page break command, position the cell pointer in the row containing the first line of data you want to be printed on a new page. Then position the cell pointer in the leftmost column of the print range and issue the /Worksheet Page command by typing **/WP.** Lotus 1-2-3 will insert a new row at the current cell's position. The double colon (::) represents the page break symbol. The page break will not occur in the report unless the page break symbol is located in the leftmost cell of the designated print range.

If you wish to force another page break at the end of a table so that only the data within the table is printed on the page, move the cell pointer to the row beneath the last row of the table and repeat this procedure. During printing, when the program encounters these page break symbols, it will advance the paper to the top of the page and begin printing the table. When it reaches the second page break, it then advances to a new page and begins printing the rest of the rows in the print range.

To delete a page break entered with this command, move the cell pointer to the row containing the page break symbol and delete the entire row by using the /Worksheet Delete Row command—type **/WDR** and press the Return key.

MACROS

If you find that you need to insert a lot of page breaks in your spreadsheet as you prepare it for printing, you may want to use the simple macro Alt-N (for new page) listed below to cut down on the keystrokes involved.

ALT-N, A MACRO TO START A NEW PAGE

Label	*Macro Contents*
'\n	**'/WP**

To use this macro, position the cell pointer in the row containing the data you want to be printed on a new page; then move it to the leftmost column of the print range, usually column A, and press Alt-N.

THE /PRINT MENU

The /Print Menu contains commands that have two purposes: to print reports from your spreadsheets and database files and to create new disk files saved in ASCII format that can be read by other software programs. After typing **/P** to activate the menu, you must tell the program whether you want to send the contents of the worksheet to the printer or to create a new print file by choosing either the Printer or the File option.

After selecting the destination, you are presented with a menu of options used to define the parameters for either type of printing. If you are interested in creating ASCII disk files containing data from your worksheets, you will primarily be concerned with the Options Margins and, for some files, the Options Other Unformatted commands.

The rest of the commands on the /Print Menu will be needed most often only when you are sending your data to the printer. Both types of printing require that you use the Range option to define the range of cells to be included before you can use the Align and Go commands either to create the new disk file or to print the report as defined.

/Print

MENUS

/Print
Printer File
Range Line Page Options Clear Align Go Quit

KEYBOARD ENTRY

/PP /PF
R L P O C A G Q

FUNCTION

The /Print Menu has two basic functions: to print hard copies of data in your worksheets using the text printer you have installed with your system and to create an ASCII version of the data in your worksheets by creating a new file. The ASCII file created from such a procedure is automatically given the file name extension .PRN.

Even without the special file name extension, this type of file is not saved in a format that can be loaded directly into Lotus 1-2-3 by using the /File Retrieve command (to load any ASCII file, whether created in Lotus 1-2-3 or not, you must always use the /File Import command). The File option is intended primarily for transferring spreadsheet data to other software programs that cannot read the Lotus 1-2-3 .WKS or .WK1 file formats. (For a discussion of the applications for copies of your spreadsheet data in ASCII format files, see Chapter 29.)

Most of the time, you will use the /Print Menu commands to set up the parameters that define the layout for your printed reports and the data to be included and to send the reports to your text printer. Lotus 1-2-3 contains default settings that will be used if you do not change them (refer to the section "The Printing Defaults" for a listing of these values), so that all you have to do is specify the cell range to be included before using the Align and Go commands to begin printing.

USAGE

Once you use the /Print command on the Lotus 1-2-3 Main Menu, you are presented with these two options:

Printer File

If you intend to use your text printer to print a report from the worksheet currently in memory, choose the Printer option. If you want to create a new text file version of all or a part of the data in the worksheet, choose the File option. If you choose the File option, you will be prompted to enter a file name. After entering the name and pressing the Return key, the following line of menu options will appear:

Range Line Page Options Clear Align Go Quit

If you choose the Printer option, this line of menu options will be displayed immediately. This menu contains a Quit command to take you back to READY mode, which allows you to cycle through its various options without having to keep typing **/PP** or **/PF**.

THE RANGE OPTION

You must use the Range option to designate the cell range to be included in the printout or new disk file. You can indicate this range by typing in the cell addresses, entering a range name, or pointing out the range. If you use pointing, you must type a period to anchor the cell pointer after positioning it in the first cell before you use the cursor keys to extend the range.

Depending on the width of the cell range, you may have to modify the right margin setting with the Options Margins command. The default value for the right margin is 76 characters with a left margin of 4. This means that the maximum line length is 72 characters. If your print range contains more columns than will fit within this line length, you will have to change either the left and right margins or use the appropriate setup string to turn on compressed printing. If you do not, Lotus 1-2-3 will print only those entire columns of information on one page.

The program remembers the print range that you designate and saves it as part of the worksheet file if you use the /File Save command before exiting the program. To clear the range, use the /Clear Range command.

The Line and Page Options

The Line and Page options are used to advance the paper in the printer either one line at a time or to the next form feed. These commands give you control over the printer from within Lotus 1-2-3 without having to use its controls. This is a nice feature: many printers require you to take the printer offline before using either the line feed or form feed controls. After using them, it is easy to forget to put the printer back on-line, resulting in a printer error the next time you try to print.

The Line option advances the paper one line and positions the printhead at the very beginning of the new line. It is used most often to advance the printer a line at a time to the top of the form. After positioning the print head at the top of the form, you will want to use the Align option before using the Go command to print your next report.

The Page option will advance the printer to the next top of form as defined with the Align option. It is used most often to advance the printer to the top of the next page after the printer has finished printing the last line of a report.

The Options Menu

The next selection, Options, is attached to this menu of choices:

Header Footer Margins Borders Setup Pg-Length Other Quit

Each of these options, with the exception of the Quit command, is discussed in the sections that follow. Typing **Q** to access the Quit command from this menu returns you to the previous level, from which you can use the Align and Go commands to begin printing. If you create a macro that sets new values using these options, remember to include a Q for the Quit command before using the AG letter combination to start the printing.

Header The Header option is used to enter a single-line heading that will be printed on each page of the document. The header line is printed on the first line below the top margin. The default top margin is two lines. Because the body of the report does not begin printing until the fifth line from the top, this leaves a spacing of two lines before the first line of the report. Although you can change the top margin setting by using the Margins Top command, you cannot change the two lines between the header and the first line of the body of the report.

To enter a header, type **H** and then the header text. You can use the vertical bar character (¦) to center or right-justify text within this header (for details on how to use this character to position header text, refer back to the section entitled "Adding Headers and Footers to Reports"). If you wish the current date to appear in the header, type the @ symbol. If you wish the page number of the report to appear in the header, type the # symbol. Otherwise, type the text header exactly as you want it to appear in the report.

Footer In addition to a report header, you can also define a footer that prints on each page. This text is placed at the bottom of the page, three lines above the end of the page (leaving two blank lines after the last line of body of the report on the page and two lines after the footer to the last line of the page). Its vertical placement can be changed by using the Margins Bottom command (although the two lines between the last line of the report and the footer cannot be changed). You can position text within the header by using the same technique used to define a header. You can also use the @ symbol to insert the current date or the # symbol to add page numbers.

Margins The Lotus 1-2-3 report defaults assume that you are using $8^1/_2 \times$ 11-inch paper. The default left and right margins are 4 and 76, respectively. The top and bottom margins are both set to 2 lines (between headers and the top of the page and between footers and the bottom of the page).

To change any of these margins, you must access the Margins option and then type the initial letter of the margin you wish to change. Once you type **M**, you will see these choices:

Left   Right   Top   Margin

After you type the initial letter, you must type in the new value to be used. As soon as you begin typing, the current value that is displayed will disappear.

Left and right margin settings are measured in characters. The value depends on the pitch in effect for printing the report. The standard pitch is pica type, which translates to 10 characters per inch. Top and bottom margins are measured in lines and depend on the lines per inch in effect. (These margins are the space between the footer and the bottom of the page, not the distance between the body of the worksheet and the edge of the paper.) The standard is single spacing, which translates into 6 lines per inch. Both the pitch and the spacing can be changed by using the appropriate setup string entered with the Setup command.

If you are using 14-inch-wide paper to print a report, you will want to use the Margins Right command to set a new right margin of 136 (140 characters in pica type is the maximum that can be accommodated, although you must set the Margin Left to 0 to obtain this line length). If you are printing your report in compressed type (see the Setup option that follows) on an 8½ × 11-inch sheet, you would also use this right margin setting.

Borders The Borders option allows you to specify headings in particular rows or columns of the spreadsheet as borders for the report, meaning that they will be printed on each page of the report. When you access the Borders option, you are presented with two additional options:

Columns Rows

If you want both a column of labels and some rows of headings to be included on each page, you would use the Borders option twice, once using the Columns option and once using the Rows option.

When you want to specify a row containing column headings that should appear in the top line of the body of the report on every page, use the Rows option. You will be prompted to enter the border rows. To do so, move the cell pointer to one of the cells in the row that contains these headings and press the Return key. If you want to designate more than one row as border rows, move the cell pointer to the first row, type a period to anchor the cell range, and use the appropriate cursor key to highlight all of the rows you want to include (you do not have to indicate the number of columns as part of this range; this is handled by the right margin setting).

When you want to specify a column containing row headings to appear on the left of each page of the report, use the Columns option. You indicate the column or columns to be designated as border columns in the same way as you do border rows.

When defining border columns, border rows, or both, be sure that you do not include these columns and rows as part of the print range. The labels and data in these border areas will automatically be printed in the report. If you include them as part of the print range, they will be printed twice on the first page of the report.

If you need to obtain a printout including the column letter and row number references along with your data, you can use the Borders option to do so. For more information on this technique, refer back to the section entitled "Printing Identifying Columns and Rows on Each Page of the Report."

Setup The Setup option is used to enter printer control codes to change such things as the pitch and line spacing, as well as other printing enhancements. Any control codes entered here affect the entire printed report.

When you define a setup string, enter its decimal code using three digits preceded by the backslash. For instance, to print a report in compressed print (17 cpi) on an IBM or Epson dot-matrix printer, you use the decimal code 15. When entering this value as a setup code in Lotus 1-2-3, you enter it as \015. If you use a printer control code to change to a smaller pitch such as compressed type, you must also remember to increase the right margin setting, or Lotus 1-2-3 will not print any more columns than it did when using a larger pitch.

You can enter as many printer control codes as you want. When using more than one code, you can enter codes after the initial Escape code as ASCII characters rather than entering their decimal equivalents preceded by the backslash and a zero, making sure that there are no spaces between them. For instance, you could enter the codes to set the pitch to 8 lines per inch on an Epson printer (Esc 0) as **\0270** or as **\027\048**. Refer to Table 25.1 to see common setup strings that control pitch changes for the IBM and Epson dot-matrix printers and the HP LaserJet.

Pg-Length The Pg-Length option is used most frequently when you are printing reports on paper longer than 11 inches. It can also be used to fit more lines per page on an $8^1/_2 \times 11$-inch page. Its default setting is 66 lines per page (with a top and bottom margin of 5 lines each, this leaves 56 lines per page when using single spacing). You can change this value to any between 1 and 100.

If you have changed the lines per inch setting with a setup code, you can adjust this value to accommodate the number of lines according to whether you have set the spacing up or down. If you are trying to fit a few more lines on a one-page report using single spacing, you should consider using the Other Unformatted option to remove page breaks and headers and footers to accommodate the extra lines.

Other The Other option is attached to a menu of choices that allow you to modify the formatting or contents of the printed report. Its menu options include the following:

As-Displayed Cell-Formulas Formatted Unformatted

The first and third options on this menu, As-Displayed and Formatted, are the defaults used by the program whenever you print a worksheet to a disk file or the printer. With As-Displayed in effect, the contents of the cells in the print range specified are printed just as they appear on the screen, except that the column and row borders are not included. With Formatted in effect, the program pages the report as specified by the Pg-Length and lines per page settings and includes all headers and footers that you have defined. The As-Displayed option is used to restore this program default whenever you have previously used the Cell-Formulas option. The Formatted option is used to restore this program default whenever you have previously used the Unformatted option.

The Cell-Formulas option causes the contents of the cells in the print range to be printed as a line listing rather than as a formatted report as displayed on the screen. The literal contents, including any formulas used, of each cell in the range are printed on a separate line of the report. This command is most often used to document the complete contents of the worksheet. In it, each cell entry is printed on an individual line across each row, down the entire worksheet.

The Unformatted option prints a copy of the report without using the Pg-Length value to break pages or the top and margin settings, including any header or footer that has been defined. This option is used most often to remove these formatting commands before printing the worksheet to an ASCII file (using /Print File as the initial command) that will be used in another application program such as a word processor.

It is also useful when printing a report that contains only a few more lines than will fit within the standard page length. Using the Unformatted option suppresses the page break at the Pg-Length setting, allowing those few extra lines of the report to fit on a single page because no space is retained for either the header or footer.

THE CLEAR OPTION

Because the program remembers all the print settings that you set up from the /Print Menu, you may find it convenient to use the Clear option when setting up a report that uses a different print range and/or different formats. When you access the Clear option, you are presented with these four additional options:

All Range Borders Format

Using All clears all print settings back to their program default values. This includes the print range, margin settings, borders defined, and formatting specified.

The Range option resets the print range that has been defined in the worksheet. If all you need to do is designate a new part of the spreadsheet to be printed, using the Clear Range option makes this easier to accomplish. It leaves all of the other formatting options in effect while freeing the cell pointer so that you can move to the new area before using the Range command to indicate the new cell range to be used.

The Borders option clears any previously set borders. It allows you to print a copy of the report using the same print range and other formatting settings but without repeating any columns or rows on subsequent pages.

The Format option returns the format settings, including the page length and the margins, to their default values. It also clears out any printer control codes that were entered by using the Setup option.

The Align and Go Options

The Align and Go options are used together when sending a report to the printer. The Align command tells the program that the printhead is currently at the top of the form. It then uses this position to page the report according to the number of lines per page (set with the Pg-Length command). The Go option actually begins the printing process. If you need to suspend printing for any reason after that, press the Ctrl-Num Lock keys. If you wish to abort the printing process, press the Ctrl-Scroll Lock keys.

If you are using the File option to create an ASCII file, you do not need to use the Align command before the Go command. ASCII files are not paged, regardless of the Pg-Length setting in effect.

MACROS

This section includes two keystroke macros that you might want to use. The first one is a second-time print macro. It can be used for quick copies of reports that do not require any range or formatting changes.

The second macro is designed to illustrate how you can create macros to automatically enter special control codes in the spreadsheet. This particular example can be used to print a single line (usually the spreadsheet title) in double-width characters if you are using either an IBM or Epson dot-matrix printer. It can easily be adapted to turn on and off other printer control codes that you might wish to use. This technique for entering setup codes directly into the worksheet to affect the printing of parts of a spreadsheet is not supported in Release 1A.

ALT-P, A SECOND-TIME PRINT MACRO

Label	*Macro Contents*
'\p	**'/PPAGPQ~**

To use this macro, you must have already defined the print range and any other formatting settings you need. To print another copy of the report as it has been previously defined, press Alt-P (it does not matter where the cell pointer is in the worksheet when you type this sequence). Make sure that your printer is on and online before using this macro.

ALT-X, A MACRO TO TURN ON ENLARGED PRINT FOR ONE LINE

Label	*Macro Contents*
'\x	**'/WIR~¦¦\027\014~**

To use this macro, position the cell pointer in the leftmost column (usually column A) of the worksheet in the row that contains the line you want to be printed in double-width (5 cpi) print. Then press Alt-X (for extra-large type). Lotus 1-2-3 will insert a new row and then enter the appropriate setup code for printing a single line of text in enlarged print on an IBM or Epson dot-matrix printer.

You can easily edit the macro contents to include another setup code that you wish to use. However, remember that unlike this code, which automatically turns itself off after printing one line, most setup codes must not only be turned on with the appropriate setup code but must be turned off with another one as well. For instance, if you were creating macros to enter the setup code for printing a section of the report in boldface type, you would create two macros—one to enter the setup code to turn double-strike on and another to turn it off.

SEE ALSO

/Worksheet Page

SUMMARY

This chapter has covered the printing commands and discussed various techniques for printing reports from both spreadsheets and Lotus 1-2-3 databases. Because the program's /Print command menu is used not only to produce printed reports but also to create copies of worksheets in ASCII format, the chapter necessarily touched on techniques for creating such .PRN files. You will find more information on the use of such files in Chapter 29, "Importing and Exporting ASCII Files," where techniques for creating text files are discussed in the context of transferring data to other software programs, especially word processors.

This chapter also dealt with creating reports from Lotus 1-2-3 database files. If you need more information on setting up and maintaining such files, see Chapters 20 and 21. In Chapter 20, you will find information on creating and adding data to a database. In Chapter 21, you will find information on extracting information from an existing database. The operations covered in this chapter are often required as a prelude to printing various reports using the information in a database.

CHAPTER 26

PRINTING AND PLOTTING GRAPHS

Printing and Plotting Graphs

In this chapter you will find information on how to use the PrintGraph program to print the graphs you have created in Lotus 1-2-3. If you need information on how to create and save graphs for printing, see Chapter 24, "Creating and Using Graphs."

The first part of this chapter covers how to start up the PrintGraph program and configure it for your hardware. You will also find discussions on how to select fonts, graph size, and colors before printing. Following these discussions on how to use the PrintGraph program, you will find a complete reference entry describing all the options on the PrintGraph Menu. If you just need specific information on how to use one of the PrintGraph options, you may want to proceed directly to this reference section and look up the menu option you need to use.

Using the PrintGraph Program

In order to print any graphs you have created and saved with the /Graph Save command, you must exit the Lotus 1-2-3 program and start up the PrintGraph utility. There are several ways to do this, depending on how you started up Lotus 1-2-3 and how much memory your computer has:

- If you started Lotus 1-2-3 by using LOTUS as the startup command, you can exit the program with the /Quit Yes command and then press the → and Return keys (or type **P**).
- If you started Lotus 1-2-3 by using 123 as the startup command, you can exit the program with the /Quit Yes command and then type **graph** (if you are using Release 1A) or **pgraph** (if you are using Release 2) at the operating system prompt.
- If you are using Release 2 and your computer has sufficient memory (use the /Worksheet Status command to check that at least 150K is available), you can use the /System command and then start up the PrintGraph program from the operating system by typing **pgraph**.

If you are running Lotus 1-2-3 on a two-disk-drive system, you will have to replace the Lotus System Disk with the PrintGraph Disk when prompted to do so. If you are running Lotus 1-2-3 on a hard disk system, the PrintGraph program will be loaded as soon as you give the command, provided you have copied its program files in the same directory that holds the Lotus 1-2-3 program files.

Configuring Your Hardware

The first time you use the PrintGraph program, you will have to configure it to work with your hardware. Figure 26.1 shows the main menu for the PrintGraph program in Release 1A, and Figure 26.2 shows the main menu of the program in Release 2. Basically, they contain the same options, though the information on the Release 2 menu has been rearranged somewhat and some of the headings have been changed.

```
Copyright 1982, 1983 Lotus Development Corp.  All Rights Reserved.          MENU
--------------------------------------------------------------------------------
Select  Options  Go  Configure  Align  Page  Quit
Select pictures
================================================================================
 SELECTED GRAPHS  COLORS               SIZE    HALF            DIRECTORIES

                  Grid:      Black     Left Margin:     .750   Pictures
                  A Range:   Black     Top Margin:      .395   B:\
                  B Range:   Black     Width:          6.500   Fonts
                  C Range:   Black     Height:         4.691   A:\
                  D Range:   Black     Rotation:        .000
                  E Range:   Black                             GRAPHICS DEVICE
                  F Range:   Black     MODES
                                                               Epson FX80/1
                  FONTS                Eject: No               Parallel
                                       Pause: No
                  1: BLOCK1                                    PAGE SIZE
                  2: BLOCK1
                                                               Length   11.000
                                                               Width     8.000
```

FIGURE 26.1: The main PrintGraph Menu options and default settings in Release 1A. This screen shows you the main menu selections and program defaults when you first start up the PrintGraph program. Unlike when using Lotus 1-2-3, the program remains in MENU mode as you select graphs to be printed and change various printing settings, so none of its commands are prefaced with / as when using Lotus 1-2-3. As you use the commands on this menu to make changes to the graph printing settings, the settings shown on this screen are updated to reflect the new values.

```
Copyright 1985 Lotus Development Corp.  All Rights Reserved.  Release 2   MENU

Select graphs for printing
Image-Select  Settings  Go  Align  Page  Exit

   GRAPH        IMAGE OPTIONS                      HARDWARE SETUP
   IMAGES        Size              Range Colors     Graphs Directory:
   SELECTED       Top        .395  X Black            C:\123\DATA
                  Left       .750  A Black          Fonts Directory:
                  Width     6.500  B Black            C:\123
                  Height    4.691  C Black          Interface:
                  Rotate     .000  D Black            Parallel 1
                                   E Black          Printer Type:
                 Font              F Black            IBM/Lo
                  1  BLOCK1                         Paper Size
                  2  BLOCK1                           Width      8.500
                                                      Length    11.000

                                                   ACTION OPTIONS
                                                    Pause: No   Eject: No
```

FIGURE 26.2: The main PrintGraph Menu and default settings in Release 2. The Select command is now called Image-Select, and the Options and Configure options have been combined in the new Settings option. Essentially the same information is shown below the menu options, although it has been rearranged slightly, with the Range Colors and Image Options column interchanged. Also, the Modes (Pause and Eject) are now called Action Options and are listed below the last column to the right, which contains the Hardware Setup information.

Before printing graphs, you must make sure that the graphics printer or plotter you are using is listed on this screen and that the directories showing where the program will look for the fonts files and your graph files are both correct. If any of these settings are not correct, you will need to change them before attempting to print any of your graphs.

Configuring the Printer and Files in Release 1A

If you are using Release 1A and you find that some of the default settings on the main PrintGraph Menu screen are not correct for your system, choose the Configure option. When you do, you will be presented with the following choices:

Files Device Page Interface Save Reset Quit

To indicate the graphics printer you will be using, select the Device option. Figure 26.3 shows the screen that then appears, listing the first group of graphics printers supported by the program. To select a new printer, use the ↓ key to move the highlight to the name of the printer to be used and press the space bar to mark it. (The listing of the graphics devices seen in this first screen is only partial. To see the rest of the printers and plotters, press the PgDn or End key to go directly to the bottom of the list.)

The PrintGraph program shows that a particular printer has been selected by placing the # symbol before its name. To select a new printer (only one device can be selected at a time), you move the highlight to it and press the space bar. After selecting the appropriate graphics device, press the Return key to return to the Configure Menu options. (If you press the Esc key, the program will return you to this menu without changing the device as you have marked it.)

```
Copyright 1982, 1983 Lotus Development Corp.  All Rights Reserved.          POINT
--------------------------------------------------------------------------------
Select graph output device

================================================================================
          Type of Graphic Output
         ----------------------------------------
   Anadex 9620A Silent Scribe Printer        [Space] bar moves mark
 # Epson FX80 Printer, Single Density Mode   [Enter] selects marked device
   Epson FX80 Printer, Double Density Mode   [Escape] exits
   Epson FX80 Printer, Triple Density Mode         without changing device
   Epson FX80 Printer, Quad Density Mode     [Home] goes to beginning of list
   HP 7470A Plotter                          [End] goes to end of list
   IBM Graphics Printer, Single Dens. Mode   [Up] moves cursor up
   IBM Graphics Printer, Double Dens. Mode   [Down] moves cursor down
   IBM Graphics Printer, Triple Dens. Mode    List will scroll if cursor moved
   IBM Graphics Printer, Quad Density Mode    beyond top or bottom of display.
   Epson MX80 or MX100, Single Dens. Mode
   Epson MX80 or MX100, Double Dens. Mode
   Epson MX80 or MX100, Triple Dens. Mode
   NEC 8023 Printer
   Okidata 82A or 83A Printer
```

FIGURE 26.3: Selecting a new graphics device to print graphs in Release 1A with the Configure Device command. This figure shows the first part of the listing of the graphics devices supported by this version of the program. Currently the Epson FX-80 printer in single-density mode is selected (shown by the # symbol that precedes its name). To change the graphics device, move the highlight to the name of the new printer or plotter in the list and press the space bar. This removes the # mark from the currently selected printer and places it before the new device. Press the Return key to return to the menu options. To save this new selection as part of the GRAPH.CNF file, you would use the Save command on the Options Menu. That way, it would remain the default device when the PrintGraph program is used in future work sessions.

If you have selected a printer that uses a serial interface instead of a parallel interface, or you have selected a parallel printer connected to another port, you will have to use the Interface option to select the appropriate interface setting. These are listed by number from 1 to 4 (refer to Table 2.5 in Chapter 2 for a listing of the type of interface and the port associated with each).

After you type the appropriate number, you are returned once again to the Configure Menu options. (If your graphics device uses a serial interface, you will also be required to specify the baud rate at which it sends data. See Chapter 2, "Configuring the PrintGraph Printer and Drive (Release 1A)" and Table 2.5 for details on how to do this.)

If you also need to change the default directories where the program looks for your graph files (referred to as Pictures in this version of Lotus 1-2-3), for the font files, or both, you will need to use the Files option on this menu. When you select this command, you will see three choices:

Pictures Fonts Quit

To change the directory where the PrintGraph program looks for the graph files, choose the Pictures command and type in the drive and directory, using the full path name if your files are stored in a subdirectory of the directory containing your Lotus 1-2-3 program files. To indicate the correct directory for the font files (usually the one containing the PrintGraph program files), choose the Fonts option and type in the directory. Then use the Quit option to return to the Configure Menu options.

Once you are back at this menu, select the Save option if you want the graphics device, Pictures directory, and Fonts directory to be made the defaults for this and future work sessions in the PrintGraph program. Selecting a new graphics printer and new file directories without using the Save command makes them the defaults only as long as you remain in the PrintGraph program. To return to the main PrintGraph Menu, use the Quit option.

Configuring the Printer and Files in Release 2

If you are using Release 2 and you find that the default graphics device and/or the Graphs or Fonts directories listed on the main PrintGraph Menu are not correct for your system, choose the Settings command. Once you do, you will be presented with these menu options:

Image Hardware Action Save Reset Quit

From this menu, choose the Hardware option. This brings up the following menu of choices:

Graphs-Directory Fonts-Directory Interface Printer Size-Paper Quit

To change the graphics device, choose the Printer option. When you do, you will see a screen listing only the printers or plotters you selected when you initially installed Lotus 1-2-3. If the devices listed on the screen do not include the graphics printer or plotter you plan to use, you will have to exit the PrintGraph program and use the Install program (see Chapter 2, "Configuring the Default Printer(s) in Release 2") to add it. Once you have added the printer or plotter by using the Install program, you can return to this menu option and select it from this screen.

If the device you want to use is listed on this screen but is not currently marked with a # symbol before its name and description, use the ↓ key to move the highlight to it. Then press the space bar to mark it. Press Return to return to the Hardware Menu options (if you press the Esc key instead, your change will not be made).

If the new graphics device you selected from the Printer option requires a different type of interface (serial as opposed to parallel) or is connected to a different port, you will also need to use the Interface option to select the correct type of interface and port (refer to Chapter 2, "Customizing PrintGraph Defaults (Release 2)" for details on how to do this). After selecting the appropriate number for your type of interface and the port, you will be returned to the Hardware Menu options.

Once back at the Hardware Menu options, you should also select the Graphs-Directory option if the directory where the PrintGraph program will look for your graph files needs to be changed. After selecting it, type in the correct directory (using the full path name if your files are kept in a subdirectory of the one containing the Lotus 1-2-3 program files) over the one currently listed and then press the Return key. Do the same thing using the Fonts-Directory option if it is not correct. Most often, this directory will be the same as the one containing the PrintGraph program files. Then use the Quit option to return to the Settings Menu options.

Once you are back at this menu, select the Save option if you want the graphics device, Graphs directory, and Fonts directory to be made the defaults for this and future work sessions in the PrintGraph program. Selecting a new graphics printer and new file directories without using the Save command makes them the defaults only as long as you remain in the PrintGraph program. To return to the main PrintGraph Menu, use the Quit option.

Selecting the Graphs to Print

Once the graphics device and directories containing your graph files and the font files are correct, you can select the graph or graphs you want to print. In Release 1A, the option you use is the Select command on the main PrintGraph Menu. In Release 2, this command has been changed to Image-Select. Both commands work identically.

After accessing the Select or Image-Select command, you are presented with a complete listing of all the graph files in the Graphs (or Pictures) directory. The only files you will see in this list are those that have been saved with the /Graph Save command and therefore carry the .PIC file name extension.

The PrintGraph program allows you to batch-print graph files by selecting them from this list. To select a graph file, move the highlight to it and mark it by using the space bar, just as you do when selecting a new graphics device. If you select a file in error, you can move the highlight to it and press the space bar again to deselect it.

If you wish to preview a graph on the screen to make sure it is the one you want before marking it for printing, move the highlight to it and press the Graph function key (F10). The graph will be displayed on the screen until you press a key to return to the selection screen.

You can select several graphs to be printed in a series, even if your printer accepts only single sheets of paper. Just be sure that you use the Settings Action Pause Yes command sequence so that the printer stops for you to change the paper. After marking all the files you want to print and pressing the Return key to select them, you will be returned to the main PrintGraph Menu. At the left of this screen below the menu options, you will see a list of the graph files you selected. They will be printed in the order they are listed here when you give the signal by using the Align and Go commands.

Selecting Fonts and Colors

Before sending the signal to print the graphs you have selected, you should check to see that the size, fonts, and color settings listed on the main PrintGraph Menu screen are as you want them. This section describes how to select different fonts and colors, if you are using a color printer. In the next section, you will find information on how to change the sizing of your graph and its orientation on the page.

The PrintGraph program allows you to choose between eleven type styles (eight in Release 1A) to be used in printing the graph. These choices are shown in Figure 26.4. When assigning type styles, you specify a type style for Font 1 and Font 2. Font 1 is a larger font that is used to print only the first title of your graph. Font 2 is a smaller type size used to print the rest of the text in the graph, including the second, X-axis, and Y-axis titles; legends; data labels; and X-axis and Y-axis scale labels. Generally, Font 1 is approximately twice as high as Font 2, regardless of the type style selected.

In the list of available type styles shown in Figure 26.4, notice that several font names are listed twice. The only difference between them is whether they are terminated with a 1 or 2. In these cases, the 2 indicates a

```
Copyright 1985 Lotus Development Corp.  All Rights Reserved.  Release 2   POINT
Select font 1

          FONT NAME       SIZE
          ------------------          [SPACE] turns mark on and off
        # BLOCK1          5737        [RETURN] selects marked font
          BLOCK2          9300        [ESCAPE] exits, ignoring changes
          BOLD            8624        [HOME] goes to beginning of list
          FORUM           9727        [END] goes to end of list
          ITALIC1         8949        [UP] and [DOWN] move cursor
          ITALIC2        11857            List will scroll if cursor
          LOTUS           8679            moved beyond top or bottom
          ROMAN1          6863
          ROMAN2         11847
          SCRIPT1         8132
          SCRIPT2        10367
```

FIGURE 26.4: Selecting a new type style for Font 1 using the Settings Image Font command from the main PrintGraph Menu in Release 2. The names of the eleven available fonts are shown on this screen. Notice that four of the names are duplicated and have been terminated with 1 and 2. The font name with the 2 is a heavier version of the same type style and will print darker on most graphics printers. To select a new font for Font 1, you move the highlight to its name and press the space bar. This automatically removes the # symbol from the currently selected font (Block1 in this figure) and places it before the new font. To complete the selection, you press the Return key. As soon as you make a new font selection for Font 1, both Font 1 and Font 2 will be changed to the new type style. If you want to print Font 2 in a different font, you must then use the 2 option and repeat the selection process.

heavier weight that prints slightly darker than its counterpart ending with a 1. However, there is no difference between the two in terms of style.

The default font for printing both Font 1 and Font 2 is Block1. If you wish to change this for either or both fonts, you must select the Settings Image Font command (in Release 1A, this command is Options Font) and then type **1** to change Font 1 or **2** to change Font 2. To select a new font, move the highlight to the name of the font you wish to use and press the space bar to select it. Then press the Return key to make the change.

You can select a different type style for Font 2 if you wish. If you want to use only the one type style you have just selected for Font 1 in printing the entire graph, you don't need to access Font 2; the PrintGraph program will automatically change both Font 1 and Font 2 to use the font name you first selected.

When choosing different type styles, you must be careful to avoid selecting fonts that don't print well on your graphics device. If you are using a dot-matrix printer to produce the graph, most fonts other than Block1 and Block2 will not be printed with sufficient resolution to be clearly legible. Even when using a pen plotter, where resolution is not a problem, you may want to stay away from the script fonts, which are very light, even when you select Script2.

If you are using a color printer, you can assign various colors to the data variables and the parts of the graph by using the Settings Image Range-Colors command (or Options Color in Release 1A). The number and type of colors available for assignment to the various parts of the graph depend on the type of graphics device you have selected (if your printer does not print in color, black will be the only choice listed).

You can assign different colors to the different data variables by selecting their letters listed on the menu (A–F). The color choice assigned to the X letter command on the menu (called the Grid option in Release 1A) determines the color used to draw the graph frame as well as all other parts of the graph besides the legends and the individual variables.

To assign a color to the X range or to the other data variables used, select the option letter, highlight one of the colors available, and press the Return key or just type the first letter of the color's name. You can repeat this procedure to assign different colors to each of the other data variables.

If you are printing a pie chart and have assigned various fill types by indicating their code numbers in a cell range defined as the B data variable, you can use the X and A–F options to assign various colors to each section of the pie as follows:

Fill Codes Used in B Range	Range-Colors Letter to Select
1	X
2	A
3	B
4	C
5	D
6	E
7	F

After you have finished assigning colors from the Range-Colors Menu, choose the Quit option to return to the Image Menu options.

Note: If you are using a plotter, the program will prompt you to load different pens in a specific order. The thickness of the pen and its ink color determine the appearance of the final printed graph.

Changing the Size and Rotation of the Graph

The PrintGraph program assumes that you will be printing your graph on an 8½ × 11-inch sheet and uses half size as its default setting. If you accept this default, you can print two graphs on a single sheet of paper. When printing graphs half size, they are printed in the same vertical orientation as they appear when previewed on the screen. If you change the setting to full size, the graph is automatically rotated 90 degrees. It also takes up the entire sheet of paper, so only one graph can be printed per sheet.

The main PrintGraph Menu screen shows the size in effect by listing the top and left margins, the width and height, and the rotation of the graph. If the size is set to half size (referred to as HALF in Release 1A), these settings will be displayed:

Left Margin:	.750
Top Margin:	.395
Width:	6.500
Height:	4.691
Rotation:	.000

If the size is set to full size, these settings will be displayed:

Left Margin:	.250
Top Margin:	.500
Width:	6.852
Height:	9.445
Rotation:	90.000

The PrintGraph program also lets you manually adjust these settings to determine the size of the graph, its margins on the page, and its rotation. To change to full size or to adjust the size settings manually, choose the Size option from among the Image Menu selections (from the Options Menu in Release 1A). Once you select the Size option, you will see three new menu choices:

Full Half Manual Quit

If you want to print your graph full size, choose the Full option and then choose Quit. When you return to the main PrintGraph Menu, you will find that the margin, size, and rotation settings on this screen have been changed to reflect the full-size values listed above.

Manually Sizing the Graph

If you wish to size and orient the graph in some other way, select the Manual option. When you do, you will see five options that you must use when resizing the graph and a Quit option to return to the previous menu:

Left Top Width Height Rotation Quit

When manually setting these values, you must be careful to maintain the proper aspect ratio, which is the ratio of the graph's width to its height. The PrintGraph program uses an aspect ratio of 1.385 for the X axis to 1 for the Y axis. When entering the width and height values, you should try to maintain these proportions. For instance, if the graph's X-axis width were to be 4 inches, the proper Y-axis height would be 4 divided by 1.385, or approximately 2.888 inches.

Be aware that the program measures height and width in relation to the page, not to the graph's axes. If you also use the Rotation option to change a graph's orientation on the page, you will have to recalculate these values to maintain the proper aspect ratio. Rotation values, which are entered in degrees, refer to the orientation of the graph's axes. At 0 degrees, the X axis is horizontal and the text reads left to right. At 90 degrees, it is vertical and the text reads up the page. At 270 degrees, it is again horizontal, but the text appears upside down as the graph comes off the printer. At 360 degrees, the graph is again vertical, only this time the text reads down the page. When you rotate a pie chart, which does not have X and Y axes, the same type of rotation takes place with regard to its titles and labels.

When you rotate a graph 90 degrees, to maintain the aspect ratio of 1.38 width to height, the length of the Y axis would be approximately 1.38 times the length of the X axis because of the way the graph has been turned. When sizing and rotating pie charts, you must maintain this aspect ratio to avoid having the circle appear as an ellipse. The PrintGraph program considers the Y axis at 0 degrees rotation to be perpendicular to the graph title.

After setting new values using the Rotation, Width, and Height options, you should then use the Left and Top options to specify these values. The margin settings will depend on the new values given to the width and height of the graph. You can set these values to position the graph as you want, as long as you leave sufficient room to print the resized graph on the page. If you are printing the graph on 8½ × 11-inch paper, to center the graph between the top and bottom of the page, subtract the new height from 11 and divide by 2 to obtain a new top margin setting. To center the graph horizontally, do the same calculation, this time subtracting the new width from 8½.

When you have finished setting these values, use the Quit option to return to the Image Menu options. To return to the Settings Menu, type **QQ**. From there, you can use the Save command to save all of the Image settings, including the size, fonts, and colors to be used. Once saved, these settings will be in effect the next time you use the PrintGraph program. To print the graphs selected with the Image-Select command, type **Q** to return to the PrintGraph Menu. All of the settings you have changed are updated on the screen as soon as you make them. You should review them before printing your graphs with the Align and Go commands.

Printing Graphs

Before giving the signal to have the graphs selected for printing sent to the printer or plotter, you may want to modify the Pause or Eject settings by using the Settings Action command (Options Pause and Options Eject in Release 1A). Both of these commands have Yes/No options attached to them.

If you want the program to stop after printing each of the graphs you have selected, choose the Yes option on the Pause command. This allows you to change the settings for the next graph to be printed or to change the paper. The PrintGraph program will beep at you continuously to indicate that it has finished printing a graph. After making the changes you need, press the space bar to print the next graph in the queue.

The Eject command determines whether the program will advance to a new sheet of paper after printing each graph. Select the Yes option to print only one graph per page. If you are using a printer that takes only single sheets, you will want to activate Pause Yes so that the program will alert you to change paper before printing the next graph. If you are using a printer that takes continuous form-feed paper, this step is unnecessary. You can allow the program to advance to the next page automatically and print all of your selected graphs without pausing. The program defaults are Pause No and Eject No.

To begin printing the selected graphs, choose the Align and Go options. The Align command works just as it does when printing spreadsheets. It tells the program that the current printhead position is the top of the form. The Go command begins the printing process. First the program reads the first graph file, then the font files, and then begins printing the first graph. Printing graphs is a much slower process than printing spreadsheets, so your printer will be occupied for some time if you have selected a number of graphs to be printed. The mode indicator flashes WAIT during the printing process. When it returns to MENU mode, you are free to quit the program and return to work with Lotus 1-2-3 or some other software program.

THE PRINTGRAPH MENU COMMANDS

The PrintGraph program is a separate utility program used to print graphs created in Lotus 1-2-3. It differs from the Lotus 1-2-3 worksheet program in that its command menu is always on the screen. This means that you do not have to preface any of its commands with the forward slash.

Note: The arrangement and some of the command names in the PrintGraph Menu system in Release 2 have been altered from the way they appear in Release 1A (compare Figures 26.1 and 26.2). Nevertheless, no new functions have been added. The command options in this reference section are presented as they appear in Release 2.

PrintGraph Commands

MENUS

Image-Select Settings Go Align Page Exit

KEYBOARD ENTRY

I S G A P E

FUNCTION

The only function of the PrintGraph program is to print graph files created in Lotus 1-2-3. In order to be printed, your graphs must have been created in Lotus 1-2-3 and saved with the /Graph Save command. All such files are given the file name extension .PIC to differentiate them from regular worksheet files.

To use the PrintGraph program, you must also have a printer or plotter capable of printing graphics attached to your system. The Lotus 1-2-3 PrintGraph program supports a wide range of graphics printers and plotters. When you install the program initially (in Release 2), you indicate which graphics printers you have attached to your system. The printers and plotters you indicate during this procedure will be the only ones you can choose from when printing your graphs with this program (for information on how to install other graphics devices, see Chapter 2).

USAGE

To use the PrintGraph program, you must exit Lotus 1-2-3. If you started Lotus 1-2-3 with the LOTUS startup command, use the /Quit Yes command to return to the Lotus Access System Menu and select the PrintGraph option from it. If you started Lotus 1-2-3 with the 123 startup command, use the /Quit Yes command to return to the operating system and then type **pgraph** (**graph** in Release 1A) at the operating system prompt. If you are using floppy disks, you will be prompted to insert your PrintGraph Disk (replace the Lotus System Disk with the PrintGraph Disk).

If you are using Release 2 and your computer has sufficient memory, you can also use the /System command to return to the operating system and then enter the appropriate startup command.

Once the PrintGraph program has been loaded into memory, you can use its menu options to select the graphs to be printed and the settings to be used to print them. The use of each of the menu options is discussed in the order in which each appears on the PrintGraph Menu.

IMAGE-SELECT

Use the Image-Select option to indicate the graph files to be printed. When you choose this option, you will be presented with a list of all the .PIC files in the current Graphs directory. To select the graphs to be printed, you move the highlight to each of them and press the space bar. This marks the file name with a # symbol.

To move to the end of the listing quickly, you can press the End key (pressing the Home key will take you back to the beginning of the list). To scroll through the list vertically, one screen at a time, use the PgDn key. To move the highlight one file at a time, use the ↓ or ↑ key to move it in the appropriate direction.

You can use this method to select as many graphs as you want to print. The PrintGraph program will print them in the order they are selected rather than in the order they are listed—in other words, if you mark the third graph file listed before you mark the second file, the third file will be printed before the second file.

If you mark a file in error, move the highlight to it and press the space bar again. This removes the # symbol from it, deselecting it for printing. When you have marked all of the graphs, press the Return key to return to the main PrintGraph Menu options. Only use the Esc key if you chose the Image-Select option in error and wish to return to this menu without marking any files for printing.

When you return to the main PrintGraph Menu, you will see a list of all the graph files you marked for printing. They will be listed in the order in which PrintGraph will print them, which corresponds to the order you marked them.

Note: To view the contents of a graph file on the screen, you can move the highlight to it and press the Graph function key. This allows you to preview the file to make sure it is one of the graphs you want to print. Press any key to return to the screen containing the graph file listing.

SETTINGS

You use the Settings option on the main PrintGraph Menu to select a new graphics device, to change the directories in which the program looks for your graph files or font files, to assign new fonts or colors, to change the size and rotation of the graph, to have the printer pause, or to keep the printer from advancing to a new page after printing each graph. When you select the Settings option, you are presented with the following options:

Image Hardware Action Save Reset Quit

The Reset option is used to reset all of the print settings back to their default values. The Save option will save all of the current settings as part of the PGRAPH.CNF file read into memory each time you start up the PrintGraph program. Use the Quit option to return to the main PrintGraph Menu.

Image Select the Image option to change the sizing and/or orientation of your graph on the page, to select new fonts (type styles) for printing the graph, or to assign colors to your graph if you are using a color printer. When you select the Image option, you are presented with this menu:

Size Font Range-Colors Quit

Use the Size option to change either the size of your graph or its orientation on the page. Use the Font option to select a new font for printing the graph. Use the Range-Colors option if you are using a color printer or plotter to assign colors to each part of the graph. The Quit option will take you back to the previous menu, where you can save your settings.

Changing the Size: The default size and orientation when you first use the PrintGraph program is half size with a rotation of 0 degrees. This means that each graph takes up half a sheet of an $8^1/2 \times 11$-inch sheet of paper and is printed in the orientation that it appears in when it is viewed on the screen. A full-size graph is automatically rotated 90 degrees so that its text reads up the page, and it takes up the entire page. (To compare the size and margin settings for these two, refer back to the section "Changing the Size and Rotation of the Graph.")

When you choose the Size command, you are presented with these menu choices:

Full Half Manual Quit

To have your graph printed full size, select the Full option. If your PrintGraph settings show that full size is in effect and you want to print the graph on half a page, select the Half option. You can also size and orient your graph to your own specifications by selecting the Manual option. Use the Quit option to return to the previous menu after you have finished making your selections.

When you choose the Manual option to set new values determining the layout and size of the graph, you are presented with these menu options:

Top Left Width Height Rotation Quit

The values that you enter for the Top and Left options determine where the graph is placed on the page by setting the printing position of the top-left corner of the graph in relation to the top-left edge of the paper. The Width and Height options determine the dimensions of the graph on the page. All four of these settings are given in inches (use decimals to indicate fractions of an inch).

The Rotation option determines the orientation of the graph on the page. It is given in the number of degrees of rotation. If you entered 90 as the new rotation value, the program would rotate the graph one quarter turn to the left. As you increase this value, the rotation continues in a counterclockwise direction. Always enter the value as a positive number, keeping in mind that degrees between 0, 90, 270, and 360 can alter the appearance of your graph. A graph that uses an X-Y coordinate system might not appear rectangular, and a pie chart might not appear circular. Refer to the discussion on aspect ratios and rotation in the section entitled "Manually Sizing the Graph" to obtain more information on manually sizing graphs and changing their orientation.

Selecting Fonts: The PrintGraph program supports eleven different fonts (type styles) that can be assigned to the graph. Each graph uses two basic sizes of fonts, called Font 1 and Font 2. Font 1 is used to produce only the first title in the graph. Font 2 is used to produce all other text in the graph. Font 1 is larger than Font 2.

To select new fonts, choose the Font option from the Image Menu options. You will then be presented with two choices:

1 2

To change the font used for Font 1, type **1**. You will then be presented with a list of the different fonts. Names that appear twice, appended with a 1 and 2, are the same type styles; the 2 indicates a heavier version.

The default font for Font 1 and Font 2 is Block1. To select another font, move the highlight to the other font and press the space bar to mark it with a # symbol. Then press the Return key to change the font. If you use the Esc key, your change will not be recorded on the Print-Graph screen.

If you want your graph to be printed in the same new font that you just selected, you do not need to select the 2 option and change it there also. The PrintGraph program automatically assigns the new font to both Font 1 and Font 2. However, if you want to mix type styles by selecting a different font for Font 2, select the 2 option and select the new font just as you did when choosing a new font for Font 1. Use the Quit option when you are finished to return to the Image Menu options.

Selecting the Colors for Each Data Variable: If your graphics device is capable of printing in color, you can use the Range-Colors command to indicate which colors to use to print each part of the graph. As soon as you select the Range-Colors option, you are presented with these menu choices:

X A B C D E F Quit

The X option controls the color of the graph frame and all other parts of the graph besides the data variables used in the graph and the legend. The letter choices A–F are used to assign individual colors to each data variable used in the graph. To assign a color, you type the appropriate letter. You are then presented with a list of the different colors available on your graphics printer. You can assign one of the available colors by moving the highlight to it and pressing the Return key or by typing the first letter of its name.

After you have finished assigning colors to each part of graph, use the Quit option to return to the Image Menu options. If you are assigning colors to a pie chart and you have set up a B data variable to control the fill types, you can use the letter options on the Range-Colors Menu to assign different colors to each segment of the pie. Refer back to the discussion section "Selecting Fonts and Colors" to see how the fill type code values are paired with the data range letters on this menu.

Using the Hardware Option The Hardware option on the PrintGraph Settings Menu is used to make current a new graphics device, graph file directory, or font file directory. It is also used to indicate that you will be using a paper size other than $8^1/_2 \times 11$ inches. If you indicated that you had more than one graphics device attached to your system when you installed Lotus 1-2-3, you can use the Printer option to switch to an alternate device. If the directory listed on the main PrintGraph Menu screen is not the one that contains the graph files you want to print, you must use the Graphs-Directory option to change the directory bcfore selecting the files to be printed with the Image-Select option.

When printing graphs, the PrintGraph program needs to read the contents of various font files. If the directory currently listed on the main PrintGraph Menu as the Fonts directory does not contain these files, the PrintGraph program will give you an error message and go into ERROR mode when you give the go-ahead to print your selected graphs. To correct the directory, you use the Fonts-Directory option on the Hardware menu.

You also use the Hardware Menu if you are printing your graphs on a paper size different from $8^1/_2 \times 11$ inches. This is done by choosing the Size-Paper option.

When you select the Hardware option on the Settings Menu, you are presented with the following choices:

Graphs-Directory Fonts-Directory Interface Printer Size-Paper Quit

The Graphs-Directory and Fonts-Directory Options: To change the directory where the PrintGraph program looks for your graph files, type **G** and the new directory, including the drive and path name. To change the directory where the program looks for the font files, type **F** and the new directory. This directory will almost always be the same one that contains the PrintGraph program files.

Using the Printer and Interface Options: To make a new graphics device current, type **P** to choose the Printer option. The program will then display a list of the graphics printers and plotters that you indicated were available to your system during installation. If you indicated a dot-matrix printer such as an IBM graphics printer or Epson dot-matrix, you will see two listings, one for low density and another for high density (in Release 1A, there are four density choices: Single, Double, Triple, and Quad Density). To produce darker graphs, choose the high-density selection for the printer you wish to make current.

To select a new device, move the highlight to it and mark it by pressing the space bar. Be sure to press the Return key to have the change recorded. Use the Esc key only to return to the Hardware Menu options without changing the graphics device.

If the new graphics device you selected does not use the same port or the same type of interface, you must use the Interface option to make the appropriate changes there before using the Quit command to leave the Hardware Menu options. When you select the Interface option, you are presented with numbers from 1 to 8. Each number is associated with a different type of port and interface. The numbers from 5 to 8 are used only when you are operating Lotus 1-2-3 on a network and need to indicate the DOS device (LPT1 to LPT4) attached to the network.

Options 2 and 4 are used when your graphics device takes a serial interface (1 and 3 are parallel interfaces connected to LPT1 and LPT2, respectively). Option 2 indicates that the serial device is connected to COM1, and option 4 indicates that the device is connected to COM2. When you choose either of these options, you must also specify the baud rate by selecting a number between 1 and 9. The baud rates associated with these numbers are as follows:

Option Number	Baud Rate
1	110
2	150
3	300
4	600
5	1200
6	2400
7	4800
8	9600
9	19200

Using the Size-Paper Option: The last option included on the Hardware Menu options before the Quit option (to return to the previous menu level) is the Size-Paper option. You use this option only when you are printing your graphs on a paper size other than 8½ × 11, which is the program default.

When you select Size-Paper, you are presented with these three menu choices:

Length Width Quit

To enter a new value for the page length, type **L** and the new value in inches, using decimal values for any fractions of an inch; then press the Return key. To enter a new value for the page width, type **W** and indicate the new value in inches, just as you did for the length. After entering both your changes, use the Quit command to return to the Hardware Menu options.

The Action Option Thc Action option is used to indicate two things: whether the program should pause between printing each graph in the queue and whether it should automatically advance to a new page after it finishes printing each graph. The two options that control these aspects are Pause and Eject. When you select the Action option, they are presented along with a Quit option in this order:

Pause Eject Quit

Both Pause and Eject are attached to Yes/No options. The PrintGraph program displays which of these settings are in effect on the screen below the main PrintGraph Menu options.

To have the printer stop after it prints each graph, select the Pause Yes sequence (Pause No is the default). Using this sequence allows you to change the paper after each graph has been printed or to change settings such as fonts, size, color, page size, and the like. After making the necessary changes during a printing pause, press the space bar to have the program resume printing the next graph in the queue.

Note: Using the Pause Yes command sequence when printing graphs on a network has no effect on the printing. The PrintGraph program pauses until you press the space bar, even though it does not stop the printing from the queue.

To prevent the program from advancing to the top of the form each time it finishes printing a graph, make sure that the Eject No setting is in effect (this is the default setting). If you have set the graph size to half size, the program will print two graphs on a page.

If you are printing your graphs on continuous form-feed paper at half size and want only one graph to a page, make sure the setting is Eject Yes. If you are using a plotter, you can still leave the Eject Yes setting in effect, because the PrintGraph program will prompt you automatically to insert a new sheet of paper.

The Save and Reset Commands You can make all of the settings chosen with the PrintGraph options the permanent program defaults by using the Save command on the Settings Menu. If you are using the PrintGraph program on a floppy disk, make sure that this disk is not write protected before giving this command. The program will save all of your setting changes as part of the PGRAPH.CNF file, which is read into memory each time you start up the PrintGraph program.

Because the PrintGraph program is not copy protected, you can make different working copies of it, each of which contains different default settings that are commonly used. That way, you can use the appropriate PrintGraph disk when starting up the program to change the default settings in effect without having to access all of the menu options individually. If you are using the PrintGraph program on a hard disk system, this system will not work without saving different versions of the PGRAPH.CNF file in different directories.

The Settings Menu also includes a Reset option that can be used to change all of the printing options back to their default values. Use this option when you want to print graphs using most, if not all, of the default settings, including size, orientation and layout, fonts, colors, printer, graph and font directories, paper size, and pause and eject set to No.

Using the Align, Go, and Page Commands

After you have made sure that all of the PrintGraph settings are correct and have selected the graph files to be used, you start the printing by selecting the Go option from the main PrintGraph Menu. Before doing so, select the Align option to set the top of form as the current position of the printhead. When you select Go, if you are using a plotter, you will be prompted to load the pens in the order they are listed on the screen. When you have loaded the pens, press the space bar to start the plotting. If you are using a graphics printer, you will not be prompted at all, but the program will mark the current printhead position as the top of form.

Once you select the Go option, the program will load the first graph file and the font files you have selected. If you need to abort the printing in progress, press the Ctrl-Scroll Lock (Break) combination key.

Note: If you are on a network and the program returns to the main PrintGraph Menu before it begins printing your first graph, select the Page option to start printing.

After your graphs have been printed, you can use the Page option to advance the printer to the next top of form (the following page if you are using continuous form-feed paper). When all of your graphs have been printed, you can select the Exit Yes command sequence to return to the operating system or to the Lotus Access System, depending on how you entered the program. Remember to type **exit** at the operating system prompt, if you entered PrintGraph by using the Lotus 1-2-3 /System command.

SEE ALSO

/Graph Save

SUMMARY

This chapter has covered PrintGraph, a separate utility program that must be used when you want to print graphs created in a Lotus 1-2-3 worksheet. For information on how to generate graphs from spreadsheets or databases, see Chapter 24, "Creating and Using Graphs."

When you use the PrintGraph program, you can change the graphics printer or plotter to be used, as long as you have configured the program to work with that printer or plotter during the installation procedure. If you add a new graphics printer, you must run the Install program again. To obtain information on how to do this, refer to Chapter 2, "Installing and Customizing Lotus 1-2-3."

PART 7

LOTUS 1-2-3 MACROS

Macros have justifiably been called the hidden power of Lotus 1-2-3. Part 7 divides this subject according to the type of macro: simple keystroke macros for automating input and command menu selection, and more complex data processing macros that make use of these techniques plus the Lotus 1-2-3 macro command language.

Chapter 27 gives you the basic guidelines for creating macros. Its discussions include how to enter your keystrokes in a macro, how to name macros, document them, access them, and terminate them. It also covers how to plan macros, locate them in the worksheet, and debug them. Finally, it discusses how to create and use a library of macros that will make building a new spreadsheet application easier.

Chapter 28 takes up where Chapter 27 leaves off by introducing the Lotus 1-2-3 macro command language. This is an area in which Release 2 has greatly augmented the capabilities introduced in Release 1A. The technique and application discussions in this chapter introduce the basic syntax of the command langugage and then group the commands by function: commands that control inputting and editing data in macros, commands that perform decision making, commands that control the screen display, those that enable you to set up custom menus, those that handle errors, and those that transfer data between worksheet and ASCII files. After these discussions, you will find reference entries for each of the macro commands listed alphabetically.

CHAPTER 27

Keystroke Macros

Keystroke Macros

This chapter introduces the creation of macros: how they are structured, named, documented, and invoked. You must be familiar with these basic rules governing macros to use the Lotus 1-2-3 macro command language, which is discussed at length in the next chapter.

In the following discussions, you will find information on how to create macros that simply store and replay your keystrokes. The majority of the macros presented along with the various Lotus 1-2-3 commands and functions introduced in other chapters are of this type. These macros save time by storing the command keystrokes and input almost exactly as you would type them in manually, but these macros play the keystrokes back very rapidly when you invoke them.

While such macros are easy to create and can help you quite a bit by automating many of the more repetitive tasks involved in editing and creating worksheets, they are by no means the only type of macros supported by the program. Lotus 1-2-3 now supports a command language that gives you much more power over processing data within the worksheet.

If you are new to macros, you will want to begin by creating keystroke macros that automate command sequences and data entry you use routinely. If you are already practiced at creating keystroke macros, you may want to go directly to Chapter 28 to obtain information on using the Lotus 1-2-3 macro command language.

Overview of Macros

Macros allow you to customize the way Lotus 1-2-3 works. Any keystroke you make from the keyboard can be stored in a macro and replayed when the macro is activated. This includes all letters, numbers, and punctuation symbols that can be entered into a worksheet cell from your keyboard.

As you know, Lotus 1-2-3 commands can be invoked by pressing the forward slash key (/) followed by the first letter of the name of each of the menu options used. In a macro, any command sequence can therefore be recorded and stored as strings of these letters preceded by a / symbol. For example, you can store the command to save a worksheet, /File Save, by entering the keystrokes **/FS**.

Other special keys on the IBM keyboard, such as the function keys, editing keys, and cursor-movement keys, can also be stored in macros, although these cannot be entered directly as can the alphanumeric and punctuation characters. Lotus 1-2-3 macros use a special representation of each of these keys. By entering the name that represents the key, you store its keystroke so that it is played back when the macro is activated, just as though you had entered it manually from the keyboard.

The Structure of a Macro

Macros consist of a set of keystrokes, special command instructions, or both, typed directly into the cells of the worksheet just as you would enter any other data. A single cell can contain one or many such instructions within it. While it is common practice to break up macro instructions at convenient points and enter them in a range of cells, this is not necessary. As long as the instructions you enter do not exceed 240 characters, they can all be entered in a single cell.

More often than not, you will want to break up a macro's instructions into different cells in the worksheet to make it as easy as possible for you to follow and understand them. This often means grouping each set of instructions that performs a single function or closely related functions in a single cell. This makes it easier to document a macro's purpose as well as to follow its function. More will be said on this subject in following discussions on entering and documenting macros.

Macro instructions that are not entered into a single cell must be entered into a cell range that consists of a single column. Lotus 1-2-3 executes macro instructions from left to right in each cell, beginning with the first cell in the range and working down the cells in the same column. It stops execution whenever it encounters a specific instruction to stop, an empty cell, a sole value entry in a cell, or a cell that contains an empty label or a string formula whose result is an empty string (Release 2 only).

It is very important that you separate the cell ranges containing instructions for individual macros with at least one blank cell. If you do not, when you invoke the first macro at the top of the column, it will execute all of the instructions for all subsequent macros until it reaches an empty cell.

Entering Keystrokes in Macros

All macro keystrokes and commands must be entered in the worksheet as labels. This means that many of your macro entries must be prefaced with an apostrophe so that they can be entered in the cell in LABEL mode. If you think about it, this is the only way you can possibly store a set of Lotus 1-2-3 menu command instructions in a cell. If you just type /, Lotus 1-2-3 will immediately go into MENU mode and present you with its list of Main Menu options.

Therefore, whenever your macro begins with a series of Lotus 1-2-3 command options, you will always have to preface it with an apostrophe in order to store the commands in the cell. Of course, this is also the case when your macro begins with any punctuation keys, numbers, or formulas that would otherwise be entered into the cell as values. As with any label, the apostrophe will not be displayed in the cell, although it will be visible in the Control Panel.

If the first character of the macro instruction that you are entering into a cell causes the program to go into LABEL mode, you do not need to preface it with an apostrophe. You will find that this is the case for all macro keywords, because they start with the left curly brace, {, which is automatically interpreted as a label character.

Note: You will see the apostrophe before many of the instructions in the Macro Contents column of example macros listed in other chapters of this book because of the requirement that macro keystrokes and commands be entered as labels in cells. Although these macros must be entered with this label prefix, it will not be displayed except in the contents of the cell in the Control Panel.

Naming Macros

Lotus 1-2-3 does not automatically recognize macro instructions entered into cells of the worksheet as a macro. To differentiate these labels from regular spreadsheet labels, you associate macros with the keys that invoke them by giving these keys as part of their range names.

Each macro is executed by holding down the Alt key, typing the single letter key by which it is named, and then releasing both keys. In order to associate an alphabetical letter with a macro, you give it a range name that consists of the letter preceded by \ (the backslash). You can think of this backslash character as representing the Alt key that is actually pressed when activating and executing the macro.

Macro range names must therefore consist of single alphabetical letters from A to Z preceded by a \ (backslash) if they are to be invoked from the keyboard. However, subroutines that are set up in separate cell ranges controlled from the main set of instructions can be given regular range names consisting of up to 15 characters without the backslash.

Note: There is one exception to this, the macro named \0 (Alt-0). A macro given this range name represents a very special macro that is automatically executed whenever the worksheet file is retrieved. See the section entitled "Creating Custom Menus" in Chapter 28 for more information on this type of macro.

Lotus 1-2-3 does not differentiate between capital and lowercase letters in range names. All range names entered in lowercase are automatically converted to their uppercase equivalents. This means that you can assign only one macro to each letter key in a single worksheet file, which effectively limits the number of individual macros per worksheet to 26 (unless you create an Alt-0 macro, making 27). You can, however, assign different macros to the same letter keys as long as these macros are entered into different worksheet files.

When you assign a range name to the set of instructions entered into a single cell or cell range in the worksheet, you can use the /Range Name Create command. When the macro instructions are entered in a range of cells, you need only indicate the address of the first cell as the range; Lotus 1-2-3 automatically reads and executes the contents of all cells down the column range.

You can also assign range names to your macros by entering the name of the macro in a cell immediately to the left of the first cell containing the macro instructions and using the /Range Name Labels Right command. This is the preferred method, because it allows you to structure the macro in a three-column layout with the first column containing the macro name, the second the macro contents, and the third comments that document the function of each set of macro instructions (see Figure 27.1 for an illustration of this layout).

When you use this system, you must also preface the macro name with an apostrophe when you enter it in its cell. This is required because the backslash is normally used in Lotus 1-2-3 to create a repeating label. For instance, if you enter the macro name as \w in a cell without an initial apostrophe, the result will be a string of w's (wwwwwwwww) across the entire width of the cell. Instead, this macro's name must appear in the cell as \w (though in the Control Panel it will appear as '\w). The only way to have it displayed as \w in the cell is to enter it as '\w.

Note: For this reason, all of the macro names under the Label column heading in the example macros shown throughout this book are prefaced with apostrophes before the backslash.

Structuring your macros in this way and using the /Range Name Labels Right command to name them is more efficient than using the /Range Name Create command, because with Labels Right you can name many macros entered in the same column in one operation. You must remember, however, to separate each individual macro with at least one blank row. This kind of arrangement is not only beneficial when you create a series of simple keystroke macros (like the construction set illustrated in Chapter 5, "Using Worksheet Construction Macros") but is also highly desirable when creating complex macros that use subroutines (each of which is given its own range name) called from within the main set of macro command instructions (covered in detail in Chapter 28).

```
Y73: [W11]                                                              READY

      Y           Z                                  AA        AB        AC
61 Macro Name Macro Contents                     Description
62 Alt-Y                                         Macro to date stamp worksheet
63 \y         @CHOOSE(@MONTH(@NOW)-1,            <- Calculate current month
64            "January","February","March",
65            "April","May","June","July",
66            "August","September","October",
67            "November","December")
68            &" "&@STRING(@DAY(@NOW),0)         <- Add space & calculate day
69            &", 19"                            <- Add comma and 19
70            &@STRING(@YEAR(@NOW),0)~           <- Calc year & enter formula
71            {EDIT}{CALC}~                      <- Convert formula to label
72
73
74
75
76
77
78
79
80
21-Oct-86  06:34 PM
```

FIGURE 27.1: Example macro illustrating the structured layout wherein the macro name is entered in one column, followed by the macro instructions in the second column and the macro documentation in the third column. In this example, the macro's name, \y (Alt-Y), is entered into cell Y63. Its purpose is to date-stamp the worksheet by taking the date from the @NOW function (@TODAY in Release 1A) and converting it into a label. All of the macro contents are located in column Z, beginning in cell Z63 next to the macro name. This makes it possible to assign the macro name \y to cell Z63 by using the /Range Name Labels Right command. The rest of the macro instructions are entered in column Z below this cell without any blank cells (which indicate the end of the macro). Notice that each set of commands is documented with explanatory comments in column AA. Because the macro begins execution in the cell named \y and automatically reads down the column, these comments will never be mistaken as part of the macro.

Documenting a Macro

This kind of macro structure makes it easier not only to give range names to your macros but also to document the functioning of each set of instructions the macro contains. It is important to document even the simplest keystroke macro, not to mention complex macros that involve many steps, each of which may contain many commands.

Because macros are executed from the first cell of the named range down the column, you can safely enter your comments to document the function of each set of instructions in the column immediately to the right. If you wish, you can place your comments in a column further over to the right, leaving a blank column or columns between the macro contents and their associated descriptions. You will, however, want to widen the column containing the macro instruction, so that all of the keystrokes and commands are visible in their cells.

Some people like to preface comment lines with an asterisk or some other symbol (you will see an arrow created by typing the greater-than symbol and a hyphen in some of the example macros in this book). This distinguishes these lines clearly as nonfunctioning comments.

When documenting a simple keystroke macro, you may have to add only a simple comment line describing the overall function of the macro rather than the function of each command. For instance, a macro that consists of the keystrokes /FS~R can be simply be described as a second-time save macro. In a more complex macro made up of several steps, you will want to document each step, either by describing its function or its relation to previous or following steps.

You may even want to document how to use the macro along with its functioning. This is usually required when new users who are unfamiliar with how to invoke and terminate the macro will be using it in creating or editing worksheets.

Invoking a Macro

Once the macro instructions have been entered in a cell range and this range has been given a range name associated with the appropriate letter key, you can invoke the macro at any time by holding down the Alt key, typing the letter, and then releasing both keys. The macro named Alt-0 is the only exception to this—this macro is invoked automatically whenever the worksheet containing it is retrieved. It cannot be invoked from the keyboard.

Before testing a macro for the first time, you should always save the worksheet by using the /File Save command. If the macro contains errors that adversely affect the data in the worksheet, you can then retrieve the worksheet file and make any necessary corrections to its contents. Of course, any time you edit the contents of a macro, you cannot be sure that you have not introduced new potentially destructive errors in the macro. You should therefore use /File Save each time you edit a macro before testing it out in its revised form.

Before invoking a macro, you must determine whether you need to reposition the cell pointer for the macro to work properly and not damage the contents of the worksheet. This depends on the function of the macro. If you are executing a macro that erases the contents of the current cell (/RE~), you will want to make sure that the cell pointer is positioned in the cell you want to delete (if the cell pointer were in the cell that contains these macro keystrokes, it would, of course, wipe them out!).

However, if you are executing a macro that prints a copy of the spreadsheet data by using previously defined parameters (/PPAG~PQQ), it would not matter where the cell pointer is located when you invoke the macro. There would be no adverse effect on the macro even if the cell pointer were still located in the cell containing these keystrokes.

Terminating a Macro

Most keystroke macros do not contain a specific command to terminate the macro. They rely instead on the blank cell that is left below the last cell containing keystroke instructions to determine where and when they stop. You can terminate any keystroke macro by pressing the Ctrl-Scroll Lock, or Break, key combination even before the macro has finished playing back the last command. If you find that your macro contains errors that cause the program to go into ERROR mode, you can terminate the macro in this way. You may then also have to press the Esc or Return key to return to READY mode.

Some keystroke macros make use of a simple looping technique: when the program reaches the end of the macro instructions, it is instructed to return to the range name given to the macro (using the {BRANCH} or '/XG commands). This causes the program to reexecute all of the instructions beginning with the first cell in the range, effectively setting up an endless loop. The only way to terminate macros containing such loops is to press the Break key combination. (The Alt-C and Alt-R macros illustrated in Figure 3.6 for doing data entry down columns or across rows with the 10-key number pad are of this type.)

Representing Keys in Macros

As stated earlier when first introducing macros, some keys on the keyboard are not entered into the contents of macros exactly as they are when actually using Lotus 1-2-3 to create or edit worksheets. These special keys include all of the cursor-movement keys, editing keys, and most of the function keys used by the program. Table 27.1 shows how these keys are represented in macros.

The device used by Lotus 1-2-3 for representing such keys is to enter their name inside a pair of curly braces. There is one very important exception to this rule—the Return key. The Return key is represented by a single character called the tilde. This key is a shifted key; it is located on the key that contains the accent mark that looks like a backward apostrophe. (On many keyboards, this key is positioned immediately to the right of the apostrophe/quote key.)

Note: If you need to enter the tilde or one of the curly braces into a macro, enclose the character in its own pair of curly braces as {~}, {{}, or {}}.

The convention of using curly braces to enclose the name given to these special keys has been extended in Release 2 to include the command keywords. Because the left curly brace is regarded as a label character, whenever a sequence of macro instructions begins with one of these keys or a command language keyword, you do not have to preface its entry into the cell with an apostrophe. (However, in Release 1A, all macro commands are prefaced with a forward slash, as in /X, which requires this initial apostrophe. In this version of the program, only the names for the special keys shown in Table 27.1 use the curly braces.)

Note: This handbook uses the convention of showing all these special keys and the Release 2 command language keywords in uppercase letters to set them apart from the data and range names that are used with them. However, they do not have to be entered in capital letters. They work as long as they are spelled correctly, regardless of whether they are entered in upper- or lowercase letters.

	KEY REPRESENTED	MACRO ENTRY
	Return (↵)	~
Cursor-movement keys	←	{LEFT}
	→	{RIGHT}
	↑	{UP}
	↓	{DOWN}
	Ctrl-←	{BIGLEFT} (Release 2 only)
	Ctrl-→	{BIGRIGHT} (Release 2 only)
	Home	{HOME}
	End	{END}
	PgUp	{PGUP}
	PgDn	{PGDN}
Editing keys	Backspace	{BACKSPACE} or {BS}
	Del	{DELETE} or {DEL}
	Esc	{ESCAPE} or {ESC}
	Ins	{INSERT} or {INS}
	Tab	{BIGRIGHT} (Release 2 only)
	Backtab	{BIGLEFT} (Release 2 only)
Function keys	Edit (F2)	{EDIT}
	Name (F3)	{NAME}
	Abs (F4)	{ABS}
	Goto (F5)	{GOTO}
	Window (F6)	{WINDOW}
	Query (F7)	{QUERY}
	Table (F8)	{TABLE}
	Calc (F9)	{CALC}
	Graph (F10)	{GRAPH}

TABLE 27.1: Macro Representation for Special Keys

Keys that Cannot Be Represented in Macros

There are a few keys used by Lotus 1-2-3 that cannot be entered into macros:

- Caps Lock
- Num Lock

- Scroll Lock
- Help (F1)
- Step (Alt-F1 in Release 1A; Alt-F2 in Release 2)
- Compose (Alt-F1, Release 2 only)

Note: In Release 2, pressing the Compose key sequence is represented by {COMPOSE}, but it is not recognized by the program as a valid macro keyword. If you use it in a macro to enter an LICS character, you will receive the error message "Unrecognized key/range name {...}" followed by the cell address that contains it in parentheses. To enter one of the LICS codes into the worksheet from a macro, use the @CHAR function instead. This function is explained in Chapter 17.

Repeating Keystrokes

It is often necessary in macros to instruct the program to repeat a keystroke more than once—for example, to move the cell pointer a specified number of times in a certain direction. To specify repetition of a key in Release 1A, you must enter its macro representation as many times as you want it repeated. In Release 2, you can simplify this by entering the number of times the keystroke is to be repeated as part of its macro representation.

For instance, to have the cell pointer moved three cells to the right in a macro, you would have to enter

{RIGHT}{RIGHT}{RIGHT}

in Release 1A. In Release 2, the same thing can be accomplished by entering

{RIGHT 3}

Entering a repetition factor as part of the macro representation in Release 2 is not limited to cursor movement. You can enter such a factor into any special key name contained in curly braces (listed in Table 27.1). For instance, if you wanted to have a macro change the cell reference that follows into a mixed reference with the column relative and the row absolute, you could enter

{ABS 2}

before the cell reference in the macro. This presses the Absolute function key (F4) twice, thus producing a mixed address with the column relative and row absolute.

When entering a repetition factor, you do not have to enter it as a constant such as 2, 3, or 4. You can also enter it as a cell reference or a range name that contains such a value or as a formula that calculates such a value. For example, if cell A2 contains the number 3, you could enter this repetition factor as

{LEFT A2}

The macro would then move the cell pointer three cells to the left. If cell A2 has been given the range name Number, you could produce the same cursor movement by entering this in the macro:

{LEFT Number}

You can also include a formula in the key representation. If cell A2 contains the number 3 and B2 contains the value 2, you could move the cell pointer up five cells by entering this into the macro:

{UP A2 + B2}

There is just one caution about using cell references, range names, or formulas to indicate the repetition factor: if any of these contain an NA or ERR value, a label, or an empty cell when the macro is invoked, the macro counts the repetition as 0.

While you can indicate repetition of the special keys enclosed in curly braces, you cannot use this technique to indicate pressing the Return key more than once. Whenever a macro requires you to press the Return key several times in succession, you must enter a tilde to represent each time the Return key is pressed. For example, to have the current cell in the worksheet formatted to Percent with 1 decimal place, you would enter

'/RFP1~~

The first tilde signifies pressing the Return key to enter the number of decimal places as 1, and the second tilde signifies pressing the Return key to accept the range to be formatted as only the current cell.

Adding Pauses for User Input

Lotus 1-2-3 macros allow you to enter a question mark enclosed in curly braces whenever you want to have the macro pause and wait until you have had a chance to input data or respond to on-screen command prompts. To continue execution of the macro, you press the Return key. Incorporating this pause often makes your keystroke macros less specific, so you can make better use of them in more varied situations.

For example, consider a macro to help you change the width of the current column by using the /Worksheet Column Set-Width command. In this situation you want to create a macro that cuts down on the amount of typing needed to enter the command while still allowing you to widen or narrow the column as the situation requires.

To create a simple keystroke macro that changes the width of the current column to 10 spaces, you could enter the following:

'/WCS10~

When invoked, this macro accesses the /Worksheet Column Set-Width command and enters 10 in response to the prompt to enter the new column width; it then presses Return to set the width.

Of course, this macro is useful only when you need to change the column width to 10 characters. It could easily be made more universal by substituting the macro pause for the actual number of characters as

'/WCS{?}~

When this macro is invoked, it also enters the keystrokes to activate the /Worksheet Column Set-Width command. Then it pauses to allow you to indicate how wide to make the current column. You can respond by using the cursor arrow keys to point or by typing in the value. As soon as you press the Return key to enter the new width, the macro resumes and presses the Return key (represented by the tilde in the macro) to set the new width.

The only thing to remember when adding pauses to your macros is that you must physically press the Return key to continue the execution of the macro. Lotus 1-2-3 does not display a prompt telling you that the macro has paused and is waiting for your input. All you will see is the appropriate command prompt or partially completed entry on the edit line of the Control Panel. The only clue you will have is the display of the CMD status indicator at the bottom of the screen, indicating that a macro is in effect and is controlling the command or data entry.

Creating Your First Macros

As you begin to create macros for your spreadsheets, there are a few things to consider. Before you create a macro to automate a command sequence or to enter data into the spreadsheet, you must determine how much time it will save in creating or maintaining the spreadsheet.

While it is possible to customize a great many of Lotus 1-2-3's menu commands and functions, turning them into simpler commands that can be invoked simply by pressing an Alt-letter combination, it may not be wise to do so. For one thing, it is very difficult to associate the overall function of all of your macros with meaningful names created from single letters of the alphabet.

For instance, if you create a macro to delete a row from the worksheet, should you name it Alt-D for delete or Alt-R for row? If you name it Alt-D but also need to create a macro to do date entry, what will you name your date macro? If you decide to name that macro Alt-D and the macro to delete a row Alt-R, and then you need to create a macro to do data entry from the 10-key number pad across a row, what will you name it? Giving meaningful single-letter names to macros can be difficult, if not impossible, depending on the number and type of commands your macros must cover.

Assuming you can create a system that makes some sense, you may find it harder to remember the keys required to perform a particular Lotus 1-2-3 command than to use the regular forward slash and multiple-letter key combinations. You may also find that you have named your macros suitably in the context of one worksheet, but you will have to rename them in another to differentiate them from new macros required there.

It becomes difficult to keep track of the function of a macro name if it varies from worksheet to worksheet. For instance, if you are accustomed to using Alt-R for doing data entry from the 10-key number pad in one worksheet environment but have reassigned Alt-R in a new worksheet to a macro that deletes a row, you may find yourself deleting data when you mean to add it.

Planning Your Macros

The first steps in creating a macro are to outline the functions of the macro, transcribe these into a set of keystroke and command instructions that can be read by Lotus 1-2-3, and then decide where to locate the instructions in the worksheet. You will often begin this process by going through the command keystrokes manually, writing down each command and prompt you encounter. After you have written this out, you can transcribe any necessary keystrokes into their Lotus 1-2-3 macro representations. This includes such keystrokes as moving the highlight in one direction a number of times or pressing the Return key to signal a response to a prompt or to complete a command.

When you first outline the functions of the macro, examine how many and what type of command sequences you want the macro to automate for you. Also estimate how often you will use these commands in the worksheet and in what contexts. Remember, because macros are entered as a part of the worksheet file, you can make them as application-specific as you deem necessary.

However, there is a trade-off: if your macros are too finely tuned to a particular spreadsheet application, you will find yourself spending a great deal of time editing the macro or even recreating it when you begin working on another, slightly different application. This brings up the question of which parts of a macro command sequence should be fully automated and which should not.

Consider the example of a simple keystroke macro to aid you in doing date entry with the @DATE function. It is clear that you will want the macro to type in **@DATE(** automatically to begin the date entry. If all of the years are the same (such as 1987), you may even want the macro to enter **87** as the first argument. Assuming the months and days all differ, you would then add two pauses so that the macro would allow you to enter these manually. After each pause, the macro enters the comma and then close parenthesis and Return to enter the serial date number in the cell. Thus far, the date macro would contain these keystrokes:

'@DATE(87,{?},{?})~

Next, you need to consider whether you want the macro to format the date for you. If you do, you must decide which date format to assign. If you want the Date 1 format, you need to decide whether you want the macro also to widen the column (assuming it is still set to the default of 9) for you to display the date. To have your date macro perform these commands, you would then add these keystrokes at the end of it:

/RFD1~~/WCS10~

Finally, you need to decide whether you want to move the cell pointer in a particular direction to prepare for the next date entry. If you are planning on doing date entry down a column, you could add the {DOWN} keystroke to it. The final date macro would then be entered into the cell as

'@DATE(87,{?},{?})~/RFD1~~/WCS10~{DOWN}

This date macro is now about as specific to the date entries you would be making in the particular spreadsheet as you can make it. However, it may not always be as efficient as you intended because of its precision.

If you find that one of the years is not 1987, you will have to edit the cell contents after the macro is completed. You can edit the contents of a cell when it is on the Control Panel. To do so, invoke the macro, backspacc to erase the 87, enter the correct digits, enter a comma, and press Return.

Also, though the macro saved some keystrokes by automatically widening the column to display the date format used, this command is not required for any of the subsequent date entries in the same column. Once the column has been set at 10 characters when entering the first date, this command sequence is no longer required. Consider too that it could even be detrimental to widen the column to 10 characters. What if you were to use this macro to enter a date in a column that has already been widened to 20 characters so that long labels in the column are displayed entirely? As soon as you enter the date in a particular cell of this column, it will automatically reset its width to 10, and you will have to widen it all over again.

One way around this kind of problem is to create macros that work in tandem. You could eliminate the /WCS10~ keystrokes if you also create a macro containing these keystrokes to widen columns for you:

'/WCS{?}~

After making the first date entry in a column of the worksheet, you could use this macro to widen the column sufficiently to display the Date 1 format.

Locating Your Macros in the Worksheet

Deciding where to locate your macros in the worksheet is as important as planning their contents. Because macros exert an influence over the spreadsheet but are not actually a part of the data and formulas used, they must be located out of the way. At the same time, they can easily be corrupted or damaged if you forget about them during spreadsheet creation and editing. Using the /Worksheet Delete Column and Row commands while creating a new spreadsheet is potentially dangerous to macros. You should use these commands with great care.

One suggestion is to give yourself ample room to enter your spreadsheet data and formulas, locating and concentrating macros in an area that is both over and down from the one where you will be doing most of your creation and editing. Another is to give a range name to the entire cell range containing all the macros you have defined, including the columns that contain the macro names, their contents, and their documentation. This makes it easier to move the macros to a new, unused area of the worksheet, should it become necessary as the spreadsheet grows. When your spreadsheet begins to spread close to the area containing the macros, you can use the /Move command to relocate them, once again over and down from the new columns and rows where you need to enter spreadsheet data.

Common Macro Errors

The most common errors made in macros are caused by typing mistakes or forgetting to include responses to all of the prompts that appear when accessing a menu command sequence. The best way to guard against either type of error is to break up the macro instructions and enter them in several cells rather than as a very long sequence of command keystrokes in one cell.

As a rule, you can break up Lotus 1-2-3 menu commands wherever you want. In other words, if the command sequence is

'/WGPE/RU{END}{RIGHT}~

it could be entered as

'/WGP
E/RU
{END}{RIGHT}~

in three cells (each directly beneath the others), without adversely affecting the functioning of the macro. Splitting the complete command sequence /WGPE onto two lines does not impair Lotus 1-2-3's ability to follow the macro and replay the correct command keystrokes. However, it may make it more difficult for you to follow its meaning and therefore catch any typing errors or omissions.

When you split macro instructions into individual cells in a column range, you cannot split any key representations enclosed in curly braces (this goes for command language keywords as well). You could not, for example, split up either the {END} or {RIGHT} instructions into four cells like this:

'/WGP
E/RU
{END}{RI
GHT}~

The {RIGHT} key name must be entered in one cell for this macro to work properly. You could, of course, place {END} in one cell and {RIGHT} in the one below it.

In terms of catching errors, especially when you are still new to macro creation, you might be better off just entering one complete sequence of commands per cell. For instance, in the example cited above, you could enter the command to turn on global protection in one cell and the commands to unprotect a range using the End and → keys to point it out in another:

'/WPGE
'/RU{END}{RIGHT}~

(Notice that when you arrange the macro in this way, you must remember to precede both sets of instructions with apostrophes.)

In terms of remembering what keystrokes must be added to respond appropriately to prompts, there are two conflicting things to remember in this macro. The first is that the /Worksheet Global Protection Enable command does not require you to press the Return key, so you do not add a tilde to terminate it. The second is that the /Range Unprotect command prompts you to indicate the cell range as soon as you type **/RU** and requires you to press the Return key after you have indicated it, so you do have to add a tilde after the {END}{RIGHT} commands. (You also have to remember that the /Range Unprotect command automatically anchors the cell range at the current cell and therefore does not require a period for anchoring.)

These subtle differences between the way various Lotus 1-2-3 commands handle Returns, anchor cell ranges, and the like are the hardest details to add correctly to macros, especially when they include sequences of commands that all behave a little differently. The best way to avoid such errors is to walk through the sequences manually, writing down the commands and prompts as they occur on the screen before entering the keystroke instructions in the macro itself.

Debugging and Editing Macros

Despite your best efforts to catch these errors, there will be many times when your macros fail to perform as intended. Remember to save the worksheet file before you try out a new macro and to move the cell pointer, if required, to an area of the worksheet where it cannot do damage to the contents of your macros.

If, when tested, the macro goes awry in some way, take the program out of CMD mode by pressing the Break key combination (Ctrl-Scroll Lock). If the program goes into ERROR mode after pressing Break, press the Return or Esc key.

Each time a macro is executed, it moves very rapidly through the command menu options (you usually see only a flicker) so that you probably will not know where the problem developed until Lotus 1-2-3 beeps at you or perhaps goes into ERROR mode. However, sometimes the macro hangs up at a particular menu prompt and just waits without causing a bona fide error. This can indicate that you forgot to enter the required keystrokes to respond to this prompt (perhaps with a tilde to press the Return key). You may also find that the macro stops at a particular prompt and that it has added some sort of illegal character such as a period or a comma. This can indicate that you added an extra period to anchor the spreadsheet pointer or a comma to delimit a function that is not required (or allowed) in responding to the command prompt.

Many times, these symptoms will not appear to alert you to the location of the problem. If, upon examining the contents of the macro, you cannot spot any typo or omission in the instructions, you can retest the macro in single-step mode.

To do this, press Alt-F1 (or Alt-F2, if you are using Release 2) before you invoke the macro a second time. You will see the STEP indicator displayed at the bottom of the screen (it changes to SST as soon as you invoke the macro). In this mode, the macro is executed a keystroke at a time, and you must press the Return key to have it advance to the next macro instruction. This allows you to move through the macro, examining what happens after each keystroke until you locate the problem (at least the first problem—your macro could easily contain many). Once you spot the place at which the macro hangs up or causes the program to go into ERROR mode, you can use the Break key combination to terminate it.

Then return to the cell range that contains the macro and locate the instructions that require editing. You edit the contents of a macro just as you do any other cell in a Lotus 1-2-3 worksheet—by moving the cell pointer to it and pressing the Edit function key (F2). This brings the contents of the macro line to the second line of the Control Panel, where they can be edited as necessary. After editing the contents of a macro, you can save the worksheet and invoke the macro again to retest it. You do not have to reactivate it by using the /Range Name Labels Right command. Because the contents of macros can be edited like any other cells in the worksheet, you can easily make modifications to a basic macro at any time.

Creating and Using Macro Libraries

There are certain macros, such as those used to make it easier to enter or edit data in the spreadsheet, that you will want to reuse in many, if not all, of the spreadsheets you create with Lotus 1-2-3. Rather than reenter individual macros as you need them in each new worksheet that you begin, you can store them together in a separate file. This file represents a macro library that can be called up whenever you start a new worksheet.

You can retrieve a macro library file with the /File Retrieve command and build your spreadsheet in it, or you can start a new worksheet file and then use the /File Combine Copy Named/Specified-Range command to bring the cell range containing the macros into it.

If you choose the former method, you must save the spreadsheet under a new name to keep the macro library file from being overwritten with the spreadsheet data and formulas you enter. If you don't pay attention and save the new worksheet file using the macro library file name, you will have to use the /File Xtract command to put the macros back into a separate file. (They will also have to named again in this new worksheet by using the /Range Name Labels Right command.)

If you choose to use the latter method, you must use the /Range Name Labels Right command to rename your macros before you can use them (range names are not transferred when you use the /File Combine commands). Also, you will have to use the /Range Name Create command if you want to assign a range name to the cell range containing your macros.

SUMMARY

This chapter has introduced you to the basic functions of Lotus 1-2-3 keystroke macros. It has provided an overview of what macros are, how they are constructed, and how they can help you in your work.

In the next chapter, you will find information on creating macros that use the Lotus 1-2-3 macro command language. This language allows you to create macros that go far beyond simple keystroke operations.

These commands extend your data processing capabilities in the worksheet to include interactive processing, controlling the path of macro execution, controlling the screen display, and creating your own Lotus 1-2-3 command menus. If you are using Release 2, you will also find commands that give you control over direct file processing, allowing you to transfer data between Lotus 1-2-3 and other applications.

CHAPTER 28

THE MACRO COMMAND LANGUAGE

The Macro Command Language

This chapter discusses the Lotus 1-2-3 macro command language and contains reference entries for each command. Release 2 has added 40 new macro commands to the Lotus 1-2-3 macro command language, 33 of which have no equivalents into Release 1A. These additional commands are the ones brought into Lotus 1-2-3 from Symphony. If you have used the Symphony macro command language, you will find that these commands are almost identical in Lotus 1-2-3.

The techniques and applications discussions in this chapter group the various command keywords by function. These discussions provide a general working knowledge of how such commands are used in macros. You will then find reference entries for each of the command keywords, listed in alphabetical order. If you are using Release 1A, you can find the particular /X command you are interested in by looking up its Release 2 equivalent at the beginning of the command language reference section.

The Lotus 1-2-3 Macro Command Language

The Lotus 1-2-3 macro command language has been greatly expanded in Release 2 of the program. It now includes 40 command keywords that form the core of what can be considered a bona fide programming language. As such, it allows you to create macros whose data processing capabilities far outstrip those possible by using keystroke storage techniques.

These macro commands perform four main functions:

- Interactive processing in macros. These commands allow macros to pause, accept user input, and continue processing based on that input. You can thus create macros that interact with the user via custom Control Panel menus.
- Control of macro execution. These commands provide for conditional data processing using IF-THEN and FOR-NEXT statements, branching, and subroutine calls with parameter passing.
- Control of the display screen. These commands allow you to freeze the keyboard, suppress the display of the Control Panel, change the

mode indicator, and sound a beep tone to gain the user's attention.

- File processing. These commands can transfer data between a worksheet file and an ASCII file without using the /File or /Print Menu commands. With these commands, you can read or write data between files a character or line at a time.

Using Range Names to Identify Data Variables

Lotus 1-2-3 macros are entered in cells; the data variables used with the various command language statements are also entered in cells. This means that you can refer to them by cell address and, therefore, do not have to name them before you use them.

However, as with any worksheet cell, you can assign range names to these cells and use the range names to identify the data variables used. It is wise to use range names to identify cells containing data variables, because even if a cell address changes, its associated range name will still refer to the appropriate cell.

For instance, if you use the Lotus 1-2-3 {LET} statement to initialize a data variable for storing a first-quarter sales figure entered in cell B5 in cell D55, you could enter this statement as

{LET D55,B5}

However, if the worksheet data is reorganized, the macro will still try to use the original cell references, which will cause an error in processing. This problem is solved if you give cells D55 and B5 range names, such as Quarter and Sales, which can then be used in the LET statement:

{LET Quarter,Sales}

If the spreadsheet data in the Quarter and Sales cells is relocated in the worksheet, Lotus 1-2-3 adjusts the cell references to reflect the new locations, which significantly reduces the possibility of invalidating the macro. As with any data input in the worksheet, you can enter a data variable either as a label or as a value.

Release 1A versus Release 2 Commands

The macro command language in Release 1A is restricted to eight commands, all of which are prefaced by /X. Each of these commands has new Release 2 equivalents (shown in Table 28.1). If you are using Release 2, you can continue to use these /X commands if you wish; this version of Lotus 1-2-3 will also recognize them.

The Release 1A macro commands form a nucleus of functions that allow you to create macros in two of the four areas discussed previously:

- Interactive processing in macros using the /XL, /XN, and /XM commands
- Control of macro execution with decision making using the /XI (IF-THEN), /XG (Goto branching), and the /XC and /XR (subroutine) commands

The Release 1A language does not allow you to control the screen display and perform direct file processing.

Syntax of Command Language Statements

Like Lotus 1-2-3 @ functions, most command language statements require arguments that you must enter in a predefined order and separate by the delimiter character in effect (this book uses the comma as the delimiter character). As with the @ functions, the command name must be spelled correctly, although it does not matter whether you enter it in lowercase, uppercase, or mixed case.

When using the Release 2 command language, each command, or keyword, must be enclosed in a pair of curly braces, just as when entering special key

RELEASE 2 KEYWORD COMMAND	RELEASE 1A OR 2 /X EQUIVALENT	FUNCTION
{IF condition}	'/XIcondition~	IF-THEN
{BRANCH location}	'/XGlocation~	Go to
{routine-name}	'/XClocation~	Call subroutine
{RETURN}	'/XR	Return from subroutine
{QUIT}	'/XQ	Terminate macro execution
{GETLABEL message,location}	'/XLmessage~location~	Display prompt for user input (label)
{GETNUMBER message,location}	'/XNmessage~location~	Display prompt for user input (value)
{MENUBRANCH location}	'/XMlocation~	Process user-defined menu

TABLE 28.1: Release 2 Macro Command Keyword Equivalents for Release 1A /X Commands

names (see Chapter 27). Further, each command, including its arguments and right brace, must be entered in a single cell. You cannot split a command into different cells as you can when entering Lotus 1-2-3 menu command keystrokes. For example, the following statement entered on two lines would not be allowed and would cause an error in your macro:

{LET Price,
Cost*1.6}

This would have to be entered in a single cell of the macro as

{LET Price,Cost*1.6}

Spaces must be used correctly. Always enter a space to set off the command keyword from its arguments, but do not include spaces between arguments. (You can enter spaces if they are part of one of the arguments; enclose these arguments in quotation marks.) If the command keyword does not take any arguments, do not enter any spaces between its left curly brace, name, and right curly brace.

When using Release 1A /X commands, you must preface them with an apostrophe to enter them as labels. This is not necessary when using a Release 2 keyword, because the left curly brace character is automatically taken as a label.

Using Range Names as the Arguments of Command Language Statements

It is always preferable to use range names instead of cell addresses in the arguments of command language statements. If a cell's address is changed, its range name will still refer to the appropriate cell. This convention is strongly urged because it minimizes the possibility of introducing errors into your macros after making layout changes to the data in the worksheet. When you assign range names to cells and cell ranges, obey the same conventions that you do when naming any cell range in Lotus 1-2-3 (see Chapter 8 for details on naming cell ranges).

Some keywords do not allow you to use range names (or cell addresses, for that matter). For instance, the {INDICATE} statement does not accept a range name. When you use this command, you must enter its argument as a literal string (that is, enclosed in a pair of quotation marks).

The use of quotes clearly marks the argument entry as something other than a range name, formula, or value of some sort. Use quotation marks to resolve any ambiguity in arguments that might lead Lotus 1-2-3 to misinterpret the argument. This is particularly important if you include a character such as a comma or curly brace in the argument; such characters could be taken as part of the command statement.

For example, if you use the {LET} command to input a data variable in a cell given the range name Total as

{LET Total,Year-to-Date}

Lotus 1-2-3 will interpret Year-to-Date as a range name and use the value stored in this cell. If, however, you entered the statement as

{LET Total,"Year-to-Date"}

Lotus 1-2-3 would enter the literal string Year-to-Date as a label in the cell named Total.

If you revised this statement to include a value such as 1000, you would enter it as

{LET Total,1000}

to have Lotus 1-2-3 enter this value in the Total cell. If, however, you enclosed this second argument in quotes, as in

{LET Total,"1000"}

Lotus 1-2-3 would enter 1000 as a string in the cell named Total.

Conventions Used in This Handbook

This handbook observes the following conventions:

- Command keywords are shown in capital letters.
- Range names are shown with the first letter capitalized. No range names containing characters such as commas, requiring the use of quotation marks, are used.
- All character strings are enclosed in quotation marks, even if those marks are not required for the macro to operate properly.

Inputting and Editing Data in Macros

You can instruct a macro to input a particular entry into a cell of the worksheet by using the {LET} or {PUT} keyword or by using keystrokes.

To illustrate this, consider the following macro statements, all of which enter the value 1500 into the first cell of a range named Subtotal:

{GOTO}Subtotal~1500~

or

{LET Subtotal,1500}~

or

{PUT Subtotal,0,0,1500}~

The first statement takes the keystroke approach: the Goto function key (F5), represented as {GOTO}, takes the cell pointer to the range named Subtotal, where the value 1500 is entered. The second statement uses the {LET} statement to enter the value 1500 directly into the range named Subtotal (it does not relocate the cell pointer).

The third statement uses the {PUT} command to accomplish the same thing. This command is used to enter information in tables. In this example, the range of cells named Subtotal makes up the table. The next two arguments (0,0) give the column and row offset from the first cell in the Subtotal range. Giving a zero offset for both the column and row directs the program to put the value 1500 in the first cell of this range (or table). The cell pointer does not have to be relocated to perform the data entry.

In addition to performing data entry, the {LET} command has another function for which it is used even more often. You can use the {LET} statement in macros that involve repetitive processing to set up and maintain counters in the worksheet that keep track of each execution. For instance, it is common to set up a cell named Count and initialize it as follows:

{LET Count,Count + 1}

If you are familiar with the BASIC programming language, you will recognize this usage of the {LET} keyword by Lotus 1-2-3 as being somewhat similar to the technique BASIC uses.

Erasing Entries in the Worksheet

You can use the macro command keyword {BLANK} in a macro to erase a cell entry. This works like the /Range Erase command in a keystroke macro. For instance, to erase the entry in the first cell of the range named Subtotal, you could use either of the following macro instructions:

{GOTO}Subtotal~/RE~

or

{BLANK Subtotal}~

Again, the major difference between these two statements is that the {BLANK} command does not require moving the cell pointer to the beginning of the range named Subtotal in order to erase its contents.

Recalculating the Spreadsheet

When you make new entries or deletions manually in a worksheet (assuming global recalculation is set to Automatic), Lotus 1-2-3 automatically updates the new values and recalculates all dependent formulas. This is not the case when controlling input and delete functions with macro command statements.

To have your new variables updated in the spreadsheet, you can add the {CALC} key name (or ~ if global recalculation is set to Automatic). There are also two other command keywords that can be added to recalculate new data variables. These are {RECALC} and {RECALCCOL}; they allow you to control the area of the worksheet that is to be recalculated at any given point in the macro's execution.

This cuts down significantly on the time it takes before the new values are calculated and the macro execution resumes. The {RECALC} command recalculates the formulas row by row in the range specified as its argument. The {RECALCCOL} command recalculates them column by column within the specified range.

Converting Values to Labels in a Macro

When you need to use a value entered in a cell as a label in your macro (as when displaying messages or concatenating strings), you do not have to use the @STRING spreadsheet function. The command language's {CONTENTS} command performs essentially the same function. However, using the {CONTENTS} keyword gives you more control over the resulting label; you can add optional arguments that control the width of the display as well as specify the display format to be used. Table 28.2 shows you the format codes that can be entered as one of these optional arguments and the corresponding numeric display format.

When you use these format codes to modify the display of the resulting label, you must specify a value for the width argument as well. The {CONTENTS} command works by taking the value (or label) from a range name given as the source range (given as the second argument) and copying it into another range defined as the destination range (given as the first argument). If you do not specify a width or display format, the program uses that of the source range argument.

For instance, if you enter the value 34566.778 in a cell named Value, you can use the {CONTENTS} command to enter it in a new cell named Label, formatted with the Currency format with two decimal places, by using this statement:

{CONTENTS Label,Value,11,34}{CALC}

The left-aligned label entered into the cell named Label would appear as

FORMAT CODE	NUMERIC DISPLAY FORMAT
0–15	Fixed with 0 to 15 decimal places
16–31	Scientific with 0 to 15 decimal places
32–47	Currency with 0 to 15 decimal places
48–63	Percent with 0 to 15 decimal places
64–79	Comma (,) with 0 to 15 decimal places
112	+/− format
113	General
114	Date 1 (DD-MMM-YY)
115	Date 2 (DD-MMM)
116	Date 3 (MMM-YY)
121	Date 4 Long Intn'l (MM/DD/YY default)
122	Date 5 Short Intn'l (MM/DD default)
119	Date 6 (HH:MM:SS AM/PM)
120	Date 7 (HH:MM AM/PM)
123	Date 8 Long Intn'l (HH:MM:SS default)
124	Date 9 Short Intn'l (HH:MM default)
117	Text format
118	Hidden format
127	Worksheet's default display

TABLE 28.2: Format Codes for the {CONTENTS} Command

$34,566.78. The format code 34 specifies the use of the Currency format with two decimal places. Note that the width value of 11 does not actually change the width of the column holding the Label cell to 11 characters (if its width is 9 characters, it will be displayed only if there is no entry in the cell on its right). Nevertheless, you must specify the width to avoid the overflow indicator (a string of asterisks) across the Label cell (11 is required because the label prefix ' is added to the 10 characters).

Decision Making in Macros

Lotus 1-2-3 allows you to control processing within the macro instructions by three commands: {IF} ('/XIcondition~ in Release 1A), {BRANCH} ('/XGlocation~ in Release 1A), and {DISPATCH} (no Release 1A equivalent). Direct branching to new macro instructions is accomplished by using the {BRANCH} or '/XGlocation~ (Goto) statements. Conditional branching is accomplished by using the {IF} or '/XIcondition~ statements. Indirect branching is accomplished by using the {DISPATCH} command.

When you invoke a macro, it begins processing each instruction from the first cell of the named range, continuing down each cell until it encounters a blank cell, a cell containing a value, or a command statement that terminates the macro. In Release 1A macros this command is entered as **'/XQ**. In Release 2 macros, you can use '/XQ or the {QUIT} command keyword to terminate execution.

Each time a simple keystroke macro is executed, it processes the same instructions in the same sequence until it reaches a quit command or blank cell. To add elements of decision making to a macro, you can use one of the branching commands. The simplest of these commands is the {BRANCH} (or '/XGlocation~) keyword. It transfers execution directly to a new set of macro instructions. This allows you to organize macro instructions according to function. When you use the {BRANCH} keyword, you indicate the location of these new instructions by entering the range name assigned to them.

Conditional branching is done by using the IF command in either its '/XIcondition~ or {IF} form. These commands work much like the @IF function in Lotus 1-2-3. If the condition stated as its argument is met, it executes the next instruction; otherwise, it skips to the instruction after that. However, unlike the @IF function, the argument contains only the condition. The instructions the macro uses, which depend on the outcome of the conditional testing, are entered separately.

For example, the {IF} command is often used with a counter to have a macro terminate after a certain number of iterations. It allows processing to continue as long as the count number entered in the {IF} condition has not yet been reached:

{IF Count = 10}{BRANCH Done}
{LET Count,Count + 1}
{BRANCH Main}

In this example, the macro branches to the cell range named Done only when the value in the cell range named Count is 10. Otherwise, it continues to process the instructions in the cells below the {IF} statement. In this example, this includes the {LET} statement to increment the counter and a {BRANCH} statement that directs execution of the macro to instructions contained in the first cell of the range named Main.

When the choices in execution involve more than two possible results, you can use multiple {IF} statements. For example, you could use multiple {IF} and {BRANCH} commands to evaluate the contents of a cell and branch to the appropriate macro instructions:

{IF Choice = "Alpha"}{BRANCH Alpha}
{IF Choice = "Beta"}{BRANCH Beta}
{IF Choice = "Gamma"}{BRANCH Gamma}

However, you can accomplish the same result in a macro by using the {DISPATCH} command, as in

{DISPATCH Choice}

This command causes the macro to evaluate the contents of the cell range named Choice and to branch automatically to the name of the cell range contained there. If Choice contains the label Alpha, the macro will branch to the cell range named Alpha, and so on.

Using Subroutines in Macros

When you create a complex macro made up of many sets of instructions, you will find it much easier to organize and document its workings if you break the macro down into distinct modules, each of which performs one set of tasks. In the Lotus 1-2-3 command language, these modules are referred to as *subroutines.*

Using subroutines offers several advantages. They keep a macro smaller, allowing you to reuse a set of instructions without repeating the instructions in the macro (in other words, subroutines can be called from anywhere in the macro). This makes a macro more efficient both in the use of computer memory and in execution. Subroutines are also easier to debug than complex macros. You can develop a subroutine and correct its errors much more easily than when there are many instructions.

Once you have entered a subroutine, you give it a range name like any other cell range in Lotus 1-2-3. Because subroutines are not invoked directly but are referred to, or *called,* from within the main set of macro instructions, you do not name them with the backslash and a single letter key.

To call a subroutine in a macro, you enter its range name in curly braces in Release 2. In Release 1A, you must use the command '/XClocation˜ , where the location argument is the range name given to the subroutine. After the macro executes the instructions in the subroutine, you can use the {RETURN} command ('/XR in Release 1A) to instruct it to return to the main body of the macro, where it will execute the next instruction below the subroutine call.

You can nest many levels of subroutines in a macro—in other words, you can call one subroutine from within another. If your macro contains a series of nested subroutines, each of which calls another, you can use the {RESTART} command to clear the subroutine chain of command (clear the stack) and return control to the original calling macro.

Repeating a Subroutine with FOR Loops When your macro requires repeated execution of a subroutine, either a specified number of times or until a particular condition is met, you can set up looping procedures in your subroutines by using the {FOR} command keyword. The {FOR} command requires several arguments:

{FOR counter-location,start-number,stop-number, step-number,starting-location}

The counter location is the cell range where the count numbers are stored. The start number is the initial value entered into this cell. The step number tells the macro how much to increment the value in the counter location each time the subroutine is executed. The stop value tells the macro at what number to stop executing the subroutine. The starting-location argument is the name of the cell range that contains the subroutine.

For example, consider the following macro instructions:

```
Count    1
'\w      {GOTO}Table~
         {FOR Count,1,5,1,Widen}
         . . . .

Widen    '/WCS15~{RIGHT}
```

In this example, the cell pointer is positioned at the beginning of the cell range named Table when the macro is invoked. The cell named Count is then initialized with the start number 1. The {FOR} statement then transfers control to the subroutine named Widen, which contains instructions to set a new column width of 15 characters and move the cell pointer one cell to the right. As soon as the macro finishes performing these instructions in the Widen subroutine, it increases the count stored in the Count cell by 1 (to 2) and reexecutes the Widen subroutine. This looping process continues until the value in the Count cell reaches the stop number of 5.

If you wish to add a condition under which the looping should be terminated before the counter reaches the stop-number value, you can add an {IF} statement followed by the {FORBREAK} keyword. For example:

```
Widen    {IF Step=2}{FORBREAK}
         '/WCS15~{RIGHT}
```

Passing Values to a Subroutine In a subroutine call statement, you can define arguments that enter data variables for the subroutine to process. By passing these values to the subroutine, you can have the subroutine use different values at different times during the macro's execution. In order to store the data variables passed to the subroutine, the first statement in the subroutine must contain a {DEFINE} command. (For examples, see the {DEFINE} reference entry.)

The arguments of the {DEFINE} command are the locations for each data variable, that is, the cell ranges where the values assigned to the data variables are stored. The {DEFINE} command also accepts optional suffix arguments, :value or :string, which define the type of data variable. If you do not use one of these type arguments, the data variable is considered to be a character string.

Controlling the Screen Display

The Release 2 macro command language has several commands that enable you to control the screen display during the execution of your macros. Whenever your macros include instructions that access the Lotus 1-2-3 menu commands, you will see a flicker as the program rapidly replays the keystrokes included. In long macros containing many such command keystrokes, you may want to suppress this flickering by using the {WINDOWSOFF} and {PANELOFF} command keywords in the macro.

The {WINDOWSOFF} command freezes the display screen so that it is not redrawn even when the macro instructions affect a part of the worksheet. Using this statement helps to speed up a macro, because Lotus 1-2-3 does not have to take time to redraw the display screen. The {PANELOFF} command clears the command entry and response lines of the Control Panel and then suppresses further display of keystrokes on the Control Panel. This is the area that causes the most flicker as the macro rapidly executes the menu command sequences.

Usually, both commands are used together in a macro to reduce the on-screen distractions caused by macro execution. They should not, however, be added to your macro until you have completed debugging it. You can use the {WINDOWSON} and {PANELON} commands to unfreeze the display screen and Control Panel later in the macro. If you do not add these statements, the {WINDOWSOFF} and {PANELOFF} commands will automatically turn off when the macro terminates its execution.

You can have a macro display your own mode indicator in the upper-right corner of the screen during the macro's execution by adding an {INDICATE} statement and entering up to five characters as an optional argument. If you do not add an argument to this keyword, Lotus 1-2-3 displays the READY indicator. Use the {INDICATE} statement with no argument at the end of a macro to suppress your own mode indicator and redisplay the READY mode indicator.

For example, you could enter this command to have the word MACRO displayed as the mode indicator.

{INDICATE "MACRO"}

Notice that the indicator display is enclosed in optional quotation marks. When you add this optional argument, you *must* enter it as a literal character string: you cannot use a cell reference or range name. If the display string contains a space, comma, or colon, you must enclose it in quotation marks.

To blank the mode indicator entirely, add an {INDICATE} statement containing an empty string:

{INDICATE ""}

The last command for controlling the screen display during macro execution, the {BEEP} command, produces an audible sound. This command is used to sound one of the four tones used by the IBM computer. It can be used whenever you want to alert the user to a change in processing, especially one that requires input, or to an error in processing. To change the tone that is produced, add a number between 1 and 4. If you do not specify a tone number, the program uses tone 1.

User Input in Macros

The Lotus 1-2-3 macro command language supports several methods for suspending execution of the macro to accept user input for processing. Both Release 1A and Release 2 will accept {?} as a pause that suspends execution until the user presses the Return key. During this pause, the user is free to access any Lotus 1-2-3 menu command or type any keyboard character.

You may often want to restrict user input in a macro to accept only a new label or value. The {GETLABEL} ('/XLlocation˜ in Release 1A) and {GETNUMBER} ('/XNlocation˜ in Release 1A) commands display the prompt message you specify on the Control Panel, stop a macro's execution, and await the user's input, which is terminated by the Return key.

The difference between the two has to do with the type of input the user is to make. If you use the {GETLABEL} keyword, the characters entered will be accepted as a label even if they consist of numbers not prefaced with an apostrophe. Use the {GETNUMBER} command when you want the user to make numeric entries in response to your prompt.

The following example uses the {GETNUMBER} command statement to allow the user to enter the number of report copies to print:

```
Num
Count
'\r       {GETNUMBER "Enter number of copies to print:",Num}
          '/PPR{?}˜Q
          {For Count,1,Num,1,Print}˜
Print     '/PPAGPQ
```

When you invoke this macro, it displays the message "Enter number of copies to print:" in the Control Panel. The number you enter on this line is stored in a cell named Num when you press the Return key. This value is used by the {FOR} command to control the number of times the Print subroutine is accessed. Notice that this macro also uses the {?} pause to allow the user to specify the print range either by cell addresses, range name, or pointing.

In addition to these commands, which accept a string of text or numeric input, Release 2 has included two new keywords, {GET} and {LOOK}, which accept only one keystroke. They are useful whenever you require the user to press a single key to designate some kind of choice.

The {GET} statement suspends macro execution and waits until the user presses a single key; it then immediately resumes execution. For example, you could have the user enter a single key to designate where the cell pointer should move next, as in

{GET Keystroke}
{IF Keystroke = "h"}{HOME}
{IF Keystroke = "e"}{END}{HOME}

The {LOOK} command works a little differently. It does not suspend the execution of a macro but merely checks whether the user has typed any character in the type-ahead buffer. If the user presses a series of keys, only the first keystroke in this buffer is stored in the range named as the command's location argument.

To suspend a macro's execution until a specified period of time has elapsed, you can use the {WAIT} command keyword. This command can also be used to delay the execution of a macro until a specific time. This is useful when creating a macro that does not begin a lengthy report printing session until after office hours.

When you want to suspend a macro's execution for a specified time, you must combine the {WAIT} statement with the @NOW and @TIME functions, as in

{WAIT @NOW + @TIME(0,1,0)}

This would suspend execution of the macro for one minute.

To delay processing until a specific hour, use the @INT(@NOW) or the @TODAY function (in Release 2.01) with the @TIME function. For example, this command will delay execution until 8:00 PM on the current day:

{WAIT @INT(@NOW) + @TIME(20,0,0)}

Creating Custom Menus

Lotus 1-2-3 macros can be set up so that they are entirely menu driven. The command menus that you create in a macro appear and work like any other Lotus 1-2-3 command menu. Setting up menus offers several advantages:

- It minimizes the chances of the user introducing errors into the macro that might interfere with its processing.
- Because it guides the user through each menu choice, even those who are inexperienced with Lotus 1-2-3 can access and use the application created by the macro.
- Because such menus appear and work like a regular Lotus 1-2-3 menu, they do not introduce a new way of interacting with the program that could confuse experienced users as they go back and forth between using your custom menus and the standard Lotus 1-2-3 command menus.

If you want to create a complex macro that completely customizes a spreadsheet or database application in Lotus 1-2-3, you can save it under the macro name \0 (backslash zero) to make it execute as soon as the worksheet file is retrieved. That way, the user performs his or her work in the file only under the control of your custom menu macro.

You can also name one worksheet file on your data disk AUTO123.WK1 (or .WKS if you are using Release 1A). This file will be retrieved automatically when you start up Lotus 1-2-3. If this file also contains an Alt-0 macro, the macro will be invoked as soon as the worksheet is loaded.

Note: Always give your Alt-0 (\0) macro another name such as Alt-M (\m) so that you can invoke it by an alternate name. This allows you to make changes to the macro and test them out without having to save and retrieve the worksheet file. Position the cell pointer in the first cell of the range containing the main menu commands and then use the /Range Name Create command to assign a new backslash-letter (\m) range name to it.

When you create menu macros, you use a special macro command to have the macro branch to the various routines that contain the menu options, option descriptions, and commands. In Release 1A this command is '/XMlocation~ . In Release 2, you can use either this command or the {MENUBRANCH} command keyword. Release 2 also includes a new keyword, {MENUCALL}, that allows you to perform a subroutine call rather than branch to the menu routine.

Follow these guidelines when creating menu macros:

- A menu cannot contain more than eight options. However, you can have as many submenus attached to the menu options as you like.

- A menu option must be entered as a label.
- Begin each menu option with a different first letter. If possible, restrict the option name to a single word. If you must use more than one word, you should place a hyphen (no spaces) between the words so that it is clear to the user that it represents only a single menu choice.

When you create a menu macro, you create a routine that first lists the name of the menu option in one cell, a label describing the function of the menu options in the cell directly beneath it, and the keystroke and macro commands to carry out the options in the cell or cells below. Figure 28.1 illustrates this layout for a menu macro that contains four main options: Update, Save, Print, and Quit.

Error Handling in Macros

A well-designed interactive macro minimizes the chance of user error that could cause it to terminate prematurely. As much as possible, you should take pains to guard against allowing the user to make incorrect entries (especially the label versus value type) by adding validation routines as part of your macro instructions. For instance, to guard against an incorrect entry, you can have the macro validate the entry in one of two ways: by using the {IF} command keyword or @LENGTH function or by using the @VLOOKUP or @HLOOKUP functions to check it against a table of acceptable entries.

Once an error occurs during macro execution, the macro terminates execution and returns control to the user, displaying a Lotus 1-2-3 error message and going into ERROR mode (see Appendix A). This can happen as a result of an input error or because the user has pressed the Break key combination (Ctrl-Scroll Lock).

If you wish to prevent the user from prematurely terminating the macro with the Break key, you can use the {BREAKOFF} command. This disables this key combination during the macro's execution. If you wish to disable the Break key only during some critical point in the macro's execution, you can enable it again by placing a {BREAKON} statement in the appropriate location in the macro.

Note: The {BREAKOFF} command should be executed only once in a macro. Repeated {BREAKOFF} statements make the macro vulnerable to

```
MACRO
/XMMENU 1~

UPDATE                          SAVE                                    PRINT                           QUIT
ACCESS UPDATE MENU              ACCESS FILE SAVE MENU                   ACCESS PRINT MENU               CANCEL MENU
/XMUPDATE~/XMMENU 1~            /XMSAVE~/XMMENU 1~                      /XMPRINT~/XMMENU 1~             /XQ

DOWN                            RIGHT                                   LEFT                            UP
MOVES CURSOR DOWN & UPDATE      MOVES CURSOR RIGHT & UPDATE             MOVES CURSOR LEFT & UPDATE      MOVES CURSOR UP & UPDATE
{DOWN}{?}~/XMUPDATE~/XMMENU 1~  {RIGHT}{?}~/XMUPDATE~/XMMENU 1~         {LEFT}{?}~/XMUPDATE~/XMMENU 1~  {UP}{?}~/XMUPDATE~/XMMENU 1~

SAVE                            EXIT                                    QUIT
SAVE & REMAIN                   SAVE & EXIT                             RETURN TO PREVIOUS MENU
/FS~R/XMSAVE~/XMMENU 1~         {HOME}/FS~R/QY/XMSAVE~/XMMENU 1~        /XMMENU 1~

PRINT SPECIFIED RANGE           PRINT IN CONDENSED                      QUIT
PRINT 10 CPI                    PRINT 17 CPI                            RETURN TO PREVIOUS MENU
/PPR{?}~AGPPQ/XMPRINT~/XMMENU 1~ /PPR{?}~OS\015~QAGPPQ/XMPRINT~/XMMENU 1~ /XMMENU 1~
```

FIGURE 28.1: This figure shows a typical menu macro that contains various suboptions attached to three of the four main menu choices: Update, Save, Print, and Quit. Each menu is laid out with the options across the first row, the menu descriptions in the second row, and the command keystrokes in the third. Notice that most of these contain menu branch statements (entered as /XMlocation~) to direct the macro either to a nested menu or back to the main menu level. In this arrangement, the user can press the Esc key to back up to the previous menu just as when using the regular Lotus 1-2-3 command menus.

the Break key, because a macro can be interrupted by Ctrl-Scroll Lock at each {BREAKOFF} instruction.

In addition to preventing the user from terminating the macro with the Break key, you can also add {ONERROR} statements that tell the macro how to recover when a particular user error occurs during execution. When you add an {ONERROR} command, you can prevent the macro's termination by having it branch to a new set of instructions designed to instruct the user in how to correct the error. You can also add an optional location argument, where the macro displays a Lotus 1-2-3 error message associated with the particular error that has occurred.

Transferring Data between Files

The Release 2 Lotus 1-2-3 command language contains a group of related command keywords that can be used to process data directly between Lotus 1-2-3 worksheet files and data files created and saved in ASCII format. They allow you to transfer data from an ASCII file into a Lotus 1-2-3 worksheet or from a Lotus 1-2-3 worksheet into some other file format without using the commands on the /File Import or /Print File menus.

These commands can process two types of files: text files, which store their data in a series of bytes divided by lines, or sequential files, which store their data as a continuous stream of bytes.

The text file is the type created by most word processing software. Each line in this type of file is terminated by a carriage-return (ASCII code 13) and line-feed character (ASCII code 10). This type of file can be processed by using the {READLN} command because this command is set up to read text into a Lotus 1-2-3 worksheet file line by line rather than character by character. Each line of text in the file is read into and stored in a separate cell of the worksheet.

To transfer Lotus 1-2-3 data line by line to another file, you use the {WRITELN} command. This command transfers the contents of a worksheet cell to a new file as a single line of text.

To process a sequential file, you use the {READ} and {WRITE} commands. These read data into a worksheet file or write worksheet data to a new file character by character. The {READ} statement can copy up to 240 bytes from a sequential file into a Lotus 1-2-3 worksheet cell. The {WRITE} statement transfers one or more characters from a worksheet cell into the current position in the new file.

When you set up macros to process data between files using such commands, you begin by entering an {OPEN} statement whose first argument specifies the complete file name of the existing file to be used (if you are transferring data from it into a Lotus 1-2-3 worksheet) or the file name of a new file (if you are transferring data out of the worksheet).

After specifying the file name, you enter a second argument that specifies the mode of transfer: either R (for read) to transfer data from the ASCII file into a worksheet file, W (for write) to transfer data from a worksheet to the ASCII file format, or M (for modify) to allow both read and write access between the open file and the worksheet (that is, to transfer in both directions).

Both text and sequential files number the position of each byte in the file beginning with the first byte at position 0 and increasing by 1 for each subsequent byte until the last byte in the file is reached. The {FILESIZE} command keyword obtains the total number of bytes in the file. The program maintains a byte pointer that indicates the current position. To obtain the current position of the pointer, you can use the {GETPOS} command. The {SETPOS} command resets the byte pointer to a new byte position in the file.

You can process data between only one worksheet and ASCII file at a time. When your macro has finished reading or writing data between the two, you must add a {CLOSE} statement before opening another file into which or out of which you will transfer data in the currently retrieved worksheet.

THE LOTUS 1-2-3 COMMAND LANGUAGE KEYWORDS

This section contains an alphabetical listing of reference entries for all of the command keywords in the Lotus 1-2-3 Release 2 command language. If you are using Release 1A, you can find information on its macro commands by looking up the corresponding Release 2 command in this section. Release 1A command keywords and their equivalent commands in Release 2 are shown in Table 28.1.

As mentioned previously, you can use any of the /X macro command keywords that originated in Release 1 in the macros that you create in Release 2. The functions and arguments of the Release 2 commands are identical to the corresponding /X commands in Release 1A, with the exceptions of the /XL and /XN commands ({GETLABEL} and {GETNUMBER} in Release 2). There is a minor but noteworthy distinction between these pairs of commands, which you can sometimes put to good use.

The general syntax of the /XL command is

/XLmessage ~ location ~

If you omit a cell address or range name for the location argument, Lotus 1-2-3 will store the user's response to the message as a label in the current cell (the cell that contains the cell pointer when the macro is executed).

The general syntax of {GETLABEL} is very similar:

{GETLABEL message,location}

However, if you omit the location argument when using the {GETLABEL} command, Lotus 1-2-3 will return an ERROR when it tries to execute this statement. The /XN and {GETNUMBER} commands also contain this disparity between the two releases.

Because of this slight variation in the operations of the two sets of commands, you may find situations where it is more efficient to use the Release 1A commands than the Release 2 versions. For example, if you are creating a data input macro that prompts the user for each field entry in a record, and you want the data to be placed directly into the database, you will want to use /XL and /XN instead of {GETLABEL} and {GETNUMBER}.

After the macro situates the cell pointer at the beginning of the first record, you can use the /XL or /XN command to prompt the user to enter the appropriate information for each field in the database. If the first field requires the entry of the user's first name, write the /XL command as follows:

/XLEnter first name: ~ ~ {RIGHT}

Because no cell location follows the first return, Lotus 1-2-3 enters the user's response to this prompt in the current cell as soon as the user presses Return. The {RIGHT} keyword then positions the cell pointer in the next field of the new record. You can continue to code the macro in this way until the entire record is entered. When you have added the commands required to fill each field, you can have the macro terminate, or reposition the cell pointer and loop back to the first /XL statement to allow the user to enter another record.

The other Release 2 commands with equivalents in Release 1A do not have this type of minor variation between releases, so there is no reason to use the /X commands unless you are more comfortable with them.

Note: In the following reference entries, optional arguments are designated by placing them in a pair of angle brackets, as in this example:

{BEEP <number>}

{BEEP}

The {BEEP} command sounds one of the four tones used by the IBM computer.

SYNTAX

{BEEP <number>}

where number is an optional argument between 1 and 4 indicating the tone to be sounded when the computer beeps. You can also specify this argument by a cell address or range name that contains such a number. If you enter 0 as the value, it will produce the same tone as entering 4. If you enter a value other than 0 to 4, the program calculates it modulo 4 and uses the resulting value as the tone.

USAGE

This command is useful when you want to gain the user's attention, especially if some input is required. It can also be used to alert the user to the end of a waiting period or that the macro has terminated. It is often combined with the {ONERROR} command to alert the user that some type of processing error has occurred.

You can enter an optional argument that tells the macro which of the four different tones made by the computer is to be used. This value can be entered as a constant between 1 and 4 or as a range name that contains such information. If you do not specify a number argument, the macro will use tone 1 (the low tone used by Lotus 1-2-3 to signify that an error has been made).

EXAMPLES

{BEEP 1}

This statement sounds tone 1 (a low tone) once.

{BEEP 3}

This statement sounds tone 3 (the highest and shortest tone) once.

{BEEP Tone}

This statement sounds the tone indicated by the number contained in the range named Tone. If this number is 2, it will sound tone 2 (a high tone). If this number is 4, it will sound tone 4 (the lowest tone).

{BLANK}

The {BLANK} command erases the contents of a cell range.

SYNTAX

{BLANK location}

where location is a cell address or cell range defined by range name.

USAGE

The {BLANK} command works like the /Range Erase command. It deletes the contents of the cells in the named range but does not affect the display format or protection settings in effect. It is more convenient than adding the command keystrokes '/RE followed by the range name because it does not require moving the cell pointer to the range. {Routine-Name}

EXAMPLES

{BLANK CalcResult}

This command statement erases the contents of the range named CalcResult.

{BLANK State}
{GOTO}State~{?}~

This command statement erases the contents of the range named State and then moves the cell pointer to that range and waits for the user to enter a new state abbreviation into it.

{BRANCH} or /XG (Release 1A)

The {BRANCH} or '/XGlocation~ command directs execution of the macro to a new set of instructions beginning in the cell location specified by the range name.

SYNTAX

{BRANCH location}

or

'XGlocation~

where location is a single-cell address or cell range defined by range name.

USAGE

This command tells the macro to go to a new cell location and execute the instructions listed there. It should not be confused with a subroutine call; the macro does not return to the original routine unless you specify another {BRANCH} statement.

When you enter a {BRANCH} command into a statement, the macro execution immediately shifts to the cell location given as its argument. This means that any instructions listed after it in the same cell will never be executed.

Using the {BRANCH} statement allows you to break up and organize the macro instructions in separate cell ranges. This makes its easier to read and debug your macros, because all of the instructions do not have to be entered in one contiguous cell range.

Note: Specifying the {BRANCH} keyword is not the same as using the {GOTO} key name. {GOTO} takes the cell pointer to the cell range but does not cause the macro to execute the instructions located there.

EXAMPLES

{BRANCH Print}

This statement causes the macro to begin executing the instructions listed in the cell range named Print.

{IF Result>100000}{BRANCH Maximum}
{BRANCH Minimum}

These statements execute the instructions in the cell range named Minimum unless the value in the Result range is greater than 100,000, in which case the instructions in the cell range named Maximum are executed. (This kind of two-way branch using the {IF} command keyword is quite common in macros.)

SEE ALSO

{Routine-Name}

{BREAKOFF}

The {BREAKOFF} statement disables the Break key (Ctrl-Scroll Lock).

SYNTAX

{BREAKOFF}

This keyword does not take an argument.

USAGE

The {BREAKOFF} command is used to prevent the macro user from prematurely terminating the execution of a macro by pressing the Break key. Once the macro executes a {BREAKOFF} command, it immediately disables the Break key. If the user presses this key combination in an attempt to halt a macro, the computer will beep. The {BREAKOFF} condition lasts until the macro encounters a {BREAKON} statement, until its execution is terminated by a {QUIT} command, or until it reaches a cell that is empty or contains a literal value.

EXAMPLES

{BREAKOFF}
{TransRec}
{BREAKON}

The {BREAKOFF} statement disables the Break key during the execution of the subroutine called TransRec. After the instructions in this subroutine are executed and the macro returns to the original routine, the {BREAKON} statement enables the Break key before the macro continues its execution.

SEE ALSO

{BREAKON}

{BREAKON}

The {BREAKON} statement is used to enable the Break key (Ctrl-Scroll Lock) in a macro after it has been disabled with {BREAKOFF}.

SYNTAX

{BREAKON}

This keyword does not take an argument.

USAGE

The {BREAKON} command must be used to restore the function of the Break key during the execution of a macro once it has been disabled with a {BREAKOFF} statement (see the previous reference entry). Enabling the Break key allows the user to interrupt a keyboard command and return to READY mode or terminate the execution of a macro before it reaches a {QUIT} command or the end of the macro instructions.

EXAMPLES

See the example for the {BREAKOFF} reference entry.

SEE ALSO

{BREAKOFF}

{CLOSE}

The {CLOSE} command closes the file previously opened with an {OPEN} statement.

SYNTAX

{CLOSE}

This keyword does not take an argument.

USAGE

The {CLOSE} statement is used to terminate any data transfer process between a Lotus 1-2-3 worksheet file and an ASCII file. It must be preceded by an {OPEN} statement to have any effect in the macro. Once the macro executes a {CLOSE} command, the data link between the two files is closed and only another {OPEN} statement can reopen it.

EXAMPLES

{OPEN "Newacct","W"}
{WRITELN YTD}
{CLOSE}

The first statement opens a text file in write mode and gives it the file name NEWACCT. The next statement writes the contents of the cell range named YTD into NEWACCT as the line appended to the end of the file. The last statement closes the file, terminating the data transfer from the worksheet to NEWACCT.

SEE ALSO

{OPEN}

{CONTENTS}

The {CONTENTS} command converts a number to a label that looks like a number.

SYNTAX

{CONTENTS destination-location,source-location,<width-number>, <format-number>}

where destination-location is the cell range where the resulting label will be entered, and source-location is the cell range that contains the number to be copied as a label.

The width-number argument is taken as though the source-location cell were set to that number of characters. It does not actually change the cell width of the destination location. The format number is taken as though the source location were formatted with that numeric display format. It adds to the resulting label whatever formatting characters are part of the display format chosen.

If no width number or format number is entered, the macro uses the width and display format of the source location. If you specify a format number, you must also include a width number.

USAGE

The {CONTENTS} command is used to copy a number contained in the worksheet and convert it into a label that appears as if it had been entered as a value. This command is very useful whenever the spreadsheet contains a calculated value that you would like to use as a label.

For instance, you could use this command in a macro that prints invoices to print a message that tells the customer how much is currently owed, such as "Please disregard this notice if your check for the balance of $345.58 has already been sent." To plug the calculated balance of $345.58 into the message string, you use the {CONTENTS} command to copy it from the appropriate cell and convert it into a label, still using the Currency format.

When you use this command, you can specify a width-number argument that determines the number of characters in the resulting string that are to be copied to the destination location. The value in this argument does not actually change the column width of the column containing the destination cell. It can, however, be used to position the label in its destination cell.

You can also add a format number to include one of the display formats in the resulting label. Table 28.2 in the discussion section "Converting Values to Labels in a Macro" contains a complete listing of these code numbers with their corresponding numeric displays. If you use a format number, you must also include a width number. Remember to make this number large enough to accommodate any characters added by the numeric display format you have designated. Otherwise, the label will contain only asterisks, indicating insufficient room to display the label in its new format.

EXAMPLES

In the following examples, assume that the cell named Value contains the number 1254.50. Also assume that its column width is set to 9 and that it has been formatted with the /Range Format Fixed 2 command.

{CONTENTS Label,Value}

This statement places the nine-character label '1254.50 into the cell named Label.

{CONTENTS Label,Value,4,66}

This statement places the four-character label **** in the cell named Label. The asterisks would be displayed because the width number of 4 is insufficient to display the number in the Comma display format with two decimal places (indicated by the 66 code).

{CONTENTS Label,Value,10,66}

This statement places the ten-character label '1,254.50 in the cell named Label.

{DEFINE}

The {DEFINE} command designates the location at which each of the arguments passed to a subroutine will be stored and sets the argument type as either a value or a string.

SYNTAX

{DEFINE location1:type1,location2:type2,...}

where location(s) is a single cell or cell range designated by range name and the type(s) is either the optional suffix :string or :value. Specifying a nonexistent range name or a type other than :string or :value will cause a macro error.

USAGE

When you use a subroutine call in a macro (see {Routine-Name}), you can specify optional arguments that contain values or labels for the subroutine to process. Before such arguments can be passed to the subroutine, they must be stored in cells in the worksheet. You use the {DEFINE} command to evaluate the type of argument and to perform this storage operation.

The arguments of the {DEFINE} statement contain the locations given as range names where the macro will store each of the arguments in the subroutine. If the named range is a cell range, the value or string argument is entered in the first cell of the range.

After defining the location, you can add a suffix to designate the type of argument, either :value or :string (you can abbreviate these to :v or :s, respectively). If you specify a value type, the argument is evaluated and then entered in the storage cell as a value. If you specify a string type, the argument is entered as a left-aligned label in the storage location. If you do not specify the type by using one of these suffixes, the program will enter it as though the :string type had been used.

To prevent a macro error when using the {DEFINE} statement, the subroutine call must include the same number of arguments as used in the {DEFINE} command. Also, the {DEFINE} command must be placed as the first statement in the subroutine instructions.

EXAMPLES

Assuming the subroutine call

{Update 6700,30*Int,Newrate}

appeared in the main macro, the following {DEFINE} statements would produce various results:

Update {DEFINE Input1,Input2,Input3}

This statement stores 6700 as a label in the cell named Input1, 30*Int as a label in the cell named Input2, and Newrate as a label in the cell named Input3.

Update {DEFINE Input1:value,Input2:value,Input3:value}

This statement stores 6700 as a value in cell named Input1, evaluates 30*Int as an expression (as long as Int has been defined as a single-cell range and contains a value) and enters the resulting value in the cell named Input2, and enters the contents of Newrate as a value in the cell named Input3. If Newrate does not contain a value, an ERR value is entered into the Input3 cell.

SEE ALSO

{Routine-Name}

{DISPATCH}

The {DISPATCH} command is used to perform indirect branching in a macro. The macro continues execution in the routine whose name appears in the cell specified in its location argument.

SYNTAX

{DISPATCH location}

where location is a single-cell address or range name containing a label or a string formula that refers to the macro routine to which the macro is to branch. If the location argument is a multiple-cell range, the {DISPATCH} command acts like a direct {BRANCH} statement.

USAGE

The {DISPATCH} command performs a branching operation (as opposed to a subroutine call) by using the range name entered into a single-cell range named in the {DISPATCH} argument. For example, assume that you have entered the label NewEntry in a cell named Next. Entering the statement {DISPATCH Next} is then equivalent to entering the statement {BRANCH NewEntry} in the macro.

The location argument most often consists of a label that refers to a range name given to a single-cell range, although it can contain a string formula. However, if the location argument contains a value (or is empty), a macro error will occur.

You can use the {DISPATCH} statement for conditional branching that depends on a variable contained in the location cell (unlike the {BRANCH} statement, where branching can never be conditional).

EXAMPLES

{LET Next,"Recalc"}
{DISPATCH Next}

This statement branches macro execution to the routine named Recalc.

> **{LET Next,@CHOOSE(Choice,"Reprint","Done"}**
> **{DISPATCH Next}**

This statement branches macro execution either to the routine named Reprint or to the routine named Done, depending on the value in the cell named Choice. If Choice contains 1, the macro branches to Reprint. If Choice contains 0, it branches to Done.

{FILESIZE}

The {FILESIZE} command enters the number of bytes in the currently open file into the cell address or cell range specified in its location argument.

SYNTAX

{FILESIZE location}

where location is a cell address or range name.

USAGE

This command is used to determine and record the size of the currently open ASCII file. The size (the total number of bytes in the file) is entered into the cell address or first cell of the cell range specified as the location argument.

If no file is currently open when the macro executes the {FILESIZE} command, the command will be ignored and processing will continue in the current cell. If the statement is executed successfully, the macro resumes execution in the cell below it.

EXAMPLES

{FILESIZE Byte-Count}

This statement enters the number of bytes in the currently open file into the cell named Byte-Count.

```
{OPEN "Newfile","W"}
{WRITELN "Confidential"}
{FILESIZE Total-Bytes}
```

The first statement opens a new file named Newfile in write mode. The second statement writes Confidential as a line of text. The third statement returns the total number of bytes in the cell named Total-Bytes as 14 (12 for Confidential plus 2 for the carriage-return and line-feed characters).

SEE ALSO

{SETPOS}

{FOR}

The {FOR} command executes a subroutine a specific number of times, depending on the start number, stop number, and step number used.

SYNTAX

{FOR counter-location,start-number,stop-number,step-number, starting-location}

where counter-location is a cell address or cell range designated by range name; the start-, stop-, and step-number arguments are literal values, formulas, or range names that contain values; and starting-location is the range name of the subroutine to be executed.

USAGE

The {FOR} command provides a convenient way to add a FOR-NEXT loop to a macro to execute a particular subroutine a specific number of times. Once the macro has executed the subroutine the number of times specified, it resumes execution in the cell below the one containing the {FOR} statement.

Five arguments are required by the {FOR} command:

1. The counter location is a cell that holds the start value when the {FOR} statement is first executed. Each time the subroutine is executed, the program updates this value by the step number.
2. The start number is a value that initializes the counter before the subroutine is first executed.
3. The stop number is the value that tells the macro when to terminate the FOR loop. When the counter exceeds this value, the macro terminates this loop and does not reexecute the subroutine.

4. The step number is the value that tells the macro how much to increment the counter each time it executes the macro.

When specifying start, stop, and step numbers, you can use negative or fractional values. If you use a negative step-number argument, the counter increases from the stop value to the start value. However, if the stop number is larger than the start number and the step number is negative, the loop will never be executed. Most of the time, it is simpler to increase the start number by the step number until it exceeds the stop value.

Note: The start, stop, and step numbers are stored internally by Lotus 1-2-3. You cannot reset them or change them from the macro. The only way to terminate a {FOR} statement prematurely is to use a {FORBREAK} or {QUIT} statement (although using {QUIT} will prevent the subroutine from being executed more than once).

EXAMPLES

{FOR Counter,1,6,1,Subtot}

This statement executes the subroutine named Subtot six times.

{FOR Counter,12,4, – 2,Subtot}

This statement executes the subroutine named Subtot four times.

{FOR Counter,1, – 6,1,Subtot}

This statement never executes the subroutine named Subtot, because the stop number is less than the start number and the step number is positive. It could work, however, if the step number were also negative, as in

{FOR Counter,1, – 6, – 1,Subtot}

This statement executes the subroutine named Subtot seven times.

SEE ALSO

{FORBREAK}

{FORBREAK}

The {FORBREAK} command immediately terminates a FOR loop, even if the stop value has not yet been reached.

SYNTAX

{FORBREAK}

This keyword does not take an argument.

USAGE

The {FORBREAK} command provides a way to prematurely terminate the repeated execution of a subroutine controlled by a {FOR} statement. It must always be placed in the subroutine being executed by the {FOR} statement. If you place it outside the subroutine instructions, it will cause a macro error (Invalid FORBREAK), and you cannot trap such an error by using the {ONERROR} command.

When the macro encounters and executes a {FORBREAK} statement, it immediately resumes execution in the cell below the one containing the {FOR} statement.

EXAMPLES

```
'/x       . . . .
          {FOR Counter,1,5,1,Accum}
          . . . .

Accum     {IF @ISERR(Subtot)}{FORBREAK}
          . . . . .
```

In this example, the {FOR} statement causes the routine named Accum to be executed five times unless the cell named Subtot contains an ERR value. In this case, the {FORBREAK} statement would cause the macro to resume execution in the cell below the one containing the {FOR} command.

SEE ALSO

{FOR}

{GET}

The {GET} command suspends the execution of the macro and records the first keystroke made by the user in the cell designated by the location argument.

SYNTAX

{GET location}

where location is a cell address or cell range designated by range name.

USAGE

The {GET} command, unlike the {LOOK} command, suspends the execution of the macro to store the first keystroke made into the typeahead buffer. If the key is one of the special function keys, editing keys, or cursor-movement keys, it is entered into the cell using its key name (refer to Table 27.1). Keystrokes that cannot be represented, such as Caps Lock and Scroll Lock, do not cause the macro to resume execution.

When the {GET} statement is executed, the keystroke entered is not automatically entered into the cell location. If the global recalculation is set to Automatic, you can add a Return (~) to have it entered. If the global recalculation is set to Manual, you add a {CALC} statement after the {GET} statement.

EXAMPLES

{GET Char}{CALC}
{IF Char = "{HOME}"}{QUIT}
. . . .

This statement suspends the execution of the macro and waits until the user presses a key. This keystroke is then recorded in the cell named Char. If the user has pressed the Home key, the macro terminates; otherwise, it continues to execute subsequent macro instructions.

SEE ALSO

{GETLABEL}
{GETNUMBER}
{LOOK}

{GETLABEL} or /XL (Release 1A)

The {GETLABEL} or '/XLmessage~location~ command suspends execution of the macro to allow the user to enter a label (in the Control Panel). When the user presses Return, the label is stored in the cell specified as the location argument, and the execution of the macro resumes.

SYNTAX

{GETLABEL prompt-string,location}

or

'/XLmessage~location~

where prompt-string (or message) is a literal character string up to 80 characters long (it cannot be a range name or cell reference), and location is a single cell address or cell range designated by range name.

USAGE

The {GETLABEL} command prompts the user to enter a label and pauses the macro to allow it to be entered. When the macro executes a {GETLABEL} statement, it displays the prompt string (message) in the first line of the Control Panel. The macro pauses, and the cursor is placed at the end of the prompt text. The user then types the label on this line and presses Return to resume macro execution.

The label is stored in the cell named by the location argument. If the location is a cell range, this label is stored in its first cell. If the user presses only the Return or Esc key, the macro will store an empty string in this cell.

After executing a {GETLABEL} statement, the macro does not automatically enter the text typed by the user into the location cell. You must add a Return (~) or {CALC} command (if the program's recalculation is set to Manual) to have the macro update the screen and enter the text.

EXAMPLES

{GETLABEL "Next, enter your first name ",Fname}

This statement enters the user's response to the prompt to enter his first name in a cell named Fname. The quotation marks are required because of the comma after Next. If this were entered without quotes, the macro would return the error message "Invalid range in GETLABEL," because it would not be able to locate a range named "enter your first name" in the worksheet.

{GETLABEL "Enter your Zip Code ",Zip}

This statement enters the user's numerical response to the prompt to enter his zip code as a label in the cell named Zip. Note that using {GETLABEL} avoids the problem of having the user type an apostrophe before entering a value as a label.

SEE ALSO

{GET}
{GETNUMBER}

{GETNUMBER} or /XN (Release 1A)

The {GETNUMBER} or '/XNmessage~location~ command suspends execution of the macro to allow the user to enter a value (in the Control Panel). When the user presses Return, the value is stored in the cell specified as the location argument, and the execution of the macro resumes.

SYNTAX

{GETNUMBER prompt-string,location}

'/XNmessage~location~

where prompt-string (or message) is a literal character string up to 80 characters long (it cannot be a range name or cell reference) and location is a single cell or cell range designated by range name.

USAGE

The {GETNUMBER} command prompts the user to enter a value and pauses the macro to allow the value to be entered. When the macro executes a {GETNUMBER} statement, it displays the prompt string (message) in the first line of the Control Panel. The macro pauses, and the cursor is placed at the end of the prompt text. The user then types the number on this line and presses Return to resume macro execution.

The user can enter a number, a range name, or a cell reference that contains a value or formula in reponse to a {GETNUMBER} prompt. If a formula involving cell references is being entered, it does not have to be prefaced with a +, as in +A2*B3. It will be accepted without any character normally used to force the program into VALUE mode (the previous formula can be entered simply as A2*B3). However, you do use a – (minus sign) before a cell reference if you want to use the negative of its current value.

The value is stored in the cell named by the location argument. If the location is a cell range, this label is stored in its first cell. If the user presses only the Return or Esc key, the macro stores an ERR value in this cell.

After executing a {GETNUMBER} statement, the macro does not automatically enter the text typed by the user into the location cell. You must add a Return (˜) or {CALC} command (if the program's recalculation is set to Manual) to have the macro update the screen and enter the text.

EXAMPLES

{GETNUMBER "Enter 1st Quarter sales total: ",Qtr1}

This statement enters the value typed by the user in response to the prompt to enter the 1st Quarter sales total in the range named Qtr1. Notice that the prompt string is enclosed in quotes to allow the use of the colon and an extra space after it.

{GETNUMBER "Enter new commission rate: ",Rate}

This statement enters the value typed by the user in response to the prompt to enter the commission rate in the range named Rate.

SEE ALSO

{GET}
{GETLABEL}

{GETPOS}

The {GETPOS} command determines the current position of the byte pointer in the open file and returns this value in the location cell given as its argument.

SYNTAX

{GETPOS location}

where location is a cell address or cell range designated by range name.

USAGE

The {GETPOS} command determines the position of the byte pointer in the currently open file and records that value in the worksheet. Byte position is counted from position 0 for the first byte in the file. The current position of the pointer is entered as a value into the cell or cell range specified as the location argument.

If no file is currently open when the macro executes the {GETPOS} command, it is ignored and the macro continues execution in the cell that contains it. If the command is executed successfully, the macro resumes execution in the cell below it.

EXAMPLES

{GETPOS Current}

This statement enters the number of the current byte pointer position in the open file in the cell named Current.

{GETPOS Current}
{WRITE "COGS"}
{SETPOS Current + 5}

The first statement records the current pointer position in the cell named Current. The second writes the label COGS at the current position, and the third statement repositions the pointer to a new position equal to the total of the value in the cell named Current plus five.

SEE ALSO

{SETPOS}

{IF} or /XI (Release 1A)

The {IF} or '/XI statement evaluates the condition entered as its argument. If the condition is true, the macro continues execution in the same cell. If it is false, the macro continues execution in the cell below.

SYNTAX

{IF condition}
or
'/XIcondition ~

where condition is a logical formula or cell address or the range name of a single cell that contains such a formula.

USAGE

The {IF} statement is used to perform two-way conditional branching in the macro. The argument contains a logical expression that is evaluated as either true or false. The outcome of this evaluation determines where the macro continues its execution.

Only if the condition is found to be true will the macro continue to execute instructions that immediately follow the {IF} statement. If the condition is false, the macro goes immediately to the first instruction in the cell directly below it. If you do not place any commands directly after the {IF} statement, the macro will execute the instructions in the cell below it, regardless of whether the condition is true or false.

The {IF} statement is often used in macros with the {BRANCH} command to have various commands carried out depending on the outcome of a calculation or some interaction between the user and the macro.

EXAMPLES

{IF Payment< =200}{BRANCH Invoice}
{Branch Start}

Because of this {IF} statement, the macro begins executing the instructions in the cell range named Invoice only if the value in the cell named Payment is below or equal to 200. Otherwise, it branches to the range named Start and begins executing the instructions there.

{IF @EXACT(Reply) = "Y"}{QUIT}
{BRANCH Continue}

Because of this {IF} statement, the macro terminates execution if the cell named Reply contains a capital letter Y. If this cell contains anything else (even a lowercase y), the macro branches to the range named Continue and begins executing the instructions there.

{INDICATE}

The {INDICATE} command is used to place your own mode indicator in the upper-right corner of the display screen during a macro's execution.

It is also used to return the mode indicator to the one currently used by Lotus 1-2-3 during the macro's execution.

SYNTAX

{INDICATE <string>}

where string is an optional argument whose content replaces the mode indicator in the upper-right corner of the screen.

USAGE

You can use the {INDICATE} command whenever you want your own mode indicator to be displayed during a macro's execution. To specify a new message, you enter an optional argument consisting of up to five characters. To avoid ambiguity, you should enclose these characters in double quotes, especially if you use spaces in the message. You cannot use a cell reference or range name to enter this optional argument.

When an {INDICATE} statement containing your own mode indicator is executed, this message replaces the various mode indicators that would normally appear during macro execution. In order to return control of this area to Lotus 1-2-3, you should enter an {INDICATE} statement with no argument before the macro terminates. This restores the mode indicator to READY.

Note: When the {PANELOFF} command is used, a subsequent {INDICATE} command will have no effect.

EXAMPLES

{INDICATE "START"}

This statement replaces the current mode indicator with START. This will remain in effect until the macro executes a subsequent {INDICATE} command, either to change the message or to return it to READY.

{INDICATE ""}

This statement blanks out the mode indicator area during macro execution.

{LET}

The {LET} command enters the value or label in the first cell of the range specified in the location argument.

SYNTAX

{LET location,number}

or

{LET location,string}

where location is a cell address or cell range designated by range name. The second argument can consist of either a number or a string. If the input is to be a value, enter a number argument as a constant, a formula, or a reference to a value. If the input is to be a label, enter a string argument as a character string enclosed in quotes, an expression that results in a character string, or a reference to such a string.

USAGE

The {LET} statement is used when you need the macro to create a value or label entry in the worksheet. The macro automatically enters this value or label in the cell in the upper-left corner of the cell range, if the range consists of more than a single cell.

The {LET} statement is not automatically calculated by the macro. To have the value or label entered in the cell, you must terminate the statement with a Return (˜) if recalculation is set to Automatic or a {CALC} if it is set to Manual.

EXAMPLES

{LET Count,Choice}

This statement enters the value or label in the cell named Choice into the first cell of the cell range named Count. If no cell range has been given the name Choice it will enter Choice as a label in the range named Count.

{LET Deduct,100}

This statement enters the value 100 in the first cell of the range named Deduct.

{LET Result, + "Gross "&Income}

This statement concatenates Gross with the label in the cell named Income and enters this new label in the first cell of the range named Result. Notice that the literal string "Gross " is prefaced with a plus sign. This is required to avoid an error. If the label in the cell named Income is Sales, the new label displayed in Result will be Gross Sales.

SEE ALSO

{PUT}

{LOOK}

The {LOOK} command enters the first character currently in the typeahead buffer into the cell specified by the location argument.

SYNTAX

{LOOK location}

where location is a cell address or cell range, designated by range name.

USAGE

The {LOOK} statement in a macro causes the program to look in the typeahead buffer and determine whether anything has been typed there during its execution. If it has, it stores the first character in the cell designated by the location argument as a left-aligned label. If the user has not touched the keyboard since the last interaction with the macro, this cell will be an empty cell with only a label prefix.

The {LOOK} statement only *copies* the first character from the typeahead buffer; it does not remove it. This means that the same character will be recorded in subsequent {LOOK} statements. If you want to remove characters from the buffer as they are recorded in a cell of the worksheet, use the {GET} command.

EXAMPLES

{LOOK Keystroke}
{IF Keystroke = "y"}{GOTO}Table~
. . . .

The first statement checks the typeahead buffer and records the first character typed, if any, as a label in the cell named Keystroke. The {IF} statement then evaluates the contents of the label. If it contains the keystroke y, the cell pointer is moved to the beginning of the cell range named Table. If it contains some other label or is blank, the macro continues executing the subsequent instructions.

SEE ALSO

{GET}

{MENUBRANCH} or /XM (Release 1A)

The {MENUBRANCH} or '/XMlocation~ command displays a custom menu in the Control Panel and branches to the routine chosen by the user.

SYNTAX

{MENUBRANCH location}

or

'/XMlocation~

where location specifies the top-left cell of the range that contains the menu macro designated by range name or by cell address.

USAGE

The {MENUBRANCH} (or '/XMlocation~) command is used to suspend the execution of a macro to allow the user to select an option from a custom menu. When the macro executes a {MENUBRANCH} statement, it displays the menu options listed in the first row of the cell range in the Control Panel. It also displays the menu descriptions entered beneath each option name in the second row of the menu macro cell range, below the menu options shown in the Control Panel.

As soon as the user chooses one of these menu options (either by highlighting it and pressing Return or by typing its initial letter), the macro executes the instructions in the menu macro range that corresponds to the menu name. These instructions are located in the third row in the same column as the one that contains the menu command name.

When you set up the cell range that contains the menu options, short descriptions, and macro instructions, keep the following in mind:

- You must enter each menu option in a single cell of the first row of the menu macro range. Each option must be entered as a label, and a menu cannot contain more than eight options. Also, do not leave any blank cells between your options, but make sure that you leave a blank cell after the last option.
- Each menu option should begin with a different character. That way the user can select it by typing this letter as well as by highlighting the name and pressing Return.
- Enter the short descriptions that you want to appear beneath each option in the menu in the appropriate column below their corresponding menu option. They, too, must be entered as labels. You cannot leave empty cells below your menu options. If you do not want a description to appear below a particular menu option, enter a blank label by pressing the space bar.
- Begin the macro instructions associated with each menu option in the third row of this menu macro cell range in the column containing the menu command name. Not all of the instructions must be entered into this one cell. You can enter groups of instructions in contiguous cells below in the same column as long as they begin in the third row.

The {MENUBRANCH} command acts like any other macro branch command in that control does not automatically return to the instructions in the main macro below the {MENUBRANCH} statement. To return control to the main macro or any other macro routine, you must enter a {MENUBRANCH} or {BRANCH} statement at the end of the command instructions. If you are using Release 2, you can use the new {MENUCALL} command to return control automatically to the calling program.

However, if the user presses the Esc key when a {MENUBRANCH} statement has been executed rather than selecting a menu option, the menu disappears and macro execution resumes in the cell directly beneath the one containing the {MENUBRANCH} statement.

EXAMPLES

```
'\m     {MENUBRANCH Main}
        {BRANCH Update}
```

Main	Print	Save	Quit
	Print Report	Save & Continue	End
	'/PPRAGPQ	'/FS~R	{BRANCH Update}

When the user presses Alt-M to invoke this macro, the {MENU-BRANCH} statement suspends macro execution and displays the three menu options Print, Save, and Quit in the second line of the Control Panel. The macro also displays the command descriptions Print Report, Save & Continue, and End beneath each menu option in the third line of the Control Panel.

The user may select any of these three options by moving the highlight to it (it is automatically positioned on the first option, Print) and pressing the Return key or by typing either **P**, **S**, or **Q**. As soon as an option is selected, the corresponding instructions listed in the third row are executed.

In the case of the Quit option, the macro executes the instructions in the routine named Update. The same thing occurs if the user presses the Esc key before making a menu selection.

SEE ALSO

{MENUCALL}

{MENUCALL}

The {MENUCALL} command displays a custom menu in the Control Panel and performs the subroutine call chosen by the user.

SYNTAX

{MENUCALL location}

where location specifies the top-left cell of the range or the cell address that contains the menu macro designated by range name.

USAGE

The {MENUCALL} command works much like the {MENU-BRANCH} command (see the previous entry) except that it performs a subroutine call based on the user's menu selection instead of merely branching to the associated instructions. That means that once the instructions are executed, control automatically returns to the instructions in the cell below the one containing the {MENUCALL} statement.

EXAMPLES

```
'\m      {Ident}
         {MENUCALL Region}
         {BRANCH Sales}
Ident    {GETLABEL "Enter name: ",Input}~
         {GOTO}Input~{DOWN}
Region   South        East         West         North
         Region       Region       Region       Region
         South~       East~        West~        North~
Sales    {GETNUMBER "Enter total sales: ",Total}~
         {DOWN}/RT{END}{UP}~Output~{GOTO}Output~
         /RNDOutput~{DOWN}/RNCOutput~~/FS~R
```

This example shows the {MENUCALL} statement being used to display a simple menu of regional choices that allows a salesperson to select his or her region and enter it into the worksheet after the salesperson's name has been input. Once the choice has been made, the macro automatically executes the {BRANCH} statement beneath {MENUCALL} statement. After the user responds to the {GETNUMBER} prompt and enters a sales total, the user's name, region, and sales are copied to a new range in the worksheet and the file is saved again.

SEE ALSO

{MENUBRANCH}

{ONERROR}

The {ONERROR} command instructs the macro to branch to a new location and execute the instructions there when a Lotus 1-2-3 error occurs.

SYNTAX

{ONERROR branch-location,<message-location>}

where branch-location is a cell address or cell range, designated by range name. The message-location argument is optional. If you use it, you enter a cell address or cell range by range name where the program places the error message associated with the particular Lotus 1-2-3 error.

USAGE

The {ONERROR} statement is used to prevent premature termination of a macro caused by a Lotus 1-2-3 error. A Lotus 1-2-3 error is any error outside the macro that normally causes the program to beep and go into ERROR mode. Some errors do not cause the program to go into ERROR mode, even though the program beeps and displays an error message on the screen. These types of errors cannot be trapped by using the {ONERROR} statement.

When you use an {ONERROR} statement and an error occurs, the program immediately branches to the routine named in the branch-location argument. Note that this is comparable to using a {BRANCH} statement; it is not a subroutine call. In fact, if the macro is executing a subroutine call at the time the error occurs, the subroutine stack is automatically cleared. This means that after the program executes the instructions included in the range named as the branch location, execution will not necessarily resume in the main macro or calling routine unless you add a {BRANCH} statement to tell it to do so.

You can add multiple {ONERROR} statements to a macro. The first one remains in effect until an error occurs or the macro terminates. If you have added several {ONERROR} statements to a macro, the first one may not be the one first used. The one used depends on the error and where the macro is when it happens.

Also, remember that pressing the Break key (Ctrl-Scroll Lock) causes the program to go into ERROR mode. An {ONERROR} command will trap such an error unless you have used the {BREAKOFF} command.

EXAMPLES

Figure 28.2 shows an example of a macro, Alt-R, whose purpose is to retrieve a new worksheet. An {ONERROR} statement has been added to ensure that the macro will not terminate because of an error caused by misspelling the worksheet file name or trying to retrieve a file that does not exist on the current directory.

In this figure, an error has occurred because the user typed in a nonexistent worksheet file name. The {ONERROR} statement then branched to the routine named ErrTrap in cell B9. This routine causes the program to beep once and then position the cursor in the cell named Message. In this example, this cell is A1. The macro adds the first line of text and then copies the Lotus 1-2-3 error message "File does not exist" from the ErrMsg cell (in B19) into the next cell below it. Two more lines of text are then added that explain the possible cause for the error.

Notice the {?} that has been added after the last line of text (telling the user to press the Return key to try the /File Retrieve operation again). Because the macro paused before it could enter this message in the current cell (A5), it appears on the data entry line.

As soon as the user presses the Return key, the macro erases all the text in the message area (cells A1 to A5) and then branches back up to the main macro (\r), where it repeats the /File Retrieve command.

```
A5:                                                                    LABEL
To try again, press the Return key when ready

     A        B        C        D        E        F        G        H
1   The following Lotus 1-2-3 error has occurred:
2   File does not exist
3   You may have mistyped the name
4   or your file may be in another directory.
5
6   \r       {ONERROR ErrTrap,ErrMsg}
7            /fr{?}~
8
9   ErrTrap  {Goto}Message~
10           {Beep 4}
11           The following Lotus 1-2-3 error has occurred: {DOWN}
12           /cErrMsg~~{DOWN}
13           You may have mistyped the name{DOWN}
14           or your file may be in another directory. {DOWN}
15           To try again, press the Return key when ready{?}~
16           {GOTO}Message~/RE{DOWN 4}~
17           {BRANCH \r}
18
19  ErrMsg   File does not exist
20
26-Oct-86  02:53 PM                      CMD
```

FIGURE 28.2: This figure illustrates how you can use the {ONERROR} command to trap a potential "File does not exist" error when using a macro to retrieve a new worksheet. It shows the macro in action at the point where the user has typed in a nonexistent file name, triggering the {ONERROR} command that directs the macro to execute the instructions in the ErrTrap routine (B9). Notice that the macro is paused. It will wait until the user presses the Return key, whereupon it will erase the message area, including the Lotus 1-2-3 error message, and will execute the /File Retrieve command again. Because the {BREAKOFF} command has not been used, if the user presses the Break key, it, too, will trigger the ErrTrap routine.

Note: The only way to terminate this macro is to retrieve a file successfully. If the user presses the Break key to try to terminate, this error will be trapped by the {ONERROR} statement.

{OPEN}

The {OPEN} command opens a new file for transferring data directly to or from a Lotus 1-2-3 worksheet file, depending on the access-mode argument used.

SYNTAX

{OPEN filename,access-mode}

where filename is literal string, string formula, or cell range that contains or results in a valid DOS file name and access-mode is either R for read, W for write, or M for modify mode.

USAGE

The {OPEN} statement must be executed successfully in a macro before the macro will be able to execute a {READ}, {READLN}, {WRITE}, or {WRITELN} statement to transfer data directly from and to the Lotus 1-2-3 worksheet file currently in memory.

The first argument must be a valid DOS file name. The file name can contain the full path name, including the drive specifier—up to 64 characters maximum. If the drive and subdirectory path are not specified, the macro will use the current directory. If the drive or directories listed do not exist, the {OPEN} statement will fail.

After specifying the filename argument, you must specify the access mode. There are three such modes:

- R for read mode. For an {OPEN} statement in this access mode to succeed, the file name given must exist in the specified directory. In read mode, you can use only the {READ} or {READLN} commands to transfer data from the open file into the worksheet.
- W for write mode. An {OPEN} statement in this access mode will succeed even if the file already exists. If it exists, the macro will delete it and create a new, empty file with its file name. In write mode, you can use only the {WRITE} or {WRITELN} commands to transfer data from the worksheet to the new file.

- M for modify mode. For an {OPEN} statement in this access mode to succeed, the file name given must exist in the specified directory. In modify mode, you can use write or read commands to transfer data to and from the worksheet.

When a file is opened with the {OPEN} statement, the byte pointer is positioned at the first byte (position 0). If another file is open when the macro executes the {OPEN} command, the program automatically closes the previously used file.

EXAMPLES

{OPEN "\ACCTS\NEWACCT","W"}

This statement opens a new file named NEWACCT in the ACCTS subdirectory in the write access mode.

{OPEN "B:\MAILLIST","R"}

This statement opens the file MAILLIST located on a disk in drive B in the read access mode. If this file does not exist on this disk, the {OPEN} statement fails.

{OPEN "B:\MAILLIST",R}{LET File,"Not Found"}{RETURN}
{LET File,"Found"}
. . . .

This statement appends the one shown above to include command statements to update a cell range named File. If the file name MAILLIST is not found on the disk in drive B, the {OPEN} statement is ignored and the macro continues to process the statements in this cell. This means that it updates the contents of the File cell with Not Found and executes the subroutine {RETURN}. If this file does exist, the File cell is updated with the label Found and the macro continues to execute the subsequent statements in this subroutine.

SEE ALSO

{CLOSE}
{READ}
{READLN}
{WRITE}
{WRITELN}

{PANELOFF}

The {PANELOFF} command freezes the Control Panel in its current state during macro execution until the macro either encounters a {PANELON} statement in a subsequent command or terminates.

SYNTAX

{PANELOFF}

This keyword does not take an argument.

USAGE

When a macro executes a number of Lotus 1-2-3 menu commands in rapid succession, you can see just a flicker from the Control Panel area as it executes these instructions. To eliminate this effect, you can enter a {PANELOFF} statement in the macro. This freezes the Control Panel until you unfreeze it with a {PANELON} statement or the macro terminates.

This command is often used with the {WINDOWSOFF} command to freeze the entire display screen during execution of particular macro subroutines. You can still use a {GETLABEL} or {GETNUMBER} command even when the Control Panel has been disabled by a {PANELOFF} statement.

EXAMPLES

```
{WINDOWSOFF}{PANELOFF}
'/WIR~\-~
'/C~.{UP}
{END}{RIGHT}{DOWN}~
{PANELON}{WINDOWSON}
```

These statements freeze the entire display screen while the macro inserts a new line and enters repeating hyphens in the new row. As soon as the macro executes the last line, the screen is redrawn and the changes are displayed.

SEE ALSO

{PANELON}

{PANELON}

The {PANELON} command reactivates the Control Panel after it has been frozen with a {PANELOFF} command so that it is redrawn and updated during subsequent macro execution.

SYNTAX

{PANELON}

This keyword does not take an argument.

USAGE

You use this command whenever you want to reactivate the Control Panel after having used the {PANELOFF} command in the macro. If you do not enter a {PANELON} statement, the Control Panel will be reactivated automatically when the macro terminates.

EXAMPLES

See the example for {PANELOFF} in the previous reference entry.

SEE ALSO

{PANELOFF}

{PUT}

The {PUT} command enters a number or a label at a particular location within a range.

SYNTAX

{PUT location,col-number,row-number,number}

or

{PUT location,col-number,row-number,string}

where location is a cell range designated by cell addresses or range name, col-number is the number of the column counting the first column of the range as zero, and row-number is the number of the row, counting the first row of the range as zero.

The last argument can consist of either a number or a string. If the input is to be a value, enter a number argument as a constant, a formula, or a reference to a value. If the input is to be a label, enter a string argument as a character string enclosed in quotes. You may also enter an expression that results in a character string or a reference to such a string.

USAGE

The {PUT} command is related to the {LET} statement in that it is used to enter values or labels in cells in the worksheet. However, unlike the {LET} statement, which enters the value or label in the first cell of the range specified as its argument, {PUT} enters it in a particular column and row of the specified range.

The first column of the range is numbered from zero when entering the column number. The first row of the range is also numbered from zero when entering the row number. If you specify a range consisting of a single cell and use any column numbers or row numbers other than zero, an error will occur. An error will also occur if you specify a column or row number outside the cell range.

The {PUT} statement, like the {LET} statement, is not calculated automatically by the macro. To have the value or label entered, you must terminate the statement with a Return (~) if recalculation is set to Automatic or a {CALC} if it is set to Manual.

EXAMPLES

{PUT Target,2,1,Payment*1.5}~

This statement enters a value equal to one and one half times the value in the cell named Payment into the cell in the third column and second row of the range named Target.

{PUT Table,3,0,"First Quarter"}

This statement enters the string First Quarter into the cell in the fourth column and first row of the cell range named Table.

{QUIT} or /XQ (Release 1A)

The {QUIT} or 'XG command immediately terminates the execution of the macro and returns control of Lotus 1-2-3 to the user.

SYNTAX

{QUIT}

or

'/XQ~

These commands do not take any arguments.

USAGE

The {QUIT} or 'XQ command is used to terminate the macro and return the program to READY mode. As soon as this statement is encountered, the macro terminates. Any instructions placed after it are ignored.

The {QUIT} command is often combined with an {IF} statement to terminate the macro only when the user specifies that the macro should not continue to process data.

EXAMPLES

{IF Choice = "Done"}{QUIT}

. . . .

This {QUIT} statement is executed and the macro's execution is terminated when the cell named Choice contains the string Done. If Choice does not contain this label, the macro continues to execute all of the following instructions.

{READ}

The {READ} statement transfers the number of bytes specified from the currently open ASCII file and copies them into the Lotus 1-2-3 worksheet in the cell range specified.

SYNTAX

{READ bytecount,location}

where bytecount is the number of bytes entered as a number, a single-cell range name, or a formula; and location is a cell or cell range designated by cell address or range name. If a cell range is specified, the macro reads the characters into the first cell of the range, the one in the upper-left corner.

USAGE

The {READ} command keyword is used when you are transferring data directly from an ASCII sequential file into a Lotus 1-2-3 worksheet. If you are transferring data from a text file that stores the data by lines, you should use the {READLN} command.

The {READ} statement begins at the current position of the pointer (see {GETPOS} and {SETPOS}) and reads the number of characters (bytes) specified as the first argument. These characters are copied as left-aligned labels into the cell designated by the location argument. The bytecount argument must be a value between 0 and 240 (negative values are taken as the equivalent of 240 characters), the maximum number that any Lotus 1-2-3 cell can contain.

If the number of characters specified in the bytecount argument is larger than the number of bytes left in the file from the current byte pointer position, the macro reads in all of the remaining characters. If the pointer is at the end of the file when the {READ} command is encountered, the macro creates an empty label containing only an apostrophe.

If no file has yet been opened with an {OPEN} statement, the {READ} statement is ignored and the macro continues to execute the instructions in the cell that contains the {READ} keyword. When the macro executes the {READ} statement, the byte pointer advances the number of bytes in the bytecount argument, and the macro resumes execution in the cell below the one containing the {READ} command.

EXAMPLES

For the following examples, assume that a sequential file has already been opened and that the byte pointer is currently positioned at the beginning of this string of data, which is located at the end of the file:

GNMA 10.64 Gvt Sec 10.13

The {READ} statement

{READ 10,Sell1}

would copy the first ten characters, GNMA 10.64, into the cell named Sell1 as a left-aligned label. It would also advance the pointer to the space between the 4 and the G in Gvt Sec in the file.

{READ 20,Sell2}

This {READ} statement would copy all of the remaining characters (the bytecount argument exceeds the number of bytes remaining in the file), Gvt Sec 10.13, into cell named Sell2 as a left-aligned label.

{READ 1,End-of-file}
{IF End-of-file = ""}{RETURN}

This {READ} statement copies the character at the byte pointer into the cell named End-of-file. Because the pointer is at the end of the file, it will create an empty label, and the condition in the {IF} statement will be true. As a result, the {RETURN} statement will terminate this read subroutine, and the macro will return to the original routine.

SEE ALSO

{GETPOS}
{READLN}
{SETPOS}

{READLN}

The {READLN} command transfers a single line (i.e., a string of characters terminated by a carriage return and line feed) from the currently open ASCII text file and copies it into the Lotus 1-2-3 worksheet in the cell range specified.

SYNTAX

{READLN location}

where location is a cell or cell range designated by cell address or range name. If a cell range is specified, the macro reads the line into the first cell of the range, the one in the upper-left corner.

USAGE

The {READLN} command copies a line of text from the current position of the byte pointer (at the beginning of the line of text) into the cell named in the location argument. All of the characters in the line, up to the carriage-return and line-feed characters, are copied into this cell as a left-aligned label. After transferring the line, the byte pointer is advanced just beyond the carriage-feed and line-feed characters.

If no text file was previously opened with an {OPEN} statement or if the pointer is at the end of the file when the macro executes the {READLN} statement, the command will fail and the macro will continue to process the instructions in the same cell. If the {READLN} statement is successful, the macro will return to the cell below the one containing the {READLN} command and continue its execution from there.

EXAMPLES

For the following example, assume that a text file has been opened and that the pointer is located at the beginning of these two lines, both of which have been terminated with carriage-return and line-feed characters:

Wickes 461,000 4 1/4 – 1/8
BAT Ind 311,400 5 1/8 + 3/8

The statement

{READLN Quote1}

reads "Wickes 461,000 4 1/4 – 1/8" into the cell named Quote1 as a left-aligned label. The pointer is then moved to the beginning of the next line containing the quotation for BAT Ind.

SEE ALSO

{OPEN}

{RECALC}

The {RECALC} command recalculates all formulas in the range specified as the location argument, starting with the cell in the upper left and proceeding row by row.

SYNTAX

{RECALC location,<condition>,<iteration-number>}

where location is a cell or cell range designated by range name. The condition and iteration-numbers are optional arguments. If you enter a condition argument, the program will recalculate the range again if the condition is found to be false. The iteration number tells the program how many times to recalculate the range. The formulas in the range will be recalculated until either the condition becomes true or the number of recalculations becomes equal to the iteration number.

USAGE

The {RECALC} command provides an alternative to using the {CALC} key name to recalculate formulas in the worksheet during the macro's execution. Unlike {CALC}, the {RECALC} command recalculates only a part of the cells in the worksheet that are designated as a cell range in the location argument.

You use the {RECALC} statement when the formula or formulas are located below and to the left of the cells in the worksheet they refer to. Use the {RECALCCOL} statement if they are located above and to the right of the cells they refer to and use {CALC} if they refer to cells located in both areas.

The appropriate recalculation command must be used if the global recalculation method is set to Manual when the macro is executed. Lotus 1-2-3 does not automatically recalculate new values for formulas when using keyword commands such as {LET}, {GETNUMBER}, and {PUT}, even if recalculation is left on Automatic.

If you use the {RECALC} statement to recalculate new values in a particular range, you will want to add a general {CALC} statement to the end of the macro before it terminates to make sure that all cell dependencies have been updated in the entire worksheet.

EXAMPLES

{LET Commission,Sales*.06}
{RECALC Salestotal}

The first {LET} statement sets the value in the cell named Commission to six percent of the value currently in the cell named Sales. The

{RECALC} statement recalculates this new value, assuming that the Commission cell is located in the range named Salestotal and that the Sales cell is located above and to the right of the Commission cell.

SEE ALSO

{RECALCCOL}

{RECALCCOL}

The {RECALCCOL} command recalculates all the formulas in the range specified as the location argument, starting with the cell in the upper left and proceeding column by column.

SYNTAX

{RECALCCOL location,<condition>,<iteration-number>}

where location is a cell or cell range designated by range name. The condition and iteration number are optional arguments. If you enter a condition argument, the program will recalculate the range again if the condition is found to be false. The iteration number tells the program how many times to recalculate the range. The formulas in the range will be recalculated until either the condition becomes true or the number of recalculations equals the iteration number.

USAGE

The {RECALCCOL} command provides an alternative to using the {CALC} key name to recalculate formulas in the worksheet during the macro's execution. Unlike {CALC}, the {RECALCCOL} command will recalculate only a part of the cells in the worksheet that are designated as a cell range in the location argument.

You use the {RECALCCOL} statement when the formula or formulas are located above and to the right of the cells they refer to. Use the {RECALC} statement if they are located below and to the left of the cells in the worksheet they refer to, and use {CALC} if they refer to cells located in both areas.

The appropriate recalculation command must be used if the global recalculation method is set to Manual when the macro is executed. Lotus

1-2-3 does not automatically recalculate new values for formulas when using keyword commands such as {LET}, {GETNUMBER}, and {PUT}, even if recalculation is left on Automatic.

If you use the {RECALCCOL} statement to recalculate new values in a particular range, you will want to add a general {CALC} statement to the end of the macro before it terminates to make sure that all cell dependencies have been updated in the entire worksheet.

EXAMPLES

{RECALCCOL Rate,Return>15000,10}

This statement recalculates the formula in the range named Rate until the value in the cell Return is greater than 15,000 or until the formula has been recalculated 10 times.

SEE ALSO

{RECALC}

{RESTART}

The {RESTART} command clears the subroutine stack so that control is not returned to the calling routine.

SYNTAX

{RESTART}

This command keyword does not take an argument.

USAGE

The {RESTART} command should not be confused with the {RETURN} statement. It is used only in nested subroutines when you do not want to return control to the calling subroutine. After the macro executes a {RESTART} statement, it continues processing the instructions in the subroutine until it reaches the end or encounters a {RETURN} statement. If it reaches the end of the subroutine signaled by an empty cell or a cell that contains a numeric constant, macro execution ends.

Note: The {RESTART} command has no effect if you use it in the main macro rather than in a subroutine.

EXAMPLES

{IF Reply = "No"}{RESTART}{BRANCH Begin}
{RETURN}

This {IF} statement executes the {RESTART} command if the cell named Reply contains No. This clears the subroutine stack so that the {BRANCH} statement is required to transfer control to the routine named Begin. If Reply contains something else besides No, the {RETURN} statement is executed and control is returned to the calling subroutine.

{RETURN} or /XR (Release 1A)

The {RETURN} or '/XR command immediately terminates a subroutine. The macro resumes execution with the statement just below the subroutine call statement.

SYNTAX

{RETURN}

or

'/XR

These commands do not take any arguments.

USAGE

The {RETURN} command is used to terminate the execution of a subroutine and return control to the calling program. It is often used with {IF} command statements to return control to the original routine conditionally.

EXAMPLES

{IF Total>125000}{RETURN}

. . . .

This {IF} statement terminates execution of the subroutine if the cell named Total contains a value greater than 125,000. Otherwise, it continues to execute the subroutine instructions in the cell below (indicated by ....).

SEE ALSO

{Routine-Name}

{Routine-Name} or /XC (Release 1A)

To call a subroutine in the macro, you can either enclose the name of the subroutine in curly braces as {Print} or use the '/XC command, as in '/XCPrint~.

SYNTAX

{routine-name <optional-argument>,<optional-argument>,...}

or

'/XClocation~

where routine-name or location is the range name of the cell range that includes the macro instructions for the subroutine.

When using the Release 2 {routine-name} statement, you can add optional arguments, the contents of which are entered into the cells specified as the location arguments of the {DEFINE} command. These are passed to the subroutine that is being called (see {DEFINE} for details on passing arguments to a subroutine).

USAGE

Using subroutines in a macro should not be confused with using {BRANCH} statements. With a subroutine, the macro automatically returns to the macro routine from which it was called (often referred to as the *original routine* or *calling program*) when it completes execution of the instructions contained in it. The macro resumes execution in the calling program in the cell directly below the one containing the subroutine statement. When you use a {BRANCH} statement, the macro does not return to the original routine unless you add another {BRANCH} statement to direct it to do so.

You can nest subroutines in a macro so that a subroutine calls another subroutine rather than returns directly to the original routine. For example, you can have the main macro call subroutinc 1, which in turn calls subroutine 2, which in turn calls subroutine 3. When subroutine 3 finishes execution, control is returned to subroutine 2; when 2 finishes, control is returned to 1; and, finally, when 1 finishes, control is returned to the main macro.

If a macro encounters an error somewhere in this chain of command, the subroutine stack is automatically cleared. You can also clear the stack of nested subroutines by using the {RESTART} command.

If no error or {RESTART} command is encountered, the macro executes the instructions in the subroutine until it encounters another subroutine call, a {RETURN} or '/XR command, a {QUIT} or '/XQ command, a blank cell, or a cell that contains a value. When the macro reaches a {RETURN} statement or the end of the subroutine, it immediately transfers control back to the calling program, resuming execution with the statement in the cell below the one containing the subroutine call.

When you specify the routine name or location argument, use a range name assigned to a cell address or cell range. Do not specify a subroutine call by entering a cell address.

EXAMPLES

{IF Total> = 15000}{Done}
{Recalc}

This {IF} statement executes the subroutine named Done if the value in the cell named Total is greater than or equal to 15,000. Otherwise, it executes the subroutine named Recalc.

```
'\t      {GOTO}Project1~
         {Sum}
         . . . .
         {GOTO}Project2~
         {Sum}
         . . . .

Sum      {END}{DOWN}{DOWN 2}
         '@SUM({UP 2}.{END}{UP})~
         {UP}\-~
```

This macro, called Alt-T, positions the cell pointer in the cell named Project1 and then executes the Sum subroutine. This subroutine totals the cells in this range and then returns to execute the instructions in the cell below it (illustrated by ....). When the macro encounters the second {GOTO}, it takes the cell pointer to the cell named Project2 and reexecutes the Sum subroutine there.

SEE ALSO

{DEFINE}
{RETURN}
{RESTART}

{SETPOS}

The {SETPOS} command is used to reposition the byte pointer in the currently open ASCII file.

SYNTAX

{SETPOS file-position}

where file-position is a number or a calculation that results in a number. This number is used to specify the character at which you want to position the pointer from the first byte of the file, numbered 0. The file-position value cannot be negative.

USAGE

This command is used to reposition the byte pointer in an ASCII file before read and write operations between a Lotus 1-2-3 worksheet and this open file. Byte position begins with the first character in the file, which is counted as zero. The value given as the file-position argument is counted from 0, not from the current pointer position (an absolute positioning, not a relative positioning).

Lotus 1-2-3 does not prevent you from specifying a file-position value beyond the last character in the open file. To determine the last character position in file, add a {FILESIZE} statement. If no file is currently open, the {SETPOS} command is ignored, and the macro continues processing in the cell that contains it. If the command is successfully executed, the macro resumes execution in the cell below it.

EXAMPLES

{SETPOS 50}

This statement sets the byte pointer to position 50 (the 51st byte in the open file).

{SETPOS Position}

This statement sets the byte pointer to the position equal to the value contained in the cell range named Position.

{FILESIZE End}
{SETPOS End}
{WRITE "*End of File***"}**

These statements determine the last position in the open file, store the value in a cell named End, use this value to set the current pointer position at the end of the file, and then write the end-of-file marker at this position.

SEE ALSO

{GETPOS}
{FILESIZE}

{WAIT}

The {WAIT} command suspends the execution of the macro until the time specified as a time serial number in its argument.

SYNTAX

{WAIT time-serial-number}

where time-serial-number is a number, a formula that results in a number, or a range name or cell address that contains such a numeric entry.

USAGE

The {WAIT} statement is used to pause the execution of a macro until a particular time. It can be used to pause the macro for a specified time, such as for a few seconds or minutes, or to delay the macro's processing until a specific hour. Unless a {BREAKOFF} statement has been used, you can use the Break key sequence to escape from a wait executed by the {WAIT} command.

The argument of a {WAIT} command must contain a valid time serial number. This is usually input into the argument of a {WAIT} statement by using the @NOW and @TIME functions to suspend execution for a specified number of seconds, minutes, or hours. To delay macro execution until a specified time, you can use the @INT(@NOW) + @TIME() paradigm. Note that Release 2.01 simulates @INT(@NOW) with @TODAY.

The {WAIT} command takes the current time from the operating system. If this time has not been set correctly, a macro processing delay will not be executed at the hour you intended. During execution of a {WAIT} statement, the on-screen clock is not updated.

EXAMPLES

{WAIT @NOW + @TIME(0,0,50)}

This statement suspends execution of the macro for 50 seconds.

{WAIT @INT(@NOW) + @TIME(13,30,0)}

This statement suspends execution of the macro until 1:30 PM of the current day.

{WAIT @NOW + @TIMEVALUE(Time-out)}

This statement suspends the execution of the macro for the period of time specified in the label contained in the cell range named Time-out. If this cell contains the label 1:00, the macro will be suspended for one hour. If it contains the label 0:24, the macro will be suspended for 24 minutes.

{WINDOWSOFF}

The {WINDOWSOFF} command freezes the screen display until the macro encounters a {WINDOWSON} statement or terminates.

SYNTAX

{WINDOWSOFF}

This keyword does not take an argument.

USAGE

Using the {WINDOWSOFF} command freezes the display window in its current state at the time the statement is encountered. The display remains frozen until the macro reaches a {WINDOWSON} statement or the macro terminates. During the time {WINDOWSOFF} is in effect, calculations to formulas made with the {CALC}, {RECALC}, or {RECALCCOL} statements will be performed, though the results will not be displayed on the screen.

Freezing the display with the {WINDOWSOFF} command speeds up macro execution because Lotus 1-2-3 does not have to take time to redraw the screen after performing various macro commands. This command is often used together with the {PANELOFF} command to reduce the amount of flicker caused as the macro executes the command menu keystroke instructions.

SEE ALSO

{PANELOFF}
{WINDOWSON}

{WINDOWSON}

The {WINDOWSON} command unfreezes the screen display initiated with a {WINDOWSOFF} statement, allowing the macro to redraw the screen during the rest of its execution.

SYNTAX

{WINDOWSON}

This keyword does not take an argument.

USAGE

When you use a {WINDOWSOFF} statement in a macro, it freezes the screen display in its current state. You use the {WINDOWSON} statement to counteract this command, if you want the screen to be updated as subsequent macro instructions are executed.

SEE ALSO

{WINDOWSOFF}

{WRITE}

The {WRITE} command directly transfers a string of characters from the Lotus 1-2-3 worksheet to an open ASCII file at the current position in that file.

SYNTAX

{WRITE string}

where string is literal string, a range name assigned to a single cell, or a calculation whose result is a string.

USAGE

The {WRITE} statement takes the string given as its argument and outputs it from the worksheet file to the currently open ASCII file at the current position of the byte pointer (see {SETPOS}). If no file has been opened with the {OPEN} command, the {WRITE} statement is ignored and the macro continues execution in the cell that contains it. If the {WRITE} statement succeeds, the macro resumes execution in the cell below it.

After executing a {WRITE} statement, the byte pointer is advanced to a new position just beyond the last character written into the file. A subsequent {WRITE} command will then be executed from this new position in the file.

EXAMPLES

{WRITE Quotes}

This statement outputs the contents of the cell named Quotes into the current position in the ASCII file that is open. If the range named Quotes consists of more than one cell, only the first cell of the range will be output.

If Quotes is not a valid cell range name, the macro will write the six-character string Quotes into the file. If Quotes is an empty cell or if it contains a value (instead of a string), this statement causes an error in the macro and terminates its execution.

{WRITE "Balance Due"}

This statement writes the literal character string Balance Due into the open file at the current position of the pointer.

SEE ALSO

{WRITELN}

{WRITELN}

The {WRITELN} command directly transfers a string of characters from the Lotus 1-2-3 worksheet to an open ASCII file at the current position in that file. It also adds carriage-return and line-feed characters to the end of the string to mark the end of the line.

SYNTAX

{WRITELN string}

where string is literal string, a range name assigned to a single cell, or a calculation whose result is a string.

USAGE

The {WRITELN} command works much like the {WRITE} command except that it automatically adds a carriage-return and a line-feed character at the end of the string output to the new file. These characters act as an end-of-line marker as used by text files.

The {WRITELN} statement takes the string given as its argument and outputs it from the worksheet file to the currently open ASCII file at the current position of the byte pointer (see {SETPOS}). If no file has been opened with the {OPEN} command, the {WRITELN} statement is ignored and the macro continues execution in the cell that contains it. If the {WRITELN} statement succeeds, the macro resumes execution in the cell below it.

After executing a {WRITELN} statement, the byte pointer is advanced to a new position just beyond the carriage-return and line-feed characters written into the file. A subsequent {WRITELN} command will then be executed from this new position in the file.

EXAMPLES

{WRITELN Title}

This statement outputs the contents of the cell named Title as a new line of text into the current position in the ASCII file that is open. If the range named Title consists of more than one cell, only the first cell of the range is output.

If Title is not a valid cell range name, the macro will write the five-character string Title into the file. If Title is an empty cell or if it contains a value (instead of a string), this statement causes an error in the macro and terminates its execution.

{WRITELN "Average Balance"}
{WRITELN "Minimum Due"}

These statements output the first literal character string, Average Balance, on one line of the open ASCII file and the second literal string, Minimum Due, on the subsequent line of the file.

SEE ALSO

{WRITE}

SUMMARY

This chapter has presented the Lotus 1-2-3 macro commands. As you have seen, Release 2 has significantly increased the number of macro commands, providing a powerful programming language in its own right. These commands can be combined to produce complex macros that can automate many types of routine tasks and save you valuable time. However, if you are new to Lotus 1-2-3 and inexperienced in programming, it will take time and patience to master this new command language and learn how best to use it to automate your work in Lotus 1-2-3.

See Chapter 27 if you need general information on how macros are constructed, organized, and debugged. Chapter 27 also contains information on creating simple keystroke macros.

Chapter 29 contains information on using the /File Import and /Print File commands to transfer data to and from your Lotus 1-2-3 worksheets. These commands can be used in your macros instead of the direct file-processing commands in the Release 2 macro command language.

PART 8

USING LOTUS **1-2-3** *WITH OTHER APPLICATION PROGRAMS*

Data sharing between application programs is becoming increasingly important as the computer becomes accessible to more people in the office. Part 8 examines data sharing from two perspectives: transferring data using the ASCII format as the medium of exchange between a Lotus 1-2-3 worksheet and some other application program, and direct translation of data by means of the Lotus 1-2-3 Translate utility or a similar translation program provided as part of the program with which you wish to share data.

Chapter 29 covers the use of the ASCII file as the first, indirect method of data sharing. This method is most often used when sharing data between a worksheet and a word processor or between a worksheet and software on a noncompatible computer system, such as a mini or mainframe computer.

In Lotus 1-2-3, this process involves using the /File Import and /Print File commands in Lotus 1-2-3, both of which are covered in the discussion and tcchniques sections. You will also find information there about using the /Data Parse command added to Release 2. It is used when importing ASCII files that contain text and numerical data. Each line of the ASCII file must be imported as character strings that are entered as long labels in single cells. The /Data Parse command provides the means for breaking up these long labels into separate cell entries.

Chapter 29 contains complete reference entries both for /File Import and for /Data Parse. (Chapter 25 in Part 4 contains the reference entry for the /Print command, including the Printer and File options.)

Chapter 30 discusses direct translation, the preferred method of sharing data between Lotus 1-2-3 and other application programs. It examines the options available on the Release 1A and Release 2 Translate utilities from the perspective of how and when they are to be used. This chapter also discusses using the translation programs that are included with the application program with which you wish to share Lotus 1-2-3 data when that program is not supported by the Lotus 1-2-3 Translate program.

CHAPTER 29

Importing and Exporting ASCII Files

IMPORTING AND EXPORTING ASCII FILES

This chapter discusses transferring data saved in ASCII (American Standard Code for Information Interchange) format into and out of Lotus 1-2-3 worksheets. You will often use the ASCII file format when transferring data between Lotus 1-2-3 and the word processor you are using in the office. You will also need to use the ASCII file transfer when downloading and uploading data from your mainframe computer database into and out of Lotus 1-2-3 worksheets. If you need to transfer data between Lotus 1-2-3 and some other data processing application, you can probably use either the Lotus 1-2-3 Translate utility or one provided with the software program you are using (see Chapter 30). Always check to make sure you can use such a translation program before using the ASCII file transfer described in the following sections.

To import data stored in ASCII code, you use the /File Import command. To export data stored in ASCII code, you use the /Print File command. In addition, Release 2 has added a new command, /Data Parse, that allows you to separate strings of ASCII data imported as long text labels in a single cell into several individual cells or fields of the worksheet.

After the techniques and applications discussion sections, you will find reference entries for the /File Import and /Data Parse commands. If you need to export spreadsheet data in an ASCII file by using the /Print File command, refer to the section "Exporting Lotus 1-2-3 Worksheets to ASCII Files" in this chapter; also refer to the /Print command reference entry in Chapter 25 for details about using its options.

IMPORTING ASCII FILES INTO LOTUS 1-2-3 WORKSHEETS

The ASCII file format provides a standardized code for representing all letters, punctuation symbols, and numbers, and many printer control codes. This code is used as the standard means of communication between almost all types of computers (IBM mainframe computers are a notable exception).

Application programs for the IBM PC also adhere to the ASCII standard, although none of them store their data files in this format (they use, instead, a more efficient binary storage format).

Converting a Word Processing Document into an ASCII File

Before you can transfer data created in another application program (such as your word processor) into a Lotus 1-2-3 worksheet file, you must translate it either directly into the Lotus 1-2-3 worksheet storage format or into ASCII format. Although a few word processors, such as WordStar 2000, provide for direct importation of Lotus 1-2-3 worksheet data into a document file, almost none can directly export their documents into the Lotus 1-2-3 worksheet file format. This means that you will have to use your word processor's facility for translating a document into an ASCII file before you can bring the word processing data into the worksheet.

This is usually done by using a special translation program that is separate from the word processor itself or by using the word processor's own print commands to print the content of your document to disk (this is the method that Lotus 1-2-3 uses with its /Print File command). When the word processor prints the document to disk rather than to your printer, it is automatically saved in ASCII format.

When the document is saved in ASCII format, special formatting characters such as those that boldface and underline text are not saved. The text, numbers, and punctuation used in the document are saved as separate lines, each terminated with a carriage-return and line-feed character. Headers, footers, and footnotes are transferred to the new ASCII file.

Note: Some word processing programs such as WordPerfect refer to ASCII format files as DOS text files. If your word processor has a facility for creating DOS text files, you will use this whenever you need to transfer data in a document into a Lotus 1-2-3 worksheet. (The name refers to the fact that you can display the contents of an ASCII file on the screen in a readable form by using the DOS TYPE command.)

Also, if your word processor is WordStar, you create an ASCII format file by opening your document in Non-document mode (choose N from the Main Menu intead of D to edit the document). After opening the document, you then save it as usual (with ^KD). Files that have been opened and saved in Non-document mode can always be converted to the regular WordStar file format by subsequently opening them in Document mode and saving them again.

Downloading Data from the Company's Database

If your company stores its data in a central database on a mainframe or minicomputer, and you wish to transfer a part of the database into a Lotus 1-2-3 worksheet, chances are that you will have to import the data into your spreadsheet in ASCII format. In order to capture data from another computer, you will have to use a communications setup, including the appropriate hardware and software, to store the data in a PC disk file. A similar process is required if you want to capture data from some on-line database such as the Dow-Jones Stock Quote Reporter service.

If you are using Release 1A and your data contains a mix of labels and values, you will want to save data as a DIF (Data Interchange Format) file, if at all possible (some mainframe software allows you to make such a conversion). This is because Release 1A lacks the built-in facility to break up long text labels into separate cell entries. (If you are using Release 2 of Lotus 1-2-3, this is less important because you can use the /Data Parse command to separate the data after importing the ASCII data into the worksheet by using the /File Import Text command.)

If this option is not available to you but your office uses dBASE II or dBASE III, you could convert the data in the ASCII data file into a dBASE file. The Lotus 1-2-3 Translate utility can import either DIF or dBASE files directly into the Lotus 1-2-3 worksheet. If neither option is available, you can set up a macro that will break up the text and numbers into separate cells. (For information on how to do this, refer to "Using /Range Justify to Parse Labels in Release 1A" in Chapter 7.)

However, if your downloaded file contains only numeric data, these steps are unnecessary; you can use the Lotus 1-2-3 /File Import Numbers command to import standard ASCII text files into your worksheet. When you use the Numbers option, Lotus 1-2-3 automatically places each numeric entry into a separate cell in the worksheet.

Using the /File Import Command

Once you have saved your data in an ASCII file, whether it was produced from a word processing document or downloaded from another computer, you use the /File Import command to take it into a worksheet. The /File Import command works much like the /File Combine command in that it reads in data from the ASCII file into the worksheet at the cell pointer's current position. This allows you to add the data to an existing spreadsheet or database. Be careful when using the /File Import command; like the /File Combine Copy command, it will overwrite any existing cell entries that are located in the range used in the import operation.

Importing ASCII Files Containing Text and Numbers

Two options are associated with the /File Import command; Text and Numbers. The Text option imports each line in the ASCII file as a long label in a single cell. The text in the line may not exceed 72 characters if you are using Release 1A or 240 characters if you are using Release 2. Each subsequent line of text in the ASCII file is put into single cells in succeeding rows of the worksheet, from the cell pointer's current position down the column it occupies.

Using Data Parse to Break Up Long Label Entries

To break a long label into separate cell entries across the same row, you then use the /Data Parse command. To illustrate the power and versatility of this command and explain how it works, consider the following scenario. The word processing department maintains a document file that contains a complete list of the vendors you use. Rather than retype this information in a new Lotus 1-2-3 database, you would prefer to import it and then add to it.

In the word processing document, the information is entered as a table using tab stops to separate the individual items, vendor number, name, city, and state into individual columns. Figure 29.1 shows this table (created in WordPerfect).

Figure 29.2 shows the resulting ASCII file created from the table. Its contents were displayed on the screen by using the DOS TYPE command. Notice that the columns are no longer properly aligned in the ASCII file. Not only have the city and state columns been shifted to the right so that they are no longer left-aligned with their column headings, but also the cities in two of the vendor entries are shifted so far to the right that their state entries are no longer aligned beneath the State column heading.

This is caused by the number of tabs that the word processing operator had to enter in order to align the entries in the table. In this ASCII file, each tab stop is stored as seven spaces. In the case of the two vendors, Oak Crest and Oak Mill, whose names were shorter than the others, the operator had to tab three times before entering their cities.

Vendor #	Vendor Name	City	State
12	Cherry Hill	Encina	CA
15	Mathers and Sons	LaJolla	CA
20	Oak Crest	Sonoma	CA
35	Avalon Mill	Salt Lake	UT
45	Genera Ltd.	Seaview	WA
51	Fine Furniture	Boise	ID
67	Oak Mill	Salem	OR
68	Piedmont Products	Whitehead	ID
88	Maple Magic	Kerry	OR

Doc 1 Pg 1 Ln 1 Pos 10

FIGURE 29.1: Vendor table created in a word processor. This figure shows a typical table containing information that is to be transferred to a Lotus 1-2-3 worksheet. Its columns were created by using tabs. After the table is saved as a document, the file is printed to disk in ASCII code because this word processor (WordPerfect) does not have an option on its translate utility for converting its data to the Lotus 1-2-3 worksheet file format. See Figure 29.2 to view the table in ASCII form.

Note: If your table were very short, like the one illustrated in Figure 29.1, you would want the word processing operator to make a copy of the document and remove all of the tabs from it before saving the file in ASCII form. However, if such a list consisted of many pages of vendors, this would not be practical or absolutely necessary. Fortunately, the /Data Parse command can deal with lines that have been formatted differently so that all of the misaligned data can be properly arranged in a spreadsheet cell range.

Figure 29.3 shows the vendor data after it has been brought into a new worksheet file by using the /File Import Text command. When accessing this command, Lotus 1-2-3 displays a line listing of all files that carry the .PRN (for print file) file extension. Because this ASCII file was not saved with any extension, it was necessary to type in the file name rather than select it from the list.

Notice that the file is brought into the worksheet with the same alignment problem that you saw in the ASCII file when it was typed to the screen (in Figure 29.2). Also, although the text appears as though it has

```
C:\123\DATA>type vendor.
Vendor #        Vendor Name             City            State
12                      Cherry Hill             Encina  CA
15                      Mathers and Sons        LaJolla CA
20                      Oak Crest                       Sonoma  CA
35                      Avalon Mill             Salt Lake       UT
45                      Genera Ltd.             Seaview WA
51                      Fine Furniture  Boise   ID
67                      Oak Mill                        Salem   OR
68                      Piedmont Products       Whitehead       ID
88                      Maple Magic             Kerry   OR

C:\123\DATA>_
```

FIGURE 29.2: This figure shows the ASCII file created from the word processing table illustrated in Figure 29.1. It has been displayed on the screen with the DOS TYPE command (one mark of an ASCII file is that its contents are legible when displayed with the TYPE command). Notice that all of the data is no longer perfectly aligned as it was in the word processor. This is because the tabs have been converted into a corresponding number of spaces in the ASCII file. When creating the table, the word processing operator had to tab three times after entering the vendor number to align the vendor names beneath the Vendor Name column heading. Also, the operator had to tab over farther when the vendor names were short to align the city entries in their column. Though it is not visible on the screen, each line in this ASCII table is terminated with a carriage return and line feed character. See Figure 29.3 to view the file after it has been brought into a Lotus 1-2-3 worksheet.

been entered into separate cells in columns A through H, all of the entries are really in the cells in column A. This can be verified by examining the contents of cell A1 in the Control Panel shown in the figure. Each vendor entry has been imported as a long text label in the column, extending from row 1 through 10.

To use this information in a Lotus 1-2-3 database, each of the items in these long labels must be broken up into single cell entries and each item (or field) placed in the same column. Because there are four distinct fields, when these labels are split up they should extend across four columns in the worksheet. This exactly what the /Data Parse command will do.

When you access the /Data Parse command, the following menu options are displayed:

Format-Line Input-Column Output-Range Reset Go Quit

The first option to use is Format-Line. When you select this command, you are presented with two suboptions:

Create Edit

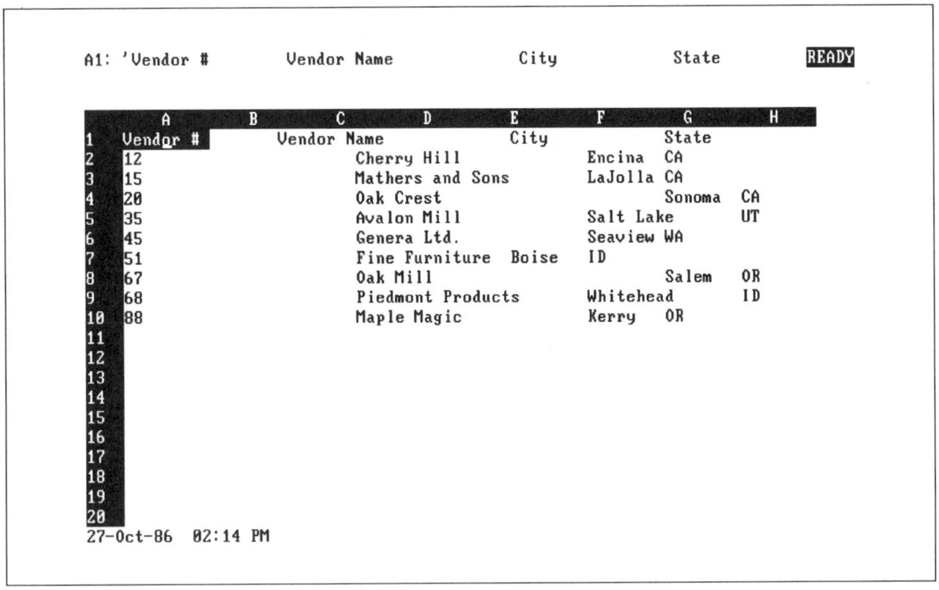

FIGURE 29.3: The vendor table ASCII file after it has been brought into a Lotus 1-2-3 worksheet by using the /File Import Text command. The appearance of the table is the same in the Lotus 1-2-3 worksheet as it was when examining the contents of the ASCII file with the TYPE command (see Figure 29.2). To preserve the labels, the Text option on the /File Import menu was used. As a result, each line of text was brought into the spreadsheet as a long label in column A (you can verify this by examining the contents of cell A1 in the Control Panel). Because this data is to be used in a Lotus 1-2-3 database, each item of information (vendor number, name, city, and state) must be entered into individual cells by using the /Data Parse command. See Figures 29.4 through 29.6 to view each step of this operation.

The Create option is used to insert a format line that shows the program where to separate each field.

With the cell pointer in cell A1, accessing the /Data Parse Format-Line Create option inserts the format line in row 1 shown in Figure 29.4. The format line in this case is actually a special kind of label entry located in cell A1. This format line entry contains a ¦ prefix that is similar to the two ¦¦ (vertical bars) used for entering printer setup codes in a row of the worksheet.

Notice that L's have been placed above each separate word in row containing the vendor table column headings. These L's, for Label, show that Lotus 1-2-3 has identified six individual fields in this row. Greater-than symbols are placed above each character in the row below, and asterisks mark the unused spaces until another label has been identified with an L.

If there were actually six separate fields in the database, this format line created by Lotus 1-2-3 would be correct. However, because two of the

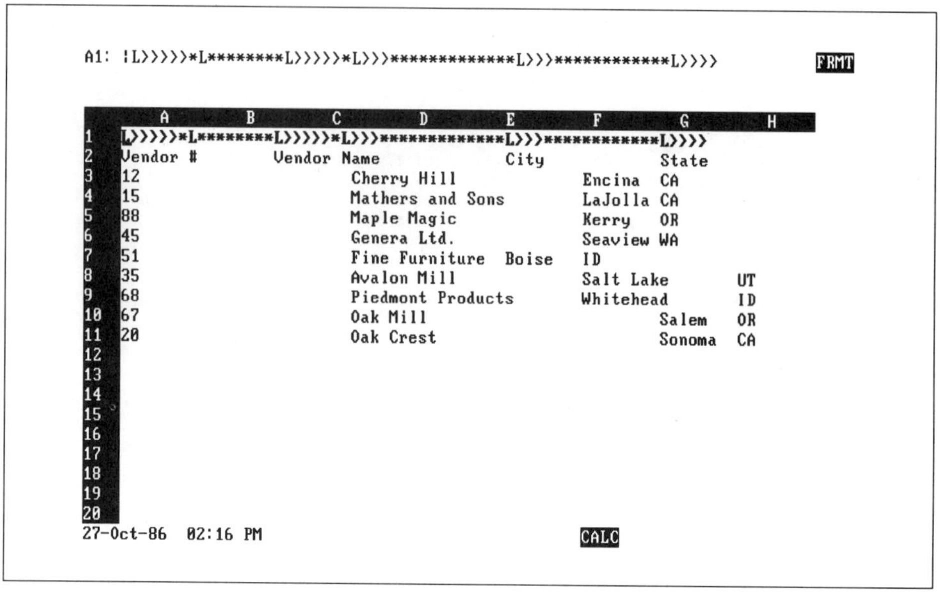

FIGURE 29.4: This figure shows the imported vendor table after the first format line has been inserted above the row containing the vendor column headings. This was done by positioning the cell pointer in the cell containing this long label (A1) and using the /Data Parse Format-Line Create command. This inserted a new row containing the format line seen here (it too is a label, now in cell A1). The L's indicate where the program has identified a block of information to be parsed. It also indicates that each of these blocks will be entered as labels. Because of the spaces between the headings Vendor # and Vendor Name, the program has incorrectly identified # and Name as starting new data blocks (fields) to be entered in separate cells. To rectify this, the format line must be edited by using the Format-Line Edit command. Figure 29.5 shows this line after it has been edited.

identified labels are part of a single field, the line must be edited. If you did not edit it, the program would place each label below an L in a separate cell in the row identified as the output range.

To edit the format line, you merely access the Format-Line option again, this time choosing the Edit instead of the Create suboption. This places the cursor on the format line in row 1 (which is displayed in double intensity on your screen). Once the cursor is on the format line, you can edit it just as though it were on the edit line of the Control Panel. There are two differences, however: the program goes into Overtype mode (shown by the OVR status indicator at the bottom of the screen), and the mode indicator displays the message FRMT (for format). If you want to edit the format line in Insert mode, press the Ins key once and the OVR indicator will disappear.

Note: You must place the cursor on the cell containing the long format line label before selecting Edit, or 1-2-3 will not recognize the line as a valid format specification.

To make the necessary changes to this first format line, you must delete the L's above the # symbol and above the Name in Vendor Name and replace the isolated * in the vendor name with a > so that the field is contiguous. To do this, move the cursor to the L's and type either > or * over it. You use > to mark a continuation of the text in the line below and * to mark unused spaces until you reach the next data block. (You only use letters, such as V, T, or D, to change the type of the data block you are marking.) After typing over these two L's, press the Return key to establish the correct format line.

Because the actual vendor numbers, names, cities, and states, are not left-aligned with each column heading, another slightly different format line must be added to determine where these fields are to be split. Notice, however, that because not all of the entries in each row line up with each other, one format line will not work for all of the data entries.

In fact, three different format lines must be added and edited before actually parsing the data. Figure 29.5 illustrates all of these format lines after they have been properly edited. Notice that vendor number entries all have a V (for Value) instead of an L above them. When the second format line was created (by placing the cell pointer in cell A3 and using the /Data Parse Format-Line Create command), Lotus 1-2-3 automatically added the V because the entries consist of only numerical data.

After you create a format line for each group of entries with different formats, the data is ready to parse. To perform this operation, you must define two ranges: an input range (via the Input-Column option of the Data Parse menu), which in this case consists of all of the cell entries and format lines in colum A, the cell range A1..A14, and an output range (using the Output Range option of the Data Parse menu). The output range can be located anywhere in the spreadsheet where there is no existing data that could be overwritten.

In this particular example, the data was copied into a cell range below the imported text labels and format lines, and the output range was designated as cell A17. As when making a many-to-many copy, you need only define the first cell of the range where you want the copied cell entries to begin. After designating both the input and output ranges, you use the Go option on the /Data Parse menu to perform the parsing.

Figure 29.6 shows the results after the column widths in columns B and C have been widened to display all of the cell entries. After the data has

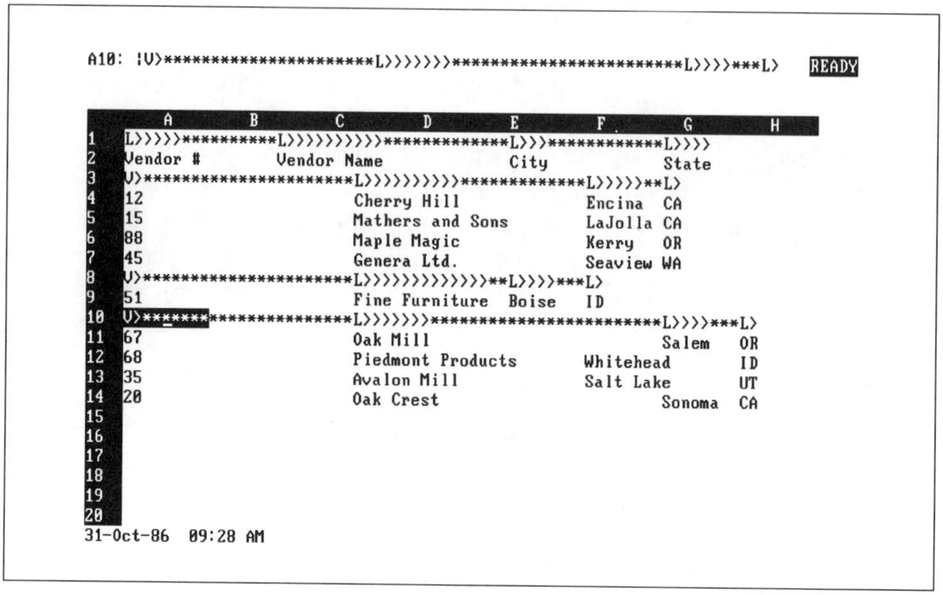

FIGURE 29.5: This figure shows the vendor table data after all format lines required to parse it properly have been added and edited. Notice that the first format line shown in Figure 29.4 has been edited by replacing the L's with the unused space symbol (*) and the continuation character symbol (>). A new format line was then created above the first line of data. In this format line, Lotus 1-2-3 correctly identified the Vendor # column entries as values (marked with V). This line was also edited to prevent a new cell entry from being created for the second part of the first vendor name (it contained an L above Hill). Not all of the data can be parsed by using this second format line. To make the data easier to format, the entries were grouped by using the /Move command. As you can see, two more slightly different format lines were required to ensure that the data is properly parsed. The fourth format line works even though not all of the city entries are left-aligned, because those to the left of L for the city field fall beneath unused spaces within the Vendor Name field. Figure 29.6 shows the data after the /Data Parse operation has been completed.

been split into separate cell entries, the original imported labels and format lines in column A can be deleted (with the /Range Erase command using the cell range A1..A14). You can then move the parsed data (now entered in the cell range A17..D26) to its final position in the database.

The /Data Parse command makes importing ASCII files that contain both labels and values a much easier operation, especially if the data is aligned more uniformly than it was in this example. If your word processor lacks data management capabilities for sorting and selecting data based on conditions you specify, you can use the /File Import Text and /Data Parse commands to prepare a mailing list database in Lotus 1-2-3. You can then use its /Data Sort and /Data Query commands to select and sort only those entries you wish to include in the mailing. The selected and sorted data in

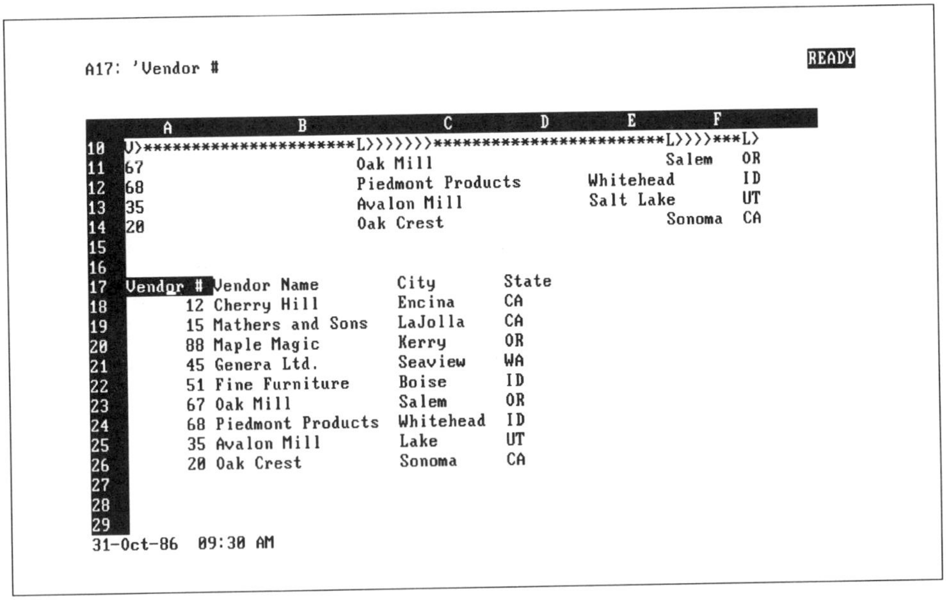

FIGURE 29.6: This figure shows all of the data in the imported vendor table after the /Data Parse operation has been completed. After creating and editing all of the required format lines (shown in Figure 29.5), the input and output ranges were defined. Because all of the format lines and data in the table are contained in long labels entered into cell in column A, the input range was one column wide, extending from cell A1 to A14. The output range was designated as cell A17. In this figure columns B and C were widened to show all of the data in the cells in these columns. All of the table items are now entered into individual cells. (You can verify this by examining the contents of cell A17 in the Control Panel: it contains only the first column heading instead of all of the headings.) These rows of data can now be used in a database application.

the /Data Query output range can then be printed to disk using the /Print File command. Finally, this ASCII text file can be used as the data file in a merge operation between it and a standard form letter created with your word processor (see the section "Sending Data to Word Processors" later in this chapter for more information).

Importing ASCII Files Containing Only Numerical Data

If your ASCII text file contains only numerical data or if you are only interested in transferring the numerical data it contains into a Lotus 1-2-3 worksheet, you would use the /File Import command with the Numbers rather than the Text option. When you use this option, Lotus 1-2-3 ignores any text characters when importing the data unless they are enclosed in double quotes. (This is a common feature of the comma-delimited or CSV ASCII file. In comma-delimited format, all text entries are enclosed in a pair of quotes, and each item in a line is preceded by a comma.) The numbers option also automatically enters each numerical entry in a separate cell of the worksheet, making it unnecessary to do any kind of parsing.

To demonstrate what does and doesn't work when importing numerical data, consider another word processing table, this one containing a list of products with vendor number, product number, and prices. Figure 29.7 shows the table as it was set up in the word processor. Because it contains column headings that would be totally ignored if the ASCII version of this file were initially imported with the /File Import Numbers command, the table is first imported with the /File Import command using the Text option. This stores each entry as a long label in a single cell.

To parse and convert the vendor numbers, part numbers, and prices to values, the /File Import Numbers command is then used with the same ASCII file and with the cell pointer in the same place, which in this

Vendor	Product	Description	Price
15	1705	24" Round dining table	278.00
20	2345	Oak Hutch	1395.00
68	4401	Straight back chair	49.50
51	1085	Captain's chair	65.00
12	2455	36" x 65" Book shelf	25.50
67	5603	48" Square dining table	265.00

Doc 1 Pg 1 Ln 1 Pos 7

FIGURE 29.7: This figure shows another table created in a word processor. It tracks product information including the vendor number, product number, price, and description. To transfer the table to Lotus 1-2-3, an ASCII file containing its data is created so that it can be brought in by using the /File Import command. Because most of the data consists of numbers, except for the column headings and the last column of descriptions, the file will be imported twice in the same area of the worksheet, first by using the Text option and then by using the Numbers option. Figure 29.8 shows the results of these operations.

example is cell A1. Figure 29.8 shows the data after it was imported a second time by using the /File Import Numbers command.

Because Lotus 1-2-3 ignores all text entries not enclosed in quotation marks, it did not overwrite the column headings that were already placed in cell A1 during the first /File Import operation using the Text option. Notice what happened to the description information when Lotus 1-2-3 imported the file using the Numbers option. It entered each number in the vendor number, product number, and price columns in individual cells in columns A, B, and C. However, it placed those description entries that began with the number giving the size in separate cells in column D, eliminating all of those descriptions that did not contain numbers.

Lotus 1-2-3 also placed part of the text for the first and last two descriptions in separate cells in column E. It did this because it interpreted the

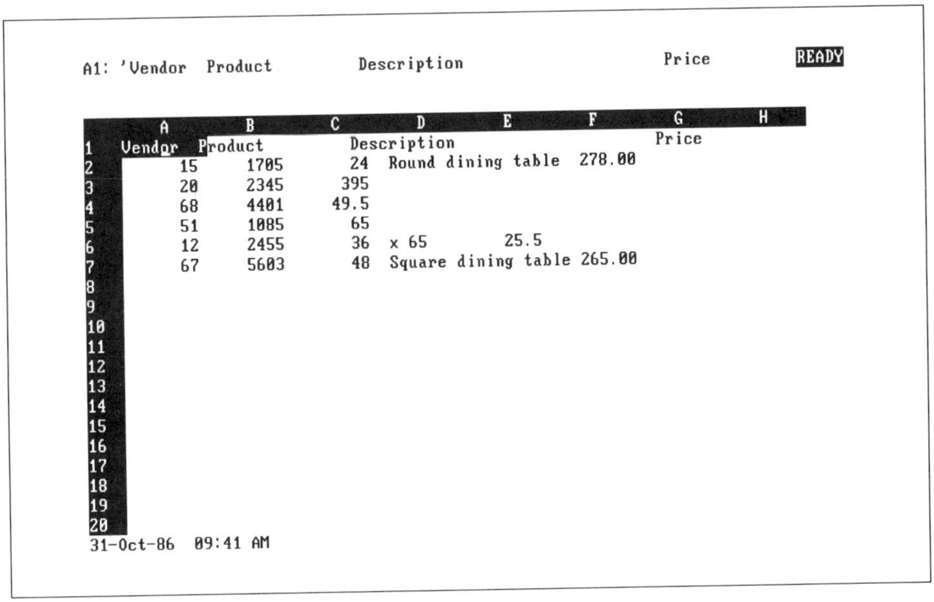

FIGURE 29.8: This figure shows the result of importing the product table shown in Figure 29.8 two times, the first time using the /File Import Text command and the second time using the /File Import Numbers command. When the Text option was used, each line of data was brought into the worksheet as long text labels in cells A1 through A7. You can see that the column headings for this table are all still contained in cell A1 by examining its contents in the Control Panel. When the Numbers option was then used, the program ignored column headings in the file (and thus did not overwrite the label in A1) and copied in the numerical entries in separate cells in the following rows. When Lotus 1-2-3 did this, it copied some of the product descriptions in which text was preceded by a double quote (used in the table as an inch mark). If the description was not preceded by a size number and did not contain a quote, it was totally ignored, as in rows 3 through 5. Importing ASCII files that contain text and data by using the Numbers option works only when all of the text is enclosed in pairs of quotes.

quotes used to indicate inches as text delineators. The second-to-last description in cell E6 contains only the text × 65 because there was a second double quote mark after 65 in the table. Only text enclosed in a pair of quotation marks is entered, so the program ignored the rest of the description beyond it.

When using the /File Import Numbers command, you must be sure either that the ASCII file you intend to import contains only lines of numeric entries or that all of the text entries are properly enclosed in double quotes. Some programs will automatically output ASCII files in the comma-delimited format, whereby all text entries are enclosed in a pair of quotes and every item in the line is separated by a comma. The /File Import Numbers command works flawlessly with this type of file, because it ignores the commas as text and copies the rest of the items into individual cells of the worksheet.

Exporting Lotus 1-2-3 Worksheets in ASCII Files

In addition to importing text and data into Lotus 1-2-3 worksheets from ASCII files, you may also need to export data generated and stored in Lotus 1-2-3 worksheets for use with other software programs. Most often, this will occur when you need either to transfer data to your word processor to be included in a report or to upload spreadsheet data to another computer system whose software does not read the DIF file format (if it does, use the Lotus 1-2-3 Translate utility).

In either case, you create the ASCII file by using the /Print File command, which creates a new file saved in ASCII code. Because the export feature is most often used to send Lotus 1-2-3 data to word processing documents, the /Print File command is discussed in the following section in that context. If you are creating an ASCII file to be used with some other type of software, you will find that most of the information on using the /Print File command relates directly to your situation.

Sending Data to Word Processors

When you need to use some of your Lotus 1-2-3 spreadsheet or database data in a word processing report, you can export it as ASCII text that the word processor can use. The primary reason for transferring the data from the worksheet rather than retyping it (aside from saving time) is that it ensures that none of the values calculated in the spreadsheet will be mistyped in the word processed report.

In fact, many users who have access to both Lotus 1-2-3 and a word processor routinely set up and calculate the figures that need to be included in reports in a worksheet table before importing it into the word processed document. Once the data is taken into the appropriate place in the report, it can be formatted by using the word processor's features.

When you export data from a worksheet into an ASCII file by using the /Print File command, the cell entries in each row are arranged on separate lines of the resulting text file. You will be prompted to enter a new file name, which does not happen when using the Printer option. This file name must obey the DOS file-naming conventions; Lotus 1-2-3 will automatically append the extension .PRN to it. This allows you to save the file under the same file name as the worksheet, if you like, because their names have different extensions.

Note: You cannot load a file printed to disk with the /Print File command and given the extension .PRN by using the /File Retrieve command. If you ever need to load such a file back into a Lotus 1-2-3 worksheet, you must use the /File Import command to do so.

After you enter the file name, just as when sending a part of the worksheet to the printer, you must use the Range option to designate all of the cells to be included in the new ASCII file. After you do this, you must make sure that the right margin is wide enough to include all the columns in the print range (use the Options Margins Right command). You will also want to set the left margin at zero (by using the Margins Left options from the Options menu). If you do not, you will usually find that all of your data is indented in the word processing document by the number of spaces set for the left margin of a Lotus 1-2-3 report.

Before using the Go option to create and save the new ASCII file, use the Other Unformatted option from the Options menu. When you create a print file with the Unformatted option in effect, Lotus 1-2-3 ignores any headers, footers, or page breaks that you may have previously specified when printing a report from the spreadsheet. You can always add this kind of page formatting to your document by using the word processor's features once you have brought the ASCII file into the document.

Some word processors, like WordStar, will load ASCII files without requiring any prior conversion. However, many—such as MultiMate and WordPerfect—require you to convert the file before it can be loaded into the word processor. This means that you will have to use the word processor's utility program or command before you can edit the file.

Note: MultiMate Advantage will also convert .DIF files into its document format. If you wish, you may use the Lotus 1-2-3 Translate utility to convert the spreadsheet data into this file format and then use MultiMate's Advance Utilities to convert it.

You will often be bringing the worksheet data stored in the ASCII file into an existing document. After you convert the .PRN file and save it, if this is required, edit the document that is to contain the Lotus 1-2-3 data, locating the cursor at the beginning of the line where it is to appear. Then use the word processor's command to bring in an external file (^KR in WordStar, Shift-F8 in MultiMate, and Alt-F10 in WordPerfect).

Once you have combined the files, you may need to edit the data, especially if it is to appear in a tabular format. It often helps to set up an appropriate ruler line before the place where you intend to bring in the Lotus 1-2-3 data. This is especially important if the line length of the data in the Lotus 1-2-3 file exceeds that of the right margin currently used in the document. You will almost always find it necessary to insert tabs (decimal tabs, most often) to format the data into columns as you want them to appear in the final printed report.

The /File Import Command

The /File Import command must be used when you wish to incorporate data saved in an ASCII file (sometimes referred to as a DOS text file) format. This command can import any text file in which the data has been saved in ASCII code where each line of text has been terminated with a carriage-return or line-feed character. If your ASCII file has been saved in the comma-delimited format (sometimes referred to as CSV for Comma Separated Value), you can use the Numbers option when importing your file to have each item of data placed into a separate cell of the worksheet during the import operation.

/File Import

MENUS

/File
Import
Text   Numbers

KEYBOARD ENTRY

/FIT /FIN

FUNCTION

The /File Import command transfers data stored in ASCII format files into Lotus 1-2-3 worksheets. It provides two options: Text and Numbers. Use the Text option when you wish to import from the ASCII file both text and numbers that have not been saved in comma-delimited format. This option imports each line of data as a left-aligned label into a single cell of the worksheet starting from the current position of the cell pointer. Each subsequent line of the ASCII file is entered into successive cells in the same column below the cell pointer.

The Numbers option ignores all nonnumeric entries unless they are enclosed in double quotes (if you use single quotes, the text will be ignored when the file is imported). The Numbers option is used when:

- The ASCII file contains only numerical entries.
- The file contains numerical and text entries that are delimited by commas, and all text entries are enclosed in double quotes.
- The numbers in the file are the only entries you want to import into the spreadsheet.

This option enters each number in its own cell as a value and each group of characters enclosed in quotes in its own cell as a left-aligned label. Each separate entry in a single line starts at the cell pointer's current position and is placed in succeeding individual columns across the row. Each subsequent line of text is placed in successive rows of the worksheet below the cell pointer.

USAGE

To use the /File Import command, locate the cell pointer at the beginning of the cell range into which you want the data from the file to be copied. Be sure that this range contains no existing cell entries that you do not wish to lose. Access the command by typing **/FI**. Choose either the Text or Numbers options by typing either **T** or **N**.

The program will then prompt you for the name of the file to import. It will display a line listing of all text files in the current directory that have a .PRN file name extension. If your file does not have this extension, you will have to type in its name (once you begin typing its name, the entry line will be cleared). If your file does have a .PRN extension, you can select it by moving the highlight to it and pressing the Return key.

Lotus 1-2-3 will read in all of the data in the ASCII file from the current position. If you used the Text option, each line of data will be stored in a single cell as a left-aligned long label. If you are using Release 2, you will probably then want to use the /Data Parse command to have each individual entry in this label entered into separate cells across each row the worksheet (see the following reference entry). If you use the Numbers option, you may have to adjust the width of the columns to display all of the data and then use the /Range Format command to display the numbers as you wish them to appear in the spreadsheet.

EXAMPLES

For examples using the /File Import command with both the Text and Numbers options, refer to Figures 29.7 and 29.8.

THE /DATA PARSE COMMAND (RELEASE 2 ONLY)

The /Data Parse command provides an easy way to split individual items that have been input as a single label in a worksheet cell (sometimes referred to as a long label). It is most often used to separate data items consisting of text and numbers that have been imported into a worksheet by using the /File Import Text command.

/Data Parse

MENUS

/Data
Parse
Format-Line Input-Column Output-Range Reset Go Quit
Create Edit

KEYBOARD ENTRY

/DP
FC FE I O R G Q

FUNCTION

The /Data Parse command allows you to create format lines that instruct the program where to split individual items contained in a cell label into separate cell entries that are placed into succeeding columns. When you create a format line (by using the Format-Line Create options on the /Data Parse menu), Lotus 1-2-3 uses different code letters to designate the different types of cell entries it identifies:

- L Label entry—converts the entries below it into left-aligned labels.
- V Value entry—converts the entries below it into a right-aligned value that can be used in calculations.
- D Date entry—converts the entries below it into a date serial number that must formatted after the parsing is completed.
- T Time entry—converts the entries below it into a time serial number that must formatted after the parsing is completed.

You can edit the format line that Lotus 1-2-3 creates to change the type of entry and the point where items are split up. The format line is entered at the cell pointer's position by inserting a new row (similar to using the /Worksheet Page or the /Worksheet Insert Row commands). The line is entered in this new row as a special long label entry (prefaced by ¦ in the literal contents of the cell) in the cell that contains the cell pointer. When you create a format line, always position the pointer in the first cell that contains the long label to be parsed.

Because the format line is itself a label entry, it can be edited either by using the Format-Line Edit options from the /Data Parse menu or by using the Edit function key (F2) if you use the Quit option on the /Data Parse menu. If you use the Edit function key, remember that you are in Insert mode, which is not true when editing a format line with the Format-Line Edit options on the /Data Parse menu. You may want to press the Ins key to turn on Overtype mode.

Using the Edit function key instead of the Format-Line Edit option on the /Data Parse menu is helpful when you must edit several different format lines that you have created. Because you do not have to use the Quit option each time you need to move the cell pointer to the next format line to be edited (and then have to type **/DPFE**), it makes this job go much faster.

The program distinguishes the type of entry in a format line by placing one of the four code letters above the first character of each separate item (identified by spaces between entries). It also places greater-than symbols above each subsequent character in this entry and asterisks to mark all of the unused spaces until the next entry is identified by code letter.

The > symbols mark only the number of characters in the row directly below the format line, so they may not match the number of characters in the same entries in subsequent lines. This will not affect the parsing of these items into separate cells as long as there are enough unused spaces (marked with asterisks) between the item entries. For example, when Lotus 1-2-3 creates the following format line above these two entries, all of its items will be correctly parsed:

```
|V>>**L>>>>>>>>**V>>**L>>>>>>
'101 Diskette 200 Reorder
'201 Diskette 1056 No reorder
```

Although the value 1 in 1056 is not aligned under the V in the format line, it will be parsed into the third column in its row just like the value 200 because there are unused spaces above it. The No reorder label will also be parsed into a cell in the fourth column of its row; the same will be done with the Reorder label for the same reason. However, if either of these misaligned characters was beneath a > symbol, it would not be correctly parsed.

When you edit a format line, you can change the type of entry by typing a new letter code over the one entered by Lotus 1-2-3. For instance, if you want an item identified as a value with a V in the format line to be entered as a label, you would move the cursor to it and type an L in its place. You must be careful when manually editing these codes because you cannot make an item that begins with a letter or punctuation symbol into a value. If you specify a type that will not work with the data being parsed, the program will go into ERROR mode when you use the Go option from the /Data Parse menu, and you will receive the error message "Invalid format line."

Note: The /Data Parse command accepts the period and the "e" or "F" used in scientific notation, provided they are used to construct real numbers properly.

You can also use the letter S as a code to indicate that Lotus 1-2-3 is to skip (ignore) the item that starts below it. Data blocks below an S will not appear in the cells when the data is parsed. You can use this code whenever you have an entry in the imported data that you do not want to keep in the worksheet.

Lotus 1-2-3 is able to translate entries only into date and time serial numbers that match one of its date or time formats. If the entries have been entered as dates such as 10/31/87, you can convert them into date serial numbers by using the D format letter code. However, if the dates were entered in the form 19871031, they would not be successfully translated into date serial numbers (they would be parsed as labels even if you use the D code).

When Lotus 1-2-3 parses labels, it copies the data that has been formatted into a new cell range in the worksheet. Each group of characters identified as distinct items in the label is entered into a separate cell. For this reason, you must identify both an input range and an output range. The input range must contain the format lines that have been created as well as all of the data below it (because these all exist in a single column of the worksheet, your input range will always be a cell range only one column wide). If you do not begin this range with the first format line you will receive the error message, "Parse input range must start format lines" when you use the Go option from the /Data Parse menu. The output range needs only to be the first cell where you want the parsed data to begin. Lotus 1-2-3 will use whatever columns and rows are required from that cell on when parsing the data into individual cells.

USAGE

To use the /Data Parse command, position the cell pointer in the first cell containing the labels you want parsed; then type **/DP**. Select the Format-Line Create options from this menu by typing **FC**. Lotus 1-2-3 will create a format line identifying where each item in the line below begins and its type. It identifies an item, or data block, when there is at least one space between the characters in the label.

These data blocks may not be identified correctly in the format line created by Lotus 1-2-3. For example, if you have a column heading that contains a two-word description, the format line will identify each of the words as separate entries to be placed in different cells.

In such a case, you would edit the format line by typing **FE** from the /Data Parse menu. This places the editing cursor on the format line. You can move the cursor to the code letter above the incorrectly identified data block and type a > symbol (used to mark a continuation of a block) over it. When you edit a format line this way, the program is in Overtype mode (indicated by the OVR status indicator at the bottom of the screen). You will also see the CALC indicator immediately to its left. (This remains on the screen until you use the Go option to perform the parse operation.) You can also edit this type of entry by typing a new code letter.

When you edit a format line, all of the editing keys work just as they do when you are editing a cell entry. Once you have finished making modifications to this format line, press the Return key to update the line and to return to the /Data Parse menu. If you wish to leave the format line without having your changes recorded, press the Break key combination. Do not press the Esc key. Doing so will erase the entire format line, leaving a blank cell, when the program returns to READY mode. If this happens, you cannot recreate the format line by using the /Data Parse Format-Line Create command without repositioning the cell pointer one cell down from the one that contains your first label to be parsed (the program will not allow you to create a format line in a blank cell).

You can create as many different format lines as you need to identify the individual items as separate data blocks in subsequent rows of data. To do so, you must use the /Data Parse Quit option, move the cell pointer to the cell containing the long label that requires different formatting, and then use the /Data Parse Format-Line Create command again by typing **/DPFC**. Once you have created other format lines, you can edit them, if required, just as you did the original one.

When you have created and edited all of the format lines needed to mark all of the separate data blocks, use the Input-Range option to identify the cell range containing both the format lines and the data to be parsed. You can indicate this range by typing the cell addresses or by pointing. If you use pointing, you will find that the range is not yet anchored, allowing you to move the pointer to the cell containing the first format line. Once you have positioned it in this cell, type a period and use the down arrow or press End and use the down arrow to mark all of the entries and subsequent format lines in that column. Then press the Return key to mark the range and return to the /Data Parse menu.

Next, you need to indicate the location of the output range. To do this, access the Output-Range option from this menu by typing **O**. You only need to indicate the first cell of the output range. To do so, you may type in the cell address or point to it. When designating the output range, make sure there is no existing data in the vicinity that could be destroyed when you give the go-ahead to have the program parse your labels.

After you indicate the output range and press Return, access the Go option to have the parsing operation performed. Once the data has been copied into separate cells, you may erase the original labels, entries, and format lines from the worksheet by using the /Range Erase command. If you wish, you can then move the newly parsed data to another place in the worksheet.

If you find that your data is not correctly parsed and you wish to use the same output range when you redo the command, first erase the existing data. Because the /Data Parse command does not work like the /Data Query Extract command by erasing the output range before writing in new data, some of the old data may still exist in the cell range even after you have changed the format lines and reissued the command.

The /Data Parse command contains a Reset option that will clear both the previously set input and output ranges. Use it if you need to parse labels in a new part of the spreadsheet during the current work session. This makes it easier when you go to define to the new input and output ranges, especially if you do this by the pointing method. For examples of applications for the /Data Parse command and examples of how it is used, refer to Figures 29.3 through 29.6.

SUMMARY

This chapter has dealt exclusively with the subject of transferring data into and out of Lotus 1-2-3 worksheets using ASCII format files. Before you create an ASCII file to be imported into a worksheet by using the /File Import command, make sure that you cannot use the Lotus 1-2-3 Translate utility to take the external file in directly.

This is especially important if the file you need to bring into the worksheet contains both text and data and you are using Release 1A where you do not have access to the /Data Parse command. If the Lotus 1-2-3 Translate utility will not convert the type of file you wish to import, the program in which it was created may offer its own translation program that will convert the file into a Lotus 1-2-3 worksheet format (see Chapter 30).

You may also sometimes need to export spreadsheet data to other application programs. See first if Lotus 1-2-3's Translate utility can convert the worksheet file into a format used by the program or if the program contains its own translate utility to convert a Lotus 1-2-3 worksheet.

If you need to transfer Lotus 1-2-3 data to a word processor, chances are that the word processor will not be able to accept the data in any format other than ASCII (WordStar 2000 is an exception—it can read in worksheet data either by complete file or by cell range). When you must use the ASCII file format as the transfer medium, you can make a copy of your worksheet or a part of its data in ASCII code by using the /Print File command. You can find more detailed information on using the /Print command in Chapter 25.

CHAPTER 30

THE TRANSLATE UTILITY

The Translate Utility

This chapter discusses transferring data files between Lotus 1-2-3 worksheets and other application software using the Lotus 1-2-3 Translate utility or, alternatively, the translation program included as part of the application program itself. Here you will find discussions on transferring Release 2 worksheets to Release 1A as well as transferring them to and from Jazz and Symphony, two other programs by Lotus Development Corporation. This chapter will also discuss transferring worksheet data to and from other popular spreadsheet and database management programs.

Direct translation of data between a Lotus 1-2-3 worksheet file and another application's own file format is easily accomplished by using a menu-driven translation utility program. Because Lotus 1-2-3 is such a standard, almost all data processing application programs for the IBM PC and compatible computers include direct translation of data to and from Lotus 1-2-3 worksheets as options in their own translate programs. This is especially true of newer application programs whose formats are not accommodated by the Lotus 1-2-3 Translate utility.

Very seldom will you find that you have to use an ASCII file as the medium of exchange between Lotus 1-2-3 and another IBM PC software product, outside of the area of word processing software.

Using the Lotus 1-2-3 Translate Utility

Releases 1A and 2 of Lotus 1-2-3 both provide separate Translate utility programs for converting files to and from the worksheet file format. Both of these programs can be accessed directly from the Lotus Access System Menu by choosing the Translate option. In addition, the Release 2 Translate program can be accessed directly from the DOS operating system by typing the command **TRANS** and pressing the Return key. You can also use the /System command to exit to DOS and start the Translate utility with this same TRANS command. Remember to type **EXIT** when you have finished your conversions and wish to return to Lotus 1-2-3.

Note: The Release 1A Translate program can be run from the DOS prompt by entering **TRANSLAT.** In Release 1A, the individual translate functions are performed by separate programs called by the TRANSLAT-.COM program menu. You can run a translation by running one of these subprograms at the DOS prompt (e.g., WKSDBF.EXE). However, this direct approach is not advisable.

If you are using Lotus 1-2-3 (either version) on a two-disk-drive system, you must replace the Lotus System Disk with a working copy of your Utility Disk when prompted to do so. If you are running Lotus 1-2-3 on a hard disk system, Lotus 1-2-3 will load the Translate program as long as its files are located in the directory that is current when you enter the TRANS startup command.

Release 2 of the program has added substantially to the number and types of formats it is able to import and export. To get an idea of the kinds of translations that are possible with both versions of the program, refer to Tables 30.1 and 30.2.

As you can see from these tables, the number of translations possible with the Release 2 Translate program has increased significantly. For one thing, this version of the Translate program allows you to convert file formats that do not even involve Lotus 1-2-3 worksheets. For example, it is possible to use this program to convert a dBASE III file to a Symphony file or a Version 1.0 Symphony to a DIF file.

If your office uses both versions of Lotus 1-2-3, you might want to use the Release 2 Translate program to perform conversions of .WKS files to other software formats that are not supported by the Release 1A Translate utility. For instance, you could use it to convert data in your worksheet

	ORIGINAL FORMAT	REQUIRED EXTENSION	MENU CHOICE	RESULTING FORMAT	EXTENSION
To import other file formats to Lotus 1-2-3 worksheets	VisiCalc DIF dBASE II	.VC .DIF .DBF	VC to WKS DIF to WKS DBF to WKS	Lotus 1-2-3 Lotus 1-2-3 Lotus 1-2-3	.WKS .WKS .WKS
To export Lotus 1-2-3 worksheets to other file formats	Lotus 1-2-3 Lotus 1-2-3	.WKS .WKS	WKS to DIF WKS to DBF	DIF dBASE II	.DIF .DBF

TABLE 30.1: Translations Possible in Release 1A

directly to a dBASE III file (the Release 1A Translate only converts to the dBASE II format). This would make it unnecessary for the dBASE user to convert the dBASE II to a dBASE III file by using its dCONVERT utility.

Translating Files Using the Release 1A Translate Utility

When using the Release 1A Translate utility, you must make sure that the file you want to convert carries the correct file name extension before

FROM	TO
Lotus 1-2-3, Release 1A	Lotus 1-2-3, Release 2 or 2.01 dBASE II dBASE III DIF Symphony, Version 1.0 Symphony, Version 1.1 or 1.2
Lotus 1-2-3, Release 2 or 2.01	Lotus 1-2-3, Release 1A dBASE II dBASE III DIF Symphony, Version 1.0 Symphony, Version 1.1 or 1.2
dBASE II and III, DIF, Jazz, and VisiCalc	Lotus 1-2-3, Release 1A Lotus 1-2-3, Release 2 or 2.01 Symphony, Version 1.0 Symphony, Version 1.1 or 1.2
Symphony, Version 1.0	Lotus 1-2-3, Release 1A Lotus 1-2-3, Release 2 or 2.01 dBASE II dBASE III DIF Symphony, Version 1.1 or 1.2
Symphony, Version 1.1 or 1.2	Lotus 1-2-3, Release 1A Lotus 1-2-3, Release 2 or 2.01 dBASE II dBASE III DIF Symphony, Version 1.0

TABLE 30.2: Translations Possible in Release 2

you use the program. DIF files must carry the .DIF extension, dBASE II files must carry the .DBF extension, and VisiCalc files must carry the .VC extension (these extensions are usually automatically appended to the file names that you assign).

If a file does not have the correct extension, you can change it or add it to the file name from the Lotus Access System's File Manager program by using the Rename option or from the DOS operating system by using its RENAME command.

For instance, if you want to translate a spreadsheet stored in a DIF format to a Lotus 1-2-3 worksheet, it must carry the .DIF file name extension. However, some files stored in this format may not carry the exact .DIF extension. If this is the case, you can simply rename the file from the operating system, as in the following example:

B>ren accts.sdf accts3.dif <Return>

After invoking up the Translate utility by choosing its option on the Lotus Access System Main Menu, you are presented with a list of menu options:

VC to WKS DIF to WKS WKS to DIF DBF to WKS
WKS to DBF Quit

Use the → and ← keys to position the highlight on the option you wish to use; then press the Return key. After you select the type of translation, you will be prompted to enter the source drive, which is the one containing the file to be converted:

A B C D E F G

Again, use the → and ← keys to position the highlight on the correct drive letter; then press the Return key. If the file you wish to use is stored on a hard disk (C, D, E, F, or G), it must be located in the current directory when you start the Translate utility. You cannot make a new directory current when specifying its drive letter.

After selecting the source drive, Lotus 1-2-3 will display a list of all the files on that drive that carry the extension appropriate for the kind of translation you selected. For instance, if you selected the WKS to DBF translation, you will see a listing of all of the files that have a .WKS extension. Use the ↓ and ↑ keys to move the highlight to the appropriate file name and press the Return key to select it.

Note: If you are translating a worksheet file to either a DIF or DBF (dBASE II) format, you will be prompted to choose between translating the entire worksheet and translating a named range after you select the file name of the worksheet. If you choose the Range option, you will then be prompted to enter the range name (the program will accept a valid range name, or the range's cell references). If you are converting a Lotus 1-2-3 database to a dBASE II file, your named range can consist of a single row of cells containing the field names. All of the records in the Lotus 1-2-3 database will be converted during translation until the program encounters a blank row in the worksheet.

After you select the file, the program will once again display the menu of drive letters A through G, and it will prompt you to select the letter of the drive where you want your translated file to be stored. Select this drive letter as you did the one for the source drive; then press the Return key.

The program will display the original file name (the source file) and the new file name (the destination file) on the screen and ask for your confirmation to perform the conversion. You will see that the source file name and destination file name differ only in extensions (if you wish to rename the translated file, do so by using the DOS RENAME command after exiting from the Translate utility after the conversion).

Choose the Yes option to have the program perform the translation. Choose the No option to return to the file selection menu to select another file for translating or another destination drive letter. Choose the Quit option if you wish to abort the translation and return to the Translate Menu. From there, you can either choose another type of translation or use the Quit option to exit the Translate program. After the translation has been completed, you will be returned to the Translate Main Menu, where you may use the Quit option to return to the Lotus Access System or begin another translation.

If you select the Yes option and are translating a DIF Format file to a worksheet, you will be prompted to choose between columnwise and rowwise translation. This refers to whether the program that created the DIF file placed the vectors (columns) definition before the tuples (rows) definition in the DIF file. If you are using the DIF file created by SuperCalc, choose the default option, Columnwise. If the choice you make is inappropriate, your spreadsheet data will be transposed when you retrieve the translated worksheet.

If you are translating a VisiCalc spreadsheet file to a Lotus 1-2-3 worksheet and the spreadsheet contains formulas that use the @CHOOSE, @NOT, @AND, and @OR functions, these will not be translated properly in the resulting worksheet. During the translation process, Lotus 1-2-3 will display the error message "Formula error" and the cell address that contains the function. It will, however, go ahead and translate these functions into labels in the new worksheet.

Also, if you are translating a dBASE II database file that contains deleted records (those marked for deletion and not yet packed), the Translate utility will ignore them and they will not be written into the resulting worksheet. If you wish them to be included, you must use dBASE to unmark them before converting the .DBF file to a .WKS file.

Translating Files Using the Release 2 Translate Utility

When you access the Translate utility in Release 2, you are presented with the list of programs shown in Figure 30.1. Here, you indicate the file format of the source file (the one you want translated to another format) by using the ↓ and ↑ keys to highlight the appropriate program option and then pressing the Return key.

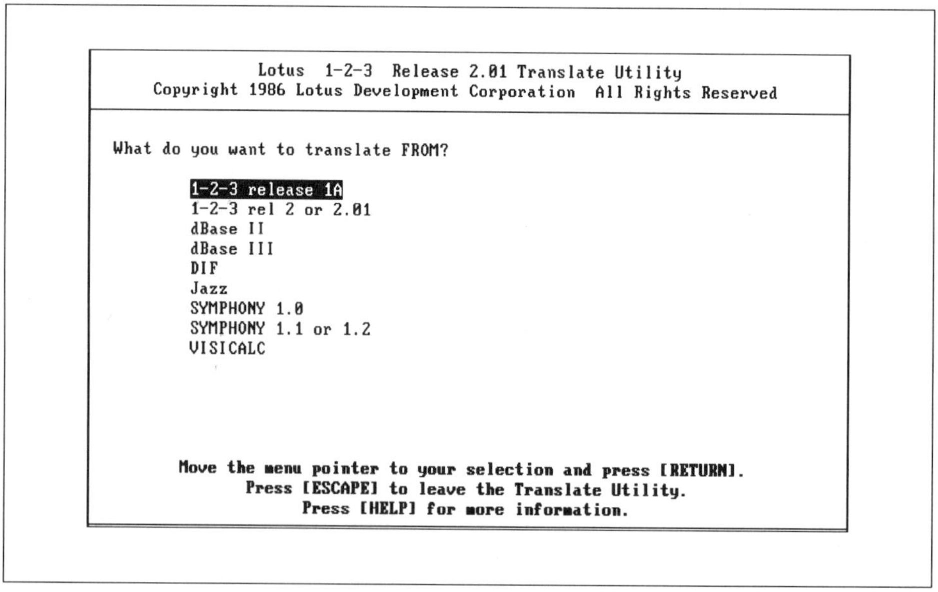

FIGURE 30.1: The menu options on the Release 2 Translate Utility ask you to indicate the format you want to translate from. From here you select the name of the program that the file to be translated was created in. The types of possible formats to which the file can be translated depend directly upon the name of the program chosen. You can refer to Table 30.2 to see the various possibilities.

After that, you are presented with a new list of application programs from which you indicate the file format of the destination file (the type you want the source file translated into). The kind and number of programs that are displayed vary, depending on the format of the source file. To see what formats are available for each source file type, refer to Table 30.2.

After you select the type of file by highlighting the appropriate program and pressing Return, the Translate program displays a screen of information outlining guidelines for a successful translation. If there is more than one screen of information, you will see the message "Press [Return] for next page" displayed at the bottom of the screen. Be sure to read all of the information screens before proceeding if you are unfamiliar with the requirements for successfully performing the type of translation you have called for.

After reading the information, press the Esc key to continue. If you wish to abort the translation operation, press the Break key combination (Ctrl-Scroll Lock) and you will be returned immediately to the first menu screen. From there, you can exit the Translate program by pressing the Esc key and typing **Y** if you need to make changes to your file before translating it.

If you wish to continue with the translation, you must choose the source file to be translated. The Translate program will display a partial listing of all of the files in the current directory that carry the extension associated with the source file type. If there are no files of this type in the current directory, you will receive the message "No files were found that match the source specification".

At this point, if the current directory is A:\ or B:\ and your file is located on a different floppy disk, you can replace the data disk and press the Return key to have the program search for files matching the source specification. If your file is located on the hard disk but the current directory is not correct, you can press the Esc key to clear the message and edit the file name. You may use the Backspace key to delete characters and then retype them. If you wish to clear the entire file name, press the Esc key again and type in the full path name. Then press the Return key to have the program search the new directory for matching files.

Once the program has listed the files, move the highlight to the file you want translated and press the Return key. The Translate program will then display the full file name of both the source and destination files. They will be the same except for their extensions. You will then be prompted to edit the file specification. If you wish to change the destination file name as well, you may do so. Press the Esc key if you want to make changes to the file name (press Esc a second time to clear the entire file name; then retype it, including its directory path). When you have finished editing the destination file name or the specification type (its file name extension)—or if you don't want to make any changes—press the Return key.

You will then be prompted to confirm the translation with three options: Yes, No, and Quit. Choose the Yes option to have the program perform the translation. Choose the No option to return to the file selection menu to select another file for translating. Choose the Quit option if you wish to abort the translation and return to the first Translate menu screen. From there, you can either choose another type of translation or press the Esc key and type Y to exit the Translate program.

After the translation has been completed, you will be returned to the first Translate menu screen where you may press the Esc key and type Y to return to the Lotus Access System or operating system. You can also begin to define another translation.

Translating Release 2 Worksheets to Release 1A

If your office uses both versions of Lotus 1-2-3, there may be times when you will need to use the Translate utility to translate Release 2 worksheets to Release 1A so that fellow workers who use Release 1A can have access to the data that you have generated. (Remember that even though the Translate utility has an option to translate Release 1A worksheets to Release 2, it is never required. You can just load a Release 1A worksheet using the /File Retrieve command.)

Because of the substantial changes to Release 2, you should be aware of problems and discrepancies that can arise before attempting the translation:

- Release 2 handles computer memory much differently from Release 1A. As a result, a worksheet that can be loaded in its original WK1 format may cause a memory-full error when you try to load the file after it has been translated to the WKS format. If this occurs, you must try to reduce the overall area of the Release 2 worksheet or delete extraneous data (perhaps graphs and range names) and try the translation a second time. As a last resort, you can also break the worksheet up into several files.
- The size of the Release 2 worksheet is much larger than that of Release 1A. If your WK1 spreadsheet contains data in rows past 2048, they will not be translated into the corresponding WKS file. If

the formulas that are successfully translated contain references to the missing data in these rows, their results will not be trustworthy and may contain ERR values.

- Release 1A does not support password-protected files; therefore you cannot translate a Release 2 file that has been password-protected until you remove the password (save the file again without a password).
- Many of the Release 2 @ functions and macro keynames and keywords have no counterparts in Release 1A. Any @ function that is not recognized will be translated as a label entry in the new file. Trying to use macros that contain Release 2 keynames or keywords will cause a macro error.
- Release 1A does not support the LICS codes. If you have entered any special characters in the Release 2 file you are translating to Release 1A, they will be represented by fall-back characters (these are illustrated on the last two help screens that are displayed when you set up a Release 2 to Release 1A translation).

Translating dBASE Files to Lotus 1-2-3

Because of the widespread use of dBASE II and dBASE III Plus as the corporate database management system, the Lotus 1-2-3 Translate utility provides for direct translation of dBASE data to and from Lotus 1-2-3 worksheet files. When translating data from a dBASE database file into a Lotus 1-2-3 worksheet, there are a few things that you need to keep in mind:

- Records in the dBASE file after record 8191 (2047 if you are using Release 1A) will not be translated.
- Labels longer than 240 characters will be truncated. Column widths greater than 72 will be truncated if the destination file is Lotus 1-2-3 Release 1A.
- If you are translating a dBASE III Plus file, any Memo fields used in the database will not be translated (these are stored in a separate text file with the extension .DBT).
- Records that are deleted in the database file (marked for deletion but not yet packed) will not be translated into the Lotus 1-2-3 worksheet.

Whenever you wish to translate a dBASE III Plus database into a Release 2 worksheet, use the Lotus 1-2-3 Translate utility rather than copying the database from dBASE. Figure 30.2 illustrates the difference between using dBASE's COPY command with WKS as the type and using the Lotus 1-2-3 Translate utility.

The first database in the cell range, A1..E7, was created by using this dBASE III COPY command:

.COPY PRODUCTS TYPE WKS

This outputs the field names and records in a .WKS worksheet file that could then be loaded directly in Lotus 1-2-3 by using the /File Retrieve command.

The second database in the cell range, A10..E16, is the translation created by the Lotus 1-2-3 Translate utility using dBASE III as the type to translate FROM and 1-2-3 Release 2 as the type to translate TO. It was then copied into the worksheet containing the first records with the /File Combine Copy command so that you could compare the results.

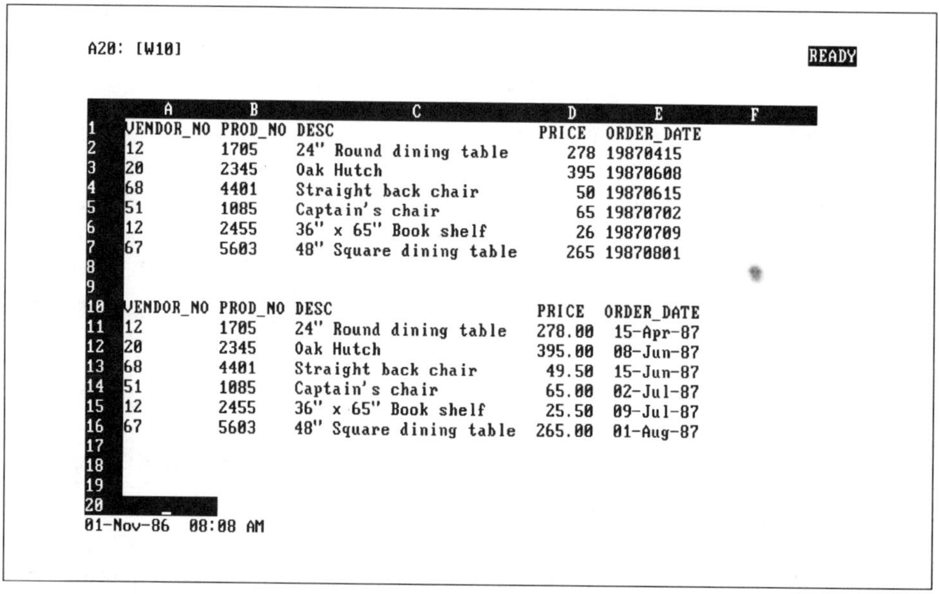

A20: [W10] READY

	A	B	C	D	E	F
1	VENDOR_NO	PROD_NO	DESC	PRICE	ORDER_DATE	
2	12	1705	24" Round dining table	278	19870415	
3	20	2345	Oak Hutch	395	19870608	
4	68	4401	Straight back chair	50	19870615	
5	51	1085	Captain's chair	65	19870702	
6	12	2455	36" x 65" Book shelf	26	19870709	
7	67	5603	48" Square dining table	265	19870801	
8						
9						
10	VENDOR_NO	PROD_NO	DESC	PRICE	ORDER_DATE	
11	12	1705	24" Round dining table	278.00	15-Apr-87	
12	20	2345	Oak Hutch	395.00	08-Jun-87	
13	68	4401	Straight back chair	49.50	15-Jun-87	
14	51	1085	Captain's chair	65.00	02-Jul-87	
15	12	2455	36" x 65" Book shelf	25.50	09-Jul-87	
16	67	5603	48" Square dining table	265.00	01-Aug-87	
17						
18						
19						
20						

01-Nov-86 08:08 AM

FIGURE 30.2: This figure compares the results of translating a dBASE III Plus file using the Release 2 Translate utility to using dBASE's COPY command with WKS as the type. The records shown in the upper range of this figure (A1..E7) were translated using the dBASE COPY command. Those in the lower cell range (A10..E16) were translated using the Translate program and then copied into the worksheet using the /File Combine Copy command. Notice that Lotus 1-2-3's Translate utility was able to do a more thorough job. It not only preserved the two-decimal formatting for the Numeric PRICE field but also (and more important) converted the date field, ORDER_DATE, into a Lotus 1-2-3 serial date number and automatically formatted it to the Date 1 format.

Notice that when you use the Translate utility, the Price and Order_Date fields are translated into forms that require no further formatting. In the dBASE III file, the Price field is a numeric field with two decimal places and the Order_Date field is a date field. When you use the Translate utility, the program interprets these field types correctly and converts them appropriately. The Price field has been given the Fixed format with two decimal places, and the Order_Date field has been translated as a serial date number automatically formatted to the Date 1 format.

By contrast, in the first database example created by dBASE, the Price field information has not kept its dBASE formatting. This data has been brought into the Lotus 1-2-3 worksheet in the General format (the global default format). A more important difference is that the dates in the Order _Date field have been brought in as label entries. dBASE keeps its date field entries in a modified Julian format rather than as date serial numbers. The COPY command in dBASE is not set up to convert these to the Lotus 1-2-3 format even when you specify the type as WKS.

While it would be easy to format the price data to display it with two decimal places, it would require a great deal more work to convert the date labels to Lotus 1-2-3 serial date numbers (you would have to create a macro that uses both the @ string and @DATEVALUE commands).

Translating Lotus 1-2-3 Worksheets to dBASE Files

When you want to translate Lotus 1-2-3 worksheets into dBASE files, you must make sure that your Lotus 1-2-3 database is organized correctly to ensure a successful translation:

- All of the data you want to be included in the dBASE file must be organized as a Lotus 1-2-3 database. If you are translating the entire worksheet, the first row of the file must consist only of the field names with succeeding rows consisting of data records. Before translating the file, delete any criterion or output ranges. You can, however, save the database under a range name and specify that it, rather than the entire worksheet, be translated. In that case, any other ranges or data outside the database proper can remain in the file.
- dBASE field names cannot be longer than 10 characters and must not contain spaces. If you have spaces in the Lotus 1-2-3 field names, replace them with underscores.

- dBASE field names must begin with a letter, and the colon is the only embedded punctuation character that can be used. If you have any field names that begin with other characters or have used other embedded punctuation characters, edit their names before attempting the translation.
- All of the data in the cells of the worksheet must be displayed so that the complete field entries will be translated (any characters not displayed will be truncated). Make sure all of the columns are wide enough to display all of the characters in every field entry before translating the worksheet.
- If you are translating a Release 2 worksheet into a dBASE II file, you can translate only the first 32 database fields into the dBASE file (the limit on the number of fields in Release 1A and dBASE II files is the same). If you are translating a Release 1A or 2 worksheet into a dBASE III Plus file, you can translate only the first 128 fields.
- The field type in the resulting dBASE file is determined by the type of entries in the first record of the Lotus 1-2-3 database. Labels are converted into character fields, values into numeric fields, and serial date numbers into date fields (in dBASE III Plus). If you have any blank fields (cells) in the first record, make sure they are formatted so that their type can be correctly interpreted during translation (better yet, put in a "dummy" value or label that can later be deleted in dBASE).

Figure 30.3 shows you a Lotus 1-2-3 database that has been prepared for translation into a dBASE III Plus file. The first row consists of only the field names with the records right beneath it. The first record was then checked for any empty fields whose type could be misinterpreted during translation. Finally, the entire database (only part of which is visible in this figure) was given the range name Data before the file was saved under a new file name (this keeps the original database worksheet intact with all of its titles).

When the translation was performed, the Range option was used and the range name Data was supplied. That way, it was not necessary to delete the criterion and output ranges that exist in the database, although it would have been if the entire worksheet had been translated.

Figure 30.4 shows the resulting structure of the new translated dBASE III Plus file, PERSONEL.DBF. The type of fields shown in the third column indicate how each entry in the first record of the Lotus 1-2-3 database was interpreted.

A1: [W12] 'Number READY

	A	B	C	D	E	F	G	H
1	Number	L:Name	F:Name	Sex	Dept	Position	Super	Salary
2	360-22-0978	Holland	Katherine	F	Acctg	Clerk	Newman	19,000
3	230-45-9512	Jones	Daniel	M	Acctg	Bookkeeper	Newman	27,500
4	458-56-8723	Newman	Paul	M	Acctg	Accountant	Pauli	55,000
5	561-34-5644	Jones	Alexander	M	Acctg	Secretary	Newman	25,000
6	567-43-2366	Langly	Sandra	F	Pers	Secretary	McKnight	24,000
7	345-14-7245	McKnight	George	M	Pers	Manager	Dorian	50,000
8	705-34-2378	Smith	Mary	F	Pers	Clerk	McKnight	18,750
9	465-25-8751	Mead	Peter	M	Sales	Acct Exec	Smithson	35,000
10	598-52-7054	Durran	George	M	Sales	Acct Exec	Smithson	30,000
11	124-15-7602	Baker	Thomas	M	Sales	Acct Exec	Smithson	32,500
12	865-12-4102	McMead	Andrea	F	Sales	Acct Exec	Smithson	38,000
13	466-52-7035	Smith	Mary	F	Admin	President		135,000
14	307-28-1251	Dorian	Alvin	M	Admin	VP Admin	Smith	62,000
15	359-78-1063	Smithson	Gena	F	Admin	VP Sales	Smith	70,000
16	253-65-2319	Pauli	Thomas	M	Admin	VP Finance	Smith	82,500
17	965-50-2344	Baker	Colin	M	Mktg	Director	Smithson	65,000
18	625-86-5139	Jones	Sylvia	F	Mktg	Secretary	Baker	28,900
19	465-10-2450	Lawson	Mark	M	Mktg	Assistant	Baker	27,500
20	306-73-2176	Clarkson	Sean	M	Mktg	Artist	Baker	25,000

01-Nov-86 08:09 AM

FIGURE 30.3: This figure shows a Lotus 1-2-3 personnel database readied for translation into a dBASE III Plus file. Before translating a Lotus 1-2-3 database into dBASE, all extraneous labels and other types of cell ranges (such as the criterion and output ranges) must be eliminated. If the entire worksheet is to be translated, the file must consist only of the database. Also, the field names cannot be longer than 10 characters, must begin with a letter, must contain no spaces (use underscores), and must use no embedded character other than the colon. The field entries in the first record must either contain data or, if they are left blank, be formatted so that their field type can be correctly interpreted. Finally, all of the columns in the database must be wide enough to display all of the characters in every field to prevent their being truncated during conversion.

Because the Salary field in the worksheet was formatted to the Comma format with zero decimal places, the SALARY field in dBASE also has no decimal places in the resulting numeric field. If they were desired, they could, however, still be added by using the MODIFY STRUCTURE command. Notice that the two date fields, HIRED and BIRTH, have been converted successfully to dBASE date fields because they were entered as serial date numbers in the Lotus 1-2-3 database with the @DATE function.

Figure 30.5 shows the first eleven records in the new PERSONEL.DBF file, displayed with the BROWSE command. The second through eighth fields (the Social Security Number field is not visible in this screen) are displayed to show the date field entries in the HIRED field. Notice that all of the data, with the exception of the date format in this field, appear exactly as they do in the Lotus 1-2-3 database (shown in Figure 30.3).

```
. use personel
. display structure
Structure for database: C:personel.dbf
Number of data records:       19
Date of last update   : 10/31/86
Field  Field Name  Type       Width    Dec
    1  NUMBER      Character     12
    2  L:NAME      Character      9
    3  F:NAME      Character     11
    4  SEX         Character      4
    5  DEPT        Character      7
    6  POSITION    Character     11
    7  SUPER       Character      9
    8  SALARY      Numeric        8
    9  HIRED       Date           9
   10  COMPANY     Numeric        8      1
   11  BIRTH       Date           9
   12  AGE         Numeric        4      2
** Total **                     102

. _
Command Line  ||<C:>||PERSONEL          ||Rec: 1/19   ||   ||

                        Enter a dBASE III PLUS command.
```

FIGURE 30.4: The structure of the new dBASE III Plus database file created from a Lotus 1-2-3 database (shown in Figure 30.3). The dBASE field types were determined by the type of data in the first record of the Lotus 1-2-3 database. As you can see, labels were converted to character fields, values to numeric fields (their display format determines the number of decimal places), and dates (entered as serial numbers) into date fields. The maximum width of each resulting field was determined by its column width in the Lotus 1-2-3 database (thus the need to make sure that each column is wide enough to display all of the field contents).

Translating Data to and from Other Lotus Products

Symphony and Jazz are both integrated programs published by Lotus Development Corporation. They incorporate word processing, spreadsheets, database management, graphics, and communications. Symphony is a very close cousin to Release 2, except that it includes word processing and communications features that are absent from Lotus 1-2-3. The @ functions and macro keynames and keywords work the same way in both programs. However, Symphony also includes some macro commands for controlling its different environments that are not in Release 2 and will not be recognized if the macros are used unedited. Jazz, on the other hand, is a Macintosh program that works quite differently from Symphony and Lotus 1-2-3.

Symphony to Lotus 1-2-3 Although the Translate utility provides options to translate Symphony Version 1.0, 1.1, and 1.2 files to Lotus 1-2-3 Release 2

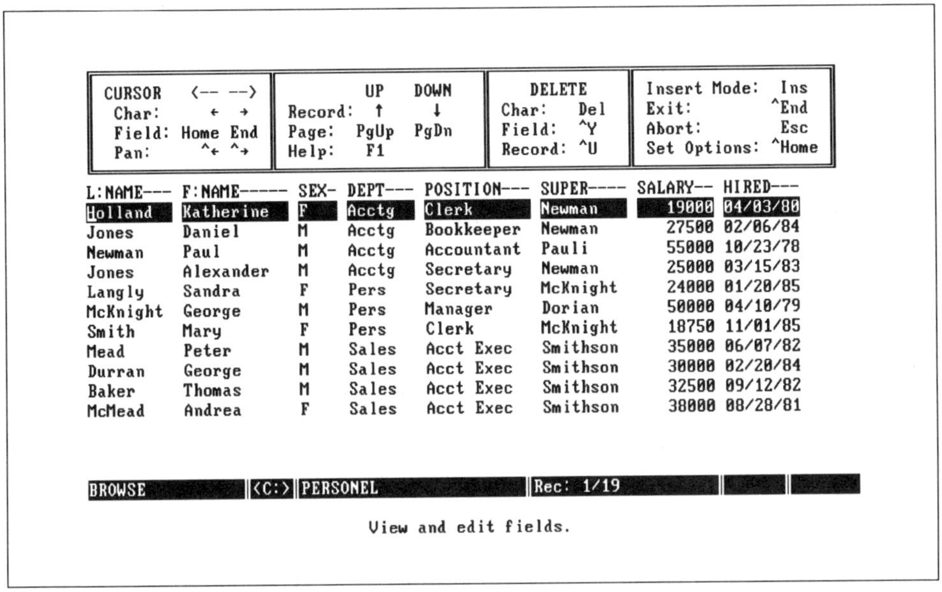

FIGURE 30.5: The first group of records in the new PERSONEL.DBF file shown with the BROWSE command. This figure shows you the data of a portion of the fields (the first field, containing the Social Security Number, is not visible on this screen). You can see that Lotus 1-2-3 dates have been correctly converted in the the dBASE file (this is the dBASE default display for date fields corresponding to the Lotus 1-2-3 Long International default date format) as have all of the rest of the data entries.

worksheets, you do not need to translate them. You can load them directly by using the /File Retrieve command. However, remember that the .WRK or .WR1 extensions given to Symphony files (depending upon the version used) will not be picked up by the file-search pattern (*.WK?) used by Lotus 1-2-3. You will therefore have to type in the full name, including the extension, to load them in Lotus 1-2-3 (you can also rename them with the DOS RENAME command).

When you want to transfer data between a Symphony worksheet and a Lotus 1-2-3 Release 1A worksheet, you must use the Release 2 Translate utility (there is no such facility in the Release 1A Translate program). The potential problems to anticipate when translating a Symphony (either Version 1.0 or 1.1) worksheet to Release 1A are essentially the same as those you must be aware of when translating a Release 2 file to Release 1A (in fact, use the same guidelines for translating Release 2 to Release 1A files enumerated in the previous section, "Translating Release 2 Worksheets to Release 1A," before attempting such translations).

Lotus 1-2-3 to Symphony When you want to use a Lotus 1-2-3 worksheet in Symphony, you do not have to translate the files using the Release 2 Translate utility under these circumstances:

- The worksheet has been created using Release 2 and the version of Symphony that will use it is Version 1.1 or 1.2.
- The worksheet has been created using Release 1A and you are using any version of Symphony (Version 1.0, 1.1, or 1.2).

You do have to use the Translate utility if you want to use a worksheet created in Release 2 with Version 1.0 of Symphony. Here, the potential problems are very similar to those of translating a Release 2 worksheet to Release 1A:

- Release 2 handles computer memory much differently from Version 1.0 of Symphony. As a result, a worksheet that can be loaded in its original WK1 format may cause a memory-full error when you try to load the file after it has been translated to the WRK format. If this occurs, you must try to reduce the overall area of the Release 2 worksheet or delete extraneous data (perhaps graphs and range names) and try the translation a second time. As a last resort, you can also break the worksheet up into several files.
- Symphony, Version 1.0 does not support password-protected files. Therefore, you cannot translate a Release 2 file that has been password-protected until you remove the password (save the file again without a password).
- The Release 2 @ functions @CTERM, @DDB, @RATE, @SLN, @TERM, and @SYD have no counterparts in Symphony Version 1.0. Any @ function that is not recognized will be translated as a label entry in the new Symphony file.

Jazz to Lotus 1-2-3 You can translate Jazz worksheet files into Lotus 1-2-3 worksheets only by using the Lotus 1-2-3 Release 2 Translate utility (you can, however, use the Jazz Convert command to bring Lotus 1-2-3 worksheet data directly into a Jazz worksheet). Because of the incompatibility between the disk formats used by the IBM PC and the Macintosh computer, your Jazz worksheet file (carrying the .JZZ extension) will have to be sent via a modem or a direct cable hookup between the computers. You can use the Jazz communications features to send the Jazz worksheet file to the IBM computer.

When translating a Jazz worksheet file to a Lotus 1-2-3 worksheet, there are a fair number of Jazz functions that cannot be properly interpreted by Lotus 1-2-3 (either version). These functions include:

CRYSGN	FCOUNT	FPAGE	FVAR	SCALE
EXP1	FIXED	FPREV	ISBLANK	SUBSTR
EXP2	FMAX	FSTD	ISREF	
FAVG	FMIN	FSUM	LN1	

Whenever cells containing these functions are encountered in the Jazz worksheet that is being translated, the corresponding cells in the new Lotus 1-2-3 worksheet will contain ERR values.

Transferring Data between Lotus 1-2-3 and Other Types of Spreadsheet Programs

Almost all other spreadsheet programs for the IBM PC offer their own translation programs that will directly convert a Lotus 1-2-3 worksheet (some older versions are not able to translate Release 2 worksheets) into the formats they use. In the rare case that the spreadsheet program will not convert Lotus 1-2-3 worksheet files, you will have to use the Lotus 1-2-3 Translate utility to convert your worksheet into a DIF file. This will also sometimes be necessary when you are sending Lotus 1-2-3 data to another type of computer (mini or mainframe) whose software can read the DIF format.

When translating a Lotus 1-2-3 worksheet to a DIF file, you must choose between two options: Columnwise or Rowwise. These choices refer to the way in which the program that will be using the DIF file expects the data to appear. Most of the time, you will be safe in choosing Columnwise, which is the default setting. In the rare instance that the program expects to see the tuples (rows) listed before the vectors (columns), the arrangement of Lotus 1-2-3 data will be transposed in the new spreadsheet.

Using Lotus 1-2-3 Data with Other Data Processing Software

If you are using other data management software that runs on the IBM PC and whose formats are not listed on the Lotus 1-2-3 Translate utility, you will have to look to their own translation programs when you want to tranfer data between them and your Lotus 1-2-3 worksheet files. Most of the time, you will find that they can both import and export Release 1A files.

However, older versions (usually the initial versions of the programs) may not support direct translation of Release 2 files. Refer to Table 30.3 to compare the type of Lotus 1-2-3 translations supported by some of the more popular data processing programs on the IBM PC.

When you use the translation utilities supplied by these programs to import Lotus 1-2-3 worksheets, most of them have requirements similar to those you encounter when translating a Lotus 1-2-3 database to a dBASE file. Database management systems like R:Base 5000, Paradox, and Reflex, like dBASE III Plus, do not require that you set up the database structure before you import the Lotus 1-2-3 worksheet data. They are also able to pick up the field names and data types and convert them into the appropriate format by interpreting the types of entries made in the Lotus 1-2-3 worksheet.

Like exporting worksheets to dBASE files, importing Lotus 1-2-3 files into these programs requires you to arrange the data in the standard Lotus 1-2-3 database format, the first row of the worksheet containing field names and succeeding rows containing the database records. Some, like Paradox, will not import a database defined by a range name. In such a case, you will have to make sure that your Lotus 1-2-3 file contains only the database, excluding any secondary cell ranges such as criterion and output ranges.

Lotus 1-2-3, Release 1A, Only	**Lotus 1-2-3, Release 1A and 2**
R:base 5000	R:BASE System V (exports to .WKS format only)
Paradox, Version 1.0	Paradox, Version 1.1
Reflex, Version 1.0	Reflex, Version 1.1
Q&A, Version 1.0	Q&A, Release 2
SuperCalc3	SuperCalc4

TABLE 30.3: Types of Lotus 1-2-3 Translations Supported by Other Data Processing Programs

SUMMARY

This chapter has discussed translating files between the two versions of Lotus 1-2-3 as well as between Lotus 1-2-3 and other types of application programs using either the Lotus 1-2-3 Translate utility or a similar utility provided by the other program. Directly translating a worksheet file into another format or vice versa using a translation program is generally a fairly straightforward process.

However, depending on the type of program you wish to use with Lotus 1-2-3, you may run across some conversion problems that will require manual reentry or editing of some of the data in the translated file. You can frequently keep these problems to a minimum by preparing the data in the file according to the guidelines offered in this chapter before performing the translation.

However, some data exchanges cannot be accomplished by using a translation utility—either Lotus 1-2-3's or the other program's—to transfer your data between Lotus 1-2-3 and another application program. In these cases, you can always use an ASCII file as the medium by which the data is exchanged between programs. If you find that the program you are using (most often a word processor) does not allow you to import or export the Lotus 1-2-3 file format directly, you should investigate how to perform the transfer with ASCII files. This topic is covered in detail in Chapter 29.

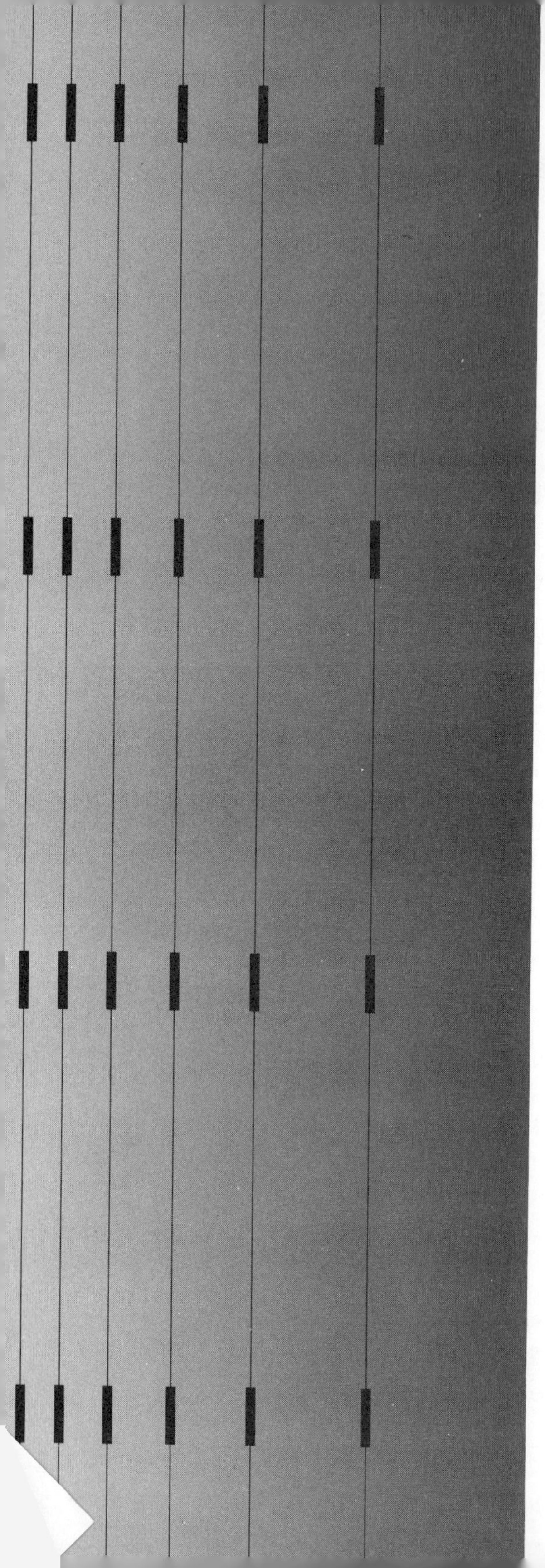

APPENDIX A
LOTUS 1-2-3 ERROR MESSAGES

Lotus 1-2-3 error messages are displayed at the bottom of the screen whenever the program is unable to process a command as you have specified it. Most of the time, this causes the program to go into ERROR mode. When the ERROR mode indicator is flashing in the upper-right corner of the screen, you can press the Return key to escape from it and return to READY mode. You should then take whatever steps are necessary to prevent the error from reoccurring before you try to invoke the same command again.

The error messages in Release 2 of the program are the same as those in Release 1A, except that Release 2 has added a number of very specific macro command error messages to the ones shown below. These macro error messages not only pinpoint the source of the problem but also tell you the cell address where it is located. To obtain more information about macro errors (which do not cause the program to go into ERROR mode), refer to the discussions and reference entries in Chapter 28. You will also find information there on how to use the {ONERROR} command to trap Lotus 1-2-3 errors whose error messages are listed in this appendix.

The following error messages are presented in alphabetical order.

Cannot create file Your disk does not have enough room to store the additional file.

Cannot delete file You have specifed a file name that does not exist on the disk from which you are trying to remove the file.

Cannot read help file You have attempted to read a Help file, and 1-2-3 was unable to do so.

Directory does not exist You have entered the /File Directory or /Worksheet Global Default Directory command, specifying a directory that doesn't exist.

Disk error Lotus 1-2-3 has failed to read from or write to the specified disk after two tries. Check to be sure that the disk is properly seated in its housing and that it is properly formatted. If these conditions are correct, the disk may be damaged, or the drive may not be functioning properly.

Disk drive not ready Check to make sure that the disk drive door is closed and that there is a properly formatted disk in the drive.

Disk full There is not enough room on the disk for the operation you requested. The /File List command will tell you how much room is left on a disk. If your worksheet is too large to fit on a single disk, you must save parts of it by using the /File Extract command. You may be able to solve the problem by replacing your current disk with a blank one that has been properly formatted.

Disk is write-protected You have issued a command to write a file to a disk that has a write-protect tab affixed to the notch on its right side. Remove the tab and try again.

File close error If you encounter this message, something may be wrong with your computer or with your system disk. If everything is working properly, this message should never appear.

File does not exist You have requested a file that does not appear on the specified disk or have mistyped its name. To check the directory of the disk, use the /File List command.

Formula computation error This error message indicates that something is wrong either with your system disk or with your computer. It should never appear under normal circumstances.

Formula too long The formula you have written exceeds either the maximum allowable length of 240 characters or the maximum allowable number of nested parentheses, which is 32. Break the formula into two or more separate formulas and enter each in a different cell.

Illegal cell or range address You have entered a range name or a set of cell coordinates that cannot be properly interpreted by 1-2-3. You may have made a typing error or you may have previously deleted the endpoint of a named range.

Illegal character in filename You have entered a file name containing characters other than letters, numbers, or underscore characters (hyphens can be used in file names only if you are using Release 2). Edit the file name.

Illegal disk name You have (probably through mistyping) specified a disk that does not exist in your system or has a drive designator higher than P:.

Illegal file format You have attempted to read a file, either through the /File Retrieve command or the /File Combine command, that is not a valid worksheet file (one that has been saved either with the /File Save or the /File Extract command).

Illegal formula When recalculating a spreadsheet, 1-2-3 encountered a formula that was not valid. After you have pressed the Return key to escape ERROR mode, the cell pointer will be on the first cell containing an invalid formula.

Illegal menu If you have used the /X Menu command in a macro, either:

1. You have specified more than eight items;
2. The combination of all your prompts contains too many characters; or
3. You have not specified any items.

Illegal number input You have entered a number that is too large, too small, or not valid for the selected command. You may have mistyped the entry.

Illegal "\nnn" code in setup string You have attempted to enter a printer setup string using a code greater than 255. Your printer setup strings must consist of numeric representations of ASCII characters, which are numbered from 0 to 255.

Input line too long A file that you have attempted to read with the /File Import Text command contains a line longer than 240 characters. This may occur if the program that generated the file does not end lines with carriage returns. You may have to edit the file in a text editor or word processor that allows you to insert carriage returns.

Justify range is full or line too long You have entered the /Range Justify command, and there is not enough room to justify the labels in the range that you specified. Press the Escape key to see the results, increase the space available for labels, and try again.

Key column is outside of sort range You have attempted to sort your data by using the /Data Sort command, and the key column you have given for sorting is not within the range of cells you want to sort.

Memory full There is no more room in your computer's memory to add to your worksheet. You may be able to increase the available memory by

1. Saving the file with the /File Save command, then clearing memory and bringing the file back with the /File Retrieve command, especially if you have been inserting or deleting rows or columns.
2. Arranging your worksheet so that it takes up the smallest possible rectangle. Locate the lower-right corner of your worksheet with the End and Home keys. Then see if you can move the data in that area upward or to the left.
3. Deleting any empty rows and columns, range names, or named graphs.

Missing or illegal configuration file Lotus 1-2-3 looked for the file called 123.CNF and could not find it. After you press the Escape key, the default setting will be used automatically. You can recreate the 123.CNF file by using the /Worksheet Global Default command, specifying your equipment, and then issuing the Update command.

Named range not found in worksheet file You have attempted to add to your present worksheet a named range that does not exist in the file you specified in the /File Combine command. Try specifying a different range name. You may have to save your present file with the /File Save command, then use the /File Retrieve command to examine the range names in the other file, and start over.

No files of specified type on disk You have issued the /File List command and there are no files of the type you specified on the selected disk.

No unprotected cells in range You selected the /Range Input command, but there are no unprotected cells in the input range for the pointer to rest on.

Not a valid worksheet file You have issued the /File Retrieve or /File Combine command specifying a file that is not a valid worksheet file.

Number stack full Something is drastically wrong. Check the Customer Service Booklet and get in touch with Lotus customer support.

Part of file is missing Either:

1. The Ctrl-Z character, which normally marks the end of a file, is not present at the end of an imported file; or
2. Your disk is damaged. You must reconstruct the file.

Printer error There is something wrong beyond the point at which the cable from the computer to the printer leaves the computer. Check to see that both ends of the cable are securely fastened, that the printer is turned on and on line, and that it is properly loaded with paper. If you have a serial printer, you may not have redirected printer output to the appropriate serial port before printing.

Protected cell You have tried to change the contents of a protected cell. You must first issue either the /Range Unprotect command for the cell or the /Worksheet Global Protection Disable command for the entire worksheet.

Range name does not exist You have specifed a named range that doesn't exist.

System error Something is wrong with the computer's operating system. Reboot immediately by pressing Ctrl-Alt-Del or by pressing the hardware reset switch.

Too many fields The criterion or output range for the /Data Query command may not exceed 32 fields. You have specified a larger range.

Too many records for output range You have issued the /Data Query Retrieve command, and the output range has too few rows to contain the number of records that match the criteria you have specified. Some of the data will be missing in the output range.

Unrecognized key name in braces You have typed something within braces { } that is not recognized by Lotus 1-2-3 as the name of a key.

Worksheet full You have either:

1. Inserted so many rows or columns that those below or to the right of them will be beyond the edge of the worksheet; or
2. Moved or copied a range of cells to a position such that some of them will be beyond the edge of the worksheet.

APPENDIX B
LICS CHART

Release 2 of Lotus 1-2-3 now supports an extended character set called the Lotus International Character Set, or LICS for short. This set represents a series of decimal codes from 0 to 255. The first 128 codes, from 0 to 127, are standard in that they conform to the ASCII codes. Those above code number 127 are unique to the Lotus software applications Lotus 1-2-3, Manuscript, and Symphony. They differ signifcantly from the Extended Graphics Character Set supported by IBM. As you can see from Table B.1, most of these higher codes represent foreign-language symbols (thus the name International Character Set).

To use one of these characters in a worksheet, you press the Alt-F1 key combination, referred to as the Compose key, release the Alt and F1 keys, and then type the two characters shown as the Compose Sequence in Table B.1. Some characters allow more than one form of the Compose Sequence. For these, all possible sequences are shown.

Note: Not all of LICS characters, such as the trademark and copyright symbols, can be represented properly on the screen. In such cases, Lotus 1-2-3 will use an approximation of the character. This approximation is referred to as *fallback monitor presentation* (see your Lotus 1-2-3 documentation for a complete list of these characters). Also, many printers cannot interpret the LICS code correctly; when you print a spreadsheet, some of the printed characters may not match what you see when the spreadsheet is displayed on your screen.

LICS Code	Character	Description	Compose Sequence
0	Ctrl-@		
1	Ctrl-A		
2	Ctrl-B		
3	Ctrl-C		
4	Ctrl-D		
5	Ctrl-E		
6	Ctrl-F		
7	Ctrl-G		
8	Ctrl-H		
9	Ctrl-I		
10	Ctrl-J	Line Feed	
11	Ctrl-K		
12	Ctrl-L	Form Feed	
13	Ctrl-M	Return	
14	Ctrl-N		
15	Ctrl-O		
16	Ctrl-P		
17	Ctrl-Q		
18	Ctrl-R		
19	Ctrl-S		
20	Ctrl-T		
21	Ctrl-U		
22	Ctrl-V		
23	Ctrl-W		
24	Ctrl-X		
25	Ctrl-Y		
26	Ctrl-Z		
27	{Escape}		
28	FS		
29	GS		
30	RS		
31	US		
32	(Space)		
33	!		
34	"		
35	#		+ +
36	$		
37	%		
38	&		
39	'	Apostrophe	

LICS Code	Character	Description	Compose Sequence
40	(		
41	)		
42	*		
43	+		
44	,		
45	-		
46	.		
47	/		
48	0		
49	1		
50	2		
51	3		
52	4		
53	5		
54	6		
55	7		
56	8		
57	9		
58	:		
59	;		
60	<		
61	=		
62	>		
63	?		
64	@		a a A A
65	A		
66	B		
67	C		
68	D		
69	E		
70	F		
71	G		
72	H		
73	I		
74	J		
75	K		
76	L		
77	M		
78	N		
79	O		

LICS Code	Character	Description	Compose Sequence
80	P		
81	Q		
82	R		
83	S		
84	T		
85	U		
86	V		
87	W		
88	X		
89	Y		
90	Z		
91	[		((
92	\		/ /
93	]		))
94	^		v v
95	_		
96	`		
97	a		
98	b		
99	c		
100	d		
101	e		
102	f		
103	g		
104	h		
105	i		
106	j		
107	k		
108	l		
109	m		
110	n		
111	o		
112	p		
113	q		
114	r		
115	s		
116	t		
117	u		
118	v		
119	w		

LICS Code	Character	Description	Compose Sequence
120	x		
121	y		
122	z		
123	{		* (-
124	¦		* ^/
125	}		*)-
126	~	Tilde	* —
127	DEL		
128	`	Uppercase grave	* ` space
129	´	Uppercase acute	* ´ space
130	^	Uppercase circumflex	* ^ space
131	¨	Uppercase umlaut	* " space
132	~	Uppercase tilde	* ~ space
133			
134			
135			
136			
137			
138			
139			
140			
141			
142			
143			
144	`	Lowercase grave	* space `
145	´	Lowercase acute	* space ´
146	^	Lowercase circumflex	* space ^
147	¨	Lowercase umlaut	* space "
148	~	Lowercase tilde	space ~
149	ı	Lowercase i without dot	i space
150	_	Ordinal indicator	_ space
151	▲	Begin attribute (display only)	b a
152	▼	End attribute (display only)	e a
153	■	Unknown character (display only)	
154	•	Hard space (display only)	space space
155	←	Merge character (display only)	m g
156			
157			
158			
159			

LICS Code	Character	Description	Compose Sequence
160	ƒ	Dutch Guilder	f f
161	¡	Inverted exclamation mark	! !
162	¢	Cent sign	c¦ C¦ c/ C/
163	£	Pound sign	L= l= L- l-
164	″	Low opening double quotes	″ ^
165	¥	Yen sign	Y= y= Y- y-
166	Pts	Pesetas sign	* P T p t P t
167	§	Section sign	S O s o S O s O
168		General currency sign	X O x o X O x O
169	©	Copyright sign	C O c o C O c O
170	ª	Feminine ordinal	a _ A _
171	«	Angle quotation mark left	< <
172	Δ	Delta	d d D D
173	π	Pi	* P I p i P i
174	≥	Greater than or equals	* > =
175	÷	Divide sign	:-
176	°	Degree sign	0
177	±	Plus/minus sign	+ -
178	²	Superscript 2	^ 2
179	³	Superscript 3	^ 3
180	″	Low closing double quotes	″ v
181	µ	Micro sign	* / u
182	¶	Paragraph sign	! p ! P
183	•	Middle dot	^ .
184	™	Trademark sign	TM Tm tm
185	¹	Superscript 1	^ 1
186	º	Masculine ordinal	o_ O_
187	»	Angle quotation mark right	> >
188	¼	One quarter	* 1 4
189	½	One half	* 1 2
190	≤	Less than or equals	* = <
191	¿	Inverted question mark	? ?
192	À	Uppercase A with grave	A `
193	Á	Uppercase A with acute	A ´
194	Â	Uppercase A with circumflex	A ^
195	Ã	Uppercase A with tilde	A ~
196	Ä	Uppercase A with umlaut	A ″
197	Å	Uppercase A with ring	* A

LICS Code	Character	Description	Compose Sequence
198	Æ	Uppercase A with ligature	* A E
199	Ç	Uppercase C with cedilla	C ,
200	È	Uppercase E with grave	E `
201	É	Uppercase E with acute	E '
202	Ê	Uppercase E with circumflex	E ^
203	Ë	Uppercase E with umlaut	E "
204	Ì	Uppercase I with grave	I `
205	Í	Uppercase I with acute	I '
206	Î	Uppercase I with circumflex	I ^
207	Ï	Uppercase I with umlaut	I "
208	Đ	Uppercase eth (Icelandic)	D -
209	Ñ	Uppercase N with tilde	N ~
210	Ò	Uppercase O with grave	O `
211	Ó	Uppercase O with acute	O '
212	Ô	Uppercase O with circumflex	O ^
213	Õ	Uppercase O with tilde	O ~
214	Ö	Uppercase O with umlaut	O "
215	Œ	Uppercase OE diphthong	* O E
216	Ø	Uppercase O with slash	O /
217	Ù	Uppercase U with grave	U `
218	Ú	Uppercase U with acute	U '
219	Û	Uppercase U with circumflex	U ^
220	Ü	Uppercase u with umlaut	U "
221	Ÿ	Uppercase Y with umlaut	Y "
222		Uppercase thorn (Icelandic)	P -
223	ß	Lowercase German sharp s	s s
224	à	Lowercase a with grave	a `
225	á	Lowercase a with acute	a '
226	â	Lowercase a with circumflex	a ^
227	ã	Lowercase a with tilde	a ~
228	ä	Lowercase u with umlaut	a "
229	å	Lowercase a with ring	a *
230	œ	Lowercase ae with ligature	* a e
231	ç	Lowercase c with cedilla	c ,
232	è	Lowercase e with grave	e `
233	é	Lowercase e with acute	e '
234	ê	Lowercase e with circumflex	e ^
235	ë	Lowercase e with umlaut	e "
236	ì	Lowercase i with grave	i '
237	í	Lowercase i with acute	i '

LICS Code	Character	Description	Compose Sequence
238	î	Lowercase i with circumflex	i ^
239	ï	Lowercase i with umlaut	i "
240	ð	Lowercase eth (Icelandic)	d -
241	ñ	Lowercase n with tilde	n ~
242	ò	Lowercase o with grave	o `
243	ó	Lowercase o with acute	o '
244	ô	Lowercase o with circumflex	o ^
245	õ	Lowercase o with tilde	o ~
246	ö	Lowercase o with umlaut	o "
247	œ	Lowercase oe diphthong	* oe
248	ø	Lowercase o with slash	o /
249	ù	Lowercase u with grave	u `
250	ú	Lowercase u with acute	u '
251	û	Lowercase u with circumflex	u ^
252	ü	Lowercase u with umlaut	u "
253	ÿ	Lowercase y with umlaut	y "
254		Lowercase thorn (Icelandic)	p -
255			

* Indicates that you must enter the compose sequence in order shown. Do not type the asterisk (*).

INDEX

In the following indexes, **boldface** page numbers show where to find the formal reference entry for a given command, function, or macro; consult the other page numbers for topical discussions and further information.

COMMAND INDEX

FUNCTION INDEX

Topical Index

A

B

C

Q

R

S

W

X

Y

Z

CURSOR KEY ASSIGNMENTS

MODE	KEY	FUNCTION
In READY or POINT mode	→	Moves cell pointer one column to right.
	←	Moves cell pointer one column to left.
	↑	Moves cell pointer up one row.
	↓	Moves cell pointer down one row.
	Home	Moves cell pointer to the first cell of the worksheet (A1 unless titles are in effect).
	End	Used with the arrow keys or the Home key. If cell pointer is in an empty cell, End moves it to the next occupied cell in the direction of the arrow. If cell pointer is in an occupied cell, End moves it to the next empty cell in the direction of the arrow. If End is used with Home, cell pointer moves to the last active cell in the worksheet.
	PgUp	Moves cell pointer up one screen.
	PgDn	Moves cell pointer down one screen.
	Tab or Ctrl-→	Moves cell pointer right one screen.
	Shift-Tab or Ctrl-←	Moves cell pointer left one screen.
In EDIT mode	→	Moves cursor one character to right.
	←	Moves cursor one character to left.
	↑	Enters contents into cell and moves cell pointer up one row.
	↓	Enters contents into cell and moves cell pointer down one row.
	Home	Moves cursor to first character.
	End	Moves cursor to last character.
	PgUp	Enters contents into cell and moves cell pointer up one screen.
	PgDn	Enters contents into cell and moves cell pointer down one screen.
	Tab	Moves cursor five spaces to right.
	Shift-Tab	Moves cursor five spaces to left.

LABEL PREFIXES

LABEL PREFIX	FUNCTION
' (apostrophe)	Left-aligned (program default unless changed)
^ (circumflex)	Centered
" (double quote)	Right-aligned (like values)
\ (backslash)	Repeats character typed after it across entire cell width.
Note: Use one of these label prefixes to force a value to be entered as a label, such as '1st Quarter.	